MARKETS IN CRYPTO-ASSETS REGULATION

This book provides a commentary on the Markets in Crypto-Assets Regulation (MiCAR), a game-changing EU regulation for crypto-assets and crypto-asset services.

Directly applicable in all EU Member States, MiCAR serves as a benchmark for future regulation in other jurisdictions, influencing rulemaking and crypto industry around the world.

In this book, leading experts in the fields of financial law, regulation and technology examine the goals, rules and operation of MiCAR. The book explores its provisions in the broader context of current market practices, technological developments, existing financial law instruments (eg MiFID II, Prospectus Regulation, Crowdfunding Regulation and Market Abuse Regulation), court cases (eg the bankruptcies of FTX and Celsius), regulatory initiatives in the USA and the UK, as well as soft law instruments.

The book is designed for anyone dealing with crypto-assets or considering entering the crypto space. This includes representatives from legal and business communities, both incumbent (banks, investment firms, investment funds) and new market players (crypto exchanges, wallet service providers, issuers of stablecoins), supervisory authorities, students and academics.

The reader will gain a deep understanding of the scope and structure of MiCAR, key terms used in it, its rationale, and the main rules for issuers of crypto-assets, crypto-asset service providers and crypto-asset services.

Hart Studies in Commercial and Financial Law: Volume 20

Hart Studies in Commercial and Financial Law

Series Editors: John Linarelli and Teresa Rodríguez de las Heras Ballell

This series offers a venue for publishing works on commercial law as well as on the regulation of banking and finance, and the law on insolvency and bankruptcy. It publishes works on the law on secured credit, the regulatory and transactional aspects of banking and finance, the transactional and regulatory institutions for financial markets, legal and policy aspects associated with access to commercial and consumer credit, new generation subjects having to do with the institutional architecture associated with innovation and the digital economy including works on blockchain technology, works on the relationship of law to economic growth, the harmonisation or unification of commercial law, transnational commercial law, and the global financial order. The series promotes interdisciplinary work. It publishes research on the law using the methods of empirical legal studies, behavioural economics, political economy, normative welfare economics, law and society inquiry, socio-legal studies, political theory, and historical methods. Its coverage includes international and comparative investigations of areas of law within its remit.

Volume 1: The Financialisation of the Citizen: Social and Financial Inclusion through European Private Law
Guido Comparato

Volume 2: MiFID II and Private Law: Enforcing EU Conduct of Business Rules
Federico Della Negra

Volume 3: Reforming Corporate Retail Investor Protection: Regulating to Avert Mis-Selling
Diane Bugeja

Volume 4: The Future of Commercial Law: Ways Forward for Change and Reform
Edited by Orkun Akseli and John Linarelli

Volume 5: The Cape Town Convention: A Documentary History
Anton Didenko

Volume 6: Regulating the Crypto Economy: Business Transformations and Financialisation
Iris H-Y Chiu

Volume 7: The Future of High-Cost Credit: Rethinking Payday Lending
Jodi Gardner

Volume 8: The Enforcement of EU Financial Law
Edited by Jan Crijns, Matthias Haentjens and Rijnhard Haentjens

Volume 9: International Bank Crisis Management: A Transatlantic Perspective
Marco Bodellini

Volume 10: Creditor Priority in European Bank Insolvency Law: Financial Stability and the Hierarchy of Claims
Sjur Swensen Ellingsæter

Volume 11: Chinese and Global Financial Integration through Stock Connect: A Legal Analysis
Flora Huang

Volume 12: The Governance of Macroprudential Policy: How to Build Regulatory Legitimacy Through a Social Justice Approach
Tracy C Maguze

Volume 13: A Socio-Legal Theory of Money for the Digital Commercial Society: A New Analytical Framework to Understand Cryptoassets
Israel Cedillo Lazcano

Volume 14: Venture Capital Investment and Government Incentives: Law, Regulation and Policy Design
Tamara Wilkinson

Volume 15: Regulating Primary Markets in the Capital Markets Union: Between Uniformity and Differentiation
Konstantinos Serdaris

Volume 16: Regulating Innovation in the Digital Age: A Demand-Centred Toolbox for the Data-Driven Economy
Nikita Divissenko

Volume 17: Digital Assets in Enforcement and Insolvency: Securing Creditor Access and Protecting Customer Interests in the Crypto World
Edited by Christian Koller and Matthias Lehmann

Volume 18: Transnational Mortgage Law: Reconstructing the Global Framework for Housing Finance
Guido Comparato and Irina Domurath

Volume 19: UNCITRAL Model Laws on Digital Trade: Electronic Transferable Records, Digital Identity and Trust Services
Luca G Castellani

Volume 20: Markets in Crypto-Assets Regulation: Law and Technology
Edited by Matthias Haentjens, Louise Gullifer and Ilya Kokorin

Markets in Crypto-Assets Regulation

Law and Technology

Edited by
Matthias Haentjens
Louise Gullifer
and
Ilya Kokorin

•HART•
OXFORD • LONDON • NEW YORK • NEW DELHI • SYDNEY

HART PUBLISHING

Bloomsbury Publishing Plc

Kemp House, Chawley Park, Cumnor Hill, Oxford, OX2 9PH, UK

1385 Broadway, New York, NY 10018, USA

Bloomsbury Publishing Ireland Limited, 29 Earlsfort Terrace, Dublin 2, D02 AY28, Ireland

HART PUBLISHING, the Hart/Stag logo, BLOOMSBURY and the Diana logo are trademarks of Bloomsbury Publishing Plc

First published in Great Britain 2025

A catalogue record for this book is available from the British Library.

A catalogue record for this book is available from the Library of Congress.

Library of Congress Control Number: 2025945722

ISBN: HB: 978-1-50997-040-7
ePDF: 978-1-50997-042-1
ePub: 978-1-50997-041-4

Typeset by Compuscript Ltd, Shannon

For product safety related questions contact productsafety@bloomsbury.com

To find out more about our authors and books visit www.hartpublishing.co.uk. Here you will find extracts, author information, details of forthcoming events and the option to sign up for our newsletters.

TABLE OF CONTENTS

LIST OF CONTRIBUTORS

Nick Campuzano is a PhD candidate at the Hazelhoff Centre for Financial Law at Leiden University, the Netherlands. His research interests include benchmarks, market abuse, and financial markets.

Simon Gleeson is a consultant to, and was a partner at, Clifford Chance in London. He is described by all of the major directories as one of the world's leading experts in financial services and banking regulation, capital markets and derivatives. His academic work focuses on the law of banking, money and payment, with particular reference to the development of the digital economy and Cryptoassets. Simon is currently a Visiting Professor at Oxford University, and a fellow of Fitzwilliam College Cambridge – he teaches at both institutions. He has lectured at Harvard, Oxford, Cambridge and Edinburgh Universities, and at King's College London, the LSE and QMW London. He is a former visiting fellow of All Souls, Oxford. In 2021 he was appointed a Deputy High Court Judge, where he sits in the Chancery Division.

Louise Gullifer KC (hon) FBA is Rouse Ball Professor of English Law at the University of Cambridge, chair of the Cambridge Law Faculty and a fellow of Gonville and Caius College, Cambridge. She is an associate member of 3VB, where she practised for a number of years, and a Bencher of Gray's Inn. She teaches and writes extensively in all areas of commercial and financial law. She is the editor of Goode and Gullifer on Legal Problems of Credit and Security and has co-authored a number of books on commercial law, debt financing, and the law of Intermediated Securities. She is a member of the UK Financial Markets Law Committee. She was the chair of the drafting group for the UNIDROIT project on Digital Assets and Private Law and is a member of the UNIDROIT working group on Principles on the Private Law of Verified Carbon Credits. She was the UK delegate to UNCITRAL working group VI during its work on secured transactions.

Matthias Haentjens holds the chair for civil law at Leiden University, the Netherlands. He also practises law as advocaat at De Brauw Blackstone Westbroek. He has been a deputy judge in the commercial law division of the Court of Amsterdam from 2019-2025. He teaches and writes extensively in all areas of commercial and financial law. He has authored articles, books and authoritative case notes on commercial law, banking law, and insolvency law. He is elected fellow of several international associations, including the International Insolvency Institute, the European Law Institute, and the European Banking Institute. Professor Haentjens was a member of the drafting group for the UNIDROIT project on Digital Assets and Private Law and is a member of the UNIDROIT working group on Bank Insolvency Law. He regularly advises national governments and international organisations on matters of financial and commercial law.

Ilya Kokorin is Assistant Professor of Law at Leiden University, the Netherlands. He is also a supervisory officer at the Dutch Authority for the Financial Markets (AFM). His research focuses on the intersection of financial, insolvency, and corporate law, with particular attention to the challenges and opportunities arising from rapid technological innovation.

Marisa Macháček is a lawyer and currently senior associate at an international law firm in Germany (focusing on Tech and Intellectual Property). She studied in Heidelberg and London, trained with BaFin in Germany and the European Commission (DG Fisma) and worked as a lawyer in securitisation and financial regulation at an international law firm. Her previous publications focused on financial technology and decentralised business models.

Heikki Marjosola is Associate Professor of Financial Law at University of Helsinki, Finland. His research focuses on corporate governance, corporate finance law and financial regulation. Previously, he was assistant professor of law at the London School of Economics and Political Science. Marjosola also acts as an independent advisor in legal matters relating to banking and finance as well as EU law.

Philipp Maume is an Associate Professor of Law at TUM School of Management, Technical University of Munich. He holds a Doctor of Laws from Augsburg University (Germany) and a Doctor of Juridical Science from La Trobe University (Australia). His main research area is fintech regulation, with a focus on DLT/blockchain. In this area, he is advising the German Government, the German Parliament and the European Parliament.

Elisabeth Noble is a Senior Policy Advisor and the principal advisor on innovation at the European Banking Authority (EBA). She leads the EBA's policy work on crypto-assets, including MiCAR implementation, and leads the team responsible for the delivery of the EBA's thematic work on innovation, encompassing AI/ML, BigTech, technology-facilitated value chain evolution, platformisation, and DeFi. She represents the EBA in EU and international standard-setter work streams relating to FinTech, financial system interconnectedness, and the regulatory perimeter. Prior to joining the EBA in 2014, Elisabeth spent 7 years at the UK's finance ministry advising primarily on the response to the 2008/9 financial crisis, including resolution measures, and the post-crisis domestic and EU regulatory reforms and adjustments to the supervisory architecture (establishment of the UK PRA and FCA, and EU Banking Union). Elisabeth has also spent some time in the private sector. Elisabeth is a Visiting Professor in Practice at London School of Economics and Political Science (LSE).

Philipp Paech is Associate Professor of Law at the London School of Economics and a Distinguished Global Professor of Law at the University of Notre Dame. He teaches and conducts research in the fields of financial regulation and the commercial law of finance. His work focuses on risk mitigation, settlement infrastructure, and innovation and technology in financial services. For over 20 years, he has contributed to international legal reform and policy projects, including work under the auspices of UNIDROIT, the OECD, the UK Foreign Office, the European Commission, the European Central Bank, and the European Parliament.

Rogier Raas is a professor in financial law at the Hazelhoff Centre of Financial Law of Leiden University, the Netherlands. He is also a partner at the law firm Stibbe in Amsterdam.

Marika Salo-Lahti is an Associate Professor of Business Law (tenure track) at the University of Vaasa, Finland. Her research interests include legal perspectives on FinTech (eg, crypto-assets, robo-advising, and crowdfunding), Legal Design, artificial intelligence, and sustainability. She leads the Business Law and Information research group.

Lodewijk van Setten is Director & Chief Risk Officer at DLT Solutions and Director & General Counsel at Trilitech, a prominent ecosystem entity of the Tezos blockchain. He specialises in traditional and blockchain powered financial services & products. His work at DLT Solutions includes serving as non-executive director for VASPs and incorporated dApp platforms. At Trilitech, he focuses on core protocol and layer 2 solutions, tokenisation techniques, DAO governance structures, NFTs across gaming & art projects, and DeFi use cases.

TABLE OF CASES

ECJ cases by number

ECJ cases by party

Hong Kong

US courts

US courts (CFTC/SEC cases)

TABLE OF LEGISLATION

European Commission

EU Directives

EU Regulations

UNIDROIT Instruments

1

Introduction

MATTHIAS HAENTJENS, LOUISE GULLIFER AND ILYA KOKORIN

Markets in Crypto-Assets Regulation: Law and Technology provides a commentary on the Markets in Crypto-Assets Regulation (MiCAR) – a major piece of EU legislation that regulates markets in crypto-assets. MiCAR was adopted on 31 May 2023 and is fully applicable in the EU as of 30 December 2024.

This book explores MiCAR's provisions within the broader context of current market practices, technological advancements, existing financial law instruments, clarifications of European Supervisory Authorities and recent market developments, including the collapses of large market players such as FTX and Celsius. It also addresses regulatory initiatives in the UK and various soft law instruments. The crypto-asset markets and the relevant regulatory framework are rapidly evolving at the moment. Thus, the context of the discussion in this book is necessarily limited to that of the time at which MiCAR came into force. Having said that, chapters eleven and thirteen of the book look to the future in relation to crypto-assets and activities that are not included within MiCAR.

The book aims not merely to describe the regulation but to explain it. It takes a critical stance to identify ambiguities, important gaps, potential difficulties in application, and areas for future improvement. It identifies themes that are likely to be critical aspects of the debate about the regulation of crypto-assets in the near and medium future. The chapters also contain recommendations on how MiCAR's provisions should be implemented in practice and outline the steps relevant market participants (eg, crypto-asset service providers) need to take to comply with the regulation. The purpose of the book is to enable its readers to gain an understanding of the scope and structure of MiCAR, the key terms it employs, its underlying rationale, and its main rules for issuers of crypto-assets, crypto-asset service providers, and crypto-asset services.

The book's structure largely mirrors that of MiCAR itself. The first four chapters address MiCAR's background, goals, structure, scope, fundamental terms, and the typology of crypto-assets. In chapter two, Ilya Kokorin discusses the background, goals and structure of MiCAR. The content and structure of MiCAR are heavily influenced by the aims of its drafters and the regulatory environment of which it will form a part. To understand the instrument, it is therefore important to understand its purpose and the perceived need for it to fit within EU financial markets regulation.

In chapters three and four, Philipp Paech examines the scope of the instrument and the key terms it employs. While the general concept of a crypto-asset is reasonably well understood, the precise scope of MiCAR is less intuitive, although, as with any regulatory instrument, it is crucial for those involved in the market to appreciate the details of its application. In chapter three, Paech discusses the types of assets covered by MiCAR, pointing out the effective departure from technological neutrality and the uneasy interaction between the ambit of assets regulated by MiCAR and those regulated under MiFID II and other financial law instruments. He also discusses the persons to whom MiCAR applies, an exercise that involves consideration not only of the relevant definitions but also how those definitions interact with the substantive provisions throughout the instrument. The precise wording of definitions of the various crypto-assets regulated by MiCAR is the subject of Paech's chapter four. Paech makes it clear that the definitions, on their face, are designed to reflect the risks posed by different types of assets (as opposed, for example, to their classification in private law). However, he questions whether this alignment with risk is entirely achieved by the wording of the MiCAR definitions.

Chapters five to ten follow the key sections of MiCAR. In chapter five, Heikki Marjosola and Marika Salo-Lahti examine MiCAR Title II, which covers the offer and admission to trading of crypto-assets other than e-money tokens (EMTs) and asset-referenced tokens (ARTs). In this chapter, Marjosola and Salo-Lahti examine which types of crypto-asset are likely to fall within Title II, specifically focusing on utility tokens. They also discuss key issues in relation to this residual category of crypto-assets, such as the requirements for an offer of these types of crypto-asset and ongoing duties owed by issuers and offerors (and how these compare to equivalent requirements and duties under MiFID II and the EU Crowdfunding Regulation) as well as the consumer law-inspired regulatory approach, including a 14-day withdrawal right. The authors question whether this right is suitable for the wide variety of crypto-assets falling under Title II MiCAR.

In chapter six, Philipp Maume examines MiCAR Titles III and IV, covering ARTs and EMTs. While not a technical term, these tokens can loosely be described as 'stablecoins', and it is the perceived risks posed by these assets (eg financial stability, consumer and investor protection, monetary policy and sovereignty) that were the original drivers for the regulation found in MiCAR. Maume critically examines MiCAR's regulatory approach to stablecoins and compares it with the approach adopted in existing financial markets regulation, asking in particular whether MiCAR will incentivise or deter market participants from issuing stablecoins in the EU. He highlights the complexity of MiCAR's rules, the privileged position of incumbent financial institutions, raises his concerns about the access of SMEs and startups to EU markets, the ambiguity of MiCAR's provisions (eg, 'referencing'), the proportionality of restrictions imposed on super-significant stablecoins, and regulatory overlaps within MiCAR and with existing financial law instruments.

In chapter seven, Ilya Kokorin discusses MiCAR Title V, which is devoted to the regulation of crypto-asset service providers (CASPs). Before the adoption of MiCAR, CASPs and their services were mainly subject to national legal frameworks, some of which did not have special rules for businesses active in crypto markets. The adoption of an EU-wide legal regime aims to create a level playing field and provide legal certainty for CASPs offering their services across the EU. In this chapter, Kokorin examines MiCAR's provisions concerning access to European crypto-markets, observing that, with the exception of a narrowly construed reverse solicitation exemption, third-country companies require MiCAR authorisation to operate in the EU. Neither equivalence nor national third-country regimes are available to them. Kokorin explores the key CASP application requirements, outlines the obligations of all crypto-asset service providers (eg prudential requirements, outsourcing, prevention and management of conflicts of interest) and highlights the obligations with respect to specific crypto-asset services (eg custody, operation of a trading platform). He emphasises the complexity of the regulation, which arises from its co-existence with existing EU law (eg, PSD2, EMD2, DORA), internal conflicts and ambiguities (eg the application of different MiCAR provisions to a single asset or relationship), as well as numerous Level 2 and Level 3 instruments seeking to clarify MiCAR's rules.

In chapter eight, Marisa Machacek discusses the concept of 'significance', which is used in MiCAR to identify AMTs, EMTs and CASPs, which are considered to require special regulatory treatment because of the potential systemic risks they pose, for example, due to their size or interconnectedness with the financial system. Machacek examines the criteria applied to determine whether a token or a CASP is 'significant' and the regulatory consequences of such a determination. These consequences include more stringent disclosure and reporting obligations and more rigorous supervision by EU authorities. Machacek argues that these far-reaching consequences could enable 'significant' market players to demonstrate that their risk profile is manageable and that their existence should therefore be permitted by regulators.

Chapter nine consists of a discussion of the MiCAR provisions on market abuse in Title VI by Nick Campuzano and Rogier Raas. These authors compare and contrast the MiCAR market abuse regime with the Market Abuse Regulation (MAR) regime. Despite the avowed aim of formulating a bespoke regime for crypto-assets, the similarities are striking. Campuzano and Raas consider the way in which the market abuse provisions are likely to operate within the crypto-asset environment, and conclude that despite the many similarities with the MAR regime, the compliance burden for market participants under MiCAR is likely to be greater.

In chapter ten Elisabeth Noble examines Title VII, which establishes the supervisory and enforcement powers available to regulatory authorities in relation to the MiCAR regime. Noble considers the nature of these powers, the interaction between competent authorities, ESMA and the EBA, and looks ahead to the challenges authorities face in exercising their powers, as well as the need for cooperation and coordination between relevant supervisors.

In chapters eleven and twelve, the wider context in which MiCAR operates is considered. Like all regulatory instruments, MiCAR has a defined scope designed to target specific risks it aims to mitigate. As a result, certain activities are expressly excluded from its coverage, and some areas of market activity fall outside its scope. In chapter eleven, Lodewijk van Setten discusses crypto-related topics which are excluded from MiCAR's scope or do not fall within it. In relation to assets, Van Setten describes different methods of tokenisation and considers whether all methods give rise to 'crypto-assets' within the definition in MiCAR. He also critically examines the express exclusion of non-fungible tokens (NFTs) from MiCAR's scope. The regulation of CASPs by MiCAR is limited to certain functions: Van Setten examines the extent to which decentralised activities, known as decentralised finance or 'DeFi', fall within MiCAR's regulatory net. It is, of course, possible that the scope of MiCAR will be extended in all these regards if unacceptable risks are deemed likely to arise.

In chapter twelve, Simon Gleeson provides a comparative discussion of the development of regulation of the crypto-asset market in a non-EU jurisdiction: the UK. Gleeson not only compares the content of the regulatory provisions in the two regimes but also analyses the fundamentally different approach of the UK compared to the EU in developing crypto-asset regulation. He distinguishes between the EU's 'pre-emptive' approach in providing reasonably comprehensive regulation for the entire (or nearly entire) crypto-asset market, and the UK's 'wait-and-see' approach, whereby specific risks are identified, examined, and debated before targeted regulation is implemented, while aiming to retain a 'level playing field' between crypto-asset activities and traditional finance.

In chapter thirteen, the editors of this volume provide a thematic analysis of the chapters in the book, drawing out what they consider to be the main criticisms of the MiCAR regime and offering some insights into future challenges and developments. A recurrent theme throughout the book is the potentially problematic interaction between MiCAR and other regulatory instruments, particularly those focused on more traditional financial markets. One prevalent technique used by the drafters of MiCAR is to 'copy-paste' existing regulation into the new instrument, raising the question as to whether MiCAR is sufficiently tailored to the crypto market (or, perhaps, in the light of the UK approach, too crypto-specific). This debate is an important but ongoing one in relation to future regulation; the discussion in this book highlights the issue and provides detailed analysis to enable the debate to continue in the light of future experience.

Comprehensive regulatory regimes often raise questions about the interaction between public (regulatory) and private law, and MiCAR is no exception. Chapter thirteen discusses the instances where this interaction has been raised in the book and points out that clarity of the application of private law to crypto-assets and service providers is an essential component of a well-functioning market: without such clarity (including clarity of conflict of laws rules), a regulatory regime cannot properly achieve its objectives. It is evident from the analysis of the provisions of MiCAR in the book that the instrument pursues a number of regulatory objectives which are balanced against each other, with the balance varying according to context. This balance is discussed in chapter thirteen, which concludes that it is not possible to make any generalised statement about the regulatory approach of MiCAR, and that any assessment should focus on specific provisions. Chapter thirteen also compares the regulatory approaches of the EU, the UK and (rather concisely) the US, noting that the more flexible, reactive and, in some instances, indeterminate approach of the US has notable disadvantages as well as advantages. Finally, chapter thirteen looks to the future, considering some of the areas that MiCAR does not cover at the moment, such as DeFi and asking how the risks raised by these should be dealt with.

The book does not follow a rigid article-by-article approach. Instead, it focuses on MiCAR's main provisions, describes them in a structured way and explains them. Some of MiCAR's provisions are self-explanatory and require little commentary, while others may necessitate more in-depth analysis and critique. The book will be interesting and useful to academics and practitioners alike. However, while this book is designed to help readers who need to apply MiCAR in practice to understand the framework of the instrument, the constant changes and development – both in the markets and in the regulatory environment – mean that practitioners are advised to consult the most recent versions of relevant documents, including adopted acts published in the Official Journal, clarifications from national competent authorities, courts and the European Supervisory Authorities.

2

MiCAR: Background, Goals and Structure

ILYA KOKORIN*

2.1. Introduction

In March 2018, the European Commission (EC) adopted the FinTech Action Plan, which seeks to create a more competitive and innovative financial market by, inter alia, enabling innovative business models and supporting the uptake of new technologies, including blockchain. The Commission points out that 'crypto-assets and the underlying blockchain technology hold promise for financial markets and infrastructures.'[1] Yet it acknowledges that their 'use also presents risks, as has been witnessed by strong volatility of crypto-assets, fraud and operational weaknesses and vulnerabilities at crypto-asset exchanges.'[2] In 2017, ESMA highlighted the risks related to investments in crypto-assets and specifically in initial coin offerings (ICOs).[3] The urgent need for regulatory intervention was clear, yet the scope of such regulation and its relationship to existing financial law was less obvious.

In the FinTech Action Plan, the EC mandated the European Banking Authority (EBA) and the European Securities and Markets Authority (ESMA) to study the applicability and suitability of the existing EU regulatory framework to crypto-assets. In its 2019 advice,[4] ESMA concluded that crypto-assets pose specific challenges to regulators and market players, particularly due to a lack of clarity as

* The views expressed in this chapter are solely those of the author and do not necessarily reflect those of the AFM.

[1] European Commission, FinTech Action plan: For a more competitive and innovative European financial sector, COM(2018) 109 final, 8 March 2018 (FinTech Action plan) eur-lex.europa.eu/legal-content/EN/TXT/?uri=CELEX:52018DC0109.

[2] ibid.

[3] ESMA, ESMA highlights ICO risks for investors and firms, 13 November 2017, www.esma.europa.eu/press-news/esma-news/esma-highlights-ico-risks-investors-and-firms. The ESAs published a joint warning in February 2018, emphasising extreme volatility and bubble risk, absence of protection (eg, no guarantee schemes), lack of exit options, intransparency of price formation, operational disruptions and the spread of misleading information.

[4] ESMA, Advice, Initial Coin Offerings and Crypto-Assets, ESMA50-157-1391, 9 January 2019 (ESMA Advice).

to how the existing rules apply to crypto-assets. Pure payment-type crypto-assets, like Bitcoin, were regarded as unlikely to qualify as financial instruments. ESMA also observed that in the absence of applicable financial law rules – for those crypto-assets not falling within the category of financial instruments – consumers were exposed to substantial risks.[5] Around the same time, the EBA published its report, in which it observed that, typically, 'crypto-assets fall outside the scope of EU financial services regulation [...] and specific services relating to crypto-asset custodian wallet provision and crypto-asset trading platforms do not constitute regulated activities under EU financial services law.'[6] Beyond legislation aimed at combatting money laundering and terrorism financing,[7] most crypto-assets fell outside the perimeter of EU financial law and were therefore not subject to provisions on consumer and investor protection, market integrity and financial stability.

In response to this legal vacuum, in 2020, the EC published a Proposal for a Regulation on Markets in Crypto-assets (Proposal for MiCAR).[8] This proposal was based on Article 114 of the Treaty on the Functioning of the European Union and was introduced as part of the Digital Finance Strategy for the EU. The European Commission stated that 'digital finance has a lot to offer, and the people and businesses of Europe are ready for it.'[9] Apart from the Proposal for MiCAR, the Digital Finance Strategy contained the proposal for a Regulation on a pilot regime for market infrastructures based on distributed ledger technology (DLT Pilot Regime)[10] and the proposal for a Regulation on digital operational resilience for the financial sector (DORA).[11] The latter two instruments pursue specific purposes and are largely outside the scope of this book.

A provisional agreement on the Proposal for MiCAR was reached on 30 June 2022. The Council's Permanent Representatives' Committee (COREPER) meeting of 5 October 2022 endorsed the final compromise text with a view to agreement.[12] On 20 April 2023, the European Parliament voted in favour of MiCAR.

[5] ibid para 8.

[6] EBA, Report on crypto-assets with advice for the European Commission, 9 January 2019 (EBA Report) p 4.

[7] Directive (EU) 2015/849 of the European Parliament and of the Council on the prevention of the use of the financial system for the purposes of money laundering and terrorist financing.

[8] Proposal for a Regulation of the European Parliament and of the Council on Markets in Crypto-assets, and amending Directive (EU) 2019/1937, COM(2020) 593 final, 24 September 2020.

[9] European Commission, Communication from the Commission to the European Parliament, the Council, the European Economic and Social Committee and the Committee of the Regions on a Digital Finance Strategy for the EU, COM(2020) 591 final, 24 September 2020.

[10] Regulation (EU) 2022/858 of the European Parliament and of the Council of 30 May 2022 on a pilot regime for market infrastructures based on distributed ledger technology. The DLT Pilot Regime entered into application on 23 March 2023. However, as of June 2024, no DLT market infrastructures have been authorised yet. See DLT Pilot Regime, www.esma.europa.eu/esmas-activities/digital-finance-and-innovation/dlt-pilot-regime.

[11] Regulation (EU) 2022/2554 of the European Parliament and of the Council of 14 December 2022 on digital operational resilience for the financial sector. DORA entered into force on 16 January 2023 and will apply as of 17 January 2025.

[12] Provisional Agreement resulting from the Interinstitutional Negotiations. Proposal for a regulation of the European Parliament and of the Council on markets in crypto-assets and amending Directive (EU) 2019/1937 (COM(2020)0593) data.consilium.europa.eu/doc/document/ST-13198-2022-INIT/en/pdf.

The Council adopted it on 16 May 2023. The final act was signed on 31 May 2023 and published in the Official Journal on 9 June 2023. MiCAR entered into force on 29 June 2023. Its provisions concerning ARTs and EMTs became applicable from 30 June 2024, while other provisions apply from 30 December 2024. In this chapter, I will introduce the main goals of MiCAR and outline its structure.

2.2. Drivers and Goals of MiCAR

2.2.1. Legal Certainty and Technological Development

The adoption of crypto-asset-specific legislation was driven by a number of important considerations or drivers. The problem tree presented in the Impact Assessment accompanying the Proposal for MiCAR clearly outlines these drivers.

Figure 2.1 Problem Tree[13]

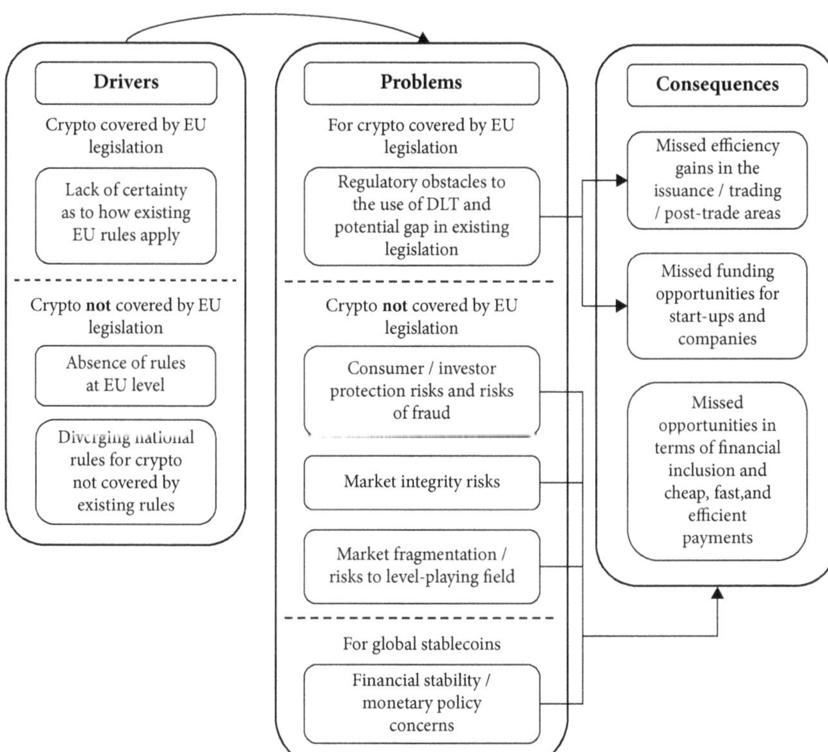

[13] This figure is based on Commission Staff Working Document, Impact Assessment accompanying the document Proposal for a Regulation of the European Parliament and of the Council on Markets in Crypto-assets and amending Directive (EU) 2019/1937, SWD(2020) 380 final (Impact Assessment) at 11, eur-lex.europa.eu/legal-content/EN/TXT/?uri=CELEX%3A52020SC0380.

As noted above, the application of the 'traditional' financial regulatory framework to the wide range of crypto-assets and services related to them has proven problematic. While it is clear that some crypto-assets – following the substance-over-form approach[14] – are likely to fall under the category of 'financial instruments' (eg, tokenised securities), other crypto-assets (eg, payment and utility tokens) do not easily fit into this category.

Additional difficulty arises from the fact that the notion of 'financial instruments', and specifically that of 'transferable security', has not been strictly harmonised under EU law. ESMA recognises that the national transposition of MiFID II, being a directive rather than a regulation, has resulted in differences across the laws of Member States. This means that 'there is no commonly-adopted application of the definition of "financial instrument" under MiFID in the EU.'[15] This problem was known previously,[16] but has become particularly topical with the proliferation of crypto-assets. Since MiFID II, the Prospectus Regulation and other EU financial law instruments were not designed with crypto-assets in mind, without tailored crypto-asset regulation and clarifications from the European Supervisory Authorities (ESAs), national competent authorities faced challenges in interpreting and applying existing instruments. This was considered to have potentially led to market fragmentation and regulatory arbitrage.[17] The adoption of MiCAR aims to bring more clarity to the delineation of regulatory spheres in EU financial law. However, some authors have expressed doubts about MiCAR's ability to set clear boundaries between crypto-assets that qualify as financial instruments and those falling within its own scope.[18]

In the absence of a harmonised EU-level framework, some Member States, such as France, Germany and Malta, had adopted bespoke rules addressing certain aspects of crypto-assets.[19] These rules often differed in scope and in the activities

[14] ESMA, Consultation Paper on the Draft Guidelines on the conditions and criteria for the qualification of crypto-assets as financial instruments, ESMA75-453128700-52, 29 January 2024, para 20, noting that the substance-over-form approach implies that 'the legal qualification of the product should not be determined by its technological envelope.'

[15] ibid p 3.

[16] J Dybiński and K Oplustil, 'Defining "Securities" in the European Capital Markets Code' in R Veil (ed), *Regulating EU Capital Markets Union: Volume I: Fundamentals of a European Code* (Oxford University Press, 2024) 263, 264, observing that 'not only the EU securities laws do not formulate a uniform definition [of a security], but also do not use the notion consistently throughout the acts.'

[17] On the concept of regulatory arbitrage with a focus on financial markets, see A Minto, S Prinz and M Wulff, 'A Risk Characterization of Regulatory Arbitrage in Financial Markets' (2021) 22 *EBOR* 719. See also D Nouy, Chair of the Supervisory Board of the ECB, 'Gaming the rules or ruling the game? – How to deal with regulatory arbitrage' (Speech at the 33rd SUERF Colloquium, Helsinki, 15 September 2017) www.bankingsupervision.europa.eu/press/speeches/date/2017/html/ssm.sp170915.en.html.

[18] P Giudici and G Ferrarini, 'Digital Offerings and Mandatory Disclosure: A Market-Based Critique of MiCA' in E Avgouleas and H Marjosola (eds), *Digital Finance in Europe: Law, Regulation, and Governance* (De Gruyter, 2022) 104, noting that 'the boundary between transferable instruments and crypto-assets as defined in the [MiCAR Proposal] is blurred, creating uncertainty as to the applicable regulation and opening numerous arbitrage opportunities to the interested parties to the extent that MiCA includes a lighter regime, for instance with regard to non-approval of the white paper by the registration authority.'

[19] Impact Assessment (n 13). For an overview of pre-MiCAR national regimes for crypto-assets, see ESMA Advice, Appendix 5.

covered, and imposed different requirements on issuers of crypto-assets and providers of crypto-asset services. As a result, a highly fragmented regulatory environment emerged, which complicated the cross-border operation of businesses involving crypto-assets. For instance, before MiCAR, there was no EU passporting regime for crypto businesses. Consequently, the obligation to seek licences under the laws of different Member States for the provision of crypto-asset services and the offerings of crypto-assets inevitably led to additional transaction costs and barriers to entry into the EU market.[20]

MiCAR, with its passporting regime (eg, Article 59(7)) and harmonised rules, seeks to eliminate market fragmentation, create legal certainty and a level playing field, and enable crypto businesses to scale up their activities across the EU.[21] This is in line with another goal articulated in MiCAR: the support of innovation and promotion of the wider use of distributed ledger technology (DLT). The latter has been recognised as a transformative and foundational technology, including in the financial sector.[22]

2.2.2. Consumer and Investor Protection

Substantial losses suffered by crypto investors as a result of failures of crypto-asset service providers,[23] hacks, collapsed or fraudulent ICOs,[24] and market abuse,[25] brought to the spotlight the issue of consumer and investor protection and market integrity. In his book *Going Infinite: The Rise and Fall of a New Tycoon* devoted to the collapse of once the third largest crypto-exchange FTX and the man behind it, Sam Bankman-Fried, Michael Lewis described the state of affairs in crypto markets as follows:

> The whole thing was odd: these people joined together by their fear of trust erected a parallel financial system that required more trust from its users than did the traditional financial system. Outside the law, and often hostile to it, they discovered many ways to run afoul of it. Crypto exchanges routinely misplaced or lost their customers' money. Crypto exchanges routinely faked trading data to make it seem as though far more

[20] Impact Assessment (n 13).

[21] MiCAR, Recitals (5) and (6).

[22] MiCAR, Recital (1). See also Impact Assessment (n 13) para 1.3., noting that '[c]rypto-assets could deliver many benefits to the economy. When used as a means of exchange, payment tokens can enhance competition in the payment market and increase the efficiency of payments (especially cross-border) in terms of cost, speed, security and user-friendliness by limiting the number of intermediaries (such as banks).'

[23] I Kokorin, 'The anatomy of crypto failures and investor protection under MiCAR' (2023) 18(4) *Capital Markets Law Journal* 500.

[24] ESMA Advice, addressing ICOs and emphasising the risks as fraud, cyber-attacks, money laundering, and market manipulation. L Hornuf, T Kück and A Schwienbacher, 'Initial coin offerings, information disclosure, and fraud' (2022) 58 Small Business Economics 1741.

[25] Chainalysis, The 2024 Crypto Crime Report, February 2024, see go.chainalysis.com/crypto-crime-2024.html.

trading had occurred on them than actually had. Crypto exchanges fell prey to hackers, or to random rogue traders who gamed the exchanges' risk management.[26]

The risks faced by investors were exacerbated by the lack of proper disclosure, the provision of exaggerated or misleading information by issuers and service providers, the high price volatility of crypto-assets, fraudulent activities and deceptive practices. The absence or inadequacy of regulation at the Member State-level was problematic. Moreover, given the international nature of crypto-asset markets, regulation at the national level – even if adopted – was unlikely to be sufficient to protect investors and safeguard market integrity. While only truly global regulation and regulatory cooperation could be effective,[27] the harmonised EU-wide regulatory framework established by MiCAR represents a significant step toward safeguarding investor rights.

MiCAR introduces a wide range of rules designed to ensure consumer and investor protection. Among them are rules mandating disclosure by means of crypto-asset white papers and marketing communications (eg, Articles 19 and 29). These rules seek to mitigate information asymmetries between issuers of crypto-assets (who naturally have more information about the offered crypto-assets) and their buyers. Adequate (ie, comprehensive, clear and concise) provision of information via a white paper should enable prospective holders of crypto-assets to make informed purchase decisions and better understand the relevant risks.

The failures of Three Arrows Capital, Voyager, Celsius, FTX, Alameda, BlockFi, Genesis, Bittrex Inc. and other crypto firms during the so-called Crypto Winter of 2022–23 exposed the fragility of their business models, the lack of accountability and sound governance, the opacity of crypto-asset operations, the concentration of trading activity in just a few large crypto exchanges, market interconnectedness, inadequate regulatory and supervisory models, and – importantly – the high risks faced by crypto investors around the world. The collapse of these firms resulted in large losses for venture capital and retail investors alike.[28] To protect future consumers and investors dealing with crypto-assets and crypto firms, MiCAR introduces detailed rules for crypto-asset service providers (CASPs) and the services they offer. These rules impose, inter alia, operational, organisational

[26] M Lewis, *Going Infinite: The Rise and Fall of a New Tycoon* (WW Norton & Company, 2023) 108.

[27] To support the consistency and comprehensiveness of regulatory approaches to crypto-asset activities, the FSB has developed the Global Regulatory Framework for Crypto-Asset Activities, 17 July 2023, see www.fsb.org/uploads/P170723-1.pdf. K Knot, President of the Netherlands Bank and Chair of the Financial Stability Board, 'The need for regulating crypto-assets – a global effort' (Speech at the Asia Securities Industry & Financial Markets Association (ASIFMA) Annual Conference, Hong Kong, 1 March 2024) www.bis.org/review/r240229h.htm, observing that 'without globally consistent implementation [of the FSB's regulatory framework], certain crypto-service providers may continue to evade regulation.'

[28] G Cornelli et al, 'Crypto shocks and retail losses' (2023) BIS Bulletin No. 69, 4 www.bis.org/publ/bisbull69.pdf, concluding that 'most global investors have probably lost money on their crypto investments.'

and prudential requirements on CASPs, address the pervasive issue of conflicts of interest, and set forth obligations concerning specific crypto-asset services (see Title V MiCAR and chapter seven of this book).

2.2.3. Financial Stability and Monetary Sovereignty

MiCAR acknowledges that markets in crypto-assets do not currently pose a threat to financial stability in the EU.[29] The Crypto Winter of 2022–2023 and the stress on crypto markets have not spilled over into traditional financial markets.[30] However, it has been observed that 'if the present trajectory of growth in the size and complexity of the crypto-asset ecosystem continues, and if financial institutions become increasingly involved with crypto-assets, then crypto-assets will pose a risk to financial stability.'[31]

MiCAR acknowledges that certain types of crypto-assets – asset-referenced tokens (ARTs) and e-money tokens (EMTs), colloquially referred to as 'stablecoins' – 'could in the future be widely adopted by retail holders, and such a development could raise additional challenges in terms of financial stability, the smooth operation of payment systems, monetary policy transmission or monetary sovereignty.'[32] The Impact Assessment, supplementing the Proposal for MiCAR, also observed that the potentially systemic nature of stablecoins implies 'significant risks for the wider financial system, thus calling for supervision that is more stringent and a ruleset that effectively minimises these risks.'[33]

That stablecoins – crypto-assets that purport to maintain a stable value by referencing an official currency, another crypto-asset, value or right – may pose specific risks is recognised globally. In 2019, the G20 mandated the FSB to examine regulatory issues raised by so-called 'global stablecoins' (GSCs) – widely adopted stablecoins with potential reach and use across multiple jurisdictions, including as a means of making payments and/or as a store of value. In 2023, the FSB published a final version of its High-level Recommendations for the regulation, supervision and oversight of GSCs.[34] These recommendations seek to promote consistent and effective regulation, supervision and oversight of GSCs to address potential financial stability risks while supporting innovation.

[29] MiCAR, Recital (5).

[30] BIS, 'Financial stability risks from cryptoassets in emerging market economies' (2023) BIS Paper No. 138 www.bis.org/publ/bppdf/bispap138.pdf.

[31] L Hermans et al, 'Decrypting financial stability risks in crypto-asset markets' (2022) Financial Stability Review, www.ecb.europa.eu/press/financial-stability-publications/fsr/special/html/ecb.fsrart202205_02~1cc6b111b4.en.html. See also P Tierno, 'The Role of Cryptocurrency in the Failures of Silvergate, Silicon Valley, and Signature Banks' (2023) Congressional Research Service Insight, crsreports.congress.gov/product/pdf/IN/IN12148.

[32] MiCAR, Recitals (5), (71) and (103).

[33] Impact Assessment (n 13) p 83.

[34] FSB, High-level Recommendations for the Regulation, Supervision and Oversight of Global Stablecoin Arrangements, 17 July 2023, www.fsb.org/wp-content/uploads/P170723-3.pdf.

One of the most famous global stablecoin arrangements was Facebook's Libra/Diem project.[35] This project was met with caution or even resentment in Europe, with German Finance Minister Olaf Scholz famously proclaiming that '[w]e cannot accept a parallel currency.'[36] The Libra/Diem project, to a significant degree, prompted the adoption of the stringent stablecoin regulation in MiCAR, and of MiCAR itself.[37] It was believed that due to the large customer base of technology companies like Facebook and because of the network effect they benefit from, stablecoins issued by them 'have the potential to gain a substantial geographical footprint'[38] and 'could pose challenges and risks to global and euro area financial markets', affecting market liquidity and asset prices.[39] Given the promised stable value of stablecoins, retail clients 'could assume that their coin holdings are as safe as bank deposits and can be transferred and spent just as easily and safely.'[40] If stablecoins were to become a preferred store of value and occupy a substantial share of the value currently held in bank deposits, 'monetary policy transmission to the real economy via banks (through official interest rates) could be undermined.'[41]

The real or perceived risks to financial stability, monetary transmission channels and monetary sovereignty shaped MiCAR's rules regarding asset-referenced tokens and e-money tokens, and prompted the inclusion of special rules for those ARTs and EMTs considered to be 'significant' (eg, Articles 43–45). These rules impose additional requirements concerning, among others, higher capital requirements and stricter liquidity management. Finally, MiCAR introduced rules for a special category of 'super-significant' stablecoins (Article 23). Becoming 'super-significant' leads to dramatic consequences: its issuer will be required to stop the issuance. According to Lehmann, '[t]his is nothing else than a prohibition of a product in the form of a hard cap that no stablecoin can surpass.'[42]

[35] On the Libra/Diem project, see DA Zetzsche, RP Buckley and DW Arner, 'Regulating Libra' (2021) 41(1) *Oxford Journal of Legal Studies* 80.

[36] Reuters, 'Germany's Scholz: We cannot accept parallel currencies such as Facebook's Libra' (19 September 2019) www.reuters.com/article/technology/germanys-scholz-we-cannot-accept-parallel-currencies-such -as-facebooks-libra-idUSKBN1W21TR/.

[37] Marco Dell'Erba, *Technology in Financial Markets: Complex Change and Disruption* (Oxford University Press, 2024) 252, observing that 'MiCAR was an attempt to respond to the political concerns originating from Libra (and then Diem).'

[38] Impact Assessment (n 13) p 20.

[39] M Adachi et al, 'A regulatory and financial stability perspective on global stablecoins' (May 2020) www.ecb.europa.eu/press/financial-stability-publications/macroprudential-bulletin/html/ecb.mpbu202005_1~3e9ac10eb1.en.html.

[40] ibid.

[41] Impact Assessment (n 13) s 2.1. See also Opinion of the European Central Bank of 19 February 2021 on a proposal for a regulation on Markets in Crypto-assets, and amending Directive (EU) 2019/1937 (CON/2021/4), para 2.1.2, observing that since 'the financial system in the euro area is predominantly based on credit institutions, abrupt shifts in the strength of the balance sheet of credit institutions can adversely affect the stability of credit institutions and their lending capacity and, with it, the transmission of monetary policy, although changes to the financial system resulting from innovation and competition are per se not undesirable.'

[42] M Lehmann, 'MiCAR – Gold Standard or Regulatory Poison for the Crypto Industry' (2024) 61 *Common Market Law Review* 699, 717.

2.2.4. MiCAR: In Search of a Balanced Approach

The previous sections highlighted different policy goals pursued by MiCAR. Among these goals are: (i) consumer and investor protection, (ii) market integrity, (iii) financial stability, and (iv) the promotion of the development and use of new technologies, such as DLT. Different rules within MiCAR may be connected to a single goal or to several goals at the same time. In principle, these goals are not mutually exclusive or contradictory. For example, by prescribing clear and detailed rules for CASPs, even if these rules impose a certain burden on them (the proportionality of such a burden can be debated in each specific context), MiCAR seeks to ensure investor protection and support the upscaling of crypto businesses. The latter point might be less obvious. However, by aiming to create clear and predictable rules and establishing a level playing field for all market participants across the EU, MiCAR strives to boost the credibility of the crypto sector, which is crucial for the success of crypto firms and the competitiveness of European enterprises on a global scale. MiCAR officially 'recognises' crypto businesses and allows them to operate within a regulated space, thus facilitating their access to the regulated financial sector.

At the same time, the goals of MiCAR sometimes have to be traded off against each other. This balancing exercise is common in financial regulation.[43] For example, the stringent regulation of stablecoins and high entry requirements (eg, authorisation as a credit institution or e-money institution for issuers of any EMTs) may prevent startups and small and medium-sized enterprises (SMEs) from entering the market. In this instance, the goals of investor protection and the protection of financial stability and monetary sovereignty take centre stage and prevail over other goals of MiCAR. As just discussed in the paragraph above, the reason for this approach stems from fears related to the proliferation of 'private money' and projects like Facebook's Libra/Diem. The question remains whether the chosen approach is proportional and strikes a fair balance between MiCAR's goals. It can be argued that the one-size-fits-all approach adopted with respect to stablecoins is hardly conducive to the further development of new technologies and the EU's DLT sector (see further chapters six and eight of this book).[44]

Another example is MiCAR's rules concerning market abuse, which aim to ensure market integrity and investor protection. On the one hand, MiCAR acknowledges that applying all the provisions of the Market Abuse Regulation (MAR) to crypto-assets falling under MiCAR would be disproportionate, particularly since issuers of crypto-assets and crypto-asset service providers are frequently SMEs.[45] On the other hand, despite its intention to adopt a tailored market abuse

[43] J Armour et al, *Principles of Financial Regulation* (Oxford University Press, 2016) 51.

[44] Lehmann (n 42) 699, 718–19, observing that in regulating stablecoins, MiCAR expresses contradictory policies and creates rules imposing a very heavy burden on stablecoin issuers, and potentially restricting technological development.

[45] MiCAR, Recital (95).

framework, MiCAR mirrors the core prohibitions and obligations present in the MAR, and, in some respects, is even more stringent than the MAR. One may therefore question whether this partial copy-and-paste approach is suitable and can support the uptake and productive use of new technologies (see chapter nine of this book).

Commenting on MiCAR's principle of 'same activity, same risk, same rule', Paech notes that a uniform, standardised approach 'could result either in excessive regulation, hampering innovation, or in insufficient regulation, exposing the financial system to unforeseen risks.'[46] Finding the right balance is undoubtedly a challenging task. MiCAR is a complex legal instrument with the potential to become a global standard for the crypto industry. Yet it will take time to be fully developed, because of the framework character of the instrument and thus will need further adjustments and clarifications, including through various Level 2 and Level 3 acts, to address specific risks and emerging developments, and possibly to correct existing imbalances. MiCAR must therefore remain flexible and adaptable to ensure it fosters innovation while safeguarding financial stability, market integrity and consumer and investor protection.

2.3. Structure of MiCAR

MiCAR consists of 119 recitals, 149 articles (divided into 9 titles) and 6 annexes. This book will largely follow MiCAR's structure.

Title I (Articles 1–3) contains provisions devoted to the subject matter, scope and definitions. It stipulates that MiCAR's subject matter includes uniform requirements 'for the offer to the public and admission to trading on a trading platform of crypto-assets other than asset-referenced tokens and e-money tokens, of asset-referenced tokens and of e-money tokens, as well as requirements for crypto-asset service providers.'[47] This title will be discussed in chapters three and four.

Title II (Articles 4–15) addresses the offer to the public and admission to trading of crypto-assets other than asset-referenced tokens and e-money tokens. We will refer to this residual category of crypto-assets as 'Title II crypto-assets' or 'Title II tokens'. The majority of the rules in this title concern the publication and notification of a specific primary market disclosure document – a crypto-asset white paper, and marketing communications. It also prescribes a special consumer protection measure – a right of withdrawal.[48] This title will be discussed in chapter five.

Title III (Articles 16–47) lays down detailed rules for ARTs and their issuers. In turn, **Title IV** (Articles 48–58) focuses on EMTs. The regulation of ARTs and EMTs (ie, 'stablecoins') is the *raison d'être* of MiCAR, as it seeks to contain the

[46] P Paech, 'New Regulations or Novel Regulation for Crypto-assets and DeFi? – The Folly of Hybrid Laws' (SSRN, 2023) 4, https://ssrn.com/abstract=457996.

[47] MiCAR, Article 1(1).

[48] MiCAR, Article 13.

rise of 'private money', which could pose substantial risk to the monetary sovereignty of the EU and its Member States. The provisions in Title III concern, among others, the authorisation of ART issuers, their obligations, and rules on reserves of assets. Title IV is less detailed, since the regulation of EMTs heavily relies on existing financial law, specifically the E-Money Directive (EMD2). This combination of rules from two distinct legal instruments, along with various exemptions, results in a complex array of rules and layers of regulation. The analysis of Titles III and IV will be provided in chapter six.

Title V (Articles 59–85) establishes a harmonised regulatory framework for the operation of crypto-asset service providers in the EU. CASPs – such as crypto exchanges, crypto brokers, and crypto custodians – play a crucial role by enabling consumers and investors to participate in the crypto economy. In regulating these market players, MiCAR addresses access to the EU crypto markets and the authorisation of CASPs, as well as obligations imposed on all CASPs (eg, the obligation to act honestly and in the best interests of clients, prudential and governance requirements). It also sets out obligations related to specific crypto-asset services (eg, custody and administration on behalf of clients, operation of a trading platform). We will explore Title V in chapter seven.

Title III, Chapter 5 (significant ARTs), **Title IV, Chapter 2** (significant EMTs) and **Title V, Chapter 5** (significant CASPs) are devoted to stablecoins and CASPs that have a certain degree of importance and potential influence, and are classified as 'significant' under MiCAR. These stablecoins and CASPs are subject to a distinct set of stringent rules and a different supervisory regime. Chapter eight of this book will explore the MiCAR-specific concept of 'significance' and examine the rules contained in the respective chapters of Titles III, IV and V.

Title VI (Articles 86–92) concerns the prevention and prohibition of market abuse involving crypto-assets. The prevention of market abuse (ie, insider dealing, market manipulation and unlawful disclosure of inside information) and the protection of market integrity are among the main goals of MiCAR. The framework of Title VI was heavily inspired by that of MAR and should ultimately instil confidence in markets in crypto-assets. The provisions of MiCAR on market abuse will be dealt with in chapter nine.

Title VII (Articles 93–138) establishes the powers available to competent authorities and to the European Banking Authority to supervise and enforce the application of MiCAR. It confers specific powers on the European Supervisory Authorities to promote supervisory convergence and consistency in the classification of crypto-assets. Title VII forms an indispensable part of the new regulatory framework for crypto-assets, equipping relevant authorities with essential powers to share information, conduct investigations and on-site inspections, and impose supervisory measures and administrative penalties in the event of suspected or identified infringements of MiCAR. It will be discussed in chapter ten.

Title VIII (Article 139) concerns the European Commission's power to adopt delegated acts to clarify and further specify certain provisions of MiCAR (eg, technical elements of the definitions in Article 3 and criteria for classifying

ARTs as significant). **Title IX** (Articles 140–149) covers a range of provisions, including those related to transitional measures, amendments to several EU laws, MiCAR's entry into force, and reporting on the application of MiCAR and recent market developments. The latter include decentralised finance (DeFi) in crypto markets, the assessment of the necessity and feasibility of regulating crypto lending and borrowing, and non-fungible tokens (NFTs). These areas of the crypto-asset market are largely outside MiCAR's current scope. This book will not separately discuss these titles, as they are either self-explanatory or primarily concern uncertain future developments and potential avenues for regulation. Nevertheless, the 'excluded' topics and their possible regulation will be analysed in chapter eleven.

Annex I specifies disclosure items in white papers for Title II crypto-assets (eg, information about the offeror/issuer, the crypto-asset project and the crypto-assets being offered). **Annex II** contains disclosure items in white papers for ARTs (eg, information about the issuer, ARTs, rights and obligations attached to the ART and the reserve of assets). **Annex III** covers disclosure items for white papers of EMTs (eg, information about the issuer, EMTs, rights and obligations attached to the EMT and the underlying technology). **Annex IV** provides for minimum capital requirements for CASPs, which depend on the assigned class of the CASP, determined with reference to specific authorised crypto-asset services. **Annex V** lists infringements referred to in Titles III and VI for issuers of significant ARTs, while **Annex VI** lists infringements of Title IV in conjunction with Title III for issuers of significant EMTs. Where relevant, these annexes will be referred to in the chapters of this book.

The book also includes a separate chapter examining the regulatory frameworks for crypto-assets and crypto-asset services in the UK (chapter twelve) – an influential jurisdiction for the crypto industry. The analysis of an alternative approach to regulating crypto businesses, and its comparison with the MiCAR regime, aims to enhance our understanding of MiCAR itself and to provide readers with a more comprehensive perspective on current regulatory developments. Moreover, to some extent, the success of MiCAR depends on its relative fitness and attractiveness compared to other competing regulatory models.

2.4. Conclusion

This chapter explains the background of MiCAR, examines its rationale and main policy goals, and outlines its structure.

The origin of MiCAR is complex, as it was developed against the background of:

(i) the ICO wave of 2017-early 2018, which coincided with thousands of new blockchain-based projects – many of which were rife with scams, such as rug pulls (where developers abandon a project after having raised the money), leading to serious consumer and investor protection concerns;

(ii) the belief expressed in the FinTech Action Plan of 8 March 2018 that blockchain/distributed ledger technologies, which underlie crypto-assets, hold promise for financial markets and infrastructures and could 'lead to a major breakthrough that will transform the way information or assets are exchanged, validated, shared and accessed through digital networks';[49]
(iii) the reports produced by the EBA and ESMA on 9 January 2019,[50] concluding that most crypto-assets fell outside the scope of EU financial services regulation and could be subject to divergent national approaches. According to these ESAs, the existing state of affairs gave rise to issues concerning consumer protection, operational resilience, market integrity and the level playing field across the EU; and
(iv) the stablecoin initiative announced by Facebook in the spring/summer 2019 – the Libra project, fears of which resulted in the stringent regulation of stablecoins under MiCAR. According to some, it is the Libra (later renamed to Diem) project that represents the very *raison d'être* of MiCAR.[51]

Thus, MiCAR's drafters considered the potential benefits and promises of new technologies and crypto-assets embracing them, such as enhanced competition in the payment market, a streamlined capital raising process for SMEs, increased efficiencies in the 'traditional' financial sector, including the ability to record information in a secure and immutable format.[52] However, they were also aware of the multiple risks posed by crypto-assets and related activities. Consequently, MiCAR pursues several general and related policy objectives. It aims to: (i) instil appropriate levels of consumer and investor protection and market integrity; (ii) support innovation and promote the development of crypto-assets and the broader use of DLT; (iii) ensure financial stability; and (iv) establish a sound legal framework that creates legal certainty and clearly defines the regulatory treatment of all crypto-assets not covered by existing financial services legislation.

As argued in this chapter, while these objectives are not necessarily mutually exclusive or conflicting, the EU legislator – when drafting MiCAR – engaged in a balancing exercise, giving more weight to one objective over another in specific contexts. For example, one could argue that by imposing stringent requirements on issuers of ARTs and EMTs, MiCAR prioritises the goals of financial stability and investor protection over the goal of supporting innovation by ensuring experimentation and market access for startups and SMEs. In any event, it will require experience in practice to say something useful about whether the chosen regulatory approach strikes a fair balance between the four major policy objectives.

[49] FinTech Action plan.
[50] ESMA Advice and EBA Report.
[51] Dell'Erba (n 37) 252, observing that 'MiCAR was an attempt to respond to the political concerns originating from Libra (and then Diem)'; P Maume, 'The Regulation on Markets in Crypto-Assets (MiCAR): Landmark Codification, or First Step of Many, or Both?' (2023) 2 *ECFR* 243, 247, observing that 'there is no doubt that this announcement [announcement of the planned launch of Facebook's own cryptocurrency called Libra] provided the main impetus for the creation of MiCAR.'
[52] Impact Assessment (n 13) para 1.3.

The entry into force of MiCAR in June 2023 is likely to be the first step in the development of a comprehensive regulatory framework for the crypto economy. Further fine-tuning is already being made by means of Level 2 legislation (ie, implementing and delegated acts) and Level 3 guidelines published by the EBA and ESMA. MiCAR itself provides for possible amendments. For example, the appropriateness of the thresholds to classify an ART or EMT as significant should be reviewed by the EC as part of its review of MiCAR's application. This review may result in a legislative proposal. Additionally, Article 142 prescribes the preparation of a report on the latest developments with respect to crypto-assets, particularly on 'excluded' topics such as DeFi, crypto lending and borrowing, and NFTs.[53] Given the recent failures of crypto lenders (eg, Voyager, Celsius),[54] the probability of new legislative initiatives or even MiCAR2, is considerable.[55] In this respect, MiCAR is a living instrument, which must be adaptable to deal with fast-changing technologies and rapidly evolving crypto-asset markets.

[53] See Joint EBA-ESMA Report on the recent developments in crypto-assets (Article 142 of MiCA), 16 January 2025.

[54] On failures of crypto lenders and possible avenues for regulation, see Kokorin (n 23) 500; E Avgouleas and A Seretakis, 'How Should Crypto Lending Be Regulated Under EU Law?' (2023) 24 *EBOR* 421.

[55] In her testimony before the European Parliament in June 2022, the ECB's president Christine Lagarde suggested that crypto-lending and borrowing required a separate regulatory response – 'MiCAR II'. Maume (n 51) 243, 275, predicting that 'MiCAR2 is already on the horizon.'

3

MiCAR Scope and Key Terms

PHILIPP PAECH

3.1. Introduction

While the various titles of MiCAR address substantively different activities,[1] they all rest on a commonly defined scope. The nominal definition of this scope appears in Title I of the Regulation. However, these rules are incomplete in isolation; to fully understand the scope, they must be read in conjunction with other provisions scattered throughout MiCAR, along with its recitals, relevant rules from the broader EU *acquis* (such as the Markets in Financial Instruments Directive (MiFID II) and the E-Money Directive (EMD2)), and documents issued by EU regulatory authorities – the European Securities and Markets Authority (ESMA) and the European Banking Authority (EBA).

MiCAR's scope is designed to encompass persons engaging in specific activities, such as the offering of crypto-assets to the public or crypto-asset exchange services, irrespective of who conducts them and whether the market participant is required to be authorised. This creates a framework that imposes obligations on anyone engaging in such activities, thus casting the widest possible personal scope.

Regarding material scope, MiCAR fills a gap that previously existed in the EU *acquis* by covering instruments resembling financial products that are neither money nor subject to MiFID II, EMD2, Undertakings for Collective Investment in Transferable Securities Directive (UCITS Directive), or other EU rules regulating financial products. The range of instruments it covers is wide. It defines two very specific and heavily regulated types of crypto-assets – asset-referenced tokens (AMTs) and e-money tokens (EMTs), with a view to addressing concerns around so-called 'stablecoins' such as USDTether and USDCircle, and a lightly regulated catch-all category of instruments encompassing anything in the form of a DLT-bound token that represents a right or value. This latter category encompasses Bitcoin and similar products, and generally every product that is a crypto-asset while not falling within the categories of ART or EMT.

[1] Notably, Titles II–VI (the so-called issuer regime for different types of crypto-assets), Title V (the crypto-asset service provider 'CASP' regime) and Title VI (the market abuse regime).

While no earlier EU financial market legislation hinges on the use of a specific technology, MiCAR does. The EU legislator apparently accepted the notion of the unique nature of '*crypto*', awkwardly limiting MiCAR's scope to instruments existing on a DLT network. This clear departure from the EU legislator's usual principle of technological neutrality could, in time, result in competitive distortions, offer space for regulatory arbitrage and create new regulatory gaps.

3.2. Personal Scope of MiCAR

The personal scope encompasses natural and legal persons, as well as certain other undertakings engaged in the issuance, public offering, and admission to trading of crypto-assets or the provision of crypto-asset services within the EU.[2] That is, the scope is defined by reference to certain types of persons (section 3.2.1) exercising certain types of activities (section 3.2.2).

3.2.1. Natural and Legal Persons, Certain Other Undertakings

The regulation casts a wide net regarding the types of persons generally falling within its purview. The inclusion of natural and legal persons ensures that every market actor is covered by the obligations and prohibitions of the law. The criteria defining natural and legal persons and their ability to engage in financial services are set by the national law of the Member States.

Personal scope and authorisation requirement. Consistent with most[3] of the EU financial services *acquis*, natural persons are precluded from significant parts of MiCAR-regulated activity, as they cannot obtain the relevant authorisation, colloquially referred to as a licence, (see Table 3.1 below) and as a consequence 'shall not […]' engage in the relevant activity.[4] This is the case even though the definitions of the terms 'issuer' and 'offeror' in Article 3(10) and (13) expressly include natural persons.

The effect of first including natural persons within the scope but subsequently excluding them from the range of potential licensees is that natural persons who *do* engage in the issuance or offering of crypto-assets nonetheless remain issuers and offerors in functional terms. In the absence of the relevant licence, they are engaging illegally in a regulated activity, yet the obligations under MiCAR continue to apply. This approach conforms to the rationales underlying MiCAR, notably its aim to protect the counterparties of offerors, issuers, and service providers. Their interests would not be served if the activity of an unlicensed natural person were

[2] MiCAR, Articles 2(1) and 3(10) and (13).

[3] An exception is the Consumer Credit Directive 2014/17/EU, which allows a regulated financial services to be provided by natural persons.

[4] MiCAR, Articles 4(1), 16(1), 48(1) and 59(1).

not regulated. They are better served by the imposition of MiCAR obligations on issuers, offerors, and service providers, even if they lack the relevant licence.

Further, this approach allows for the seamless transfer of ongoing crypto-asset activity (ie, issuance, offering, or services) from an (unlicensed) natural person to a (licensed) legal person, where the relevant parties work towards healing non-compliance with the licensing requirement. This seems particularly suitable to avoid any regulatory vacuum in situations where there is uncertainty regarding the status of a partnership of natural persons. Such partnerships can, in principle, obtain a licence as an 'other undertaking' for some of the MiCAR-regulated types of activities (see below). In the event of any uncertainty regarding the authorisation status of a relevant partnership, it is clear that its activity remains subjected to MiCAR, as the natural persons constituting the partnership fall within the personal scope of the MiCAR rules.

DeFi. The anchoring of the personal scope on the term 'person' also bears consequences with regard to so-called decentralised finance ('DeFi') applications. It has the effect that computer algorithms which autonomously issue crypto-assets, offer them to the public, or seek their admission to trading, or that provide crypto-asset service functions, are not subject to MiCAR rules. They are not 'persons' under Article 2(1), and hence the regulation does not apply to them due to the lack of a suitable addressee. Activities performed by DeFi applications therefore remain unregulated.[5] However, this exclusion does not apply to functions that are 'DeFi in name only', ie, those applications that are described or perceived as autonomous but which are *de facto* controlled or controllable by persons.[6]

Further, where the market activity is partly decentralised, for instance, where issuance is purely algorithmic, but crypto-asset services are provided by persons, MiCAR applies to those persons, but not to the purely algorithmic activity.[7] These persons are encompassed within MiCAR's scope, and authorisation for relevant activities is consequently necessary, following an approach that prioritises substantial analysis over branding or marketing.[8] For a detailed discussion of decentralisation in the context of MiCAR, see chapter eleven of this book.

Certain other undertakings. MiCAR acknowledges that Member States' laws recognise a variety of business organisations not structured as legal persons, but rather as partnerships of natural persons or combinations of natural and legal persons. Depending on the jurisdiction, such organisations may, under national law, undertake regulated activities, such as the provision of certain financial services. Maintaining this practice, MiCAR introduces as a third category of

[5] See also MiCAR, Recital (22); see also MiCAR, Article 142.

[6] See Danish Financial Supervisory Authority, 'Decentralised finance and the markets for crypto-assets: When is your offering exempt from regulation?' (25 June 2024) www.dfsa.dk/news/2024/jun/crypto-assets_250624.

[7] See P Maume, 'The Regulation on Markets in Crypto-Assets (MiCAR): Landmark Codification, or First Step of Many, or Both? (2023) 20(2) *European Company and Financial Law Review* 244, 266.

[8] See ESMA, Draft technical Standards specifying certain requirements in relation to conflicts of interest for crypto-asset service providers under the Markets in Crypto Assets Regulation (MiCA), ESMA18-72330276-1634, 31 May 2024.

market actor 'certain other undertakings'.[9] This category allows the competent national authority to licence such actors for specific types of MiCAR-regulated activity, provided that the relevant type of undertaking meets requirements ensuring a level of safeguards comparable to those offered by the national legal framework governing legal persons.[10] This approach is consistent with the approach taken in MiFID II.[11]

The following Table 3.1 illustrates which type of market actor can exercise the different MiCAR-regulated activities.

Table 3.1 Crypto-asset activities and persons engaging in them

Relevant provision	**Activity**	**Personal scope**
Title II		
Article 4(1)	Offering Title-II crypto-assets to the public	Legal person
Article 5(1)	Seeking admission to trading of Title-II crypto-assets	Legal person
Title III		
Article 16(1) first and third subparagraph, Article 17	Offering ARTs to the public or seeking their admission to trading[12]	Legal person, or certain other undertaking with similar safeguards, or credit institution
Title IV		
Article 48(1) first and second subparagraph, Recital (66)	Offering of EMTs to the public or seeking their admission to trading	Credit or e-money institution
Title V		
Article 59(1) and 3	Provision of crypto-asset services	Legal person, or certain other undertaking with similar safeguards, or credit institution or certain other types of regulated financial institution
Title VI		
Article 86(1)	Market abuse prohibition	Person

[9] MiCAR, Recital (22) and Article 2(1)).

[10] MiCAR, Articles 16(1) and 59(3).

[11] See MiFID II, Article 4(1)(1)).

[12] The third sub-paragraph of MiCAR Article 16(1) states that other undertakings 'may issue' ARTs only if their legal form ensures an equivalent level of protection. The reference to the activity of *issuance* is, however, confusing, as Article 16(1) otherwise only regulates the offering and admission

As shown in Table 3.1, a notable divergence exists between offerors of Title-II crypto-assets, who must be legal persons, and offerors of ARTs, which may include 'other undertakings' provided equivalent safeguards are in place. Although the rules on ARTs under Title III are comprehensive and complex – reflecting the significantly higher systemic and consumer protection risks associated with ARTs – Article 16(1) permits 'certain other undertakings' to be authorised as ART issuers or offerors. By contrast, such undertakings are prohibited from acting as offerors of the less stringently regulated Title-II crypto-assets. This distinction arises because ART offerors, or those seeking admission for ART trading, must be authorised. This authorisation process enables the competent authority to review and assess the governance structures of the undertaking, ensuring conformity with relevant standards. In the case of Title-II crypto-assets, where no authorisation requirement applies, governance standards can only be assured by mandating that the offeror or person seeking admission is organised as a legal person.

The precise delineation between 'natural persons' and 'certain other undertakings' is not specified in MiCAR itself, but rather falls under the national law of the competent Member State. Nevertheless, MiCAR imposes significant limitations on which other types of undertakings can issue ARTs or obtain an authorisation as a crypto-asset service provider. It requires that their legal form must ensure a level of protection for third parties equivalent to that afforded by legal persons, and that they are subject to equivalent prudential supervision appropriate to their legal form.[13] As MiCAR is a regulation, its rules are applied directly by national authorities and ultimately interpreted by EU courts. However, the assessment of whether the relevant requirements for equivalence are fulfilled may create fringe cases, inviting differing viewpoints between market participants and authorities. Consequently, some residual uncertainty regarding which undertakings can be authorised under Titles III and V will be likely to persist for a period and potentially constitute an opportunity for regulatory arbitrage.

Article 48(1) allows for different interpretations as to who can offer EMTs to the public or seek their admission to trading. The second subparagraph derogates from subparagraph 1 in that unspecified 'other persons' may offer to the public or seek admission to trading of EMTs. Even though the second subparagraph does not make clear to which of the offeror-criteria in the first subparagraph it refers, it must be read as only referring to the words 'unless that person is the issuer'. The requirement in Article 48(1)(a) remains applicable, ie, only credit institutions or e-money institutions are allowed to offer EMTs to the public or seek their admission to trading.

to trading. The intention of the legislator was probably to clarify that other undertakings that issue ARTs may offer them or seek their admission to trading only if their legal form provides the relevant level of protection.

[13] MiCAR, Articles 16(1) and 59(3).

3.2.2. Activities

Article 2(1) MiCAR sets out the two strands of activities determining the regulatory architecture of MiCAR.

First, MiCAR applies to persons engaged in the creation of crypto-assets and their initial distribution, as expressed in Article 2(1) by reference to:

- issuance of crypto-assets;
- offering them to the public; or
- seeking[14] admission of them to trading.

This bundle of activities is broadly analogous to activities on the traditional primary capital market. The logic of the triad of issuer, offeror and person seeking admission is partly copied from the Prospectus Regulation.[15] The rules govern the entirety of these activities and are often referred to as the 'issuer regime'. The issuer regime is described in section 3.2.2.1.

Second, MiCAR also applies to persons that provide services related to crypto-assets, termed 'crypto-asset service providers' or 'CASPs'. This activity is broadly comparable to services on the secondary capital market offered by investment firms, trading venues and other well-known types of service providers. For the list of relevant services, see Article 3(1)(16)). Many of the rules governing the activities of CASPs are inspired by the MiFID II/MiFIR regime. The set of rules governing these activities is often referred to as the 'CASP regime'. It is analysed in section 3.2.2.2.

Following Article 2(2), certain persons are excluded from the scope of the issuer or CASP regimes. This limitation of the personal scope is discussed in section 3.2.2.3. Article 2(1) does not mention the market abuse regime introduced by MiCAR Title VI, which has a universal personal scope. This regime will be covered in section 3.2.2.4.

3.2.2.1. Persons Engaging in Issuance, Offering or Seeking Admission to Trading of Crypto-assets (Titles II–IV)

The rules of the so-called issuer regime are laid down in MiCAR Titles II–IV. They address persons that the law distinguishes on the basis of the functions they perform, notably, the issuance of crypto-assets, and the subsequent initial distribution of the relevant crypto-assets in the market, which comprises

[14] See further section 3.2.2.1.

[15] Prospectus Regulation, Articles 11(1), 20(2). Note the different wording: 'person *asking* for admission'. The notable difference between these two regimes is that MiCAR hinges on the authorisation of the crypto-asset issuance without separately approving the white paper, whereas the Prospectus Regulation hinges on the approval of the relevant prospectus, see also Maume (n 7) 256.

the offering to the public and the seeking of admission to trading of these crypto-assets.

Distinguishing the three functions. The functions of issuing, offering to the public and seeking admission to trading are not necessarily performed by different actors. The issuer can itself offer the crypto-assets it issues to the public or seek their admission to trading. This is, in the understanding of MiCAR, the standard case for ARTs and EMTs, as a person shall not make an offer to the public or seek the admission to trading of an ART or EMT, unless that person is the issuer of the respective tokens.[16] The issuer can, however, permit via a written consent other persons to cater for, or participate in, the initial distribution by allowing them to offer the crypto-assets to the public or seek admission to trading.[17] Therefore, the term 'issuer regime' is slightly misleading, as the rules addressing those who offer crypto-assets to the public or seek their admission to trading may not necessarily be limited in application to those issuing crypto-assets, but may also apply to other persons who will be covered by the relevant rules of Titles II–IV.

The drafting of the personal scope of MiCAR oscillates between functional language and language that appears to refer to specific types of entities instead. Notably, the frequent references to 'issuer' and 'offeror' throughout MiCAR complicate the understanding of the rules, as they appear to be referring to different types of persons, whereas the function alone is the relevant criterion for the application of the relevant material rules. The limited reference made in MiCAR to the person that 'engages in the issuance/offer' or 'issues/offers', or to the 'person seeking admission' is closer to the functional logic of the rules.

3.2.2.1.1. Issuer

The wording 'person [that is] engaged in the issuance [...] of crypto-assets' is used for purposes of defining the scope of MiCAR in Article 2(1). Throughout the remainder of the text that person is referred to as the 'issuer'.

The issuer (who potentially also offers the relevant crypto-assets and seeks their admission to trading, see sections 3.2.2.1.2 and 3.2.2.1.3) is the main addressee of the rules of Titles III and IV on ARTs and EMTs.[18] Issuance of Title-II crypto-assets is not regulated, and, hence, the issuer, issuance or issuing are not addressed in Title II. Table 3.2 below lists the rules that address the issuer with respect to the function of issuing crypto-assets. Note that the same person may be subjected to additional rules if it also offers crypto-assets or seeks their admission to trading (see the following sections).

[16] MiCAR, Articles 16(1) and 48(1).
[17] MiCAR, Articles 16(1) second subparagraph and 48(1) second subparagraph.
[18] cf different opinion Maume in ch 6, s 6.2.1.2 of this book: 'MiCAR does not regulate issuing ART, but introducing them to the EU market [...].'

Table 3.2 Obligations of issuers under MiCAR

Relevant provision	**Obligation**
Title III	
Article 16	Acquire authorisation to offer ARTs to the public and to seek their admission to trading
Article 19 with Article 26	Draw up crypto-asset white paper for ARTs according to requirements
Article 22	Reporting to competent authority on ARTs
Article 23	Restrictions on issuance of ARTs used widely as means of exchange
Article 25(1)	Notification of competent authority of any major changes or material modifications concerning ARTs or ART issuer[19]
Article 25(2)	Draw up a modified white paper
Article 26(1)	Liability for information in a white paper
Article 27	Obligation of ART issuer to act honestly etc.
Article 28	Publication of white paper by ART issuer
Article 29	Requirements for marketing communication relating to an offer to the public of an ART, or to the admission to trading of such ART
Article 30	Ongoing information to holders of ARTs
Article 31	Complaints handling procedures by ART issuer
Article 32	Identify, prevent, manage and disclose conflicts of interest
Article 33	Notify changes to management of ART issuer
Article 34	Establish robust governance arrangements
Article 35	Comply with own funds requirements
Article 36–38	Set up reserve of assets
Article 39	Right of redemption against issuers of ARTs
Article 40	Prohibition to pay interest in relation to ARTs
Article 44 (voluntary)	Apply for voluntary classification as significant ART
Article 45	Additional obligations for issuers of significant ART
Article 46	Draft and maintain a recovery plan
Article 47	Draft and maintain a redemption plan

(continued)

[19] cf Article 18: the authorisation is originally sought by the person offering crypto-assets or seeking their admission to trading.

Table 3.2 ***(Continued)***

Relevant provision	Obligation
Title IV	
Article 49(3)	Issue EMTs at par value
Article 49(4)	Redeem the monetary value of the EMT at par at any time in funds
Article 49(5)	Prominently state redemption conditions
Article 49(6)	Not demand a fee for redemption
Article 50(1)	Not grant interest on an EMT
Article 51 with Article 52	Draw up crypto-asset white paper for EMT according to requirements
Article 54	Requirements regarding the investment of funds received by issuers
Article 58	Observe risk management and governance standards from ART regime (Articles 36, 37, 38 and 45) if EMT issue is 'significant'

Determining the issuer. The definition of 'issuer' of crypto-assets refers to a 'person [...] who issues crypto-assets'.[20] In its circularity, it is in line with other EU instruments, such as the Capital Requirements Directive (CRD), Market Abuse Regulation (MAR) and the Prospectus Regulation. Once authorisation has been granted in accordance with Article 21, the person of the issuer is clearly identified. However, on the way there, the authority may have to decide whether the person named as 'issuer' in the application[21] is *de facto* the issuer of the relevant crypto-asset.

MiCAR does not provide a catalogue of criteria to establish who this person is, nor does it expressly deal with the situation that more than one person is involved in the initial creation and distribution of crypto-assets, such as in a 'consortium of issuers'. Therefore, the description of the role of the issuer as the entity that has control over the creation of crypto-assets (MiCAR, Recital (20)) is not clear enough.

It is also potentially misleading, considering that issuance is highly regulated in respect of ARTs and EMTs in MiCAR Titles III and IV. The logic of Titles III and IV requires resorting to traditional financial law concepts (which also apply across the remainder of the EU *acquis*), identifying the issuer as the person that is obliged towards the holder of the relevant asset. In the context of ARTs, that person would be the person obliged to pay the sum of money ('funds') equivalent to the market value of the relevant ART.[22] In the context of EMTs, the issuer

[20] MiCAR, Article 3(1)(10).
[21] MiCAR, Article 18(2).
[22] MiCAR, Article 39(1).

is the person against whom holders of e-money tokens have a claim at par.[23] In both cases, this person should be identifiable from the white paper[24] and the authorisation register and, hence, is to be regarded as the issuer for purposes of MiCAR. The identification of the obligor, central to the character of the issuer, therefore, also determines who is subject to all other issuer-related obligations.

The case of Title-II crypto-assets is slightly more complex, as these vary in nature. Many Title-II crypto-assets, including utility tokens,[25] also aim to provide the holder with a right (whether the right is sufficiently linked to the crypto-asset is a matter of applicable private law). However, as these rights can be very different in nature and directed against different obligors, they are not a suitable criterion when it comes to identifying the issuer. Other Title-II crypto-assets, such as Bitcoin, do not encompass any rights at all. Therefore, the criterion set out in Recital (20) may serve at least as a fallback. In any case, Title II does not regulate issuance, and hence, the identification of the issuer is not important for its application.

3.2.2.1.2. Offeror

Activity. Offering crypto-assets means engaging in their initial distribution to holders. The term 'offering' describes the provision of the pertinent information to prospective holders. The precise meaning of 'offeror' and 'offer to the public' is outlined in Articles 3(1)(12) and 3(1)(13) MiCAR and is a 'communication to persons in any form, and by any means, presenting sufficient information on the terms of the offer and the crypto-assets to be offered so as to enable prospective holders to decide whether to purchase those crypto-assets'. Contrary to what the wording 'purchase' may suggest, it need not be a transaction that involves any kind of consideration, and, hence, 'acquire' would have been the better term here.

'Offering' encompasses the initial communication on the terms of the crypto-asset issuance, as would be done typically, but not necessarily, by the issuer, notably by way of including the relevant information in the white paper or through marketing communication. Specific rules on the content of the white paper and on marketing communication are included in Titles II, III and IV and are examined in chapters five and six of this book.[26]

Offering – Placing. There can only be one single offeror per crypto-asset issue. All activity relating to further dissemination of that information is qualified as 'placing', ie, the 'marketing, on behalf of or for the account of the offeror or a party related to the offeror, of crypto-assets to purchasers'.[27] Specific rules on the content

[23] MiCAR, Article 49(2) and 3.
[24] MiCAR, Article 19(1)(d) and Annex II Part D(2) and (9).
[25] See ch 4 on typology of crypto-assets.
[26] MiCAR, Articles 6, 7, 19, 29, 51 and 53.
[27] MiCAR, Article 3(1)(22).

of the white paper and on marketing communications are included in Titles II, III and IV and are examined in chapters five and six of this book.

To the public. The wording of the definition of 'offer to the public' is particularly broad; it does not require more than 'a communication to persons'.[28] No specific intent is required, and no further criteria on the circle of addressees are provided that could flesh out the idea of 'to the public'.[29] Following the definition, a small number of addressees seem to suffice for a person to be considered an 'offeror'. This may result in slight divergences stemming from the national context of supervisory practice. However, considering this issue in respect of the definition's precursor in the EU prospectus regime, Moloney emphasises that the broad, principles-based definition of 'offer to the public' under the prospectus regime was resilient since its introduction in 2003, despite initial concerns that it could create uncertainty.[30] It had also proven effective in defining the scope of the prospectus regime and in creating desired deterrent effects in relation to pre-offer communications by analysts connected to the issuer (who, as a consequence, had to take care not to trigger the prospectus requirements with their communications), also as a result of ESMA's efforts in respect of supervisory convergence.

It is often claimed that market structure and market practice in the traditional capital markets and the market for crypto-assets diverge in terms of reach ('global'), market structure ('decentralised') and communication methods ('social media') and that concepts adopted from pre-existing legislation could not be transposed into crypto-asset regulation. However, these differences, to the extent that they exist, are only gradual and do not imply that concepts borrowed from pre-existing regulation *per se* do not deliver the desired results.

Sufficient information. Similar to the issue just discussed, the necessary content of the communication for it to qualify as 'offering' is largely unspecified. The definitions of 'offeror' and 'offer' ultimately hinge on the expectations of the prospective buyer ('[…] so as to enable prospective buyers to decide […]'). This is not a very clear criterion and may set the bar for qualifying as an offering very low, given that crypto investors, at least at the moment of writing, often content themselves with rudimentary information before buying. However, this openness only exists in the context of defining the offeror. Materially, the required content of the white paper and of marketing communications is subject to detailed rules.[31] Separate exemptions are also provided for offerings to fewer than 150 persons per Member State, small and subsequent offers (see chapter five of this book).

Obligations. Table 3.3 below lists the rules that are directed at the offeror (which may or may not be the issuer) of crypto-assets.

[28] MiCAR Article 3(1)(12) and (13).

[29] On 'the public' see EBA 2013 report on definition of credit institution.

[30] N Moloney, *EU Securities and Financial Markets Regulation*, 4th edn (Oxford University Press, 2023) section II.4.3.2.

[31] See further chs 5 and 6 of this book.

Table 3.3 Obligations of offerors under MiCAR

Provision	Obligation
Title II	
Article 4	Be a legal person; draw up a white paper; comply with marketing obligations (see Articles 6 and 7)
Article 8(1) and (6)	Notify the white paper, notify targeted host Member States via home Member State
Article 9	Publish the white paper
Article 10	Publish the number of crypto-assets issued
Article 12	Modify the white paper and marketing materials and notify about these modifications
Article 13	Inform on right of withdrawal
Article 14	Comply with conduct requirements (eg, act honestly, communicate in a fair manner)
Article 15	Liability for information in a white paper
Title III	
Articles 16 and 18	Be a legal person and be authorised
Article 29	Comply with requirements regarding marketing communications
Title IV	
Article 48	Be a credit or e-money institution and notify relevant authority
Article 53	Comply with requirements regarding marketing communications

Offerors other than the issuer. Other persons than the issuer, including crypto-asset service providers, can act as offerors,[32] provided they comply with the relevant requirements.[33] Those persons that offer crypto-assets to the public, and which are not at the same time the issuer of the relevant crypto-assets, have to comply with certain rules directed at the issuer. Notably they are subjected to conduct rules,[34] must comply with standards regarding marketing communications,[35] and are prohibited from granting interest to holders of EMTs and ARTs.[36] This logic does

[32] See MiCAR, Article 5(2), Article 16(1) second subparagraph, Article 48(1) second subparagraph.
[33] See EBA statement, 5 July 2024, www.eba.europa.eu/regulation-and-policy/asset-referenced-and-e-money-tokens-micar.
[34] See eg MiCAR, Article 27.
[35] MiCAR, Articles 29 and 53.
[36] MiCAR, Articles 40 and 50.

not apply to the offering to trading of Title-II crypto-assets, as their issuance is not regulated by MiCAR and all material rules from the outset address the offeror or person seeking admission to trading.

3.2.2.1.3. Person Seeking Admission to Trading

Article 1(2)(a) refers to 'admission of crypto-assets to trading on a trading platform for crypto-assets'. Article 2(1) refers to persons that are engaged in the 'admission to trading of crypto-assets'. Neither of these mentions amounts to a dedicated definition, which could normally be expected in Article 3.

Terminology. Remarkably, Articles 1 and 2 use wording that differs from the material rules in Titles II–IV, which refer to 'seeking' admission to trading of crypto-assets. The terminology in Articles 1 and 2, and consequentially the precise nature of the relevant activity (ie, seeking admission *or* admission as such), therefore, appear to be unclear. Here, it is helpful to consider the context: the activity of 'admitting to trading' is a function of the trading platform.[37] 'Admitting to trading' is hence part of the activities regulated in the CASP regime in MiCAR Title V as 'operating a trading platform', see chapter seven.[38] By contrast, the activity addressed in the context of the initial distribution of crypto-assets is the 'seeking admission to trading', as the issuer, or its representative, envisages the distribution of the relevant crypto-assets through a trading platform.[39]

The wording chosen in Articles 1(2)(a) and 2(1) therefore appears incongruous. The relevant activity, which is also discussed in this section, is 'seeking admission to trading'. This is also in line with the logic followed in the Prospectus Regulation.

Delineating the activity. The concept of 'admission to trading' is borrowed from MiFID and also used in other EU financial services instruments, including the MAR and the Prospectus Regulation. Under this concept, the operator of a trading venue verifies compliance with relevant standards required for being admitted to that specific trading venue, thereby adding a layer of checks, with a view to contributing to higher standards in investor protection and market integrity. The activity of the person 'seeking' admission to trading on a crypto-asset trading platform accordingly involves providing the relevant information to the operator of that platform alongside the request to admit the crypto-assets to trading.[40]

Obligations. Persons seeking admission of crypto-assets to trading are subject to a number of obligations, some of which are specific to this activity, whereas most obligations are identical to those applying to the activitiy of offering crypto-assets to the public (see section 3.2.2.1.2).

[37] MiCAR, Article 3(1)(18). See also MiFID II, Article 51.
[38] MiCAR, Article 76(1)(a).
[39] MiCAR, Articles 5(1), 16(1) and 48(1).
[40] MiCAR, Article 76(2).

Table 3.4 Obligations of persons seeking admission to trading under MiCAR

Provision	Obligation
Title II	
Article 5	Be a legal person; draw up a white paper; comply with marketing obligations requirements (see Articles 6 and 7)
Article 8(1) and (6)	Notify the white paper, notify targeted host Member States via home Member State
Article 9	Publish the white paper
Article 12	Modify the white paper and marketing materials and notify about these modifications
Article 14	Comply with conduct requirements (eg, act honestly, communicate in a fair manner)
Article 15	Liability for information in the white paper
Title III	
Articles 16 and 18	Application for authorisation (see section 3.2.1)
Article 29	Comply with requirements regarding marketing communications
Title IV	
Article 48	Requirements for the offer to the public or admission to trading of EMTs (issuer authorisation and notification of a white paper)
Article 53	Comply with requirements regarding marketing communications

In line with requirements applicable to offerors (see section 3.2.2.1.2), persons that seek admission of crypto-assets to trading and which are not at the same time the issuer of the relevant crypto-assets, have to comply with certain rules aligned with those for the issuer. Notably, they are subjected to conduct rules,[41] must comply with standards regarding marketing communications,[42] and are prohibited from granting interest to holders of EMTs and ARTs.[43]

3.2.2.2. *Persons Providing Crypto-asset Services (Title V)*

The general scope of MiCAR Title V is set out in Article 2(1) MiCAR, which states that the regulation applies to 'persons that provide services related to crypto-assets'. The definitions of the different types of crypto-asset services can be found in Article 3(1)(16)–(26) MiCAR. The primary consequence of an activity being

[41] MiCAR, Article 27.
[42] MiCAR, Article 29 and 53.
[43] MiCAR, Articles 40 and 50.

qualified as one of these services is that the service shall not be provided within the EU, unless authorised.[44]

Crypto-asset services. The scope for the authorisation requirement flows from a combination of the scope provision, definitions and the authorisation requirement.[45] It is very wide, as it encompasses any activity that materially matches one of the definitions of services contained in the list provided in Article 3(1)(17)–(26). Article 59 stipulates that a person must not provide crypto-asset services within the EU, unless properly authorised. There is no requirement that the relevant market participant engages in that activity in the course of a business, or that the activity is exercised regularly or provided on a professional basis for it to constitute a crypto-asset service under MiCAR. Hence, exercising these activities – even occasionally – triggers the authorisation requirement of Article 59(1).

Crypto-asset service provider. Crypto-asset service providers are persons whose occupation or business is the provision of one or more crypto-asset services to clients on a professional basis.[46] This definition is borrowed, with minor modifications, from the definition of 'investment firm' in MiFID II.[47]

However, it is not the definition of a crypto-asset service *provider* that defines the scope of MiCAR. This follows, on the one hand, from the wording of the scope provision in Article 2(1) (see section 3.2.2) and, on the other hand, from the fact that an existing authorisation according to Article 59 is a constitutive element of the classification as a crypto-asset service provider.

Constitutive authorisation. Article 59(1)(a) states that a person shall not provide crypto-asset services unless it is authorised as a crypto-asset service provider. The relevant authorisation is provided pursuant to Articles 62 and 63. The authorisation requirement is constitutive, ie, without this permission, a person providing relevant services is not a crypto-asset service provider who lacks permission but rather an actor engaging in an illegal activity. This flows directly from the wording of Article 59(1) when read together with Article 3(1)(15). Additionally, Article 59(5) stipulates that a person who is not a crypto-asset service provider shall by no means pretend to be one or create confusion in that respect.

This makes the remaining criteria mentioned in Article 3(1)(15) – ie, 'business or occupation' and 'on a professional basis' – difficult to understand. *Before* an actor has obtained authorisation under Articles 59 and 63 MiCAR, it is not a 'crypto-asset service provider', precisely because it lacks authorisation. It is irrelevant whether the service is provided as 'business or occupation' and 'on a professional basis'. *After* an actor has obtained the authorisation, the criteria of 'occupation or business' and 'on a professional basis' are also irrelevant, as they

[44] MiCAR, Article 59(1).
[45] MiCAR, Article 2(1), Article 3(1)(16)–(26) and Article 59(1).
[46] MiCAR, Article 3(1)(15)).
[47] MiFID II, Article 4(1)(1).

would have already been considered during the approval process and hence play no further role once authorisation has been granted.

The literal scope of the MiCAR crypto-asset service-related provisions, as just described, and the ensuing prohibition to provide unauthorised services, therefore extend to anyone providing relevant services, even occasionally and on a non-professional basis.

In practice, however, it is unlikely and impractical that national competent authorities will implement the prohibition without any minimum threshold regarding regularity, professionality or profit motive. This is best illustrated by considering the example of 'providing advice on crypto-assets'.[48] This activity clearly needs such a minimum threshold before the authorisation requirement and the specific requirements regarding the conduct of business[49] are triggered. These minimum intervention thresholds will be a matter of national supervisory practice, and a certain degree of divergence on this question can be expected, with room for guidance from the EBA or ESMA, for example, in the context of their Q&A tools.

Notification regime for authorised financial services providers. For specific types of financial service providers which are authorised under other EU regimes – notably, credit institutions, central securities depositories (CSDs), investment firms, e-money institutions, UCITS management companies, alternative investment fund (AIF) managers and MiFID II market operators – a notification regime applies instead of the authorisation regime.[50]

For credit institutions, the range of crypto-asset services they can provide, subject to prior notification, is unrestricted.[51] For all other types of regulated institutions, however, the range of crypto-asset services they can provide under the notification regime is tailored to align with their general activity and authorisation, and thus is restricted, largely to crypto-asset services which are equivalent to services they already provide in relation to funds and financial instruments.[52]

The firms covered by the notification regime can thus provide relevant crypto-asset services. As soon as they begin providing them, they are within the scope of the relevant MiCAR rules. However, it is not immediately obvious whether or not they are crypto-asset service providers in the sense of Article 3(1)(15) or whether the crypto-asset service would, after notification, be considered an ancillary activity covered by their original licence. The wording in Article 60 appears incoherent, as it uses different terms for the financial services provider in question: 'applicant crypto-asset service provider', 'crypto-asset

[48] MiCAR, Article 3(1)(16)(h).
[49] MiCAR, Articles 59(1), 81.
[50] MiCAR, Article 60.
[51] MiCAR, Article 60(1).
[52] MiCAR, Article 60(2)–(6).

service provider', or 'entity'.[53] However, regulated and authorised financial institutions continue to operate under their existing licences and do not need to obtain a separate CASP authorisation, since the authorisation regime does not apply to them.[54] Consequentially, they are not crypto-asset service providers in the sense of MiCAR.

The material rules of Title V are nevertheless triggered whenever crypto-asset services are provided. As a result, these rules also apply to actors covered by the notification regime. MiCAR only exempts them from the Title V requirements as regards prudential requirements, and from the rules on the acquisition of crypto-asset service providers.[55] The reason for this exemption lies in the fact that these rules are potentially incongruent with corresponding prudential and governance rules and acquisition requirements under the legal frameworks governing these financial service providers, such as CRD, MiFID II, EMIR, etc – to which they are already subjected.

Financial service providers planning to provide crypto-asset services therefore fall within the scope of MiCAR, and the crypto-asset services they provide after successful notification are within the scope of Title V. They are not authorised crypto-asset service providers but instead authorised credit institutions, investment firms, CSDs, etc, whose original authorisation extends to the provision of relevant crypto-asset services, as from the moment of successful notification. That said, it could be that the intention to begin crypto-asset services constitutes a material change to the business model for which a supervisory consent or non-objection is required under the relevant entity's original licensing regime.

3.2.2.3. Persons Excluded from the Scope

According to Article 2(2), MiCAR does not apply to the following:

(a) persons who provide crypto-asset services exclusively for their parent companies, for their own subsidiaries or for other subsidiaries of their parent companies;
(b) a liquidator or an administrator acting in the course of an insolvency procedure, except for the purposes of Article 47;
(c) the ECB, central banks of the Member States when acting in their capacity as monetary authorities, or other public authorities of the Member States;
(d) the European Investment Bank and its subsidiaries;
(e) the European Financial Stability Facility and the European Stability Mechanism;
(f) public international organisations.

Following Article 2(2)(a), the provision of intra-group crypto-asset services (Title V) is exempt from the scope, whereas intra-group activity covered in Titles II–IV and in Title VI is included in the scope of MiCAR.

[53] MiCAR, Article 60(7)(a), (8) third subparagraph, and (9).
[54] MiCAR, Article 60(1), with Articles 62–64.
[55] MiCAR, Articles 67 and 83–84.

MiCAR does not apply to a liquidator or an administrator acting in the course of an insolvency procedure. Yet the rule in Article 2(2)(b) provides for the applicability of Article 47, which means that an insolvency administrator is bound by the redemption plan that had been drawn up previously by the ART issuer.

The exemptions of the European Central Bank (ECB), European Investment Bank (EIB), European Financial Stability Facility (EFSF) and European Stability Mechanism (ESM) and of public international organisations in general relate to the entirety of MiCAR (Article 2(3)(c)–(f)).

3.2.2.4. Persons Engaging in Market Abuse (Title VI)

Title VI, examined in chapter nine of this book, addresses the prevention and prohibition of market abuse involving crypto-assets. It applies to 'any person', ie, natural persons, legal persons, and any form of undertakings recognised under the laws of Member States, such as partnerships. This includes persons who are otherwise excluded from the scope of MiCAR, ie, the application of Titles II–V. Algorithms which are not controlled or controllable by a person do not fall within the scope of Title VI due to lack of an addressee 'person'. As a consequence, a truly autonomous algorithm would not be covered by the market abuse prohibition.

3.3. Material Scope

Following Article 2(1), the material scope of MiCAR is rooted in the concept of 'crypto-asset', a term defined in Article 3(1)(5) in a relatively open manner, using technological instead of functional criteria. It encompasses, in a first step, a wide range of products (section 3.3.1). The regulation, however, excludes a number of them from the scope in a second step. First, 'unique and non-fungible' crypto-assets, colloquially called 'non-fungible tokens' or 'NFTs', are outside the scope of MiCAR[56] (section 3.3.2). Second, certain types of financial products are not captured by the scope of MiCAR even if they qualify as crypto-assets, for instance financial instruments (share, bond, derivatives, etc.), deposits, or certain other products[57] (section 3.3.3).

Crypto-assets which are not excluded from the scope are divided into three categories.[58] First, the highly regulated ARTs and EMTs for which the law sets

[56] MiCAR, Article 2(3).
[57] MiCAR, Article 2(4).
[58] See MiCAR, Recital (18).

out detailed rules in Titles III and IV. The legislator's intention to curb the rise of so-called 'stablecoins' has been cited as the main driver for the introduction of MiCAR.[59] They are discussed in chapters four and six.

Further, MiCAR provides rules in Title II which absorb the remainder of crypto-assets, ie, those crypto-assets that are not excluded from the scope and are neither ARTs nor EMTs. These crypto-assets are clunkily termed 'crypto-assets other than asset-referenced tokens or e-money tokens'. They are not defined in Article 3. Rather, this residual category is introduced at the beginning of Title II. They will be called 'Title-II tokens' or 'Title-II crypto-assets' in the following, and are discussed in chapters four and five. Within that category of Title II tokens, some are identified as 'utility tokens' as they promise access to goods or services. Utility tokens are not a category of crypto-assets in their own right but are Title-II tokens to which a handful of specific rules regarding the inherent promise apply. They are discussed in chapters four and five.

3.3.1. Crypto-asset

A crypto-asset is defined in MiCAR as a 'digital representation of a value or of a right that is able to be transferred and stored electronically using distributed ledger technology or similar technology'.[60]

With a view to the application of specific rules, MiCAR works with the three aforementioned subcategories of crypto-assets (asset-referenced tokens, e-money tokens, Title-II tokens and the subset of utility tokens) which all share, as a common basis, this definition of crypto-asset.

Digital representation. The term 'representation' appears ill-chosen in this definition, as its linguistic understanding suggests a dichotomy between the crypto-asset on the one hand, and the value or right it purportedly represents on the other hand. This understanding would imply that the definition covers crypto-assets that reference external values or have underlying assets. While this accurately describes many crypto-assets (such as ARTs and EMTs, which are backed by reserves, or utility tokens, which entitle their holder to a service), it could fail to encompass, if taken literally, other crypto-assets which do not represent anything, notably Bitcoin, Ether, and many others. These asset types derive their value from market attribution rather than representing any external right or value beyond their digital manifestation.[61]

[59] M Lehmann, 'MiCAR – Gold Standard or Regulatory Poison for the Crypto Industry?' (EBI Working Paper No 160, European Banking Institute 2024) SSRN, ssrn.com/abstract=4692743, 3; Maume (n 7) 247.

[60] MiCAR, Article 3(1)(5).

[61] See UNIDROIT Principles on Digital Assets and Private Law (2023) Principle 4 and its commentary.

Value or right. The concept of a *right* inherently necessitates the existence of an obligor, which may or may not be the issuer of the crypto-asset. This obligor can be a natural person, legal entity, or any other identifiable undertaking. However, numerous crypto-assets, including prominent examples like Bitcoin and Ether, do not confer any rights upon their holders against any party. Instead, their value is purely a function of market dynamics – the consideration that participants are willing to pay for a scarce crypto-asset, akin to collectibles.

The inclusion of the term *value* in the definition therefore serves a crucial purpose. It ensures that the absence of a *right* does not automatically exclude such crypto-assets from MiCAR's purview. This extends the scope to include assets whose worth is derived solely from market perception and demand, rather than from anything underlying it. This finding extends to cases where crypto-assets have only immaterial value, as this may still be a strong enough driver for the relevant crypto-assets being exchanged. Crypto-assets that have neither material nor immaterial value are not exchanged on a 'market' at all, and are, hence, not included in the scope of MiCAR. This includes tokens that have a mere technical function and as such no value. No interest beyond their technical function exists primarily in contexts like blockchain test environments, or system operations. Examples include Ethereum testnet tokens, such as those on Goerli, used solely for testing smart contracts and transactions; these tokens are distributed for free.[62]

No issuer. The definition of 'crypto-asset' does not include the feature of an identifiable issuer.[63] MiCAR, therefore, applies to both crypto-assets for which an issuer can be identified and those for which this is not possible. Recital (22) excludes crypto-assets which do not have an identifiable issuer from the application of Titles II, III and IV and affirms the applicability of Titles V and VI, thereby implicitly confirming that also products without identifiable issuer can be crypto-assets in the sense of MiCAR.[64]

Transferability. From a linguistic perspective, it seems incongruous to suggest that a *representation* can be *stored* and *transferred*.[65] The intended meaning is likely to refer to the storage of relevant digital information on a DLT database, where each crypto-asset is associated with a specific address. The idea of transfer refers to the right or value which moves from the alienator to the acquirer. The digital information itself remains within the same database, instead, it is the informational value of the database that changes – a process which would have been more aptly described (using the MiCAR terminology) as *changing a record* in the

[62] See K Dwyer, 'Ethereum's Testnets Explained [2024] Holešky, Goerli, Sepolia, and More' (9 November 2023) www.ankr.com/blog/ethereum-testnets-ultimate-guide/?utm_source=chatgpt.com.

[63] cf different opinion: ch 5, s 5.2.

[64] Lehmann (n 59) 4.

[65] See MiCAR, Article 3(1)(5).

distributed ledger.[66] This terminological confusion arises from the legislator's reliance on vocabulary borrowed from the physical world, which proves inadequate for describing digital phenomena. The result is a definition of crypto-assets that relies heavily on intuitive recognition – a 'you know it when you see one' approach – rather than precise legal criteria.

The delineation between transferable crypto-assets and non-transferable ones is important as it limits the scope of MiCAR. Non-transferable crypto-assets encompass a right or value which can only be realised against the issuer or offeror,[67] and whose technical arrangements are such that they cannot be transferred to third parties. From the perspective of the purpose of MiCAR, and following the logic of financial regulation more generally, it makes sense to exclude these non-transferable products from the scope of application, as their risk profile is markedly different from transferable products, notably as regards liquidity risk, and the lower potential for speculation, money laundering and market abuse. Recital (17) makes clear that for an asset to fall outside the definition of crypto-asset, the transfer to third parties must be technically excluded, hence, the contractual exclusion of a transfer, or the pure *de facto* absence of a secondary market, are not enough to make a crypto-asset non-transferable, and thereby exclude it from the scope of application of MiCAR.

Stored electronically using DLT. MiCAR's material scope is delineated by referencing a specific database technology – namely, 'distributed ledger technology or similar technology'. An aggregate reading of the relevant five definitions contained in the text[68] results in a definition of DLT as technology that enables the operation and use of a distributed ledger, ie, an information repository that keeps records of transactions and that is shared across, and is synchronised between devices or processes ('network nodes') that are part of a network and that each hold a complete or partial replica of records of all transactions on the relevant distributed ledger and that use rules and procedures by which an agreement is reached, among the network nodes, that a transaction is validated.

Article 3(1)(2) refers expressly to the feature of distributed record keeping, so that crypto-assets are distinct from other financial products held in centralised or decentralised databases, such as, in particular, traditional holdings of financial instruments or funds, even if they are organised on a purely electronic basis. Further, the definition expressly refers to the characteristic of using a consensus mechanism to validate transactions.[69] By contrast, it does not refer to specific encryption methods typically used in the market at present, notably, there is no reference to the 'block' and 'hash' elements that inspired the technology's original

[66] See MiCAR, Article 3(1)(3).

[67] MiCAR, Recital (17).

[68] MiCAR, Article 3(1)(5), with the definition of DLT set out in Article 3(1)(1)–(4).

[69] MiCAR, Article 3(1)(3), it would have been more suitable to refer to 'changes to the record', for reasons discussed in this section.

name, blockchain. The apparent reason for this is the commitment of the legislator to keep the regulation 'future-proof' and define the scope 'as widely as possible'[70] and the 'blocks' of blockchain are already today regarded as one of several ways of organising a DLT. Recital (16) keeps owing an explanation why the characteristics of distributed record and consensus mechanism are regarded as future proof, and why crypto-assets follow rules different from assets created in other types of electronic databases.

Technological neutrality. This open question leads to the wider point of why the legislator departed from the principle of technological neutrality underlying general regulatory strategy in the EU,[71] and hailed in Recital (9), when conceiving the basic approach of MiCAR. The principle of technological neutrality aims to ensure that similar or analogous activities and assets are subject to similar standards and rules regardless of the (technological) form they take.[72] Technological neutrality could therefore be seen as part of the 'same risk, same rule' equation.[73] MiCAR, however, could 'hardly be any more technology specific'.[74]

First, the focus on DLT is potentially harmful to innovation as the market could be disincentivised to develop financial products based on technologies that lack one of the features required for MiCAR to apply (distributed ledger, consensus mechanism, etc), such as those based on a centralised database.[75] Mere doubts whether relevant technological criteria would be met are already sufficient to hamper market development in this direction.

Second, and connected to the foregoing, the technology-centred approach creates regulatory frictions and potentially opportunities for regulatory arbitrage. Products which are functionally identical and create comparable risks fall within the ambit of formally and materially different laws. If a MiFID II financial instrument, for instance, a collective investment undertaking (CIU), which is excluded from the scope of MiCAR,[76] is compared with an ART-type crypto-asset, which is governed by MiCAR Title III, it can be seen that the record-keeping method for what is functionally a financial instrument does not have any influence on the classification as MiFID II-governed financial instrument. Products that fit the definition of 'financial instrument' are within the ambit of MiFID II even

[70] See MiCAR, Recital (16).

[71] See European Commission, Digital Finance Strategy for the EU (2020), eur-lex.europa.eu/legal-content/EN/TXT/PDF/?uri=CELEX:52020DC0591, 9; European Commission, Final report of the Expert Group on Regulatory Obstacles to Financial Innovation: 30 recommendations on regulation, innovation and finance (2019), finance.ec.europa.eu/publications/final-report-expert-group-regulatory-obstacles-financial-innovation-30-recommendations-regulation_en, 12.

[72] ESMA, Consultation paper on draft Guidelines on the conditions and criteria for the qualification of crypto-assets as financial instruments, ESMA75-453128700-52, 29 January 2024, p 10.

[73] EU Commission, Expert Group on Regulatory Obstacles to Financial Innovation (ROFIEG), 30 Recommendations on Regulation, Innovation and Finance (2019) Recommendation 13, 67–69, finance.ec.europa.eu/document/download/98a331c4-6700-4355-b545-cb97a49f13c2_en?filename=191113-report-expert-group-regulatory-obstacles-financial-innovation_en.pdf.

[74] Lehmann (n 59) 7; similar Maume (n 7) 254.

[75] Lehmann (n 59) 8.

[76] MiCAR, Article 2(4)(a).

without the clarification of MiCAR Article 2(4)(1). The latter merely clarifies that the relevant products do not (also) fall within the scope of MiCAR, should they happen to be recorded on a DLT. By contrast, the regulatory status of an ART-type product may vary based primarily on the relevant database structure. ART-type products recorded on a DLT database come under MiCAR, while the regulatory status of an identically structured product for which a different type of database is used and that does not fall within the definition of crypto-asset[77] would be unclear. This distinction lacks justification from the perspective of regulatory goals, notably market efficiency, systemic stability, crime prevention, or consumer protection.

Third, and lastly, paradoxically, the definition's vagueness allows for the inclusion of very inefficient databases that merely conform to the loose criteria in the definition. The best example of the effect of this approach is the validation mechanisms of certain DLT databases, notably Bitcoin, which is notoriously excessively energy-hungry.[78] MiCAR approaches the issue of efficiency from the angle of disclosure alone: crypto-asset white papers have to provide relevant information to the market.[79] The idea is that the market will price in relevant information, thereby making inefficient products less attractive. However, as long as relevant inefficiencies can be allocated to non-adjusting third parties (in the case of energy-hungry applications: society at large), disclosure as a regulatory tool remains ineffective.

The legislator takes a markedly more prescriptive stance on comparable issues, notably on operational resilience. In this regard, the rules on digital operation resilience (DORA) impose on CASPs (see chapter seven), and issuers of ARTs and EMTs[80] (albeit not on issuers of Title II tokens) the use of ICT systems that are appropriate, reliable and technologically resilient and have sufficient capacity.

Overall, the technology-centric regulatory framework adopted for MiCAR by the legislator does not effectively serve the general rationales underlying financial regulation. Its adoption can potentially be explained by an amalgam of motives.

First, MiCAR is certainly an attempt to be 'competitive' and attract relevant business by creating a framework dedicated to the 'crypto sector'.[81] Certain parts of that market have been favourable to some (light) regulation for some time prior to MiCAR's introduction, as operating in a regulated space opens new opportunities, including facilitated access to the regulated financial sector. The legislator may have felt that a visibly attractive framework would need to be centred around the relevant technology itself.

[77] MiCAR, Article 3(1)(1)–(4).

[78] See Cambridge Bitcoin Electricity Consumption Index, ccaf.io/cbnsi/cbeci.

[79] See MiCAR, Recital (7), Articles 6(1)(j) and (12), 19(1)(h) and (11), 51(1)(g) and (6), 66(5)–(6).

[80] Regulation (EU) 2022/2554 of the European Parliament and of the Council of 14 December 2022 on digital operational resilience for the financial sector, Article 2(1)(a), (f).

[81] See Maume (n 7) 250.

Second, the legislator may have eyed the first-mover's advantage,[82] combined with the perceived benefits of the 'Brussels Effect',[83] ie, the EU's quasi-power to regulate global markets in this area. A novel, bold, supposedly future-oriented approach may have appeared to it as the best way to create this effect and reap the associated benefits.

Third, the legislator may have considered the introduction of a novel type of regulation as the best way to close regulatory gaps that have emerged as a consequence of the emergence of a new market,[84] such as, in particular, newly emerging needs to protect significant numbers of consumers from financial harm. However, even assuming such a regulatory gap existed, it remains unclear whether a technology-centred approach to legislation was the only or most suitable way to close it, considering that it is not the use of DLT itself that creates the risks driving MiCAR's introduction.

3.3.2. Exclusion of Unique and Non-fungible Crypto-assets

Article 2(3) excludes from the scope crypto-assets that are unique and not fungible with other crypto-assets. The reason for this exclusion is the fact that crypto-assets that do not have a value which can be ascertained by reference to a market (as opposed to value which is attributable to their unique characteristics) have no financial use and therefore carry less risk.[85]

It remains a case-by-case analysis whether MiCAR's scope extends to crypto-assets that are materially identical and accepted by the market as interchangeable, whilst differing in formal features which render each of them specific – a question well known from banknotes with serial numbers. Such crypto-assets would not be excluded from the scope of MiCAR, as the attribution of an identifying feature is not, in and of itself, sufficient to classify the relevant crypto-asset as unique and non-fungible.[86] As long as one crypto-asset could be substituted for another systemically without changing the value, any identifying feature remains without effect on the question of fungibility, and the relevant crypto-assets are fungible. Any value discrepancy negates the characteristic of fungibility for this crypto-asset, consequently excluding it from MiCAR's scope. This question also remains open in relation to 'large series or collections' that Recital (11) seeks to include within the scope. Beyond the question of what constitutes a 'large series or collection',[87] it will always remain decisive whether the relevant single fractions

[82] See Maume (n 7) 250.

[83] See A Bradford, *The Brussels Effect: How the European Union Rules the World* (Oxford University Press, 2019) xiv.

[84] See EBA, Report on crypto-assets (9 January 2019) 12–19, www.eba.europa.eu/publications-and-media/press-releases/eba-reports-crypto-assets.

[85] See MiCAR, Recital (10).

[86] MiCAR, Recital (11), third sentence.

[87] Maume (n 7) 261.

or items can be substituted, in the view of the market, for one another without changes in value.

The criteria for fungibility are justiciable, potentially leading to fringe cases where fungibility is unclear due to questionable interchangeability. Defining 'fungibility' within MiCAR would not help mitigate the ensuing uncertainty. The question of whether an asset is fungible, ie, can be substituted for another without changes in value, is a factual question which depends on the view of the market,[88] and it will be within the purview of courts to establish what that view is.

3.3.3. Exclusion of Financial Instruments, Deposits and Other Financial Products

Any product meeting the criteria set out in Article 3(1)(1)–(5) on its face is a crypto-asset under MiCAR. However, MiCAR excludes from its scope certain types of product. In addition to excluding non-fungible crypto-assets, MiCAR further excludes from its scope all crypto-assets that qualify as certain regulated financial products, as enumerated in the list contained in Article 2(4)(a)–(j). This list includes financial instruments, deposits, funds and a range of other financial products, referring to their respective definitions in relevant EU legislative instruments.[89] That is, even if such a financial product meets the definition of crypto-asset, its issuer, offeror or person seeking admission to trading, as well as market participants providing services in its regards, are not regulated by MiCAR but exclusively under other applicable EU legislative instruments. Following this approach, MiCAR ensures that existing regulatory frameworks remain intact, and that only regulatory lacunas, which opened with the emergence of novel crypto-assets, are filled.[90]

3.3.3.1. General Considerations

The excluded financial products are defined by reference to relevant EU legislative instruments.

Exclusion from scope. For most financial products excluded from MiCAR, the source of the relevant definition is a directive, for instance, the MiFID II definition of financial instruments. However, definitions in EU directives are implemented

[88] See E McKendrick (ed), *Goode and McKendrick on Commercial Law*, 6th edn (LexisNexis and Penguin Books, 2020) 2.89.

[89] For financial instruments, deposits and funds, listed in Article 2(4)(a)–(c) MiCAR, the pertinent references to other EU instruments are found in Article 3(1)(14) and (49)–(51) MiCAR. In Article 2(4)(d)–(j) MiCAR, relating to securitisation positions, insurance and pension products and social security schemes, the relevant references are directly incorporated.

[90] See D Zetsche and J Sinnig, 'The EU Approach to Regulating Digital Currencies, Law and Contemporary Problems' (2024) 87(2) *Law and Contemporary Problems* 4.

into the law of Member States, which automatically leads to a certain level of fragmentation,[91] the significance of which depends on the level of ambiguity of the definition in the directive, some of which are very detailed, while others are more open.

Consequently, in these cases, there will be 27 subtly distinct approaches to, for example, differentiating MiFID II financial instruments from MiCAR-governed crypto-assets with direct consequences as regards the applicability of MiCAR.[92] This could cause uncertainty and open opportunity for regulatory arbitrage between Member States.[93] In relation to MiFID II financial instruments, national interpretations are meant to converge based on relevant guidelines issued by ESMA. Even on the basis of these (non-binding) guidelines, Member States' competent authorities retain room for interpretation.[94] No such guidelines are anticipated for other types of financial products excluded from the scope of MiCAR and which are defined in EU directives, including deposits, life and non-life insurance, occupational pension schemes and individual pension products.[95] In the absence of guidelines, divergences comparable to those described in relation to financial instruments are natural and may even be more pronounced. In relation to deposits, relevant differences in interpreting the term have been documented early on.[96]

The scenario differs for financial products defined in relevant EU *regulations*, particularly concerning securitisation positions, pan-European pension products and social security schemes.[97] Whilst interpretations by national competent authorities may still vary, these products are ultimately governed by a single European rule emerging directly from the relevant regulation. Therefore, this single approach to definition and interpretation provides a much more harmonised, if not fully uniform, delineation of these financial products from functionally similar crypto-assets governed by MiCAR.

[91] See eg EBA, Crypto-assets need common EU-wide approach to ensure investor protection, 9 September 2019 www.esma.europa.eu/press-news/esma-news/crypto-assets-need-common-eu-wide-approach -ensure-investor-protection.

[92] See Zetsche and Sinnig (n 90), referring to official surveys revealing differing regulatory interpretations amongst EU regulators of six different types of financial instruments.

[93] ibid.

[94] See MiCAR, Article 2(5); ESMA, Guidelines on the conditions and criteria for the qualification of crypto-assets as financial instruments, Final Report, ESMA75-453128700-1323, 17 December 2024 www.esma.europa.eu/sites/default/files/2024-12/ESMA75453128700-1323_Final_Report_Guidelines_on_the_conditions_and_criteria_for_the_qualification_of_CAs_as_FIs.pdf. See s 4.2, inviting Member States to report to ESMA whether they do, do not but plan to, or, do not and intend not to comply with the guidelines.

[95] MiCAR, Article 2(4)(b), (c), (e)–(h).

[96] See EBA, Opinion of the European Banking Authority on elements of the definition of credit institution under Article 4(1), point 1, letter (a) of Regulation (EU) No 575/2013 and on aspects of the scope of the authorisation, EBA/OP/2020/15, 18 September 2020 www.eba.europa.eu/publications-and-media/press-releases/eba-flags-eu-commission-elements-definition-credit.

[97] MiCAR, Article 2(4)(d), (i) and (j).

3.3.3.2. Tokenised Financial Instruments

Tokenised financial instruments are financial instruments in crypto-asset form.[98] MiCAR does not apply to such instruments. Instead, relevant products and services are exclusively governed by the regulatory framework for financial instruments, ie, the vast EU securities regulation rulebook. It includes, in particular, MiFID II/ MiFIR, the Prospectus Regulation, the Market Abuse Regulation, the Money Market Fund Regulation, the UCITS Directive, the Short Selling Directive, the European Market Infrastructure Regulation, the Central Securities Depositories Regulation, amongst others, and the respective national implementations (where applicable), plus complementary autonomous national law of the Member States.

Consequently, clear criteria are needed, enabling market participants and regulators to determine under what conditions a crypto-asset qualifies as a financial instrument as compared to a MiCAR-scope instrument. This necessity is less relevant in relation to crypto-assets which constitute 'plain-vanilla' manifestations of the concept of a share, a bond, etc. Clarity is needed to uphold legal certainty and avoid regulatory arbitrage in borderline cases. The delineation between the MiCAR-regulated ARTs and the UCITS Directive-regulated CIUs is a case in point.

While the issue of delineation does already exist in relation to traditional ('non-crypto') financial instruments, the problem of uncertainty and regulatory arbitrage becomes particularly apparent in relation to tokenised financial instruments, for two reasons. First, novel forms of contractual relationships between issuers and holders emerge due to unsubstantiated confidence in the viability of highly creative crypto-asset-based business models (which may even be opaque at times). These relationships may defy traditional classification as, eg, derivative, money market instrument or other financial instrument. Second, issuers may deliberately attempt to structure their products in a way that avoids classification as financial instruments in order to benefit from supposedly lighter regulation under the MiCAR regime. The ability to clearly identify tokenised financial instruments therefore becomes an urgent necessity.

This determination of what constitutes a tokenised financial instrument falls within the purview of competent authorities and is justiciable based on the 27 national implementations of the MiFID definition of financial instrument.[99] As the EU legislator has not availed itself of any opportunity to amend the MiFID II/ MiFIR framework in this respect, the varying national implementations of the MiFID II definition of financial instrument[100] continue to inevitably affect the determination of the applicable regulatory framework for those crypto-assets the nature of which raises the question of whether they are financial instruments.

[98] See MiFID Article 4(1)(15).

[99] ESMA, Legal qualification of crypto-assets – survey to NCAs, January 2019, ESMA50-157-1384. MiFID II lack of harmonisation is a problem in this context.

[100] MiFID II, Article 4(1)(15) with Annex I, Section C.

Effect of ESMA Guidelines. This continuing lack of legal certainty, creating space for regulatory arbitrage, has led to ESMA being tasked with developing guidelines to define the conditions and criteria under which crypto-assets qualify as financial instruments, with the aim of enhancing legal certainty and ensuring uniform application.[101] However, given that the root issue – the 27 divergent implementations of the definition of financial instruments – has been entrenched since MiFID II's inception, this task is very difficult.

And, in fact, the ESMA guidelines and associated examples largely fail to substantially improve legal certainty or predictability in this regard. From a substantive law perspective, the ESMA Guidelines have no effect on national implementations of the MiFID II definition. From a formal perspective, Member States are required only to 'make every effort to comply' with the guidelines, and report whether they comply, intend to comply, or do not intend to comply.[102]

However, even confirmation that Member States comply with the guidelines will not entirely remove divergence. This is because, first, Member States' competent authorities will still read the guidelines against the background of their own national law, and, second, because the additional interpretative value of the guidelines is very low, and they may, in some instances, even add to uncertainty because of poor quality of drafting.

The ESMA Guidelines seek to unify the interpretation of the subcategories of financial instruments. As baselines, they correctly propagate a technologically neutral and substance-over-form interpretation,[103] and imply the need for a case-by-case analysis for each crypto-asset. The structure of the document is modelled on the relevant list of financial instruments contained in MiFID II, Annex I, Section C, notably transferable securities, money market instruments, units in collective investment undertakings, different types of derivative contracts, and emission allowances. For nearly all types of financial instruments, the guidelines stress the central role of the rights and obligations conferred upon the issuer and holder, or seller and buyer, in the case of derivatives, of the relevant financial instrument.[104]

3.3.3.3. *Tokenised Deposits*

Deposits are excluded from the scope of MiCAR,[105] similar to financial instruments, as described in the previous section. As a consequence, MiCAR does not

[101] See ESMA (n 94).
[102] See Regulation (EU) No 1095/2010 of 24 November 2010 establishing the European Securities and Markets Authority, Article 16(3).
[103] See ESMA (n 94) paras 11, 12 and 14.
[104] See ESMA (n 94) paras 21 (nature of shares), 25 (nature of bonds), 34 (nature of money market instruments), 37 (nature of units in collective investment undertakings), alone, the characterisation of derivative contracts is misguided, see para 44; see also M Lehmann and F Schienerl, 'The Concept of Financial Instruments – Drawing a borderline between MiFID and MiCAR' (2024) EBI Working Paper series 171.
[105] MiCAR, Article 2(4)(b).

apply to 'tokenised deposits', ie, instruments that are crypto-assets while also falling within the definition of a deposit. Instead, tokenised deposits are governed solely by the EU regulatory framework that applies to deposits generally, including the CRD,[106] Capital Requirements Regulation (CRR),[107] the Deposit Guarantee Schemes Directive (DGSD)[108] and their national implementations (where applicable), as well as complementary autonomous law of the Member States.

The EBA Report. The EBA has pointed out that the term 'deposit' is not harmonised across the EU[109] and has highlighted the continued relevance of this shortcoming, including with respect to the delineation between tokenised deposits and crypto-assets that have similar functions but are not deposits, notably EMTs.[110]

As opposed to the ESMA Guidelines (see section 3.3.3.2), the EBA report does not attempt to nudge Member States to a more harmonised interpretation of the relevant core definition. Instead, the EBA report sets out elements that can facilitate the assessment to be carried out by national competent authorities, which must be based, like in the case of tokenised financial instruments, on a case-by-case analysis.[111] It identifies the continuity of the contractual relationship and the lack of transferability in the secondary market as strong indicators in favour of a classification as tokenised deposits, as opposed to EMTs. First, according to the report, the ownership of a (tokenised) deposit was typically linked to the identity of the account holder, whereas the ownership of an EMT is linked to the control over the token itself. Second, in case of (tokenised) deposit, the claim on the bank took the form of nominative bank account balances that could not be transferred. A payment using tokenised deposits involved destruction of the claim on the bank of the sender, and creation of a new claim on the bank of the receiver, regularly involving interbank clearing mechanisms. Differently, EMTs were private liabilities transferrable to others, without altering the claim on the issuing bank, and the balance sheet of the latter was only updated upon redemption.

At the time of writing, the EBA had identified one single 'live' tokenised deposit scheme across the EEA but noted that 17 per cent of banks responding to the relevant survey were expecting to engage in deposit taking in tokenised form within a two-year horizon.[112] While legal certainty in respect of the delineation between

[106] Directive 2013/36/EU of 26 June 2013 on access to the activity of credit institutions and the prudential supervision of credit institutions.

[107] Regulation (EU) 575/2013 of 26 June 2013 on prudential requirements for credit institutions.

[108] Directive 2014/49/EU of 16 April 2014 on deposit guarantee schemes. It contains in Article 2(3) a partial definition of deposit which applies within its scope and that of the CRR.

[109] EBA, Report on the Perimeter of Credit Institutions established in the Member States, 27 November 2014.

[110] See EBA, Report on Tokenised Deposits, December 2024, at 5 and 10 www.eba.europa.eu/sites/default/files/2024-12/4b294386-1235-463f-b9b5-08f255160435/Report%20on%20Tokenised%20deposits.pdf.

[111] ibid 17–19.

[112] ibid 11.

tokenised deposits and EMTs is therefore highly relevant, the current legal framework is fragmented and unclear, and offers room for regulatory arbitrage, quite comparable to the weaknesses in the framework governing tokenised financial instruments.

3.3.4. Inclusion of E-money

While most regulated financial products are excluded from MiCAR's scope as per the list in Article 2(4), electronic money, as defined in the EMD2, is notably absent from this list and thus is not excluded. As a consequence, there is an overlap of scope of the relevant two EU instruments. Electronic money and EMTs, and the relationship between EMD2 and MiCAR, will be discussed in chapter six.

3.4. Geographical Scope

MiCAR's geographical scope is defined in Article 2(1), following which MiCAR applies to all persons engaging in relevant activities 'in the Union'. The relevant provisions of Titles II, III, IV and V provide for similar wording:

- a person shall not make an offer to the public of [Title-II tokens] in the EU, unless [white paper has been drafted, notified and published, etc];[113]
- a person shall not make an offer to the public, or seek the admission to trading, of an ART in the EU, unless [authorised, etc];[114]
- a person shall not make an offer to the public, or seek the admission to trading of an EMT in the EU, unless [authorised, etc];[115]
- a person shall not provide crypto-asset services in the EU, unless [authorised, etc].[116]

In the Union (EU). The criterion 'in the EU' means within the geographical boundaries of the EU Member States. It focuses on whether the activities, ie, offering crypto-assets or relevant services, are directed at or accessible to residents of the EU. MiCAR does not define the precise meaning of 'in the Union' but Article 61(1) uses the criterion of 'clients established or situated in the Union'. This includes marketing efforts of any kind targeted at EU residents, regardless of where the service provider is located, and the making available of relevant crypto-assets or services to EU residents, even if the offering originates from outside the EU.

[113] MiCAR, Article 4(1).
[114] MiCAR, Article 16(1).
[115] MiCAR, Article 48(1).
[116] MiCAR, Article 59(1).

Third-country residents present on EU territory. According to the wording 'situated', MiCAR also targets issuers, offerors and those seeking admission to trading, as well as service providers that target residents of third countries not established in the EU but temporarily present on EU territory, unless they had been offered the relevant product or service already before entering EU territory.

EU residents present on the territory of third countries. The scenario of EU residents temporarily travelling to third countries without being resident in that country but who receive an offer that is directed to residents of that third country, is not covered by the scope of MiCAR. This may change where communication in the third country is specifically directed at EU residents. Relevant indicators include the language chosen, or a specific relation between the offered product or service to one or more EU countries.[117]

Reverse solicitation. 'Reverse solicitation' refers to a situation where a potential client of a crypto-asset service within the EU initiates the contact with a service provider outside the EU, rather than the service provider soliciting the client. This concept is included in a number of EU instruments, including the Prospectus Regulation, AIFMD, MiFID II, MiFIR and others.

MiCAR introduces this concept in Article 61(1), in relation to the provision of crypto-asset services. Following this rule, where a client initiates, at its own exclusive initiative, the provision of crypto-asset services or activity by a third-country firm, the requirement for authorisation of that service provider under Article 59 does not apply to the provision of that crypto-asset service.

The defining characteristic of reverse solicitation is that the initial request for services or information comes from the client within the EU, not from the provider or issuer.[118] This can occur through unsolicited inquiries or requests for information about products or services. The understanding of reverse solicitation needs to be narrow and specific. To rely on reverse solicitation as a defence or exemption, providers would need to demonstrate that the request was indeed unsolicited and initiated by the client. This may require clear documentation of the client's request and the absence of any prior solicitation or advertising targeting the EU market. Further, an exemption can only apply to the particular service or product requested and does not cover subsequent offers or services.

Whereas Title V includes a specific rule on reverse solicitation in Article 60(1), there is no such rule regarding Titles II–IV. However, the concept of 'offer in the Union' already contains the relevant elements of the logic underlying reverse solicitation, so that a specific rule is not necessary.

[117] Maume (n 7) 261–62, referencing a press release issued in 2022 by the German competent authority BaFin that informed about the violation of German financial regulation by a Singapore-based issuer which had targeted German customers by communicating in German and using a '.de'-domain.

[118] See ESMA, Consultation paper on the draft guidelines on reverse solicitation (29 January 2024) at 18–20 www.esma.europa.eu/sites/default/files/2024-01/ESMA35-1872330276-1619_Consultation_Paper_on_the_draft_guidelines_on_reverse_solicitation_under_MiCA.pdf.

3.5. Temporal Scope

Titles III and IV apply since 30 June 2024 (Article 149(3)). This must also apply to relevant definitions and other indispensable elements.[119] From 30 December 2024, the entirety of MiCAR applies (Article 149(2)), including Titles II and V.

Issuance, offering and seeking admission to trading of ART and EMT before 30 June 2024, and issuance of Title II tokens before 30 December 2024 are excluded from the scope of the Regulation.[120]

3.6. Conclusion

The rules on the scope of MiCAR achieve the main legislative objective of closing key regulatory gaps. Products in the form of crypto-assets, and related services, that historically were outside the perimeter of EU regulation are now firmly within the regulators' purview. Relevant rules aiming at consumer protection and systemic stability therefore apply.

However, it is less clear whether the scope has been shaped in a way that contributes to legal certainty, predictability and efficiency more generally, for two reasons.

First, the larger part of MiCAR, notably Titles III, IV and V, replicates preexisting EU law, notably MiFID II, Prospectus Regulation, EMD2 and others, albeit with divergences of varying significance. It is not obvious which considerations motivated these divergences – most importantly, there does not seem to be a connection between these divergences and the presumed novelty of crypto-assets, grounded in the use of a specific technology. In other words, MiCAR extends to certain products, seemingly because they are structured using DLT, and subjects them to a separate set of rules which, however, does not appear to be motivated by the specific characteristics of that technology nor indeed the economic characteristics of the products themselves.

Against this background, the regulatory framework would have been clearer and more efficient if the legislator had adapted existing legislation, in particular EMD2, Money Market Funds Regulation, UCITS Directive, Prospectus Regulation and MiFID II/MiFIR to safely include the issuance of ARTs and EMTs and the provision of crypto-asset services, and would have restricted the new law to the minimum necessary, in particular, by catering for products currently covered in Title II. Such an approach could have also provided a historic opportunity to address the well-known issue of the imperfect harmonisation of the notion of 'financial instrument' for the purposes of MiFID II and other overdue fixes.

[119] Lehmann (n 59) 1.
[120] Lehmann (n 59) 4.

Second, the delineation between MiFID II-governed financial instruments and MiCAR-governed ARTs, on the one hand, and between CRD-governed deposits and MiCAR-governed EMTs (where issued by a bank) on the other hand is highly impracticable and will cause significant uncertainty when it comes to classification. Further issues relate to the intersection between MiCAR and PSD2 (outside the scope of this chapter) regarding EMTs (as compared to traditional e-money) also create substantial practical difficulties.

4

Typology of Crypto-Assets

PHILIPP PAECH

4.1. Introduction

MiCAR was conceived in response to the emergence of so-called 'stablecoins',[1] products that share, or purport to share, some characteristics of money, specifically value storage for use as a means of payment. This development exposed an undesirable regulatory lacuna at the intersection of the regulation of fiat and commercial bank money, e-money, and money market funds.[2] In other words, the legislator was wary of instruments functionally akin to day-to-day financial products with payment and value-storage functions, characterised by a stable value, high liquidity, and transferability, absent a clear regulatory regime.

As Facebook promoted the proposal for the *Libra* coin,[3] central banks and regulators realised that 'stablecoins' could be adopted *en masse* across markets, at a scale that might pose risks to consumer welfare, monetary policy transmission and financial stability.[4]

[1] The term 'stablecoin' is a marketing term and does not describe a homogeneous market practice, nor is it legally defined. While some of the relevant products have maintained relative stability since their inception (in particular the *USDC* and *USDT* coins), other 'stablecoins' were decidedly unstable and even failed entirely, causing total losses to their holders (eg, the *Terra Luna* coin). Therefore, while the term serves as a useful shorthand in debate, it is good practice to keep it in inverted commas.

[2] D Arner, R Auer and J Frost, 'Stablecoins: risks, potential and regulation' (2020) BIS Working Paper No. 905, www.bis.org/publ/work905.htm; W Bolt, V Lubbersen and P Wierts, 'Getting the Balance Right: Crypto, stablecoin and CBDC' (2022) DNB Working Paper No. 736, www.dnb.nl/media/jo3h1dlu/working_paper_no-_736.pdf.

[3] Facebook has 4 billion weekly active users, which could easily have become users of Libra. For early takes on Libra, see A Croce, M Langiulli and G Marocchi, 'The weight of a Libra: are stablecoins a new challenge for external statistics compilers?' (2020); IFC Conference on external statistics, 'Bridging measurement challenges and analytical needs of external statistics: evolution or revolution?', www.bis.org/ifc/publ/ifcb52_08.pdf; O Read and S Schäfer, 'Libra Project: Regulators Act on Global Stablecoins' (2020) 55 *Intereconomics* 392, www.intereconomics.eu/contents/year/2020/number/6/article/libra-project-regulators-act-on-global-stablecoins.html; J Cunliffe, Former Deputy Governor of the Bank of England for Financial Stability, 'Money and payments: a 'black ships' moment?' (Speech at the Economics of Payments XII Conference at the Federal Reserve Board, Washington DC, 26 October 2023, www.bankofengland.co.uk/speech/2023/october/jon-cunliffe-speech-at-the-economics-of-payments-xii-conference.

[4] See Explanatory memorandum to MiCAR, eur-lex.europa.eu/legal-content/EN/TXT/HTML/?uri=CELEX:52020PC0593.

First, 'stablecoins' may constitute significant risk to consumer welfare and, in turn, financial stability in a scenario where confidence collapses in an issuer's ability to redeem, ie, to reconvert the stablecoins into cash or other forms of money.[5] Such consequential loss of trust could trigger a run-like market reaction, potentially spilling over from the crypto-asset market to other products, including deposits held in the banking system. This situation is likely to cause systemic instability.[6]

Second, should 'stablecoins' be widely adopted in the long term, they may partly replace money circulating within the banking system, thereby undermining the effectiveness of central banks' monetary policy and diminishing liquidity in the banking system.[7]

Third, a potential displacement of funds held in deposit accounts to non-bank issuers may impede the ability of banks to lend. This may result in the non-bank financial sector serving an ever-larger segment of the lending market. This also poses risks to the prudential resilience of the financial system due to the relatively 'lighter' regulatory regimes applicable to non-bank lenders compared to banks.[8]

Fourth, concerns may arise with regard to the operational resilience of the technology used for custody and transfer, potentially exposing users (including consumers) to various risks.

These concerns explain why the European legislator felt compelled to regulate the market for 'stablecoins'.[9] However, not all 'stablecoin' business models require regulation – only those with the potential to create the aforementioned risks fall within the regulatory scope. The legislator has identified two categories of stablecoins which are subject to MiCAR's material rules: e-money tokens (EMTs), which purport to maintain their stability in one way or another by referencing a single official currency (eg, a crypto-asset whose marketing suggests that its value is backed by or pegged to the US dollar), and asset-referenced tokens (ARTs), which purport that their stability is connected in one way or another to another value or right, or a combination thereof (eg, a crypto-asset whose marketing suggests that it is designed to maintain a stable value by referencing the value of a basket of government debt or a basket of currency reserves, or a real estate portfolio).

[5] ESMA, 'Crypto-assets and their risks for financial stability', ESMA50-165-2251 (4 October 2022) www.esma.europa.eu/sites/default/files/library/esma50-165-2251_crypto_assets_and_financial_stability.pdf; R Ahmed, I Aldasoro and Chanelle Duley, 'Public information and stablecoin runs' (2024) BIS Working Paper No. 1164, www.bis.org/publ/work1164.pdf.

[6] See L Galati and F Capalbo, 'Silicon Valley Bank bankruptcy and Stablecoins stability' (2024) 91 *International Review of Financial Analysis* 103001.

[7] IMF-FSB Synthesis Paper: Policies for Crypto-Assets (7 September 2023) www.fsb.org/uploads/R070923-1.pdf.

[8] For an overview of the non-bank financial system, see the annual monitoring exercises of the Financial Stability Board (FSB), Global Monitoring Report on Non-Bank Financial Intermediation (16 December 2024) www.fsb.org/2024/12/global-monitoring-report-on-non-bank-financial-intermediation-2024/.

[9] See Explanatory memorandum to MiCAR; FSB, Final Report, 'High-level Recommendations for the Regulation, Supervision and Oversight of Global Stablecoin Arrangements' (17 July 2023) www.fsb.org/uploads/P170723-3.pdf.

It is however not the factual stability or any factual legal and economic structure of 'stablecoins' that brings them within the scope of MiCAR Titles III and IV. Already the attempt to create an impression ('purport') of stability is enough to make a crypto-asset 'EMT' or 'ART' in the sense of MiCAR. Working out the details of this novel way to define a financial product is the first purpose of this chapter.

The partial functional convergence of traditional financial products – particularly fiat and commercial bank money, e-money, and money market fund instruments with EMTs and ARTs – naturally leads to definitional overlap and challenges in clearly delineating one category from another – a crucial prerequisite for legal certainty and the avoidance of regulatory arbitrage. The scope of MiCAR is structured in a way that allows uncertainty in this regard to persist. Notably, the distinction between EMTs and e-money, as well as between EMT-related crypto-asset services and PSD2 payment services, remains unclear.[10] With regard to ARTs, questions arise concerning their differentiation from money market funds in certain cases. The proper delineation of these products from one another is the second purpose of the analysis below.

Innumerable crypto-assets which are not ARTs or EMTs are present on the market, most famously Bitcoin. The range of underlying business models is very wide. These crypto-assets are regulated under MiCAR Title II and hence termed 'Title-II tokens', or 'Title-II crypto-assets' in this book. MiCAR sets out substantially fewer comprehensive rules in Title II as compared to Titles III and IV, reflecting the perception of the special status of EMTs as an alternative means of payment, and ARTs as potentially having this characteristic.[11]

The catch-all category of Title-II tokens is based on the definition of crypto-assets and is otherwise defined only by way of exclusion ('crypto-assets other than asset-referenced tokens or e-money tokens'). Utility tokens also fall into this category. However, as they present a different risk profile, a few provisions in Title II are modified in their application to them.[12] Both Title-II crypto-assets and the subcategory of utility tokens are discussed in this chapter.

4.2. E-money Tokens

EMTs are functionally akin to other financial products, notably fiat money, commercial bank money and e-money instruments. The legislator recognises this similarity, particularly between EMTs on the one hand, and e-money in the sense

[10] European Commission, Letter, 'Subject: Interplay between MiCA and PSD2 – Possible "no action letter" by the EBA', 6 December 2024.

[11] See in particular Recitals (18) to (20) and (4), and the 'cap' on ARTs used widely as a means of exchange (Article 23 MiCAR).

[12] See, in particular, Article 4(3)(c) MiCAR.

of the EMD2, on the other hand, and also sees EMTs as a likely surrogate for coins and notes, expecting them to be used as a means of payment.[13]

On the basis of the principle of technological neutrality, the legislator should recognise the functional similarity and regulate EMTs exclusively in relation to the peculiarities and specific risks that flow from the use of DLT, as this is what distinguishes the two products. Beyond that, the legislator would be expected to keep regulation the same.[14] However, that is not the case here, albeit the regulatory outcomes are broadly aligned.

Definition of EMT. In the case of EMTs, the legislator has opted to create a materially different class of regulated product. Whereas e-money is defined in the EMD2 as 'electronically stored monetary value as represented by a claim on the issuer which is issued on receipt of funds for the purpose of making payment transactions',[15] MiCAR defines an e-money token as a 'crypto-asset that purports to maintain a stable value by referencing the value of one official currency'.[16] Even though e-money and EMTs are functionally extremely similar (MiCAR even states that EMTs are 'deemed'[17] electronic money), the definitions of the two products could not be more different.

The EMD2 definition of e-money, on the one hand, employs criteria that relate to the factual economic and legal structure of the product. The MiCAR definition of EMTs (and ARTs), on the other hand, hinges on the criterion that the relevant product attempts to create an impression of stability ('purport') but does not require any factual criteria to be fulfilled.[18] In other words, to enter the scope of MiCAR Title IV, the product does not need to be stable, and there does not need to be any factual connection between the token and the referenced currency or between the holder and the issuer (as is the case regarding e-money evidencing a specific claim against the issuer). It is sufficient for the product, or rather the communication accompanying it, to assert these facts to qualify as an EMT in the sense of MiCAR. As a result, even so-called algorithmic stablecoins could fall within the scope of EMT.[19]

This addressee-focused approach to shaping the scope (ie, communication of the purported stability) disregards the factual traits of the relevant product and leads to an extremely wide application of Title IV. It can be explained by the

[13] MiCAR, Recital (18).

[14] This approach has also been termed the 'same function, same risk, same regulation' principle, see Expert Group on Regulatory Obstacles to Financial Innovation (ROFIEG), 30 Recommendations on Regulation, Innovation and Finance, December 2019.

[15] EMD2, Article 2(2).

[16] MiCAR, Article 3(1)(7).

[17] MiCAR, Article 48(2).

[18] See MiCAR, Recital (41).

[19] P Maume, 'The Regulation on Markets in Crypto-Assets (MiCAR): Landmark Codification, or First Step of Many, or Both?' (2023) 20(2) *European Company and Financial Law Review* 244, 258, comes to same result but referring to the different types of operational set up, which, however, seems irrelevant for the offeror 'purporting' the stable value.

experience that the market for crypto-assets easily accepts assertions by market actors in respect of the value of a token,[20] and therefore uncritically adopts products as means of exchange, payment or for storing value, without there being any meaningful assurance regarding the products' stable value, such as the existence of a claim or redemption right against the issuer or, indeed, any legal right at all. Such elements may be demanded by the regulation based on the qualification of the token but do not flow from the MiCAR definitions of the product.[21] From a regulatory perspective, it therefore makes sense to define EMTs solely based on the impression that a product seeks to create regarding its stability. The scope thus can include those products that pose the greatest risk, notably the ones that make relevant promises without, absent the application of the regulation, having the appropriate economic and legal fundamentals.[22]

The criterion for whether a product *purports* to be stable by reference to one single currency is thus the core of the provision defining the scope of Title IV. It is a criterion open to interpretation even though the question of whether or not a product does comply with this criterion is absolutely crucial. In concrete terms, compliance with this criterion determines whether a crypto-asset falls within the scope of the comprehensive prudential regulation in Title IV (if the criterion is complied with), or falls within the remit of significantly lighter, disclosure-focussed regulation of Title II (if it is not complied with).

The decision of when a crypto-asset 'purports to be stable [etc]' has to be taken by the national competent authority in the context of the classification of the crypto-asset for regulatory purposes. These authorities can seek non-binding opinions from the European Supervisory Authorities (ESAs) on the regulatory classification of a crypto-asset under Article 97(3) MiCAR. Fierce debates between regulators and regulatees can be expected. The comprehensive prudential regulatory framework of Title IV is incompatible with most crypto-asset business models. Therefore, numerous attempts of regulatory arbitrage can be expected to take place. Thus, an accompanying communication, notably the white paper, may make specific assertions regarding the asset's value, trying to tread a fine line between suggesting stability without falling within the definition of EMT and, hence, being subject to the comprehensive prudential requirements of Title IV.

[20] Z Vardai, 'Investors claim Tether's $118B reserves may face audit and liquidity risks' (*Cointelegraph*, 20 September 2024) cointelegraph.com/news/tether-transparency-business-structure-118b-ftx-concern.

[21] The *Libra* coin, in particular, was structured so as to exclude a redemption right against the issuer. Ledger Insights, 'Libra EC Response: Redemption, E-Money & Regulations' (*Ledger Insights*, 4 May 2020) www.ledgerinsights.com/libra-ec-response-redemption-e-money-regulations/.

[22] Once these products are within the scope of Title IV, the substantive rules impose compliance with these economic and legal fundamentals, notably a repayment claim at par, the keeping of an appropriate reserve, and a set of governance rules. EMTs that do not comply with the requirements of Title IV cannot be authorised, and their distribution on EU territory would therefore be illegal (see ch 6 of this book).

The decision of the relevant national competent authority is justiciable. With a view to promoting harmonisation in the classification of crypto-assets by national competent authorities, the ESAs have issued Guidelines including a 'standardised test' for classification,[23] and, in addition to being potentially requested to prepare non-binding opinions on a crypto-asset classification,[24] must report annually on classification challenges.[25] These mandated tasks under MiCAR are without prejudice to other actions the ESAs could take to promote convergence (eg, via own initiative guidelines) in exercise of their general powers pursuant to their Founding Regulations (see chapter ten).[26]

The benchmark of what is necessary for a product to be considered to be purporting stability is not specified in MiCAR. The communication, in particular through the white paper that comes with the product needs to be capable of creating a relevant expectation within the addressee.

MiCAR provides a framework as to the factual elements that form part of the impression that the product communication is able to create. Notably, it must have the potential to provoke an impression of 'stable value' by 'referencing the value of one official currency' (in the case of EMTs), or by referencing 'another value or right or a combination thereof, including one or more official currencies' (in the case of ARTs).

An EMT purports to maintain a stable value by referencing the value of one official currency. The term 'referencing' is to be understood broadly and encompasses any suggestion that a crypto-asset has a stable value, while reference is made to an official currency to substantiate that claim. This reference can be specific, for instance, employing formulae such as 'backed by', 'tracking', 'pegged to', or 'stabilised by'. For the discussion of the terms 'referencing' and 'pegging', including the need to distinguish referencing for regulatory law purposes from any private law considerations and underlying assets, see further chapter six of this book.

However, relevant communications can be unspecific or even implicit. The core criterion employed by the definition ('purport') is unspecific, and the relevant benchmark cannot be what message the issuer intends with the relevant communication, but must be how potential addressees perceive it. If the communication accompanying the crypto-asset has the potential to create the impression of

[23] Article 97(1) MiCAR. ESAs, Guidelines on templates for explanations and opinions, and the standardised test for the classification of crypto-assets, under Article 97(1) of Regulation (EU) 2023/1114, 10 December 2024 www.eba.europa.eu/activities/single-rulebook/regulatory-activities/asset-referenced-and-e-money-tokens-micar/esas-guidelines-templates-explanations-and-opinions-and -standardised-test-classification-crypto.

[24] Article 97(3) MiCAR and, in the case of purported ARTs, Article 20(5) MiCAR (EBA and ESMA only).

[25] Article 97(4) MiCAR. This report must, among other things, identify difficulties in the classification of crypto-assets and divergences in the approaches of the competent authorities.

[26] Such findings may be taken into account in European Commission reports on the application of MiCAR (Article 140 MiCAR, see specifically para (1)(q)).

the existence of a relationship between the crypto-asset and the relevant single currency that ensures stability, the criterion of 'purport' is fulfilled.

The referenced currency can be the official currency of any country,[27] see Article 3(1)(8). It is not a requirement that the currency itself be stable in value. As soon as reference is made to a basket of currencies or a basket of mixed assets, the EMT framework in Title IV does not apply. In that case, it is relevant to consider whether the ART framework in Title III might.

Relationship between EMT and E-money. EMTs are conceptually similar to ARTs but also fit into the concept of 'electronic money', a well-established category of financial product under EU law, regulated under the EMD2. An EMT can only be issued by a credit institution or electronic money institution acting in conformity with Title IV MiCAR,[28] notably strict prudential requirements, including a requirement for redemption at par[29] and associated conditions regarding safeguarding and reserves. As a consequence, an authorised EMT does factually mimic the value of a specific currency and, hence, comes very close to the economic and legal structure of traditional e-money.

Against this background, the legislator has opted for a regulatory framework either complementing or combining EMD2 and MiCAR rules. Depending on details, many EMT issues might fall into the definition of e-money and, therefore, be subject to the rules of the EMD2. From a substantive perspective, there are three different types of products in the sphere of these legislative measures:

- Products within Article 2 EMD2, and outside the scope of Article 3(1)(7) MiCAR ('traditional' e-money).
- Products within Article 2 EMD2 and which are also crypto-assets and hence qualify as EMTs following Article 3(1)(7) MiCAR, thereby entering the scope of Title IV. Article 49(1) disapplies large parts of the EMD2.
- Products outside Article 2 EMD2 but which qualify as EMTs following Article 3(1)(7) MiCAR, which enter the scope of Title IV and are then, critically, also deemed as 'electronic money' (Article 48(2) MiCAR).

As a baseline, the EMD2 framework remains unchanged, ie, the rules applicable to ('non-tokenised') e-money stay unaltered. EMTs, many of which would already fall under the EMD2, are incorporated into the MiCAR framework via the EMT definition. Concerning the prudential elements of EMT issuance – including initial capital, own funds, permitted activities, and fund safeguarding – MiCAR stipulates in Article 48(3) that Titles II and III of the EMD2 apply unless explicitly stated otherwise. Adding another layer of complexity, MiCAR's own rules

[27] See UN Operational Rates of Exchange, treasury.un.org/operationalrates/OperationalRates.php.

[28] MiCAR, Article 48(1).

[29] MiCAR, Article 49(4).

subsequently override the EMD2 regulations on issuance and redeemability to which it initially referred, Article 49(1) MiCAR. This intricate design is not only hard to follow but raises three issues.[30]

As a further example of the consequences of abandoning technological neutrality,[31] it appears that those EMTs which would already qualify as electronic money as they enter the scope of the EMD2 (second group), are not governed by the same rules as 'traditional' electronic money, contributing to frictions and creating potential for regulatory arbitrage.

Additionally, the reference to Titles II and III of the EMD2 seems to elevate a text that is not originally directly applicable – the EMD2, being a directive, necessitates national transposition – to one that *is* directly applicable. MiCAR is difficult to interpret in any other manner. Notably, this resulting fragmentation, which lacks a clear rationale, is solely the outcome of employing different technologies for what is functionally the same product. The asset category of 'electronic money' is thus divided into 28 separate regulatory regimes (27 national transpositions of the EMD2 for traditional electronic money, and the MiCAR regime directly applicable to EMTs), the boundary between which remains ill-defined. This setup poses significant challenges in terms of predictability, applicability, and international compatibility, lacking the clarity and consistency needed to set international standards.

Finally, by deeming all EMTs 'electronic money', MiCAR brings relevant activities involving such tokens into the scope of EU payments regulation (PSD2),[32] resulting in overlap between MiCAR and the PSD2 in some cases (notably in the context of the Title V MiCAR service of transferring crypto-assets).[33]

4.3. Asset-referenced Tokens

The ART category of crypto-assets encompasses a substantially broader range of crypto-assets than the EMT category. An asset-referenced token is defined as 'a type of crypto-asset that is not an electronic money token and that purports to maintain a stable value by referencing another value or right, or a combination thereof, including one or more official currencies'.[34]

[30] See P Paech, 'New regulations or novel regulation for crypto assets? – the folly of hybrid laws' (Revue Banque & Droit, October 2024) (www.revue-banque.fr/sommaire/-/meta/banque-et-droit-n-hs-2024-2).

[31] See ch 3.

[32] See further Recital (93) MiCAR.

[33] In view of this overlap, the EBA, in close coordination with ESMA, has been invited to consider issuing a 'no action letter' regarding the interplay of PSD2 and MiCAR to address practical issues stemming from the application of the two regimes. See Letter 'Interplay between MiCA and PSD2 – Possible "no action letter" by the EBA' (n 10). This approach risks moving legal uncertainty within the material rules to the enforcement stage.

[34] MiCAR, Article 3(1)(6).

Crucial elements of the EMT definition, as discussed above, apply accordingly in the context of the ART definition. Also here, the question of whether a crypto-asset 'purports to maintain a stable value [etc]' determines whether it is regulated under Title II or the significantly more stringent Title III. Equally, the question of which conditions apply to such crypto-assets in order for them to be authorised for public offering and admission to trading is separate from the question of the definition – these material rules are set out in MiCAR Title III and discussed in chapter six of this book.

The material difference between the definition of ARTs and EMTs lies solely in the object which is referenced in the communication: a single currency in the case of EMTs, any value or right, or a basket thereof, including one or more currencies, in the case of ARTs. Based on this difference, the European legislator attaches different regulatory treatment depending on whether the relevant issue could be seen as a direct substitute for a specific currency (in which case the asset is an EMT, regulated in Title IV), or not (in which case the asset is an ART, regulated in Title III), notwithstanding that the latter may be potentially used at scale as a means of exchange[35]).

Crypto-assets that purport to maintain a stable value by referencing an object other than values or rights do not fall within the definition of ARTs. That would be the case, for example, in relation to a token that purports to be stable because it is 'morally supported' by the President of the USA.

The definition of ART does not restrict the type of value or right to which the relevant ART may purport to maintain stability. Examples could include a Libra-style reference to a value consisting of a blend of official currencies, or a reference to commodities or precious metals, as in the case of *TetherGold*,[36] or a basket of other crypto-assets.[37]

At the time of writing, 1 million new crypto-assets are reported to be created weekly,[38] many of which will promise to be valuable in one way or another, by reference to a great variety of 'things'. While the identification of the referenced object for the purpose of the EMT definition is simple (an existing official currency), the openness of the ART definition causes challenges, as the question of what constitutes a 'value or right' invites debate. Consequently, crypto-assets purporting a stable value by referencing values, rights, or a basket thereof, fall within this definition even if the rights or values are not stable by themselves. Therefore, on the basis of the wording alone, 'value or right' could include anything from a portfolio of government bonds to a basket of lottery tickets. Indeed, MiCAR implies a broad interpretation of these terms.[39]

[35] MiCAR, Article 23.

[36] See eg TetherGold, gold.tether.to/.

[37] See eg DAI, makerdao.com/en/whitepaper#introduction.

[38] O Hawkins, E Hemingway and N Asgari, 'Donald Trump's memecoin copycats spark fears for investors' *Financial Times* (7 February 2025) www.ft.com/content/831919a9-47b0-4ac3-bcdd-5154c27d9f9c, citing Brian Armstrong, chief executive of Coinbase.

[39] See MiCAR, Recital (2), (18), (41).

4.4. Title II Tokens

There is no separate definition in Article 3 for this broad category of crypto-assets. Instead, the material scope of Title II is set out in Article 4, by reference to 'a crypto-asset other than an asset-referenced token or e-money token'.

The category of Title II crypto-assets encompasses any product that falls within the definition of crypto-asset (Article 3(1)(5)) except those that qualify as ARTs or EMTs. The material rules of Title II are significantly less onerous than those applicable to ARTs and EMTs. They mainly draw on disclosure mechanisms, including by introducing an obligation to publish a white paper, to ensure investor protection and mandate basic governance mechanisms to identify and mitigate conflicts of interest. The in-depth discussion of rules applicable to Title II crypto-assets is carried out in chapter five of this book.

Still, the class of Title II tokens comprises important crypto-assets, notably *Bitcoin* and similarly structured crypto-assets, albeit in that specific case the material rules may not be applicable in the absence of a 'person' (issuer) to whom the rules are addressed. This latter finding corresponds with the statement in Recital (22), following which crypto-assets with no identifiable issuer shall not fall within the scope of Titles II, III and IV. However, the provision of services with regard to 'crypto-assets',[40] including Title II crypto-assets, engages Title V. This point was also noted in chapter three of this book.

Crypto-assets that purport to be stable without reference to a single currency or another value or right, or crypto-assets that are just perceived by market participants as stable without referencing anything, are also within the Title II category, instead of falling within the scope or the comprehensive regulatory framework set out in MiCAR Titles III and IV. The legislator apparently assumed that the deceptive potential regarding the stable value of such crypto-assets cannot have the same ramifications as the potential of EMTs and ARTs, most probably due to the fact that such crypto-assets are likely to be perceived to be speculative investments, rather than as a means of exchange. As such, these crypto-assets are subjected to the disclosure-focused rules of the Title-II regime.

4.5. Utility Tokens

'Utility token' is defined in Article 3(1)(9) as a crypto-asset 'that is only intended to provide access to a good or a service supplied by its issuer'. This group of tokens is a subset of Title-II tokens.[41] The only reason for the special mention of utility tokens in MiCAR is that their risk profile is deemed structurally different due to

[40] See MiCAR, Article 3(1)(5).
[41] See MiCAR, Recital (18).

the limited (and often 'one time') use to which they may be put. Therefore, MiCAR modifies the rules that otherwise apply to Title II tokens. Notably, utility tokens:

- are exempt from Title II if the service or good to which they provide access already exists, unless the offeror makes known its intention to seek admission to trading for these utility tokens;[42]
- should not exceed the offer period beyond 12 months from the date of publication of the crypto-asset white paper, if goods and services do not yet exist or are not yet in operation;[43]
- trigger an obligation to mention in the white paper the risk that they may not be exchangeable against the good or service as promised, in particular, in the case of the default of the issuer.[44]

In all other contexts, utility tokens are treated as regular Title-II crypto-assets.

However, these modifications cannot apply where a crypto-asset combines the utility function with some other function, as the general regulatory framework must apply in this regard. Therefore, a crypto-asset is only a utility token if it is 'only intended' to provide access to goods or services supplied by its issuer. This delineation is important, for instance, in the context of identifying crypto-assets that are MiFID II financial instruments. 'Hybrid' tokens may consist of a component comparable to shares and a right to access services or goods,[45] a phenomenon that was common during the boom of so-called Initial Coin Offerings (ICOs) in 2016–2018, for instance, with expectations of a return on the value of a crypto-asset in the event the project to which the initial fund-raising relates succeeds (eg, a start-up brewery) plus access to a good (eg, a barrel of beer).

4.6. Conclusion

The typology of crypto-assets in the sense of MiCAR is divided along the demarcation line of systemic effect vs financial harm.

Crypto-assets that have the potential to gain systemic importance by being used at scale as a store of value and means of exchange, and potentially weakening the transmission of monetary policy, are subjected to the most stringent requirements, including the comprehensive prudential frameworks of Title III and Title IV (the latter in combination with the EMD2). This approach also recognises the implications of potential 'run-like' behaviours of token holders should they wish to redeem *en masse* in the event of a crisis of confidence in an issuer or

[42] MiCAR, Article 4(3)(c) and (4) and Recital (26).

[43] MiCAR, Articles 4(6). See also Article 12(8) concerning changes made in the modified crypto-asset white paper.

[44] MiCAR, Article 6(5)(d) and Recital (30).

[45] See Maume (n 19) 257.

wider market strains. By contrast, Title II crypto-assets are subject to substantially lighter disclosure and conduct of business requirements designed to ensure that investors are made aware of the key features and risks posed by the crypto-assets in question.

The ART and EMT frameworks apply to crypto-assets that formally fall within the relevant (very wide) definitions, even if they do not materially pose any of the mentioned risks. Any crypto-asset purporting to maintain a stable value by referencing currency, rights or values, will be covered by one or the other definition. However, in a traditionally compliance-immature sector, few such crypto-assets may meet the stringent requirements of Title III or Title IV (as applicable), should the tokens be offered to the public or sought admission to trading in the EU. Therefore, the MiCAR regime is potentially creating a great number of cases in which crypto-asset issuers are de-facto non-compliant with Titles III and IV, respectively, and their offering on EU territory illegal, as a consequence. This situation can only be addressed on the side of rigorous enforcement of the rules. That said, in line with a risk-based approach to market surveillance and supervision, national competent authorities are likely only to pursue enforcement action in cases where the potential damage of an ART or EMT exceeds the threshold of materiality in the authority's Member State. However, that threshold is not defined, neither at the level of Member States nor at EU level in the case of potential coordinated actions of national supervisors, absent an EU-wide supervision mechanism, save for those authorised ARTs and EMTs determined to be significant. The consequences for legal certainty and market efficiency are severe.

MiCAR casts its net also extremely widely in relation to Title II crypto-assets. Even though regulatory obligations are significantly lighter, relevant enforcement must follow a risk-based approach, under which the national competent authorities prioritise enforcement in relation to those tokens that pose a material risk. Again, the consequences for legal certainty and market efficiency will be tangible.

5

Offer and Admission to Trading of Crypto-Assets Other than ARTs and EMTs

HEIKKI MARJOSOLA AND MARIKA SALO-LAHTI

5.1. Introduction

This chapter focuses on Title II of MiCAR[1] (Articles 4 to 15), which concerns the offer to the public of crypto-assets other than asset-referenced tokens (ARTs) or e-money tokens (EMTs) as well as the admission to trading of such crypto-assets. Under MiCAR, the offering to the public and admission to trading of Title II crypto-assets[2] are regulated activities, which means that several requirements must be met, and steps completed, before either of the activities can be carried out in the EU. Title II encompasses a mix of regulatory strategies. On the one hand, Title II of MiCAR stands out from the rest of MiCAR by focusing primarily on information regulation. The majority of the rules concern the publication and notification of a specific primary market disclosure document (ie, crypto-asset white paper) and marketing communications. These rules differ little in substance from the regulation of ordinary capital raising in the EU,[3] except by being less prescriptive. On the other hand, Title II includes a consumer protection measure that is less familiar in capital markets law. Under Article 13 of MiCAR, all retail holders who purchase Title II crypto-assets directly from an offeror, or from a crypto-asset service provider (CASP) placing crypto-assets on behalf of the offeror, have 14 calendar days to withdraw from the agreement.

[1] Regulation (EU) 2023/1114 of the European Parliament and of the Council of 31 May 2023 on markets in crypto-assets, and amending Regulations (EU) No 1093/2010 and (EU) No 1095/2010 and Directives 2013/36/EU and (EU) 2019/1937, OJ L 150, 9.6.2023, pp 40–205.

[2] We use the term 'Title II crypto-assets' throughout this chapter to refer to all crypto-assets falling under MiCAR's Title II.

[3] For the primary market, see, eg, Regulation (EU) 2017/1129 of the European Parliament and of the Council of 14 June 2017 on the prospectus to be published when securities are offered to the public or admitted to trading on a regulated market, and repealing Directive 2003/71/EC, OJ L 168, 30.6.2017, pp 12–82 (Prospectus Regulation).

Title II also includes principles-based conduct of business obligations, such as the duty to act honestly, fairly and professionally (Article 14(1)(a)), that are similar to those applicable to investment firms under the Markets in Financial Instruments Directive 2014/65/EU (MiFID II).[4]

In this chapter, we present a systematic picture of MiCAR Title II and analyse its key features. In section 5.2, we discuss the scope of Title II, which is carefully tailored but also somewhat ambiguous, particularly with respect to the type of assets falling under its remit. Section 5.3 goes through the key duties and rights of holders of Title II assets and persons offering them and seeking admission to trading. To better understand the nature of these rules, we will highlight certain similarities and dissimilarities with existing EU financial regulation such as MiFID II, the Prospectus Regulation, the Transparency Directive,[5] and the Crowdfunding Regulation.[6] Section 5.4 discusses the remedies and enforcement powers designed to ensure the effectiveness of Title II rules. In section 5.5, we provide analytical commentary, focussing particularly on the hybrid nature of Title II rules, which combine elements from traditional financial law and consumer law, and the critical role of investor disclosure as a regulatory strategy. The chapter also includes a brief comment on the potential role of technology in enhancing investor protection and how MiCAR Title II might help enabling it. Section 5.6 concludes.

5.2. The Scope of Title II

The personal scope of Title II is relatively straightforward. Except for explicitly exempted entities listed under Article 2(2) MiCAR, Title II applies to all persons or undertakings that offer to the public crypto-assets other than EMTs or ARTs or who seek admission to trading of such assets.[7] Natural persons are prohibited from engaging in either of the activities; both the persons offering to the public of crypto-assets and the persons seeking their admission to trading must be legal persons.[8] Offerors are defined as persons who offer crypto-assets to the public, ie, communicate to persons in any form, and by any means, 'presenting sufficient information on the terms of the offer and the crypto-assets to be offered so as to enable prospective holders to decide whether to purchase those crypto-assets'.[9]

[4] Article 24 of Directive 2014/65/EU of the European Parliament and of the Council of 15 May 2014 on markets in financial instruments, OJ L 173, 12.6.2014, p 349 (MiFID II).

[5] Directive 2004/109/EC of the European Parliament and of the Council of 15 December 2004 on the harmonisation of transparency requirements in relation to information about issuers whose securities are admitted to trading on a regulated market and amending Directive 2001/34/EC, OJ L 390, 31.12.2004, pp 38–57 (Transparency Directive).

[6] Regulation (EU) 2020/1503 of the European Parliament and of the Council of 7 October 2020 on European crowdfunding service providers for business, OJ L 347, 20.10.2020, pp 1–49.

[7] MiCAR, Article 2(1).

[8] MiCAR, Article 4(1) and Article 5(1).

[9] Article 3(1)(12)–(13). The definition under Article 3(1)(12) trails closely the definition of an 'an offer of securities to the public' in Article 2(i)(d) of the Prospectus Regulation.

The offeror and the issuer of Title II crypto-assets can be the same entity,[10] but this is not necessary.

The material scope of Title II, ie, type of crypto-assets to which it applies, is defined in exceptionally broad terms. The asset must first of all fulfil the general qualities of crypto-assets as defined in MiCAR, ie, represent value or a right in a digital format and to be able to be transferred and stored electronically using distributed ledger technology or similar technology.[11] If the asset fulfils those qualities, and it does not qualify as an ART or EMT, it falls as a rule under Title II. By defining Title II crypto-assets in such open-ended and residual manner, MiCAR ensures that it is future-proof and captures 'all types of crypto-assets that currently fall outside the scope of Union legislative acts on financial services.'[12]

In contrast to its open-ended scope, Title II explicitly identifies only one specific type of crypto-asset that falls under it: utility tokens. The term 'utility token' is defined broadly as a crypto-asset intending 'to provide access to a good or a service supplied by its issuer'.[13] Utility tokens represent the part of the token economy having the clearest connection to the real economy, in that their basic purpose is to 'provide consumptive rights on services and products through a blockchain-based platform.'[14] Utility tokens are therefore designed to support a productive enterprise.

By regulating the issuance and marketing of utility tokens more leniently than other types of crypto-assets, MiCAR seeks to support innovative and inclusive financing methods, particularly in relation to the financing of small and medium-sized enterprises (SMEs).[15] The universe of utility tokens is diverse and expanding. Established utility tokens include, inter alia, Filecoin (FIL), which provides access to a decentralised storage network, and Basic Attention Token (BAT), which facilitates the functioning of a blockchain-based private ad platform. Utility tokens may also entail governance rights which allow holders to influence, typically by casting votes, certain decisions by the issuing entity.[16] An example is UNI, which allows voting within the Uniswap decentralised exchange protocol. Although primarily a 'governance token', UNI also facilitates the functioning of the exchange by enabling their staking within the Uniswap liquidity protocols. The most important utility tokens are those that facilitate transactions on blockchain networks such as Solana (SOL), Ethereum (ETH), or Binance (BNB) where the tokens are used, eg, to pay for transaction fees.

[10] For instance, in so-called initial exchange offerings (IEOs), where the asset is admitted to trading on the operator's own initiative, the rules on admission to trading under Article 5(1) apply to the operator of a crypto-asset trading platform. See MiCAR, Article 5(2).

[11] MiCAR, Article 3(1)(5)).

[12] MiCAR, Recital (16).

[13] MiCAR, Article 3(1)(9)).

[14] H Benedetti, C Caceres and L Abarzúa, 'Utility Tokens' in HK Baker, H Benedetti, E Nikbakht and SS Smith (eds), *The Emerald Handbook on Cryptoassets: Investment Opportunities and Challenges* (Emerald Publishing Limited 2021) 79–92, dx.doi.org/10.2139/ssrn.4088568.

[15] MiCAR, Recital (2).

[16] DA Zetzsche et al, 'The Markets in Crypto-Assets regulation (MiCA) and the EU digital finance strategy' (2021) 16(2) *Capital Markets Law Journal* 203, 206.

MiCAR's rules on offering of crypto-assets under Title II are more calibrated to ensure that they are proportionate and risk-based. Title II sets out a threefold structure: Some crypto-asset offers are subject to all the requirements imposed in Title II; certain offers are exempted entirely from Title II; and, certain other offers are exempted only from the requirement to draw up and publish a crypto-asset white paper and marketing communications.[17] These three categories are illustrated in Table 5.1 below.

Table 5.1 The scope of MiCAR Title II rules on offers of crypto-assets

Entire Title II applies	**Title II applies in part (Article 4(2))**	**Title II does not apply (Article 4(3))**
All crypto-assets other than EMTs or ARTs that • have an identifiable issuer (Recital 22); • are not unique and are fungible (Recital 10); • are not captured by other relevant EU legislation (notably MiFID II and Prospectus Regulation); and • do not qualify for specific exemptions under MiCAR. For instance: • utility tokens; • algorithmic crypto-assets that do not aim to stabilise their value by referencing one or several assets (Recital 41); • unique physical assets that have been tokenised and issued in fractional parts (Recital 11).	The requirement to draw up, notify and publish (along with marketing communications) a crypto-asset white paper does not apply to: • Offers to fewer than 150 persons per Member State where such persons are acting on their own account; • Small offers (total consideration does not exceed 1 million EUR per 12 months); • Offers made solely to qualified investors; • Subsequent offers of the same crypto-asset where MiCAR-compliant white paper has already been published and relevant consents are received (Article 4(7)).	No requirement of Title II applies where any of the following conditions are met: • The crypto-asset is offered for free;[18] • The crypto-asset is automatically created as a reward for maintaining/validating tasks related to the distributed ledger; • The offer concerns a utility token that provides access to an already existing good or service; • The crypto-asset gives the holder the right to use it only in exchange for goods and services in a limited network of merchants with contractual arrangements with the offeror.

The first column of Table 5.1 again reflects the open-ended scope of Title II. But it also confirms that there are several important crypto-assets that fall entirely

[17] As set out under Article 4(1) points (b), (c), (d) and (f).

[18] The second subparagraph of Article 4(3) further clarifies that 'a crypto-asset shall not be considered to be offered for free where purchasers are required to provide, or to undertake to provide, personal data to the offeror in exchange for that crypto-asset, or where the offeror of a crypto-asset receives from prospective holders of that crypto-asset any fees, commissions, or monetary or non-monetary benefits in exchange for that crypto-asset.'

outside MiCAR. The crypto-asset must first of all be such that it has an identifiable issuer. As Recital 22 of MiCAR explains:

> Where crypto-asset services are provided in a fully decentralised manner without any intermediary, they should not fall within the scope of this Regulation [...]. Where crypto-assets have no identifiable issuer, they should not fall within the scope of Title II, III or IV of this Regulation.

MiCAR is not entirely clear on what types of activity fall under the 'issuance' of crypto-assets. Unlike the case with EMTs and ARTs, Title II does not directly regulate the issuance of crypto-assets. The term 'issuer' is defined tautologically under Article 3(1)(10) as someone 'who issues crypto-assets'. Recital (20) further clarifies that issuers are 'entities that have control over the creation of crypto-assets.' However, the exclusion of crypto-assets without an identifiable issuer from the scope of Titles II, III and IV of MiCAR does not exempt them from other provisions of MiCAR, including those applicable to CASPs providing services with respect to such crypto-assets.

Another important asset class completely excluded from MiCAR's scope is unique and non-fungible crypto-assets. According to MiCAR's reasoning, such assets are excluded because they cannot have 'financial use'.[19] However, the designation of an asset by the issuer is of no definitive legal consequence: following the substance over form approach, a crypto-asset designated as a non-fungible token (NFT) can *de facto* have features that make it fungible or not sufficiently unique, and thus it would be captured by MiCAR's substantive scope.[20] To be excluded, both the issued token and the underlying right or asset must be unique and non-fungible. Where a crypto-asset does not meet these requirements – for instance where the underlying asset is unique but it is tokenised in fractional parts – the crypto-asset falls under MiCAR.

The third excluded asset class is financial instruments such as shares, debentures, units in collective investments schemes and derivatives. Whether tokenised or not, they remain regulated under existing EU financial markets law.[21] This respects the key principle of 'same activities, same risks, same rules' and technological neutrality.[22] MiCAR provides little guidance on what distinguishes Title II crypto-assets from financial instruments covered by the MiFID regime.[23] The responsibility for the correct classification of crypto-assets lies primarily with the offerors or persons seeking admission to trading, but this is subject to oversight by the ESAs and national competent authorities.[24] The classification can be challenged

[19] According to MiCAR, Recital (10), non-fungible and unique crypto-assets 'are not readily interchangeable and the relative value of one such crypto-asset in relation to another, each being unique, cannot be ascertained by means of comparison to an existing market or equivalent asset.'

[20] MiCAR, Recitals (10)–(11).

[21] MiCAR, Recital (9). MiCAR also excludes e-money, deposits, and structured deposits and securitised assets. See ESMA, Consultation Paper, On the draft Guidelines on the conditions and criteria for the qualification of crypto-assets as financial instruments, 29 January 2024, ESMA75-453128700-52.

[22] See MiCAR, Recital (9).

[23] Zetzsche et al (n 16) 219–20.

[24] MiCAR, Recital (14).

by the competent authorities, also after the offer has been concluded.[25] Competent authorities can request opinions from the ESAs on the classification of crypto-assets.[26] Resolving such classification questions in a consistent and predictable way throughout the EU will be challenging, and regulatory arbitrage risks are evident.[27] The task is made more challenging by the fact that the assets themselves continue to evolve with their native ecosystems.[28] To cope with such uncertainty, MiCAR calibrates the perimeter of Title II rules in a way that is familiar to EU financial law, ie, mandating ESMA to develop guidelines on the conditions and criteria for the qualification of crypto-assets as financial instruments (Article 2(5)).[29]

Columns 2 and 3 of Table 5.1 include the qualified exemptions provided under Articles 4(2) and 4(3) MiCAR regarding the offering of Title II assets. Exempting certain types of offer based on their size (small offers) or the quality or number of targeted investors (qualified investors; fewer than 150 persons per Member State) is in accordance with the EU's prospectus regime,[30] and the general goal of the Capital Market Union to ease access to capital market funding, particularly for SMEs.[31]

The full exemptions listed in column 3, which relate eg, to free token offers and certain automatically created tokens (including mining rewards), are more idiosyncratic. The fact that Article 4(3) exempts these activities and crypto-assets entirely from Title II is not as radical as it seems. No exemptions provided under Article 4, including those listed in 3 of Table 5.1, apply where the offeror or its agent 'makes known in any communication its intention to seek admission to trading' of the asset in question.[32] Where such intent is signalled, the offeror will be subject to Title II in its entirety. And if the offered asset in question is already admitted to trading, the offer will fall under Article 5 of MiCAR which regulates admissions to trading.[33] Under Article 5, the person seeking admission will be exempted from the duty to draw-up, notify and publish a crypto-asset white paper only when there already exists a white paper drawn up and updated in accordance

[25] ibid. See also DA Zetzsche, RP Buckley, DW Arner and MC van Ek, 'Remaining regulatory challenges in digital finance and crypto-assets after MiCA', Policy Department for Economic, Scientific and Quality of Life Policies Directorate-General for Internal Policies. PE740.083 – May 2023, 112. Zetzsche et al. propose the introduction of a default rule, under which all crypto-assets would be at first deemed as 'transferable security'.

[26] MiCAR, Recital (14).

[27] T Tomczak, 'Crypto-Assets and crypto-assets' subcategories under MiCA Regulation' (2022) 17(3) *Capital Markets Law Journal* 365, 370–71.

[28] For various use cases, functions, organisational models, and tokenomics designs of utility tokens, see HK Baker et al (eds), *The Emerald Handbook on Cryptoassets: Investment Opportunities and Challenges* (Emerald Publishing Limited, 2023). CoinMarketCap lists prices for 10,097 active crypto-assets. See CoinMarketCap, 'Today's Cryptocurrency Prices by Market Cap', www.coinmarketcap.com.

[29] On 29 January 2024, ESMA published a Consultation paper 'On the draft Guidelines on the conditions and criteria for the qualification of crypto-assets as financial instruments', which proposes guidelines for determining whether a crypto-asset is a financial instrument.

[30] See Prospectus Regulation, Article 1(3)–(4).

[31] N Moloney, *EU Securities and Financial Markets Regulation* (Oxford University Press, 2023) 95–96.

[32] MiCAR, Article 4(4).

[33] MiCAR, Article 5(1)(b)–(d).

with Articles 6 and 12 of MiCAR. In addition, the person responsible for drawing up such a white paper must give a written consent to its subsequent use. As noted above, the application of these rules, along with the rest of Title II, nevertheless requires that a specific entity in control of the issue can be identified. It might be hard to predict when this is the case, given that the degree of decentralisation varies significantly between different systems.

5.3. Key Duties and Rights under Title II

5.3.1. Risks and Rationales

Crypto-assets are a risky asset class. This has not gone unnoticed by financial regulatory authorities, who have issued regular warnings to customers over the past decade.[34] In its 2022 warning, the European Supervisory Authorities (ESAs) listed the following key risks associated with crypto-assets: extreme price movements; misleading information, lack of protection; product complexity; fraud and malicious activity; market manipulation; lack of price transparency; low liquidity; hacks, operational risks; and security problems.[35] To counter such risks, MiCAR subjects crypto market participants to a wide range of disclosure duties, organisational requirements and prudential rules.

Title II of MiCAR nevertheless stands out from the rest of MiCAR by focusing primarily on information regulation. The focus on disclosure is not surprising, given that in terms of risks such as fraud, misrepresentation, product complexity and lack of transparency, markets for Title II crypto-assets are not that different from traditional financial markets. Accordingly, the rationales for regulation are also similar.[36] At the same time, the risks posed by Title II crypto-assets are both different and less substantial compared to the market integrity, financial stability and monetary policy risks potentially created by EMTs and ARTs. Accordingly, Title II does not include any entry restrictions (authorisation and licensing requirements)[37] or prudential rules such as own funds or reserve requirements.[38]

[34] The EBA issued its first warning on virtual currencies in 2013. See EBA, 'Warning to Consumers on Virtual Currencies', EBA/WRG/2013/01 (2013). See also, eg, ESAs, 'ESMA, EBA and EIOPA Warn Consumers on the Risks of Virtual Currencies' (2018).

[35] The European Supervisory Authorities (ESAs), 'EU financial regulators warn consumers on the risks of crypto-assets'. ESAs 2022, 2, www.esma.europa.eu/sites/default/files/library/esa_2022_15_joint_esas_warning_on_crypto-assets.pdf.

[36] Zetzsche et al (n 25) 42.

[37] During Trilogues the European Parliament added an authorisation requirement: 'subparagraph (ba) was added to Article 4(1) and it imposes the requirement of authorization from a competent authority.' See Tomczak (n 27) 379. See the relevant European Parliament document from 17 March 2022, www.europarl.europa.eu/doceo/document/A-9-2022-0052_EN.pdf. The Compromise Text from 5 October 2022 data.consilium.europa.eu/doc/document/ST-13198-2022-INIT/en/pdf, and the final version of MiCAR do not include subparagraph (ba) and therefore do not impose authorisation requirements for offerors of crypto-assets other than EMTs and ARTs.

[38] MiCAR, Recitals (6), (18) and (49). See also Tomczak (n 27) 377–80.

Also, whereas MiCAR imposes stricter requirements for significant ARTs (Title III) and significant EMTs (Title IV), as well as for significant crypto-asset service providers (Title VI), it does not recognise significant Title II crypto-assets.

As in EU securities regulation, the rules concerning offering and admission to trading of Title II crypto-assets are primarily designed to mitigate information asymmetries between issuers (and insiders) and investors. The main information regulation is contained in Articles 6 and 12, which regulate the content and form of the crypto-asset white paper (including its summary), and Article 7, which concerns marketing communications. In the following section we will compare these rules with similar regulation in MiFID II and the Prospectus Regulation. An analysis of the disclosure regime in MiCAR Title II would be incomplete without examining the rules mandating ongoing disclosure of material information. Therefore, we will briefly look at the rules requiring public disclosure of inside information (Article 88), although these fall outside Title II. Finally, we will analyse the key customer protection measure of MiCAR Title II, that is, the right of withdrawal under Article 13.

5.3.2. Crypto-asset White Papers

In primary securities markets, where securities are first offered to investors, disclosure rules are designed to reduce the risk of fraud and misrepresentation while also supporting issuers in signalling their quality and thus mitigating the 'market for lemons' effect.[39] Quality signalling problems have been particularly ubiquitous in crypto-markets where fraud has been prevalent. The historical data shows that initial coin offerings (ICOs) have a high rate of failure.[40] Many ICOs have been reported where the issuer was either non-existent or disappeared soon after the ICO.[41] The US Consumer Financial Protection Bureau reported in 2022 that of the more than 8,300 crypto-asset-related consumer complaints since 2018, roughly 40 per cent were frauds and scams.[42] Another problem has been the lack of standardisation. The content, length and structure of unregulated white papers have been diverse, making it difficult for investors to compare different crypto-assets.[43]

The disclosure rules of MiCAR Title II follow the general logic of securities regulation. Their core function is to reduce information asymmetries by providing

[39] Moloney (n 31) 73–74.

[40] P de Andrés, D Arroyo, R Correia and A Rezola, 'Regulatory and market challenges of initial coin offerings' (2019) ECGI Law Working Paper No. 461/2019.

[41] ESMA 2019, Advice, Initial Coin Offerings and Crypto-Assets, 14 www.esma.europa.eu/sites/default/files/library/esma50-157-1391_crypto_advice.pdf.

[42] Consumer Financial Protection Bureau, Complaint Bulletin – An analysis of consumer complaints related to crypto-assets, November 2022.

[43] See eg J Thewissen, P Shrestha, W Torsin and AM Pastwa, 'Unpacking the black box of ICO white papers: A topic modelling approach' (2022) 75 *Journal of Corporate Finance* 102225.

investors with the information necessary to make informed decisions. The information disclosed should be correct, and there should be enough of it. The economic rationale is simple. Due to externalities and public good problems, offerors, if unregulated, would disclose a sub-optimal amount of information, or would provide the information in a form that the market participants could not effectively use. Mandatory disclosure corrects incentive problems, prevents free-riding and promotes standardisation, which is considered a public good.[44] The emphasis on primary market disclosure is particularly justified in the case of SMEs where there might be little historical data, or none at all, to evaluate the possible performance of the project.

The disclosure rules in MiCAR Title II also follow EU capital markets law in that there is a standardised document at the centre, a 'crypto-asset white paper', that is designed to give investors the core information about the characteristics, functions and risks of the crypto-assets. The white paper is 'an information document containing mandatory disclosures'.[45] The required content and form of the crypto-asset white paper and the publication process are broadly similar to the EU prospectus regime. The obligation to draw up, notify and publish a white paper is associated with the acts of offering to the public of crypto-assets or the admission of crypto-assets to trading.[46] The original MiCAR proposal referred instead to 'issuance' and 'issuers' of crypto-assets, which departed from the wording used in the Prospectus Regulation. This received well-founded criticism and the proposal was subsequently amended.

As noted by Zetsche et al, the terms 'offeror' and 'offerings', unlike the term 'issuer', are well-established terms in EU financial law.[47] The entity offering crypto-assets to the public or the entity seeking their admission to trading is not necessarily the same entity that issued the crypto-assets. However, the lack of a clear definition of the term 'issuer' remains problematic because it is a key term for setting MiCAR's perimeter.[48]

The white paper must contain general information, including:[49]

(1) Information about the issuer, offeror or another person (eg, the operator of the trading platform) seeking admission to trading. This includes such information as the name, legal form, registered office, registration date, legal entity identifier, contact telephone number, email address, etc.
(2) Information about the crypto-asset. This covers the crypto-asset type and a brief, clear and non-technical description of the characteristics of the

[44] See eg Luca Enriques and Sergio Gilotta, 'Disclosure and Financial Market Regulation' in N Moloney, E Ferran and J Payne (eds), *The Oxford Handbook of Financial Regulation* (Oxford University Press, 2015).
[45] MiCAR, Recital (24).
[46] MiCAR, Articles 4(1) and 5(1).
[47] Zetzsche et al (n 16) 222.
[48] As noted above, Titles II, III and IV of MiCAR only apply to crypto-assets with an identifiable issuer.
[49] MiCAR Article 6(1) and Recital (24).

crypto-asset, including its functionality. If a white paper relates to utility tokens, the relevant information should cover the quality and quantity of goods or services to which the utility tokens give access.

(3) Information about the crypto-asset project to be carried out. Such information should generally include the name of the crypto-project and of the crypto-asset, a brief description of the crypto-asset project, an indication as to whether the project concerns utility tokens, and where applicable, the planned use of any funds or other crypto-assets collected.

(4) Information about the offer of the crypto-asset to the public or its admission to trading. This information should cover, inter alia, the amount of the offer, including, where applicable, any minimum and maximum target subscription goals, issue price of the crypto-asset and subscription fees, the total number of crypto-assets to be offered, refund mechanism and timeline, etc.

(5) Information about the rights and obligations attached to the crypto-assets. This includes information about rights and obligations (if any) of the purchaser, procedure and conditions for the exercise of those rights and conditions, if any, under which these rights and obligations may be modified, etc.

(6) Information about the underlying technology. This encompasses information about the DLT and its functioning, protocols and technical standards, incentive mechanisms to validate transactions and applicable fees, etc.

(7) Information about the related risks. These generally include issuer-related risks (eg, its financial situation, business activity and industry, legal and regulatory risks, internal control risks, ESG risks), crypto-assets-related risks, project implementation-related risks and technology-related risks.

(8) Information about the adverse climate and environmental effects of the consensus-mechanism. The content, methodologies and presentation of information in respect of sustainability indicators in relation to adverse impacts on the climate and other environment-related adverse impacts must be laid down in draft regulatory technical standards by ESMA.[50]

Apart from points (6) and (8), which address risks that are more idiosyncratic to crypto-assets, the other elements resemble those found in the Prospectus Regulation.[51] Article 6 MiCAR also lists more specific disclosure items, such as statements about possible lack of liquidity and transferability, as well as the risk that the crypto-asset may lose its value.[52] Any speculation about the future value of crypto-assets is prohibited.[53] White papers should be concise and comprehensible and present information in a fair, clear and not misleading way.[54]

[50] MiCAR, Recital (7) and Article 6(12). See also ESMA, Consultation Paper, Technical Standards specifying certain requirements of Markets in Crypto Assets Regulation (MiCA) – second consultation paper, 5 October 2023, ESMA75-453128700-438.

[51] Prospectus Regulation, Article 6.

[52] MiCAR, Article 6(5).

[53] MiCAR, Article 6(4).

[54] MiCAR, Article 6(2).

White papers must be published together with marketing communications, if any, on the website of the offeror. The publication must be made at 'a reasonable time in advance of, and in any event before the starting date of, the offer to the public of those crypto-assets or the admission to trading of those crypto-assets.'[55] Just as in the prospectus regime, MiCAR Title II requires that the white paper be accompanied by a summary. This instrument, which addresses the specific needs of retail buyers, will be discussed in more detail below.

MiCAR also replicates the distinction found in the Prospectus Regulation between primary and secondary issuances. Secondary issues can be subject to significantly lighter disclosure requirements or even no requirements at all.[56] Although the first paragraph of MiCAR Article 4(7) provides that 'any subsequent offer to the public of the crypto-asset [...] shall be deemed a separate offer [...]', the second paragraph of the same provision exempts such offers from the duty to draw up and publish an additional white paper. This is largely in line with Article 1(5)(a) of the Prospectus Regulation.

White papers and marketing materials, where applicable, must be modified 'whenever there is a significant new factor, material mistake or material inaccuracy that is capable of affecting the assessment of the crypto-assets' (Article 12(1)). Unlike prospectuses, which are not amended but 'supplemented' following a process outlined in Article 23 of the Prospectus Regulation, the modified crypto-asset white paper must be notified and published in its entirety, together with amended marketing communications, where applicable.[57] Somewhat confusingly, MiCAR Article 12(1) provides that the requirement to modify the white paper 'applies for the duration of the offer to the public or *for as long as the crypto-asset is admitted to trading*' (emphasis added). The intention has probably not been to extend the obligation beyond the point in time when trading on the market begins.[58] If applied throughout the entire trading period, such an obligation to modify the crypto-asset white paper would constitute a cumbersome way of implementing a type of continuous disclosure obligation. By contrast, in Article 23 of the Prospectus Regulation, the time period for supplements is defined as being the time between 'when the prospectus is approved and the closing of the offer period or the time when trading on a regulated market begins, whichever occurs later.' This type of definition would be preferable also in MiCAR.

Not only is the time span for updating the information defined differently in MiCAR compared to the Prospectus Regulation, but the time span for keeping the information publicly available is also different. According to Article 9 MiCAR, crypto-asset white papers and, where applicable, the marketing communications shall remain available for as long as the crypto-assets are 'held by the public'. Article 21 of the Prospectus Regulation, in contrast, states that all prospectuses

[55] MiCAR, Article 9(1).

[56] See Article 14 of the Prospectus Regulation for the simplified disclosure regime for secondary issuances.

[57] MiCAR, Article 12(6).

[58] The wording appears consistent in MiCAR's other language versions, such as Finnish, Swedish and German.

approved shall remain publicly available for at least 10 years after their publication. This timeframe for public availability is aligned with that of annual and half-yearly financial reports under the Directive 2004/109/EC.[59]

In terms of the content of the offering document, the MiCAR white paper requirements are generally more flexible and less prescriptive than their Prospectus Regulation counterparts. The Prospectus Regulation and its relevant annexes describe categories of information for different prospectus types in a fair amount of detail. The nearly 200 pages-long Prospectus delegated regulation sets out a granular list of further requirements.[60] Beyond MiCAR's Annex I, which describes in broad terms the disclosure items required under Article 6, the form and content of the crypto-asset white papers are left to be developed by market practice. The provision mandates neither the ESAs nor the Commission to develop delegated or implementing acts specifying further the content and form of the crypto-asset white papers. However, ESMA, in cooperation with the EBA, must develop draft implementing technical standards to establish standard forms, formats and templates for the purposes of ensuring that white papers are machine readable (Article 6(11)). The scope of ESMA's mandate is, however, limited by the items to be included in the white paper, as set out in Annex I of MiCAR. ESMA, therefore, cannot provide for additional disclosure requirements, at least in a form that would become binding EU law.

Another crucial difference between the prospectus and MiCAR regimes is that MiCAR does not set out a 'materiality standard' comparable to Article 6(1) of the Prospectus Regulation. According to the latter, 'a prospectus shall contain the necessary information which is material to an investor for making an informed assessment.' In the prospectus regime, this standard is used as the main benchmark for assessing the issuer's liability for negligent or fraudulent prospectus disclosure in national private law systems.[61] In terms of materiality of information, MiCAR only provides a negative standard according to which the white paper should 'not contain material omissions'.[62] It further explains in its preamble that the white paper 'should not contain a description of risks that are unforeseeable and very unlikely to materialise.'[63] It is not evident that this approach supports the effective enforcement of issuer liability as regards misrepresentations (see section 5.4 below) or the general obligation under MiCAR to present the crypto-asset white paper 'in a concise and comprehensible' form.[64]

The most significant difference to the prospectus regime is that MiCAR Title II does not require prior approval by national competent authorities of crypto-asset white papers, or related marketing communications, before their publication

[59] Prospectus Regulation, Recital (63).
[60] Commission Delegated Regulation (EU) 2019/980 of 14 March 2019.
[61] Moloney (n 31) 111.
[62] MiCAR, Article 6(2).
[63] MiCAR, Recital (24).
[64] MiCAR, Article 6(2).

(Article 8(3)).[65] As a rule, an offeror, a person seeking admission to trading, or an operator of a trading platform for Title II crypto-assets must only notify the white paper to the competent authority of their home Member State.[66] Here the treatment of Title II crypto-assets is again more lenient than in the case of ARTs, which can be offered to the public or admitted to trading only after the competent authority has approved the relevant crypto-asset white paper.[67] The notification must explain why the crypto-asset described in the white paper falls under MiCAR Title II, ie, why the asset is neither an EMT nor an ART or some other excluded asset, such as a financial instrument falling outside the scope of MiCAR.[68]

Offerors and persons seeking admission to trading of Title II crypto-assets benefit from a 'European passport'. Upon publishing the crypto-asset white paper in accordance with MiCAR Title II rules, the crypto-assets may be offered throughout the EU and be admitted to trading on any trading platform in the EU.[69] As is usually the case in EU financial law, the passporting right is subject to prior notification. MiCAR's two-stage notification procedure for cross-border offers and admissions, set out in Article 8(6), is innovative. In the first stage, offerors and persons seeking admission to trading of Title II crypto-assets must provide their home Member State's competent authority, together with the initial white paper notification, a list of the host Member States where they intend to offer their crypto-assets or seek admission to trading. This notification must also include information on the starting date of the intended offer or intended admission to trading. In the second stage, the competent authority notifies the relevant authorities of the host Member States of the intended offer or the intended admission to trading, together with the corresponding crypto-asset white paper.

5.3.3. Ongoing Disclosure Rules

Since Title II crypto-assets are transferable assets that can be admitted to trading in a secondary market, there is an obvious need for disclosure after the publication of the crypto-asset white paper and, where applicable, the commencement of trading.

[65] For a critical view, see Zetzsche et al (n 16) 212, noting that 'mere ex post enforcement and accountability through liability does not really seem sufficient to ensure adequate levels of integrity and confidence in the market.' According to Zetzsche et al., 'Only public authorities' ex ante review – coordinated by ESMA – can ensure a harmonized application of MiCA.'

[66] Under MiCAR Article 3(1)(35) 'competent authority' means one or more authorities (a) designated by each Member State in accordance with Article 93 of MiCAR concerning offerors, persons seeking admission to trading of Title II crypto-assets, issuers of asset-referenced tokens, or crypto-asset service providers; and (b) one or more authorities designated by each Member State for the application of Directive 2009/110/EC concerning issuers of e-money tokens.

[67] See MiCAR, Recital (43).

[68] MiCAR, Article 8(4).

[69] MiCAR, Article 11.

In secondary markets for securities, mandatory disclosure rules serve various goals and rationales. Disclosure mitigates information asymmetries and associated agency problems, such as excessive compensation, self-dealing and other forms of managerial (and blockholder) opportunism.[70] The need to incentivise disclosure with mandatory rules has been linked to the public good nature of information, positive externalities related to corporate disclosure (which also incentivises free-riding), and the need to standardise information and subsidise informed traders.[71]

In EU securities law, the relevant rules mandating disclosure are included in the EU Transparency Directive 2004/109/EC, which sets obligations relating to periodic financial reporting, and the Market Abuse Regulation 596/2014 (MAR),[72] which mandates, inter alia, the prompt disclosure of inside information. MiCAR Title II contains, in contrast, no rules concerning ongoing disclosure of material information. The only exception is Article 10(2), according to which offerors of crypto-assets that do not set a time limit on their offer must publish on their website on an ongoing basis and at least monthly the number of units of the crypto-assets in circulation. The omission seems odd, not least because MiCAR mandates issuers of ARTs to disclose 'any event that has or is likely to have a significant effect on the value of the asset-referenced tokens [...].'[73] The shortcoming is nevertheless partly compensated by MiCAR's general rules on inside information, which apply to Title II crypto-assets as well. Under MiCAR Article 88, all issuers, offerors and persons seeking admission to trading must inform the public as soon as possible of inside information[74] that directly concerns them, in a manner that enables fast access as well as complete, correct and timely assessment of the information by the public.[75] Disclosure can be delayed, largely in line with the approach in MAR, where certain legitimate reasons exist.[76]

Issuers of Title II crypto-assets will not be subject to specific duties regarding periodic financial or non-financial reporting. Such issuers – typically blockchain startups – are rarely publicly traded companies, which means that they are not subject to the Transparency Directive's reporting requirements.[77]

[70] See P Mahoney, 'Mandatory Disclosure as a Solution to Agency Problems' (1995) 62 *University of Chicago Law Review* 1047.

[71] A good overview of the debate is provided in Enriques and Gilotta (n 44).

[72] Regulation (EU) No 596/2014 of the European Parliament and of the Council of 16 April 2014 on market abuse, OJ L 173, 12.6.2014, pp 1–61 (MAR).

[73] MiCAR, Article 30(3).

[74] Largely in line with MAR, inside information is defined under MiCAR Article 87(1)(a) as 'information of a precise nature, which has not been made public, relating, directly or indirectly, to one or more issuers, offerors or persons seeking admission to trading, or to one or more crypto-assets, and which, if it were made public, would likely have a significant effect on the prices of those crypto-assets or on the price of a related crypto-asset.'

[75] MiCAR, Article 87(1).

[76] MiCAR, Article 88(2). On the prevention and prohibition of market abuse involving crypto-assets, see Title VI MiCAR and Chapter 9 of this book.

[77] For criticism of this omission, see Zetzsche et al (n 25) 84, arguing that issuers of crypto-assets should be required to publish ongoing information through semi-annual and annual reports.

There is a broader and worthwhile debate to be had as to what extent the above-discussed goals and rationales for mandatory disclosure in securities markets are consistent with the specific information needs of the markets for utility tokens and other Title II crypto-assets. This complex issue will be briefly discussed in section 5.5.

5.3.4. Marketing Communications

When it comes to practical investor decision-making, marketing information may be even more important than the official disclosure in the white paper. According to recent consumer research conducted by the UK's Financial Conduct Authority (FCA), social media plays a significant role in crypto-asset advertising, especially among young people (aged 18–24), 44 per cent of whom heard of crypto-assets for the first time through social media.[78] However, online news, including blogs and forums, is still the most common channel for people to hear of crypto-assets for the first time.[79] The dominant role of marketing can be problematic, as the ESAs have explicitly warned consumers about the misleading advertisements concerning crypto-assets, including via social media and influencers.[80]

The increasing regulation of marketing materials (and the recognition of consumer protection risks relating to new marketing channels such as social media) is part of a larger consumerist trend in the EU financial services regulation. The Commission has emphasised the need to strengthen consumer protection in the context of its digital finance[81] and retail investment strategies.[82] For instance, the recent proposal for an Omnibus Directive as regards the EU retail investor protection rules aims at adapting the framework to the increasing use of digital market channels such as social media for retail investing.[83]

MiCAR's approach to investor protection with respect to marketing communications mainly relies on disclosure obligations. No specific intervention powers or monitoring duties are given to ESMA or national authorities with regard to online marketing activities by third parties.[84] The most important prohibition

[78] M Aju and T Burrell, 'FCA – Research Note: Cryptoassets consumer research 2023' (Wave 4, 8 June 2023) 14. This result was for crypto-asset users. For non-crypto-asset users, traditional media, such as TV and newspapers, was the most common channel to hear of crypto-assets for the first time.

[79] ibid 16–17.

[80] The European Supervisory Authorities (ESAs), EU financial regulators warn consumers on the risks of crypto-assets. ESAs 2022 15 (2022).

[81] Commission Communication on a Digital Finance Strategy for the EU, Brussels, 24.9.2020 COM(2020) 591 final, eur-lex.europa.eu/legal-content/EN/TXT/?uri=CELEX%3A52020DC0591.

[82] See Commission, Retail investment strategy (24 May 2023) finance.ec.europa.eu/publications/retail-investment-strategy_en.

[83] See Commission Proposal for a Directive as regards the Union retail investor protection rules, COM/2023/279 final. (the Omnibus directive proposal) eur-lex.europa.eu/legal-content/EN/TXT/?uri=CELEX:52023PC0279.

[84] Compare the Omnibus directive proposal, Recital (32).

concerns the distribution of marketing communications before the publication of the crypto-asset white paper, where such is required.[85] According to Article 7(1)), all marketing communications, including materials disseminated through digital channels such as social media platforms,[86] should be fair, clear and not misleading and be consistent with the information provided in the white paper. All marketing communications must also be clearly identifiable as marketing, and they should state that no authority has reviewed or approved them (Article 7(1)).

Unlike crypto-asset white papers, which must always be notified to the competent authority of the home Member State, marketing communications must be notified only upon request from the competent authorities of the home Member State or the host Member State.[87] The competent authority of the Member State where the marketing communications are disseminated has the power to assess the compliance of the marketing communications with Article 7(1) content requirements (Article 7(3)).

The MiCAR rules on marketing may seem lenient, particularly compared to the recent initiatives under the EU's retail investment strategy. However, the strong right of withdrawal under Article 13, examined below, safeguards investors, also against aggressive marketing via digital and other channels.[88]

5.3.5. General Conduct of Business Obligations

Article 14 includes general conduct of business obligations for offerors and persons seeking admission to trading. These largely resemble traditional EU financial services law and include a duty: to act honestly, fairly and professionally; to communicate with token holders in a fair, clear and not misleading manner; and to identify, prevent, manage and disclose potential conflicts of interest. These duties have their counterparts, for instance, in MiFID II.[89] Reflecting the idiosyncratic technological risks of crypto-asset markets, MiCAR also requires that offerors and persons seeking admission to trading of crypto-assets maintain their systems and security access protocols in conformity with the appropriate EU standards.[90]

MiCAR duties are nevertheless more relaxed and simpler than MiFID II duties. The duty to act in the best interest of holders and to treat them equally matches MiFID II requirements.[91] In MiCAR, however, this duty can be exempted if the preferential treatment and reasons for it are disclosed in the crypto-asset

[85] MiCAR, Article 7(2).
[86] MiCAR, Recital (24).
[87] MiCAR, Article 8(2). According to Article 3 of MiCAR, 'host Member State' means the Member State other than the home Member State where an offeror or person seeking admission to trading has made an offer to the public of crypto-assets or is seeking admission to trading.
[88] See section 5.3.6.
[89] MiFID II, Articles 23, 24(1) and (24(3).
[90] MiCAR, Article 14(1)(d).
[91] MiFID II, Article 24(1).

white paper as well as marketing communications.[92] Again, the responsibility lies squarely with the investor who should know what they are buying. As another example, MiFID II imposes rather strict governance requirements in its Article 16 on investment firms (eg, duties related to compliance, product approval process, and record-keeping), which must also understand the products they offer and recommend to clients, and provide appropriate information to clients 'in good time'.[93] MiCAR imposes no governance duties, whether corporate governance or product governance related, on issuers of Title II crypto-assets.

MiCAR Title II requirements are also more relaxed than those applicable to ARTs and EMTs. For example, Title II does not impose prudential requirements on issuers. In contrast, MiCAR Article 35 imposes own funds requirements for issuers of ARTs and Article 36 provides a requirement to maintain a reserve of assets. According to Article 34, issuers of ARTs must also establish, among other things, governance arrangements, including policies and procedures to ensure compliance with MiCAR, a business continuity plan, and a complaints-handling procedure. These ART-related requirements will be elaborated in chapter six of this book.

5.3.6. Right of Withdrawal

As the general obligations of Article 14 aim to safeguard investors at a broad level, Article 13 introduces a more direct, consumer law-type tool that seeks to protect retail holders: the right of withdrawal. Retail holders who have purchased Title II crypto-assets directly from an offeror or a crypto-asset service provider placing crypto-assets on behalf of an offeror, have 14 calendar days in which they can withdraw from their crypto-asset purchase without any costs and without giving any reasons. 'Retail holder' is defined as 'any natural person who is acting for purposes which are outside that person's trade, business, craft or profession.'[94] There is no withdrawal right if the crypto-asset has been admitted to trading prior to their purchase (Article 14(4)). No withdrawal rights are available for the purchasers of ARTs and EMTs.

The 14-day right of withdrawal is familiar in EU consumer law, but less typical in financial law.[95] Article 9 of the Consumer Rights Directive 2011/83/EU[96]

[92] MiCAR, Article 14(2)).

[93] See MiFID II, Section II.

[94] MiCAR, Article 3(1)(37).

[95] But see Article 23(2) of the Prospectus Regulation that gives investors two working days to withdraw their acceptances when a supplement to the prospectus has been published and certain other conditions are met.

[96] Directive 2011/83/EU of the European Parliament and of the Council of 25 October 2011 on consumer rights, amending Council Directive 93/13/EEC and Directive 1999/44/EC of the European Parliament and of the Council and repealing Council Directive 85/577/EEC and Directive 97/7/EC of the European Parliament and of the Council.

gives consumers 14 days in which they can withdraw from a distance or off-premises contract, without giving any reasons and without any costs. Article 14 of the Consumer Credit Directive 2008/48/EC[97] also gives a 14-day withdrawal period for consumer credit agreements. The New Consumer Credit Directive, which will repeal and replace the Directive 2008/48/EC, also includes a right of withdrawal.[98]

In contrast, the EU Crowdfunding Regulation gives non-sophisticated investors a 'pre-contractual reflection period', during which they can revoke their offer to invest without giving any reasons and without any penalty.[99] This right expires after four calendar days, which is much shorter than the right of withdrawal period in MiCAR and in consumer law. A 14-day withdrawal period is also included in the Distance Marketing of Consumer Financial Services Directive 2002/65/EC.[100]

5.4. Remedies and Enforcement

As in EU capital markets law generally, the primary responsibility to spot and act on non-compliance with MiCAR rules lies with authorities. Although national competent authorities under MiCAR do not play a gatekeeper role comparable to that under the EU prospectus regime, where authorities scrutinise and approve prospectuses prior to the admittance of securities to public trading, their powers and responsibilities are far from negligible in MiCAR. The supervisory and investigatory powers are set out in Article 94. The national competent authority (NCA), duly notified of the crypto-asset white paper and of the marketing communications, may require the offeror or person seeking admission to trading to amend the crypto-asset white paper or the marketing materials where they fail to comply with the information requirements specified in Articles 6 and 7.[101] The NCA may also have the power to suspend an offer to the public or an admission to trading of crypto-assets for a maximum of 30 consecutive working days

[97] Directive 2008/48/EC of the European Parliament and of the Council of 23 April 2008 on credit agreements for consumers and repealing Council Directive 87/102/EEC.

[98] Directive (EU) of the European Parliament and of the Council of 18 October 2023 on credit agreements for consumers and repealing Directive 2008/48/EC, Article 26.

[99] Regulation (EU) 2020/1503 of the European Parliament and of the Council of 7 October 2020 on European crowdfunding service providers for business, and amending Regulation (EU) 2017/1129 and Directive (EU) 2019/1937, Article 22(2).

[100] It has been argued that the Distance Marketing Directive even applies to equity crowdfunding. See M Meoli and S Vismara, 'Information manipulation in equity crowdfunding markets' (2021) 67 *Journal of Corporate Finance* 101866. However, this directive has recently been repealed with the Directive concerning financial services contracts concluded at a distance (EU) 2023/2673, which confirms that this is not the case. See eg Recital (18), which explicitly states that where an EU act governing specific financial services gives consumers time to consider the implications of the contract signed, only those specific rules will be applied unless otherwise provided. The precedence of specific legislation is not affected by the term used. Instead of right of withdrawal, the right can be called eg, a 'cancellation period' or a 'reflection period'.

[101] MiCAR, Article 94(1)(i) and (j).

where there are reasonable grounds for suspecting that MiCAR obligations have been infringed.[102] Where MiCAR rules have already been infringed, or where there exist reasonable grounds for suspecting that they will be infringed, an offer or admission to trading can be prohibited.[103] Also, marketing communications can be suspended or prohibited.[104] For the purpose of 'naming and shaming', any infringement can also be made public.[105]

Additionally, MiCAR empowers ESMA to impose temporary prohibitions or restrictions on the marketing, distribution and sale of Title II crypto-assets, and on activities and practices related to them, where, for example, a significant investor protection concern so requires.[106] Substantively similar 'product intervention powers' are given to NCAs.[107]

The decentralised nature of certain crypto market infrastructures presents its own distinct enforcement challenges. Traditional financial law is based on the presumption that an intermediary in charge and liable for complying with law can always be identified, even when tasks have been outsourced or delegated.[108] The more decentralised the financial infrastructure, the more difficult it is to determine which court has jurisdiction and which laws, if any, apply.[109] For MiCAR Title II, decentralised finance does not present an enforcement challenge, if only because it falls out of its scope entirely.[110]

MiCAR Title II also stands out by enabling effective delegation of responsibilities. Unlike crypto-asset service providers, who cannot outsource services or activities to third parties without remaining fully responsible for discharging all of their obligations under MiCAR,[111] an operator of a trading platform may effectively assume, by way of a contract entered in accordance with Article 5(3), the obligations set out under MiCAR Article 5(1), which normally apply to the entity that seeks admission of the crypto-assets to trading. These obligations include, inter alia, the key duties to draw up, notify and publish the crypto-asset white paper. Where such a contract is concluded, the person seeking admission to trading remains responsible only for matters not delegated to the operator of the trading platform, or when it has provided misleading information to the operator.[112] This could in principle help avoid the creation of ambiguous hierarchies of liability and accountability.[113] But where a dispute arises as to what has

[102] MiCAR, Article 94(1).
[103] MiCAR, Article 94(1)(m).
[104] MiCAR, Article 94(1)(p).
[105] MiCAR, Article 94(1)(r).
[106] MiCAR, Article 103.
[107] MiCAR, Article 105.
[108] Zetzsche et al (n 25) 46–52.
[109] ibid 49.
[110] See n 113 below.
[111] MiCAR, Article 73.
[112] MiCAR, Recital (32).
[113] D Zetzsche, D Arner and R Buckley, 'Decentralized Finance' (2020) 6(2) *Journal of Financial Regulation* 172.

been delegated, or whether the operator has assumed the responsibilities based on misleading information, enforcement could become cumbersome.

The effectiveness of private enforcement under MiCAR is more questionable. Just as Article 11 of the Prospectus Regulation, Article 15 MiCAR seeks to ensure that offerors and persons seeking admission to trading are responsible for the information provided in the crypto-asset white paper under Member States' civil liability rules. An offeror or a person seeking admission to trading, and the members of their administrative, management or supervisory bodies, can therefore be held directly liable for publishing a white paper that contains information that is misleading, incomplete, unfair or unclear.[114] However, Article 15(4) ensures that the burden of proof will be on the holder of the crypto-asset, who must first establish that Article 6 requirements have been infringed, and then show that they relied on the information when deciding to purchase, sell or exchange the crypto-asset.[115] The Prospectus Regulation, which contains no such provision, leaves more leeway to national private law systems on crucial issues such as burden of proof. As argued by Ferrarini and Giudici, by placing the burden of proof squarely on the claimant or a sanctioning entity, MiCAR may erect insurmountable hurdles to establishing liability.[116]

For issuers of Title II crypto-assets, there is no requirement to establish complaints-handling procedures as is the case with ARTs.[117]

5.5. Assessing Title II and Looking Ahead

5.5.1. Between Consumerism and Efficiency

MiCAR borrows its logic from both capital markets law and consumer law.[118] Its disclosure obligations are functionally similar to those laid down in securities

[114] MiCAR, Article 15(1).

[115] MiCAR, Article 15(4).

[116] G Ferrarini and P Giudici, 'Digital offerings and mandatory disclosure: A market-based critique of MiCA' in E Avgouleas and H Marjosola, *Digital finance in Europe: Law, Regulation, and Governance* (De Gruyter, 2021) 87–107.

[117] MiCAR, Article 31.

[118] In order to systematise the overall regulatory logic of MiCAR, we could also use the 5-I's Model developed by Salo-Lahti and Annola to systematise crowdfunding regulation. The five I's in the model refer to the main regulatory objects in MiCAR: Investor, Investment, Information, Intermediary and Issuer. 'Investor' refers to the protective elements of financial market regulation that are based on the characteristics of investors. An example of this category is client classification: financial market regulation typically safeguards especially retail investors. In MiCAR, 'retail holders' have some specific rights, such as the right of withdrawal. 'Investment' in the model refers to the regulatory tools that relate to the investment itself. In MiCAR, the classification of crypto-assets determines their legal treatment. 'Information' includes disclosure requirements which are typical investor protection tools in financial market law. 'Intermediary' refers to the service providers, such as crypto-asset exchanges and wallet providers. In contrast to crowdfunding regulation, the role of issuers is strong in the crypto-asset regulation. As a result, the fifth 'I' – 'Issuer' – has been added to the original 4-I's Model of crowdfunding in

regulation, even if narrower in scope.[119] At the same time, MiCAR adopts a strong consumer law measure – the withdrawal right – that is unfamiliar to other spheres of financial market regulation.[120]

Utility tokens, which provide access to a good or a service supplied by its issuer, have features of consumer products, which arguably justifies the consumerist approach. One purpose of the right of withdrawal has been to give consumers an opportunity to try the goods or services in order to assess their value before making the final decision about committing.[121] The right is therefore particularly useful for so-called 'experience goods', whose quality can be observed only after the good has been consumed.[122] However, as acknowledged in MiCAR, utility tokens generally refer to goods that do not yet exist or services that are not yet in operation. In fact, Article 4(3)(c) of MiCAR Title II exempts utility tokens that provide access to an already existing good or service entirely from its scope.[123] It would therefore be more accurate to describe Title II crypto-assets as 'credence goods', whose quality may be known only years later.[124] In this sense, they are similar to financial products and services.[125] In other words, a purchaser of a utility token issued by a blockchain startup is unlikely to be able to ascertain within two weeks whether the purchased token, or the future service or functionality it gives access to, is worth the price paid.[126]

The right of withdrawal – a deviation from the contract law principle of *pacta sunt servanda* – can also have significant and unpredictable behavioural consequences. It may increase the willingness to conclude transactions, as consumers can later withdraw from irrational decisions. The right generates confidence by helping to overcome lack of trust towards the trader or the goods and services provided. But it may also encourage irrational decision-making without

order to better serve as a systematisation tool for MiCAR. Although, as already mentioned, there may not always be any issuer. See M Salo-Lahti and V Annola, 'Investor protection strategies in crowdfunding regulation' in P Kalmi, T Auvinen and M Järvenpää (eds), *Responsible Finance and Digitalization: Implications and Developments* (Routledge, 2022); M Salo-Lahti, 'Regulating Crypto-Assets: Investor Protection Strategies and the 5-I's Model' (2023) 34(4) *European Business Law Review* 585.

[119] See sections 5.3.2 and 5.3.3 above.

[120] See section 5.3.6 above.

[121] O Bar-Gill and O Ben-Shahar, 'Regulatory Techniques in Consumer Protection: A Critique of European Consumer Contract Law (2013) 50 *Common Market Law Review* 109, 120; JA Luzak, 'To Withdraw Or Not To Withdraw? Evaluation of the Mandatory Right of Withdrawal in Consumer Distance Selling Contracts Taking Into Account Its Behavioural Effects on Consumers' (2014) 37 *Journal of Consumer Policy* 91, 95.

[122] On different type of goods and quality disclosure, see A Ogus, *Regulation: Legal Form and Economic Theory* (Bloomsbury Publishing, 2004) 132–33.

[123] This exemption does not apply, however, where the offeror, or another person acting on the offeror's behalf, makes known in any communication its intention to seek the token's admission to trading. See MiCAR, Article 4(4).

[124] Ogus (n 122) 133.

[125] On financial products as credence goods, see J Armour et al, *Principles of Financial Regulation* (Oxford University Press, 2016) 56–57.

[126] MiCAR's Recital (26) notes that 'no requirements [of MiCAR] should apply to offers of utility tokens providing access to an existing good or service. Likewise, according to Article 4, Title II shall not apply to offers of such utility tokens.

appropriate and diligent risk assessment, behaviour that is contrary to the type of informed decision-making that capital market regulation aims to promote. Indeed, consumer psychology research indicates that a withdrawal right may encourage consumer laziness when it comes to gathering information before purchasing.[127] The right of withdrawal may also lead to cost inefficiency if traders compensate their losses by raising prices.[128]

The withdrawal right may also encourage speculation. Although the value of purchased and unlisted tokens would not fluctuate during the two weeks withdrawal period, the value of monies or assets used as means of payment could change considerably – especially if the payment has been made in volatile cryptocurrencies. The offeror should nevertheless be able to mitigate such risks contractually: the second paragraph of Article 13(2) provides that the 'reimbursement shall be carried out using the same means of payment as that used by the retail holder for the initial transaction, *unless the retail holder expressly agrees otherwise* [...]' (emphasis added).

Issuers and offerors may also exploit the withdrawal right. Here the early experiences from crowdfunding are noteworthy. As mentioned earlier, the EU Crowdfunding Regulation includes a four-day pre-contractual reflection period.[129] One study has shown that this reflection or 'cooling-off' period may be manipulated to increase the bid's attractiveness.[130] Members of crowdfunding platforms are much more likely than other investors to withdraw their investments before the end of the offering.[131] The practice is reasonable in crowdfunding markets dominated by small and unsophisticated investors who are more likely to 'herd' after early participants.[132] The behaviour of peer investors has an important signalling function also in crypto-markets. This is especially the case with utility tokens or similar platform-specific tokens where network effects are significant.[133] To counter risks of abuse, in our view, investors should be given information on the ratio of cancelled offers before the end of the withdrawal period.

Beyond such consumerism, the fact that Title II crypto-assets can be – and often are – submitted to public trading warrants a more market-oriented approach.[134] However, market efficiency, which is hardly mentioned in MiCAR's

[127] Luzak (n 121) 105.
[128] ibid.
[129] EU Crowdfunding Regulation, Article 22(2).
[130] Meoli and Vismara (n 100).
[131] ibid.
[132] See J Armour and L Enriques, 'The promise and perils of crowdfunding: between corporate finance and consumer contracts' (2018) 81(1) *Modern Law Review* 51, 84, noting that this means that 'the collective decision actually gets made on the basis of less information than the investors may have possessed at the beginning.'
[133] In plain terms, 'the more users the platform has, the easier it is for any user to find a transaction counterparty, and the more useful the tokens are'. LW Cong, Y Li and N Wang, 'Tokenomics: Dynamic Adoption and Valuation' (2021) 34(3) *Review of Financial Studies* 1105, 1106.
[134] L Hornuf, T Kück and A Schwienbacher, 'Initial Coin Offerings, Information Disclosure, and Fraud' (2022) 58 *Small Business Economics* 1741, 1755.

provisions or recitals, is clearly not among its primary concerns. In this, MiCAR departs significantly from modern securities regulation, which protects investors primarily via promoting market efficiency.[135] For instance, although retail investors may be unable or disincentivised to digest the wealth of disclosed information in securities prospectuses, this information is still useful for various information intermediaries such as analysts, underwriters and professional investors. The activities of such intermediaries and informed traders ensure that prices of financial instruments reflect all available information.[136] The rationale, in short, is that 'in an efficient stock market, unsophisticated investors are already protected by market prices'.[137]

The lesser emphasis on efficiency in MiCAR Title II probably reflects fundamental differences in the traded assets themselves. The valuation and pricing of crypto-assets – an emerging topic within financial economics or tokenomics – differ significantly from traditional securities.[138] Title II crypto-assets cannot entail dividend rights or other rights in the project's cash flows (otherwise, they risk being classified as financial instruments).[139] The value of a utility token is based on capitalisation of platform growth and the practical or functional utility of a token within a DLT-based ecosystem rather than the discounted value of future cash flows, as is the case with securities like shares.[140]

The evolving crypto market structure is also different. There are neither 'informed investors' on whom unsophisticated investors could free ride nor established information intermediaries supporting accurate pricing. Therefore, instead of efficiency concerns, the main rationale for mandatory disclosure in the case of Title II crypto-assets stems from the need to mitigate various agency problems and conflicts of interest between principals (holders) and agents (offerors).[141]

The final difference between traditional securities and Title II crypto-assets concerns user groups. Whereas capital markets offer financing for mature companies, Title II crypto assets are more frequently used by young companies and SMEs for funding specific projects. Just as in crowdfunding, utility tokens are

[135] Moloney (n 31) 73–77.

[136] Enriques and Gilotta (n 44).

[137] Enriques and Gilotta (n 44) 515.

[138] Cong et al (n 133) 1106, noting that '[i]n contrast to financial assets whose values depend on cash flows, tokens derive value by enabling users to conduct economic transactions on the digital platform, making them a hybrid of money and investable assets.' On valuation of crypto-assets, see eg T Kostoula, 'Valuation of cryptoassets in EU insolvency: Challenges and prospects' (2023) 32(1) *International Insolvency Review* 8.

[139] See AS Kavuri and A Milne, 'Trading and Regulation of Cryptocurrencies, Stablecoins and Other Cryptoassets' in K Thomas Liaw (ed), *The Routledge Handbook of FinTech* (Routledge, 2021) 147–62, criticising the creation of a parallel regime for crypto-assets as unnecessary and, at worst, counterproductive, possibly resulting in regulatory arbitrage and weakening of the existing regime for financial instruments.

[140] Cong et al (n 133) 1106.

[141] We ignore here Decentralised Autonomous Organisations (DAOs) that lack management bodies and might thus avoid agency problems by design – at least those between management and token holders.

used by start-ups to raise capital from a large number of unsophisticated individuals who typically invest only small sums.[142] The need for more cost-effective and flexible regulation – typical of the regulation of technological innovations – is therefore a key goal for both crypto-assets and crowdfunding. But in terms of investor protection measures, MiCAR falls short of EU crowdfunding rules. The EU Crowdfunding Regulation requires service providers to carry out a thorough appropriateness assessment of prospective non-sophisticated investors, including an entry knowledge test.[143] In the context of crowdfunding, it has even been suggested that the role of the service providers should be extended to include ensuring the accuracy of the provided information, especially when supervisory authorities are not involved in the assessment of the key investment information sheet (KIIS).[144] MiCAR Title V includes no such provisions.[145]

To conclude, in the case of Title II crypto-assets, there exists neither gatekeeper-intermediaries comparable to crowdfunding markets nor information intermediaries protecting investors via the pricing mechanism. Risks are therefore primarily managed by unsophisticated investors themselves, making judgments based on regulated disclosure documents – and having two weeks to change their mind for whatever reason (where the tokens are not listed). The following section will assess the role of disclosure in more detail.

5.5.2. The Disputed Role of Investor Disclosure

Information disclosures are crucial for reducing information asymmetries and related agency problems. However, their contribution to better investor decision-making is often disputed. The European Commission study on investor disclosures found that disclosure is 'a necessary but insufficient means' in helping retail investors in their decision-making.[146] The Commission found that disclosure templates were not 'engaging', that is, they did not encourage investors to read them. This is a serious problem because engagement serves as a foundation for comprehension, and subsequent informed decision-making. Investor information documents that are too long, densely worded, and complex do not serve

[142] On crowdfunding, see Armour and Enriques (n 132) 52.

[143] EU Crowdfunding Regulation, Article 21(1). Macchiavello has nevertheless noted that the ECSPR seems to trust investors more to evaluate projects and manage risks compared to other financial regimes, despite at least equally serious information asymmetry. See E Macchiavello, 'The European Crowdfunding Service Providers Regulation: The Future of Marketplace Lending and Investing in Europe and the "Crowdfunding Nature" Dilemma' (2021) 32(3) *European Business Law Review* 557, 586.

[144] P Staikouras, 'The European Union Proposal for a Regulation on Cross-Border Crowdfunding Services: A Solemn or Pie-Crust Promise?' (2020) 31(6) *European Business Law Review* 977, 1098–1099.

[145] See ch 7 in this book for further analysis. According to Article 140, by 30 June 2027, the Commission shall present a report containing an evaluation of the possibility of introducing appropriateness tests in Articles 78, 79 and 80 'in order to better protect clients of crypto-asset service providers, especially retail holders'.

[146] European Commission, Disclosure, inducements, and suitability rules for retail investors study. Final Report. May 2022 – corrected in February 2023, 14.

their intended purpose and can have negative effects on consumers.[147] In its retail investment strategy, the Commission accordingly notes that 'retail investors have difficulties accessing relevant, comparable and easily understandable investment product information to help them make informed investment choices.'[148]

These risks are pertinent in crypto markets as well. Thewissen et al found that among the sample of 5210 white papers they surveyed, the median length of a white paper was 30 pages, while the lengths varied from three pages to 167 pages.[149] Due to disclosure requirements brought by MiCAR, both the document length and the level of technical detail can be expected to keep rising. Assessing the offered instruments is even more demanding for crypto investors who may have to understand both the technical and financial sides of crypto-assets to manage risks effectively. Cyber-attacks and thefts remain persistent features of the crypto-markets. Due to the strict technology dependency, complications relating to the underlying technology can have adverse effects on market value. This emphasises the role of non-financial information related to issues such as IT architecture, system design and stability. It is therefore welcome that Article 6 of MiCAR lists 'information on the underlying technology' as one of the content requirements for a white paper. But further emphasis needs to be put on presenting such information in a clear and comprehensible manner. According to a study by the FCA, the understanding of the underlying technology is not strong among crypto-asset owners, and less than half (47 per cent) believe they have a good understanding of how the underlying technology works.[150]

To alleviate the problems of overly lengthy and technical investor disclosures, the EU financial market legislation has introduced several simplified investor disclosure documents. A good example is the EU Crowdfunding Regulation and its KIIS. According to its Article 23, a KIIS must be fair, clear and not misleading and must not contain footnotes. Its maximum length has been restricted to six sides of A4-sized paper if printed.[151] Much attention is paid to the understandability of information in a KIIS. Information must be presented in a way that is 'easy to read' and that facilitates understanding.

There are several similarities between a KIIS and Title II crypto asset white papers. First, information on the project funded is at the core. The information

[147] ibid.

[148] See Commission proposal for Omnibus directive, Brussels, 24.5.2023, COM(2023) 279 final, eur-lex.europa.eu/legal-content/EN/TXT/?uri=CELEX:52023PC0279.

[149] Thewissen et al (n 43). The white papers in the sample were published between 2015–2020. The most discussed topics in the white papers were the ICO's blockchain application and platform development. Interestingly, topics related to legal features and risk management were the least discussed.

[150] Financial Conduct Authority (FCA), Research Note: Cryptoassets consumer research 2023 (8 June 2023) 43.

[151] ESMA has also developed a standardised KIIS model that must be followed. See ESMA, Final Report. Draft technical standards under the European crowdfunding service providers for business Regulation (10 November 2021), ESMA35-42-1183, elaborating the requirements and models for presenting the information in the KIIS, including the presentation of certain risks, financial ratios and costs and charges.

provided under Title II crypto-asset white papers should be fair, clear and not misleading and it should be presented in a concise and comprehensible form.[152] Second, both disclosure documents start with similar disclaimers, warning investors that the documents have not been approved by competent authorities. This is an important difference compared to more traditional financial disclosures, where an approval by competent authorities is more important in enhancing trust. In both Title II of MiCAR and the Crowdfunding Regulation, more emphasis is put on cost-efficiency. By not requiring prior approval from competent authorities, start-ups and SMEs can be offered cheaper and faster access to crypto or capital markets.[153] Unlike with a KIIS, however, Title II crypto-asset white papers must be notified to the relevant competent authorities.[154]

Both KIIS and Title II crypto-asset white papers must also include similar warnings, such as warnings of the risk of losing all invested money, problems with liquidity, and the lack of coverage by investor compensation schemes and deposit guarantee schemes. However, there are also some differences. Technology and environment related risks should be included in a crypto-asset white paper but are not mandatory for a KIIS. One remarkable feature in the Crowdfunding Regulation is that in the standardised risk warning of the KIIS, investors are advised not to invest more than 10 per cent of their net worth in crowdfunding projects. Such crude investment limit suggestions, which were not adopted in MiCAR, are a peculiar novelty in EU financial market law.

Simplified investor information documents existed already before the Crowdfunding Regulation's KIIS. For UCITS funds, key investor information documents (KIIDs)[155] replaced their predecessors, simplified prospectuses (SPs),[156] in 2012. KIIDs are restricted to only two A4 pages and must contain illustrations to foster understanding. The EU Regulation on key information documents for packaged retail and insurance-based investment products (PRIIPs Regulation)[157] introduced a similar type of disclosure item, namely, key information documents (KIDs) for packaged retail and insurance-based products.[158]

[152] MiCAR, Article 6(2).

[153] See eg EU Crowdfunding Regulation, Recital (54).

[154] MiCAR, Article 8.

[155] Directive 2009/65/EC of the European Parliament and of the Council of 13 July 2009 on the coordination of laws, regulations and administrative provisions relating to undertakings for collective investment in transferable securities (UCITS) (UCITS IV Directive).

[156] Simplified prospectuses were introduced in the UCITS III Directive. See Directive 2001/107/EC of the European Parliament and of the Council of 21 January 2002 amending Council Directive 85/611/EEC on the coordination of laws, regulations and administrative provisions relating to undertakings for collective investment in transferable securities (UCITS) with a view to regulating management companies and simplified prospectuses.

[157] Regulation (EU) No 1286/2014 of the European Parliament and of the Council of 26 November 2014 on key information documents for packaged retail and insurance-based investment products (PRIIPs).

[158] See eg M Salo and H Haapio, 'Putting Financial Regulation to Work: Using Simplification and Visualization for Consumer-Friendly Information' 4. JusletterIT, 25 February 2016.

Simpler and shorter investor disclosures increase cost-efficiency and generally reflect the idea that, especially from the perspective of retail investors, the emphasis should be on quality over quantity of information. However, existing research indicates that simplified investor disclosure documents and standardised risk warnings do not always have the intended effect due to persistent biases and motivational and perceptual limits.[159] The increased retail orientation has also faced criticism within the EU, particularly in the context of the prospectus regime. The critics have noted that since public offers are rarely targeted at retail investors, prospectuses should primarily be designed to the needs of professional investors and information intermediaries. Issuers must also be able to make technical and detailed disclosures to manage litigation risks. It has become clear, then, that prospectuses cannot fully address the problems of retail market accessibility.[160] Instead of trying to make the prospectus fit the needs of both retail and professional investors, the most recent amendments to the prospectus regime introduced a parallel disclosure document – a prospectus summary – designed primarily to meet the needs of retail investors. The prospectus summary, which follows the 'key investor information' concept, has been described 'as a reasonable compromise'.[161]

A similar compromise was adopted in MiCAR Title II, although crypto-asset white papers could be rarely targeted at professional investors. Article 6(7) of MiCAR requires that each white paper must be accompanied by a summary which provides 'in brief and non-technical language' key information about the offer to the public of the crypto-asset or its intended admission to trading. The white paper summary should be easily understandable and presented in a clear and comprehensive format, using characters of readable size, to help prospective holders of the crypto-asset to make an informed decision. Again, the requirements under MiCAR Article 6(7) are much less prescriptive compared to the Prospectus Regulation, which regulates the prospectus summary in a fair amount of detail.[162]

5.5.3. Enabling Technology

Going forward, the authorities and legislators should bear in mind that the comprehensibility of information can also be enhanced by technological means. Natural language processing (NLP) has already been used to predict the likelihood

[159] See eg M Mercer, AR Palmiter and AE Taha 'Worthless warnings? Testing the effectiveness of disclaimers in mutual fund advertisements' (2010) 7(3) *Journal of Empirical Legal Studies* 429. For an overview of literature, see G Helleringer, 'Retail Investors and Disclosure Requirements' in K Mathis (ed), *European Perspectives on Behavioural Law and Economics* (Springer, 2015) 193–209.

[160] For discussion of criticism, see Moloney (n 31) 135–37.

[161] ibid 136.

[162] Prospectus Regulation, Article 7. See also Moloney (n 31) 137, noting that the 'level of specification is immensely granular.'

of success of ICOs, but it can also help analyse the content of white papers. Camassa studied the white paper contents of 'other than' category of crypto-assets, referring to MiCAR Title II, and explored the possibilities of using NLP. She argues that in the future, NLP models, especially large language models (LLMs) such as GPT and BERT, could bring several benefits. They could be used to check automatically if a white paper complies with MiCAR requirements. Another possibility could be to identify which regulatory norms are relevant in each part of the text. LLMs could also be used to prepare drafts of white papers. Investors would also benefit from the possibility to ask questions on the content of white papers, which could enhance their understanding of the project and risks related to it. Another helpful feature of LLMs is their ability to summarise information contained in long and dense texts.[163]

To this end, the requirement under MiCAR Article 6(10) that crypto-asset white papers must be made available in a machine-readable format is welcome. MiCAR also mandates ESMA, in cooperation with the EBA, to develop draft implementing technical standards to establish standard forms, formats and templates to facilitate machine-readability. On 5 October 2023, ESMA published a Consultation Paper, which includes a section devoted to machine readability of white papers.[164] ESMA observes, inter alia, that 'PDF and html are not consistent with MiCA requirements […].'[165] ESMA identified two formats as fulfilling the machine-readability requirement, namely xHTML with Inline XBRL tags (for simplicity, iXBRL) and XML,[166] with the former being more preferable.[167] At the time of writing, no final position has been taken on this issue. Once such standards are finalised, it should be clearer how strictly the structure of white papers will be standardised in terms of content, form and length.

Legal experts are nevertheless needed to develop AI applications that could be used in the MiCAR context, given the specific and precise meaning of legal terms.[168] However, the challenges related to the specificity of legal language can be overcome, and there are already many AI applications in the legal field, such as Codify AI,[169] Spellbook[170] and ContractPodAi's Leah Legal Copilot.[171]

[163] C Camassa, 'Legal NLP Meets MiCAR: Advancing the Analysis of Crypto White Papers' (2023) arxiv.org/pdf/2310.10333.pdf. On the possibilities of AI to help both readers and writers of legal information, see also M Salo-Lahti, M Ranta and H Haapio, 'AI Tools for Sustainability – Actionable Information for both Humans and Machines', JusletterIT, 30 March 2023.

[164] ESMA, Consultation Paper, Technical Standards specifying certain requirements of Markets in Crypto Assets Regulation (MiCA) – second consultation paper, 5 October 2023, ESMA75-453128700-438.

[165] ibid para 226.

[166] ibid para 227. See also ESMA's proof of concept illustrating a concrete application of the proposed format requirements, www.esma.europa.eu/document/mica-white-papers-poc#ft2.

[167] ESMA, Consultation Paper, Technical Standards specifying certain requirements of Markets in Crypto Assets Regulation (MiCA) – second consultation paper, para 244.

[168] Camassa (n 163).

[169] Codify AI, www.codifyai.com.

[170] Spellbook by Rally, 'Draft Contracts 3x Faster with AI', www.spellbook.legal.

[171] ContractPodAi, 'Generative AI Legal Assistant, Leah Legal Copilot' contractpodai.com/leah-copilot-ai-legal-assistant.

5.6. Conclusion

The legal framework established in MiCAR Title II aims to support innovation and fair competition, while also protecting investors and the integrity of crypto-asset markets. It pursues these objectives with a hybrid set of rules combining elements from traditional financial law and consumer law. As capital raising instruments, utility tokens and other Title II crypto-assets bear family resemblance with other forms of capital raising regulated by EU law, such as traditional financial instruments and crowdfunding. As most financial instruments, they are transferable and can be admitted to public trading. But just as in crowdfunding, utility tokens are used by start-ups to raise capital from a large number of unsophisticated individuals who typically invest only small sums.

Given fundamental differences in users, assets and market structures, we argued that the goals and rationales for mandatory disclosure in securities markets are only partly consistent with the specific information needs of the markets for utility tokens and other Title II assets.[172] Instead of efficiency concerns, the main rationale for Title II disclosure rules is to address issues such as inadequate disclosures, misrepresentations and fraud, which are still prevalent in crypto-markets.[173] To address such risks effectively, however, more is needed than publication of white papers and marketing materials, particularly when the tokens are submitted to public trading. Much also depends on how MiCAR's rules on the disclosure of inside information will be applied and enforced.

In contrast to disclosure rules, the 14-day withdrawal right under Article 13 of MiCAR is transplanted from EU consumer contract law. Apart from the EU Crowdfunding Regulation, which grants investors a four-day 'pre-contractual reflection period' to revoke an investment offer, such measures are alien to EU financial law. One possible reasoning for adding such an instrument in Title II is that utility tokens – the only non-referenced crypto-asset recognised and defined by Title II – provide access to goods and services. But investors are unlikely to use the right based on the quality of the goods or services, which are unlikely to exist when the right expires. The withdrawal right also risks inviting unintended behaviour, such as manipulation of demand to increase the offer's attractiveness prior to listing. Experiences from crowdfunding markets are not encouraging in this respect. It is also doubtful whether the withdrawal right is suitable for the 'wide variety of crypto-assets'[174] falling under Title II of MiCAR (ie, all crypto-assets other than ARTs or EMTs).

Beyond addressing risks, MiCAR also aims to promote innovation. Whether this succeeds depends on MiCAR's regulatory costs. Meeting MiCAR's disclosure requirements will result in significant direct costs even if the requirements

[172] Armour and Enriques (n 132) make a similar argument in the context of crowdfunding.
[173] Zetzsche et al 2021 (n 16) 211.
[174] MiCAR, Recital (18).

on white papers and marketing communications are less onerous than their Prospectus Regulation counterparts. Indirect costs might also fall if more standardised and comprehensive information reduces under-pricing of issued tokens.[175] The most significant costs are likely to accrue on those issuers who decide to go public, ie, seek listing of their tokens. It has been estimated that the requirement to continuously publish inside information will put significant regulatory burden on small and medium-sized issuers, which might opt for non-EU markets with less demanding rules.[176] The experiences from rapidly evolving crowdfunding markets suggest that relative regulatory costs affect geographic patterns of market evolution.[177]

The two-weeks withdrawal period will also result in unpredictable costs that will be difficult to measure. The EU Crowdfunding Regulation shows more awareness of the potential effects of the right to revoke an offer on the costs of raising capital and thus mandated the Commission to assess 'whether the reflection period should be shortened to allow for a more efficient capital raising process without harming investor protection.'[178] The Commission would be wise to carefully assess regulatory costs also in the case of MiCAR.

[175] David Florysiak, 'Utility Tokens, Markets in Crypto Assets Regulation (MiCAR), and the Costs of Being Public' (11 December 2022) 14, ssrn.com/abstract=4295913.
[176] ibid.
[177] Armour and Enriques (n 132).
[178] Crowdfunding Regulation, Recital (48).

6

Regulation of ARTs and EMTs, and their Issuers

PHILIPP MAUME

6.1. Scope and General Approach of Stablecoin Regulation under MiCAR

6.1.1. Overview of this Chapter

The perceived threat presented by global stablecoins such as Meta's Libra/Diem project was one of the key drivers for the creation of MiCAR; the regulation of stablecoins has been called by commentators MiCAR's '*raison d'être*'.[1] Not surprisingly, MiCAR devotes Titles III and IV to their regulation.[2] It is an ironic footnote that the Libra/Diem project has been stopped whilst MiCAR is in force.[3]

This chapter examines the regulation of stablecoin issuers. As many of the rules are extremely detailed and descriptive, it cannot discuss every single issue or obligation but will instead try to focus on the essential law and give the 'big picture'. The key element of the MiCAR approach is the distinction between asset-referenced

[1] M Lehmann, 'MiCAR – Gold Standard or Regulatory Poison for the Crypto Industry?' (2024) EBI Working Paper Series 2024/160, 15, papers.ssrn.com/abstract_id=4692743.

[2] For overview of the final MiCAR version (each with parts on Titles III and IV), see eg F Annunziata, 'An Overview of the Markets in Crypto-Assets Regulation (MiCAR)' (2023) EBI Working Paper Series No. 2023/158, papers.ssrn.com/abstract_id=4660379; P Maume, 'The Regulation on Markets in Crypto-Assets (MiCAR): Landmark Codification, or First Step of Many, or Both?' (2023) 20 *European Company and Financial Law Review* 243; Lehmann (n 1); on the MiCAR Draft, see DA Zetzsche, F Annunziata, DW Arner and RP Buckley, 'The Markets in Crypto-Assets Regulation (MICA) and the EU Digital Finance Strategy' (2020) EBI Working Paper Series 2020/77, papers.ssrn.com/abstract_id=3725395; specifically on MiCAR stablecoins S Cichon, 'All That Glitters Is Not Gold: The Regulation of Stablecoins under the MiCA Regulation – Between Innovation and Risk Mitigation' (2024) 9 *Cambridge Law Review* 79; with a focus on stablecoins under MiCAR based on the MiCAR Draft, see ED Martino, 'Regulating Stablecoins as Private Money between Liquidity and Safety. The Case of the EU "Market in Crypto Asset" (MiCA) Regulation' (2022) Amsterdam Law School Legal Studies Research Paper No. 2022-27, papers.ssrn.com/abstract_id=4203885.

[3] There is little doubt that Libra/Diem would have qualified as an ART under MiCAR; see also Zetzsche et al (n 2) 13.

tokens (ART) as set out in Article 3(1)(6) and e-money tokens (EMT) as set out in Article 3(1)(7).[4] In short, EMTs are crypto-assets that are referencing (only) one official currency. They can thus be seen as the equivalent of this currency in the crypto space. ARTs on the other hand are all other crypto-assets that reference values or rights – this could be a combination of currencies, or commodities.

In section 6.1, this chapter will first introduce the regulatory approach taken by MiCAR in Titles III and IV. It will also explain the different mechanisms behind both ART and EMT, as they are important for understanding the regulatory concepts. Section 6.2 will focus on issuers of ART, covering the authorisation regime (6.2.1), the crypto-asset white paper (6.2.2), ongoing requirements (6.2.3) and the rules regarding the reserve of assets (6.2.4). Section 6.3 will outline the specifics of EMT regulation in Title IV, where they deviate from the ART framework in Title III.

6.1.2. Overall Regulatory Approach

Titles III and IV are a combination of different regulatory elements. The first is an authorisation requirement,[5] a well-known element from the regulation of investment firms, credit institutions, e-money institutions and payment service providers. The authorisation procedure is roughly based on MiFID II and has been modified to accommodate the specific requirements of the token economy. However, MiCAR is combining this with the obligation to draw up a white paper and ongoing disclosure and reporting requirements.[6] To some extent, this is straightforward because the same requirement applies to crypto-assets falling under Title II MiCAR. The structurally remarkable element is the combination of a disclosure requirement with the authorisation requirement. In other words, MiCAR treats issuers of ART and EMT not just as issuers, but also as investment firms or banks. Consequently, they even need to treat token holders as clients. In the eyes of the MiCAR drafters, this is justified because stablecoins could be widely used by holders to transfer value or as a means of exchange, potentially posing increased risks for crypto-asset holders and to market integrity.[7] In fact, the events of the crypto winter have aptly demonstrated the danger that stablecoins might pose to the (crypto) system.[8] In case of further growth of the crypto-markets, disturbances might create threats to the systemic stability of the financial system as a whole.

The regulation of stablecoins (and in particular, Title III) is the part of MiCAR that deviates most from the established concepts of financial markets regulation.

[4] For more on the typology of crypto-assets under MiCAR, see ch 4 of this book.

[5] Although for credit institutions only a notification procedure applies.

[6] See also Annunziata (n 2) 48: transparency regime supplemented by a licensing regime; Maume (n 2): mix of regulatory mechanisms.

[7] MiCAR, Recital (40).

[8] Annunziata (n 2) 48.

In contrast to the other Titles, there is no straight blueprint from existing financial markets regulation that could be followed, making it a bit of a conceptual novelty.[9] At the same time, the new framework meets an industry that is still fledgling, but by no means new. It will be interesting to see how the markets develop as soon as the MiCAR framework applies. At the time of writing this chapter, the two global market leaders Tether (USDT) and USD Coin (USDC) had a market capitalisation of about USD 100 billion and USD 30 billion,[10] while the next biggest coins DAI and Ethena were significantly smaller (about 3–5 billion USD). Euro-based stablecoins are insignificant, the ECB estimating that only 0.2 per cent of the global stablecoin market is referencing the Euro.[11] The share of other EU currencies is even smaller. In other words, the current stablecoin market is essentially a market that carries on the dominance of the US Dollar (with all its advantages and disadvantages) into the crypto world.

An important question is if the MiCAR approach will be able to facilitate an EU system for stablecoin payments or cut off the EU crypto-payments area from the international stage. Trying to create a regulatory environment from scratch has been aptly described as 'legal certainty as the foundation for innovation in the crypto sector'[12] in the EU. But at the time of writing this chapter, market insiders wonder if the leading global stablecoin Tether will even bother to apply for a MiCAR-licence or simply forgo the EU market.[13] A lot will depend on whether and how the US will introduce its own stablecoin regulation.[14] Thus, the success of MiCAR does not only depend on MiCAR itself. That said, in July 2024, Circle, a global financial technology firm and the issuer of USDC and EURC, reported that it had secured an Electronic Money Institution licence from the French authority (*Autorité de Contrôle Prudentiel et de Résolution*) – a precondition for the issuance of the MiCAR-compliant EMTs.

As of 11 June 2025, not a single authorisation for ART has been granted by national regulators, while 17 EMT have been listed in the ESMA database. However, this needs to be seen in the context of the authorisation requirement for ART in Article 16 MiCAR (see below section 6.2.1), which requires a comprehensive assessment by the national competent authority. In contrast, offerors of EMT

[9] Maume (n 2) 266.

[10] All numbers taken from www.coinmarketcap.com, as at 21 June 2024. It has to be noted that even the market leader Tether's market capitalisation is 'only' about 10% of the Bitcoin market capitalisation.

[11] ECB, 'The international role of the euro' (June 2022), 34, www.ecb.europa.eu/pub/pdf/ire/focus/ecb.irebox202206_05~9f49f44d15.en.pdf.

[12] Cichon (n 2) 83.

[13] M Shahidullah, 'Will MiCA regulation end Tether's dominance in the EU?' (3 April 2024) crypto.news/will-mica-regulation-end-tethers-dominance-in-the-eu; C Bergmann, 'Tether-CEO: "Wir haben Europa im Grunde aufgegeben"' (16 April 2024) bitcoinblog.de/2024/04/16/tether-ceo-wir-haben-europa-im-grunde-aufgegeben.

[14] It is to be expected that the US will sooner or later introduce crypto-asset regulation. In April 2024, US senators introduced a bipartisan stablecoin bill (the Lummis-Gillibrand Payment Stablecoin Act); for overview, see J Cieplak et al, 'US Senators Introduce Comprehensive Stablecoin Bill' (Latham & Watkins Global Fintech & Digital Assets Blog, 16 May 2024) www.fintechanddigitalassets.com/2024/05/us-senators-introduce-comprehensive-stablecoin-bill/.

need to be authorised as credit institutions or e-money institutions (see below section 6.3.2). Under MiCAR, they only need to notify the crypto-asset white paper to the national regulator (which is much less time consuming). Thus, the discrepancy in numbers might be caused by the differing procedural requirements.

6.1.3. A Privilege for Incumbent Banks?

The MiCAR approach to stablecoins has been criticised as overly strict. From a regulatory point of view, it is only logical that the EU has imposed a legal framework on stablecoins and their issuers. It is a different question, however, whether this framework strikes the right balance between market and investor protection on the one hand and the promotion of innovation on the other.

Stablecoins are functionally much closer to traditional payment instruments (mostly due to their alleged stability) than to decentralised payment tokens. This stability can only be achieved if the issuer takes certain measures. Thus, it is understandable that the EU lawmakers put stricter regulatory requirements on these issuers than on other market participants, such as 'regular' issuers. The aim is to prevent collapses of stablecoin providers and major crashes such as Terra/ Luna in 2022,[15] which triggered the so-called 'crypto winter'.[16] There is also a strong resemblance to the regulatory treatment of issuers of e-money (ie, electronic money institutions) under Directive 2009/110/EC (EMD2): in both cases a private entity issues means of exchange that can be used like money (without being money). Thus, the regulation of ART-/EMT-issuers can be viewed from two very different angles: first, standing in the shoes of fintech start-ups and prospective smaller issuers it can be seen as a piece of overregulation; second, through the lens of financial services and payments regulation, it can be seen as a coherent application of well-established regulatory principles.[17]

Simply put, Title III creates a privileged position for incumbent banks and investment firms.[18] While 'pure' crypto issuers have to undergo authorisation (see section 6.2.1), credit institutions are subject to a mere notification procedure. The regulatory rationale seems clear – credit institutions are already subject to a strict (national) authorisation procedure established by Directive 2013/36/EU (CRD IV),[19] meaning that another authorisation regime would result in regulatory duplication.[20] Credit institutions also already have their own regulators to supervise them.[21] However, although banks will find it easier to transpose their existing

[15] For overview of so-called 'crypto-failures' (including stablecoins), see Ilya Kokorin, 'The anatomy of crypto failures and investor protection under MiCAR' (18) 2023 *Capital Markets Law Journal* 500.

[16] Annunziata (n 2) 47.

[17] Similarly Cichon (n 2) 93: 'adaptation of pre-existing mechanisms'.

[18] Lehmann (n 1) 24.

[19] MiCAR, Recital (44).

[20] Maume (n 2) 266.

[21] Annunziata (n 2) 48.

compliance systems and internal organisation to the crypto space, they are acting outside their own 'turf'[22] when it comes to the underlying technology. Until now, the drivers for the evolution of crypto in Europe have been smaller (often young) companies; the incumbent banks waited for long (or are still waiting) to jump on the bandwagon. In other words, the market participants with crypto experience and expertise have to undergo authorisation whilst the 'newcomers' from the traditional financial sector only need to notify the competent authorities. To make matters worse, if national authorities take a conservative stand, new market participants might find it difficult to satisfy the statutory requirements, for example, the necessary experience for members of the management body (section 6.2.5.2). Finally, the high requirements for own funds (=capital requirements, section 6.2.8) could essentially prevent smaller start-ups from entering the market.

However, there is a second effect that is directly linked to the evolution of MiCAR. Bigtech companies not based in the EU will find it difficult to issue ART in the EU. It will be impossible for them to issue ARTs as a side business. At the very least, they would have to set up an EU-based subsidiary, which would then have to comply with the MiCAR framework. This would, for example, require the respective Bigtech to equip the subsidiary with all the necessary means to issue the stablecoins (which would need to be moved from the mother company to the subsidiary, at potentially high cost) while establishing a legal barrier between mother company and subsidiary (which would make the use and transfer of data under the GDPR more difficult). It would also render enforcement much more effective for national regulators in the EU.

The MiCAR stance on EMTs in Title IV is even stricter. Only banks and electronic money institutions can issue these under MiCAR; there is no exception for large investment firms or crypto-asset service providers. This greatly reduces the number of potential issuers and is arguably a death sentence for smaller market participants.[23] The MiCAR archetype of a stablecoin issuer generally does not seem to be an agile start-up – Recital (52) states that ART issuers are usually at the centre of a network of entities that ensure the issuance of such crypto-assets. This suggests that, in the eyes of MiCAR, issuers of stablecoins are typically large entities and not smaller fintechs. The MiCAR approach obviously prioritises stability through business size over the innovative power of start-ups.

6.1.4. What is Stability and How is it Achieved?

To understand stablecoins (and in a second step: the regulatory mechanism underlying Titles III and IV) it is important to distinguish between two issues: what stability is and how it is achieved.

[22] Lehmann (n 1) 25.
[23] Maume (n 2) 266.

As a starting point, it is necessary to clarify the use of the term 'referencing'. MiCAR uses it in the definitions for both EMT and ART,[24] but unfortunately without defining it. This is problematic because 'referencing' could mean different things. First, it can be used for a stablecoin that is supposed to have the same value as a real-life asset or currency (however this is achieved). This is often referred to as the token being 'pegged' to the asset or currency. A typical example would be a US Dollar stablecoin such as Tether. In this context, 'referencing' is about the situation or outcome in the market (so the link between the price of the token and the 'referenced' asset). It is a fair assumption that the term 'in relation to', which is used commonly in the MiCAR recitals,[25] means the same thing as 'referencing'. Second, referencing can relate to the assets that the issuer owns to achieve the stability of the token. In this context, 'referencing' would not be about the market side and token price, but about the underlying assets. Although both meanings are, strictly speaking, accurate, the ambiguity can create confusion in a debate on MiCAR stablecoins. In the light of this ambiguity, this chapter will use the following terminology: the terms 'referencing' and 'referenced' are used for the asset or currency whose market value the stablecoin tries to match. This is to be distinguished from underlying assets that the issuer of the stablecoin is owning.

The best way to understand the mechanisms of a stablecoin is through the meaning of 'stability'. Again, this can refer to two different things: The first one is the token's value that remains as stable as possible, which is usually achieved by choosing a mix of underlying assets that in combination will retain a stable value. This mix of assets should be independent of singular events and drivers, for example by including assets whose price movements might cancel each other out.[26] This would be desirable for a stablecoin that is supposed to form a new standard of payment independent from current (volatile) currencies. From the perspective of many businesses, this is a desirable outcome because it reduces risks. In particular, it reduces the need for measures against exchange rate fluctuations (that also affect EMT). Conceptually, ARTs that do not just represent one single real-world asset would usually fall into this category. The failed Libra project would also have been a typical example.

The second meaning of stability could be stability *in relation* to the real-life asset. This could be a stablecoin that ideally has the same or nearly the same market value as the respective currency (it is 'pegged' to the currency, see above), for example Tether (USDT) in relation to the US Dollar.[27] Such a coin would mirror the overall acceptance of a real-world fiat currency in the crypto space. The fact that

[24] See discussion in ch 3 of this book.

[25] It seems that the term 'in relation to' is used in recitals that have not been included in the Commission Draft and that were added later, see for example MiCAR, Recitals (5), (6), (41).

[26] For example, increasing central bank interest rates typically result in a decreasing gold price – which can be countered by owning certain money-market instruments with a market price that responds to the increasing interest rates.

[27] See discussion in ch 3 of this book.

the currency may be itself volatile does not change the fact that such a stablecoin is stable in relation to it.

In the next step, either of these two forms of stability can be achieved by two very different approaches. The classical one is to maintain a stable value by owning physical, financial or crypto-assets ('asset-linked stablecoins').[28] This comes with a major disadvantage. In a similar way to the issuance of e-money, this approach ties up many resources – users will only trust in the stability of the coin if the issuer owns or otherwise controls significant amounts of the assets that the crypto-assets purports to reference. For example, Tether claims that all USDT tokens issued are 100 per cent covered by reserves.[29] Similarly, Libra was supposed to achieve price stability through a basket of currencies backing the coin.

The second mechanism is algorithmic. These 'algorithmic stablecoins' maintain their value via specific protocols adjusting supply in response to a change in demand.[30] The idea is to create stability without the need for expensive reserve assets. Although several algorithmic stablecoins have failed in recent years, most notably Terra/Luna in 2022,[31] MiCAR does not prohibit their issuance per se. Any issuer of a crypto-asset that attempts to maintain a stable value not using underlying assets but an algorithm is also subject to Titles III and IV.[32] This includes compliance with the rules on the reserve of assets (section 6.2.9), which is anathema to the business case behind algorithmic stablecoins and effectively thwarts the business case. The only exception is algorithmic crypto-assets that do not aim to stabilise their value by referencing assets (read: that are not stablecoins), which are not subject to Title III (section 6.2.1.3).

6.2. Asset-referenced Tokens (ART)

6.2.1. Authorisation Requirement

6.2.1.1. General Introduction

The authorisation regime for ART is contained in Chapter 1 of Title III, named 'Authorisation to offer asset-referenced tokens to the public and to seek their admission to trading'. Accordingly, it contains rules on authorisation and its requirements (Articles 16–18), its assessment and the decision (Articles 20–21), and its withdrawal (Article 24). It also includes rules on the crypto-asset white paper and respective liability (Articles 19, 25, 26).

[28] Martino (n 2) 28.

[29] Tether website, 'Transparency', tether.to/en/transparency/?tab=reports.

[30] Martino (n 2) 28; see also MiCAR, Recital (41) second sentence.

[31] For discussion, A Briola, D Vidal-Tomás, Y Wang and T Aste, 'Anatomy of a Stablecoin's Failure: The Terra-Luna Case' (2023) 51 *Finance Research Letters*.

[32] MiCAR Recital (41), second sentence.

However, the lines between authorisation requirements, governance and organisational requirements and other ongoing obligations are not clear. For example, Chapter 1 also contains ongoing reporting obligations (Articles 22–23) while we find an obligation to keep the ART-holders informed (Article 30) or how to publish the white paper (Article 28) in Chapter 2. The duty to modify the crypto-asset white paper in case of significant changes to the issuer's business model is set out in Article 25 (Chapter 1), although it has little to do with the initial authorisation. At the same time, some ongoing requirements, such as the good repute of the management body or risk management procedures, need to be met and explained in the initial application for authorisation.[33] This unclear structure not only makes it difficult to find a suitable shape for this book chapter but also complicates a structured approach to the construction and application of the rules in practice.

6.2.1.2. Issuer Authorisation

The key provision for the authorisation of ART is Article 16, according to which an offer to the public (Article 3(1)(12)) or the application for admission of such to an EU crypto trading venue (Article 1(2)(a)), requires authorisation from the competent national authority in accordance with Article 21. Thus, MiCAR does not regulate issuing ART, but introducing them into the EU market, either via an offer to the public or admitting them to a trading venue. However, it is still possible for investors to acquire ARTs that were issued on a trading venue outside the EU, or in a peer-to-peer transaction.[34]

The offer or application must be made by the issuer, which must be established in the European Union. Alternatively, under the second paragraph of Article 16(1), a third party may offer to the public or seek admission to trading with the written consent of the issuer.[35] This focus on the issuer is supposed to ensure proper supervision and monitoring,[36] and, although not mentioned expressly, also enforcement. An issuer from a third country must therefore first establish a subsidiary in a Member State. The negative phrasing 'no person shall [...] unless that person is the issuer' makes it clear that ARTs that do not have an issuer (ie, are offered via a DeFi solution)[37] cannot be publicly offered or introduced to a regulated crypto trading venue in the EU. This is a stricter approach than the one taken in Title II, where the person making the offer does not have to be the issuer.

[33] Although the latter is also the case for the comparable regime under MiFID II.

[34] Maume (n 2) 266.

[35] These persons are then subject to the obligation to act honestly, fairly and professionally (see section 6.2.4.2), must provide information on an ongoing basis (see section 6.2.6.2) and are prohibited from grating interest (see section 6.2.9.6).

[36] MiCAR, Recital (42).

[37] This could be the case if an ART is automatically issued by a smart contract protocol without an issuer being involved or being identifiable. This construct is particularly attractive for algorithmic stablecoins that do not rely on a reserve of assets. On DeFi under MiCAR, see Maume (n 2) 253 et seqq.

The authorisation regime also applies the idea of EU passporting, as the approval granted by the competent authority is valid for the entire EU according to Article 16(3). Other Member States cannot impose additional requirements if authorisation has been granted by another Member State.[38] As with the authorisation regime set out in Title V, it remains to be seen if the competent authorities in all Member States will apply the same level of care, knowledge and diligence. If not, then this might pose a serious threat for the fledgling crypto markets in the EU. The problem is that if a national regulator grants authorisation for issuing stablecoins[39] prematurely or even unlawfully, the other Member States are bound by this decision. Thus, as soon as one of the Member States applies a 'laissez-faire' approach to attract issuers and thus business, this could undermine the whole MiCAR system.[40]

According to Article 16(2), no authorisation is required for offers below a token value of EUR 5,000,000 over 12 months and for offers that are solely addressed to qualified investors (Article 3(1)(30)). However, in these cases the obligation to draw up a white paper remains.

6.2.1.3. *Application to Algorithmic Stablecoins*

In principle, the authorisation requirement also applies to algorithmic stablecoins. MiCAR Recital (41) second sentence states that so-called algorithmic stablecoins (see section 6.1.4) that aim to maintain a stable value in relation to an official currency or to one or several assets via protocols are subject to Title III and Title IV (including the authorisation requirement). This is a logical continuation of the first sentence, which states that the rules apply 'irrespective of how the issuer intends to design the crypto-asset, including the mechanism for maintaining the stable value of the crypto-asset.' However, the consequence of being subject to Title III and Title IV is being subject to the requirement of having a reserve of assets – which effectively destroys the business case for algorithmic stablecoins (see section 6.2.9).

In contrast, Recital (41), third sentence, states that '[o]fferors or persons seeking admission to trading of algorithmic crypto assets that do not aim to stabilise the value of the crypto-assets by referencing one or several assets should in any event comply with Title II.'[41] In other words, algorithmic crypto-assets that are not

[38] MiCAR, Recital (45).

[39] The same problem arises for CASP authorisations.

[40] For example, the Baltic states have seen huge money-laundering scandals between 2018 and 2020 due to weaknesses in their supervisory agencies (see eg K McNaughton, 'The tale of the Baltics: Experiences, challenges, and lessons from reforming their national Financial Intelligence Units (FIUs)' (2024) 5 *Journal of Economic Criminology* 100080); another example is Malta's attempt to establish a crypto-hub in the EU in 2017/2018, much to the chagrin of the European Commission. See M Reel, 'Why the EU Is Furious With Malta' (11 September 2018) www.bloomberg.com/news/features/2018-09-11/why-the-eu-is-furious-with-malta.

[41] MiCAR Title II sets out the disclosure obligations when offering crypto-assets other than EMT or ART. The main difference is that Title II does not contain any authorisation requirements (and no need for a reserve of assets).

stablecoins need to comply with Title II. This could, for example, be crypto-assets that are based on DeFi protocols (thus being 'algorithmic'). They do not have an issuer but might still be traded at a crypto-asset trading platform. Essentially, Recital (41), third sentence, only emphasises what Article 4 already stipulates.

6.2.1.4. *Application Procedure*

The application procedure is set out in Article 18. The application needs to contain, inter alia, comprehensive information about the issuer, its management body and its business model, descriptions of various policy and governance arrangements for compliance with Article 34, information on the good repute and competence of its management body (section 6.2.5.2), the crypto-asset white paper (section 6.2.2), a legal opinion that the token is not excluded under Article 2(4) and is not an EMT, etc. If the applicant has formerly been authorised in respect of an ART, it does not need to submit identical information again (Article 18(3)). In contrast to the corresponding Article 7 MiFID II, these rules are much more detailed, but not as detailed as those in Delegated Regulation (EU) 2017/1943, which fleshes out Article 7 MiFID II.[42] At the time of writing this chapter, the EBA was still consulting on draft regulatory technical standards to further specify the information referred to in Article 18(2).[43] The competent authority has to refuse authorisation on objective and demonstrable grounds, including where the business model of the applicant might pose a serious threat to market integrity.[44]

The timeline for a decision on the application is complicated. The competent authority must confirm receipt of the application in no more than two days (Article 18(4)). According to Article 20(1), the competent authority assesses whether the application, including the white paper, contains all the required information within 25 days of receipt of the application. Within 60 working days of receipt of the full application, the competent authority must assess if the application meets all the requirements and then take a fully reasoned draft decision granting or refusing authorisation (Article 20(2)).

This draft decision is to be transmitted to the EBA, ESMA and the ECB (Article 20(4)),[45] who then comment within another 20 working days on the legal opinion regarding the legal classification of the token to be issued (EBA,

[42] Commission Delegated Regulation (EU) 2017/194 of 14 July 2016 supplementing Directive 2014/65/EU of the European Parliament and of the Council with regard to regulatory technical standards on information and requirements for the authorisation of investment firms.

[43] EBA, 'Consultation Paper – Draft Regulatory Technical Standards on information for application for authorisation to offer to the public and to seek admission to trading of asset-referenced tokens and Draft Implementing Technical Standards on standard forms, templates and procedures for the information to be included in the application, under Article 18(6) and (7) of Regulation (EU) 2023/1114' (EBA/CP/2023/15, 12 July 2023).

[44] MiCAR, Recital (45).

[45] In Member States where the currency is not Euro, the drafts also need to be transmitted to the national central bank.

ESMA) and the potential risk posed by the token to financial stability, the smooth operation of payment systems, monetary policy transmission and monetary sovereignty (ECB). The competent authority shall then, within 25 working days of receiving the opinions, make a fully reasoned decision granting or refusing the authorisation, and notify the applicant within another five days (Article 21(1)). If authorisation is granted, the submitted crypto-asset white paper is deemed to be approved. The result is a total maximum of 90 working days (= 18 weeks) for reviewing and assessing the application. This seems ambitious, especially because MiCAR is new and the competent authorities still need to gain experience with the technology and business models and require respective resources.[46]

The nature of the 'opinions' voiced by ESMA, the EBA and the ECB is rather unclear. On the one hand, Article 20(5) states expressly that these opinions are non-binding. However, the competent authority shall 'duly consider' these opinions. It is unclear how much leeway this 'due consideration' leaves the competent authorities to deviate from the opinions. In case of a negative opinion of the ECB on grounds of a risk posed to the smooth operation of payment systems, monetary policy transmission, or monetary sovereignty, the competent authority must refuse the authorisation. In other words, the assessment of the ECB (but not of ESMA or the EBA) is de facto binding for a national competent authority. Since the aforementioned grounds for a 'negative opinion' are fundamental to the whole EU financial area, it is understandable that this decision is made at the EU level and not at the Member State level. However, it raises the question why the decision on granting the authorisation lies with the national competent authority anyway.

The pronounced role of the ECB also creates a substantial procedural problem. Article 263(1) TFEU stipulates that opinions of the Council, the Commission and the ECB are not within the scope of legal review by the CJEU. Yet the drafters of MiCAR felt the necessity to point out that it is for the CJEU to interpret that provision (ie, Article 263(1) TFEU) in light of the substance and effects of an ECB opinion.[47] Article 263(1) TFEU assumes that opinions (such as Q&A documents) are usually not binding for EU citizens and market participants. The provision stipulates that any act taken by these EU institutions that creates legally binding effects is subject to judicial review[48] – which is de facto the case for ECB opinions within the framework of Article 20(5). Thus, the respective ECB opinions should arguably be subject to legal review by the CJEU, too.[49]

[46] The problem is that stablishing a supervisory regime for MiCAR is not just a matter of duplicating the existing structures of financial markets supervision. Instead, the staff members in charge need extensive know-how on issues that are crypto-specific. In other words, some regulators would need to build up an internal structure from scratch within a very limited timeframe.

[47] MiCAR, Recital (46).

[48] See eg Case C-60/81 *IBM v Commission* ECLI:EU:C:1981:264, [1981] ECR 2639, para 9; Case C-76/01P *Eurocoton v Council* ECLI:EU:C:2003:26, [2003] ECR I-10091, para 54.

[49] Decisions made by the competent authority are of course subject to review in the national courts; the problem only relates to the ECB opinion that the decision is based on. In these cases, the national court has to apply for a preliminary ruling under Article 263 TFEU.

6.2.1.5. *Withdrawal of Authorisation*

Similar to other authorisation regimes under EU law, Article 24 allows the competent authority to withdraw the authorisation previously granted. If the authorisation is withdrawn, the issuer has to implement the redemption plan procedure under Article 47 (Article 24(5)). The grounds for withdrawal are very similar to Article 8 MiFID II and include (Article 24(1)):

- not engaging in business activities for six or not using the authorisation for twelve consecutive months;
- obtaining the authorisation by irregular means, in particular by making false statements in the application;
- not meeting the conditions under which the authorisation was granted;
- serious infringements of Title III.

Despite some minor deviations in wording, competent authorities are most likely to draw on established practices under MiFID II.

However, Article 24 also contains more crypto-specific grounds, such as the issuer being subject to a redemption plan according to Article 47 (Article 24(1)(e)), if the issuer's activity poses a serious threat to market integrity, financial stability or the payment system (Article 24(1)(g)), if the ECB issues a negative 'opinion' (section 6.2.4.1) (Article 24(2)), if a third-party entity involved in handling the reserve assets (section 6.2.9) loses its authorisation (Article 24(4)), if certain occurrences have affected the good repute of the members of the management body or shareholder/members that have qualifying holding in the issuer (Article 24(5)), or if there is an indication of failure of the governance arrangements or internal control mechanisms as set out in Article 34 (Article 24(5)).

6.2.1.6. *Notification Procedure for Credit Institutions*

Article 17 provides a less restrictive regime for credit institutions (Article 3(1)(28)). Instead of obtaining authorisation from the competent authority, the credit institution needs to notify the respective competent authority at least 90 working days before issuing (not offering) the ART (Article 17(1)(b)). In comparison to Article 18, the notification needs to comprise significantly less information. While credit institutions also need to submit a legal opinion, information on the business case and on compliance with Article 34, there is no requirement to submit information on the issuer and the management body. Because of the nature of a notification requirement, no formal decision by the competent authority is required. However, the credit institution may not make an offer to the public or seek admission to trading as long as the notification is incomplete. The notification procedure also includes the obligation to draw up a crypto-asset white paper.

The requirement to submit documentation on crypto-asset-specific aspects, such as the arrangements regarding the reserve of assets, their custody, transaction mechanisms and protocols as set out in Article 34(5), remains and this documentation also needs to be included in the notification.

6.2.1.7. Restrictions on ART Used as Means of Exchange

Article 23 sets out a mechanism that is rather unique in financial markets regulation.[50] The background is that under Article 22 (see section 6.2.6.1), ART issuers with an issue value of more than EUR 100 million must report various data to the competent authority, including the average number and average aggregate value of transactions during the relevant quarter of the year – including an estimate of the number and average aggregate value of transactions in which the ART has been used as a means of exchange, or in other words, used like money. These reporting requirements appear somewhat similar to EU payment services law.[51]

As soon as the quarterly average number of transactions is higher than 1 million and the aggregated value is higher than EUR 200 million, an issuer has to stop issuing the token (Article 23(1)(a) and, within 40 days, must submit a plan to the competent authority to ensure that transaction numbers and value stay below the threshold (Article 23(1)(b). This means that Article 23(1) effectively places a ceiling on the volume of business of the issuer. This raises various questions about its compatibility with the general principles of economic freedom.[52]

6.2.1.8. Transitional Provisions

Transitional provisions are set out in Article 143. If an ART has been issued by a non-bank before 30 June 2024, the issuer may continue to do so until an authorisation has been granted (or refused) under Article 21. The prerequisite is that the issuer applied for authorisation before 30 July 2024 (Art. 143(4)). Credit institutions simply need to notify the national competent authority under Article 17 before 30 July. They are allowed to continue issuing the tokens until the crypto-asset white paper has been approved or not approved (Article 143(5)). This carries forward the distinction between banks and non-banks under Title III. It would be an excellent indicator as to whether existing issuers are interested in issuing MiCAR tokens in the future. However, this information is not publicly available.

[50] Annunziata (n 2) 53: 'a true unicum'.
[51] Lehmann (n 1) 16.
[52] Annunziata (n 2) 54.

6.2.2. Crypto-asset White Paper

6.2.2.1. Content and Form

The obligation to publish a crypto-asset white paper is built on the idea that decreasing information asymmetry by disclosure of relevant information facilitates efficient and fair markets. Like the disclosure obligation in Title II, Article 19 is similar to the EU prospectus regime as set out in the Prospectus Regulation.[53] The requirements for the content and form of the crypto-asset white paper for ART are listed in Article 19 and further specified in Annex II. In comparison to Article 6,[54] issuers of ART also need to include information on the stabilisation mechanism, on the investment policy of the reserve assets and the respective custody arrangements, and on the rights provided to ART holders.[55] Similar to Article 6, the crypto-asset white paper must contain a summary with a warning about the potential loss of investment (Article 19(6)) and information on the principal adverse impacts on climate of the consensus mechanism (Article 19(1)(h)). The white paper must be made available in a machine-readable format (Article 19(10)). At the time of writing this chapter, ESMA and the EBA were conducting a consultation on the two latter issues.

Once the crypto-asset white paper is approved by the competent authority, it must be published on the issuer's website (Article 28). It must be publicly accessible from the starting date of the offer and remain available for as long as the ART is held by the public (not: offered to the public).

6.2.2.2. White Paper Modifications

Article 25(1) requires ART issuers to modify and update their crypto-asset white papers of any intended change to their business model likely to have a significant influence on the purchase decision of any holders or prospective holders. The requirement of a change to be 'significant' seems to be taken from Article 10 Prospectus Regulation, although the wording is slightly different.[56] However, it is likely that the scope of both provisions is identical.

The placement of Article 25 in Chapter 1 of Title II is remarkable, as this obligation clearly is not an authorisation requirement, but an ongoing obligation, suggesting that it should be in Chapter 2 of Title III. It is possible that the MiCAR

[53] Martino (n 2) 37.

[54] For detailed discussion, see ch 5 of this book.

[55] MiCAR, Recital (47).

[56] Article 10(1) Prospectus Regulation: 'Where … there has been a *significant* new factor, material mistake or material inaccuracy relating to the information included in the registration document which is capable of affecting the assessment of the securities' vs. Article 25(1): 'any intended change of their business model likely to have a *significant* influence on the purchase decision of any holders or prospective holders of asset-referenced tokens'.

drafters wanted the provision to be close to the related Articles 19 (content and form of white paper) and 26 (liability for white papers).

The modified crypto-asset white paper needs to be reviewed and approved by the competent authority (Article 25(2)). This triggers another round of consultations with the EU regulators. If the competent authority considers that the modifications are potentially relevant for the smooth operation of payment systems, monetary policy transmission and monetary sovereignty, it must consult the ECB under Article 25(3). The competent authority 'may' also consult the EBA and ESMA. This indicates that EU lawmakers consider the subsequent change in legal classification (eg, into a financial instrument or EMT) a rather unlikely event. The issuer must notify the competent authority about the modification at least 30 working days before the intended changes take effect (Article 25(1)). The competent authority must give its decision within 30 working days. Non-compliance with Article 25 is a ground for withdrawal of the authorisation according to Article 24(1)(b).

Corresponding modification rules are set out in Article 12 for crypto-assets that are neither ARTs nor EMTs, and in Article 51(12) for EMTs. Like its counterparts, Article 25 creates a significant deviation from the Prospectus Regulation. In classical financial markets regulation, there is a strict separation between the primary market (the offering of financial instruments to the public for the first time) and the secondary market (financial instruments trading and settlement). Disclosure of relevant information in the primary market is effectuated by the Prospectus Regulation. Subsequent disclosure is accomplished by continuous reporting obligations under Directive 2004/109/EC (Transparency Directive) and ad hoc disclosure obligations subject to Article 17 of Regulation (EU) No. 596/2014 (MAR). Changes to the prospectus ('supplements') within the meaning of the Prospectus Regulation are only required if significant new factors arise between the time the prospectus was approved and the closing of the offer (Article 10(1) and 23(1) Prospectus Regulation). After the closing, all important changes are covered by reporting and ad-hoc disclosure, rather than disclosure in the prospectus.

The MiCAR approach is blurring the boundaries between primary and secondary markets, since it requires the modification of published crypto-asset white papers. This is not a mere conceptual issue. For example, Article 88 sets out an obligation to disclose inside information as soon as possible, which is equivalent to Article 17 MAR. This applies to all varieties of crypto-assets, including ARTs and EMTs, which are admitted to trading on a regulated crypto-asset trading platform (Article 1(2)(a)).

The two provisions (ie, modification and disclosure) overlap because the 'significant deviation' will in many cases also constitute 'inside information'[57]

[57] The definition of 'inside information' in Article 87 MiCAR is essentially a copy of Article 7 MAR. However, it seems likely that in the context of crypto-assets, new archetypes of inside information will develop (eg, problems with the blockchain code) that would not be covered by MAR.

within the meaning of Article 87.[58] While Article 88(2) contains rules for delaying disclosure if it is in the legitimate interest of the issuer, there is no equivalent possibility under Articles 25 and 26. This is highly contradictory, and neither Title III nor Title VI provides any clue as to how this should be resolved. On the one hand, it would be coherent with existing capital markets regulation if Articles 25 and 26 did not apply to ARTs that are admitted to trading. On the other hand, at the very least, the exceptions set out in Article 88(2) should be applied accordingly to Article 25 for ARTs that are admitted to trading. In other words, if the immediate modification of the white paper is likely to prejudice the legitimate interests of the issuer, and the delay of disclosure is not likely to mislead the public, and the issuer is able to ensure the confidentiality of the information, the modification may be delayed. In any event, the competent authority would need to be informed (cf. Article 88(3)). However, there is no basis for this in the wording of Article 25, and it is also a fair assumption that Article 25 is a provision that was specifically designed for ARTs (whereas Article 88 was not). It will be interesting to see if and how regulators and courts use the legal interpretation toolbox to reconcile the application of these two provisions.

6.2.3. White Paper Liability

6.2.3.1. General Approach

One of the most controversial issues of the ART regime is the potential liability for flawed crypto-asset white papers under Article 26.[59] Civil liability is one of the typical tools in EU capital markets regulation to increase compliance. The most popular example (which is obviously the role-model for Article 26) is claims for damages brought under national law based on Article 11 Prospectus Regulation. If information in a white paper is not complete, fair or clear, or if it is misleading, the issuer is liable to the crypto-asset holder for any loss incurred due to the infringement (Article 26(1)). This applies to original crypto-asset white papers as well as to crypto-asset white papers that were modified under Article 25. Any contractual exclusion or limitation of civil liability is void (Article 26(2)). The burden of proof lies with the ART holder (Article 26(3)).

Article 26 is built on the existence of a crypto-asset white paper, which under MiCAR must be complete, fair, clear, etc. Thus, it does not cover the case of a missing white paper. However, the approval of the white paper is linked to the grant of authorisation (Article 21(1)). For ARTs there is little risk that an issuer/offeror simply ‘forgets’ about the white paper. In any event, it is likely that the competent authority would send a stern reminder. This means that the risk of

[58] The same goes for the related transparency obligation in Article 30(3) (see section 6.2.6.2).

[59] Article 26 is nearly identical to Article 52 (for EMTs) and Article 15 (for crypto-assets other than ARTs and EMTs). Thus, the following deliberations apply to these provisions too.

missing white papers is somewhat lower than it is under Article 15 built on a mere notification regime. However, it is highly advisable for national lawmakers to close this gap when applying MiCAR or implementing[60] its provisions into their domestic laws.[61]

A conceptual difference with Article 11 Prospectus Regulation is that Article 26 (and the corresponding Articles 15 and 52) creates a basis for civil liability directly in EU law. This goes one step further than the blueprint in Article 11(2) Prospectus Regulation, which only obligates the Member States to 'ensure that their laws, regulations and administrative provisions on civil liability apply to those persons responsible for the information given in a prospectus'. This does not only reduce the potential arbitrage caused by deviating implementations of EU law into national laws (cf. Article 11 Prospectus Regulation).[62] It also moves the prime responsibility for the interpretation of these highly relevant provisions to the EU level. If national courts are uncertain about the application of Article 26, they have to initiate proceedings under Article 267 TFEU. The question is why the crypto markets are policed with a structurally different – and as will be discussed in the next paragraphs – much stricter private law than the equivalent situations[63] of classical financial markets.[64]

6.2.3.2. Personal Liability

Article 26(1) MiCAR extends the liability to members of the administrative, management or supervisory board. Through the lens of effectiveness, this is logical because companies which issue crypto-assets are often young and do not have much capital, resulting in crypto-asset holders typically being unable to realise their claims due to the issuer's limited assets in case of an infringement. At the same time, these young companies are often owned and controlled by their founders. Thus, at first glance, extending liability to management might close a factual gap in investor protection.[65] However, although this could be a sensible rationale for other categories of crypto-assets, it is less convincing in the context ARTs because issuing the latter is subject to an authorisation regime, including stringent capital requirements, etc.

[60] Of course, a regulation does not per se require implementation into national law. However, like other EU regulations, MiCAR requires national member states to fill some gaps, mostly in areas that are not subject to EU legislation. A typical example are the powers of the national competent authorities (see Art. 111(1): 'Member States shall, in accordance with national law, provide for competent authorities to have the power to …'). Another typical example is the national private liability regime.

[61] For example, the draft of German legislation (*Kryptomärkteaufsichtsgesetz*, KMAG) provides a liability for missing white papers in section 19.

[62] See also Cichon (n 2) 96: 'advantageous'.

[63] Of course there are other rules in EU financial markets law that provide liability clause, for example Article 35a of Regulation (EC) No 1060/2009 on create rating agencies. However, these rules have no equivalent in the crypto-markets.

[64] Lehmann (n 1) 15.

[65] P Zickgraf, 'Primärmarktpublizität in der Verordnung über die Märkte für Kryptowerte (MiCAR) – Teil 2' (2021) *Zeitschrift für Bank- und Kapitalmarktrecht* 362, 365; Maume (n 2) 264.

The result is a de facto personal liability for board members. This is in conflict with the idea that directors of companies are (unless there is a case of insolvency) not liable to outsiders for breaches of their duties. It can also create a disincentive against issuing ARTs (and EMTs). If a bank issued a stablecoin on a large scale, members of the management body could be personally liable if things go awry. Even though this might be mitigated by Directors and Officers (D&O) Insurance, this liability threat may be a potential show-stopper for issuing ARTs or EMTs in the EU. The situation is even worse for members of the supervisory board because they are not involved in everyday decision-making and might thus have no way to influence the token issue, but nevertheless may face personal liability.

6.2.3.3. Negligence Requirement

Article 26 does not set out any negligence requirements. The question arises if this provision (and the corresponding provisions of Article 15 and Article 52) creates a strict liability regime. This is a tricky issue, as this is typically a matter of national liability law; overriding established principles for determining liability in national law might cause severe frictions and contradictions.[66] For example, the German equivalent of Article 11 Prospectus Regulation (sections 9, 12 of the German *Wertpapierprospektgesetz* (Securities Prospectus Act)) limits liability to cases where the issuer was either aware of the flaws in the prospectus or was unaware of the flaw due to gross negligence. A strict liability under Article 26 would be a significant increase in liability risk, exceeding nearly all other situations of liability under German law. Taking into consideration the personal liability of board members (see above), the result would be an extremely harsh liability regime.

On the one hand, Article 26 does not provide Member States with the express opportunity to curb liability under Article 26 through national legislation. On the other hand, it states in Article 26(5) that the Article is 'without prejudice to any *other* civil liability pursuant to national law'. The wording does not refer to stricter liability (which would be hard to imagine anyway) but uses the term 'other'. Although it is a long shot, this could be interpreted as some kind of opening. In sum, there is significant legal uncertainty about the application of Article 26 with potentially serious consequences. It is very likely that the CJEU will need to clarify this via preliminary ruling (Article 267 TFEU).

6.2.4. Ongoing Requirements

6.2.4.1. General Approach

Chapter 2 of Title III (Articles 27–35) is named 'Obligations of issuers of asset-referenced tokens'. This is slightly imprecise because Chapter 1 also contains

[66] For detailed discussion in the German literature: Zickgraf (n 65) 365–66.

several provisions that constitute ongoing obligations for issuers. Most of the provisions in Chapter 2 are copies or adaptations of existing rules under MiFID II or other EU banking and payment regulation. The low level of conceptual novelty is demonstrated by the fact that only seven Recitals address Chapter 2, most of them merely copying or paraphrasing parts of the regulation itself. Apparently, the need for explaining the Chapter 2 framework was not considered high.

6.2.4.2. *Obligation to Act Honestly, Fairly and Professionally*

Article 27 sets out the two key principles for ART issuers in their dealing with ART holders. First, issuers shall act honestly, fairly and professionally, and communicate with the holders accordingly (Article 27(1)). Second, they must act in the best interests of the holders (Article 27(2)). The same obligation can be found in Article 66(1) for crypto-asset service providers (CASPs) and their clients, and has its origin in Article 24(1) MiFID II. The odd consequence is that ART issuers must treat token holders like clients. This is not just unusual (general capital market rules such as the Prospectus Regulation do not prescribe similar rules for issuers), but also peculiar because in many cases the issuers would not necessarily know the identity of the current ART holders. In any event, despite this friction, practitioners and regulators will probably draw on the established practices under Article 24(1) MiFID II and their national equivalents.

Interestingly, Article 27(2) also contains an obligation to treat ART holders equally. This will be relevant for the holders' access to information. It resembles the obligation to treat shareholders equally as it is known in company law.[67] This adds another regulatory principle to the mix.

Unlike the liability for information given in crypto-asset white papers in Article 26, MiCAR does not prescribe any civil liability for breaches of Article 27. It is for Member States to decide whether they want to create the possibility for holders to initiate civil proceedings for breaches of Article 27.

6.2.4.3. *Conflicts of Interest*

6.2.4.3.1. A (Very Bad) Adaptation of the MiFID II Regime

ART issuers must implement and maintain effective policies and procedures to identify, prevent, manage and disclose conflicts of interest (Article 32(1)). This is a typical expression of a fiduciary duty as it is often found in financial markets regulation.[68] Article 32(1) complements Article 27(2), which states that the ART issuer must act in the best interest of the holder. These provisions are modelled after

[67] See eg Article 4 of Directive 2007/36/EC of 11 July 2007 on the exercise of certain rights of shareholders in listed companies.

[68] See eg P Latimer and P Maume, *Promoting Information in the Marketplace for Financial Services* (Springer, 2014) 88 et seq.

Article 23 and Article 16(3) MiFID II and have a rough equivalent in Article 72 for CASPs.

Article 32(2) highlights a particular focus on conflicts of interest arising from the management and investment of reserve assets under Article 36. Consequently, the scope of the provision not only includes conflicts of interest between the issuer and shareholders, members of the management body, employees, etc., but also covers 'any third party providing one of the functions as referred in Article 34(5), first subparagraph, point (h)', that is, third-party entities involved in operating, investing and custody of the reserve assets.

However, the list is not a well-thought-out adaptation of the wording of its role model. Article 23(1) MiFID II consists of two poles: (i) the investment firm and its affiliates ('conflicts of interest between themselves, including their managers, employees and tied agents, or any person directly or indirectly linked to them by control'), and (ii) the customer side ('and their clients or between one client and another'). There needs to be a conflict between these two poles. Article 32(1), on the other hand, lists just the issuer on the one side, and all other stakeholders, including token holders, on the other side. This does not make much sense, because it is not clear why an issuer would need to disclose a conflict of interest with their shareholders or managers. The correct approach would be if the issuer (including its shareholders and managers) would need to disclose a conflict of interest with the interests of the token holders or between themselves.

Obviously, the EBA has picked up on this contradiction. In the applicable Draft RTS,[69] the definition of 'connected person' is introduced. This includes 'any of the persons referred to in Article 32(1), points (a) to (d) and point (f)', but not point (e), which is the holder. In other words, the holder of the ART is not a connected person. The ensuing provisions then set out potential conflicts between a connected person and the ART holder. This would be the equivalent of the MiFID II logic but has little to do with Article 32(1). In other words, the Draft RTS attempt to rectify a major mistake in the construction of Article 32.

6.2.4.3.2. Definition of 'Conflict of Interest'

For the definition of 'conflict of interest', practitioners should be able to draw on the principles developed under fiduciary law and, in particular, under MiFID II.[70] In addition, the Draft RTS,[71] for the purposes of identifying the types of conflicts of interest, list in Article 2(1) and Article 2(2) examples where a 'connected person'

[69] EBA, 'Consultation Paper – Draft Regulatory Technical Standards specifying the requirements for policies and procedures on conflicts of interest for issuers of asset-referenced tokens under Article 32(5) of Regulation (EU) 2023/1114' (EBA/CP/2023/37, 7 December 2023) www.eba.europa.eu/publications-and-media/events/consultation-draft-rts-requirements-policies-and-procedures-conflicts.

[70] ibid.

[71] ibid.

(that is, a person listed in Article 32(1) with the exception of token holders, see above) is in any of the following situations:

- potential gains or avoids losses at the expense of the holder;
- has an interest in the outcome of an activity which is distinct from the interest of the holder;
- carries out the same business as any holder;
- receives third party inducements (monetary or non-monetary) that may damage the interest of the holder.

Although this is nearly a verbatim copy of Article 33 of Delegated Regulation (EU) 2017/565, this again shows that extending the established canon of fiduciary duties to the ART issuers comes with frictions: how is an issuer supposed to identify the businesses of the respective token holders? At least the wording of Article 2(1) Draft RTS suggests that there is some leeway for its application in practice because the issuer merely 'shall take into account' these elements. Thus, it seems likely that the listed situations typically (but not necessarily) constitute a conflict of interest. In addition, for the management and investment of reserve assets, Article 3(1) of the Draft RTS[72] lists different situations in which a connected person (see above) is in a conflict of interest with regards to investing and managing the reserve of assets (section 6.2.9).

6.2.4.3.3. Consequences

The regulatory role model in Article 23 MiFID II applies to conflicts 'that arise in the course of providing any investment and ancillary services'. In other words, the conflict must exist when the service is provided, which depends on the nature of the investment service. For an ongoing service such as portfolio management under Article 4(1)(8) MiFID II, Article 23 creates an ongoing obligation. In contrast, as soon as the investment service has been concluded (for example, investment advice under Article 4(1)(4) has been provided and no further relationship exists), there are no further obligations under Article 23 MiFID II. Since Title III of MiCAR creates or purports to create an ongoing relationship, Article 27(2) consequently creates ongoing obligations regarding conflicts of interest, rather than just for the token sale itself. The EBA seems to be holding the same view because the Draft RTS address in Article 2(1) 'types of conflicts of interest that arise in the course of *issuing, processing and redeeming* [ART] or of *investing or managing* the reserve of assets' (emphasis added).[73] Thus, the conflict of interest obligations apply to the whole lifecycle. However, Article 4(4) of the Draft RTS differentiates between conflicts of interest that 'persist and need to be managed permanently and conflicts of interest that occur with regard to a single event'.

[72] ibid.
[73] ibid.

Similar to Article 23 MiFID II, Article 32 does not prohibit conflicts of interest. Instead, it creates a procedure for addressing them. The phrase 'identify, prevent, manage and disclose conflicts of interest' is to be read literally, with identification being the first and disclosure the ultimate step if the conflict cannot be prevented or otherwise managed. Unlike in Article 23(2) MiFID II, this idea of 'last resort'[74] is not expressly stated in Article 32 or the Draft RTS,[75] but there is little doubt that EU lawmakers had a procedure in mind that resembles its MiFID II counterpart. This suggested approach would also be coherent with the most likely solution for the parallel issue in Article 72 for CASPs.[76]

An important difference between Article 23 MiFID II and Article 32 MiCAR is that Article 23 MiFID II only requires disclosure of conflicts of interest if the measures taken 'are not sufficient to ensure, with reasonable confidence, that risks of damage to client interests will be prevented'. Neither Article 32 MiCAR nor the Draft RTS contains any comparable rule. Only Recital (8) of the Draft RTS states that the 'steps taken to mitigate conflicts of interest, in accordance with Article 32(3) [...] should ensure with reasonable confidence that risks of damage to holders of asset-referenced tokens' interests or to the issuer of asset-referenced tokens will be appropriately mitigated.' If we assume that the drafters of MiCAR tried to establish a mechanism roughly comparable to MiFID II, this would involve limiting the disclosure obligation to cases where there is a risk of the interests of the holders being adversely affected. This interpretation would be in line with the general idea of conflicts of interest disclosure. Being in a conflict does not mean that the ensuing action by an investment firm is bad for the client (or here: the action taken by the ART issuer is bad for the token holder). Distinguishing between the harmful and harmless conflicts of interest and taking appropriate steps as a consequence is meant by the expression 'to [...] manage [...] conflicts of interest'[77] as it is also used in Article 32(1).

6.2.5. Governance Arrangements

6.2.5.1. General Approach

Article 34 is the key provision for the issuer's internal governance, including compliance. The amalgamation of additional tasks and obligations results in a canon of organisational duties and governance standards that is stricter than general company law but is usual for finance and banking law. The contents of

[74] See expressly Article 34(4) and Recital 48 of Delegated Regulation (EU) 2017/565.

[75] EBA (n 69).

[76] See ch 7 of this book.

[77] For the same interpretation in the MiFID II context, see P Maume, 'Robo-advisors – How do they fit in the existing EU regulatory framework, in particular with regard to investor protection?' (Study for the European Parliament ECON committee, 30 June 2021), 35 www.europarl.europa.eu/thinktank/en/document/IPOL_STU(2021)662928.

Article 34 are mostly taken from Article 9 and Article 16 MiFID II and then partly rephrased. To the extent that Article 34 does not address crypto-specific issues (such as Article 34(5)), regulators and practitioners will probably take cues from the established standards under MiFID II and other authorisation regimes in banking and payment services laws. Interestingly, Article 34(13) only empowers the EBA to issue guidelines on the minimum content of governance arrangements set out in Article 34(8)–(10) and Article 34(12). For the rest of Article 34, ART issuers will need to work with the existing wording, however vague it may be in parts.

Meeting the governance arrangements in Article 34 is one of the main requirements for authorisation under Article 16 (section 6.2.1). Conversely, competent authorities shall withdraw the authorisation if the good repute of members of the management body is negatively affected (section 6.2.1.5) or if there is an indication of a failure of the governance requirements or internal control mechanisms under Article 34 (Article 24(5)). According to the wording ('shall'), this decision is not subject to the competent authority's discretion.

Article 34 applies the principle of proportionality. This means that ART issuers only need to maintain internal mechanisms and procedures that are necessary for achieving the regulatory goals, but no more. This is demonstrated by the use of the terms 'sufficient', 'adequate', 'proportionate' and 'appropriate'. On the bright side, this is a safeguard against regulatory excess. However, it provides for uncertainty in its application in practice, at least until competent authorities and market participants have established best practices for the crypto-specific elements of Article 34 (for the general requirements, the MiFID II regime should provide sufficient guidance).

Article 34(1) stipulates the general obligation to 'have robust governance arrangements, including a clear organisational structure with well-defined, transparent and consistent lines of responsibility, effective processes to identify, manage, monitor and report the risks to which they are or might be exposed, and adequate internal control mechanisms, including sound administrative and accounting procedures.' This is essentially an elaboration of the general principles of corporate governance. In addition, Article 34(3) – quite obviously – states that the effectiveness of all policy arrangements and procedures needs to be reviewed and assessed periodically.

6.2.5.2. Management Body

According to Article 34(2), members of the management body of ART issuers must be of sufficiently good repute and possess the appropriate knowledge, skills and experience. This 'fit and proper' test is a key element of financial markets intermediary regulation and can also be found in Article 91(1) CRD IV and Article 9(4) MiFID II. Article 34(2) also states that members may not be convicted of offences relating to money laundering or terrorist financing, although other offences could also affect the good repute. Article 34(4) extends the requirement of good repute to shareholders and members that have qualifying holdings, which refers to a direct or indirect holding in the issuer which represents at least 10 per cent of the capital or of the voting rights (Article 3(1)(36)). In addition, Article 33 requires ART issuers to notify the competent authority immediately about all changes to the management body, and provide all the necessary information to assess compliance with Article 34(2).

In most cases, practitioners will be able to draw on the established ESMA/EBA guidelines in relation to Article 91 CRD IV and Article 9 MiFID II.[78] However, it will be interesting how the national competent authorities will interpret the requirements of 'knowledge, skill and experience'. The problem is that in new lines of business such as issuing stablecoins, it is difficult for applicants to demonstrate sufficient experience – simply because organising the emission of stablecoins has little to do with organising traditional banking. Thus, the established criteria[79] will not be reliable in many situations. This is a well-known problem in the area of fintech regulation and has been a serious obstacle for young and fledgling fintechs.[80] It has to be hoped that the competent authorities apply a pragmatic approach in this regard, otherwise applicants might be put at a further disadvantage in comparison to incumbent financial players, like banks (section 6.1.3). This would be in line with Recital (51), stating that the obligations under Article 34 'aim to ensure the protection of holders of asset-referenced tokens [...] while not creating unnecessary barriers.'

In addition to the powers under Title III, competent authorities also have the power to require the removal of a natural person from the management body of an ART issuer. Article 94(1)(y) obligates Member States to create respective 'removal' powers for the competent authority under national laws.

6.2.5.3. *Organisational Compliance*

Article 34(5) sets out organisational requirements that follow from the nature of the regulated activity. ART issuers must establish, maintain and implement policies and procedures on most of the obligations set out in Articles 31–45. This includes, inter alia, the reserve of assets (Article 36), its custody (Article 37), the right of redemption (Article 39), conflicts of interest procedures (Article 32) and complaints handling (Article 31), as well as the functioning of the DLT used. This list might appear redundant at first glance as it simply repeats these obligations. However, by referring to policies and procedures, Article 34(5) in effect clarifies that they all need to be part of a structured approach, ie, compliance system.

[78] For example, ESMA/EBA, 'Guidelines on the assessment of the suitability of members of the management body and key function holders' (EBA/GL/2021/06 and ESMA35-36-2319 of 2 July 2021) www.esma.europa.eu/sites/default/files/library/joint_eba_and_esma_gl_on_the_assessment_of_suitability.pdf.

[79] ibid 20, 21.

[80] See eg P Maume, 'Financial Services Regulation' in P Maume, L Maute and M Fromberger, *The Law of Crypto-Assets* (Beck Hart Nomos, 2022) 239.

Article 34(6) extends this obligation to systems, resources and procedures to ensure the continued and regular performance of services and activities. If the issuer decides to discontinue 'the issue' of the ART, it has to submit a plan to the competent authority for approval (Article 34(7)). The drafting of this provision is somewhat odd, in that 'issue' does not appear to refer to the issuance of new tokens (the usual meaning of the word), but to the continued activity of having the issued ART circulating in the market (ie, 'being the issuer'). It would not make sense to require approval from competent authority to *not* issue additional tokens. Conversely, the discontinuation of a token could adversely affect current holders, which is why an approval requirement seems reasonable.

6.2.5.4. *Risk Management and Operational Resilience*

According to Article 34(8), ART issuers have to identify operational risks and minimise them through appropriate systems, controls and procedures. MiCAR does not define 'operational risk', but the meaning should be identical to Article 4(1)(52) of Regulation (EU) No. 575/2013 (CRR).[81] Accordingly, operational risk is 'the risk of loss resulting from inadequate or failed internal processes, people and systems or from external events, and includes legal risk'.

Article 34(9) addresses the specific risk of an interruption of the ICT systems. In this regard, the issuer has to ensure the preservation of essential data and functions and the maintenance of their activities. Article 34(10) combines these two elements to operational risks in regard of ICT. For this purpose, ART issuers must have internal mechanisms and effective standards within the meaning of Regulation (EU) 2022/2554 (DORA). This includes, under Article 34(11), systems and procedures that are adequate to safeguard the availability, authenticity, integrity and confidentiality of data as required under DORA.

These systems and procedures have to be in line with Regulation (EU) 2016/679 (GDPR) as also set out in Article 34(11). This does not only mean that ART issuers have to comply with EU data protection laws. The intriguing consequence is that the competent authority, as defined in MiCAR, is also made responsible for supervising and enforcing matters of data protection law.

6.2.5.5. *Complaints Handling*

Article 31(1) obligates the ART issuer to establish and maintain effective and transparent procedures for the prompt, fair and consistent handling of complaints received from token holders. Thus, Article 31 sets out a specific organisational duty for the issuer. The issuer must also establish procedures for handling complaints between

[81] The EBA has taken the same view, see EBA, 'Consultation Paper on EBA Draft Guidelines on the minimum content of the governance arrangements for issuers of asset-referenced tokens (EBA/CP/2023/23, 20 October 2023) 14, www.eba.europa.eu/publications-and-media/events/consultation-draft-guidelines-internal-governance-arrangements.

holders and third-party entities under Article 34(5)(h), which refers in this case to the distribution of the ARTs to the public. The issuer and, if applicable, third-party entities, must develop and make available templates for lodging these complaints (Article 31(3)) and investigate and communicate the outcome of the investigation to the complainant (Article 31(4)). All complaints have to be free of charge (Article 31(2)). Further details will be set out in a Delegated Regulation (Article 31(5)).

6.2.6. Ongoing Reporting Obligations

6.2.6.1. Reporting to the Competent Authority

Title III clearly displays the MiCAR drafters' concern in relation to stablecoins that have become overly popular, or, in other words, that have achieved a high level of market capitalisation. According to Article 22, if an ART reaches an issue value that is higher than EUR 100 million, the issuer is subject to a quarterly reporting obligation to the competent authority. This must be seen in conjunction with Article 23, which is supposed to limit the use of ARTs that are used as a means of exchange (section 6.2.1.7). Surprisingly, this mechanism is found in Chapter 1 of Title III, although it is clearly an ongoing obligation and not an authorisation requirement. Another purpose of Article 22 is to monitor the market for potentially significant ARTs (Article 43 et seq).

According to Article 22(1), the reporting must include the number of holders, the value of the ART and the size of the reserve of assets and the average number and average aggregate value of transactions per day during the relevant quarter. Issuers also need to give an estimate on the respective figures for transactions that are associated with the ART's use as a means of exchange within a single currency area. At the time of writing this chapter, the ECB and the EBA were in the process of consultation regarding the reporting procedure and the assessment methodology in this respect (Article 22(6) and (7)).

Article 22(1) states that '[f]or the purposes of points (c) and (d) of the first subparagraph, "transaction" shall mean any change of the natural or legal person entitled to the asset-referenced token as a result of the transfer of the asset-referenced token from one distributed ledger address or account to another.' In other words, the reporting obligation only refers to on-chain transactions and does not cover their off-chain equivalent.[82] A possible explanation is that issuers would find it extremely difficult to monitor off-chain transactions that take place on crypto-exchanges because they only occur in the books of the exchange operator.

[82] The term 'on-chain' means that a transaction is directly recorded in the respective blockchain whilst an 'off-chain' transaction only takes place in a ledger of an intermediary (eg, a crypto exchange). For the dichotomy on-chain/off-chain, see M Fromberger, 'Technical and Factual Background' in P Maume, L Maute and M Fromberger, *The Law of Crypto-Assets* (Beck Hart Nomos, 2022) 27 et seq with further references.

However, for the purposes of this regulation, this should not be problematic, because the ECB is essentially interested in how many ARTs are used for 'regular' payment purposes. This is underlined by the ensuing statement that '[t]ransactions that are associated with the exchange for funds or other crypto-assets with the issuer or with a crypto-asset service provider shall not be considered associated to uses of the asset-referenced token as a means of exchange, unless there is evidence that the asset-referenced token is used for the settlement of transactions in other crypto-assets.'

This means that the MiCAR drafters are only interested in ART trading volume if these tokens are used in comparable ways to money. This does not include crypto-to-crypto transactions that are typical for crypto-exchanges and very often occur off-chain, unless they are used as a means of settlement.

6.2.6.2. Ongoing Provision of Information to ART Holders

Article 30(1) stipulates that ART issuers must publish on their website the amount of tokens in circulation, and the value and composition of the reserve of assets (section 6.2.9). This needs to be updated at least monthly. Article 30(2) adds an obligation to publish a summary of the audit report and a full, unredacted audit report in relation to the reserve of assets. These are sensible transparency requirements.

Article 30(3) is another bad case of regulatory overlap within MiCAR. It states that ART issuers shall as soon as possible disclose on their website any event that is or is likely to have a significant effect on the value of the token or on the reserve of assets. The MiCAR drafters realised the obvious overlap with Article 88 and the duty to disclose price relevant inside information if the ART is admitted to trading on a regulated trading platform (Article 1(2)(a)). Article 30(3) addresses this overlap by stating that the obligation exists 'without prejudice', which means that both provisions apply simultaneously. In contrast, Article 30(3) does not address the overlap with the obligation to publish a modified white paper (Article 25) on the issuer's website (Article 28). The second overlap does not seem to be overly problematic because it should be relatively easy to update crypto-asset white paper and website in one step. What is more problematic, however, is that Article 30(3), just like Article 25, does not provide for any exception from the transparency requirement in cases where it is in the interest of the issuer to delay the disclosure (cf. Article 88(2)). The consequence is that, if Articles 30(3) and 28 were interpreted literally, the exceptions in Article 88(2) would be rendered meaningless for ARTs admitted to trading in many cases (for details, see section 6.2.2.2).

6.2.7. Marketing Communications

Article 29 complements the extensive transparency and disclosure regime for ART issuers with rules on marketing communications. The term 'marketing communications' is not defined in MiCAR, but essentially covers all types of advertising. The rules on marketing communications are particularly relevant because communication via the internet and social media is the primary communications channel in the crypto industry, replacing or at least complementing the prospectus/whitepaper as the traditional disclosure instrument.

Article 29 mostly copies the rules found in Article 7 for crypto-assets other than ARTs and EMTs.[83] Interestingly, Article 29 does not require the marketing communications to contain a warning statement that the communication has not been reviewed and approved by the competent authority. The probable background is that Title II (and thus, Article 7) does not foresee an authorisation procedure for issuers. If an ART issuer was communicating in a misleading way, its authorisation might be at stake, which should be a clear deterrent against misbehaviour. Such a mechanism does not exist for Title II crypto-assets and their issuers.

In terms of content and time, marketing communications are tied to the crypto-asset white paper. According to Article 29(1)(c), the information in the marketing communication must be consistent with the white paper. In addition, no marketing communication shall be disseminated prior to the publication of the white paper. Unfortunately, these restrictions might be rather toothless because the issuer's liability under Article 26 does not extend to marketing communications. On the one hand, this can be seen as a wise self-restraint of the EU legislator because advertisement and marketing are not the same as a prospectus or white paper. It is widely accepted that advertisements are trying to depict the company in the best possible manner, which might be considered misleading if the rules of prospectus were applied. On the other hand, the absence of a special civil enforcement mechanism raises questions about the effectiveness of Article 29 in practice. It remains to be seen if national legislators will apply stricter rules here. It also has to be noted that misleading marketing communications might be subject to Directive 2005/29/EC on unfair business-to-consumer commercial practices, which means that MiCAR is not the only regulatory tool in this regard.

6.2.8. Own Funds Requirements

Article 35(1) sets out a dynamic system of own funds (referred to as 'own funds requirements' in the heading and numerous times in the Recitals). Like in other areas of prudential regulation, special requirements for own funds are supposed to make the supervised entity more resilient, indirectly increasing the stability of the whole financial system.[84] The required own funds also serve as a starting point for new companies, making sure that they have sufficient capital available to build their regulated business. Thus, the requirements have to be met when applying for

[83] For details, see ch 5 of this book.
[84] See also MiCAR, Recital (53).

authorisation (see Article 35(1): 'at all times'). According to Article 17(4), banks are not subject to Article 35, but rather to the capital requirements in the CRR. In contrast to the reserve of assets in Chapter 3 (section 6.2.9), own funds cannot be used for investment purposes.[85]

ART issuers must have own funds equal to an amount of at least the highest of the following: (a) EUR 350,000, (b) 2 per cent of the average amount of the reserve of assets referred to in Article 36 (section 6.2.9), and (c) a quarter of the fixed overheads of the preceding years. Article 35(3) gives the competent authority the power to increase the resulting amount by up to 20 per cent. The idea of this flexible approach is that the funds requirements should be proportionate to the issuance size of the ART,[86] showing again the principle of proportionality in crypto-asset regulation. If either the total amount of tokens or the costs while issuing the ART grow, so do the own funds requirements. Thus, it is likely that the EUR 350,000 will only apply to smaller token issues or at the start of the issuance process, therefore forming the bottom line of own funds requirements. This dynamic approach is known from EU banking regulation, in particular in Article 92 CRR which sets out capital ratios. In contrast, EU financial intermediaries regulation under MiFID II applies fixed own funds requirements.

However, even the EUR 350,000 as the minimum requirement appears to be quite high in comparison to requirements for other regulated activities. For CASPs, Annex I of MiCAR sets out minimum capital requirements between EUR 50,000 and EUR 150,000. For investment firms under MiFID II, Article 9 of Directive (EU) 2019/2034 on the prudential supervision of investment firms (IFD) prescribes EUR 75,000 and EUR 150,000 for most services; only for dealing on own account and the operation of an organised trading facility (which are both deemed to be particularly dangerous for clients) the capital requirement is EUR 750,000. This shows that the minimum requirement of EUR 350,000 for ART issuers is at the upper end of the scale. For smaller companies, this probably is a very steep hurdle. This is another reason why the stablecoin sector in the EU will hardly feature any start-ups.[87]

6.2.9. Reserve of Assets

6.2.9.1. Conceptual Framework

One of the key features of MiCAR stablecoin regulation is the requirement that the issuer should hold a reserve of assets (Title III, Chapter 3). The idea is that a significant part of the money or other assets that the ART receives in the course of the token sale is kept separate, invested only subject to specific rules, and is not used

[85] Zetzsche et al (n 2) 14.
[86] MiCAR, Recital (53).
[87] Lehmann (n 1) 18.

for other company-related purposes or distributed amongst the shareholders.[88] These 'reserve assets' are not necessarily the same (type of) assets as the assets which the ART is referencing. The mechanism is supposed to ensure that the issuer is at any time able to meet its obligation if the holder exercises the right of redemption under Article 39 (section 6.2.9.5).

For this purpose, the reserve assets must be fully segregated from the issuer's assets; they must not be encumbered or pledged as collateral to third parties, and the issuer must have prompt access to these assets.[89] This regulation aims to prevent the contamination of the reserve of assets – the issuer's creditors should have no claim on the reserve assets, especially in the event of insolvency.[90] It has to be noted that Chapter 3 does not automatically render these assets immune in the case of insolvency; the issuer has to ensure that such assets are legally separated. To what extent this separation is effective remains a question of national property and insolvency laws, which might need to be amended while implementing MiCAR.

A second effect of the reserve of assets is that it facilitates the ART's stability. The bigger and more reliable the bucket of assets is, the higher the holders' confidence in the ART will be, arguably reducing its price volatility. Choosing specific assets will also align the ART's market price with the market price of these assets. However, the side effect of a mandatory asset reserve is that it puts issuers of algorithmic stablecoins at a disadvantage. Algorithmic stablecoins that are referencing real-life assets (ie, that aim to maintain a stable value in relation to one or several assets via protocols) are subject to Title III (section 6.2.1.3). This means that they have to comply with all rules and obligations imposed, including by Chapter 3. The need to keep sufficient assets in reserve to cover all claims for redemption essentially destroys the business case of these algorithmic stablecoins.[91]

The rules on the reserve of assets are complemented by Title III, Chapter 6. Article 46 introduces recovery plans that ART issuers must prepare. A recovery plan must contain measures to be taken by the issuer to restore compliance with the requirements for the reserve of assets in cases where the issuer fails to comply with those requirements. It is essentially an emergency procedure to get the reserve of assets back on track without triggering insolvency proceedings. Article 47 contains the requirement for drafting and maintaining redemption plans. These plans should support an orderly redemption of ARTs, and are to be implemented upon a decision by the competent authority that the issuer is unable or likely to be

[88] For different approaches and also overview of the MiCAR regime see Kokorin (n 15). The requirement of a reserve of assets applies as well to electronic money (e-money) institutions issuing EMTs that are significant by virtue of Article 58(1) MiCAR. Furthermore, Article 58(2) envisages the possibility that competent authorities may impose that requirement to e-money institutions issuing EMTs that are not significant.

[89] MiCAR, Recital (55); see also Article 37(1).

[90] Annunziata (n 2) 52.

[91] Similar Lehmann (n 1): 'offering these kinds of stablecoins in the EU will be impossible' (focusing on synthetic stablecoins); Martino (n 2): 'algorithmic stablecoins will be, de facto, not issued in the EU because of the impossibility to comply with the ART regulatory regime'.

unable to fulfil its obligations, including in the case of insolvency, or in the case of withdrawal of authorisation of the issuer.

6.2.9.2. General Obligations

The ART issuer must ensure that the issuance and redemption of ARTs is always matched by a corresponding increase or decrease in the reserve of assets (Article 36(6)). The aggregate value of the reserve of assets must be at least equal to the aggregate value of redemption claims against the issuer (Article 36(7)). This is intended to ensure that the issuer can meet the ART holders' claims for redemption under Article 39 (section 6.2.9.5) at all times (including in insolvency),[92] but is also intended to stabilise the issuer in general.[93] MiCAR does not set out the required size and composition of reserve assets. Instead, the EBA must develop draft regulatory standards by 30 June 2024 at the latest which are then to be cast into a Delegated regulation by the Commission (Article 36(4)). Thus, Article 36 itself only sets out the general principles regarding the reserve of assets. The important exception under Article 36(4) is that the minimum amount in each official currency referenced to be held in deposits in credit institutions cannot be lower than 30 per cent of the amount referenced. Since these deposits are de facto unproductive capital, this requirement lowers the potential returns that issuers of ART can generate.

The asset reserve shall be composed and managed in such a way that 'the risks associated with the assets referenced by the ART are covered', and that 'the liquidity risks associated to the permanent rights of redemption of the holders are addressed' (Article 36(1)). The reserve of assets shall be legally and operationally segregated from the issuer's estate, and also segregated from the reserve of assets of other ARTs if more than one ART has been issued (Article 36(2) and (3)). The pools of reserve assets for different ARTs must be managed separately (Article 36(5)).

6.2.9.3. Custody of Reserve Assets

The second key policy of Chapter 3 is that the assets are not just separated from the issuer's assets but kept in custody by a third party (ie, different from the issuer), which itself must be a regulated entity under MiCAR, MiFID II or CRR.[94] This ensures (on paper) not only that the custodian is subject to regulatory standards and supervision. The consequence is also that the custodian is an entity registered in the European Union.

Under Article 37(3), credit institutions may take custody of all types of reserve assets (ie, cash, crypto-assets, securities, commodities). They are the only type of custodian that is allowed to hold money in custody. CASPs, providing custody

[92] MiCAR Recital (54).
[93] Maume (n 2) 267.
[94] MiCAR Recital (55).

and administration of crypto-assets on behalf of clients under Article 75, can only take custody of reserve assets in the form of crypto-assets. Investment firms that provide the ancillary service of safekeeping and administration of financial instruments under MiFID II can take custody of the reserves comprising financial instruments, including crypto-assets that classify as financial instruments.

Article 37 imposes various obligations on the issuer and the custodian. The issuer must establish, maintain and implement custody policies, procedures and contractual agreements to achieve the regulatory aims (Article 37(1)). This includes the obligation to avoid concentrations of custodians (Article 37(1)(d)). Thus, the issuer should, if possible, spread the custodial services among several contractual partners. The contractual agreements between the issuer and the custodians need to regulate, inter alia, the flow of information between the parties (Article 37(7)) and also ensure that the reserve assets held in custody are protected against claims of the custodians' creditors.[95] The custodians are under an obligation to act honestly, fairly, professionally, independently and in the interest of the issuers of the ARTs and the holders of such tokens (Article 37(8)), which is the equivalent of Article 27 (section 6.2.4.1). They also must identify, monitor, manage and disclose conflicts of interest of the issuers to whom they are providing custody services (Article 37(9)).

6.2.9.4. Investment of Reserve Assets

Article 38 sets out the rules for investing reserve assets. Allowing the investment of reserve assets per se is sensible because they would otherwise remain unused and thus 'dead' capital. Due to inflation, the reserve of assets could also lose in value in comparison to the asset the ART is referencing. The rules on investing reserve assets resemble, to a certain extent, the mechanism known from collective investment schemes;[96] the issuer receives funds in the ART sale and invests them in other assets. However, the main purpose of these reserve assets is not to generate yields for the client (like in a collective investment scheme), but to safeguard the rights of the token holders.[97] To further protect the reserve of assets and thus the ART holders, all profits or losses in the investment process and any counterparty or operational risks that result from the investment of the reserve of assets shall be borne by the issuer (Article 38(4)).

At first glance, it seems odd that Article 38 only refers to investment in financial instruments, while Article 37 expressly lists three categories of assets (crypto-assets, financial instruments and other assets such as funds, section 6.2.9.3). The logic is that holding a reserve in fiat currencies or crypto-assets (unless they are financial instruments) is not an 'investment' within the meaning of Article 38.

[95] It is often overlooked that there is not only the danger of insolvency of the issuer, but also of the custodian or wallet provider.
[96] Annunziata (n 2) 50–51.
[97] Annunziata (n 2) 52.

The EBA seems to share this understanding, stating in the respective consultation paper that 'the reserve of assets shall be composed of the assets that the issuer receives and keeps when issuing the tokens (e.g. deposits with credit institutions, commodities, financial instruments …) **and** by the highly liquid financial instruments the issuer may invest in' (emphasis added).[98] The question is if this effectively prohibits issuers from acquiring (new) assets other than financial instruments. This would not make sense. For example, if the basket to which the ART is referenced includes five currencies and three commodities, the obvious way of securing the token holders would be to acquire exactly these assets – in this case, the reserve of assets would be an exact match of the token holders claim if they exercised their right of redemption. Forcing the issuer to invest in financial instruments, which by their very nature come with market risk, would be against the overall thrust of Chapter 3. Thus, acquisitions that are required to maintain the stabilisation mechanism should not be considered 'investments' within the meaning of Article 38. Identifying these assets would not be difficult as they would need to be listed in the policy describing the stabilisation mechanism as required under Article 36(8)(a). Anything other than these assets would be subject to the limitations as set out in Article 38.

According to Article 38(1), reserve assets shall only be invested in highly liquid financial instruments with minimal market risk, credit risk and concentration risk. This also means that all investments have to be in financial instruments. The investments must be capable of being liquidated rapidly with minimal adverse price effect. This is likely to increase investor confidence.[99] Units in an undertaking for collective investment in transferable securities (UCITS) are considered investments with minimal risk within the meaning of Article 38(1) if the UCITS invests solely in assets as further specified by EBA in a draft technical standard (Article 38(2) and (5)).

6.2.9.5. *Right of Redemption*

The main protection mechanism for ART holders is found in Article 39(1). ART holders have a right of redemption at all times against the issuer. Upon request, the issuer must redeem either by paying an amount in funds (other than electronic money) equivalent to the market value of the assets referenced by the ART, or by delivering the assets referenced by the token (Article 39(2)). The second option protects holders if, for whatever reasons, the market value of the token is lower than the value of the underlying asset. This rule seems to limit the number and nature of the underlying assets which the ART references. If we imagine an ART

[98] EBA, 'Consultation Paper – Draft RTS to specify the highly liquid financial instruments with minimal market risk, credit risk and concentration risk under Article 38(5) of Regulation (EU) 2023/1114' (EBA/CP/2023/24, 8 November 2023) para 2, www.eba.europa.eu/publications-and-media/events/consultation-rts-specify-highly-liquid-financial-instruments-reserve.

[99] Lehmann (n 1) 18.

composed of a 'basket' of 25 different assets, including currencies and commodities, the consequence would be that these commodities would have to be 'delivered' to the token holder, which seems unrealistic. On the other hand, if the basket is only made up by a few currencies or financial instruments, delivery seems a viable (if complex) option.

The redemption needs to be free of charge (Article 39(3)). If the issuer accepts payment denominated in an official currency, it is required to offer the option to redeem the token in the same official currency (Article 39(2)). ART issuers must establish policies laying down, inter alia, the conditions to exercise the right, the mechanisms that ensure redemption, the principles of valuation, and the conditions for settlement (Article 39(2)).

6.2.9.6. Prohibition of Granting Interest

Finally, issuers must not grant interest in relation to ARTs. This is a well-known principle from e-money regulation.[100] It aims to reduce the attractiveness of ARTs as a store of value.[101] It also highlights the similarity of ARTs to e-money, sharing its specific character as an electronic surrogate for coins and banknotes, which is to be used for making payments, usually of limited amount, and not as a means of saving.[102] A second purpose is to prevent the circumvention of EU securities laws, because an ART yielding interest shares many similarities with a bond.[103]

6.3. E-money Tokens (EMT)

6.3.1. General Framework

The regulation of e-money tokens (EMTs) within the meaning of Article 3(1)(7) in Title IV follows a very similar pattern to the regulation of ARTs in Title III. However, the eligibility for issuing EMT is restricted to credit institutions and e-money institutions (Article 48(1)(a)). The consequence is that many provisions in Title III do not require an equivalent in Title IV because, for example, the internal governance and capital requirements are already set out in the authorisation regimes for credit institutions and e-money institutions. The result is that Title IV (and also this part of the chapter) is much more concise than Title III.

In addition, EMT regulation draws on the E-Money Directive (EMD2). First, all EMTs shall be deemed 'electronic money' according to Article 48(2), but not vice versa. Titles II and III of the EMD2 apply to EMTs unless otherwise stated in

[100] See also EMD2, Article 12.
[101] MiCAR, Recital (58).
[102] EMD2, Recital (1).
[103] Zetzsche et al (n 2) 17.

Title IV of MiCAR, reducing the length of Title IV even further. In other words, Title IV creates an amalgamation of crypto-asset and e-money regulation. As this book specifically addresses MiCAR, the rules following from the EMD2 will not be discussed any further.

6.3.2. Indirect Authorisation Regime

Article 48(1) does not provide for a separate authorisation procedure for EMTs. However, indirectly, Article 48 relies on authorisation. The main difference with the ART regime is that Article 48(1) limits the public offer and the admission to trading of EMTs to authorised credit institutions and electronic money institutions under the E-Money Directive. The provision highlights the deep concern of EU policymakers about private 'currencies'. Whereas ARTs seem to be considered sufficiently different from official currencies (in particular, the Euro), EMTs are similar enough that only credit institutions and e-money institutions in the EU should be able to issue them. This is also reflected in other pieces of EU regulation. For example, settlement and clearing of DLT-based financial instruments under Regulation (EU) 2022/858 (DLT Pilot Regime) are possible using MiCAR-regulated EMTs, but not ARTs.[104] Yet again, this option is limited to commercial banks (ie, credit institutions) according to Article 5(8) DLT Pilot Regime. On the one hand, this is reassuring because EU lawmakers seem to believe EMTs can play a pivotal role in digital payment and settlement systems. On the other hand, however, the consequences appear to be overly strict. It would have been possible to come up with a less strenuous regulatory framework, leaving the door open for financial service providers.

The EMT issuer also needs to draw up a crypto-asset white paper in accordance with Article 51. As in case of ARTs, the issuer must notify the competent authority. However, unlike for ARTs, there is no clause comparable to Article 21(1), stating that the crypto-asset white paper is deemed to be approved when the authorisation is granted. This resembles the regime in Title II for tokens other than ART/EMT.

According to Article 48(2), an EMT referencing an official currency (Article 3(1)(8)) of an EU Member State is deemed to be offered in the European Union. MiCAR thus establishes a worldwide claim to regulate all EMTs pegging not just the Euro, but all other EU currencies. This raises the issue of enforcement if such an EMT is established in a third country. That said, at the time of writing this chapter, this seems a rather theoretical situation, because only 0.2 per cent of the global stablecoin market is pegging the Euro (section 6.1.2).

If third parties wish to offer EMTs or seek admission to trading, they must obtain the written consent of the issuers (ie, a credit institution). They are also

[104] For discussion, see P Maume and F Kesper, 'The EU DLT Pilot Regime for Digital Assets' (2023) 20 *European Company Law Journal* 118.

subject to the prohibition to grant interest (Article 50), and must comply with the requirements concerning marketing communications (Article 53).

6.3.3. Issuance and Redeemability

Like ART holders, EMT holders have a redemption right against the issuer (Article 49(2)). In this regard, Article 49(1) declares Article 11 of the EMD2 on the issuance and redeemability of e-money inapplicable, making MiCAR is sole applicable source of regulation. The redemption must be free of charge (Article 49(6)), unless it occurs as part of a recovery plan under Article 46.

Again, since the structure of an EMT is simpler than that of an ART, the rules are much more straightforward. Issuers of e-money tokens shall issue e-money tokens at par value and on the receipt of funds (Article 49(3)) within the meaning of Article 4(25) of Directive (EU) 2015/2366 (PSD II), hence including banknotes, coins, scriptural money or electronic money. Interestingly, redemption can also happen in funds, but other than electronic money (Article 49(4)). In other words, the issuer has to open the door for the holder to get back into the world of fiat money.

6.3.4. Investment

Unlike with ARTs, the funds received by EMT issuers from EMT holders are not protected by a bespoke system of reserve assets (section 6.2.9). Instead, the safeguarding requirements in Article 7 EMD2 apply (Article 54). In addition, at least 40 per cent of the funds must be deposited in separate accounts in (other) banks, and the remaining funds received are invested in secure, low-risk assets that qualify as highly liquid financial instruments with minimal market risk, credit risk and concentration risk in accordance with Article 38 (section 6.2.9.4).

6.3.5. Rules Parallel to ART Regulation

The rest of Title IV strongly resembles (although being much shorter than) Title III. Article 50 prohibits granting interest (see Article 40 and section 6.2.9.6). Article 51 prescribes in combination with Annex III the required content and form of the white paper (see Article 19 and section 6.2.2). Marketing communications must be clearly identifiable as such, must be fair, clear and not misleading, and consistent with the white paper (see Article 29, section 6.2.7). EMT issuers including their administrative, management or supervisory bodies are also liable for information in the white paper that is not complete, fair or clear, or that is misleading (Article 52(4)). The recovery and redemption plans in Title III, Chapter 6 apply mutatis mutandis (Article 55).

6.4. Conclusion

The regulation of stablecoins under MiCAR comes with significant risks. It is possible that strict regulation will help building healthy and resilient market structures, promoting investor confidence and growth. On the other hand, the EU might be cut off from international crypto-payment structures if the leading global stablecoin issuers decide not to bother with undergoing the MiCAR authorisation requirements. On a more practical level, Title III in particular is vastly complex and nearly impossible to navigate. Issuers, regulators and also the courts will have a hard time making sense of all the little mistakes and contradictions that can be found throughout Titles III and IV. Only after some years we will be able to ascertain if the 'innovation by legal certainty' approach was successful.

7

Regulation of Crypto-Asset Service Providers and Crypto-Asset Services

ILYA KOKORIN*

7.1. Introduction

Crypto-asset service providers (CASPs) play a crucial role in crypto markets. The Bank for International Settlements (BIS) reports that, '[a]lthough crypto operates under the banner of decentralisation, in practice new centralised intermediaries have played a key role in channelling funds into the crypto universe and intermediating within it.'[1] According to some estimates, eight crypto platforms (Binance, Coinbase, Kraken, OKX, KuCoin, Bybit, Binance.US, and Bitfinex) control over 90 per cent of the crypto market's liquidity.[2] In line with these findings, ESMA observes that 10 exchanges process around 90 per cent of all trades, while the largest exchange (Binance) accounts for almost half of global trading volumes.[3] Given this 'intermediated' reality, it is not surprising that MiCAR devotes significant attention to the regulation of CASPs.

In 2022–2023, the global crypto-asset markets experienced the failure of several providers of crypto-asset services. The collapse of Three Arrows Capital, Voyager, Celsius, FTX, Alameda, BlockFi, Genesis, Bittrex Inc. and other crypto enterprises raised important questions relating to the fragility and economic viability of their business models, market integration and interconnectedness, corporate governance failures, inadequate regulatory frameworks and the high risks faced

* The views expressed in this chapter are solely those of the author and do not necessarily reflect those of the AFM.

[1] BIS, 'The crypto ecosystem: key elements and risks: Report submitted to the G20 Finance Ministers and Central Bank Governors' (July 2023), www.regulationtomorrow.com/eu/bis-report-on-the-crypto-ecosystem-key-elements-and-risks/#:~:text=On%2011%20July%202023%2C%20the,the%20options%20for%20addressing%20them.

[2] C Medalie and D Aubert, 'The Crypto Liquidity Concentration Report' (*Kaiko*, 7 September 2023) research.kaiko.com/insights/the-crypto-liquidity-concentration-report.

[3] M Calissano, F Giuglini and P Reiche, 'Crypto assets: Market structures and EU relevance' (2024) ESMA TRV Risk Analysis, 10 April 2024, www.esma.europa.eu/sites/default/files/2024-04/ESMA50-524821-3153_risk_article_crypto_assets_market_structures_and_eu_relevance.pdf.

by crypto-asset investors around the world. On the one hand, the regulation of CASPs under MiCAR seeks to foster their growth and development by allowing them to scale up their activities on a cross-border basis and facilitating their access to banking services.[4] On the other hand, MiCAR aims to ensure the integrity of crypto markets, protect investors and consumers, promote financial stability and the smooth operation of payment systems.[5]

Before the adoption of MiCAR, crypto-asset service providers and the services they offered were mainly subject to national legal frameworks, some of which did not have special rules for businesses active on crypto markets. This resulted in a highly fragmented regulatory landscape governing the crypto-asset sector. By imposing operational, organisational and prudential requirements for CASPs, MiCAR introduces a harmonised and dedicated legal regime for all Member States of the EU. In many respects, this legal regime is similar to that of the Markets in Financial Instruments Directive II (MiFID II),[6] Markets in Financial Instruments Regulation (MiFIR),[7] Investment Firm Regulation (IFR)[8] and Investment Firm Directive (IFD)[9] albeit for small and non-interconnected investment firms.

The EU legislator, when adopting the rules of MiCAR, has been guided by the principles of 'same activities, same risks, same rules' and of technology neutrality.[10] This means that when businesses operate in markets for crypto-assets where the risk profile of their activities is similar to that of businesses offering services or performing activities in respect of other types of assets (eg, financial instruments, cash payments), the legislator aimed to adapt the legislative framework for CASPs to that of the existing framework for incumbent businesses, most importantly the rules of MiFID II.

Nevertheless, some important differences remain and will be discussed in this chapter. The combination of the harmonisation of market entry requirements and the ability of CASPs to offer their services across the EU without the need to comply with additional (national) licensing hurdles furthers one of MiCAR's goals, namely the promotion of the development of transformative technologies in the financial sector. This has the potential to create economic growth and new employment opportunities.[11]

[4] MiCAR, Recital (6).

[5] MiCAR, Recitals (5), (73).

[6] Directive 2014/65/EU of the European Parliament and of the Council of 15 May 2014 on markets in financial instruments and amending Directive 2002/92/EC and Directive 2011/61/EU (recast), OJ L 173, pp 349–496.

[7] Regulation (EU) No 600/2014 of the European Parliament and of the Council of 15 May 2014 on markets in financial instruments and amending Regulation (EU) No 648/2012.

[8] Regulation (EU) 2019/2033 of the European Parliament and of the Council of 27 November 2019 on the prudential requirements of investment firms and amending Regulations (EU) No 1093/2010, (EU) No 575/2013, (EU) No 600/2014 and (EU) No 806/2014, OJ L 314, pp 1–63.

[9] Directive (EU) 2019/2034 of the European Parliament and of the Council of 27 November 2019 on the prudential supervision of investment firms and amending Directives 2002/87/EC, 2009/65/EC, 2011/61/EU, 2013/36/EU, 2014/59/EU and 2014/65/EU, OJ L 314, pp 64–114.

[10] MiCAR, Recital (9).

[11] MiCAR, Recital (1).

The paragraphs below largely follow the structure of Title V MiCAR. Section 7.2 discusses access to the EU crypto market and authorisation of CASPs (Articles 59–65). Section 7.3 addresses obligations imposed on all CASPs (Articles 66–74 and 83–84). Section 7.4 considers obligations of CASPS in relation to specific crypto-asset services (Articles 75–82). Section 7.5 concludes.

7.2. Access to the EU Crypto Market

7.2.1. Authorisation and Notification of Crypto-asset Service Providers

If a legal person or other undertaking wishes to provide crypto-asset services in the EU, it must comply with the authorisation requirements for CASPs (Chapter 1 of Title V MiCAR). Before discussing MiCAR's authorisation regime, it is important to note that MiCAR introduces a transition regime or a 'grandfathering clause', according to which CASPs that provided their services in accordance with applicable (national) law before 30 December 2024 may continue to do so until 1 July 2026 or until they are granted or refused authorisation under MiCAR.[12] Many pre-MiCAR national legal frameworks for CASPs are based on anti-money laundering (AML) legislation and only partially regulate the conduct of business by CASPs.

The rules of the national frameworks served to implement the revised scope of application of the AML Directive.[13] Since 2018, this Directive included within its scope natural or legal persons acting in the exercise of their professional activities who were engaged in exchange services between virtual currencies and fiat currencies and custodian wallet providers. These rules were less comprehensive than MiCAR and did not prescribe detailed market entry procedures, but focused on the core obligations in the context of AML laws, namely, the required know-your-customer processes when on-boarding clients and transaction monitoring.

With respect to CASPs falling under the (temporary) transition regime, ESMA warned that because of it, clients of CASPs may not benefit from the full rights and protections offered by MiCAR and may be subject to limited and uneven protections.[14] That said, Member States have the option not to apply the transition regime or to reduce its duration if they consider that their national regulatory

[12] MiCAR, Article 143(3).

[13] Directive (EU) 2015/849 of the European Parliament and of the Council of 20 May 2015 on the prevention of the use of the financial system for the purposes of money laundering or terrorist financing, amending Regulation (EU) No 648/2012 of the European Parliament and of the Council, and repealing Directive 2005/60/EC of the European Parliament and of the Council and Commission Directive 2006/70/EC, OJEU L 141, pp 73 and further.

[14] ESMA, ESMA clarifies timeline for MiCAR and encourages market participants and NCAs to start preparing for the transition, ESMA74-449133380-441, 17 October 2023.

framework is less strict than MiCAR (Article 143(3)).[15] They can also establish a simplified authorisation procedure between 30 December 2024 and 1 July 2026 for entities previously authorised under national regimes.[16]

A 'crypto-asset service provider' is defined as a 'legal person or other undertaking whose occupation or business is the provision of one or more crypto-asset services to clients on a professional basis, and that is allowed to provide crypto-asset services […].'[17] Crypto-asset services are defined in Article 3(1)(16) to cover services akin to the 'investment services' under MiFID II (Annex I, A), but with additional services included in the definition, particularly related to the exchange of crypto-assets for funds or for other crypto-assets and transfer services.

MiFID II makes a distinction between 'investment services', on the one hand, and 'investment activities', on the other hand. The latter includes the activities of: (i) dealing on own account, (ii) operating a multilateral trading facility (MTF), and (iii) operating an organised trading facility (OTF). This distinction between services and activities is not maintained in MiCAR. Instead, the activity of operating a trading platform for crypto-assets is included in the definition of 'crypto-asset service' (Article 3(1)(16)(b) MiCAR). It may be helpful to reflect on whether the decision to bring together various services and activities under a single definition in MiCAR was the most effective approach.

There would be a strong case for making a clear distinction between the rules applicable to service providers with a 'more limited' risk profile and those firms operating a complex trading facility, large-scale or otherwise. What could be problematic is the lack of separate rules for proprietary traders. The distinct regime for proprietary traders in financial instruments pursuant to the MiFID II legislative framework, as compared to the regime for those solely acting as intermediaries, plays a prominent role in the delineation of issues such as the prevention of conflicts of interest. Moreover, under MiFID II there is an enhanced prudential regime of the IFR and IFD for proprietary traders (compared to the general regime) related to the increased impact on financial stability. There is a strong argument that the increased risk related to proprietary traders is also present in crypto markets, and that, accordingly, a separate and more robust regime may be warranted under MiCAR or a future extension of it.[18]

[15] See ESMA, List of grandfathering periods decided by Member States under Article 143 of MiCAR www.esma.europa.eu/sites/default/files/2024-12/List_of_MiCA_grandfathering_periods_art._143_3.pdf.

[16] MiCAR, Article 143(6).

[17] MiCAR, Article 3(1)(15).

[18] This is not to say that there are no rules at all taking into account proprietary trading in crypto-assets. Reference is made, for instance, without being exhaustive, to the rules of Article 60(3) MiCAR which provides that the activity of exchanging crypto-assets for cash and other crypto-assets, when carried out by investment firms, shall be deemed to constitute proprietary trading within the meaning of Section A, point (3) of Annex I MiFID II, which of course refers to activities of investment firms and not a CASP. Furthermore, there are the rules of Article 70 MiCAR on the safekeeping of client crypto-assets and funds, where attention is drawn to the prohibited commingling of client crypto-assets and funds with those of the CASP itself.

Unlike an issuer of Title II crypto-assets (discussed in Chapter 5), a CASP must always have close ties with the territory of the EU. For that reason, a CASP must have a registered office in a Member State where it carries out at least part of its crypto-asset services.[19] Additionally, it must have its place of effective management and at least one of the directors residing in the EU.[20] The reason for mandating a close connection to the EU (also referred to as 'substance') is given in Recital (74), which explains that such a connection is necessary 'in order to avoid undermining effective prudential supervision and to ensure the enforcement of requirements under this Regulation intended to ensure investor protection, market integrity and financial stability.' In other words, the presence of a registered office, effective management,[21] and at least one director who is resident in the EU is required to ensure effective supervision and enforcement of EU law.[22] Thus, if a legal entity is registered in one of the EU Member States, but is merely a shell or letter-box company without an appropriate level of management and control in the EU, or is fully reliant on non-EU group members, such a company cannot be authorised as a CASP.

A CASP can be an undertaking that is neither a legal person nor a natural person. However, such an undertaking is allowed to provide crypto-asset services only if its 'legal form ensures a level of protection for third parties' interests equivalent to that afforded by legal persons' and only if it is 'subject to equivalent prudential supervision appropriate to [its] legal form.'[23] MiCAR mentions a commercial partnership as a form of an undertaking that can be authorised as a CASP (Recital (74)). If crypto-asset services are provided in a fully decentralised manner – without any intermediary, such services fall outside MiCAR's scope (see Chapter 11 of the book). But if the crypto-asset services are only partly performed in a decentralised manner, they remain fully in scope of MiCAR (Recital (22)).

In practice, most crypto-asset services are provided by legal entities, such as limited liability companies. Once authorised and following the notification procedure in Article 65, a CASP is entitled to provide crypto-asset services across the EU, either through the establishment of a branch or through the freedom to provide services (on a cross border basis), see Article 59(7) MiCAR. Any physical presence in a Member State where such services are provided on a cross-border basis (ie, a host Member State) is not required. Thus, a MiCAR authorisation in a single Member State is valid through the passporting regime for the entire EU.

[19] MiCAR, Article 59(2).

[20] ibid.

[21] The 'place of effective management' is defined as 'the place where the key management and commercial decisions that are necessary for the conduct of the business are taken.' See MiCAR, Recital (74).

[22] These requirements go further compared to MiFID II, which does not mention the requirement of director's residence. See MiFID II, Article 5. However, in many Member States, such actual physical presence of the management in the Member State is a requirement of national law. For instance, this is the case for the Netherlands. Interestingly, the initial proposal for MiCAR only contained the registered office requirement.

[23] MiCAR, Article 59(3).

The same approach is followed in other financial and banking laws, including MiFID II (for investment firms), PSD2 (for payment institutions) and CRD IV[24] (for banks). The passporting regime simplifies the provision of cross-border crypto-asset services. The establishment of a branch that will offer crypto-asset services or the cross-border provision of crypto-asset services is subject to the provision of information to the competent authority of the home Member State and the receipt of the communication indicating that such information has been notified to the competent authorities of the host Member State (Article 65 MiCAR).

Certain financial entities (eg credit institutions, central securities depositories, investment firms, electronic money institutions) can also offer crypto-asset services. The authorisation granted to such financial entities extends to the provision of crypto-asset services as well (Articles 59(1)(b) and 60). For example, a bank does not need a separate authorisation to provide crypto-asset services. Instead, it must simply notify the competent authority of its home Member State (ie, the competent authority in the Member State of the authorisation) before providing those services for the first time.[25] This notification must contain specific information relevant to the provision of crypto-asset services (Article 60(7)).[26] Such information includes, but is not limited to, a programme of operations setting out the types of crypto-asset services to be provided, technical documentation of the ICT systems and security arrangements, a description of the procedure for the segregation of clients' crypto-assets and funds,[27] a description of the internal control mechanisms, policies and procedures to ensure compliance with the AML Directive, and a detailed description of the notifying entity's business continuity plan.[28]

At the same time, MiCAR does not prescribe additional prudential and general governance requirements to the financial entities concerned, as the prevailing prudential and governance requirements imposed on such entities based on their authorisation cover the additional activities. For instance, credit institutions are, since 1 January 2025, subject to the transitional regime for capital

[24] Directive 2013/36/EU of the European Parliament and of the Council of 26 June 2013 on access to the activity of credit institutions and the prudential supervision of credit institutions and investment firms, amending Directive 2002/87/EC and repealing Directives 2006/48/EC and 2006/49/EC, OJ L 176, pp 338–436.

[25] MiCAR, Article 60(1).

[26] According to Article 60(13)–(14) MiCAR, ESMA is tasked to develop (i) draft regulatory technical standards (RTS) to specify information to be notified to an NCA, and (ii) draft implementing technical standards (ITS) establishing standard forms, templates and procedures for the notification. At the time of writing (25 March 2024), such draft RTS and ITS have been published by ESMA but have not yet been adopted by the European Commission. See ESMA, Final Report, Draft technical Standards specifying certain requirements of the Markets in Crypto Assets Regulation (MiCA) – first package, ESMA18-72330276-1634, 25 March 2024 (First Package Report).

[27] First Package Report, para 12, clarifying that 'CASPs that are electronic money institutions, payment institutions or credit institutions need not provide in their application file the information required in relation to the segregation of funds.'

[28] MiCAR, Article 60(7).

requirements concerning crypto-assets found in Article 501d CRR[29] and the disclosure requirements in Article 451b CRR regarding crypto-asset exposures and related activities.

A competent authority of a Member State (NCA) receiving a notification of the intention of the financial entity (already authorised) to offer crypto-asset services must assess whether all required information has been provided. If the notification is considered incomplete, the NCA must immediately inform the notifying entity and set a deadline for providing the missing information. The notifying entity is not permitted to provide crypto-asset services as long as the notification is incomplete (Article 60(8)).

Other types of financial entities (ie, not banks) are allowed to provide crypto-asset services only if such services are deemed 'equivalent' to the services and activities for which they have been previously authorised. Consequently, since under MiFID II an investment firm is permitted to provide the ancillary service of 'safekeeping and administration of financial instruments for the account of clients', it should be able (upon complying with the notification requirements) to provide the service of 'custody and administration of crypto-assets on behalf of clients'.[30] The exchange of crypto-assets for funds and other crypto-assets is deemed equivalent to dealing on own account under MiFID II.[31]

While the notification obligation entails a certain regulatory burden and the information to be provided to a NCA is quite extensive, it is nevertheless a lighter burden than the full authorisation procedure applicable to non-financial entities, discussed below. In other words, MiCAR offers a notable advantage to incumbent market participants who have already gone through the licensing process. In this way, it strives to avoid any duplication.[32] It is presumed that such entities are generally capable of providing crypto-asset services.[33] This presumption, as well as the rationale and consequences of offering the privilege to incumbent financial entities, has been criticised in the literature.[34]

This critique may be particularly relevant for financial entities offering services or developing products in less complex segments, like ordinary share trading. On the other hand, larger firms with the capacity to hire sufficient expertise and a history

[29] Regulation (EU) No 575/2013 of the European Parliament and of the Council of 26 June 2013 on prudential requirements for credit institutions and amending Regulation (EU) No 648/2012, OJ L 176, pp 1–337.

[30] MiCAR, Article 60(3).

[31] MiFID II, Annex I, Section A.

[32] MiCAR, Recital (78).

[33] ESMA, Consultation Paper, Technical Standards specifying certain requirements of the Markets in Crypto Assets Regulation (MiCA), ESMA74-449133380-425, 12 July 2023, para 8.

[34] See M Lehmann, 'MiCAR – Gold Standard or Regulatory Poison for the Crypto Industry?' (2024) European Banking Institute Working Paper Series 160, pp 24–26, questioning whether traditional financial institutions have enough expertise and experience to deal with crypto assets and whether they will be willing to (and indeed whether they should) enter crypto markets, given the significant risks. See also First Package Report, para 5, stating that 'ESMA is of the view that CASP advice and portfolio management services are sufficiently different from traditional investment advice and portfolio management to require CASP notifier elaborate on why its personnel is sufficiently qualified to provide such services.'

of developing complex products – such as those involved in structured finance or derivatives – may have less difficulty moving into the crypto-asset markets, including the application of the underlying technology. In some respects, crypto-asset markets do not differ drastically from traditional financial markets, as the latter also rely on complex, specialised technological applications. This is particularly evident in payment markets, where the underlying technological infrastructure is highly complex. This complexity facilitates global clearing and settlement and ensures the harmonisation of technological standards to achieve interoperability. The payments industry's agility in adopting advanced technologies has undoubtedly driven significant strides in innovation and functionality within a short time frame. A notable example is the introduction of instant payment functionalities, underpinned by an exceptionally complex technological environment.[35]

7.2.2. Provision of Crypto-asset Services by Third-country CASPs

7.2.2.1. 'Reverse Solicitation' Exemption

A large number of crypto firms are based outside the EU territory, with some in offshore jurisdictions. For example, FTX Trading Ltd, which conducted business through the FTX.com crypto exchange platform, was incorporated in Antigua and Barbuda and had its headquarters in the Bahamas. KuCoin, one of the world's largest crypto exchanges, is based in Seychelles. This is in line with the general trend towards 'deterritorialisation' of financial services.[36]

MiCAR strictly regulates the provision of crypto-asset services within the EU by third-country firms. In principle, third-country firms are prohibited from offering crypto-asset services in the EU unless they comply with its laws and regulations, including the requirement to obtain authorisation. The only exception is where crypto-asset services are provided at the exclusive initiative of the client. According to Article 61, where 'a client established or situated in the [EU] initiates at its own exclusive initiative the provision of a crypto-asset service or activity by a third-country firm, the requirement for authorisation […] shall not apply […].' This is known as the 'reverse solicitation exemption', under which a third-country service provider does not have to comply with EU authorisation requirements when providing services to EU clients, as long as such services are requested on the exclusive initiative of the client. The same exclusion from applicability can be

[35] See for more information, European Payments Council, SEPA Instant Credit Transfer (SCT Inst) www.europeanpaymentscouncil.eu/what-we-do/sepa-instant-credit-transfer.

[36] A Enria, Chair of the Supervisory Board of the ECB, 'Regulating crypto finance: taking stock and looking ahead' (Speech at the Conference on MiCAR, jointly organised by Ca' Foscari University of Venice and Banca d'Italia, Venice, 14 November 2023) www.bankingsupervision.europa.eu/press/speeches/date/2023/html/ssm.sp231114~fd1b2cc234.en.html.

found in MiFID II.[37] The rationale for this exemption is that clients shall not be excluded from using third-country firms if they choose to do so without having been solicited by such service firms.

'Reverse solicitation' means that the foreign service provider must not solicit clients or potential clients in the EU, regardless of the means of communication used for solicitation, promotion or advertising of its services. Determining whether a third-country firm has engaged in soliciting EU clients requires a comprehensive assessment of all relevant factors. While MiCAR does not provide a list of such factors, it clarifies that this assessment should be carried out 'notwithstanding any contractual clause or disclaimer purporting to state otherwise, including any clause or disclaimer that the provision of services by a third-country firm is deemed to be a service provided on the client's own exclusive initiative.'[38]

In December 2024, ESMA published the Guidelines on reverse solicitation under MiCAR ('RS Guidelines'), which follow largely, 'but not in all regards', the established practice under the MiFID II framework.[39]

- RS Guideline 1 confirms that the solicitation of clients should be construed broadly and in a technologically neutral way. Solicitation includes the promotion, advertisement or offer of crypto-asset services or activities to clients or prospective clients in the EU by any means. Paragraph 12 of the RS Guidelines contains a non-exhaustive list of methods of solicitation, which include advertisements, internet commercials, messaging platforms and other 'traditional' methods to promote the crypto-asset services.
- RS Guideline 2 addresses the persons soliciting, emphasising that the solicitation may be carried out by the third-country firm or any person acting on its behalf or having close links with the third country firm. This, for instance, includes solicitation by influencers and other celebrities.[40] The determination whether a third-country firm did engage in the solicitation of clients in the EU needs to be done on a case-by-case basis and should involve the assessment of all relevant facts and circumstances.
- RS Guideline 3 confirms that the exclusive initiative of the client is a matter of interpretation of facts, and that contractual arrangements or disclaimers cannot supersede contrary facts. A third country CASP can only rely on the exception for the crypto-asset services related to the products or crypto-assets for which the client took the initiative, and should not be allowed to offer the client further crypto-asset services subsequently, even if such services are of the same type as the one originally requested, unless they are offered in the

[37] MiFID II, Recital (111) and Article 42.

[38] MiCAR, Article 61(1).

[39] ESMA, Final Report On the guidelines on reverse solicitation under the Markets in Crypto Assets Regulation (MiCA), ESMA35-1872330276-1899, 17 December 2024.

[40] See DA Zetzsche, RP Buckley, DW Arner and MC van Ek, 'Remaining regulatory challenges in digital finance and cryptoassets after MiCA', Study requested by the ECON Committee, May 2023, pp 107–108.

context of the original transaction. ESMA has clarified that, for example, if the client contacts the third-country firm to purchase crypto-asset X, the firm is permitted to market similar crypto-assets to the client at that time. However, the third-country firm is not authorised to market additional transactions involving crypto-asset X or similar crypto-assets to the client a month later. This time-related clarification can have far-reaching implications in practice.

- In RS Guideline 4, further clarifications are provided as to when a crypto-asset or a crypto-asset service is of the same type as another one. In this respect ESMA provides that the categorisation of crypto-assets and crypto-asset services or activities a third-country firm uses should be granular enough to ensure that the reverse solicitation exemption cannot be used to circumvent the authorisation requirements under Article 59 (see para 31 of the RS Guidelines), discussed in section 7.2.3 below. ESMA offers in para 32 a non-exhaustive list of pairs of crypto-assets which should not be considered as belonging to the same type of crypto-assets for the purpose of the reverse solicitation exception.

In sum, while the reverse solicitation exception exists under MiCAR, it seems to offer an extremely narrow window for third-country firms to provide crypto-asset services to clients in the EU. We expect EU and NCAs to be particularly strict when evaluating whether the exception applies in each case involving a foreign firm.

7.2.2.2. Equivalence and National Third Country Regimes

MiCAR introduces a harmonised and relatively rigid regime for accessing EU crypto markets. Setting aside the reverse solicitation exception, a third-country firm wishing to provide crypto-asset services to EU clients must be registered and authorised as a crypto-asset service provider in the EU. This one-way street approach somewhat mirrors the approach adopted for third-country investment firms seeking to provide investment services and activities in the EU.[41] This is certainly the case since Brexit where, particularly with regard to UK firms offering investment services or performing investment activities within the EU, the EU has tightened the application of rules in this respect. The major difference between the offering of crypto-asset services by third-country firms, on the one hand, and investment services or investment activities by investment firms, on the other hand, lies in the differentiation of protection levels based on the client's capacity. While MiCAR does not differentiate the level of protection based on the client's status (the approach criticised by some commentators), MiFID II adopts a more nuanced approach, offering reduced protection if the client qualifies as a professional client or an eligible counterparty.

[41] See M Louisse and M van Rijn, 'The Third Country Regime for Investment Firms' (2024) 25 *EBOR* 183; D Busch and M Louisse, 'MiFID II/MiFIR's regime for third-country firms' in D Busch and G Ferrarini (eds), *Regulation of the EU Financial Markets: MiFID II and MiFIR*, 1st edn (Oxford University Press, 2017).

Under the legal regime applicable to investment firms (ie, MiFID II and MiFIR), a third-country investment firm can provide investment services or perform investment activities for professional clients throughout the EU if the European Commission (EC) has adopted a decision in relation to that third country, stating that its legal and supervisory arrangements ensure that firms authorised there comply with legally binding prudential and business conduct requirements which have an equivalent effect to the requirements set out in EU law.[42] This decision is referred to as the 'equivalence decision'. If such a decision is made, the third-country investment firm is allowed to offer services to professional clients without establishing a subsidiary or branch in the EU. Despite the fact that the equivalence regime has been open since January 2018, as of the writing date, the EC has not granted any equivalence decisions for third-country investment firms.

In the absence of an equivalence decision, the access of third-country investment firms to the markets of EU Member States can be based on national third-country regimes. The laws of EU Member States can allow third-country firms to provide investment services or perform investment activities for eligible counterparties and professional clients in their territories in accordance with national regimes.[43] EU law also provides an optional regime under which EU Member States can grant a third-country firm access to retail clients, provided that such a firm establishes a branch in the Member State concerned and obtains an authorisation for that branch.[44] The branch of a third-country firm remains under the exclusive supervisory responsibility of the competent authorities of this Member State.[45]

MiCAR does not establish an equivalence regime. Nor does it allow Member States to grant access to third-country firms under national legal regimes in the manner described above and thereby bypass the strict market entry approach established by MiCAR. This strict approach takes into account the potential risks posed by crypto-asset services, ensures a level playing field for all CASPs, and aims to achieve a coherent application of MiCAR rules and equal protection for investors and consumers across all Member States.

7.2.3. Application for Authorisation as a CASP

7.2.3.1. Key Application Requirements

An application for authorisation must be submitted to the NCA of a home Member State – that is, a Member State where the CASP has its registered office.[46]

[42] MiFIR, Articles 46–47.
[43] MiFIR, Article 46(4).
[44] MiFID II, Article 39.
[45] ESMA, Draft technical standards on the provision of investment services and activities in the Union by third-country firms under MiFID II and MiFIR, Final Report, ESMA35-43-2424, 28 September 2020, p 8.
[46] MiCAR, Article 3(1)(33).

Some national competent authorities have already set up a dedicated section on their websites devoted to processing licence applications.[47] In some jurisdictions, companies were allowed to apply for authorisation before the relevant MiCAR rules became fully applicable (ie, before 30 December 2024). That said, such authorisation could only take effect as of 30 December 2024.

The paragraphs below describe a number of key requirements imposed by MiCAR on applicants seeking a CASP licence. These requirements are extensive and aim to protect clients from various risks, including fraud, mismanagement, misinformation and cyberattacks. Some of these risks have led to the crypto failures mentioned in section 7.1. At the same time, the requirements aim to foster trust in market players (eg, crypto exchanges, crypto brokers, crypto custodians), which in turn could facilitate investments in crypto-assets.[48] The MiCAR authorisation-related provisions will be clarified and supplemented by regulatory technical standards (RTS) and implementing technical standards (ITS) developed by ESMA and the EBA, as well as further guidelines issued by these and national authorities.[49]

Article 62(2)(a) to (s) MiCAR lists the requirements for the application for authorisation as a CASP. Briefly, it may be noted that the requirements set out in Article 62(1)(a) to (m) and (p) to (s) are similar to the authorisation requirements for MiFID II investment firms or payment institutions subject to PSD2. Here, the European legislator has followed a template applicable to financial firms with an establishment in the EU. What is different about MiCAR compared to MiFID II is that the relevant authorisation rules are contained in an EU regulation, rather than in an EU directive. We can see a general trend from directives to regulations in recent EU legislative instruments relating to other types of players subject to supervision, including credit rating agencies, trade repositories pursuant to EMIR and securitisation repositories pursuant to the Securitisation Regulation.

On balance, the authorisation requirements for CASPs are generally similar to those applicable to investment firms and other types of financial institutions supervised in the European Union. More detailed requirements are discussed below.

[47] See eg Dutch Authority for the Financial Markets (*Autoriteit Financiële Markten*, AFM), Requirements and licences www.afm.nl/en/sector/cryptopartijen/vereisten-en-vergunningen, stating that the application for a CASP permit or notification can be submitted from 22 April 2024 and, if approved, can be used from 30 December 2024.

[48] ESMA, Consultation Paper, Technical Standards specifying certain requirements of the Markets in Crypto Assets Regulation (MiCA), ESMA74-449133380-425, 12 July 2023, paras 23–24.

[49] The Final Report Draft Technical Standards specifying certain requirements of the Markets in Crypto Assets Regulation (MiCA) – first package (ESMA18-72330276-1634) of 25 March 2024 – contains the final draft RTS prepared in accordance with ESMA's mandate based on Article 62(5) MiCAR (the 'Authorisation RTS') and the final draft ITS prepared in accordance with ESMA's mandate based on Article 62(6) MiCAR (the 'Authorisation ITS'). To date (at closure of this manuscript on 25 December 2024), the relevant Authorisation RTS and Authorisation ITS have not been published in the Official Journal. The market should therefore base its authorisation requests on the final drafts of these RTS and ITS as published by ESMA on 25 March 2024.

The application for authorisation must contain, among other elements, the name, the website operated by the CASP, a contact email address, telephone number, physical address and the type of crypto-asset to which crypto-asset services relate. The recent collapses of crypto firms have revealed complex and opaque group structures and the lack of clear divisions between group entities, which hampered effective governance and risk management arrangements.[50]

To address the opacity of corporate structures, intra-group dependencies, linkages and other concerns, MiCAR states that the application must include a programme of operations, further elaborated in relevant Level 2 acts (ie, the group structure and strategy, a list of jurisdictions, both in and outside the EU, in which the applicant plans to provide crypto-asset services, types of prospective clients, outsourcing arrangements (including intra-group outsourcing),[51] planned marketing and promotional activities, etc.[52]), the types of crypto-asset services that the applicant intends to provide and a description of governance arrangements (ie, organisational structure, personal details of the heads of internal functions, record-keeping arrangements, conflicts of interest policy, etc[53]).

The application must also contain information showing that the CASP's management is of sufficiently good repute and possesses the appropriate knowledge, skills and experience to manage the CASP.[54] The requirement of 'sufficiently good repute' equally applies to shareholders with qualifying holdings in the applicant CASP.[55] Neither members of the board nor shareholders should have been convicted of any offence in the field of money laundering or terrorist financing or of any other offence that would affect their good repute.[56] The screening of the management body and shareholders imposes an ex ante scrutiny of market access to ensure the integrity, safety and soundness of crypto markets.

Other documents include, inter alia, a description of the applicant's internal control mechanisms, policies and procedures to identify, assess and manage risks,

[50] See I Kokorin, 'Who's your debtor? Group insolvency and the curious case of Celsius' (2023) 40 *Banking & Finance Law Review* 143.

[51] For the requirements concerning outsourcing arrangement, see Article 73 MiCAR.

[52] Draft Authorisation RTS pursuant to Article 62(5) MiCAR, Article 2.

[53] Draft Authorisation RTS pursuant to Article 62(5) MiCAR, Article 4.

[54] MiCAR, Article 62(2). MiCAR, Article 63(11), mandating ESMA and EBA to issue guidelines on the assessment of suitability of the members of the management body and of the shareholders of CASPs. Joint Guidelines on the suitability assessment of the management body of CASPs and shareholders and members with qualifying holdings in CASPs were published on 27 June 2024.

[55] MiCAR, Article 3(1)(36), defining 'qualifying holding' as 'any direct or indirect holding in [...] a crypto-asset service provider which represents at least 10% of the capital or of the voting rights, [...] or which makes it possible to exercise a significant influence over the management of the [...] management of the crypto-asset service provider in which that holding subsists.' This definition corresponds to the definition of qualifying holding found in Article 4(1)(31) MiFID II and Article 4(1)(36) CRR. See section 7.3.9 for the specific procedure on acquiring and holding of qualifying interests.

[56] MiCAR, Recital (81). This recital also mentions that competent authorities should have the power to address the risks in cases where the influence exercised by shareholders is likely to be prejudicial to the sound and prudent management of the CASP 'taking into account, amongst others, their previous activities, the risk of them engaging in illicit activities, or the influence or control by a government of a third country.'

including money laundering (ML) and terrorist financing (TF) risks. The goal is to ensure compliance with the provisions of national law transposing the AML Directive,[57] and Regulation (EU) 2023/1113 on information accompanying transfers of funds and certain crypto-assets (the revised Transfer of Funds Regulation or TFR).[58]

Further clarifications concerning detection and prevention of ML and TF come from the EBA[59] and the RTS.[60] These clarifications seek to provide common EU standards on the development and implementation of policies, procedures and controls for the implementation of restrictive measures. The EBA notes that CASPs should use their ML/TF exposure assessment to decide which screening system they will use. Such a system needs to be adapted to the size and complexity of the CASP's business.[61]

In line with this, the application for authorisation must contain the applicant's AML and CTF procedures and policies. It must indicate the applicant's assessment of the inherent and residual risks of ML and TF associated with its business in view of its customer base and services provided. It must also specify measures to prevent ML/TF by clarifying the risk assessment process, customer due diligence requirements, and the policies and procedures to detect and report suspicious transactions or activities.

Additionally, a business continuity plan and the technical documentation of the ICT systems and security arrangements must be attached.[62] These requirements aim to contribute to the maintenance of orderly markets by limiting, as far as possible, undue losses for clients of CASPs in the event of a disruptive incident, such as a hack or exploit. The measures that CASPs are required to take should be adequate to address any new operational or security risks posed by CASP-specific business models, including with respect to the DLT infrastructure relied upon by the CASP. It should be noted that the MiCAR provisions in this respect are

[57] From 10 July 2027 these rules will be addressed in Regulation (EU) 2024/1624 of the European Parliament and of the Council of 31 May 2024 on the prevention of the use of the financial system for the purposes of money laundering or terrorist financing, OJ L, 2024/1624, of 19 June 2024.

[58] Regulation (EU) 2023/1113 of the European Parliament and of the Council of 31 May 2023 on information accompanying transfers of funds and certain crypto-assets. This Regulation applies from 30 December 2024.

[59] EBA, Final Report, Two sets of Guidelines on internal policies, procedures and controls to ensure the implementation of Union and national restrictive measures, EBA/GL/2024/14, 14 November 2024.

[60] Draft Authorisation RTS pursuant to Article 62(5) MiCAR, Article 6.

[61] EBA, Final Report, Two sets of Guidelines on internal policies, procedures and controls to ensure the implementation of Union and national restrictive measures, EBA/GL/2024/14, 14 November 2024, para 23, noting that '[w]here appropriate based on the volume and number of transfers of crypto-assets, CASPs should consider incorporating blockchain analysis for transaction monitoring purposes into the existing framework.'

[62] MiCAR, Article 62(2)(j). Also, ESMA, Consultation Paper, Technical Standards specifying certain requirements of Markets in Crypto Assets Regulation (MiCA) – second consultation paper, ESMA75-453128700-438 (5 October 2023) (Second Consultation Paper), containing draft RTS on measures that crypto-asset service providers must take to ensure continuity and regularity in the performance of services.

supplemented by the requirements of the Digital Operational Resilience Act (DORA)[63] which fully applies to CASPs from 17 January 2025.[64]

Additional information must be provided by applicants that intend to offer specific services, such as custody and administration of crypto-assets on behalf of clients, operation of a crypto trading platform, crypto advice, etc. For example, an applicant that intends to provide custody and administration of crypto-assets on behalf of clients must attach a description of its custody and administration policy, including how it safeguards client money and crypto-assets.[65] An applicant who plans to operate a crypto-asset trading platform must include a description of the operating rules of the trading platform and of the procedure and system to detect market abuse.[66]

7.2.3.2. The Grant and Withdrawal of CASP Authorisation

The assessment of applications for authorisation as a CASP is governed by Article 63 MiCAR. Upon receipt of a CASP application, an NCA must promptly, and in any event within five working days, acknowledge receipt in writing. Within 25 working days of receipt of the application, the NCA must assess whether the application is complete. If it is not, the NCA shall set a deadline by which any missing information must be provided. Once the application is complete, the NCA must notify the applicant promptly. The NCA has 40 working days from the date of receipt of the complete application to assess whether the applicant complies with Title V and to adopt a fully reasoned decision granting or refusing authorisation as a CASP.

The competent authority must notify the applicant of its decision within five working days of the decision date. Therefore, in the case of a complete application, the entire application process should take approximately five months. However, this process could be longer if, during the 40-day period, the NCA requests additional information necessary to complete the assessment. In such a case, the assessment period is suspended for a maximum of 20 working days.[67] This timeline aligns with that applicable to the authorisation of investment firms under MiFID II.[68]

The CASP authorisation must be refused where there are objective and demonstrable grounds that the management body of the applicant poses a threat to its effective, sound and prudent management and business continuity or exposes the applicant to a serious risk of ML/TF, or where the management does not meet

[63] Regulation (EU) 2022/2554 of the European Parliament and of The Council of 14 December 2022 on digital operational resilience for the financial sector and amending Regulations (EC) No 1060/2009, (EU) No 648/2012, (EU) No 600/2014, (EU) No 909/2014 and (EU) 2016/1011, OJ L 333, pp 1–79.

[64] See the scope of application provision of Article 2(1)(f) DORA.

[65] MiCAR, Article 62(2)(m).

[66] MiCAR, Article 62(2)(n).

[67] MiCAR, Article 63(12).

[68] MiFID II, Article 7(3), stating that the applicant shall be informed of the application outcome within six months of the submission of a complete application.

the requirements related to good repute, appropriate knowledge and skills.[69] The authorisation must also be refused if the applicant 'fails to meet or is likely to fail to meet any of the requirements' of Title V.[70] The latter 'catch-all' provision grants the NCA a broad mandate to refuse authorisation if it is not satisfied with the submitted information, prudential or organisational requirements contained in MiCAR.

Article 64 MiCAR deals with the withdrawal of authorisation. The CASP authorisation must be withdrawn, for example, if the authorisation has not been used within 12 months of the authorisation date, if crypto-asset services have not been provided for nine consecutive months, if the application contained false statements, if the CASP no longer meets the conditions for authorisation and has not taken remedial action, or if it has seriously infringed MiCAR, including its rules on the protection of clients or market integrity.[71]

The NCA may limit the withdrawal of authorisation to a particular crypto-asset service.[72] To ensure the orderly and timely transfer of clients' crypto-assets and funds to another CASP in the event of an authorisation withdrawal, MiCAR requires that CASPs establish and implement adequate procedures for that purpose.[73]

7.3. Obligations of All Crypto-asset Service Providers

7.3.1. Obligation to Act Honestly, Fairly and Professionally in the Clients' Best Interests

Title V of MiCAR contains two chapters dealing with the obligations of CASPs. Chapter 2 (Articles 66–74) covers general obligations applicable to all CASPs. Chapter 3 (Articles 75–82) sets out obligations in respect of specific crypto-asset services. Among the general obligations is the foundational, fiduciary-like duty to act honestly, fairly and professionally in the best interests of clients and prospective clients (Article 66). A similar obligation applies to investment firms under MiFID II[74] and fund managers under AIFMD.[75] This obligation makes clients' interests paramount. It shapes the professional conduct of CASPs and serves as the backbone of specific conduct of business rules, including rules on marketing

[69] MiCAR, Articles 63(10)(a)–(b) and 68(1).

[70] MiCAR, Article 63(10)(d). A similar provision can be found in MiFID II, Article 7(1), according to which the NCA shall not grant authorisation as an investment firm 'unless and until such time as it is fully satisfied that the applicant complies with all requirements under the provisions adopted pursuant to' MiFID II.

[71] MiCAR, Article 64(1).

[72] MiCAR, Article 64(4).

[73] MiCAR, Article 64(8).

[74] MiFID II, Article 24. L Enriques and M Gargantini, 'The Expanding Boundaries of MiFID's Duty to Act in the Client's Best Interest: The Italian Case' (2017) 3 *The Italian Law Journal* 485.

[75] AIFMD, Article 12(1).

communications (Article 66(2)), safekeeping clients' assets and not using them for CASPs' own account (Article 70), conflicts of interest (Article 72), best execution of orders (Article 78), and suitability assessment (Article 81).

Article 66 further specifies that CASPs must:

- Provide clients with information that is fair, clear and not misleading, including in marketing communications, which shall be identified as such. Specifically, CASPs shall not mislead clients in terms of the real or perceived advantages of any crypto-assets.[76] Clearer and fairer promotions should enable clients to be better informed to make appropriate decisions aligned with their needs and risk profile (see also chapter twelve for UK's approach to crypto promotions).[77]
- Warn clients of the risks associated with transactions in crypto-assets. Such risks include, for instance, price volatility of crypto-assets, product complexity, disruption in the underlying technology, fraud and malicious activities on crypto markets.[78]
- When operating a trading platform for crypto-assets, exchanging crypto-assets for funds or other crypto-assets, providing advice on crypto-assets or managing a portfolio of crypto-assets, provide clients with hyperlinks to any crypto-asset white papers for the crypto-assets in relation to which they are providing those services.[79]
- Make their policies on pricing, costs and fees publicly available in a prominent place on their website.[80]
- Make publicly available, in a prominent place on their website, information related to the principal adverse impacts on the climate and other environment-related adverse impacts of the consensus mechanism used to issue each crypto-asset in relation to which they provide services.[81] This requirement was not included in the original proposal for MiCAR and may create challenges for CASPs.[82]

[76] MiCAR, Article 66(2).

[77] The UK has introduced a special regime applicable to crypto-asset financial promotions. See FCA, Financial promotion rules for cryptoassets, Policy Statement PS23/6, June 2023; FCA, Finalised non-handbook guidance on Cryptoasset Financial Promotions, FG23/3, November 2023.

[78] MiCAR, Article 66(3). See also ESMA, EBA and EIOPA, 'EU financial regulators warn consumers on the risks of crypto-assets' (17 March 2022) www.esma.europa.eu/press-news/esma-news/eu-financial-regulators-warn-consumers-risks-crypto-assets.

[79] MiCAR, Article 66(3).

[80] MiCAR, Article 66(4).

[81] MiCAR, Article 66(5).

[82] In the Second Consultation Paper, ESMA recognises the challenges associated with collecting granular data on sustainability matters in light of the global and decentralised nature of activities related to crypto-assets. It proposes to focus on the validation of transactions and assumes that such validation is conflated with the issuance of a crypto-asset, suggests that the assessment should relate to the cumulative sustainability impacts of the set of DLT network nodes active in reaching an agreement that a transaction is validated (eg, energy consumption of each node, their location and devices used), and indicates that CASPs should be allowed to benefit from the best efforts clause in case of limited data availability.

7.3.2. Prudential Requirements

To promote the resilience of CASPs and ensure consumer protection, MiCAR establishes prudential requirements (Article 67). Under MiCAR, a CASP must have in place prudential safeguards equal to an amount of at least the higher of the following two amounts: (i) the amount of permanent minimum capital requirements, which ranges from EUR 50,000 to EUR 150,000 depending on the type of the crypto-asset services provided,[83] or (ii) 25 per cent of the fixed overheads of the preceding year.[84] Fixed overheads are costs that remain constant every month and do not change with changes in business activity levels. They may include, for example, office rental charges and fixed staff salaries. Notably, in its advice, the Securities and Markets Stakeholder Group (SMSG) argued that prudential requirements 'do not appear to be fully related to the potential riskiness of CASPs as they do not take into account, eg, the value of the assets in custody or the value of the crypto-assets placed or traded.'[85]

The prudential safeguards prescribed by MiCAR must take one of two forms or a combination thereof. The first form is that a CASP must hold own funds, consisting of Common Equity Tier 1 (CET1) items and instruments under the CRR (paid-in capital instruments such as shares, retained earnings, etc).[86] CET1 capital is considered to be the highest quality of regulatory capital, capable of immediately absorbing losses when they occur. The CASP must submit the appropriate documentation to evidence that the relevant capital requirements are being met. In practice, this requires the submission of a pro forma balance sheet of the company in which the amount of capitalisation and the capital items are set out, so as to enable the NCA to verify that the prudential requirements are met.

Alternatively, the second form is that the CASP must obtain an insurance policy covering the territories of the EU where crypto-asset services are provided, or a comparable guarantee.[87] Detailed requirements for such an insurance policy are listed in Article 67(5) and include, among others, that it must have an initial term of not less than one year and that it must be provided by a third-party entity that is an insurance undertaking. The insurance must protect against a number of risks, including loss of documents, acts or omissions in breach of legal and regulatory obligations, failure to establish and implement procedures to prevent conflicts of

[83] See MiCAR, Annex IV.

[84] MiCAR, Article 67(1). According to Article 67(2), CASPs that have not been in business for a year shall use, for the purpose of calculating the fixed overheads, the projected fixed overheads included in their projections for the first 12 months of service provision, as submitted with the application for authorisation. MiCAR's approach to calculating prudential safeguards for CASPs largely follows the one adopted for Class 3 investment firms, being the smaller and non-interconnected investment firms that are not subject to the stricter so-called K-Factor requirements for Risk-to-Client, Risk-to-Market and Risk-to-Form. See for further details the IFR and IFD.

[85] First Package Report, Annex II, p 49.

[86] CRR, Articles 26–30.

[87] MiCAR, Article 67(4).

interest, losses arising from business disruptions and system failures, and liability towards clients who deposited their crypto-assets with a CASP in the context of crypto custody (Article 75(8)).[88] A copy of the subscribed insurance policy and insurance agreement incorporating these elements is part of the application for authorisation.

Given the significant costs associated with obtaining insurance coverage,[89] it is likely that many CASPs will choose to fulfil the prudential requirements through firm capitalisation, in line with the levels and qualitative requirements discussed above.

7.3.3. Governance Arrangements

Some recent collapses of crypto firms can be attributed to failures in governance and internal control systems. In a declaration accompanying the FTX Chapter 11 petition, the newly appointed CEO, John J Ray III, described the governance regime of the failed crypto exchange as follows: 'Never in my career have I seen such a complete failure of corporate controls and such a complete absence of trustworthy financial information as occurred here. From compromised systems integrity and faulty regulatory oversight abroad, to the concentration of control in the hands of a very small group of inexperienced, unsophisticated and potentially compromised individuals, this situation is unprecedented.'[90] Incompetence, conflicts of interest,[91] agency risks, inadequate disclosure of information to clients and regulators, lack of appropriate risk management and outright mismanagement, often led to disastrous outcomes. This is why good governance arrangements are key to protecting clients, facilitating market integrity, and ultimately building a robust crypto ecosystem. In broad terms, governance requirements for CASPs contained in MiCAR can be divided into three categories.

The first category concerns the requirements applicable to members of the management body,[92] shareholders and members with qualified holdings, as well

[88] MiCAR, Article 67(6).

[89] Payment institutions are also permitted to obtain insurance coverage to address risks related to the safeguarding of payment services users' monies, see Article 10(1)(b) PSD2 (*Safeguarding requirements*). However, in most cases payment institutions choose to meet the safeguarding requirements through the application of Article 10(1)(a) PSD2, which is particularly related to the almost uninsurable risk and the draconic costs associated with insurance coverage.

[90] Declaration of John J Ray III in Support of Chapter 11 Petitions and First Day Pleadings, *In re FTX Trading LTD et al*, Case No 22-11068 (JTD) (17 November 2022), para 5.

[91] See SEC Complaint against Binance Holdings Limited et al., Civil Action No. 1:23-cv-01599, 13 (5 June 2023) www.sec.gov/files/litigation/complaints/2023/comp-pr2023-101.pdf.

[92] 'Management body' is defined in Article 3(1)(27) as 'the body or bodies of an issuer, offeror or person seeking admission to trading, or of a crypto-asset service provider, which are appointed in accordance with national law, which are empowered to set the entity's strategy, objectives and overall direction, and which oversee and monitor management decision-making in the entity and include the persons who effectively direct the business of the entity.'

as personnel employed by CASPs.[93] In MiCAR, these requirements are described in relatively abstract terms. They do not prescribe a specific governance structure comparable to that required for other financial sector firms. The provisions of MiCAR are drafted in this respect in a corporate law neutral way, allowing the implementation of governance in accordance with the applicable corporate law (for instance, there is neutrality as to the establishment of a one-tier board or two-tier board structure).

According to Article 68, the management – which includes both executive and (non-executive) supervisory board members – must be of sufficiently good repute and must possess the appropriate skills, knowledge and experience to perform their duties. Personnel employed by the CASP must have sufficient knowledge, skills and expertise. The European Supervisory Authorities (ESAs) observe that robust governance arrangements of CASPs contribute to trust in the financial system, facilitate confidence in crypto-asset services and support the 'development of an ecosystem of crypto assets.'[94] Among other points, the ESAs note that appropriate knowledge, skill and experience cannot be determined solely by having worked for a period of time in a certain position or by having a specific educational degree but should be assessed on a case-by-case basis, guided by the overarching principle of proportionality.[95]

The relevant 'good repute' criteria for the management concern, among others, the absence of a criminal record and the absence of any sanctions under commercial, insolvency, administrative, tax and financial services law or in relation to ML/TF. They also include the absence of sanctions, embargoes and similar measures; prior defaults, negative credit history and personal bankruptcy, etc.[96] As for 'appropriate knowledge, skills and experience', the ESAs mention the level and profile of the education, particularly in finance, economics, law, accounting, auditing and IT, and relevant practical experience, including relating to financial instruments, crypto-assets, risk management, digital operational resilience for the financial sector, AML/CTF, data protection, and strategic planning.[97] Finally, the members of the management body must be able to commit sufficient time to perform their functions and responsibilities. This includes being able to commit sufficient time in light of other obligations they might have, including with respect to other group entities to which the CASP is affiliated.

[93] MiCAR, Article 68(1)–(3) and (5), and Recital (81).

[94] Final report on Joint EBA and ESMA Guidelines on the suitability assessment of shareholders and members, whether direct or indirect, with qualifying holdings in issuers of asset-referenced tokens and in crypto-asset service providers, EBA/GL/2024/09 ESMA75-453128700-10 of 27 June 2024.

[95] Joint EBA and ESMA Guidelines on the assessment of the suitability of the members of the management body of issuers of asset-referenced tokens and of crypto-asset service providers, EBA/GL/2024/09, ESMA75-453128700-10 of 4 December 2024.

[96] ibid C.2. Notions of suitability under Articles 34(2) and 68(1) of MiCA, sub-para C.2.1. Sufficient good repute.

[97] ibid C.2. Notions of suitability under Articles 34(2) and 68(1) of MiCA, sub-para C.2.2.Individual appropriate knowledge, skills and experience.

The second category of requirements covers general organisational requirements. For example, Article 68(4) stipulates that CASPs are required to adopt policies and procedures that are 'sufficiently effective to ensure compliance' with MiCAR. Relatedly, CASPs must 'arrange for records to be kept of all crypto-asset services, activities, orders, and transactions undertaken by them.'[98] This record-keeping provision mirrors an equivalent provision of Article 16(6) of MiFID II. This is why certain clarifications, formats, content and reporting instructions applicable in the context of securities regulation are useful for CASPs.

That said, the requirements under MiCAR and the MiFID/MiFIR regime are not fully identical. For example, under MiCAR, there is no requirement to regularly report transactions to competent authorities equivalent to Article 26 MiFIR. In other words, MiCAR does not impose a general transaction reporting obligation but provides for the general record-keeping obligation. On top of the general record keeping obligation, MiCAR requires CASPs operating a trading platform to keep data relating to all orders in crypto-assets that are advertised through their systems and to ensure that such data contains the characteristics of an order, including those that link the order with the executed transactions that stem from that order (Article 76(15)). The same article allows CASPs to give NCAs direct access to their records. The records kept by CASPs must be sufficient for effective supervision by NCAs, must be kept for at least 5 years and should be provided to clients upon request.

ESMA published the Final Report for the RTS[99] on record-keeping by CASPs. To minimise the implementation burden, promote standardisation and ensure consistency and comparability of data, ESMA proposed defining the format of the records by referring, where possible, to well-established international standards, including standards on financial messaging. For this reason, the RTS[100] specify both the content of the transaction details to be maintained by CASPs and the standards and formats to be used when providing such data to NCAs.

In principle, recorded data should allow NCAs to reconstitute each key stage of the processing of each service, activity, order or transaction involving a CASP.[101] Among the relevant data elements, the RTS indicate information on the identity of counterparties (eg, Legal Entity Identifier, national personal identity identifiers),[102] and information that should allow NCAs to both identify the individual crypto-asset being traded and classify it according to internationally established principles,

[98] MiCAR, Article 68(9).

[99] Final Report Draft Technical Standards specifying certain requirements of the Markets in Crypto Assets Regulation (MiCA) – second package, ESMA75-453128700-1229, 3 July 2024.

[100] Commission Delegated Regulation (EU) 2025/1140 of 27 February 2025 supplementing Regulation (EU) 2023/1114 of the European Parliament and of the Council with regard to regulatory technical standards specifying records to be kept of all crypto-asset services, activities, orders and transactions undertaken.

[101] RTS on record-keeping by crypto-asset service providers, Article 2.

[102] ibid Articles 9 and 14.

as long as this digital asset identifier meets the international ISO 24165 standard,[103] or an equivalent unique identifier defined at the EU level.[104]

The third category of operational requirements relates to CASPs' duty to ensure continuity and regularity in the performance of their crypto-asset services. To that end, CASPs are required to employ appropriate resources and procedures, including resilient and secure ICT systems as prescribed by DORA.[105] CASPs must have a business continuity policy, including ICT business continuity plans and ICT response and recovery plans. The latter aim to ensure – in case of interruption to their ICT systems and procedures – the preservation of essential data and functions, and the maintenance or timely recovery of crypto-asset services.

Based on Article 68(10)(a), the relevant RTS have been adopted.[106] These RTS largely follow the standardised rulebook seen in other sectoral laws (eg, MiFID II) and related standards.[107] Furthermore, they supplement the provisions of DORA and the RTS adopted to further specify the requirements for business continuity.[108] At the same time, they seek to maintain a balance between building resilient CASPs and protecting their clients, on the one hand, and avoiding disproportionate and burdensome requirements that can affect market access by new entrants like start-ups and SMEs, on the other hand. For this purpose, it is proposed that business continuity requirements for CASPs are to be determined by means of robust 'self-assessment', and that CASPs should not be obliged to create a dedicated business continuity function within their organisation. In the context of self-assessment, the following criteria must be taken into account:

- the nature of the CASP and its role in the financial system;
- the business scale of the CASP, including the number of clients it has and the average value of their assets held in custody, the volume of trading executed on the platform, the number of orders and transfers, the number of countries in which the CASP undertakes its business activity;

[103] ISO 24165-1:2021, Digital token identifier (DTI) – Registration, assignment and structure www.iso.org/standard/80601.html.

[104] RTS on record-keeping by crypto-asset service providers, Article 15 (Identification of crypto assets).

[105] MiCAR, Article 68(7).

[106] Commission Delegated Regulation (EU) 2025/299 of 31 October 2024 supplementing Regulation (EU) 2023/1114 of the European Parliament and of the Council on markets in crypto-assets with regard to regulatory technical standards on continuity and regularity in the performance of crypto-asset services.

[107] Commission Delegated Regulation (EU) 2017/584 of 14 July 2016 supplementing Directive 2014/65/EU of the European Parliament and of the Council with regard to regulatory technical standards specifying organisational requirements of trading venues.

[108] Commission Delegated Regulation (EU) 2024/1774 of 13 March 2024 supplementing Regulation (EU) 2022/2554 of the European Parliament and of the Council with regard to regulatory technical standards specifying ICT risk management tools, methods, processes, and policies and the simplified ICT risk management framework, OJ 2024/1774 of 25 June 2024.

- the level of complexity that may be affected by the organisational structure of the CASP;
- the CASP's outsourcing arrangements; and
- the number and types of distributed ledgers used by the CASP.[109]

CASPs fall within the scope of DORA,[110] which provides for standard back-up and redundancy requirements.[111] The redundancy requirements are that a financial entity should have backup options or alternative methods available to ensure the smooth functioning of services (eg, settlement of transactions) in case of a failure or downtime of the primary system. According to DORA, financial entities, including CASPs, must set up backup systems that can be activated in accordance with the backup policies and procedures, as well as restoration and recovery procedures and methods.[112] However, compliance with these requirements may be difficult for CASPs, given the limits of interoperability across DLT networks, which can make it problematic to find back-up options in case of a systemic disruption (eg, ETH-based transactions are only settled on Ethereum). Another technology-related element that might affect business continuity is a certain level of unpredictability in decision-making as part of permissionless decentralised governance arrangements with multiple 'decision-makers' (eg, validating nodes) that are not controlled or influenced by the CASP. If the distributed ledger technology relied on by a CASP is experiencing downtime or some other disruption, a CASP operating a trading platform might not be able to initiate the final settlement of client transactions on-chain within the prescribed time limit of 24 hours (Article 76(12) MiCAR).[113] In any case, such risks should be communicated to clients and potential clients pursuant to Article 66 MiCAR.

7.3.4. Safekeeping of Clients' Crypto-assets and Funds

The bankruptcy of crypto intermediaries during the so called Crypto Winter of 2022–2023 revealed high-volume asset diversions,[114] frequent commingling of clients' assets with the assets of crypto platforms,[115] loss of ownership rights by

[109] Draft RTS pursuant to Article 68(10)(a) of MiCA, Annex (Criteria for the self-assessment of crypto-asset service providers).

[110] DORA, Article 2(1)(f).

[111] DORA, Article 12.

[112] DORA, Article 12(2).

[113] The risk of potential delays and interruptions in on-chain settlements is recognised in Recital (84) MiCAR, acknowledging that 'in the case of an on-chain settlement, the settlement might take longer as it is not controlled by the crypto-asset service provider operating the trading platform.'

[114] DW. Arner, DA Zetzsche, RP Buckley and J Kirkwood, 'The Financialization of Crypto: Lessons from FTX and the Crypto Winter of 2022–2023' (2023) UNSW Law Research Paper No. 23-31, p 14.

[115] See eg Notice of Filing Second Interim Report of John J. Ray III to the Independent Directors: The Commingling and Misuse of Customer Deposits at FTX.COM, *In re FTX Trading Ltd et al.*, Case No. 22-11068 (JTD) (Bankr. D. Del. 26 June 2023), arguing that 'from the inception of the FTX.com

CASPs' clients,[116] and the unauthorised reuse of clients' assets without consent or disclosure.[117]

To mitigate these risks, MiCAR provides for a general obligation concerning safekeeping of clients' crypto-assets and funds (Article 70). This general obligation is supplemented by a special one related to custody and administration of crypto-assets on behalf of clients, discussed below. According to Article 70, CASPs 'that hold crypto-assets belonging to clients or the means of access to such crypto-assets [eg, private keys] shall make adequate arrangements to safeguard the ownership rights of clients, especially in the event of the crypto-asset service provider's insolvency, and to prevent the use of clients' crypto-assets for their own account.' This provision applies both to entities specialised in crypto custody services and to those entities that hold clients' crypto-assets and funds as an ancillary activity.

The notion of 'safekeeping' plays a crucial role also in other areas of financial regulation.[118] It has been pointed out that while there is no uniform and clear-cut definition of 'safekeeping', the common aspect of safekeeping duties regarding financial assets that can be held in custody 'is the mere fact of holding those assets in custody under the custodian's name on behalf of the client.'[119] MiCAR does not have a definition of 'safekeeping' and mentions it only as part of the definition of the service of 'providing custody and administration of crypto-assets on behalf of clients'.[120] The latter means 'safekeeping or controlling, on behalf of clients, of crypto-assets or of the means of access to such crypto-assets […].'

'Control' is another term not defined by MiCAR. However, Recital (83) indicates that a client might keep control over their crypto-assets or transfer full control to a CASP. In the former case – the case of pure self-custody – the client has exclusive access to the private key and is alone empowered to dispose of crypto-assets. Arguably, if the client of a CASP maintains full and exclusive control over the crypto-asset (ie, the ability to initiate and execute a transaction with respect to that crypto-asset), so that the CASP does not have any control (either positive or negative), the safekeeping obligations do not apply to such a CASP.[121] This mirrors Principle 10 of the Principles on Digital Assets and Private Law, according to which a custodian needs to have control of the digital asset. Conversely, if the CASP has control over clients' crypto-assets (whether positive or negative,

exchange, the FTX Group commingled customer deposits and corporate funds, and misused them with abandon.'

[116] I Kokorin, 'Crypto Insolvencies and the Limits of a Contract and Contract Law' (2023) 31(6) *European Review of Private Law* 1245; J Woxholth, DA Zetzsche, R Buckley and D Arner, 'Competing Claims to Cryptoassets' (2023) UNSW Law Research Paper No. 23–26, papers.ssrn.com/sol3/papers.cfm?abstract_id=4394952.

[117] Zetzsche, Buckley, Arner and van Ek (n 40) 47. FSB, FSB Global Regulatory Framework for Crypto-Asset Activities (17 July 2023), pp 5–6.

[118] See eg AIFMD, Article 21(8); UCITSD, Article 22(1); MiFID II, Article 16(8); PSD2, Article 10.

[119] D Zetzsche and A Nikolakopoulou, 'Crypto Custody and Crypto Wallets – An Empirical Assessment' (2024) SSRN, 12, papers.ssrn.com/sol3/papers.cfm?abstract_id=4769396.

[120] MiCAR, Article 3(1)(17).

[121] This mirrors the position of UNIDROIT DAPL, Principle 10.

the latter involving the ability to prevent the client from initiating or executing a transaction), inter alia, as part of custodial wallet services, Article 70 MiCAR should apply. Situations of 'shared' control (eg, multi-sig wallets) are more complicated and should be assessed on a case-by-case basis, taking account of the level of control exercised or potentially exercised by the CASP.[122]

The duty of a CASP to make adequate arrangements to safeguard the ownership rights of clients, especially in the case of insolvency, is similar to that applicable to investment firms under MiFID II.[123] This duty under MiFID II is further elaborated in Delegated Directive 2017/593,[124] pursuant to which investment firms must keep records and accounts enabling them at any time and without delay to distinguish assets held for one client from assets held for any other client and from their own assets.[125] A similar provision is proposed in the draft RTS specifying records to be kept of all crypto-asset services, activities, orders and transactions undertaken.[126] Such records must allow for the ready identification of the balances of crypto-assets and funds held for each client. They must also include details of the accounts in which client funds are held, details of the accounts opened with third parties holding crypto-assets for the CASP, as well as agreements relevant to establishing client ownership over crypto-assets and funds.[127] These rules under MiCAR and MiFID II are administrative in nature, and a breach may be sanctioned by a public authority.[128] They seek to ensure proper record-keeping and operational management (ie, operational segregation) by CASPs with respect to their clients' assets. Nevertheless, they aim to achieve a private law result by requiring that client ownership rights in crypto-assets be safeguarded. I will examine this intersection between regulatory and private law further when discussing the MiCAR rules relating to the custody of crypto-assets (see section 7.4.1 below).

As for the safekeeping of funds, MiCAR provides that where the business model of a CASP requires it to hold funds as defined in Directive (EU) 2015/2366 (PSD2) in the form of banknotes, coins, scriptural money (money held in bank accounts) or e-money belonging to its clients, it must promptly place such funds with a credit institution or a central bank.[129] Client funds should be placed in an

[122] D Zetzsche, J Sinnig and A Nikolakopoulou, 'Crypto Custody' (2024) SSRN, 15, papers.ssrn.com/sol3/papers.cfm?abstract_id=4713409, arguing that situations where no conduct on the side of a CASP alone is sufficient to obtain control over crypto-assets do not qualify as 'control' under MiCAR.

[123] MiFID II, Article 16(8).

[124] Commission Delegated Directive (EU) 2017/593 of 7 April 2016 supplementing Directive 2014/65/EU of the European Parliament and of the Council with regard to safeguarding of financial instruments and funds belonging to clients, product governance obligations and the rules applicable to the provision or reception of fees, commissions or any monetary or non-monetary benefits.

[125] ibid Article 2(1).

[126] Final Report second package, 3 July 2024, Draft RTS on record-keeping by crypto-asset service providers, Article 5(f).

[127] ibid Article 5(2).

[128] M Haentjens, 'European Harmonisation of Intermediated Securities Law: Dispossession and Segregation in Regulatory and Private Law' in L Gullifer and J Payne (eds), *Intermediation and Beyond* (Hart Publishing, 2019) 272.

[129] MiCAR, Recital (82) and Article 70(3).

account separate from the account used by the CASP for holding its own funds. These duties do not cover e-money tokens,[130] and the discussed MiCAR rules do not apply to CASPs that are e-money institutions, payment institutions or banks as they are subject to their own sectoral rules on safeguarding client monies.[131]

Importantly, where CASPs provide payment services with EMTs – since EMTs are deemed to be electronic money (Article 48(2) MiCAR) and because they fall within the definition of 'funds' under Article 4(25) PSD2 – such CASPs must either hold a licence as a payment service provider under PSD2, or partner with a licensed payment service provider (see also section 4.2 of this book).[132] The interplay between MiCAR and PSD2 is complex and problematic for two reasons. First, what can be seen as 'payment services' related to EMTs and 'payment transactions' involving EMTs is not entirely clear. Second, the requirement to hold dual authorisation (ie, under MiCAR and PSD2) may result in a substantial regulatory burden, both for CASPs (especially SMEs) and NCAs supervising them. The lack of clarity and the high costs might lead to regulatory arbitrage and raise investor protection concerns.

Recognising these problems, Director-General Berrigan at the European Commission sent a letter to the EBA and ESMA requesting that they explore the possibility of issuing a 'no action letter' 'with regard to the enforcement of the requirements on authorisation in PSD2 as regards services with EMTs provided by CASPs […] that may be inadvertently covered by the PSD2, eg where EMTs are not used as a means of payment or for P2P payment transactions, but rather for investment or trading purposes.'[133]

7.3.5. Complaints-handling Procedures

Given the frequency and intensity of interactions between CASPs and their clients, one can expect that the number of conflicting situations and complaints will be significant. Many existing crypto firms have created their own dedicated procedures and web pages for client complaints.[134] MiCAR introduces harmonised rules, mandating CASPs to have complaints-handling procedures in place.

According to Article 71(1), CASPs must 'establish and maintain effective and transparent procedures for prompt, fair and consistent handling of complaints

[130] Note that according to Article 48(2) of MiCAR, e-money tokens are deemed to be electronic money. E-money tokens are included as electronic money in the definition of funds in the Proposal for a Regulation on payment services in the internal market and amending Regulation (EU) No 1093/2010 (PSD3).

[131] MiCAR, Article 70(5). See eg Article 10 PSD2 (*Safeguarding requirements*).

[132] MiCAR, Recital (93).

[133] European Commission, Letter, 'Subject: Interplay between MiCA and PSD2 – Possible 'no action letter' by the EBA', 6 December 2024.

[134] See eg Kraken, Complaint Handling Process: A Complete Guide support.kraken.com/hc/en-us/articles/complaint-handling-process; Bitpanda Complaints management, www.bitpanda.com/en/complaints.

received from clients and shall publish descriptions of those procedures.' Clients should be able to file complaints without any charges. Additionally, CASPs are required to inform their clients about the possibility of filing a complaint, make available a relevant template, investigate all complaints in a timely manner and communicate an outcome to their clients.

ESMA drafted the RTS specifying the requirements, templates and procedures for the handling of client complaints.[135] Among other things, these RTS clarified that clients should be able to file complaints in the languages used by the CASP to market its services or communicate with clients, as well as in the official languages of the home and host Member States that are official EU languages.[136] This clarification aims to ensure the accessibility of the complaints-handling mechanisms for the wider client base of CASPs.

Interestingly, in its detailed and prescriptive approach to the regulation of complaints-handling procedures for CASPs, ESMA differs from the EBA. The EBA has drafted the RTS on complaints handling procedures for issuers of ARTs.[137] The EBA's approach is more high-level and principle-based. Commenting on this divergence in approaches, ESMA referred to differences in the business models of CASPs and issuers of stablecoins, noting that the former are likely to attract a higher number of complaints.

7.3.6. Prevention and Management of Conflicts of Interest

Article 72(1) provides that CASPs 'shall implement and maintain effective policies and procedures, taking into account the scale, the nature and range of crypto-asset services provided, to *identify, prevent, manage and disclose* conflicts of interest [...].' (emphasis added). Conflicts of interest may arise between a CASP and its shareholders, persons directly or indirectly linked to the CASP or its shareholders, members of the management body, employees and clients. They may also occur in a situation where the CASP has two or more clients with mutually conflicting interests, or where it is vertically integrated and offers a wide range of crypto-asset services. The assessment, identification and management of conflicts of interest must take into account the business model and crypto-asset services offered by the CASP. This is why it is impossible to describe every situation that leads to conflicts of interest.

[135] Commission Delegated Regulation (EU) 2025/294 of 1 October 2024 supplementing Regulation (EU) 2023/1114 of the European Parliament and of the Council with regard to regulatory technical standards specifying the requirements, templates and procedures for the handling of complaints by the crypto-asset service providers.

[136] ibid Article 3.

[137] EBA, Final Report, Draft Regulatory Technical Standards to specify the requirements, templates and procedures for handling complaints under Article 31 of the Regulation (EU) 2023/1114 on Markets in Crypto-assets.

MiCAR refers to the prevention, management and disclosure of conflicts of interest. A question may arise about the relationships between these elements. In this respect, ESMA clarifies that conflicts of interests should be prevented or managed.[138] Thus, a separately mentioned disclosure obligation (Article 72(2))[139] does not constitute an alternative to the prevention and management. In addressing conflicts of interest, ESMA closely follows the approach adopted for investment firms under MiFID II.[140]

In its Policy Recommendations, the International Organization of Securities Commissions (IOSCO) points out that conflicts of interest could arise from the fact that many CASPs engage in multiple functions and activities under 'one roof', such as trading, exchange, execution and custody. In other words, many CASPs operate as multifunction crypto-asset intermediaries.[141] The accumulation of various functions in a single business entity or a group of closely related entities is frequently driven by economic incentives, including network effects, cost-efficiency, economies of scale and scope.

As an example of a potential conflict of interest, IOSCO refers to front-running, whereby a CASP 'front-runs' client orders in favour of its own transaction or that of a related party. A conflict with customers can occur in situations where 'a CASP that operates an order-matching service [...] is also making markets or otherwise trading as principal against other users in that market', or where a 'CASP that allows margin trading [offers] margin to an affiliate on terms better than it offers to other users.'[142] IOSCO suggests that where conflicts of interest cannot be mitigated and where disclosures are ineffective in protecting markets and investors, a regulator may have to prohibit a CASP from combining certain functions in a single legal entity or group of affiliated entities. This can result in a ring-fencing strategy, involving the delegation of specific functions to separate legal entities 'with separate board and management teams and practical separation when operating the separate legal entities.'[143]

[138] ESMA, Final Report, Draft Technical Standards specifying certain requirements in relation to conflicts of interest for crypto-asset service providers under the Markets in Crypto Assets Regulation (MiCA), ESMA18-72330276-1634, 31 May 2024, at 22.

[139] According to this provision, CASPs must, 'in a prominent place on their website, disclose to their clients and prospective clients the general nature and sources of conflicts of interest [...] and the steps taken to mitigate them.'

[140] See Commission Delegated Regulation (EU) 2017/565 of 25 April 2016 supplementing Directive 2014/65/EU of the European Parliament and of the Council as regards organisational requirements and operating conditions for investment firms.

[141] IOSCO, Policy Recommendations for Crypto and Digital Asset Markets, Consultation Report, CR01/2023, May 2023. Significant risks arising from CASPs combining a wide range of crypto-asset services, products, and functions have been highlighted by the FSB. See FSB, The Financial Stability Implications of Multifunction Crypto-asset Intermediaries (28 November 2023) www.fsb.org/2023/11/the-financial-stability-implications-of-multifunction-crypto-asset-intermediaries.

[142] ibid (IOSCO) at 16.

[143] ibid at 17.

7.3.7. Outsourcing

The dynamic landscape of the crypto-asset market necessitates robust frameworks to ensure operational integrity and regulatory compliance. CASPs often outsource certain functions to third parties to streamline operations, enhance efficiency, and leverage specialised expertise. However, such outsourcing must be carefully managed to mitigate additional operational risks and maintain compliance with regulatory requirements. Article 73 of MiCAR contains an elaborate set of rules concerning the outsourcing of services or activities by CASPs. While outsourcing operational functions can offer significant advantages, it also introduces potential risks that require vigilant management.

The following list outlines the essential conditions that CASPs must meet to ensure that their outsourcing practices do not compromise their responsibilities and obligations.

- In accordance with Article 73(1)(a), CASPs must ensure that outsourcing arrangements do not lead to a transfer of their core responsibilities. While third-party service providers may execute specific tasks, ultimate accountability for those tasks remains with the CASP. This stipulation ensures that the integrity and accountability of CASPs are upheld, regardless of any external partnerships.
- Article 73(1)(b) requires that outsourcing relationships not alter the CASP's relationship with the client. Clients' expectations and the nature of services provided should remain consistent, ensuring that the outsourcing does not negatively impact the client experience or the CASP's service quality. Moreover, CASPs must continue to honour their obligations towards clients, maintaining transparency and accountability.
- In accordance with Article 73(1)(c), CASPs must ensure that outsourcing does not affect their authorisation status. Any outsourcing arrangement must comply with the regulatory conditions under which the CASP was authorised. This requirement ensures that the fundamental conditions of operation for CASPs are not compromised by external engagements.
- To ensure effective oversight of third-party service providers, Article 73(1)(d) grants competent authorities rights of access and cooperation. Third parties involved in outsourcing must cooperate with the CASP's home Member State NCA and must not impede supervisory functions. This includes allowing on-site access and providing relevant information. Outsourcing agreements must require such cooperation to maintain regulatory oversight and enable authorities to fulfil their duties.
- CASPs must, in accordance with Article 71(1)(e), maintain the necessary expertise and resources to evaluate and supervise outsourced services. This requirement ensures that CASPs can continuously assess the quality and performance of third-party services, address any issues promptly and manage

associated risks effectively. Retaining in-house capabilities is crucial for sustained operational control and risk mitigation.

- CASPs must have unrestricted access to all pertinent information related to outsourced services. This direct access is essential for real-time monitoring and effective oversight. It ensures that CASPs can promptly respond to any issues or irregularities, maintaining service integrity and operational transparency. This follows from the requirement set out in Article 71(1)(f) MiCAR.
- Data protection is a paramount concern in outsourcing arrangements. CASPs must ensure that third-party service providers comply with the EU's data protection standards pursuant to Article 71(1)(g). These standards must be explicitly stated in written agreements to safeguard client data and maintain regulatory compliance, which will form an important part of the mandatory written agreements that must be established by CASPs in accordance with Article 71(3).

CASPs must formalise their outsourcing arrangements through detailed written agreements, so that the conditions described above can be effectively implemented. These agreements should clearly outline the roles, responsibilities, and expectations of both the CASP and the third-party service provider. Specifically, they should include provisions related to data protection, access to information, and cooperation with regulatory authorities, including the right of audit by competent authorities. Effective outsourcing management requires continuous monitoring and evaluation. CASPs should establish robust oversight mechanisms to regularly assess the performance and compliance of third-party providers. This includes conducting periodic audits, reviewing service level agreements and implementing key performance indicators to measure service quality and adherence to regulatory standards.

Outsourcing inherently introduces additional risks, which must be proactively managed. CASPs should conduct comprehensive risk assessments before entering into outsourcing agreements and develop risk mitigation strategies. This involves identifying potential risks, evaluating their impact, and implementing control measures to minimise adverse effects.

Compliance with regulatory reporting requirements is essential for maintaining transparency and accountability. CASPs should establish processes for timely and accurate reporting to relevant authorities. This includes providing information on outsourcing arrangements, third-party performance, and any incidents or breaches that may occur. The requirements included in Article 73(4) extend the compliance requirements in this respect to any requirement set out in Title V MiCAR, thereby putting a burden on the CASP to ensure the contractual outsourcing arrangements encompass all the requirements following from this framework.

Outsourcing can offer significant advantages to crypto-asset service providers by enhancing operational efficiency and enabling access to specialised expertise. This is especially true for CASPs outsourcing certain functions to other group members, many of which may have already been operational at the time of EU authorisation. However, it is imperative that CASPs meticulously manage their outsourcing arrangements to avoid additional operational risks and ensure compliance with regulatory obligations. By adhering to the outlined conditions, maintaining robust oversight mechanisms, and fostering a culture of continuous improvement, CASPs should be able to successfully navigate the complexities of outsourcing while safeguarding client interests and maintaining operational integrity.

It must be noted that Article 73 is, in essence, a watered down version of the more detailed requirements set out in DORA on the management of risks when using third-party ICT providers. Once the outsourcing relationship of a CASP falls within the domain of DORA, the CASP is also obliged to fully conform to the provisions of Chapter V DORA (Key principles for a sound management of ICT third-party risk). Among other things, this requires compliance with the detailed rules set out in the regulatory technical standards in respect of the management of this risk.[144]

7.3.8. Orderly Wind-down of Crypto-asset Service Providers

Crypto-asset service providers play a crucial role in the digital economy, offering a range of services that facilitate the use, trade, and management of crypto-assets. Given the volatility and rapid evolution of the crypto-asset markets, it is imperative for these service providers to have a robust plan in place to ensure an orderly wind-down of their activities, should such a necessity arise. This plan is essential not only for the stability of the financial system but also for protecting the interests of clients and maintaining market confidence.

According to Article 74, CASPs that provide the services referred to in Articles 75 to 79, such as custody and the operation of a trading platform, are required to develop and maintain a comprehensive wind-down plan. This plan must be tailored to support the orderly cessation of their activities in compliance with applicable national laws.

One of the primary objectives of the wind-down plan is to ensure the continuity or recovery of any critical activities performed by the service provider. In this respect, wind-down plans can be compared to the resolution plans developed by credit institutions pursuant to the BRRD. Critical activities are those that, if disrupted, could cause significant economic harm to clients or broader financial instability. This includes, but is not limited to, maintaining client accounts, executing transactions, and safeguarding crypto-assets.

[144] Commission Delegated Regulation (EU) 2024/1773 of 13 March 2024 supplementing Regulation (EU) 2022/2554 of the European Parliament and of the Council with regard to regulatory technical standards specifying the detailed content of the policy regarding contractual arrangements on the use of ICT services supporting critical or important functions provided by ICT third-party service providers, OJ 2024/1773 of 25 June 2024.

The plan must demonstrate the ability of the CASP to wind down its operations without causing undue economic harm to its clients. This involves detailed strategies for managing client funds, processing outstanding transactions, and providing clear and timely communication to clients about the wind-down process. The aim is to mitigate any adverse impacts on clients, ensuring that they have sufficient time and information to make alternative arrangements for their crypto-assets.

CASPs must conduct a thorough assessment of their critical functions and identify potential risks associated with their discontinuation. This assessment should include an evaluation of interdependencies with other financial institutions and service providers, as well as any systemic risks that could arise from the wind-down. The plan must include measures to ensure the operational continuity of critical functions. This may involve maintaining a core team of staff to manage essential operations, securing access to key systems and data, and implementing contingency plans to address potential disruptions.

A clear governance structure must be established to oversee the implementation of the wind-down plan. This includes assigning roles and responsibilities to senior management and board members, ensuring that there is adequate oversight and accountability throughout the wind-down process. Effective communication is vital during the wind-down process. For this reason, CASPs must develop a comprehensive communication strategy that outlines how they will inform clients, regulators, and other stakeholders about the wind-down. This strategy should include regular updates and provide clear instructions to clients on how to manage their assets during the transition.

Service providers must demonstrate their financial resilience to support the orderly wind-down. This includes maintaining sufficient capital and liquidity to cover the costs associated with the wind-down process, as well as any potential liabilities that may arise.

In conclusion, the orderly wind-down of crypto-asset service providers is a critical component of ensuring the stability and integrity of the EU crypto-asset market. By developing and maintaining a comprehensive wind-down plan, CASPs can safeguard their clients' interests, minimise economic harm, and uphold market confidence. This preparatory and proactive approach not only mitigates risks but also reinforces the resilience and sustainability of the digital financial ecosystem.

The relatively concise provision on the wind-down of CASPs in MiCAR reflects the light-touch regulatory approach adopted for this segment of the crypto-asset ecosystem. This approach can be partly attributed to the limited systemic impact observed from CASP failures to date. Unlike traditional financial institutions, CASPs – particularly those not engaged in stablecoin issuance – have not posed significant contagion risks to the broader financial system. In contrast, MiCAR imposes far more stringent requirements on issuers of ARTs and EMTs, reflecting their potential to function as money-like instruments and their closer nexus with financial stability. These entities are subject to robust prudential, governance, and reserve management obligations, designed to ensure stability and the capacity to meet redemption demands (see chapter six). If a bank, investment firm, or payment institution offers crypto-asset services, it would be subject to its own sectoral rules on recovery and (orderly) wind-down procedures, which impose detailed and comprehensive requirements on such financial firms.

7.3.9. Acquiring and Holding Qualifying Holdings in CASPs

CASPs are subject to the structural supervision of their owners, similar to other financial entities such as credit institutions, investment firms, insurance undertakings, and payment institutions. This supervisory regime stems from the so-called Antonveneta Directive,[145] named after the takeover bid launched in 2005 by the Dutch bank ABN AMRO for Banca Antonveneta. It was introduced to provide harmonised rules for the assessment by competent authorities of the intention to acquire and hold a so-called 'qualifying holding'. The regime serves a dual purpose: (i) ensuring the integrity of markets by verifying that business owners meet good repute standards, and (ii) ensuring that the ownership structure does not undermine the financial stability of the CASP. The latter includes a prudential assessment of the owner's financial background and their ability to provide sufficient financial support in times of distress.

The rules on good reputation are scattered across several provisions of MiCAR. As discussed earlier in this chapter, the good repute test for holders of qualifying holdings is also prescribed in the authorisation requirements for CASPs (see Article 62(2)(h)). Further requirements are contained in Article 84(1)(a), which relate to the reputation of the (proposed) acquirer of a qualifying holding. This requirement rather concerns the profile of the individual or business in respect of the appropriateness of its conduct of business, for instance, the absence of adverse media coverage. The 'repute' requirements under Article 62(2)(h) particularly concern the absence of criminal records, sanctions by public authorities, disputes with tax authorities and similar factors.

It must be borne in mind that the rules on the acquisition of qualifying holdings in CASPs are heavily based on the existing framework for other financial institutions. For instance, when determining whether a group of shareholders, individuals, or entities are 'acting in concert' – such that their (share-)holdings in the CASP must be aggregated to establish a 'qualifying holding' – one can take into account the criteria for the assessment as outlined in the Joint Guidelines on the prudential assessment of qualifying holdings, as established by the ESAs.[146] More recently, the EBA and ESMA have published Joint Guidelines on the

[145] Directive 2007/44/EC of the European Parliament and of the Council of 5 September 2007 amending Council Directive 92/49/EEC and Directives 2002/83/EC, 2004/39/EC, 2005/68/EC and 2006/48/EC as regards procedural rules and evaluation criteria for the prudential assessment of acquisitions and increase of holdings in the financial sector, OJ L 247, pp 1–16.

[146] Final Report Joint Guidelines on the prudential assessment of acquisitions and increases of qualifying holdings in the financial sector, JC/GL/2016/01, 20 December 2016.

suitability assessment of shareholders and members, whether direct or indirect, with qualifying holdings in issuers of asset-referenced tokens and in crypto-asset service providers.[147]

A 'qualifying holding' is defined in Article 3(1)(36) as:

> any direct or indirect holding in an issuer of asset-referenced tokens or in a crypto-asset service provider which represents at least 10% of the capital or of the voting rights, as set out in Articles 9 and 10 of Directive 2004/109/EC of the European Parliament and of the Council, respectively, taking into account the conditions for the aggregation thereof laid down in Article 12(4) and (5) of that Directive, or which makes it possible to exercise a significant influence over the management of the issuer of asset-referenced tokens or the management of the crypto-asset service provider in which that holding subsists.

The reference to Directive 2004/109/EC (Transparency Directive)[148] serves the objective of establishing a harmonised approach to assessing shareholdings in the EU. For instance, this might concern the assessment of certain contractual arrangements where an individual or entity has obtained an optional right to acquire shares in the capital of the legal entity as constituting the ownership of a qualifying holding. It could also concern arrangements where shareholders make provisions regarding voting rights by means of proxies. In practice, the question of whether an individual or entity holds a 'qualifying holding' is often sensitive, as the thresholds for meeting the definition are quite low. This is intended to prevent the circumvention of the rules regarding the scrutiny of ownership in firms.

It is important to emphasise that the rules regarding the acquisition of a qualifying holding apply at the start of the firm's 'existence' as a supervised entity – in other words, at the time of the authorisation process. This means that the rules regarding the acquisition of a qualifying holding in a CASP under Articles 83 and 84 MiCAR must already have been applied at the time of the application for authorisation. The procedure for the approval of acquisition of a qualified holding is therefore a parallel procedure to be followed, with the understanding that the primary addressee of these rules is not the CASP itself, but its shareholders or other owners. In practice, however, both processes are handled by the same team, partly because the application for permission to acquire the qualifying holding will require the inclusion of important sections concerning the CASP's business itself.

In most Member States, the approval process for the authorisation of the (financial) firm and the approval of the holding of a qualifying holding are vested in the same authority. However, in some Member States, such as the Netherlands, these processes are handled by different regulators (ie, AFM and DNB).

A further point to be made concerns the threshold regime. Each time the qualifying holding exceeds certain thresholds, the holder of that qualifying holding

[147] EBA and ESMA, Final Report on the Assessment of Suitability, EBA/GL/2024/09, 27 June 2024.

[148] Directive 2004/109/EC of the European Parliament and of the Council of 15 December 2004 on the harmonisation of transparency requirements in relation to information about issuers whose securities are admitted to trading on a regulated market and amending Directive 2001/34/EC, OJ L 390, pp 38–57.

must reapply to increase the size of the qualifying holding. Those thresholds are set out in Article 83(1) and are 20 per cent, 30 per cent or 50 per cent. In practice, compliance with this requirement is often overlooked, and it can lead to complex issues regarding the supervision of such companies. A breach of these obligations immediately raises a question regarding the 'reputation' of the shareholder in question, especially if the breach is enforced by the regulator. Therefore, it is crucial to comply carefully with the relevant provisions.

The criteria applied by the reviewing competent authority are contained in Article 84(1) and are almost identical to the applicable regimes for credit institutions, investment firms, payment institutions and other financial institutions. They relate to:

(a) The reputation of the proposed acquirer.
(b) The suitability of the persons who will direct the business of the target undertaking as a result of the acquisition. This criterion should be read narrowly, as this test is applied in cases where the firm's shareholders have an active involvement in the policy and management of the CASP. If they are passive owners (in other words, if the equity participation is intended solely as a passive investment), this criterion will be subject to a lesser degree of scrutiny.
(c) The financial soundness of the proposed acquirer. An important factor in this assessment is, for example, the extent to which the new owner has financed the acquisition of the stake with debt, which could exert pressure on the CASP's dividend policy. If the holder of the qualifying holding depends on the dividend stream to meet its own obligations under external financing, this may create vulnerabilities regarding the financial soundness of the CASP. Such leveraged financing structures usually attract regulatory scrutiny.
(d) The ability of the target undertaking to comply, or continue to comply, with the applicable prudential requirements.
(e) The absence of any suspicion of a risk of money laundering or terrorist financing. This criterion has a long history, having entered EU regulation following the major money laundering scandal involving the Bank of Credit and Commerce International (BCCI).[149] In essence, it is designed to prevent regulated entities in the financial system from being used as vehicles for money laundering operations.

All things considered, it can be observed that the qualifying holding regime for CASPs sets the bar at a similar level as for other financial entities. The relevant procedures are complex and require considerable attention from those to whom these standards are addressed. The regime aims to promote the integrity of the markets, but also to combat financial vulnerabilities as much as possible by allowing financially sound shareholders to enter the system.

[149] M Potts, N Kochan and R Whittington, 'Dirty Money: BCCI – The Inside Story of the World's Sleaziest Bank' (1992) US Office of Justice Programs, NCJ Number 139005, www.ojp.gov/ncjrs/virtual-library/abstracts/dirty-money-bcci-inside-story-worlds-sleaziest-bank.

7.4. Obligations in Respect of Specific Crypto-asset Services

7.4.1. Custody and Administration of Crypto-assets on Behalf of Clients

7.4.1.1. Introduction

Under MiCAR, 'custody and administration of crypto-assets on behalf of clients' is defined as 'safekeeping or controlling, on behalf of clients, of crypto-assets or of the means of access to such crypto-assets, where applicable in the form of private cryptographic keys.'[150] The term 'custody' is commonly used to describe a legal relationship or service involving the safekeeping of assets by one person (custodian) for or on behalf of another person (customer).[151]

Multifunction crypto-asset intermediaries, such as crypto exchanges and trading platforms, usually engage in crypto-asset services that can be classified as custody and administration of crypto-assets on behalf of their clients, even if this is not their main service. For example, to buy crypto-assets, clients often register with a CASP and open an account to which the purchased crypto-assets are 'credited'. To be able to trade, clients are often required to pre-fund their accounts. While the terms and conditions of the CASP might state that the client 'owns' these crypto-assets, control over them typically rests with the CASP. The transfer of control to the CASP can lead to abuses, whereby the CASP uses customer assets for its own account – disposing of them without authorisation. The FTX case demonstrates such a risk.

According to the Terms of Use of the now-defunct FTX exchange, 'Title to your Digital Assets shall at all times remain with you [customer] and shall not transfer to FTX Trading. [...] None of the Digital Assets in your Account are the property of, or shall or may be loaned to, FTX Trading.'[152] These terms are unambiguous and state that customers of the exchange are and remain owners of deposited crypto-assets. Nevertheless, soon after the collapse of the FTX group, it was established that customer assets were diverted by FTX to an affiliated cryptocurrency trading firm Alameda. The US Commodity Futures Trading Commission (CFTC) observed that after the FTX empire collapsed, 'FTX customers and the world at large discovered that FTX, through its sister-company Alameda, had been

[150] MiCAR, Article 3(1)(17).

[151] See UNIDROIT Principles on Digital Assets and Private Law (UNIDROIT DAPL), Commentary to Principle 10 (Custody), noting that 'custody', 'broadly speaking, is where a person (usually a legal person, which may be a regulated entity), maintains a digital asset on behalf of and for the benefit of another, a client (which may be another custodian), in a manner that gives the client special protection against unauthorised dispositions of the asset and against the insolvency of the custodian who maintains the digital asset.'

[152] FTX Terms of Use (13 May 2022), para 8.2.6, gighustlers.com/wp-content/uploads/2022/11/httpshelp.ftx_.comhcarticle_attachments9719619779348FTX_Terms_of_Service.pdf.

surreptitiously siphoning off customer assets for its own use – and over $8 billion in customer assets were now missing.'[153] The SEC noted that customer assets were used by Alameda to make 'undisclosed venture investments, lavish real estate purchases, and large political donations.'[154] If the factual pattern described by the CFTC and the SEC is accurate, this would mean that FTX breached its contractual obligations and infringed upon its clients' property rights by reusing deposited crypto-assets – by means of lending them to Alameda – without disclosure or the consent of the owners.[155]

The vulnerable position of clients who deposit their crypto-assets with CASPs and thereby entrust their assets with a service provider, as well as the wave of crypto failures of 2022–2023 exposing large-scale asset misappropriations, necessitate regulation. In addition to misappropriation, the loss of client assets could also result from cyber-attacks, hacks, loss of private keys and system malfunctions. MiCAR seeks to address these risks in Article 75, which deals with crypto-custody.

7.4.1.2. Agreement with Customers

MiCAR states that CASPs providing custody and administration of crypto-assets on behalf of clients must conclude an agreement with their clients with certain mandatory provisions. Such an agreement should include, at a minimum, the following information: (i) identity of the parties, (ii) nature of the crypto-asset service(s) provided and its description, (iii) custody policy, (iv) means of communication between the CASP and clients, (v) description of the security systems used by the CASP, (vi) fees, costs and charges applied by the CASP, and (vii) the applicable law.[156]

These requirements are fully justified. A recent study of terms and conditions of major crypto firms reveals that customer agreements tend to be lengthy, complex, ambiguous, subject to frequent and material unilateral modifications, and may contain internal inconsistencies.[157] Although the requirement to include the identity of parties may appear self-evident, in practice, determining which legal entity acts as the contractual counterparty to the clients of a crypto-platform is not always easy. Consider the case of the failed crypto-lender Celsius. In that case, the US bankruptcy court observed that two conflicting interpretations of the terms of use were equally possible, and that reliance on extrinsic evidence was therefore necessary to determine the actual counterparty.[158] Clarity regarding the

[153] *CFTC v Samuel Bankman-Fried and others*, Complaint for Injunctive and Other Equitable Relief (21 December 2022) at p 3, www.cftc.gov/media/8021/enfftxtradingcomplaint122122/download.

[154] *SEC v Samuel Bankman-Fried*, Complaint (13 December 2022) www.sec.gov/litigation/complaints/2022/comp-pr2022-219.pdf.

[155] Kokorin (n 116) 1245, 1258.

[156] MiCAR, Article 75(1).

[157] Kokorin (n 116) 1245. See also Zetzsche and Nikolakopoulou (n 119).

[158] Memorandum Opinion Regarding Which Debtor Entities Have Liability for Customer Claims under the Terms of Use, *In re Celsius Network LLC et al.*, Case No. 22-10964 (MG) (Bankr. S.D.N.Y. 9 March 2023) www.nysb.uscourts.gov/sites/default/files/opinions/312902_2205_opinion.pdf.

services provided by CASPs, which is likely to have a direct impact on (the nature of) customers' rights, is equally important. For example, the Terms of Use of Binance,[159] the largest crypto exchange ranked by volume, do not specify whether Binance acts as a custodian, nor do they clarify what rights customers have in relation to crypto-assets transferred to Binance accounts. This lack of clarity of the terms results in legal uncertainty. It should be crystal clear to customers what rights they have in deposited crypto-assets, how these crypto-assets are held by the CASP (custody policy, segregation mechanisms, etc.) and what would happen to those crypto-assets in the event the CASP enters insolvency proceedings.

The insolvencies of several crypto firms during the Crypto Winter highlighted both the pertinence of the issue related to the nature of relationships between CASPs and their clients (eg, custody, lending), and the fact that customer agreements often played a decisive role in determining the outcome of the disputes.[160] This is why it should be considered good practice for agreements between CASPs and their clients to include a clear and comprehensive description of the service(s) provided, information on who has control over crypto-assets, transparency and disclosures on the rights and duties of the parties to the custodial agreement, client (ownership) rights, custodian's safeguarding arrangements, permissibility of reuse, and outsourcing (ie, sub-custody).

Notably, while regulatory frameworks such as MiCAR can impose requirements on the form and content of agreements, they do not determine the legal nature of the client's rights or remedies. These remain matters of private law, governed by the applicable legal system, which typically distinguishes between personal rights arising under contract and proprietary rights in the relevant assets. Clarifying this distinction is essential to understanding the actual legal position of clients in the event of insolvency or dispute.

7.4.1.3. Segregation Requirements

Asset segregation is a widely adopted method aimed at safeguarding the rights of customers whose assets are held by an intermediary, so that proprietary rights of customers are protected under applicable private law. The rules on asset segregation can be found in several EU regulatory laws that cover a wide range of financial assets and instruments.[161] These rules are aimed at increasing the protection of the investor.[162]

[159] Binance, Terms of Use, Last Updated on 11 September 2023, www.binance.com/en-AE/terms.

[160] *Re Gatecoin Ltd (in liquidation)* [2023] HKCFI 914; *In re Celsius Network LLC*, 647 B.R. 631 (Bankr. S.D.N.Y., 2023); *In re BlockFi Inc.*, Case No. 22-19361 (MBK) (Bankr. D.N.J. May 17, 2023) (No. 923).

[161] See eg MiFID II, Article 16(8)-(9); AIFMD, Article 21(8)(a); UCITS Directive, Article 22(5)(a)(ii).

[162] CPSS/IOSCO Recommendations for securities settlement systems, 2001, para 3.62, noting that '[i]deally, a customer's securities are immune from claims made by third-party creditors of the custodian. Although the ideal is not realised in all circumstances, when the entities through which securities are held are performing their responsibilities effectively, the likelihood of a successful legal claim made on a customer's securities by a third-party creditor is minimised.'

MiCAR introduces two separate sets of rules regarding asset segregation. The first set includes provisions on segregation and custody of reserve assets – the basket of assets securing the claim of ART-holders against the issuer of ARTs.[163] These reserve assets are meant to contribute to the stability of a stablecoin's value and protect stablecoin holders. The second set of rules governs the safekeeping and custody of client assets by CASPs. The objective of these rules is to mitigate the risk that client assets are used by the custodian (although they do not prevent loss per se) or become part of its insolvency estate. The risk of these occurrences is commonly referred to as intermediary or custody risk.[164] Under some applicable laws, segregation is a necessary precondition for the client to have a proprietary right in the assets. Additionally, segregation makes it factually easier to discover when there is unauthorised use or loss and to trace what has happened to the assets as a matter of fact. This section only addresses the second set of segregation rules – segregation by CASPs.

Recital (83) provides that CASPs which hold crypto-assets belonging to their customers should ensure that those crypto-assets are not pledged or otherwise used for their own account. Article 70, discussed above, adds that CASPs that hold crypto-assets belonging to their clients shall make adequate arrangements to safeguard the ownership rights of clients and to prevent the use of clients' crypto-assets for their own account. The question may arise whether these rules strictly prohibit any sort of reuse by CASPs, even if such reuse is expressly agreed to by the parties.[165] An obligation to safeguard client crypto-assets can be interpreted as a rule against reuse or as a rule requiring any reuse to be compatible with an obligation to safeguard.

To ensure compliance with Article 75 and to promote safekeeping of customer assets, crypto-asset service providers must adopt a custody policy with internal rules and procedures.[166] The custody policy must be intended to minimise the risk of a loss of clients' assets or rights due to fraud, cyber threats or negligence.[167] Every CASP should therefore identify sources of operational and IT risks for the safekeeping and control of custodial crypto-assets, and set procedures, systems and controls to manage these risks. Additionally, MiCAR lays down a number of specific rules related to book-keeping and asset segregation.

First, Article 75(2) stipulates that CASPs must 'keep a register of positions, opened in the name of each client, corresponding to each client's rights to the crypto-assets.' This rule mandates the execution of accurate and up-to-date

[163] MiCAR, Articles 36–38. See section 6.2.9.2 of this book.

[164] C Twemlow, 'Why are Securities Held in Intermediated Form?' in Gullifer and Payne (n 128) 101.

[165] Zetzsche, Sinnig and Nikolakopoulou (n 122) 207, 224, observing that 'a battle will inevitably be fought over the extent to which the consent of clients allows for treatment different than that provided for under Article 75 MiCA. However, where reuse hinges on the client's consent, what implicit limits exist with regard to the reuse? Is there any compensation to be offered to clients, as a precondition for a valid consent? What are the legal requirements for a valid consent to the reuse?'.

[166] MiCAR, Article 75(3).

[167] ibid.

book-keeping, so that it is possible to determine the 'balances' of crypto-assets belonging to clients. In other words, crypto-assets or means of access to the crypto-assets of the clients should be clearly identified as such. This identification, made possible via internal records, can serve as evidence of client entitlements in case of a dispute. CASPs are obliged to maintain an internal register of customer assets (eg via an Excel spreadsheet) and ensure that crypto-assets are not combined with CASPs' own assets, either off-chain or on-chain. The latter requirement is facilitated through operational and technological segregation discussed below. Clients are entitled to request from their service provider a statement of position of the crypto-assets recorded in their name (Article 75(5)). Such a statement must contain information about the client's crypto-assets, their balance, value and any transfers made during the period concerned.

Second, Article 75(7) states that CASPs must ensure that the crypto-assets held in custody are operationally segregated from the CASPs' own estate. MiCAR does not clarify what is meant by '*operational segregation*'. In the context of securities regulation, segregation in an operational or administrative sense has been interpreted as meaning that 'intermediaries must have securities registered on accounts, so that these securities can be identified as belonging to clients (either collectively in omnibus accounts, or in separate accounts) or to the intermediary itself.'[168] Operational segregation in itself does not mandate specific technological requirements for the segregation of clients' and CASP's own crypto-assets. However, in practice, apart from the internal record keeping of customer crypto-assets (ie, a register of positions, corresponding to each client's rights to the crypto-assets at any given moment), such crypto-assets will have to be 'registered' (or 'placed') via (a) blockchain address(es), separate from that used by the CASP to hold its own assets.[169] This is in line with the obligation of technological segregation discussed below.

Third, in addition to 'operational segregation', Article 75(7) requires '*technological segregation*'. Operational segregation may be difficult to achieve in practice if customer and CASP's own crypto-assets are held on the same (omnibus) blockchain addresses. This is due to the technological aspects of many blockchains, where crypto-assets on one blockchain address are selected randomly for future transactions involving that same blockchain address.[170] This is why MiCAR

[168] M Haentjens, 'European Harmonisation of Intermediated Securities Law: Dispossession and Segregation in Regulatory and Private Law' in Gullifer and Payne (n 128) 268.

[169] See UNIDROIT DAPL, Principle 11(3)(d), according to which a custodian's duty to its clients may include the duty to separate the digital assets maintained for clients from the digital assets maintained for its own account. Commentary at para 11.12 adds that this is the duty to separate client assets from house assets (ie, the custodian's own assets). A custodian can segregate clients' digital assets from its own by using separate private keys or distinct sub-custodian accounts. The legal effect will ultimately depend on the applicable law.

[170] M Haentjens, T de Graaf and I Kokorin, 'The failed hopes of disintermediation: crypto-custodian insolvency, legal risks and how to avoid them' (2020) *Singapore Journal of Legal Studies* 526, 559, observing with respect to bitcoin that 'the wallet used by the crypto-custodian chooses randomly or arbitrarily which unspent transaction outputs are used as inputs for new transactions.' Therefore, if the same blockchain address is used to hold crypto-assets belonging to customers and a CASP, there is a high risk of reuse.

explicitly requires CASPs to ensure that, on the distributed ledger, customer crypto-assets are held separately from their own assets. Notably, this rule of technological segregation does not prescribe the use of separate blockchain addresses for each customer (ie, one blockchain address per customer).[171] Implementing such a requirement, while possible,[172] would undoubtedly result in significant compliance and operational costs for CASPs. This means that crypto-assets can be administered using 'pooled' or omnibus blockchain addresses, as long as these addresses are not used by CASPs to hold and trade their own crypto-assets.[173] This also means that if there is a shortfall on such an omnibus blockchain address (eg, due to a hack), customers whose crypto-assets were stored via this blockchain address, may have to share the loss proportionately. The latter, however, would need to be determined by applicable (property) law.[174]

Fourth, MiCAR imposes the requirement of '*legal segregation*'. There is no definition of 'legal segregation'. It is, however, relatively clear that asset segregation should achieve a specific result under private law. For the protection of crypto investors, it is not sufficient that crypto-assets are operationally and technologically segregated, if in insolvency these assets become part of the CASP's insolvency estate. Legal segregation ensures that crypto-assets held in custody do not fall into the estate of the CASP, especially if the latter becomes insolvent. Notably, the consequences of legal segregation are expressed functionally (no recourse from custodian's creditors, protection from custodian's insolvency) rather than in concrete legal terms (eg, that the client has a proprietary right in the assets and the custodian has none).

Operational and technological segregation does not automatically lead to legal segregation. MiCAR provides that crypto-assets held in custody 'shall' be legally segregated from the estate of a CASP, 'so that creditors of the crypto-asset service provider have no recourse to crypto-assets held in custody by the crypto-asset service provider, in particular in the event of insolvency.'[175] This rule thus functionally requires that a certain result under private law be achieved without prescribing the precise means, which are apparently left to the applicable national (property) law. It is unclear, however, what the sanction for a breach of this rule would be. Probably, a breach would be sanctioned under administrative law, as it is formulated as an instruction directed at the CASP ('shall').[176]

[171] For a similar position, see UNIDROIT DAPL, Principle 11(2) and commentary in paras 11.6 and 11.7.

[172] See eg Gemini Custody Agreement, Last Updated on 31 July 2023, providing that 'Your Custody Account will have one or more associated unique Blockchain Addresses in which your Assets will be (i) segregated from any and all other assets held by us and (ii) directly verifiable via the applicable blockchain.'

[173] An unresolved issue is whether the assets of companies belonging to the CASP's group can be commingled with the assets of the CASP's clients. Caution should be exercised with such commingling, as it could create a risk of bypassing the segregation rules prescribed by Article 75.

[174] See UNIDROIT DAPL, Principle 13(7) and commentary in paras 13.7–13.9.

[175] MiCAR, Article 75(7).

[176] See MiCAR, Article 111(1)(d), under which the violation of Article 75 can lead to the imposition of administrative penalties and other administrative measures.

Another rule whose effect would need to be achieved through private law (which may vary from one Member State to another) is the 'substitution rule' found in Article 75(4), according to which, where there are changes to the underlying DLT which create or modify clients' rights, 'the client shall be entitled to any crypto-assets or any rights newly created on the basis and to the extent of the client's positions at the time of the occurrence of that change or event', unless a valid agreement between the CASP and its clients expressly provides otherwise.

To the extent that the four rules outlined above ensure that crypto-assets deposited by customers with a CASP are not mixed up with the assets of the CASP, and in this way mitigate the risk of reuse, MiCAR is capable of enhancing the protection of crypto investors' private law property rights. Segregation reduces the operational risk. That said, the effectiveness of customer protection relies on two key factors. The first factor is the efficient enforcement and supervision by national and EU authorities to prevent debacles similar to FTX from occurring. The second factor concerns the ramifications of asset commingling. Typically, private law outcomes of commingling are governed by national property law (see further below).[177]

The objective of MiCAR is clear – it seeks to preserve proprietary rights in crypto-assets, even if such assets are held in pooled or omnibus blockchain addresses (which is very common in practice), and accordingly cannot be individualised and traced back to an individual customer. Nevertheless, it is important to note that MiCAR operates as an administrative (regulatory) law and does not directly impact national private law.[178] The exact way to achieve the preservation of client proprietary rights in crypto-assets (ie, the ultimate goal of legal segregation) will depend on the applicable law.

For example, the Dutch regulator (ie, AFM) clarifies that Dutch law does not provide for a basis 'on which crypto-assets held in custody are segregated from CASPs' assets, as there is for banks and investment firms under the Securities (Bank Giro Transactions) Act (*Wet giraal effectenverkeer*).'[179] As a result, according to the AFM, there are only two ways to achieve legal segregation under Dutch law: (i) via a special purpose vehicle – a foundation (*Stichting*) – holding customer assets and separated from the CASP and its creditors,[180] and (ii) holding customer assets with

[177] P Paech, 'Market needs as paradigm – breaking up the thinking on EU securities law' in P-H Conac, U Segna and L Thévenoz (eds), *Intermediated Securities: The Impact of the Geneva Securities Convention and the Future European Legislation* (Cambridge University Press, 2013) 31–34, describing how different jurisdictions adopted 'insular' approaches to define the legal position of account holders and account providers in respect of intermediated securities.

[178] For the discussion of property law aspects of crypto-assets, see J Woxholth, DA Zetzsche, RP Buckley and DW Arner, 'Competing claims to crypto-assets' (2023) 28 *Uniform Law Review* 226.

[179] AFM, Contact and frequently asked questions, www.afm.nl/en/sector/cryptopartijen/contact-qa. The AFM clarifies that if a CASP creates and uses a separate entity (SPV) for the purposes of compliance with segregation requirements, no separate CASP licence is required for such an SPV, because the latter merely serves as an 'extension' of the CASP.

[180] This practice is common for custody of securities. See T Struycken, 'Netherlands' in H Motani, K Wallin-Norman and T Struycken, 'Intermediated securities: Views from Europe' in L Gullifer and J Payne (eds), *Intermediated Securities: Legal Problems and Practical Issues* (Hart Publishing, 2010), observing that '[m]any large Dutch banks have each created a special purpose vehicle (*effectenbewaarbedrijf*) which, in a tripartite relationship between the investor, the bank and its special purpose

a foreign CASP, whose law does not necessitate the creation of a separate entity to achieve segregation. Regarding the second option, the AFM adds that this option should only be used if a Dutch CASP can demonstrate that this construction is, as a minimum, equivalent to the protection clients must have under Dutch law and that clients are clearly informed about the method of asset segregation and their rights in the event of loss of crypto-assets.[181]

To establish a firm foundation for customers' proprietary interests in intermediated crypto-assets, it may thus be essential for a state to supplement MiCAR with a comprehensive private law framework that enables legal segregation of intangible, indistinguishable and fungible crypto-assets, like bitcoin.[182] Belgium has recently amended its Civil Code so that the category of 'assets' or 'property' is broad and should be able to encompass incorporeals, including IP rights and crypto-assets.[183] The German Banking Act (*Kreditwesengesetz*) provides that '[t]he cryptographic instrument held for a customer within the framework of a qualified crypto custody transaction shall be deemed to belong to the customer.'[184] French law addresses the issue via administrative law – the Monetary and Financial Code (*Code monétaire et financier*).[185]

7.4.1.4. *Custodian Liability*

Article 75(8) contains the liability rule under which a CASP providing custody services shall be liable to its clients for the loss of any crypto-assets as a result of an incident that is attributable to it. While a situation where the tort is 'created' by

vehicle acts as intermediary for the benefit of the investors.' However, it should be noted that if client assets are transferred to a foundation, legal title to those assets is transferred to the foundation. This means that clients have *in personam* claims against the foundation. The protective effect is achieved only if the foundation has no creditors other than those whose assets were transferred for custody purposes.

[181] AFM, Contact and frequently asked questions. AFM seems to assume that property law effects are determined on the basis of the law of a Member State where a (foreign) CASP is located. However, one should keep in mind that this is not necessarily the case. The determination of property law applicable to crypto-assets is complicated by their (intangible and decentralised) nature and may not coincide with the CASP's registered office.

[182] M Dubovec, *The Law of Securities, Commodities and Bank Accounts: The Rights of Account Holders* (Edward Elgar Publishing 2014) 32, observing with respect to intermediated securities that '[i]n contemporary securities holding systems, [depositor proprietary interest] is classified differently in various jurisdictions in the catalogue of existing property rights and includes a co-ownership right in the pool of fluctuating assets, a co-possessory right to an immobilised security, and an equitable right that is based on a trust relationship or a security entitlement.' For the position of English law, The UK Law Commission, Digital Assets: Final Report. Law Com No 412 (2023), para 7.55, noting with respect to intermediated holding of crypto-assets on a consolidated unallocated basis that 'the best way to understand the interests of beneficiaries under such trusts are as rights of co-ownership in an equitable tenancy in common.'

[183] V Sagaert, 'The background and general principles of the new Belgian property law' (2021) 10(1) *European Property Law Journal* 3, 6.

[184] *Gesetz über das Kreditwesen (Kreditwesengesetz – KWG)*, § 46i. This provision adds that it shall not apply 'if the customer has given consent to dispose of the deposited asset for the account of the institution or third parties.'

[185] See *Code monétaire et financier*, Articles L54-10-1 and L552-2.

EU regulatory law may seem odd, it is not without precedent.[186] The custodian liability is capped at the market value of the lost crypto-assets at the time such loss occurred. Recital (83) specifies that CASPs should also be held liable 'for any losses resulting from an incident related to information and communication technology ('ICT'), including an incident resulting from a cyber-attack, theft or any malfunctions.' The same recital clarifies that this liability rule (and the whole MiCAR) does not apply to hardware and software providers of non-custodial wallets – wallets in which private keys remain in full control of the user and are not shared with or controlled by the service provider.

In principle, a CASP is only liable for losses arising from incidents that are attributable to it.[187] In civil law, a distinction is made between 'technical attribution' (ie, there must be *condicio sine qua non* causality as a prerequisite for liability) and 'normative attribution' (not only must there be *condicio sine qua non* causality, but the damages must also be normatively attributable, typically due to fault). Strict liability refers to damages that must be reimbursed because those damages are technically attributable, even if they are not normatively attributable. MiCAR does not create a strict liability regime. Attributable events are considered to be those that occur 'in the realm of the custodian's operations that the latter controls or may control.'[188] For example, among such events could be the loss of private keys due to hacks or exploits in the CASP's operations, the malfunction of the CASP's cybersecurity mechanisms, failure of hardware or software used by the CASP to 'store' client crypto-assets, failure to implement segregation measures, and the reuse of client assets.[189]

Incidents that are not technically and normatively attributable to the CASP include 'any event in respect of which the crypto-asset service provider demonstrates that it occurred independently of the provision of the relevant service, or independently of the operations of the crypto-asset service provider, such as a problem inherent in the operation of the distributed ledger that the crypto-asset service provider does not control.'[190] ESMA has interpreted this provision to mean that CASPs using permissionless DLT infrastructure, which they do not control or manage, are exempt from liability related to any loss connected to the operation of the underlying DLT.[191] As a result, losses arising from forks, bugs in the underlying distributed ledger, unpredictable governance decisions in decentralised arrangements, which are usually outside the control of the CASP should not be attributed to such a CASP.[192] Equally, events fully attributable to the negligence of the client

[186] See eg Regulation (EC) No 1060/2009 of the European Parliament and of the Council of 16 September 2009 on credit rating agencies, Article 35a (Civil liability).

[187] A similar liability regime is established in Article 21(12) AIFMD and Article 24 UCITS Directive.

[188] Zetzsche, Sinnig and Nikolakopoulou (n 122) 23.

[189] ibid.

[190] MiCAR, Article 75(8).

[191] Second Consultation Paper, para 62.

[192] In practice, a question may arise whether parties may agree on broader liability of CASPs (ie, non-fault liability). In our view, MiCAR only sets a baseline rule and does not prevent the parties from agreeing to a higher level of private law liability than is set out in Article 75(8).

(eg, a client gives away the password to his account, loses his phone with the saved password to his account, or instructs the CASP to transfer crypto-assets to a wrong blockchain address) should not trigger the liability of the CASP.

ESMA also observes that there is no legal basis to consider a permissionless DLT used by a CASP as a third-party provider, for which the CASP may be responsible under the outsourcing regime (see Article 73). According to ESMA, a permissionless DLT might be viewed as a type of 'common good' resource, whereas permissioned DLT operated by a commercial enterprise could constitute a product provided by a third-party provider.[193]

7.4.2. Operation of a Trading Platform for Crypto-assets

7.4.2.1. Introduction

MiCAR lays down a comprehensive framework for the operation of trading platforms for crypto-assets. According to Article 3(1)(18) MiCAR, operation of a trading platform for crypto-assets means 'the management of one or more multilateral systems, which bring together or facilitate the bringing together of multiple third-party purchasing and selling interests in crypto-assets, in the system and in accordance with its rules, in a way that results in a contract, either by exchanging crypto-assets for funds or by the exchange of crypto-assets for other crypto-assets'.

Given the significant role of crypto-asset trading platforms, the potential risks of money laundering and market abuse associated with their operation, the accumulation of substantial client assets in custody, and other factors, the regulation of CASPs operating trading platforms is extensive. MiCAR's rules cover the trading of crypto-assets that do not qualify as 'financial instruments' under existing financial regulations (ie, MiFID II). In recent years, the market for crypto-assets has seen significant activity concerning the establishment of crypto-asset trading platforms. Major regulated markets have also played an essential role in the emergence of various services related to crypto-assets. For instance, the Chicago Mercantile Exchange – an important derivatives marketplace – introduced trading in Bitcoin futures several years ago,[194] which was a crucial step towards integrating crypto-assets into traditional financial markets. This development has led to broader acceptance and increased trading opportunities for crypto-assets, providing investors with new options to diversify and take advantage of this emerging market.

The operation of a trading platform for crypto-assets can be compared to the operation of a stock exchange in traditional financial markets. This is why certain clarifications published by ESMA, such as those on the trading venue perimeter,

[193] Second Consultation Paper, para 63.
[194] CME Group, www.cmegroup.com/markets/cryptocurrencies/bitcoin/bitcoin.html.

are of relevance for the interpretation of MiCAR rules on trading platforms for crypto-assets.[195] Under MiCAR, a CASP operating a trading platform for crypto-assets must adhere to a stringent set of operating rules, detailed in Article 76. MiCAR's specific operating rules are designed to maintain transparency, fairness, and efficiency in the trading environment. These rules encompass various aspects, including customer due diligence (CDD) to address money laundering and terrorist financing concerns, the admission of crypto-assets, excluded categories of crypto-assets, fee structures, participation criteria, and conditions for trading suspension. In its regulatory approach, MiCAR shares some similarities with the MiFID II framework for regulated markets and multilateral trading facilities. Both aim to foster a secure, equitable, and well-regulated trading ecosystem.

7.4.2.2. Operating Rules

CASPs operating a crypto-asset trading platform are required to design and implement clear and transparent operating rules,[196] which must include the following key areas:

The *first key area* (Article 76(1)(a)) concerns the admission of new clients seeking to trade their crypto-assets on the trading platform operated by the CASP. The CASP's operating rules must include comprehensive CDD requirements aligned with the AML Directive. CDD must be rigorously enforced before any crypto-asset is admitted to the trading platform and must apply to persons wishing to become clients of the trading platform so as to make their assets eligible for trading. It is important to note that this required 'admission' process not only involves strict scrutiny by the CASP to verify the identity of potential clients (ie, 'client identification and verification process' within the CDD framework) but, as stipulated in the second subparagraph of Article 76(1), also mandates CASPs operating a trading platform to properly investigate the availability of a crypto-asset white paper. In the absence of such a white paper meeting the requirements of MiCAR (when the publication of the white paper is required under MiCAR), the crypto-asset should not be admitted for trading. This requirement closely parallels the obligations imposed on regulated markets when securities are first admitted for trading, which necessitate the drafting and publication of a prospectus compliant with the Prospectus Regulation.

Importantly, Article 76(1) states that a crypto-asset is not to be admitted to trading where no corresponding crypto-asset white paper has been published 'in the cases required by this Regulation'. In practice, a question will arise with regard to crypto-assets without an identifiable issuer (eg, Bitcoin) that might not have a MiCAR-compliant white paper.[197] For the purpose of providing information to

[195] ESMA, Final Report on ESMA's Opinion on the Trading Venue Perimeter, ESMA70-156-6360, 2 February 2023, clarifying, among other things, the concept of a 'system' and 'multiple third-party purchasing and selling interests'.

[196] MiCAR, Article 76(1).

[197] F Mendes Correia, 'Blockchain, Currency and Systemic Issues' in D Moura Vicente, R Soares Pereira and A Alves Leal (eds), *Legal Aspects of Autonomous Systems: A Comparative Approach* (Springer, 2024)

clients of the trading platform, a good argument can be made in favour of requiring it to publish a white paper for a crypto-asset without an identifiable issuer. Such a white paper should focus on the technical features, risks, and functionality of the crypto-asset and present information clearly and fairly. Finally, if a crypto-asset was admitted to trading on a trading platform before 30 December 2024 and continues to be traded thereafter, MiCAR grants a transitional exemption and provides trading platforms with a grace period until 31 December 2027 to comply with the white paper requirements.[198]

The *second key area* (Article 76(1)(b)) relates to the categories (if any) of crypto-assets that are ineligible for trading on the platform. These categories should be explicitly outlined and justified. For instance, the CASP should ensure that crypto-assets that may represent other types of (regulated) asset categories (such as financial instruments) are not eligible for trading on its platform.[199] Additionally, EMTs and ARTs issued by unauthorised issuers must not be admitted to trading.[200] If there is uncertainty about how a crypto-asset should be classified, the CASPs are expected to seek clarification from their NCAs. With this requirement, the gate-keeper role of the CASP is emphasised to prevent the trading platform from being used for trading instruments that by their nature would be subject to another set of rules and for the trading of non-compliant crypto-assets. Article 76(3) adds a limitation on the trading of crypto-assets with an inbuilt anonymisation function (so-called 'privacy tokens') like Monero (XMR) and Zcash (ZEC).

The *third key area* (Article 76(1)(c)) concerns the development and documentation of specific policies, procedures, and fee structures (if applicable) associated with the admission of crypto-assets to the trading platform. This includes transparent criteria for fee determination. These rules should also promote transparency regarding the economic model of the trading platform, enhancing the comparability of the services provided by the CASP with those offered by competing businesses.

The *fourth key area* (Article 76(1)(d)) pertains to the establishment of objective and non-discriminatory rules, along with proportionate criteria for participation in trading activities. These rules should facilitate fair and open access to the trading platform for all clients wishing to engage in trading, ensuring that no undue barriers to entry are imposed.

366, arguing that MiCAR's rules on offer and admission to trading on a trading platform, including a rule requiring the publication of a white paper, do not apply crypto-assets without an identifiable issuer. The reason for this is that Article 4(3)(b) excludes from Title II crypto-assets automatically created as a reward for the maintenance of the distributed ledger or the validation of transactions.

[198] MiCAR, Article 143(2)(b).

[199] See ESMA, Final Report, Guidelines on the conditions and criteria for the qualification of crypto-assets as financial instruments, ESMA75453128700-1323, 17 December 2024.

[200] ESMA, Public Statement on the provision of certain crypto-asset services in relation to non-MiCA compliant ARTs and EMTs, ESMA75-223375936-6099, 17 January 2025, stating that 'CASPs operating a trading platform for crypto-assets are expected to stop making all crypto-assets that would qualify as ARTs and EMTs but for which the issuer is not authorised in the EU ('non-MiCA compliant ARTs and EMTs') available for trading.'

The *fifth key area* (Article 76(1)(e)) of the mandatory rule book for trading platforms operated by CASPs concerns perhaps the most complex area: a comprehensive set of rules for non-discretionary and standardised procedures for the trading of products. These rules aim to ensure fair and orderly trading. The objectives of implementing non-discretionary and standardised procedures are manifold:

- First, these procedures aim to ensure a fair and orderly market where all participants have equal opportunities to trade. By removing discretionary decisions that could lead to biases or unfair advantages, these standardised rules promote transparency and foster trust in the trading environment.
- Second, non-discretionary procedures under MiCAR include the establishment of objective and transparent criteria for the admission and trading of crypto-assets. These criteria are designed to minimise the risk of market manipulation and ensure that only compliant and reliable crypto-assets are traded.[201] For instance, the requirement for a crypto-asset white paper akin to a prospectus in traditional securities markets ensures that all relevant information is disclosed to potential investors, fostering informed decision-making and addressing ubiquitous information asymmetries.
- Third, standardised procedures encompass clear guidelines for the settlement of trades, addressing potential settlement failures, and other contingencies. This ensures that all trades are executed efficiently and without undue delay, maintaining the smooth functioning of the market.
- Fourth and finally, the rules should set objective criteria to ensure the efficient execution of orders, minimising the potential for market manipulation and other unfair practices.

The rules concerning non-discretionary and standardised procedures are especially important in the context of crypto-assets, where the market is rapidly evolving and prone to high volatility. In this regard, MiFID II provides a relevant precedent. MiFID II emphasises the need for robust and transparent trading systems.[202] It mandates that trading venues operate under clear and consistent rules to prevent manipulative practices and ensure market integrity. By aligning the operating rules for crypto-assets with the principles and standards set forth in MiFID II, MiCAR aims to create a level playing field, protect investors and ensure market integrity.

The *sixth key area* (Article 76(1)(f)) concerns the conditions necessary to maintain the accessibility of crypto-assets for trading, including liquidity thresholds and periodic disclosure requirements. These conditions are crucial to maintaining the viability and transparency of the trading environment and are

[201] On the MiCAR's market abuse framework, see ch 9. See also ESMA, Final Report, Draft technical Standards specifying certain requirements in relation to the detection and prevention of market abuse under the Markets in Crypto Assets Regulation (MiCA), ESMA75-453128700-1278, 17 December 2024.

[202] MiFID II, Article 48.

particularly important to prevent certain crypto-assets from becoming effectively untradeable on the platform due to insufficient liquidity. Harmonising these rules should allow CASP-operated trading platforms to position themselves as markets offering consistently liquid trading in all listed assets, without exceptions. In practice, this requires the ongoing monitoring of the liquidity of traded crypto-assets and, where necessary, the temporary suspension of trading under Article 76(1)(g), should liquidity constraints arise for specific crypto-assets or entire categories thereof.

The *final key area* (Article 76(1)(g)) concerns the establishment of robust procedures to ensure the efficient settlement of both crypto-assets and funds. These should include mechanisms to address settlement failures and other contingencies.

As those familiar with the rules for organising trading platforms for financial instruments will notice, the requirements for a CASP's 'rule book' are largely inspired by the corresponding rules under MiFID II. This raises the question of whether it would have been better for the legislator to create rules specifically tailored to the unique features of the crypto-asset market. For example, the regulation on settlement procedures seems rather superficial, especially given the significant differences in how settlement works in crypto-asset markets, as compared to traditional financial markets. Settlement in financial instruments typically involves multiple intermediaries, such as central counterparties (CCPs), central securities depositories (CSDs), custodians, and payment systems. In contrast, trading platforms for crypto-assets may settle transactions off-chain or on-chain (ie, directly on the blockchain),[203] without the need for CCPs or CSDs. In many setups, the trading venue itself also acts as custodian and settlement agent.

It is also questionable whether a uniform (legal) framework already exists across all jurisdictions. In some jurisdictions, scholars argue for the classification of certain crypto-assets (depending on how the claim is recorded) as bearer assets, whereas in others, the body of legal thought in this area is far less developed. For discussion of custodian arrangements, see section 7.4.1.

The operating rules, in accordance with Article 76(4), must be drawn up in an official language of the home Member State or in a language customary in international finance. If the operation of a trading platform for crypto-assets is provided in another Member State, the operating rules must be drawn up in an official language of the host Member State or in a language customary in international finance.[204]

[203] Settlement of transaction on blockchain raises the issue of settlement finality. On this issue, see H Nabilou, 'Probabilistic Settlement Finality in Proof-of-Work Blockchains: Legal Considerations' (2022) SSRN publication, papers.ssrn.com/sol3/papers.cfm?abstract_id=4022676, arguing that 'given the decentralized nature of cryptocurrencies, defining the moment of finality in PoW blockchains, which may require a minimum level of institutional infrastructures and centralization to support the credibility of the finality, may face insurmountable challenges.'

[204] According to Recital (25), English is considered to be the language customary in the sphere of international finance.

7.4.2.3. Admission Procedures

Before admitting a crypto-asset to trading, CASPs operating a trading platform are required to ensure that the crypto-asset complies with the platform's operating rules and assess its suitability.[205] As part of this assessment, the CASP must evaluate the reliability of the technical solutions employed and any potential association with illicit or fraudulent activities, taking into account the experience, track record, and reputation of the issuer and its development team. Additionally, the CASP must assess the suitability of the crypto-asset, provided that it is neither an ART nor an EMT. This suitability assessment is general and concerns the admission of the crypto-asset to the platform. In this respect, it differs from the suitability assessment mandated by the rules concerning the provision of crypto advice and portfolio management, discussed below.[206]

As noted above, the operating rules of a trading platform must prevent the admission of crypto-assets with an inbuilt anonymisation function unless the holders of those crypto-assets and their transaction history can be identified by the CASP.[207] MiCAR does not provide a definition of an 'anonymisation function', but seems to suggest that such a function should be inbuilt in the crypto-asset itself. The limitation imposed on 'privacy tokens' extends to the settlement and exchange of funds in connection with the trading of the crypto-asset in question. In other words, if the settlement procedures of the platform allow funds to be cleared through crypto-assets, the purchaser of the crypto-asset traded on the platform must not be permitted to conceal their identity through the use of anonymous transactions related to the funds transfer.

7.4.2.4. No Dealing on Own Account by CASP Operating a Trading Platform

To manage the inherent conflicts of interest between proprietary trading activities and the operation of a trading platform for third parties, CASPs operating a trading platform for crypto-assets must, in accordance with Article 76(5), refrain from dealing on their own account on the platform they operate, including when they provide the exchange of crypto-assets for funds or other crypto-assets. Additionally, the rules regarding matched principal trading (which bear similarities to proprietary trading) establish clear boundaries, as set out in Article 76(6), and align with those set out in MiFID II. Article 4(1)(38) MiFID II defines 'matched principal trading' as follows:

> a transaction where the facilitator [the investment firm] interposes itself between the buyer and the seller to the transaction in such a way that it is never exposed to

[205] MiCAR, Article 76(2).

[206] MiCAR, Article 81. See also ESMA, Final Report, Guidelines specifying certain requirements of the Markets in Crypto Assets Regulation (MiCA) on investor protection – third package, ESMA35-1872330276-1936, 17 December 2024.

[207] MiCAR, Article 76(3).

market risk throughout the execution of the transaction, with both sides executed simultaneously, and where the transaction is concluded at a price where the facilitator makes no profit or loss, other than a previously disclosed commission, fee or charge for the transaction.

A matched principal trader faces significant operational and market risk. The need to conclude both sides of a transaction simultaneously requires an efficient process. Any errors can make the firm liable to clients and expose it to market risk. Although similar to firms executing orders, matched principal traders face additional operational and market risks.[208] Consequently, CASPs operating a trading platform are subject to strict requirements regarding matched principal trading. CASPs may only engage in matched principal trading with client consent. They must provide their home NCA with information explaining their use of matched principal trading, either on the occasion of the authorisation or at a later stage if the matched principal trading business is an extension of the business model that had been approved by the NCA at authorisation. The NCA shall specifically monitor the engagement of providers in such trading, ensuring compliance with the definition and the absence of conflicts of interest between service providers and their clients.

7.4.2.5. Requirements Concerning Trading Systems

In accordance with Article 76(7), additional requirements regarding the operation of trading platforms are imposed on CASPs. These requirements reflect those outlined in DORA while significantly complementing DORA's provisions. They are aligned with similar requirements for operators of MiFID II trading venues and incorporate lessons learned from managing trading platforms for financial instruments.

CASPs must ensure that their trading systems are resilient, designed to withstand and quickly recover from any operational disruption. This includes implementing robust infrastructure, redundancy measures, and the ability to manage various types of failures without significantly impacting the trading process.[209] The trading systems must also be capable of handling the maximum expected volume of orders and messages, particularly during peak trading times.[210] This requires adequate bandwidth, processing power, and scalability to accommodate sudden surges in activity without causing delays or system crashes.

Crypto-asset service providers must ensure that their systems can maintain orderly trading conditions even during periods of market stress.[211] This includes implementing mechanisms to prevent excessive volatility, effectively manage

[208] BJ Nieuwenhuizen, 'Prudential regulation of investment firms in the European Union' (ZIFO nr. 32) (2021), para 2.1.2.3.
[209] MiCAR, Article 76(7)(a).
[210] MiCAR, Article 76(7)(b).
[211] MiCAR, Article 76(7)(c).

liquidity, and ensure fair execution of trades, protecting the interests of all market participants. This suggests that the trading environment must be sufficiently scalable to address sudden growth in the number of trades, especially in times of high volatility and severe market stress. Additionally, trading systems should have safeguards to automatically reject orders that exceed established volume or price limits or that contain errors.[212] This helps prevent market manipulation, trading errors, and ensures that trading activities remain within acceptable boundaries, promoting market integrity.

CASPs must rigorously test their trading systems to ensure that they meet relevant operational and regulatory requirements.[213] This includes conducting stress tests, scenario analyses, and regular updates to software and hardware components to address potential vulnerabilities and enhance system performance. In the event of a system failure, service providers must have comprehensive business continuity arrangements in place to safeguard the uninterrupted provision of their services.[214] These arrangements include backup systems, disaster recovery procedures, and crisis management protocols to mitigate the impact of any disruptions and restore normal operations swiftly. In addition, MiCAR imposes a related requirement on CASPs operating a trading platform to maintain sufficient resources to enable them to report to their NCA at all times.[215]

CASPs must implement advanced monitoring and surveillance tools to prevent and detect any form of market abuse, such as insider trading or market manipulation.[216] This involves real-time analysis of trading patterns, anomaly detection algorithms, and robust reporting mechanisms to ensure compliance with regulatory standards. Trading systems must be designed to prevent their exploitation for illegal activities such as money laundering or terrorist financing.[217] This requires stringent CDD, transaction monitoring and reporting of suspicious activities to the relevant authorities. It should be noted that the last requirement diverges from the rules of MiFID II. This divergence stems from the significant concerns of EU authorities regarding the misuse of crypto-asset trading for money laundering and terrorist financing purposes.

7.4.2.6. Pre-trade and Post-trade Transparency

A high level of transparency is crucial to ensure that investors have accurate and sufficient information about the real and potential volume of transactions involving crypto-assets on trading platforms run by CASPs. Such transparency also helps

[212] MiCAR, Article 76(7)(d).
[213] MiCAR, Article 76(7)(e).
[214] MiCAR, Article 76(7)(f).
[215] MiCAR, Article 76(14).
[216] MiCAR, Article 76(7)(g). See also ESMA, Final Report, Draft technical Standards specifying certain requirements in relation to the detection and prevention of market abuse under the Markets in Crypto Assets Regulation (MiCA), ESMA75-453128700-1278, 17 December 2024.
[217] MiCAR, Article 76(7)(h).

maintain a fair competitive environment among trading platforms, preventing the fragmentation of liquidity from distorting the price discovery process for specific crypto-assets and putting investors at a disadvantage. Paragraphs (9) and (10) of Article 76 address pre- and post-trade transparency requirements imposed on operators of trading venues.[218]

CASPs that operate trading platforms are required to publicly disclose bid and ask prices, as well as the depth of trading interests at those prices (ie, volume or number of buy (bid) and sell (ask) orders placed at specific price levels on a trading platform), as advertised on their trading platforms.[219] This ensures market transparency, enabling all participants to view the prices at which others are willing to buy and sell crypto-assets. By providing this information to the public continuously during trading hours, CASPs contribute to a more open and equitable trading environment. This transparency is crucial for price discovery, as it allows market participants to make well-informed decisions based on the current supply and demand dynamics.

A CASP operating a trading platform is also required to make public the price, volume, and time of transactions executed in respect of crypto-assets traded on their platforms.[220] This means that every trade, regardless of its size, must be disclosed with its corresponding details. The purpose of this requirement is to ensure that all market participants have access to accurate and timely information about market activities. By making these transaction details public as close to real-time as technically possible, the providers help to maintain market integrity and prevent market manipulation. This real-time transparency allows participants to track market trends and activities, thereby promoting a more efficient and trustworthy trading environment.

The landscape of financial markets has evolved significantly, driven by the imperative for transparency and efficiency. One of the key developments has been the emergence of publication platforms that facilitate pre- and post-trade transparency. These platforms have not only enhanced market integrity but also paved the way for more in-depth regulations and the establishment of consolidated data tapes. A consolidated tape integrates data from various Authorised Publication Arrangements (APAs) into a single venue. This integration ensures that all market participants have access to a comprehensive and unified view of market activities, enhancing transparency and efficiency.[221] Consolidated data tapes are designed to provide a single, comprehensive source of real-time market data. This includes

[218] See further, Commission Delegated Regulation (EU) 2025/417 of 28 November 2024 supplementing Regulation (EU) 2023/1114 of the European Parliament and of the Council with regard to regulatory technical standards specifying the manner in which crypto-asset service providers operating a trading platform for crypto-assets are to present transparency data.

[219] MiCAR, Article 76(9).

[220] MiCAR, Article 76(10).

[221] See E Rogge, 'The MiFIR Review and a European Consolidated Tape: the next step towards a Capital Markets Union' (2023) 24 *ERA Forum* 119, highlighting that the objective of a consolidated tape is to provide a single reference source of information for transactions and therefore reduce fragmentation and information asymmetries.

information on pre-trade transparency (such as bid and ask prices and trading interests) and post-trade transparency (such as transaction prices, volumes, and times). By consolidating this data from multiple APAs, a consolidated tape ensures that market participants can access accurate and timely information, regardless of the trading venue.

While the requirement for consolidated tapes has become an integral part of traditional financial markets, it is not yet applicable to trading platforms in crypto-assets. Under MiCAR, CASPs are required to make public bid and ask prices, as well as transaction details, to ensure transparency and market integrity. However, the consolidation of this data into a single venue has not been mandated. As the crypto-asset market continues to grow and mature, the need for a unified and comprehensive view of market activities will become increasingly important. Implementing consolidated tapes for crypto-assets will enhance transparency, prevent market manipulation, and promote a more efficient and trustworthy trading environment.

7.4.2.7. Final Settlement (Finality of Transactions)

In accordance with Article 76(12), CASPs operating trading platforms are required to initiate the final settlement of a crypto-asset transaction on the distributed ledger within 24 hours of the transaction being executed on the trading platform.[222] This requirement underscores the importance of prompt settlement in maintaining market stability and trust among participants. The 24-hour settlement initiation window ensures that transactions are recorded and finalised swiftly, reducing the risk of discrepancies and potential disputes. That said, Recital (84) clarifies that 'the settlement might take longer as it is not controlled by the crypto-asset service provider operating the trading platform.' The actual settlement time would depend on the technological aspects of the blockchain used.

In cases where transactions are settled outside the distributed ledger (ie, off chain), CASPs are required to initiate the final settlement by the end of the day. This provision accommodates scenarios where off-ledger settlements are necessary while maintaining a strict timeline to uphold the principles of transparency and accountability. Settling transactions by the end of the day mitigates the risk of overnight exposure and potential market fluctuations that could impact the transaction's value. Additionally, enforcing strict timelines minimises counterparty risk, which is particularly crucial in the volatile crypto-asset market.

7.4.2.8. Transparent and Fair Fee Structures

CASPs operating a trading platform must uphold a high standard of transparency, fairness, and non-discrimination in their fee structures. This requirement is pivotal

[222] See also MiCAR, Recital (84).

for maintaining market integrity and fostering trust among market participants. Similar rules apply to trading venues under MiFID II.[223]

In accordance with Article 76(13), CASPs are obligated to clearly disclose all fees associated with their services. This includes, but is not limited to, transaction fees, withdrawal fees, deposit fees, and any other charges that may be levied on users. The goal is to ensure that traders and investors have a comprehensive understanding of the costs involved, allowing them to make informed decisions. Transparency in fee structures helps eliminate hidden charges and provides clarity, contributing to a more open and trustworthy trading environment.

Fairness in fee structures means that fees must be equitable and justifiable. This includes ensuring that fees are proportionate to the services provided and that there is no undue burden placed on any particular group of users. CASPs must avoid favouritism and ensure that all users, regardless of their trading volume or frequency, are subject to the same fee structures. This helps to prevent any competitive disadvantages and promotes a level playing field for all market participants. Non-discriminatory fee structures are essential to prevent any form of bias or preferential treatment. CASPs must ensure that their fees do not discriminate against any user based on factors such as the size of the transaction, the type of crypto-asset being traded, or the geographical location of the user.

A crucial aspect of transparent, fair, and non-discriminatory fee structures is their role in preventing disorderly trading conditions and market abuse. CASPs must ensure that their fee structures do not incentivise behaviour that could lead to market manipulation or other abusive practices. This includes avoiding fee models that encourage excessive trading, the placement of frivolous orders, or the cancellation and modification of orders in a manner that could disrupt the market. Transparent, fair, and non-discriminatory fee structures not only protect individual traders but also uphold the overall integrity of the crypto-asset market.

7.4.2.9. Record Keeping and Data Storage

CASPs operating trading platforms, in accordance with Article 76(15), are required to adhere to stringent data retention and accessibility standards to support regulatory oversight. They must ensure that all relevant data relating to orders in crypto-assets advertised and executed through their systems is kept available to the NCA for a minimum period of five years. This obligation is crucial for enabling effective monitoring of trading activities and ensuring market integrity.

The relevant data that CASPs are required to retain must encompass comprehensive details about each order. This includes, but is not limited to, the characteristics of the order, such as price, volume, and order type, as well as timestamps for order

[223] MiFID II, Article 48(9). See also Commission Delegated Regulation (EU) 2017/573 of 6 June 2016 supplementing Directive 2014/65/EU of the European Parliament and of the Council on markets in financial instruments with regard to regulatory technical standards on requirements to ensure fair and non-discriminatory co-location services and fee structures.

submission, modification, and execution. Furthermore, CASPs must maintain data linking each order with the executed transactions resulting from that order, providing a clear audit trail that facilitates the tracking of trading patterns and behaviours.

To enhance regulatory oversight, CASPs must either store this data in a readily accessible format or provide the competent authority with direct access to their order book. This access allows the authority to monitor trading activity in real time, thereby enabling the early detection and prevention of potential market abuses such as insider trading, market manipulation, and other forms of fraudulent activity.

7.4.3. Exchange of Crypto-assets for Funds or Other Crypto-assets

According to Article 3(1)(19) and Article 3(1)(20) MiCAR, the exchange service entails the conclusion of purchase or sale contracts concerning crypto-assets with clients for funds or other crypto-assets using proprietary capital. A reference to 'proprietary capital' means that the CASP trades on its own account and with its own capital rather than merely facilitates trades between clients or executes client orders on third-party platforms. The CASP buys and sells crypto-assets directly from or to clients using its own holdings, rather than simply matches buy and sell orders between third parties. This creates an increased risk exposure for the CASP, as it is taking on the risk of holding crypto-assets and participating directly in the market rather than acting merely as a facilitator or intermediary. This risk is counterbalanced by the right of the CASP to determine the price, as discussed further below.

The crypto-asset service of 'exchange of crypto-assets for funds or other crypto-assets' is unique and specific to MiCAR. It can be compared to the activity of currency exchanges. Indeed, Recital (87) notes that 'in exchanging crypto-assets for funds or other crypto-assets, the price for such exchanges is freely determined by the crypto-asset service provider as a currency exchange.' Notably, the same recital clarifies that the exchange of crypto-assets for funds or other crypto-assets when made by the issuer or offeror should not be a crypto-asset service.[224] Nevertheless, such an issuance or offer remains subject to the relevant provisions of MiCAR (eg, Title II for crypto-assets other than ARTs and EMTs).

To ensure customer protection, CASPs that provide exchange services to their clients must publish either a firm price of the crypto-assets (ie, firm quotes) or a method for determining the price of the crypto-assets that they propose to exchange for funds or other crypto-assets, and any applicable limit determined

[224] By excluding issuers or offerors from the scope of 'exchange services', MiCAR aims to avoid overregulation of issuance activities while maintaining regulatory oversight over the trading of crypto-assets.

by that CASP on the amount to be exchanged.[225] Publication of relevant prices or a clear methodology for their determination is crucial for transparency, market efficiency and integrity, and for safeguarding clients' interests. CASPs must ensure that exchange prices and methodology are available and visible in a prominent place on their website at all times, without registration.[226] CASPs must also establish a non-discriminatory commercial policy that indicates, in particular, the type of clients they agree to transact with and the conditions that shall be met by these clients.[227]

Client orders must be executed at the prices displayed at the time when the order for exchange is final. Crypto-asset service providers shall inform their clients of the conditions for their order to be deemed final.[228] MiCAR requires post-trade transparency. For CASPs offering exchange services, this means that information about the transactions concluded by them (ie, transaction volume and prices) must be published.[229] This requirement lacks sufficient detail, compared to the post-trade transparency requirements for CASPs operating trading platforms, which are required to make transaction details (ie, price, volume and time of transactions) public as close to real time as is technically possible.[230] Information published by CASPs should remain public for a sufficient time, and in any case, at least until midnight of the following business day.[231]

7.4.4. Execution of Orders for Crypto-assets on Behalf of Clients

According to Article 3(1)(21), this service means 'the conclusion of agreements, on behalf of clients, to purchase or sell one or more crypto-assets or the subscription on behalf of clients for one or more crypto-assets, and includes the conclusion of contracts to sell crypto-assets at the moment of their offer to the public or admission to trading'. This crypto-asset service entails the execution of buy/sell transactions on behalf of clients. Recital (87) points out that when a CASP executing orders for crypto-assets on behalf of clients is the client's counterparty, there might be similarities with the services of exchanging crypto-assets for funds or other crypto-assets. However, in the case of the execution of orders service, the CASP must always ensure that it obtains the best possible result for its client, including when it acts as the client's counterparty, in line with its best execution

[225] MiCAR, Article 77(2).
[226] See AFM, Study into advertisements and information disclosure on costs by CASPs, January 2025, observing that in some cases, CASPs did not display any policies on pricing, costs and/or fees on the public website, while in other instances this information was spread across the website as opposed to being posted on one single page.
[227] MiCAR, Article 77(1).
[228] MiCAR, Article 77(3).
[229] MiCAR, Recital (85) and Article 77(4).
[230] MiCAR, Article 76(10).
[231] ESMA, MiCAR Q&A, ESMA_QA_2181, 14 May 2024.

policy.[232] This is the key requirement that distinguishes this crypto-asset service from the previously discussed exchange service, where the price is determined solely by the CASP.

CASPs that execute orders for crypto-assets on behalf of clients must draw up an execution policy and always aim to obtain the best possible result for their clients, including when they act as the client's counterparty.[233] This requirement also applies in situations where a CASP executes the order on a trading platform operated by another CASP. The best-possible-result requirement under MiCAR is similar to the requirement found in Article 27 MiFID II, which imposes on investment firms an obligation to execute orders on terms most favourable to their clients. Article 78(1) mentions among the relevant factors the price, costs, speed, likelihood of execution and settlement, size, nature and conditions of custody of the crypto-assets or any other consideration relevant to the execution of the order. These factors may be disregarded if the client gives specific execution-related instructions.

When a CASP executes a client order, selecting the right execution venue involves evaluating a variety of factors, including the price of the relevant crypto-asset, the liquidity available at the venue, and the transaction costs charged by the venues. As such, choosing the appropriate execution venue is a critical task for the CASP in order to achieve the best possible outcome for clients. This decision is made even more complex by the fragmented nature of the crypto-asset market, which often results in a broad choice of venues where a CASP can send an order to buy or sell a crypto-asset.

To ensure compliance with the best-possible-result requirement, CASPs must establish and implement effective execution arrangements.[234] This includes the establishment and execution of an order execution policy, which must, among other things, provide for the prompt, fair and expeditious execution of client orders and prevent the misuse by the CASPs' employees of any information relating to client orders.[235] This is in line with the prohibition of market abuse, and specifically the prohibition of insider dealing (see further chapter nine of this book). When a CASP transmits clients' orders to other CASPs as part of the execution arrangements, it needs to implement procedures for the prompt and proper sending of those orders and must not receive any monetary or non-monetary benefits for transmitting those orders to any particular trading platform for crypto-assets or any other CASP.[236]

[232] When interpreting and applying this requirement and given the similarity with Article 27 MiFID II, one should take into account ESMA's Final Report, Technical Standards specifying the criteria for establishing and assessing the effectiveness of investment firms' order execution policies, ESMA35-335435667-6253, 10 April 2025.

[233] MiCAR, Recital (86).

[234] MiCAR, Article 78(2).

[235] CASPs are subject to an ongoing obligation to monitor the effectiveness of their order execution arrangements and order execution policy in order to identify and, where appropriate, correct any deficiencies in that respect. In particular, they shall assess, on a regular basis, whether the execution venues included in the order execution policy provide for the best possible result for clients or whether they need to make changes to their order execution arrangements. See MiCAR, Article 78(6).

[236] MiCAR, Recital (86).

This limitation aims to guarantee compliance with the best-possible-result rule, and to minimise risks of collusion and market abuse. On this point, ESMA stressed that competent authorities should pay particular attention to situations in which CASPs engaged in brokerage activities involving executing orders on behalf of clients use platforms (execution venues) that are part of the same group.[237] It also observed that where an execution venue might enable the CASP to obtain the best possible result for one crypto-asset, that same execution venue may result in worse execution quality for other crypto-assets. Therefore, a CASP should, 'initially and periodically, be aware of the available execution venues and assess the benefits and additional costs, that would be passed on to its clients, of adding additional execution venues.'[238] It will usually be the case that transactions are executed on trading platforms. Nevertheless, client orders can be executed outside a trading platform. Yet, in such a case, CASPs must obtain express consent from their clients before proceeding with order execution.[239]

Further, to promote transparency, CASPs are subject to an obligation to provide appropriate and detailed information to their clients on their order execution policy and any material change with respect to such policy.[240] This information should be both clear and sufficient, so that the clients can understand how their orders will be executed. At the client request, CASPs must be able to demonstrate that they have executed client orders in full compliance with their order execution policy.[241]

CASPs offering the execution services to their clients are subject to an ongoing obligation to monitor the effectiveness of their order execution arrangements and order execution policy. This monitoring should allow them to identify and, where appropriate, correct any deficiencies in that respect. They must assess, on a regular basis, whether the execution venues included in the order execution policy provide for the best possible result for clients or whether they need to make changes to their order execution arrangements.[242]

7.4.5. Placing of Crypto-assets

According to Article 3(1)(22), 'placing of crypto-assets' refers to 'the marketing, on behalf of or for the account of the offeror or a party related to the offeror, of crypto-assets to purchasers.' This service is considered equivalent to the underwriting or placing of financial instruments, whether on a firm commitment basis or not.[243]

[237] ESMA, Opinion to support the convergent application of MiCA, ESMA75-453128700-1048, 31 July 2024.

[238] ibid.

[239] MiCAR, Article 78(5). This consent can be either in the form of a general agreement or with respect to individual transactions.

[240] MiCAR, Article 78(3).

[241] MiCAR, Article 78(4).

[242] MiCAR, Article 78(6).

[243] MiCAR, Article 60(3)(e).

In traditional financial markets, the placing of financial instruments is often used to raise capital or facilitate the distribution of securities.[244] Thus, this service relates to the phase of the offering of assets on the market – 'the phase in which issues relating to the protection of investors arise more directly, such as: transparency, conflicts of interest, appropriateness and suitability, inducements, etc.'[245]

Before entering into an agreement for the placing of crypto-assets, a CASP must communicate specific information to the offeror, the person seeking admission to trading, or any third party acting on their behalf. This information includes: (a) the type of placement under consideration, including whether a minimum amount of purchase is guaranteed or not, (b) an indication of the amount of transaction fees associated with the proposed placing, (c) the likely timing, process and price for the proposed operation, and (d) information about the targeted purchasers.[246]

If the placing of crypto-assets is combined with other crypto-asset services (eg, crypto advice, execution of orders for crypto-assets on behalf of clients), there is heightened risk of conflicts of interest (see section 7.3.6). This is why, to protect clients' interests, a CASP offering placing services must establish specific and adequate procedures to identify, prevent, manage, and disclose any conflicts of interest.[247] These conflicts may arise, for example, when the CASP places crypto-assets with its own clients, when the proposed price for the placing of crypto-assets is overestimated or underestimated, or when incentives (monetary or non-monetary) are paid or granted by the offeror to the CASP, thereby potentially influencing pricing or market access.[248] In cases where a CASP cannot manage a conflict of interest by way of implementing appropriate procedures, it must not engage in the operation.

7.4.6. Reception and Transmission of Orders for Crypto-assets on Behalf of Clients

According to Article 3(1)(23), the reception and transmission of orders (RTO) for crypto-assets on behalf of clients refers to 'the reception from a person of an order to purchase or sell one or more crypto-assets or to subscribe for one or more

[244] MiFID II, Annex I, Section A, (6) and (7).

[245] F Annunziata, 'Investment services and investment funds', in F Fabbrini and M Ventoruzzo (eds), *Research Handbook on EU Economic Law* (Edward Elgar, 2019) 487.

[246] MiCAR, Article 79(1).

[247] See Draft RTS pursuant to Article 72(5) of MiCAR, www.esma.europa.eu/sites/default/files/2024-05/ESMA35-1872330276-1670_MiCA_Final_report_on_RTS_on_CoIs.pdf. ESMA, Opinion on regulatory technical standards specifying certain requirements in relation to conflicts of interest for crypto-asset service providers under the Markets in Crypto-Assets Regulation (MiCA), ESMA35-1872330276-2021, 24 January 2025, www.esma.europa.eu/sites/default/files/2025-01/ESMA35-1872330276-2021_Opinion_on_amendments_to_RTS_on_CoIs_of_CASPs_under_MiCA.pdf.

[248] MiCAR, Article 79(2).

crypto-assets and the transmission of that order to a third party for execution'. This crypto-asset service is deemed equivalent to the reception and transmission of orders in relation to one or more financial instruments.[249]

This service involves a CASP receiving client orders to buy or sell crypto-assets and then transmitting them to another party for execution. Unlike the execution of orders on behalf of clients (section 7.4.4), the reception and transmission of orders does not involve directly executing trades but rather forwarding orders to another entity that executes them. In other words, the CASP does not itself carry out the execution of the transaction on behalf of the client. Instead, the CASP acts as a conduit, forwarding the client's order to a third party – such as another CASP – that performs the actual trade. The intermediary role of the CASP under RTO is therefore more limited in scope and responsibility compared to execution services. RTO is also distinct from the placing of crypto-assets (see section 7.4.5), since placing involves the marketing of crypto-assets on behalf of or for the account of the offeror, while RTO concerns secondary market order flow without promotional activity. Unlike crypto advice (see section 7.4.7.1), RTO is a non-advisory service and does not involve the provision of personal recommendations to the client. A clear distinction should also be made between RTO and the operation of a trading platform for crypto-assets (see section 7.4.2). More specifically, trading platforms should not be authorised as RTO but as trading venues. In particular, systems broadcasting trading interests to multiple clients, with those clients being able to interact within the system or through the software with those trading interests, are likely to constitute a trading platform for crypto-assets in the MiCAR sense.

According to Article 80(1), CASPs receiving and transmitting orders for crypto-assets on behalf of clients must 'establish and implement procedures and arrangements that provide for the prompt and proper transmission of client orders for execution on a trading platform for crypto-assets or to another crypto-asset service provider.' To avoid conflicts of interest and protect clients, CASPs offering this service are prohibited from receiving any remuneration, discount or non monetary benefit in return for routing orders received from clients to a particular trading platform for crypto-assets or to another crypto-asset service provider.[250] This is commonly referred to as a 'payment for order flow' (PFOF) prohibition – a measure aimed at eliminating incentives that may undermine client trust. The prohibition is broadly aligned with MiFID II and MiFIR principles on inducements and fair treatment of clients.[251]

[249] MiCAR, Article 60(3)(f).

[250] MiCAR, Article 80(2).

[251] MiFIR, Article 39(a), according to which investment firms 'shall not receive any fee, commission or non-monetary benefit from any third party for executing orders from those clients on a particular execution venue or for forwarding orders of those clients to any third party for their execution on a particular execution venue ('payment for order flow').'

Article 80(2) adds that CASPs engaged in the reception and transmission of orders must not misuse information relating to pending client orders, and must take all reasonable steps to prevent the misuse of such information by any of their employees. This requirement seeks to reduce the risks of price manipulation and preferential treatment, both of which can amount to market abuse prohibited under MiCAR (eg, front-running). In this respect, Chapter nine of this book explains that trading information, including information related to orders, may present significant value. A substantial purchase or sale order can drive the price up or down, particularly when the trading volume of the relevant crypto-asset is low.

7.4.7. Providing Advice on Crypto-assets and Providing Portfolio Management of Crypto-assets

7.4.7.1. Crypto Advice

The service of providing advice on crypto-assets refers to 'offering, giving or agreeing to give personalised recommendations to a client, either at the client's request or on the initiative of the crypto-asset service provider providing the advice, in respect of one or more transactions relating to crypto-assets, or the use of crypto-asset services'.[252] This definition highlights the personalised and tailored nature of the service, indicating that the advice is not general or standard but is specific to the client's individual circumstances. This type of service is treated as equivalent to investment advice under MiFID II.[253] As such, the positions taken by ESMA on investment advice under MiFID II may be relevant to the interpretation and application of MiCAR.[254]

The main obligation of CASPs providing crypto advice is to assess whether the crypto-asset services or crypto-assets are *suitable* for their clients or prospective clients. The suitability assessment aims to enable CASPs to act in the best interests of their clients. They must take into account clients' knowledge and experience in investing in crypto-assets, their investment objectives, including risk tolerance, and their financial situation, including their ability to bear losses.[255]

To carry out the suitability assessment, CASPs need to obtain relevant information from their clients or prospective clients. This ensures that the advice is based on a comprehensive understanding of the client's background, financial situation and risk appetite. This information should cover: (i) knowledge of, and experience

[252] MiCAR, Article 3(1)(24).

[253] MiCAR, Article 60(3)(g).

[254] ESMA, Supervisory Briefing on understanding the definition of advice under MiFID II, ESMA35-43-3861, 11 July 2023, highlighting, among other things, that it is important 'to take into account whether it would be reasonable to think that a personal recommendation is being made in determining whether investment advice is being given.'

[255] MiCAR, Article 81(1).

in, investing, including in crypto-assets (hence, investments in other assets, such as financial instruments should also be considered), (ii) investment objectives, including risk tolerance, (iii) financial situation, including ability to bear losses, and (iv) basic understanding of the risks involved in purchasing crypto-assets.[256] In any case, CASPs must warn their clients or prospective clients that: (a) the value of crypto-assets might fluctuate; (b) there could be partial or total losses related to crypto-assets; (c) the crypto-assets might be illiquid; (d) (where applicable) the crypto-assets are not covered by investor compensation schemes; (e) the crypto-assets are not subject to a deposit protection scheme.[257]

CASPs are also required to inform prospective clients whether the advice is provided on an independent basis (ie, based on the assessment of a wide range of crypto-assets available on the market, which must be sufficiently diverse to ensure that the client's investment objectives can be suitably met) or on a non-independent basis (ie, entailing a restricted analysis of different crypto-assets, including where the advice is limited to crypto-assets issued or offered by entities having close links with the CASP).[258] In the latter case, the CASP is allowed to receive inducements from a third party, provided that such inducements are designed to enhance the quality of the relevant service, and that they do not impair compliance with the CASP's duty to act in the client's best interests.[259] Thus, clients benefit from independent advice, because it gives them access to a potentially wider selection of products or services.

ESMA has pointed out that there are increased risks of dealing with crypto-assets arising from clients' insufficient knowledge (especially among retail investors), increased accessibility of crypto-asset services, constant and swift creation of new crypto-assets, and high volatility of their value. This is why, ESMA stressed that 'it is crucial that staff of [CASPs] who give advice on crypto-assets or information about crypto-assets or crypto-asset services possess, and also maintain, an appropriate level of knowledge and competence to fulfil their obligations set out under MiCA, such as the requirement to act in the best interests of clients.'[260]

If the suitability assessment shows that a specific crypto-asset or a category of crypto-assets, or a crypto-asset service is unsuitable for a client, or should the information provided by the client or potential client be insufficient to make an adequate determination of suitability, the CASP must refrain from recommending it to the client.[261] If the suitability assessment is positive, the CASP must provide its client with the report on suitability specifying the advice given and how that advice

[256] MiCAR, Article 81(8).
[257] MiCAR, Article 81(9).
[258] MiCAR, Article 81(2)–(3).
[259] MiCAR, Article 81(6).
[260] ESMA, Consultation Paper, Guidelines for the criteria on the assessment of knowledge and competence under the Markets in Crypto Assets Regulation (MiCA), ESMA35-1872330276-2004, 17 February 2025.
[261] MiCAR, Article 81(11).

meets the preferences, objectives and other characteristics of the client.[262] This report serves as a record of the advisory process, helping ensure accountability and transparency for the client and the CASP. It is also important for supervisory purposes.

7.4.7.2. Portfolio Management

According to Article 3(1)(25), 'providing portfolio management of crypto-assets' refers to 'managing portfolios in accordance with mandates given by clients on a discretionary client-by-client basis where such portfolios include one or more crypto-assets'. This definition closely resembles the one found in Article 4(1)(8) MiFID II. In both cases, portfolio management is characterised by the discretionary nature of the mandate between the client and the firm. This means that investment decisions are implemented without any intervention by the client, other than the mandate in place stipulating the nature and details of the discretionary service to be provided. This is the key difference between portfolio management and other services covered by the MiCAR/MiFID II.

For example, under 'crypto advice' service, discussed above, the advisor only provides personal recommendations, whereas the final investment decision rests with the client. If client action is required prior to each transaction, the activity performed by the firm should not be qualified as portfolio management. This clarification should play a central role in determining the relevant type of crypto-asset service. Take, for instance, 'copy trading services', also referred to as 'auto trading services'.[263] If the CASP offers clients an opportunity to choose one or more third parties that provide trade signals and transforms each individual signal received into a buy or sell order executed by the CASP itself – without further intervention from the client, this arrangement is likely to fall within the service of 'portfolio management'. This is because the CASP exercises investment discretion by automatically executing the trade signals of third parties. Where no automatic order execution occurs because client action is required prior to each transaction being executed, the activity will not amount to portfolio management and, depending on the interaction with the client, other crypto-asset services could still be relevant (eg, investment advice, RTO, execution of orders). The assessment should be made on a case-by-case basis.

There are notable similarities between portfolio management and crypto advice. This is why both portfolio management and crypto advice are governed by the same article in MiCAR – Article 81. The decision to subject both types of crypto-asset services to the same article was made for efficiency reasons, as some

[262] MiCAR, Article 81(13).

[263] See MiFID Questions and Answers, Investor Protection & Intermediaries, 2012, Question 9: Article 4(1)(9) of MiFID – Automatic execution of trade signals; Supervisory Briefing on supervisory expectations in relation to firms offering copy trading services, 2023.

rules apply to both types of services. Among these rules are the rules on the suitability assessment[264] and the obligation to provide relevant warnings.[265]

Other provisions, however, are unique to portfolio management, and their inclusion in the same article as crypto advice may be questioned from the perspective of legislative drafting. For example, CASPs offering this service are prohibited from accepting any fees, commissions or any monetary or non-monetary benefits provided by an issuer, offeror, person seeking admission to trading, or any third party, in relation to the provision of portfolio management of crypto-assets to their clients.[266] Another specific requirement for CASPs offering portfolio management is that they must provide their clients with periodic statements of the portfolio management activities carried out on their behalf. MiCAR states that these statements must be provided every three months, unless the clients have access to an online system with up-to-date valuations of the portfolio and updated information on the suitability assessment, *and* there is evidence that the client has accessed the valuation at least once during the relevant quarter.[267]

7.4.8. Providing Transfer Services for Crypto-assets on Behalf of Clients

MiCAR defines 'providing transfer services for crypto-assets on behalf of clients' as 'providing services of transfer, on behalf of a natural or legal person, of crypto-assets from one distributed ledger address or account to another'. This service is frequently offered in combination with other crypto-asset services, such as custody, exchange of crypto-assets for funds or other crypto-assets, or the execution of orders on behalf of clients.[268] In practice, CASPs will often require an authorisation to provide transfer services to be able to offer these other services.[269]

The key requirement for CASPs offering transfer services is the conclusion of an agreement with the client specifying their duties and responsibilities. Such an agreement must contain at least the following: (a) identities of parties to the agreement; (b) description of the modalities of the transfer service provided; (c) description of the security systems used by the CASP; (d) fees applied by the CASP; and (e) applicable law.[270]

In its Guidelines, ESMA sets information requirements for CASPs offering transfer services. It covers information to be provided: (i) before entering into an

[264] MiCAR, Article 81(1).
[265] MiCAR, Article 81(9).
[266] MiCAR, Article 81(5).
[267] MiCAR, Article 81(14).
[268] MiCAR, Recital (93).
[269] See ESMA, ESMA_QA_2071, 20 June 2024, noting the self-standing nature of transfer services and clarifying that 'if the provision of a service falls under the definition of providing transfer services, despite being regarded as part of another crypto-asset service, it is subject to Article 59 on authorisation and Article 82 on providing transfer services, including the guidelines developed under Article 82(2).'
[270] MiCAR, Article 82(1).

agreement with a client, (ii) after receipt of an instruction to transfer crypto-assets, but before the execution of the transfer of crypto-assets, and (iii) after execution of individual transfers for crypto-assets.

- First, CASPs are expected to establish, implement and maintain adequate policies and procedures to ensure that, in good time before the client enters into any agreement for the provision of transfer services, they provide the client, in an electronic format, with the information and conditions related to the transfer services for crypto-assets. Such policies should include, inter alia, a description of the form of and procedure for initiating or consenting to a transfer of crypto-assets and withdrawing an instruction or consent; conditions under which the CASP may reject an instruction to carry out a transfer of crypto-assets; maximum execution time for the provision of transfer services; the means and time period within which the client is to notify the CASP of any unauthorised or incorrectly initiated or executed transfers of crypto-assets as well as the crypto-asset service provider's liability, including maximum amount thereof, for unauthorised or incorrectly initiated or executed transfers, etc.[271]
- Second, CASPs should establish, implement and maintain adequate policies and procedures to ensure that, after receiving an instruction to transfer crypto-assets but before executing the transfer, the CASPs provide their clients with specific information, such as a brief and standardised warning as to whether and when the crypto-asset transfer will be irreversible or sufficiently irreversible.[272]
- Third, following the execution of individual transfers for crypto-assets, CASPs should provide their clients with information concerning the names of the originator and the beneficiary, distributed ledger addresses of the originator and beneficiary, the amount and types of crypto-assets transferred or received, etc.[273]

Importantly, CASPs engaged in transfer services must take into account and fully comply with the revised Transfer of Funds Regulation (TFR).[274] This regulation lays down obligations of CASPs dealing with the originator of a transfer, the transfer's beneficiary and those acting as an intermediary (so-called 'travel rule').[275] These obligations mainly relate to the request and collection of information.

[271] ESMA, Guidelines on the procedures and policies, including the rights of clients, in the context of transfer services for crypto-assets under the Markets in Crypto Assets Regulation (MiCA) on investor protection, ESMA35-1872330276-2032, 26 February 2025, para 5.1.

[272] ibid para 5.2.

[273] ibid.

[274] Regulation (EU) 2023/1113 of the European Parliament and of the Council of 31 May 2023 on information accompanying transfers of funds and certain crypto-assets and amending Directive (EU) 2015/849.

[275] ibid Chapter III.

Their primary objective is 'to make the abuse of funds and certain crypto-asset transfers for terrorist financing and other financial crime purposes more difficult, and to enable relevant authorities to fully trace such transfers where this is necessary to prevent, detect or investigate money laundering and terrorism financing (ML/TF).'[276] In line with TFR, CASPs must adopt risk-based procedures to determine whether a transfer should be executed, rejected, or suspended in light of these objectives.

Finally, as noted above, it is important to point out that, depending on the precise features of the services associated with the transfer of EMTs, such services could fall under the definition of payment services under PSD2. In such cases, those transfers should be provided by an entity authorised to provide such payment services in accordance with PSD2.

7.5. Conclusion

CASPs are key players in the crypto markets. In current practice, CASPs typically perform multiple functions and offer various services: custody, execution of orders, etc. In fact, as noted earlier, centralised firms accumulate most of the liquidity in the crypto markets. This is why their regulation occupies a major place in MiCAR. The regulation of CASPs under Title V is comprehensive and aims to ensure a robust framework for the supervision of various crypto-asset services. In this chapter of the book, we examined the rules covering the access of firms to the EU crypto-markets, discussed general requirements applicable to all crypto-asset service providers, and examined the obligations of CASPs offering specific services.

The legislator intentionally and substantially limited the access of third-country firms to the EU crypto-asset service market. As a general rule, firms must be authorised by a national authority before they start providing services in the European Union. Once authorised, they fall within the European 'passport system'. This system enables the establishment of branches in other EU Member States and the provision of crypto-asset services across borders, without the need for a separate authorisation (yet subject to applicable notification requirements). The authorisation process is designed to ensure that only entities meeting the standards of competence, integrity, and financial soundness are permitted to operate. But once they are considered in compliance with these standards, they are able to establish a regional (EU) footprint in a relatively flexible way. This system is instrumental in promoting a more integrated and efficient crypto-asset market, fostering competition and innovation.

[276] EBA, Guidelines on information requirements in relation to transfers of funds and certain crypto-assets transfers under Regulation (EU) 2023/1113, EBA/GL/2024/11, 4 July 2024.

The effectiveness of the described system depends on a strict interpretation of the reverse solicitation exemption (section 7.2.2.1), which must be closely monitored. As ESMA has noted, it is important to be vigilant regarding the practice of global crypto giants accessing the EU market through an authorised firm (eg, a CASP offering execution services as a crypto broker), while executing orders on a trading platform registered and operated offshore. In such cases, groups of companies can acquire access to EU clients while minimising the impact of MiCAR – and its safeguards for market participants – on their activities.[277]

The regulation of CASPs under MiCAR is complex. This complexity stems from the novelty of business models adopted by CASPs, the technological aspects of the provision of crypto-asset services, uncertainties regarding the scope and classification of services, and the potential overlap or simultaneous application of multiple legal instruments, such as MiCAR, PSD2, EMD2, DORA and TFR. Crypto-asset services provided by CASPs must be assessed and qualified on a case-by-case basis. Potential challenges may arise in delineating specific services and assigning the correct legal qualification to them. This should be a priority when establishing a harmonised approach to the application and interpretation of MiCAR. Another priority should be the creation of coherent supervisory practices across all Member States.

[277] See ESMA, Opinion to support the convergent application of MiCA, ESMA75-453128700-1048, 31 July 2024.

8

Significant ARTs, EMTs and CASPs

MARISA MACHACEK

8.1. Introduction

This chapter will take a closer look at tokens and participants in the crypto space that will be considered 'significant' under the new rules of MiCAR. The idea of 'significance' – meaning that these instruments and market players hold a certain level of importance and considerable influence – has, to some degree, been a response to discussions prompted by the Libra/Diem stablecoin project. This project could have potentially reached a wide audience through the social media platform Facebook. MiCAR therefore introduces this 'significance' concept in Title III, Chapter 5 (significant ARTs), Title IV, Chapter 2 (significant EMTs) and Title V, Chapter 5 (significant CASPs). These particular tokens and CASPs are subject to a specific set of rules and a different unified supervisory regime.

This chapter will address the MiCAR-specific concept of 'significance'. Though many of the regimes and supervisory mechanisms in MiCAR have been inspired by, or even 'copied' from, other legislative acts such as MiFiD II, the 'significance' regime is rather unique. However, the experience of other comparable regimes, such as those set out in the Single Supervisory Mechanism (SSM) and Single Resolution Mechanism (SRM), should be considered, as such may have been taken into account by the drafters of MiCAR.

In the Impact Assessment accompanying the Proposal for MiCAR (Impact Assessment), the European Commission, supported by the assessments of the European Central Bank (ECB), identifies the potentially significant impact of globally used asset-referenced tokens (also referred to as 'global stablecoins'). These tokens, if successful in reducing price volatility, could become highly influential and widely used as both a means of payment and a store of value.[1] A crypto-token can become 'significant' either because asset holders place an enormous amount of trust in it, because of its high level of integration into financial markets, or due to its extensive reach, such that any action or failure by its issuer would have a substantial impact on the wider public and economy.

[1] Impact Assessment (SWD(2020) 380 final), 24 September 2020, para 2.2.5.

In order to address various risks posed by significant crypto-tokens, MiCAR introduced special rules for significant ARTs (Articles 43 to 45) and significant EMTs (Articles 56 to 58). While the articles on significant ARTs have served as a blueprint for the rules on significant EMTs, special attention was required to avoid conflicting rules applicable to e-money institutions and credit institutions. This chapter aims to guide readers through the classification procedures for ARTs and EMTs, as well as the then applicable supervisory structure and shed light on the transparency and reporting obligations of significant CASPs (Article 85).

All relevant chapters of MiCAR provide for the collection of data, allowing EU supervisory authorities to gain better insight into the developments of the crypto-market. The collected data will then help the European Supervisory Authorities (ESAs) issue further guidance on the application of MiCAR or even aid the European Commission in drafting future legislation in this area. The implementations and practices developing across Member States will also be interesting to watch (eg, Germany has included the new principles in its draft Financial Market Digitisation Act). In particular, with respect to significant tokens or service providers, different approaches by competent authorities (NCAs) or the development of varying levels of expertise may impact the attractiveness of a Member State as a hub for such ventures or even future 'unicorns'.

8.2. Regulation of Significant ARTs

8.2.1. Introduction: Risks and the Need for Regulation

Prompted by the Commission's FinTech Action Plan from 2018,[2] which recognises the rapid development of technologies and their integration into the financial sector, MiCAR aims to break down barriers within the EU to facilitate the expansion of new business models and foster innovation. However, initiatives such as the blockchain-based cryptocurrency project 'Diem' (formerly 'Libra'), initiated by the internet giant Meta (formerly Facebook), served as the first trigger for intense discussions among European supervisory authorities[3] when the initial concept papers were published in 2019.[4] This marked the first time a highly influential non-crypto player showed interest in entering the crypto space, which at the time represented only a small portion of the investment landscape.[5] The development of

[2] FinTech Action Plan: For a more competitive and innovative European financial sector, 8 March 2018, finance.ec.europa.eu/publications/fintech-action-plan-more-competitive-and-innovative-european-financial-sector_en.

[3] P Hansen and H Bauer, 'MiCA's Significance Regime for Stablecoins – A Sledgehammer to Crack a Nut?' (2024) SSRN publication, papers.ssrn.com/sol3/papers.cfm?abstract_id=4699043.

[4] Facebook-funded cryptocurrency Diem winds down, BBC (1 February 2022) www.bbc.com/news/technology-60156682.

[5] A Verbeek, M Lundqvist, 'Artificial intelligence, blockchain and the future of Europe: How disruptive technologies create opportunities for a green and digital economy' (2021), Innovation Finance

the most popular decentralised token, Bitcoin, further signalled the extent of public acceptance of alternative currencies. Bitcoin, as a decentralised crypto-token, is accepted as a form of payment by some retailers and has grown in popularity over the years.[6] Only recently, the private equity giant BlackRock issued a Bitcoin-based exchange-traded fund (ETF), which was launched in January 2024 and exceeded USD 10 billion in March 2024.[7]

As cryptocurrencies have already arrived and claimed their place in today's financial (token-) economy and have become integrated into many financial services, failing to address their potential influence in an instrument like MiCAR would have been grossly negligent. Recognising the opportunities presented by a borderless and highly accessible digital financial system, and observing its rapid growth and potential, EU regulators faced the challenge of addressing the risk of monopolistic structures. This led to the introduction of the concept of 'significance', a notion already familiar from the Single Supervisory Mechanism Regulation (applicable to credit institutions) and the Digital Markets Act (for dominant players in the platform sector).[8]

As of 18 June 2024, the market capitalisation of crypto-assets was estimated at USD 2.36–2.49 trillion.[9] The risks posed by an unregulated and unsupervised market of this scale must not be ignored, especially as it becomes more integrated with payments and investments. In its 2020 consultative document on 'global stablecoin arrangements', the Financial Stability Board (FSB) noted that stablecoins 'have the potential to enhance the efficiency of the provision of financial services, but may also generate risks to financial stability, if they are adopted at a significant scale.'[10] With reference to the FSB's position, the Commission pointed out in its Impact Assessment that an asset-referenced token (then referred to as a 'stablecoin') with a global dimension carries major risks.[11] These risks primarily

Advisory, Main Report, 4, pointing out that in 2019 'the funding volume provided by the EU27 venture capital market to AI and blockchain SMEs (€1.75 billion) was considerably smaller than the equivalent volumes in the United States (€16 billion) and China (€4 billion).' CR Harvey et al, 'An Investor's Guide to Crypto' (2022) SSRN publication, ssrn.com/abstract=4124576.

[6] For example, in March 2021, Tesla Inc. announced that it would accept Bitcoin as a form of payment for its cars. Yet in May 2021 it suspended vehicle purchases using Bitcoin due to climate change concerns. Even in Spain certain players were exploring the functionality of blockchain to accept cryptocurrency as a means of payment for its services. See S Goschenko, 'Spanish Airline Vueling to Accept Cryptocurrency as Means of Payment' (*Bitcoin.comNews*, 17 January 2023) news.bitcoin.com/spanish-airline-vueling-to-accept-cryptocurrency-as-means-of-payment/.

[7] W Schmitt, 'Bitcoin rally pushes BlackRock ETF over $10bn in record time' *Financial Times* (10 March 2024) www.ft.com/content/1bb8413e-b974-4e05-933e-7ffedec62bdb.

[8] Regulation (EU) 2022/1925 of the European Parliament and of the Council of 14 September 2022 on contestable and fair markets in the digital sector and amending Directives (EU) 2019/1937 and (EU) 2020/1828 (Digital Markets Act).

[9] CoinMarketCap, coinmarketcap.com/ and CoinGecko, www.coingecko.com/.

[10] FSB, 'Addressing the regulatory, supervisory and oversight challenges raised by "global stablecoin" arrangements', Consultative document, 14 April 2020, www.fsb.org/wp-content/uploads/P140420-1.pdf. See also FSB, High-level Recommendations for the Regulation, Supervision and Oversight of Crypto-Asset Activities and Markets, Final Report (FSB Recommendations), 17 July 2023, www.fsb.org/wp-content/uploads/P170723-2.pdf.

[11] Impact Assessment (SWD(2020) 380 final), 24 September 2020, 19–23.

stem from the structural weaknesses of such tokens, including conflicts of interest, fraud, cyber incidents and potential liquidity bottlenecks. These issues become more evident as digital projects and infrastructures expand and become more accessible to consumers. Another risk arises from the growing linkages and interdependencies between the crypto economy and the traditional financial system, which could impact both financial stability and the enforcement of monetary policy.

The main risks associated with significant stablecoins according to FSB are as follows:[12]

- There is a risk that the referenced assets, which are intended to 'stabilise' the market value of a stablecoin, might lose value, leading to a decline in the reserves backing the stablecoin, thus jeopardising its value stability.
- If there is a sudden loss of confidence in the issuer, for example, due to unforeseen market events, and if all or a large number of token holders attempt to sell their tokens simultaneously in a so-called 'run on the bank', there would be a significant risk to the issuer's liquidity.
- In the absence of state control and safety nets, liquidity bottlenecks could trigger market fallout. The collapse of a significant token can result in substantial financial losses for token holders.
- If consumers were to switch to using a significant token as an alternative means of saving, fewer deposits would be made in fiat currency with banks. As a result, banks would lose access to capital inflows and might be forced to engage in riskier refinancing strategies to maintain their day-to-day operations.
- The political structure could become unstable if a significant token were to become the preferred store of value, and consequently, the majority of assets currently held as bank deposits are bundled into it. This shift away from traditional intermediaries like banks could undermine the transmission of monetary policy and fiscal stimulus to the real economy (eg, through the base interest rate). The widespread use of a significant token could also influence deposit and lending rates within the domestic currency financial system, thereby diluting the effectiveness of the interest rate channel of monetary policy. In the worst-case scenario, this could result in a loss of control by governing bodies and destabilisation of financial policy with unprecedented consequences; to put it bluntly, a step towards 'monetary anarchy'.

In addition to the identified systemic risks concerning the entire monetary system, the need to protect investors and consumers who might rely on cryptocurrency as they would on state currency – despite the lack of state safety nets – was also

[12] ibid 19 ff. FSB Recommendations, at 2. See also ECB Crypto-Assets Task Force. Stablecoins: Implications for monetary policy, financial stability, market infrastructure and payments, and banking supervision in the euro area, Occasional Paper Series No. 247, September 2020, www.ecb.europa.eu/pub/pdf/scpops/ecb.op247~fe3df92991.en.pdf.

strongly emphasised by the Member States during discussions on the first draft of MiCAR. This emphasis reflects the central role consumer protection plays in the political agendas of several Member States.

The need to ensure consumer and investor protection, guarantee market integrity and preserve financial stability[13] should not overshadow the stated intention to support innovation and the development of new technologies. It is vital that the goal of risk mitigation does not impede the objective of promoting innovation, especially since the crypto market is still relatively young, developing, and far less established than the market in financial instruments. MiCAR therefore aims to balance multiple objectives: ensuring the integrity of crypto markets, protecting investors and consumers, promoting financial stability and the smooth operation of payment systems, while fostering innovation and supporting the digital economy.[14] Balancing these at times conflicting goals is challenging and has yet to be tested in the field and MiCAR shall only be the first attempt at reaching such goals.

8.2.2. The Concept of 'Significance' and an Overview of Title III, Chapter 5

The FSB report recommended creating a customised regulatory framework to address the identified risks, described above.[15] In response to these potential risks, a separate chapter on significant ARTs was introduced, namely Title III, Chapter 5.[16] Significant stablecoins were then labelled 'global stablecoins' or GSCs. Chapter 5 primarily focuses on: (i) setting appropriate thresholds for assessing significance; (ii) establishing an informed assessment procedure; and (iii) enabling an appropriate supervisory structure based on the principles of cooperation, coordination, and information exchange. Given the geographical scope and borderless nature of any significant token, effective supervision can only be achieved within a legal framework that extends beyond national borders. This approach would enable a unified supervisory mechanism and support the goal of cohesive and effective financial supervision within the EU, as already established for traditional financial services and products.[17]

The borderless nature of the digital economy and its potential impact on monetary transmission channels and monetary sovereignty can only be adequately addressed at the EU level. Therefore, the European Banking Authority (EBA) was entrusted with the task of supervising the issuers of significant asset-referenced

[13] MiCAR, Recitals (71) and (102).

[14] MiCAR, Recitals (5), (73).

[15] FSB Recommendations.

[16] This consists of Articles 43–45.

[17] See eg Council Regulation (EU) No 1024/2013 of 15 October 2013 conferring specific tasks on the European Central Bank concerning policies relating to the prudential supervision of credit institutions.

tokens (ARTs). Given that this assignment of responsibility is made in response to the specific nature of the risks posed by these crypto-assets, it should not serve as a 'precedent' for future regulation of financial services.[18] The following paragraphs provide a concise overview of the rules in Title III, Chapter 5.

Article 43 outlines the criteria for categorising an ART as 'significant', as well as the procedure making this determination. Furthermore, the role of the EBA as the supervising authority at the EU level is introduced. Therefore, Article 43 plays a central role within the regulatory framework for significant ARTs. The criteria for classifying asset-referenced tokens as significant are set out in Article 43(1) and must be (or are already) further specified by the Commission through delegated acts.[19] In sum, the significance regime under MiCAR has two effects. First, it establishes more stringent requirements for issuers of significant ARTs. Second, it transfers supervision to the EU level.

As mentioned previously, the qualification as 'significant' is not an entirely new concept in EU financial regulation. Under the SSM Regulation[20] and the SSM Framework Regulation[21] (together, SSM Regulations), credit institutions are categorised as 'significant' if they meet certain criteria related to size, relevance to the EU or a Member State, and the importance of cross-border activities. The SSM Regulations aim to identify which market players are systemically important based on their market strength and integration. Title III, Chapter 5 seeks to achieve the same goal in relation to crypto-tokens (as opposed to market players, which are dealt with later in this chapter). Although the regulatory approaches of the SSM Regulations and MiCAR are not entirely comparable, there are some conceptual similarities, particularly regarding the classification criteria.

It is also believed that the oversight framework for electronic payment instruments, schemes, and arrangements (PISA) and its exemption criteria may have influenced the ART regime.[22] The exemption criteria serve to identify which payment schemes and arrangements have too little relevance for the overall payment system to warrant oversight at the European level. For this purpose, factors such as size, market penetration in terms of value and volume, and geographical relevance are taken into account.[23] PISA, being focused mainly on payment schemes and arrangements that have gained importance for the euro area and may therefore pose a risk to EU markets, distinguishes between

[18] MiCAR, Recital (102).

[19] MiCAR, Article 43(1) and (11).

[20] Council Regulation (EU) No 1024/2013 of 15 October 2013 conferring specific tasks on the European Central Bank concerning policies relating to the prudential supervision of credit institutions.

[21] Regulation (EU) No 468/2014 of the European Central Bank of 16 April 2014 establishing the framework for cooperation within the Single Supervisory Mechanism between the European Central Bank and national competent authorities and with national designated authorities (SSM Framework Regulation).

[22] See ECB, Eurosystem oversight framework for electronic payment instruments, schemes and arrangements, November 2021, www.ecb.europa.eu/paym/pdf/consultations/ecb. PISApublic consultation202111_1.en.pdf.

[23] ibid.

national and pan-European schemes and arrangements based on specific criteria. Although PISA has a different objective than MiCAR, there are some conceptual parallels.[24]

Article 44 provides an alternative, voluntary route for classifying ARTs as significant. To ensure uniform supervision and allow continuity in supervision, an issuer of ARTs can apply directly for classification under the supervisory regime for significant ARTs when submitting its application in accordance with Article 18 or submitting the crypto-asset white paper under Article 17 (see chapter six of the book), if it can already foresee that the criteria for 'significance' will be met. This option will be particularly relevant for ARTs that are already established by the time MiCAR comes into force in such a way that they already meet the relevant thresholds. For such ARTs, there will be sufficient data to demonstrate compliance with the relevant criteria when they first become subject to MiCAR. After all, blockchain-based token trading has been around for over 10 years. However, authorities are likely to rely heavily on reports produced by issuers when collecting data for their assessment of significance (Article 22).[25] Due to the lack of IT-specific standards and the sheer speed of conducting business using DLT, it is nearly impossible for authorities to collect reliable data on their own. One of MiCAR's guiding principles is close cooperation with market participants. MiCAR was developed in parallel with the regulatory sandbox initiative of the DLT Pilot Regime Regulation. Article 44 reflects this integrative principle.

Lastly, Article 45 establishes additional obligations for issuers of significant ARTs, particularly concerning their risk management. Issuers of significant ARTs are more influential and potentially more exposed to market risks than issuers of non-significant ARTs. Consequently, they are of particular importance to the risk profile of an ART and must meet higher requirements than 'ordinary' issuers to protect consumers who invest in such tokens and to preserve financial stability. For example, higher capital requirements apply, along with obligations related to interoperability and liquidity management. These standards are, however, familiar to some market participants, as they are partially inspired by the Capital Requirements Regulation (CRR) and Capital Requirements Directive (CRD) framework applicable to credit institutions and investment firms. Furthermore, as noted in other chapters of this book, many concepts in MiCAR follow those of MiFID II. Lessons learned from events that have occurred in traditional financial markets are being applied to new business models, and the obligations of ART issuers appear aligned with those of traditional financial market players. Ultimately,

[24] Hansen and Bauer (n 3).

[25] EBA, Draft Implementing Technical Standards on the reporting on asset-referenced tokens under Article 22(7) of Regulation (EU) No 2023/1114 (MiCAR) and on e-money tokens denominated in a currency that is not an official currency of a Member State pursuant to Article 58(3) of that Regulation, 19 June 2024, 16, according to which 'Article 22(1) of MiCAR is the only provision that includes specific, harmonized reporting requirements for the issuers, and should ensure that [competent authorities] receive the information needed to perform their supervisory and other statutory activities.'

significant tokens can have similar structures and pose comparable risks to those of traditional regulated securities and other financial instruments.[26]

The Commission is responsible for continuously reviewing and monitoring market events and incorporating findings into the ongoing development of the regulatory framework, particularly through delegated acts. To this end, Title III, Chapter 5 imposes multiple reporting obligations to aid supervisory efforts. Market participants can anticipate the introduction of MiCAR II.

8.2.3. Qualification of ARTs as 'Significant'

8.2.3.1. Process of Classification

If at least three of the criteria in Article 43(1) are cumulatively fulfilled within the timeframe set in Article 43(2), the ART will be categorised as significant by the EBA in accordance with Article 43(9). The applicable timeframe or relevant period according to Article 43(2) shall be either: (i) the period from the authorisation or approval of the white paper until the first report submitted under Article 43(4) by the NCA of the issuer's home Member State to the EBA and the ECB, or (ii) any period covered by at least two consecutive reports submitted pursuant to Article 43(4).[27] Article 56 outlines a similar procedure for the classification of EMTs, with paragraph 1 directly referencing the criteria in Article 43(1). As a result, the criteria for classifying ARTs as significant also apply to EMTs.

The consequence of the classification of an ART as 'significant' is the transfer of supervision from NCAs to the EBA.[28] Conversely, supervision should be transferred back if an ART ceases to be 'significant' in the subsequent assessment period.

The data used for the assessment will be obtained from the information and reports received in line with Article 43(4) from national competent authorities. However, when processing this information, the EBA is not solely reliant on the 'goodwill' of the issuers subject to reporting obligations under Article 22. It can also take certain supervisory measures under Article 130(1) in conjunction with Annex V, as outlined in Title VII, Chapter 5, and discussed in Chapter 10 of this book. If multiple issuers jointly issue an ART, the data from their respective reports must be summarised and assessed in aggregated form.[29] The assessment of significance focuses on the specific token and its systemic relevance, rather than on the individual issuer.

[26] See IOSCO, Global stablecoin initiatives, Public Report, OR01/2020 (March 2020) www.iosco.org/library/pubdocs/pdf/IOSCOPD650.pdf.

[27] MiCAR, Article 43(1)(4) provides that competent authorities of the issuer's home Member State must report to the EBA and the ECB information relevant for the assessment of the fulfilment of the significance criteria at least twice a year.

[28] MiCAR, Article 43(10).

[29] MiCAR, Article 43(3).

The EBA is responsible for assessing whether the criteria for 'significance' are satisfied and must prepare a draft decision to classify an ART as significant.[30] Before a final decision is made, this draft must first be circulated for consultation to the issuer of the ART, the competent authority of the issuer's home Member State, the ECB and the central bank of a non-euro Member State, if the issuer is established in a Member State whose official currency is not the Euro. Relevant stakeholders must have the opportunity to comment on the draft decision. They have 20 days to submit their written remarks, which must be 'duly considered' by the EBA (which is more than merely 'taking note'). Within 60 days following the first provision of the draft decision, the EBA has to submit its final decision and notify the issuer and its NCA.[31] This decision must be revisited annually.[32] Should the EBA determine that the criteria for 'significance' are no longer met, it must issue a draft decision to no longer classify the ART as significant for consultation. The final decision must be made (including the 20-day consultation period) within 60 days of the first provision of the draft decision to relevant stakeholders.

As noted above, MiCAR also establishes a voluntary route for classifying ARTs as significant. According to Article 44, the issuer of an ART may apply on its own initiative to have its ARTs classified as 'significant'. This can be done via their application for authorisation or notification (for credit institutions). In such cases, the NCA must immediately notify the applicant issuer's request to the EBA, the ECB and, in the cases referred to in Article 43(4), to the central bank of the Member State, considering potential monetary policy implications associated with the respective token. The request must include a detailed programme of operations that indicates whether and how the issuer is likely to meet at least three of the criteria for 'significance' listed in Article 43(1). The EBA has already issued a draft delegated regulation that provides some assistance on the requirements of a programme of operations (comparable to a 'business plan') in its Article 4.[33] As according to EBA, an application that also requests classification as significant requires a higher level of information in order to adequately reflect the risk profile,[34] the draft delegated regulation sets in its Article 7(1)(i) requirements relating to the provided

[30] MiCAR, Article 43(5).

[31] MiCAR, Article 43(6).

[32] MiCAR, Article 43(8).

[33] EBA, Draft Regulatory Technical Standards on information for application for authorization to offer to the public and to seek admission to trading of asset-referenced tokens and Draft Implementing Technical Standards on standard forms, templates and procedures for the information to be included in the application, under Art. 18(6) and (7) of Regulation (EU) 2023/1114 (EBA/RTS/2024/03, 7.5.2024), p 19.

[34] EBA, Draft Regulatory Technical Standards on information for application for authorization to offer to the public and to seek admission to trading of asset-referenced tokens and Draft Implementing Technical Standards on standard forms, templates and procedures for the information to be included in the application, under Art. 18(6) and (7) of Regulation (EU) 2023/1114 (EBA/RTS/2024/03, 7.5.2024), p 7, 10.

information and contains in its Annex 1 a form to explicitly request classification as 'significant'.[35]

8.2.3.2. 'Significance' Criteria in Detail

8.2.3.2.1. Open Norms and Evolving Rules

The criteria set out in Article 43(1) establish a distinct threshold that has to be met for an ART to be classified as 'significant'. As the crypto market is fast evolving and technological developments might lead to new phenomena, one may wonder whether it is possible to fully specify all the 'significance' criteria in the text of MiCAR.[36] Acknowledging this, MiCAR states that the thresholds will be reviewed by the Commission as part of the review of its application, as MiCAR represents only the first step in the regulation of the crypto industry, and not the end of the discussion.[37]

Some of the criteria are relatively open-ended (eg, 'significance of the activities'[38] and 'interconnectedness' with the financial system[39]), allowing for unforeseen circumstances to be considered and ensuring that MiCAR remains future-proof. These criteria have been further detailed in the delegated acts.[40] In general, clearly defined criteria promote predictability and legal certainty, reducing the concern among issuers that they could change significantly in the future. There is a need for a certain degree of continuity and predictability in supervision.

The criteria must further be applied sensibly and in a proportionate manner, as the supervisory regime for significant ARTs should not be applied too rigidly. Consistent with the principle of proportionality, the adopted approach should reflect and address the specific risks posed by ARTs. It should not lead to a hasty shift of supervisory activities away from NCAs but rather only to a shift to EU supervision in exceptional cases of particular systemic importance.

The criteria in Article 43(1) serve to determine the (potential) degree of adoption and use of the token, as this could indicate the potential effects on 'financial stability, monetary policy transmission or monetary sovereignty'. The FSB notes that due to the multiple uses to which a token could be put (eg, means of payment

[35] EBA, Draft Regulatory Technical Standards on information for application for authorization to offer to the public and to seek admission to trading of asset-referenced tokens and Draft Implementing Technical Standards on standard forms, templates and procedures for the information to be included in the application, under Art. 18(6) and (7) of Regulation (EU) 2023/1114 (EBA/RTS/2024/03, 7.5.2024), p. 36, to be adopted as delegated regulation (EU) 2025/305.

[36] P Maume, 'The Regulation on Markets in Crypto-Assets (MiCAR): Landmark Codification, or First Step of Many, or Both' (2023) 2 *ECFR* 243, 267, sharing concerns that the criteria of significance and the relevant thresholds are laid down in MiCAR instead of delegated legislation.

[37] Recital (59). This and other recitals hint that there will likely be MiCAR II in the (near) future.

[38] MiCAR, Article 43(1)(e).

[39] MiCAR, Article 43(1)(f).

[40] Commission Delegated Regulation (EU) 2024/1506 of 22 February 2024.

or store of value), it is necessary to consider these potential uses across different jurisdictions using multiple criteria.[41] In light of this, the FSB proposes specific recommendations as to which criteria can be used, such as the number and type of stablecoin users, number and value of transactions, the size of asset reserves, and the value of stablecoins in circulation.[42] These criteria are generally aligned with those contained in MiCAR, which are discussed below.

8.2.3.2.2. Number of ART Holders

The first criterion requires a minimum of 10 million holders of the ART. This quantitative criterion serves to assess the ART's market acceptance and distribution. A large number of holders indicates a broad customer base, which could lead to a significant impact and elevate the overall risk profile.[43]

It is important to note that the term 'holder' was chosen for this criterion. This term is not explicitly defined in MiCAR. This seems to be a weakness in the drafting, showing that the Regulation does not take sufficient notice of possible private law concepts. In this context, this term should refer to persons who own ARTs (ie, beneficial owners), whether they are held via custodial or non-custodial wallets. That said, in technological reality, holding means holding the private key, which enables the holder to conduct any kind of transfer with crypto-assets.[44] The rights of holders are protected by MiCAR, inter alia, by means of the right of redemption (see chapter six). The holding of ARTs by third parties on behalf of ART owners – custodial or intermediated holding – should not affect the calculation of 'end holders' for the purposes of determining the 'significance' of the ART. MiCAR requires CASPs to provide issuers with the information that they need to report the number of holders.[45] This should help issuers determine the number of holders.

The criterion referring to the number of holders does not require holders to use tokens for a specific purpose (eg, store of value, means of exchange), but will primarily relate to those token holders who use a token as a store of value and 'park' values. It also does not require the ART to be used in any transactions, as transactions are covered by a separate criterion under Article 43(1)(c). The specifics of determining this threshold within the relevant timeframe will be subject to a proportionate approach by the EBA.

[41] FSB Recommendations, at 16.

[42] ibid.

[43] MiCAR, Recital (59); FSB Recommendations.

[44] D Skauradszun, 'Das Internationale Privatrecht der Kryptowerte, elektronischen Wertpapiere und Kryptowertpapiere' (2022) *Zeitschrift für die gesamte Privatrechtswissenschaft* (*ZfPW*) 56, 61.

[45] EBA, Draft Implementing Technical Standards on the reporting on asset-referenced tokens under Article 22(7) of Regulation (EU) No 2023/1114 (MiCAR) and on e-money tokens denominated in a currency that is not an official currency of a Member State pursuant to Article 58(3) of that Regulation, 19 June 2024, para 19.

8.2.3.2.3. Value of Issued ART, Market Cap and Asset Reserves

For the classification of 'significance', the value of the tokens issued, their market capitalisation, or the size of the issuer's asset reserve must exceed EUR 5 billion.[46] This quantitative criterion aims to determine the value of ARTs already available on the market, also to be understood as the trading volume, market liquidity or 'market power' of the token.

The market capitalisation of an asset-referenced token is calculated by multiplying the number of such tokens in circulation by the current market price of a single token. Hence, the market cap of an ART is based on both its customer base (ie, the acceptance and distribution of an ART) and its value. MiCAR does not specify how and at what point the value of an ART should be determined. In the Draft Implementing Technical Standards on the reporting on ARTs, the EBA refers to the value at reporting reference date and the minimum, maximum and average values over the preceding quarter.[47] According to the EBA, these values provide information to the competent authorities on the fluctuation and stability of the token's value. Yet, it proposes to use 'the average value over the preceding quarter' for the purposes of determining reporting obligations. It remains to be seen whether the same approach will be adopted for the purpose of applying the significance criterion.

For the purposes of applying the 'value criterion', the geographical distribution of tokens and the significance of cross-border activity do not play a role. The value of ARTs in circulation, or their market capitalisation, also reflects the issuer's size and provides a good indication of the size of reserve assets. The value of the reserve assets must be determined by the issuer by using market prices (Article 36(7)). Their aggregate value must be at least equal to the total value of the claims against the issuer from holders of the ART in circulation. Information about the reserve assets must also be included in the crypto-asset white paper (Article 19(1)(g)).

As discussed in chapter six, the reserve assets back the value of the tokens. They represent the issuer's 'security assets' and serve the dual purpose of ensuring the stability of the ART's value and protecting the rights of ART holders. The volume of reserve assets is likely to be correlated with the significance of the ART and the size of its issuer, indicating its ability to operate and its level of market involvement. The active assets of a credit institution are indicative in the same way.

The value threshold of EUR 5 billion is fairly high, considering that in its Impact Assessment, the Commission estimated the total market capitalisation of all stablecoins in existence in 2019 to be EUR 4.3 billion.[48] The market capitalisation of tokens falling under the definition of ARTs is likely to be even lower. This shows that only truly significant ARTs will fall under MiCAR's rules for significant ARTs.

[46] MiCAR, Article 43(1)(b). Note that, pursuant to Article 22(2), if the value of the issued token is higher than EUR 100 million, the issuer is subject to the mandatory reporting to the competent authority on a quarterly basis.

[47] EBA (n 45) 24.

[48] Impact Assessment (SWD(2020) 380 final), 24 September 2020, 2.2.5.

A large customer base and a high market capitalisation of an ART lead to a greater impact and risks.[49] The threshold value of EUR 5 billion had already been chosen in Article 6(4) of the SSM Regulation as a threshold for the minimum value of a credit institution's active assets, ie, the assets actively available to the credit institution. Hence, it is not an unfamiliar benchmark, although in the SSM Regulation, there is an explicit reference to the context of cross-border activities to reach the threshold. This is not the case with MiCAR. That said, cross-border activity is inherent in the nature of cryptocurrencies,[50] which are archetypal instruments in a borderless digital economy. Therefore, this requirement was not explicitly included in the wording of this criterion. This accords with criticism voiced by some Member States early in the negotiations. They were concerned that the criteria were not overly restrictive, so cross-border activity should not be decisive, as even one token prevalent at the national level can have an impact on the stability of the entire Euro area, if its volume is sufficiently high.

8.2.3.2.4. Average Number and Aggregate Value of Transactions

MiCAR acknowledges that large volumes of payment transactions using ARTs can pose serious risks to monetary transmission channels and monetary sovereignty within the EU.[51] This is why MiCAR includes a separate 'transaction criterion' aimed at capturing the significance of the use of ARTs for payments and remittances on an international scale.[52]

The 'transaction criterion' for determining token significance requires that the average number and average aggregate value of transactions in an ART per day during the relevant period exceed 2.5 million transactions and EUR 500 million, respectively. These are relatively high thresholds. To put them into perspective, bitcoin transactions peaked in December 2023 and still only amounted to 724,000 per day.[53] To determine whether MiCAR thresholds have been reached, the EBA can rely on reports from the NCAs and information submitted by the issuers in accordance with Article 22(1). The latter must include the number of token holders, the value of the ART issued, the size of the reserve of assets, and the average number and average aggregate value of transactions per day during the relevant quarter.[54]

[49] MiCAR, Recital (59).
[50] MiCAR, Recital (100).
[51] MiCAR, Recital (102).
[52] EBA, EBA's Technical Advice in response to the European Commission's December 2022 Call for Advice on two delegated acts under MiCAR concerning certain criteria for the classification of ARTs and EMTs as significant and the fees that are to be charged by EBA to issuers of significant ARTs and EMTs, 29 September 2023, 20.
[53] Number of daily network transactions on the blockchain of Bitcoin from January 2009 to 2 June 2024, www.statista.com/statistics/730806/daily-number-of-bitcoin-transactions.
[54] MiCAR, Article 22(1). For the purposes of reporting, 'transaction' means 'any change of the natural or legal person entitled to the asset-referenced token as a result of the transfer of the asset-referenced token from one distributed ledger address or account to another.' Thus, transfers between different addresses or accounts belonging to the same person do not qualify as a 'transaction' under MiCAR.

A question may arise regarding the exact scope and type of transactions that should be counted. In this respect, MiCAR adopts a broad approach, requiring the monitoring of both on-chain transactions (those settled on a distributed ledger) and off-chain transactions (those settled outside the distributed ledger), including transactions between clients of the same CASP.[55] Arguably, monitoring the latter may prove challenging. According to the German translation, the transaction criterion requires only an 'estimated' aggregate value of transactions (*geschätzte aggregierte Wert der Geschäfte*). However, the English version refers to the 'average' aggregate value of transactions, which appears to have a different meaning. It is unclear whether this discrepancy in language is merely a mistake or whether it grants the EBA discretion to make its own estimates. In our view, NCAs and the EBA should not be bound solely by the information and figures provided by ART issuers but should instead perform their own analysis and assessment.

8.2.3.2.5. ART Issuer as a Gatekeeper under the DMA

An ART issuer that has access to a large amount of data and a substantial user base, as do providers of core platform services such as Meta, Apple, and Amazon,[56] could quickly achieve considerable market power or gain acceptance among users solely due to its platform effect.[57] Recital (3) of Regulation (EU) 2022/1925 (Digital Markets Act or DMA) states that some of these companies control entire platform ecosystems in the digital economy. Given this structural advantage, it is extremely difficult for even the most innovative and efficient existing or new market participants to compete with or challenge these companies' dominant positions.

To be classified as a 'gatekeeper' under the DMA, a digital platform must meet certain criteria related to the number of users, turnover, or capitalisation. If an issuer is a 'gatekeeper' in accordance with the DMA, it can be presumed to have a large user base and a strong economic position in the market. A detailed analysis of the gatekeeper criteria in the DMA supports this conclusion. For example, an undertaking is presumed to satisfy the respective requirements for a gatekeeper if it provides a core platform service that in the last financial year has at least 45 million monthly active end users established or located in the EU.[58]

This criterion is clearly linked to the Diem/Libra project announced by Facebook in 2019. Based on the enormous number of users of Facebook alone, and the associated potential reach for the token, the ECB estimated that, in an extreme scenario, the global size of the Libra Reserve could reach almost EUR 3 trillion in assets under management.[59] Given Facebook's established user networks, the

[55] MiCAR, Recital (60).
[56] Gatekeepers, digital-markets-act.ec.europa.eu/gatekeepers_en.
[57] DMA, Recital (3).
[58] DMA, Article 3(2)(b).
[59] M Adachi et al, 'A regulatory and financial stability perspective on global stablecoins' (2020) *ECB Macroprudential Bulletin*, www.ecb.europa.eu/press/financial-stability-publications/macroprudential-bulletin/html/ecb.mpbu202005_1~3e9ac10eb1.en.html.

Diem/Libra project could have easily achieved mass adoption across multiple jurisdictions,[60] raising reasonable concerns among regulators. It is unclear whether a project similar to the Diem/Libra experiment is likely to be attempted again in the future.

8.2.3.2.6. Significance of Issuer's Activities at International Level

According to Article 43(1)(e), the 'significance' of an ART can be determined with reference to the significance of the ART issuer's activities on an international scale. ARTs could be used to transfer value or as a means of exchange, and the criterion for international activities encompasses payments and remittances on a global level.

This criterion clearly leaves room for interpretation, because 'significance' can be interpreted in a number of ways and be based on a number of factors. In this respect, the Commission further clarified this criterion via the Delegated Regulation 2024/1506 of 22 February 2024.[61] What is clear is that a reference to an 'international scale' implies that significance should be achieved in the context of at least two countries. Hence, domestically active ARTs lacking an international element will not meet this criterion.

The open wording of Article 43(1)(e) might suggest that it is sufficient for the issuer's activities to be internationally significant, even if they may not be such within EU borders. However, the EBA, in its technical advice, states that the cross-border dimension should cover cases where either the payer or the payee is located in the EU, but not situations where both the payer and payee are outside the EU.[62] According to Delegated Regulation 2024/1506, the core indicators of the significance of the issuer's activities on an international scale include:

- Market share of the value of cross-border transactions in an ART into and from the EU (ie, inflows and outflows).[63]
- Market share of cross-border transactions into and from the EU in an ART that are associated with uses as a means of exchange. The reporting obligations under Article 22(1)(d) are expected to capture cross-border transactions with ARTs used as a means of exchange.[64]

[60] D Arner, R Auer and J Frost, 'Stablecoins: risks, potential and regulation' (2020) BIS Working Papers No 905, 4 www.bis.org/publ/work905.pdf.

[61] Commission Delegated Regulation (EU) 2024/1506 of 22 February 2024 supplementing Regulation (EU) 2023/1114 of the European Parliament and of the Council by specifying certain criteria for classifying asset-referenced tokens and e-money tokens as significant. See also EBA, EBA's Technical Advice in response to the European Commission's December 2022 Call for Advice on two delegated acts under MiCAR concerning certain criteria for the classification of ARTs and EMTs as significant and the fees that are to be charged by EBA to issuers of significant ARTs and EMTs, 29 September 2023 (EBA's Technical Advice).

[62] EBA's Technical Advice, para 63.

[63] Delegated Regulation 2024/1506, Article 2(1)(a).

[64] ibid Article 2(1)(b).

- Market capitalisation on an international scale of an ART on the last calendar day of the relevant period.[65]
- Market capitalisation on an international scale of all ARTs and EMTs issued by the issuer on the last calendar day of the relevant period.[66]

Delegated Regulation 2024/1506 also introduces two sub-indicators related to inflow and outflow transactions, 'since the effects of each type of transaction on financial stability and monetary sovereignty can be different.'[67] Interestingly, in its Technical Advice, the EBA proposed an ancillary indicator that can be used when the core indicators do not yield a conclusive determination of significance. This indicator includes the ratio of the total value of cross-border transactions with an ART used as a means of exchange compared to the total value of cross-border payment transactions into and from the EU. According to the EBA, the use of ARTs as a means of payment could introduce and enhance risks to financial stability. This is why it proposed to assess these risks by comparing the total value of ART payments with the total value of payments processed by traditional payment providers and systems, or with the total value of payment transactions processed and reported by authorised payment service providers (eg, banks, e-money institutions) under PSD2.[68]

8.2.3.2.7. Interconnectedness of the ART or its Issuer with the Financial System[69]

The term 'interconnectedness' can have different meanings, but it generally aligns with the FSB-recommended criterion of 'interconnectedness with financial institutions and the broader economy' suggested for determining GSCs.[70] While the Crypto winter of 2022–2023 and the significant volatility of crypto-asset prices have not resulted in contagion or any notable defaults by financial institutions, it has been pointed out that 'greater involvement of financial institutions could fuel the growth of crypto-assets even further and increase financial stability risks.'[71]

The FSB has outlined the following transmission channels through which vulnerabilities arising in crypto markets could have implications for financial stability:

- Financial sector exposures to crypto-assets, related financial products and entities that are financially impacted by crypto-assets.
- Wealth effects, such as the degree to which fluctuations in the value of crypto-assets can impact their investors, which in turn can have a knock-on effect on the financial system.

[65] ibid Article 2(1)(c).
[66] ibid Article 2(1)(d).
[67] ibid Recital (4).
[68] EBA's Technical Advice, paras 77–82.
[69] MiCAR Article 43(1)(f).
[70] FSB Recommendations, at 16.
[71] L Hermans et al., 'Decrypting financial stability risks in crypto-asset markets' (2022) *ECB Financial Stability Review* 113, 117.

- Confidence effects, including the impact of the developments in crypto markets on investment confidence in both crypto and traditional markets.
- The extent of crypto-assets' use in payments and settlements.[72]

Article 43(1)(f) does not specify what is meant by 'financial system'. In this regard, the EBA proposes (and we agree) that a broad approach should be adopted and that connections with a wide range of financial institutions (banks, insurance companies, investment firms, pension funds, investment funds, etc.) have to be considered.[73] There can be various links between these institutions and ARTs and their issuers. Without attempting to cover all these links, it is important to highlight that they can work both ways. A failure of an ART issuer or an ART can pose risks to a financial institution (eg, through investments in such assets). Conversely, a failure of a financial institution (eg, acting as a custodian for the reserve assets backing the ART or issuing securities that are used as reserves backing the ART) is likely to have a contagion effect on the ART issuer and undermine holders' trust in the stability of the ART itself.[74] This is why, for instance, MiCAR prescribes that ART issuers must ensure that concentrations of the custodians of reserve assets are avoided.[75]

Among the core indicators of interconnectedness with the financial system, the Delegated Regulation 2024/1506 lists:

- The significance of the share of non-deposit reserve assets of an ART that are financial instruments issued by financial institutions. Distress in financial institutions whose financial instruments are included in the reserve assets by the ART issuer could affect the value of these reserve assets, which back the ART holders' claims on the issuer for token redemption. This creates a direct connection between a financial institution and the ART issuer.[76]
- The significance of the share of the issuer's asset holdings relative to the total supply of specific financial instruments (ie, the total value of financial instruments issued by financial institutions that are part of the reserve assets of the ART, divided by the total supply of that type of financial instrument).[77] This reflects an indirect interconnectedness between issuers of ARTs and the financial system. Such an indirect connection might impact the traditional financial system, particularly if the issuer of an ART is forced to 'fire sell' its assets due to financial distress. This sell-off could drive down the value of those assets and

[72] FSB, Crypto-asset markets: potential channels for future financial stability implications, October 2018; FSB, Assessment of Risks to Financial Stability from Crypto-assets, 16 February 2022.

[73] EBA's Technical Advice, 12.

[74] See F. Helmore, 'USD Coin value falls after revealing $3.3bn held at Silicon Valley Bank' *The Guardian* (11 March 2023) www.theguardian.com/technology/2023/mar/11/usd-coin-depeg -silicon-valley-bank-collapse.

[75] MiCAR, Article 37(1)(d).

[76] Delegated Regulation 2024/1506, Article 3(1) and Recital (7).

[77] Delegated Regulation 2024/1506, Article 3(1).

indirectly affect financial institutions by decreasing the value of the assets they hold.[78]

The Delegated Regulation also lists several sub-indicators, including the share of non-deposit reserve assets of an ART that are derivatives.[79] The data required to carry out the assessment of this indicator and other indicators can be derived from the disclosures made by the issuers of ARTs that describe the composition of their asset reserves (Article 36(9)–(10)). Interestingly, the Delegated Regulation does not explicitly mention, as a form of interconnectedness, the share of ARTs or EMTs issued that are held by financial institutions. This indicator was previously proposed by the EBA.[80]

In addition, the following ancillary indicators are set out: the ownership structure of the issuer of an ART (eg, financial institution as a shareholder), the concentration of custody of the issuer's reserve assets (eg, concentration of reserve assets among a small number of financial institutions), and the portfolio overlap of the issuer's reserve assets with those of other ARTs and EMTs, as such issuers can also be considered part of the 'financial system'.[81] These ancillary indicators should be assessed when the EBA's evaluation of the core indicators does not allow it to conclusively determine whether the significance criterion has been met.

The criterion of financial interconnectedness will become increasingly important now that major institutions, such as large investment firms like BlackRock and internationally significant banks, have begun implementing infrastructure to participate in the token economy and focus on providing digital or tokenised assets. The aspect of technological interoperability is the first step towards interconnectedness, which had already been taken, as was observed by the FSB in 2019.[82] However, such technological perspective has not been reflected as an indicator in the Delegated Act.

8.2.3.2.8. At Least One Additional Token and at Least One Crypto-asset Service

To fulfil this criterion, set out in Article 43(1)(g), an issuer must offer at least one other ART or EMT and provide at least one crypto-asset service. Such an issuer

[78] Delegated Regulation 2024/1506, Recital (8).

[79] ibid Article 3(2). Counterparties of derivatives are often credit institutions and therefore a margin call on them could have significant effects on the financial system.

[80] EBA's Technical Advice, 16. The goal of this indicator is to cover holdings of ARTs by financial institutions that would capture potential contagion effects that might arise, for instance, in a situation of a sudden decline in the market value of an ART that will have a negative effect on the asset side of a financial institution. See BCBS, Prudential treatment of cryptoasset exposures, December 2022, www.bis.org/bcbs/publ/d545.pdf. Basel III reforms: new EU rules to increase banks' resilience to economic shocks (30 May 2024) www.consilium.europa.eu/en/press/press-releases/2024/05/30/basel-iii-reforms-new-eu-rules-to-increase-banks-resilience-to-economic-shocks/. Along with the on-going developments at Basel Committee level, CRR 3 introduced a transitional prudential treatment for credit institutions' exposures to crypto-assets, taking into account MiCAR. This transitional prudential treatment is applicable until the adoption of the new regulatory framework as referred to in Article 501d(1) of the CRR 3.

[81] ibid Article 3(4).

[82] Recommendations by the FSB 2019, p 2.

is likely to be an established player in the digital economy, with access to users through the provision of a crypto-asset service and another product (ie, an ART or EMT). ESMA and the FSB refer to such players as 'multifunction crypto-asset intermediaries' (MCIs).[83] Through the connection of a token with the provision of a crypto-asset service, there could be a greater incentive for existing users to sign on and use the token to further benefit from the issuer's services. This criterion of 'significance' is based on a version of the platform effect. Interestingly, the initial proposal for MiCAR did not contain this criterion of significance.

8.2.4. Additional Obligations for Issuers of Significant ARTs

8.2.4.1. General Framework

Article 45 in its entirety deals with additional obligations imposed on issuers of ARTs classified as significant. These obligations are more comprehensive and extensive compared to those applicable to non-significant ARTs. This intensification of requirements has not been without criticism.[84]

Significant ARTs are associated with higher risks due to their larger scale of use, greater exposure and stronger presence in the market. Therefore, they are subject to stronger supervisory measures and regulatory obligations. The application of stricter standards to significant players in the financial system is well-known. For example, the criteria for determining whether a bank is considered significant – and thus subject to additional requirements and the ECB's direct supervision – are set out in the SSM Regulations.[85]

Given the failure of Terra/Luna and others and the high concentration in the stablecoin markets (with USDT and USDC playing leading roles), the need for additional requirements for significant ART (and EMT) issuers is clear. The additional obligations for significant ARTs and their issuers concern: (i) remuneration policy, (ii) fair, reasonable and non-discriminatory custody and diversification of custodians, (iii) liquidity necessary for redemption purposes, (iv) regular stress testing, and (v) reserve requirements. We will discuss these obligations below. Every issuer involved in a significant token must fulfil those obligations individually.

[83] ESMA, Opinion to support the convergent application of MiCA, 31 July 2024, www.esma.europa.eu/sites/default/files/2024-07/ESMA75-453128700-1048_Opinion_on_broker_models.pdf; FSB, FSB assesses risks of multi-function crypto-asset intermediaries, 23 November 2023, defining MCIs as 'individual firms, or groups of affiliated firms – such as FTX (prior to its failure) – that combine a broad range of crypto-asset services, products, and functions typically centred around the operation of a trading platform.'

[84] Hansen and Bauer (n 3), arguing that the threshold for significance under MiCAR is too low and that the MiCAR's approach of a straightforward dichotomy ('yes or no') on the significance question lacks nuance and does not respond to the relative systemic risk posed by an institution.

[85] ECB, Supervisory Manual (January 2024) www.bankingsupervision.europa.eu/ecb/pub/pdf/ssm.supervisory_guides202401_manual.en.pdf.

8.2.4.2. Remuneration Policy

The financial crisis of 2007–2008 prompted supervisory and regulatory authorities to recognise the role that remuneration systems in large financial institutions played in encouraging risky behaviour.[86] Because these systems significantly affect an institution's risk profile, extensive guidelines and rules were established to set requirements for remuneration systems. CRD III and subsequent legal instruments, particularly those concerning financial service providers and credit institutions, outline requirements for the remuneration policies of supervised institutions.[87] The concept of 'sound and effective risk management', relevant to remuneration policies, was introduced in CRD III[88] and retained in CRD IV,[89] representing a core element of the regulatory framework for financial institutions. This concept serves as the basis for Article 45(1).

According to Article 45(1), issuers of significant ARTs must 'adopt, implement and maintain a remuneration policy that promotes the sound and effective risk management of such issuers and that does not create incentives to relax risk standards.' A similar wording can be found in the Investment Firms Directive (IFD).[90] The EBA Guidelines on sound remuneration policies under IFD specify that remuneration requirements should not incentivise excessive risk-taking and should be aligned with the long-term interests of investment firms across the EU.[91] The guidelines observe that for certain staff members, the alignment of the variable remuneration with the risk profile of the investment firms or the assets they manage is crucial. In view of the need to ensure a level playing field and cross-sectoral consistency, these considerations are likely to be relevant for issuers of significant ARTs as well.

Furthermore, for issuers of significant ARTs, examining the ESMA guidelines on remuneration policy requirements under the MiFID framework,[92] along with the FSB Principles for Sound Compensation Practices and their Implementation Standards developed for large financial institutions,[93] can provide valuable insights and an outlook into the likely direction of the EBA's standards to be developed and applied under Article 45.

[86] See Recitals of the Directive 2010/76/EU of the European Parliament and of the Council of 24 November 2010 amending Directives 2006/48/EC and 2006/49/EC as regards capital requirements for the trading book and for re-securitisations, and the supervisory review of remuneration policies (CRD III, no longer in force). For example, Recital (1) observes that '[w]hile the causes of such risk-taking are many and complex, there is agreement by supervisors and regulatory bodies, [...] that the inappropriate remuneration structures of some financial institutions have been a contributory factor.'

[87] See MiFID II, Article 9(3)(c); CRD IV, Article 92 and EBA Guidelines on sound remuneration policies under Directive 2013/36/EU, EBA/GL/2021/04, 2 July 2021, EBA/GL/2021/13, 21 November 2021.

[88] CRD III, Recitals (1) and (3) and Annex I.

[89] CRD IV, Recital (62), Article 74.

[90] Directive (EU) 2019/2034 of 27 November 2019 on the prudential supervision of investment firms, Article 30.

[91] EBA, Final Report on Guidelines on sound remuneration policies under Directive (EU) 2019/2023, 3.

[92] ESMA guidelines on certain aspects of the MiFID II remuneration requirements, ESMA35-43-3565, 3 April 2023.

[93] FSF Principles for Sound Compensation Practices, 2 April 2009; FSB Principles for Sound Compensation Practices: Implementation Standards, 25 September 2009.

On 6 June 2024, the EBA published Draft Regulatory Technical Standards (RTS) on the minimum content of the governance arrangements on the remuneration policy under Article 45.[94] These RTS outline key governance processes for the adoption and maintenance of the remuneration policy and the main elements that should be included in that policy. These elements include requirements designed to ensure the long-term risk alignment of variable remuneration, such as a maximum ratio between variable and fixed remuneration, a link between variable remuneration and the performance of the ART issuer and its staff, and the payment of variable remuneration partly in issued tokens.

8.2.4.3. *Fair, Reasonable and Non-discriminatory Custody*

Issuers of significant ARTs are required to create conditions for the custody of these tokens by various CASPs, (i) which are authorised for the custody and administration of crypto-assets under MiCAR, and (ii) which do not belong to the same group as the issuer, as defined in Article 2(11) of the Accounting Directive.[95] This provision requires ART issuers to establish interoperability – the ability of ARTs to be placed in custody with different third-party custodians, and, therefore, partly constitutes a technical requirement.

CASPs are further expected to provide custody and administration of significant ARTs in a 'fair, reasonable, and non-discriminatory' manner. Similar wording can be found in MiFID II.[96] However, under MiCAR, issuers of significant ARTs must ensure that CASPs adhere to these principles and are therefore indirectly responsible for compliance (eg, through the design of the token and choice of CASPs). For the purpose of interpretation of the general principles, MiFiD II and related RTS may be useful (eg, for non-discriminatory market making schemes).[97]

8.2.4.4. *Assessment and Supervision of Liquidity*

It is the responsibility of an ART issuer to create a robust liquidity profile of the reserve assets through appropriate strategies and liquidity management procedures to ensure that requests for the redemption of ARTs by token holders can be met

[94] EBA, Draft Regulatory Technical Standards on the minimum content of the governance arrangements on the remuneration policy under Article 45 of Regulation (EU) 2023/1114 www.eba.europa.eu/sites/default/files/2024-06/4998fc26-cc88-4ada-835c-292f831a4ccd/Final%20report%20on%20draft%20RTS%20on%20governance%20arrangements%20for%20remuneration%20under%20%20MICAR.pdf.

[95] Directive 2013/34/EU of the European Parliament and of the Council of 26 June 2013 on the annual financial statements, consolidated financial statements and related reports of certain types of undertakings, Article 2(11) defining a 'group' as 'a parent undertaking and all its subsidiary undertakings'.

[96] MiFID II, Article 48(8)–(9).

[97] Commission Delegated Regulation (EU) 2017/578 of 13 June 2016 supplementing Directive 2014/65/EU of the European Parliament and of the Council on markets in financial instruments with regard to regulatory technical standards specifying the requirements on market making agreements and schemes, Article 7.

(Article 45(3)). Article 45(7)(b) specifies that the minimum amount of deposits in each official currency must not fall below 60 per cent of the amount referenced in that currency. The ultimate goal is to guarantee that the reserve assets maintain a resilient liquidity profile, allowing the issuer of a significant ART to continue operating normally, even during periods of liquidity stress.

The liquidity management requirements address the risk of a 'run on the bank' due to a loss of confidence in the issuer (see section 8.2.1). Although these requirements may limit the issuer's operational and investment flexibility, they aim to foster trust in crypto markets (one of MiCAR's goals) and could encourage wider public adoption of tokens.

The EBA, in collaboration with ESMA, prepared Draft RTS to specify the minimum contents of the liquidity management policy and procedures.[98] These RTS state that the 'composition and management of the reserve assets, particularly the degree to which they could be liquidated rapidly at or close to prevailing market prices, is of key importance.'[99] This is to ensure that in case of large-scale redemptions, the reserve assets can be quickly liquidated in large volume without suffering significant value loss due to a 'fire sale'.[100]

The liquidity management policy and procedures need to include, inter alia: the issuer's liquidity risk management framework (outlining processes for identifying, measuring, managing and reporting liquidity risk); the issuer's strategy for managing the reserve assets in an effective and prudent manner (including the determination of the minimum size of the asset reserves, criteria to determine their market value, concentration limits, correlation between referenced assets and the reserve assets); a liquidity contingency plan (including strategies for addressing liquidity shortfalls, liquidity risk mitigation tools, triggers for early reaction); a description of the custody policy ensuring prompt access to the reserve assets; and a description of the liquidity stress testing framework in accordance with Article 45(4).

8.2.4.5. Liquidity Stress Tests

Article 45(4) requires issuers of significant ARTs to conduct liquidity stress tests on a regular basis to test whether their systems and reserves are 'robust' enough to withstand large-scale redemptions. The risks to be evaluated through these stress tests include not only redemption risk but also risks related to deposits with credit institutions, market risk and volatility, and de-pegging risk.

[98] EBA, Draft RTS to specify the minimum contents of the liquidity management policy and procedures under Article 45(7)(b) of Regulation (EU) 2023/1114.

[99] ibid para 6.

[100] On the liquidity of reserve assets, see EBA, Draft Regulatory Technical Standards to specify the highly liquid financial instruments with minimal market risk, credit risk and concentration risk under Article 38(5) of Regulation (EU) 2023/1114, EBA/RTS/2024/11, 13 June 2024; EBA, Draft Regulatory Technical Standards to further specify the liquidity requirements of the reserve of assets under Article 36(4) of Regulation (EU) 2023/1114, EBA/RTS/2024/10, 13 June 2024.

The stress testing exercise will enable the EBA to collect more information, representing another example of collaboration between market participants and regulatory or supervisory authorities in testing the applicability of MiCAR and gathering data. Based on the outcome of the liquidity stress test, the EBA or, where applicable, relevant NCA, may decide to strengthen the issuer's liquidity requirements, for example, by setting up a higher reserve asset amount, increasing diversification of asset composition, or reducing the maturity of invested assets.[101]

8.2.4.6. *Own Funds Requirement*

According to Article 45(5), issuers of significant ARTs must adhere to a 3 per cent own funds ratio in their reserves, compared to 2 per cent for all other issuers (Article 35(1)). In other words, such issuers are required to hold higher amounts of own funds, which shall be at least 3 per cent of the average amount of the reserve assets. This requirement is also directed at building trust in the capital strength of the issuer and mitigating the risk of large losses for token holders. Yet, even this seemingly small increase in the amount of own funds (from 2 per cent to 3 per cent) has faced criticism in the literature.[102] In an earlier draft proposal, an increase to 25 per cent was suggested, which would almost certainly have crippled issuers.

8.2.5. Supervisory Structure

The classification of a token as a significant ART results in a transfer of supervisory powers and duties to the EBA, the supranational European financial supervisory authority.[103] The role of the EBA and its extended powers under MiCAR are set out in detail in Title VII and are discussed in chapter ten of this book. Specifically, Article 117 lists the EBA's supervisory tasks in relation to issuers of significant ARTs and significant EMTs.

Notably, in this instance, supervision is assigned to the EBA, rather than the ECB. The ECB, as the primary supervisory authority for traditional financial market players, would have seemed the more obvious choice. This decision sparked criticism before MiCAR's finalisation.[104] A key discussion point was whether the ECB's

[101] EBA, Guidelines establishing the common reference parameters of the stress test scenarios for the liquidity stress tests referred in Article 45(4) Regulation (EU) 2023/1114, EBA/GL/2024/08, 19 June 2024.

[102] Hansen and Bauer (n 3).

[103] On a brief overview of the ESAs, see European system of financial supervision, finance.ec.europa.eu/regulation-and-supervision/european-system-financial-supervision_en.

[104] H Schelling et al, 'ECB issues opinion on Markets in Crypto Assets Regulation (MiCA) and European Parliament Rapporteur tables own changes' (16 March 2021) www.dentons.com/en/insights/articles/2021/march/16/ecb-issues-opinion-on-markets-in-crypto-assets-regulation-eu-parliament-rapporteur-tables-changes.

role within MiCAR might be too insignificant, given its mandate to protect the currency and maintain monetary stability.[105] The ECB has extensive expertise in safeguarding financial stability. Under MiCAR's allocation of roles, the supervisory powers between the EBA and the ECB need to be coordinated, in particular, if a major credit institution issues a significant token and must be supervised under different regulatory schemes. In such a case, concentrating powers in the ECB, given its existing structures, might have been advantageous and easier to navigate. The EBA arguably has more expertise in setting technological standards, which will be useful to navigate the technological hazards of the crypto-asset market.

The transfer of supervision to the EBA may be seen as an intrusion into the competences of NCAs. Since a purely local token could be subject to supervision by the EBA if deemed significant, this transfer of power was criticised during negotiations with Member States. According to Recital (66) of the Proposal for MiCAR, this strategic decision was intended to prevent supervisory arbitrage across Member States and to centralise supervision within the EBA. Standardised supervision must be applied with a focus on systemic relevance. As an EU agency, the EBA is better equipped to address risks at this higher level.

8.3. Regulation of Significant EMTs

8.3.1. Introduction

As discussed earlier, an e-money token (EMT) is a type of crypto-asset that purports to maintain a stable value by referencing the value of one official currency ('fiat' currency). The EMT issuer is obliged to redeem each issued EMT at par value at any time. Due to the EMT's reference to one official currency and the additional safety for the users through the redemption option, the Commission considered the risk of EMTs being widely adopted as a means of payment to be high, even higher than for ARTs. Such widespread adoption could potentially disrupt financial stability in the Euro area and lead to systemic risks, similar to those posed by significant ARTs.

Therefore, if an EMT fulfils certain significance requirements, it should as well be subjected to a specific significance regime. Only e-money institutions and credit institutions are allowed to issue EMTs. This requires balancing the regulatory frameworks for credit institutions and e-money institutions with the newly introduced significance regime under MiCAR. Due to the correlation and overlap with e-money, and the potential for regulatory conflicts, special consideration has been given to the situation of e-money institutions issuing EMTs.

[105] Opinion of the European Central Bank of 19 February 2021 on a proposal for a regulation on Markets in Crypto-assets, and amending Directive (EU) 2019/1937, eur-lex.europa.eu/legal-content/EN/TXT/?uri=CELEX%3A52021AB0004.

In the Impact Assessment, the Commission considered whether the E-Money Directive (EMD2) should apply to stablecoins in general. Ultimately, this approach was rejected, as the provisions of EMD2 were not considered to be appropriate. This was particularly due to the absence of provisions for e-money that becomes systemically relevant. In other words, EMD2 lacks the significance regime. However, the Commission recognised the need for such a regime and a special set of rules, which were implemented in Title IV, Chapter 2.

Although the EU legislator decided against the complete application of EMD2 to EMTs, there are still some parallels, overlaps and interdependencies, which can result in regulatory complexity. The special obligations of Article 58 do not apply to credit institutions, since they are not subject to similar obligations under the E-Money Directive. Another parallel is that issuers of EMTs will generally be supervised by the same authorities as those under the E-Money Directive.

8.3.2. Classification and Regulation of Significant EMTs

According to Article 56, the criteria of Article 43(1) are applied to EMTs to assess whether they are significant. Since the criteria for determining whether an e-money token is to be regarded as 'significant' under MiCAR are the same as for asset-referenced token, we will not discuss them in great detail here. These 'significance' criteria are meant to determine if an EMT poses or can potentially pose serious risks to financial stability that justify additional regulatory burden. When several issuers issue the same EMT, the fulfilment of the criteria shall be assessed after aggregating the data from those issuers (Article 56(2)).

The procedure for classification follows the same rules as those that apply to the classification of ARTs as 'significant', as outlined in Articles 43 and 44. As with significant ARTs, there is a procedure for the voluntary classification of EMTs as significant (Article 57). In such cases, the competent authority must immediately notify the EBA and the ECB of the issuer's request.

8.3.3. Supervision of Significant EMTs

Supervision of significant EMTs is transferred from national authorities to the EBA (Article 56(6)). The competent authority must cooperate with the EBA to ensure a smooth transition of supervisory competences. However, there is an exception in Article 56(7). An EMT that references only one currency, particularly if used as a medium of exchange and for settling large-volume transactions, could increase systemic risk for the Member State whose currency it references. Recognising this, and aiming to keep national competent authorities as involved as possible, Article 56(7) contains an exemption from the rule of supervisory power transfer.

The supervisory responsibilities with respect to issuers of significant EMTs denominated in an official currency of a Member State other than Euro, where at least 80 per cent of the holders and transaction volumes are concentrated in the home Member State, will not be transferred to the EBA. Since the risks do not extend to the entire eurozone but are concentrated in one Member State, transferring supervision would not be feasible. In such cases, the national competent authorities will retain their supervisory responsibilities. The risks may be less noticeable in the eurozone compared to the risks posed to the financial system of the Member State concerned. For the purposes of determining whether the exception applies, a transaction is considered to take place in the home Member State (ie, the Member State of the issuer) when either the payer or the payee is established in that Member State. If the exception in Article 56(7) applies, the competent authority must report information about the significant EMT to the EBA annually. Besides, the EBA retains supervisory powers under Article 130, governing supervisory measures in a situation of infringement.

The exception in Article 56(7) applies only if an EMT references an official currency of a Member State other than the Euro. As of now, there are very few such EMTs, and even fewer of them could potentially become significant. The largest stablecoins likely to be qualified as significant EMTs are denominated in USD (which is not an official currency of any EU Member State) and therefore will not be subject to the exception. This means that significant EMTs referencing USD and falling within MiCAR scope will be directly supervised by the EBA. This is reasonable. One of the risks considered particularly high for significant EMTs is that of a 'run on the bank'. If an EMT assumes a currency-substituting function without the corresponding security and safety net that an official currency has, this could lead to major losses for users in the event of inadequate management of asset reserves and liquidity bottlenecks. Increased requirements must therefore be implemented to protect consumers – holders of significant EMTs, reflecting the consumer protection idea behind many of the rules in MiCAR.

8.3.4. Additional Obligations for Issuers of Significant EMTs

The Commission assumes that EMTs have a higher chance of being adopted in the same way as an official currency – due to the referencing of a currency and 'digital money' appeal – and could fulfil a similar function as money. Therefore, their issuers must be subject to increased scrutiny. However, to date, no digital currency has achieved such widespread acceptance and extensive adoption by consumers.[106]

Article 58(1) establishes additional obligations for issuers of EMTs, including significant EMTs. While these obligations (by default) only apply to e-money institutions issuing significant EMTs, they can also be extended to those issuing

[106] Not even the Digital Euro project by the ECB has been able to garner such support and widespread acceptance, despite being an official project led by the ECB. Due to the high complexity and general scepticism towards digital payments, particularly in Germany, it is difficult to implement such a new concept of money or value, and this certainly cannot happen 'overnight'.

non-significant EMTs if a competent authority of a home Member State so requires (Article 58(2)). Finally, Article 58 extends the application of specific rules to EMTs denominated in a non-EU currency (eg, USD). Among these rules is an important provision imposing major restrictions on the issuance of tokens used widely as a means of exchange (Article 23).

Recital (71) explains that significant EMTs could pose greater risks to financial stability, and that e-money institutions issuing them are therefore subject to additional requirements. These issuers must comply with higher capital requirements than other EMT issuers, be subject to interoperability requirements, and establish a liquidity management policy. Among the rules applicable to e-money institutions issuing significant EMTs are those listed in Article 45 and covered in the preceding sections (eg, remuneration policy, liquidity management policy and procedures, liquidity stress testing). These requirements take precedence over the obligations of EMD2. These issuers must also comply with some of the same requirements that apply to issuers of ARTs concerning the reserve of assets, such as those on custody and investment of the reserve of assets (Articles 36–38).

As noted above, if an e-money institution issues significant EMTs, the requirements in relation to the asset reserve (Article 36), its safekeeping (Article 37) and the guidelines on how it might be invested (Article 38) of MiCAR apply. Furthermore, the additional obligations set for issuers of significant ARTs under Article 45(1)–(4) also apply to such e-money institutions. In accordance with Article 58(1), these institutions must fulfil all of these requirements instead of fulfilling Article 7 EMD2. The latter contains certain safeguarding requirements with respect to the funds that have been received in exchange for the issued e-money. The received funds should either be placed in a designated separate bank account or invested in secure, liquid, and low-risk assets held in a separate account with a custodian.

Also, pursuant to Article 58(1)(b), the capital requirements applicable to e-money institutions issuing significant EMTs are not governed by Article 5 EMD2 (which states that the own funds of an electronic money institution for the activity of issuing electronic money shall amount to at least 2 per cent of the average outstanding electronic money), but by Article 35(2),(3) and (5) and Article 45(5) MiCAR, which stipulates a capital ratio of 3 per cent of the amount of the reserve assets for issuers of significant ARTs. This means that there is a higher own funds requirement compared to those established under EMD2, reflecting the higher risk profile of issuers of significant EMTs. Hence, MiCAR takes precedence over EMD2, as the latter was not designed to address the specific risks posed by significant EMTs. This is consistent with the recommendations of the FSB regarding stablecoins in general, without differentiating between ARTs and EMTs.[107]

[107] FSB, Cross-border Regulatory and Supervisory Issues of Global Stablecoin Arrangements in EMDEs, 23 July 2024, www.fsb.org/uploads/P230724.pdf, listing among concerns caused by global stablecoins risks related to 'financial stability, illicit finance, data privacy, cyber-security, consumer and investor protections, market integrity, fiscal stability, and macroeconomic stability.'

As the threshold qualifying as a significant EMT is high, and not many EMTs will be able to meet it, there should also be the possibility of applying increased security requirements to 'less significant' EMTs, as the Commission identified the risks of EMTs to be of a general nature and not only connected to the significance aspect. Therefore, pursuant to Article 58(2), NCAs of the Member States where the relevant e-money institutions are located may decide to apply the stricter requirements outlined in Article 58(1) to EMTs that do not reach the significance threshold. This can be done if necessary 'to address the risks that those provisions aim to address, such as liquidity risks, operational risks, or risks arising from non-compliance with requirements for management of reserve of assets.' This also aligns with the policy goal of enhancing consumer protection for such EMTs and holding e-money institutions accountable to high standards of risk assessment and management.

8.4. Regulation of Significant CASPs

8.4.1. Introduction

CASPs are also subject to close monitoring under the MiCAR regime. As the 'platform effect' was already recognised in the regime of significant ARTs, a similar observation can be made with respect to CASPs. Service providers may gain significance due to a large customer base, offering of services across national borders and a combination of various activities and services under the same 'roof'. As a result, a CASP might gain significant influence in the EU area. Recent examples, such as the collapses of Three Arrows Capital, Voyager, Celsius, FTX, Alameda, BlockFi, Genesis, Bittrex Inc., and other crypto enterprises, have shown that CASPs with such colossal reach can have a huge impact on consumers, especially in light of numerous cyber risks, the prevalence of hacks, and instances of fraud. In the aftermath of these crypto failures, discussions have centred around the fragility and economic viability of some of their business models, market integration and interconnectedness, corporate governance failures, inadequate regulatory frameworks, and the high risks faced by crypto investors. Large CASPs accumulate and control vast amounts of data and assets and carry out a substantial number of transactions. Therefore, the creation of a separate regime for significant CASPs in Title V, Chapter 5, is fully justified.

The provision concerning the identification of significant crypto-asset service providers (Article 85) was only introduced to MiCAR at the last minute and is not found in the earlier MiCAR Proposal. The article first appeared in 2022, when it was proposed in the Provisional Agreement resulting from interinstitutional negotiations dated 5 October 2022.[108] It introduces the 'significance' qualification

[108] Provisional Agreement resulting from interinstitutional negotiations, subject: Proposal for a regulation of the European Parliament and of the Council on markets in crypto-assets and amending Directive

for CASPs. Although the risks potentially arising from the activity of a significant CASP could be substantial, MiCAR only establishes additional notification and information obligations. For significant CASPs, ESMA is involved in the monitoring. Information collected during the first years of MiCAR will be used to prepare for revised regulation and to ensure the future ability of the European supervisory authorities to act to the extent necessary. MiCAR currently focuses on 'transparency and reporting obligations'. Any future regulation may be expanded to include new obligations or requirements for significant CASPs.

8.4.2. Classification of a CASP as Significant

8.4.2.1. Criteria for a Significant CASP and Assessment

According to Article 85(1), a CASP should be deemed significant if it has in the EU 'at least 15 million active users, on average, in one calendar year, whereby the average is calculated as the average of the daily number of active users throughout the previous calendar year.' Thus, the classification of significant CASPs is based on the number of their active users (ie, minimum of 15 million per calendar year). The concept of an 'active user' is discussed below.

Compared to the 'gatekeeper' classification under the DMA, the MiCAR threshold appears lower. Pursuant to Article 3(2) DMA, a gatekeeper must provide 'a core platform service that in the last financial year has at least 45 million monthly active end users established or located in the Union and at least 10,000 yearly active business users established in the Union [...].' However, it must be kept in mind that Article 85 fulfils the purpose of gathering information and therefore serves a different purpose than the regulation of gatekeepers in the Digital Markets Act. A lower threshold is thus justified but should still only apply to CASPs that have gained significant importance in the EU market. To put this number into perspective, the most widely used worldwide online social network Facebook counted roughly three billion monthly active users in the second quarter of 2023.[109] Should the MiCAR threshold turn out to be unfit, it can be revisited in the future.

Further, the concept of 'active users' should be understood as an autonomous concept under EU law. Similar concepts can be found in the Digital Services Act (DSA)[110] and the DMA. These acts may have provided inspiration, given that they were finalised around the time Article 85 was introduced to MiCAR. The DSA

(EU) 2019/1937 (COM(2020) 0593 – C9-0306/2020–2020/0265(COD)) (Provisional Agreement) www.europarl.europa.eu/RegData/commissions/econ/inag/2022/10-05/ECON_AG(2022)737216_EN.pdf.

[109] Facebook: quarterly number of MAU (monthly active users) worldwide 2008–2023 (21 May 2024) www.statista.com/statistics/264810/number-of-monthly-active-facebook-users-worldwide/#:~:text=With%20roughly%20three%20billion%20monthly,years%20to%20reach%20this%20milestone.

[110] Regulation (EU) 2022/2065 of the European Parliament and of the Council of 19 October 2022 on a Single Market For Digital Services and amending Directive 2000/31/EC.

refers to 'active recipients' and the DMA uses the term 'active end users'. Both concepts are meant to accurately reflect actual usage, counting only users who actively engage with the platform's services.

The DMA includes an Annex that sets out how to properly count relevant users, taking into account data such as registered user accounts and IP addresses to reduce duplication risks. The DMA calculates monthly active end users 'based on the average number of monthly active end users throughout the largest part of the financial year.'[111] This is a different approach from the one used in MiCAR, which references the average daily users over the previous calendar year.

The DSA refers to 'active recipients' of the relevant services. These recipients should actually engage with an online platform 'by being exposed to information disseminated on the online interface of the online platform, such as viewing it or listening to it, or by providing information, such as traders on an online platforms allowing consumers to conclude distance contracts with traders.'[112] While the DMA puts more emphasis on spotting 'fake accounts' or 'bots' by trying to minimise a risk of duplication, the DSA prioritises active user engagement, shifting focus onto the 'services' part.

The approaches taken in the DMA and DSA are highly relevant for Article 85. Many crypto-asset services can be offered that do not require any further active action or engagement by the user. These include, for instance, the safekeeping of client's crypto-assets or other custodial services, and reception and transmission of orders for crypto-assets on behalf of clients. Thus, it initially seems appropriate to primarily use the number of registered accounts with a CASP to assess the number of users – persons using services of a CASP. This approach also serves to avoid double counting. However, relying solely on this figure may not sufficiently fulfil the requirement of 'active' users, especially on a daily basis. As the daily average is to be determined, those users must be counted who receive the corresponding service on a given sample day. This means that such a user should not only be counted on a day when a request for the service is made, but also on any other day when such service is performed or, in the words of the DSA, when the user is 'exposed' to the information provided by the CASP. The ongoing, uninterrupted provision and use of a service that does not require daily active interaction must also be covered in accordance with the purpose of the provision. In this case, the users will still come into contact with the information provided by the CASP. Only a purely inactive user account would be insufficient and should not be counted.

There is no distinction to be made between private and business users. However, the users must be located in the EU for the purposes of MiCAR. The number of active users must be recorded and calculated by the CASP itself. As soon as the threshold of Article 85(1) is reached, the CASP must within two months report to

[111] DMA, Annex, B(2).
[112] DSA, Recital (77).

the competent authority. If the competent authority agrees with the determination of the number, it must notify ESMA.[113]

However, as the number of users is to be calculated as an average based on the users over the entire previous calendar year, the question remains as to when this reporting deadline should actually begin. The figures for the previous year will only be available to the CASP after the end of the entire calendar year, once the internal processes of counting and calculation have been completed, and only then can an average be calculated. Consequently, this means that the CASP must report its results within two months of determining and calculating the number of users – in the best case, at the beginning of each calendar year. However, this also means that such a deadline could be pushed back if the relevant CASP has inefficient internal processes that delay the internal assessment of such data. As no absolute deadline has been set, it is to be seen whether the CASPs will act in good faith, trying to provide such numbers efficiently within a reasonable timeframe, or whether some may delay the reporting to avoid any possible scrutiny by ESMA.

8.4.2.2. Role of ESMA in the Supervision of Significant CASPs

A leading supervisory authority for significant CASPs is ESMA.[114] Pursuant to Article 85, ESMA is given a monitoring, and to a certain extent, supervisory role in overseeing significant CASPs. NCAs remain responsible for the general supervisory tasks, unlike in the supervision of significant tokens. NCAs should engage in extensive and regular exchanges of information with ESMA, which is required to pool the information from all Member States.

It was already agreed in the Provisional Agreement that ESMA should assume a leading position in the supervision of significant CASPs. This decision is based on the fact that the EBA is already responsible for the supervision of issuers of significant ARTs and EMTs (Articles 43 and 56) and that pursuant to Articles 63 and 109, ESMA had already been awarded certain responsibilities concerning CASPs (ie, keeping the general register of CASPs). It was therefore a natural decision to pool all information on CASPs, including significant ones, with ESMA. ESMA further retains the general competences it was awarded in accordance with Articles 29, 30, 31 and 31b ESMA Regulation and can make use of them under the regime of significant CASPs, to the extent necessary.[115] This includes the possibility of taking measures beyond Article 85 and becoming more active should the need arise. For example, it could issue an opinion to NCAs and, hence, assume a more coordinating role.

This could, for example, be done by a briefing. A briefing does not amount to hard or soft law, though, it does send a clear message to the NCAs and will

[113] MiCAR, Article 85(2).

[114] On the role and powers of supervisory authorities within the MiCAR framework, see ch 10 of this book.

[115] MiCAR, Article 85(5).

help steer a common approach in the right direction. This does also accord with Article 106 MiCAR, which states that ESMA 'shall perform a facilitating and coordinating role in relation to measures taken by competent authorities'. Through its measures, ESMA 'shall ensure that measures taken by a competent authority are justified and proportionate and that a consistent approach is taken by competent authorities, where appropriate.'[116] For this purpose, under Article 103, ESMA is also awarded further powers for 'temporary intervention' and may even prohibit certain activities related to crypto-assets (therefore also an activity of a CASP) on its own and override the NCA.

ESMA may initially seem like a toothless tiger for significant CASPs, but that perception changes upon closer examination. The aim of the significance regime for CASPs is, first and foremost, to collect information. First, CASPs must report their figures to the relevant authorities. Second, national competent authorities are obliged to report to ESMA within the framework of Article 85. According to Article 85(3), these reports should include information on: (i) ongoing or concluded authorisations, (ii) ongoing or concluded processes of withdrawal of authorisations, and (iii) the exercise of supervisory powers set out in Article 94(1) (b), (c), (e), (f), (g), (y) and (aa). The reporting topics concern measures that the NCAs can take in relation to significant CASPs. Specifically, they can include requesting documentation, ordering the suspension of the provision of the service for up to 30 days, and prohibiting the provision of the service.

When deciding on these measures, ESMA's Board of Supervisors could informally support the competent authority as part of the exchange of views under Article 85(4). This procedure adheres to the principle of collaboration and close coordination with the NCAs, which is a leading principle underpinning the rules and regulations introduced for significant tokens and significant CASPs. One important difference, however, is that, unlike issuers of significant ARTs or EMTs, which are supervised primarily at the EU level, significant CASPs remain under the supervision of national authorities. Article 85 seeks to promote an active exchange and collaboration among supervisory authorities without aiming to interfere with the sovereignty of Member States.

8.5. Conclusion

The concept of 'significance' appears in several chapters of MiCAR and is one of the few original concepts exclusive to this regulation. It stems from the same motivation that led to the creation of MiCAR in the first place: to monitor an evolving digital financial ecosystem independent of traditional institutions, which could be replaced by a new category of market players, and independent of official currencies, which may be replaced by various coins and tokens. Also in light of CBDC

[116] MiCAR, Article 106(1).

initiatives, the possible interactions between privately issued tokens and CBDC will become more relevant and evolvement of a token economy is undisputed.

As most parts of the digital and crypto markets continue to evolve, one of the main objectives of MiCAR is to collect data and information, as reflected by multiple reporting obligations. The objective is not to hinder market development to foster technological advancement but to be prepared to intervene when necessary to protect consumers, financial stability, or the monetary system itself.

It is worth noting that, by and large, the FSB's and other recommendations have been followed. Market participants should also closely monitor reports such as those of the FSB and any published data for future developments. In the current MiCAR environment, legislative bodies appear open to allowing the possibility of highly influential players in the crypto space, which was not guaranteed following the extremely cautious response to the Meta/Facebook proposal. Thus, the existing legislative framework presents an opportunity to collaborate closely and demonstrate to regulatory and supervisory bodies that the risk profile of significant players and stablecoins is manageable and can be adequately addressed.

9

Prevention and Prohibition of Market Abuse Involving Crypto-Assets

NICK CAMPUZANO AND ROGIER RAAS

9.1. Introduction

This chapter addresses Title VI MiCAR, which concerns the prevention and prohibition of market abuse involving crypto-assets. Preventing market abuse in relation to crypto-assets is one of the main goals of MiCAR.[1] According to the European Commission (EC), rules to deter market abuse are necessary to ensure the integrity of, and confidence in, markets in crypto-assets.[2] Although the EC's intention was to design a distinct and specific market abuse framework for crypto-assets, the resulting framework outlined in Title VI is almost identical to the corresponding prohibitions and obligations in the existing market abuse regime for financial instruments as laid down in Regulation (EU) No 596/2014 (hereafter: the 'Market Abuse Regulation' or 'MAR').[3]

Title VI MiCAR consists of Articles 86–92. Article 86 determines the scope of MiCAR's market abuse regime. Article 87 provides the definition of 'inside information'. Article 88 contains the obligation for issuers and others to publicly disclose inside information. Articles 89, 90 and 91, respectively, prohibit insider dealing, unlawful disclosure of inside information, and various forms of behaviour qualifying as market manipulation. Article 92 contains certain obligations for the detection and prevention of market abuse.

In the following sections, we will review the scope of MiCAR's market abuse regime, the various prohibitions and the obligations in relation to the prevention of

[1] See MiCAR, Article 1(2)(e).

[2] MiCAR, Recital (95). See also – the nearly identical – Recital (65) of the MiCAR Proposal.

[3] See Recital (95) MiCAR, which states: '(…) as issuers of crypto-assets and crypto-asset service providers are very often SMEs, it would be disproportionate to apply all of the provisions of [the MAR] to them. It is therefore necessary to lay down specific rules prohibiting certain behaviours that are likely to undermine user confidence in markets in crypto-assets and the integrity of those markets, including insider dealing, unlawful disclosure of inside information and market manipulation related to crypto-assets.'

market abuse involving crypto-assets under MiCAR. Section 9.2 sets out the scope of MiCAR's market abuse regime. Section 9.3 focuses on the concept of 'inside information'. Sections 9.4–9.7 address the duty to disclose inside information and various prohibitions found in Title VI. Section 9.8 discusses the obligations for the prevention and detection of market abuse. Section 9.9 concludes this chapter. For each of these topics, we will provide a descriptive analysis, including explanations of the relevant provisions in MiCAR and their substantive content. Although Title VI's market abuse regime was expressly designed as a distinct and dedicated framework for regulating crypto-assets, the undeniable resemblance between MiCAR and MAR justifies turning to MAR for interpreting specific provisions within Title VI. Ultimately, we will offer general commentary on the pertinent provisions and present some observations.

9.2. The Scope of Title VI

9.2.1. General Scope

The scope of MiCAR's market abuse regime is defined by Articles 2, 3, and 86. Articles 2 and 3 establish MiCAR's general scope. Both provisions have been thoroughly discussed in previous chapters.[4] Consequently, this chapter will only touch upon certain aspects of these provisions that are most relevant to the analysis of the rules on market abuse central to it.

MiCAR's market abuse regime in Title VI draws significant inspiration from MAR. A hint of this inspiration can already be detected in the determination of MiCAR's general scope of application in Article 2. The broad territorial scope set out in this article resembles a mix of the territorial scopes of various financial market regulations.[5] Article 2 delineates the general scope of MiCAR, restricting its application to 'natural and legal persons and certain other undertakings that are engaged in the issuance, offer to the public and admission to trading of crypto-assets or that provide services related to crypto-assets'.[6] The determining factor that is clearly derived from MAR is the 'admission to trading'.[7] This is also the main determining factor in Article 86, which sets out the scope of MiCAR's market abuse rules and will be further explored below.

[4] See chs 2, 3 and 4.

[5] See P Maume, 'The Regulation on Markets in Crypto-Assets (MiCAR): Landmark Codification, or First Step of Many, or Both?' (2023) 2 *European Company and Financial Law Regulation* 243, 261, observing that 'This is essentially an amalgamation of the territorial scope stipulated in MiFID2 (provision of services in the Union), in the MAR (admission to trading) and the Prospectus Regulation (issuance and offer to the public).'

[6] MiCAR, Article 2(1).

[7] See MAR, Article 2(1).

Article 2 also lists situations in which MiCAR does not apply.[8] According to this article, MiCAR does not apply to crypto-assets that qualify as financial instruments.[9] This exception underscores the rationale and necessity for a distinct market abuse regime, as crypto-assets subject to MiCAR are not covered by MAR, as MAR only regulates (crypto-assets qualifying as) 'financial instruments'.[10]

Article 3 provides the definitions used in MiCAR, thereby determining the material scope. For the market abuse regime, the most (and arguably the only) relevant definition in Article 3 is the definition of 'crypto-asset'. This key definition relies on additional definitions, which combined amount to the following:

> a digital representation of a value or of a right that is able to be transferred and stored electronically using a technology that enables the operation and use of an information depository that keeps records of transactions and that is shared across, and synchronised between, a set of DLT network nodes using rules and procedures by which an agreement is reached, among DLT network nodes, that a transaction is validated.[11]

9.2.2. Specific Scope of MiCAR's Rules on Market Abuse

Article 86 delineates the specific scope of MiCAR's rules on market abuse in Title VI, building upon the general scope outlined in Article 2.[12] Article 86(1) MiCAR establishes that the rules on market abuse are applicable to actions performed by any person concerning: (i) crypto-assets that are admitted to trading or (ii) crypto-assets in respect of which a request for admission to trading has been made.

Concerning crypto-assets that are 'admitted to trading', the Proposal for MiCAR initially specified that its provisions on market abuse would apply to 'crypto-assets admitted to trading on a trading platform for crypto-assets operated by an authorised crypto-asset service provider [...]'.[13] The final version of MiCAR,

[8] See MiCAR, Article 2(2)–(5).

[9] MiCAR, Article 2(4)(a). The definition of a 'financial instrument' is provided in Article 3(1)(49) MiCAR, which refers to Article 4(1)(15) MiFID II.

[10] Financial instruments as defined in Article 4(1)(15) of Directive 2014/65/EU of the European Parliament and of the Council of 15 May 2014 on markets in financial instruments and amending Directive 2002/92/EC and Directive 2011/61/EU (OJ L 173) (MiFID II).

[11] The definition of 'crypto-assets' is 'a digital representation of a value or of a right that is able to be transferred and stored electronically using distributed ledger technology or similar technology' (Article 3(1)(5)). The definition of 'distributed ledger technology' or 'DLT' is 'a technology that enables the operation and use of distributed ledgers' (Article 3(1)(1)). The definition of 'distributed ledger' is 'an information repository that keeps records of transactions and that is shared across, and synchronised between, a set of DLT network nodes using a consensus mechanism' (Article 3(1)(2)). Lastly, a 'consensus mechanism' means the 'rules and procedures by which an agreement is reached, among DLT network nodes, that a transaction is validated' (Article 3(1)(3)). See for more on these definitions ch 3 of this book.

[12] See section 9.2.1.

[13] Compare Recital (95) MiCAR with Recital (65) of the Proposal for MiCAR. The part 'on a trading platform for crypto-assets' is left out of the final version, arguably because 'admission of crypto-assets to trading on a trading platform for crypto-assets' is abbreviated to 'admission to trading' in Article 1(2)(a). See also Recital (23).

however, abbreviates this to 'admission to trading' in Article 1(2)(a). Although the definition of a 'trading platform for crypto-assets' is not explicitly provided, it can be inferred from the definition of the 'operation of a trading platform for crypto-assets' found in Article 3(1)(18). From this position, it follows that a trading platform for crypto-assets is a 'multilateral system [...], which bring[s] together or facilitate[s] the bringing together of multiple third-party purchasing and selling interests in crypto-assets, in the system and in accordance with its rules, in a way that results in a contract, either by exchanging crypto-assets for funds or by the exchange of crypto-assets for other crypto-assets'.[14] Importantly, a trading platform for crypto-assets has to be authorised under Article 76 MiCAR.

The applicability of MiCAR's market abuse regime to crypto-assets traded on non-authorised platforms remains uncertain. By deviating from the wording in the MiCAR Proposal and using the broader term 'admitted to trading' in Article 1(2)(a) of the final version, the European Commission may have intended to suggest that market abuse rules could apply to crypto-assets traded on non-authorised platforms as well. However, it is doubtful whether MiCAR aims to offer the same level of protection to investors on non-authorised platforms as it does to those on authorised platforms. Doing so could undermine investors' incentives to trade on authorised platforms and reduce the incentive for trading platforms to comply with MiCAR and receive authorisation status. Additionally, the discretion granted to operators of authorised platforms in setting criteria for admitting crypto-assets suggests that MiCAR's market abuse rules are intended only for assets that meet those criteria (thus have been approved by an authorised operator).[15] Therefore, it seems unlikely that the market abuse regime aims to cover crypto-assets traded on non-authorised platforms. Also, from a practical perspective, it seems unlikely that MiCAR's market abuse rules would extend to crypto-assets admitted to trading on non-authorised platforms, as these platforms may lack the necessary systems to prevent and detect market abuse effectively.[16] Although the MiCAR's market abuse regime's applicability to crypto-assets traded on non-authorised trading platforms remains to be clarified, it is unlikely that those crypto-assets are covered.

As for crypto-assets for which 'a request for admission to trading has been made', this part extends the market abuse rules to actions and omissions even before the crypto-asset is formally admitted to trading. This anticipatory inclusion makes sense given the heightened risk of market abuse during highly volatile events, such as the admittance to trading (also known as 'Initial Exchange Offering' or 'IEO').[17] The risk of market abuse during an IEO process is exceptionally high in the period before being formally admitted to trading. A person can only request admission to trading

[14] MiCAR, Article 3(1)(18). For the definition of 'exchange of crypto-assets for funds', see Article 3(1)(19). For the definition of 'exchange of crypto-assets for other crypto-assets', see Article 3(1)(20).

[15] MiCAR, Article 76(2).

[16] CASPs operating a trading platform must have systems in place to detect and prevent market abuse. See MiCAR, Article 76(7)(g).

[17] For other aspects that increase the vulnerability to abuse, see section 9.7.1.

of a crypto-asset if he complies with the requirements in Article 5(1). While MiCAR does not specify when a request for admission to trading is considered made, CASPs operating trading platforms are obliged under Article 76(1)(c) to establish policies, procedures, and fees for admission to trading. This indicates that the determination of when 'a request for admission to trading has been made' is left to the discretion of the relevant trading platform and requires case-by-case consideration.[18]

Article 86(2) extends the market abuse rules to transactions, orders, or behaviour related to crypto-assets in Article 86(1), regardless of whether these actions occur on a trading platform.[19] This means that MiCAR's market abuse regime encompasses any such actions, whether conducted on a trading platform or in other formats, such as face-to-face or over the phone. Although Article 86(2) extends the reach of the market abuse rules to a broader range of actions related to the legal object mentioned in Article 86(1) – crypto-assets that are admitted to trading or in respect of which a request for admission to trading has been made – it does not appear to extend the scope of the legal object itself. For example, Article 86(2) does not seem to extend the reach of the market abuse rules to crypto-assets that are not admitted to trading or that have been admitted to trading on a non-authorised platform.

Article 86(3) clarifies that the market abuse rules are applicable to actions and omissions within the EU and third countries concerning crypto-assets mentioned in paragraph 1. This provision clarifies two aspects. Firstly, it confirms the extraterritorial application of MiCAR rules for market abuse, meaning that actions outside the EU could fall within its scope. For instance, spreading false rumours in the US about a crypto-asset admitted to trading in the EU would be covered by MiCAR's market abuse regime. Secondly, it clarifies that the rules apply to both actions and *omissions*, a distinction not explicitly addressed in Article 86(1), which only mentions 'acts' carried out by any persons.

9.2.3. Observations and Commentary

9.2.3.1. Proportionality of Scope is Questionable

The EC deliberated on the prospect of applying all the provisions of MAR to crypto-assets falling within the scope of MiCAR. It ultimately concluded that such an approach would be disproportionate, particularly given that issuers of crypto-assets and CASPs are frequently small and medium-sized enterprises (SMEs).[20] However, it remains unclear which specific provisions of MAR the European Commission

[18] This interpretation of the lack of a specific explanation when a request has been made is also consistent with the approach prescribed for regulated markets under MiFID II. See eg MiFID II, Article 51 and Recital (122).

[19] See MiCAR, Articles 86(1) and 86(2).

[20] See MiCAR, Recital (95). See also the nearly identical Recital (65) Proposal for MiCAR.

considered disproportionate and why. Neither MiCAR nor its Proposal, including the accompanying Impact Assessment, provides a clear explanation for why applying all provisions of MAR is deemed disproportionate. Therefore, the validity of the EC's conclusion is questionable.

Nevertheless, the conclusion that applying all MAR provisions would be disproportionate prompted the introduction of a market abuse regime tailored specifically for crypto-assets covered by MiCAR.[21] Yet, despite the intention of adopting a tailored approach, Title VI of MiCAR closely mirrors the core prohibitions and obligations of MAR. It incorporates analogous prohibitions concerning insider dealing, unlawful disclosure of inside information, and market manipulation, echoing the regulatory framework of MAR.[22] Furthermore, Title VI of MiCAR imposes similar obligations to prevent and detect market abuse as those stipulated in MAR.[23] However, in contrast to MAR, which accommodates certain exemptions, such as an exemption in the provisions on market manipulation for buy-back programs and stabilisation, Title VI takes a more stringent stance by not providing any exemptions whatsoever.[24] By including most of the MAR's prohibitions and obligations while excluding any of its exemptions, the EC may have inadvertently made MiCAR's market abuse regime significantly more disproportionate than it initially communicated.

9.2.3.2. Inconsistencies due to Copy/Paste Approach

Article 86(1) represents a modified version of MAR's scope, where the term 'financial instrument' is replaced with 'crypto-assets'.[25] A notable difference is that MAR applies to 'financial instruments,' while Article 86(1) applies to 'acts carried out by any person concerning crypto-assets', rather than to the crypto-assets themselves. Although the rationale behind this deviation remains unclear, it appears to be a more concise formulation. The wording of Article 86(1) has undergone minimal changes since its inclusion in the initial Proposal for MiCAR.

In contrast, Article 86(2), which states that '[t]his Title shall also apply to any transaction, order or behaviour concerning crypto-assets as referred to in

[21] See MiCAR, Recital (95) and Recital (65) Proposal for MiCAR.

[22] For the prohibition of insider dealing, compare Article 89 MiCAR with Articles 14(a) and 8 MAR. See also section 9.5. For the prohibition of unlawful disclosure of inside information, compare Article 90 MiCAR with Articles 14(c) and 10 MAR. See also section 9.6. For the prohibition of market manipulation, compare Article 91 MiCAR with Articles 15 and 12 MAR. See also section 9.7.

[23] Compare Article 92 MiCAR with Article 16 MAR.

[24] In addition to each prohibitions' specific exemptions, MAR provides four general exemptions for the prohibitions of insider dealing and unlawful disclosure of inside information (Article 14 MAR) and market manipulation (Article 15 MAR). Article 5 MAR provides the first two exemptions that relate to (i) buy-back programs and (ii) stabilisation programs. Article 6 provides the third and fourth exemptions for monetary, public debt management, and climate policy activities.

[25] In particular, see Article 2(1)(a) MAR, which reads: 'This Regulation applies to the following: (a) financial instruments admitted to trading on a regulated market or for which a request for admission to trading on a regulated market has been made.'

paragraph 1, irrespective of whether such transaction, order or behaviour takes place on a trading platform', is directly copied from MAR.[26] Interestingly, this provision was not part of the initial Proposal for MiCAR.[27] While the explicit reason for its addition has not been provided, it is presumed that it is to prevent the circumvention of market abuse rules. However, the necessity and value of Article 86(2) are questionable, particularly since the language of Article 86(1) ('acts carried out by any person concerning crypto-assets that are admitted to trading or in respect of which a request for admission to trading has been made') seems broad enough to encompass acts beyond those occurring directly on a trading platform. Consequently, the purpose of Article 86(2) remains unclear, and the legislative decision to deviate from MAR's wording in Article 86(1) while replicating it in Article 86(2) introduces inconsistencies.

Moving to Article 86(3), like Article 86(2), this provision is borrowed directly from MAR,[28] and was not part of the initial Proposal for MiCAR.[29] Article 86(3) serves to clarify two aspects: (i) scope beyond the EU, and (ii) inclusion of omissions. While the first aspect could be inferred from Article 86(1), the expansive territorial scope should benefit from this additional clarification. The second aspect, addressing omissions, adds value, particularly due to the inconsistency in wording between Article 86(1), which only mentions 'acts', and Article 86(3).

9.3. Inside Information – Article 87 MiCAR

9.3.1. General Framework

The prevention of market abuse under MiCAR is based on four key provisions: the prohibitions on insider dealing, unlawful disclosure of inside information, market manipulation, and the obligation for issuers to publicly disclose inside information as soon as possible. The regimes covering insider dealing, unlawful disclosure of inside information and the mandatory public disclosure of inside information rely on a common concept of 'inside information'. Under the relevant provisions, it is prohibited to make use of inside information that has not yet been disclosed. Also, inside information may not be shared with others unless there is a valid reason to do so. To prevent the prolonged existence of inside information in the first place, issuers have the obligation to share this information with the public as soon as possible.

[26] MAR, Article 2(3).

[27] This part was not included in the initial Proposal for MiCAR. Article 86(2) was added at a much later stage, after the European Parliament's first reading. See Proposal for a Regulation of the European Parliament and of the Council on Markets in Crypto-assets, and amending Directive (EU) 2019/1937 – Outcome of the European Parliament's first reading (Strasbourg, 17 to 20 April 2023), ST 8349 2023 INIT.

[28] MAR, Article 2(4).

[29] Article 86(3) was added at the same stage as Article 86(2).

The definition of 'inside information' is set out in Article 87 MiCAR. Inside information within the meaning of MiCAR is 'information of a precise nature, which has not been made public, relating, directly or indirectly, to one or more issuers, offerors or persons seeking admission to trading,[30] or to one or more crypto-assets, and which, if it were made public, would likely have a significant effect on the prices of those crypto-assets or on the price of a related crypto-asset'.

This somewhat daunting and multi-layered definition is not new. It is, in fact, a modified version of the EU market abuse regime that entered into force 20 years earlier.[31] The EU Market Abuse Directive[32] (informally abbreviated to 'MAD' and not to be confused with the currently applicable Directive 2014/57/EU[33]) contained a very similar definition. MAD entered into force on 12 April 2003, with 12 October 2004 as the transposition deadline. When MAD was replaced by MAR on 3 July 2016, the essence of the definition remained the same. Therefore, unlike most of the other sections of MiCAR, users of Title VI of MiCAR can benefit from a wealth of literature, case law and guidance on one of its key concepts.

For a better understanding of the definition, it is useful to take a closer look at its core components: (i) precise nature; (ii) information which has not been made public; (iii) relating, directly or indirectly to one or more issuers, offerors or persons seeking admission to trading; and (iv) likely to have a significant effect on the price.

9.3.2. Precise Nature

For information to qualify as inside information, it must be sufficiently precise. The idea behind this is to ensure that investors and issuers alike do not have to concern themselves with information about potential occurrences that are highly uncertain or speculative. The mere theoretical possibility of a relevant event or occurrence does not amount to information of a precise nature. For the purposes of MiCAR, information is sufficiently precise if it indicates a set of circumstances which exists or which may reasonably be expected to occur, 'where it is specific enough to enable a conclusion to be drawn as to the possible effect of that set of circumstances or event on the price of crypto-assets.'[34]

For information to qualify as sufficiently precise, two cumulative conditions must be met. First, the event must have occurred or be reasonably expected to

[30] The market abuse provisions of Articles 87 and 88 MiCAR apply to 'issuers, offerors and persons seeking admission to trading'. In this chapter, references to issuers within the meaning of Articles 87 and 88 are also deemed to include offerors and persons seeking admission to trading.

[31] Directive 2003/6/EC of the European Parliament and of the Council of 28 January 2003 on insider dealing and market manipulation (market abuse), *OJ* 2003, L96/16, Article 1(1).

[32] ibid.

[33] Directive 2014/57/EU of the European Parliament and of the Council of 16 April 2014 on criminal sanctions for market abuse (market abuse directive), *OJ* 2014, L173/79.

[34] MiCAR, Article 87(2).

occur. Second, the information must be specific enough to predict whether there would be an effect on the price. This raises the question of whether, for information to qualify as sufficiently precise, it is necessary that the direction (up or down) of that potential effect on the price is already known. In the *Lafonta* judgment,[35] the ECJ confirmed that this is not the case. In this case, the French listed company Wendel did not disclose the fact that Wendel had concrete plans to acquire a significant holding in another company. The French *Autorité des marchés financiers* imposed a fine of EUR 1.5 million on Wendel and its chairman for failing to comply with the obligation under the then-applicable Market Abuse Directive (2003/6/EC) to disclose inside information as soon as possible. Wendel's chairman argued that Wendel did not violate the disclosure obligation because, at the relevant time, it was not yet known whether the proposed investment would ultimately lead to an increase or decrease in Wendel's stock price. This argument, however, was not successful. The ECJ held:

> The increased complexity of the financial markets makes it particularly difficult to evaluate accurately the direction of a change in the prices of those instruments, as was stated in recital 1 to Directive 2003/124, which refers to several factors likely to affect those prices in a given situation. In those circumstances – which can lead to widely differing assessments, depending on the investor – if it were accepted that information is to be regarded as precise only if it makes it possible to anticipate the direction of a change in the prices of the instruments concerned, it would follow that the holder of that information could use an uncertainty in that regard as a pretext for refraining from making certain information public and thus profit from that information to the detriment of the other actors on the market.[36]

Another complexity that arises when making a 'precise nature' assessment is how to deal with events that develop and mature over time. Examples include the acquisition of, or merger with, another company, or the stepping down of the CEO of the company. Typically, such situations start with exploratory talks, which may or may not gradually evolve into more concrete and relevant developments. In such cases, it may be difficult to identify the exact moment when the 'sufficiently precise' threshold is crossed. In a landmark decision involving the resignation of the CEO of the German automotive group Daimler AG, the ECJ provided guidance on the 'precise nature' assessment in these kinds of circumstances.[37] At the time when Daimler formally announced its CEO's resignation, Daimler's stock price rose sharply. An investor who had sold his shares before the announcement initiated proceedings against Daimler, claiming that Daimler should have communicated the intention or expectation that the CEO would resign before the end of his term earlier than it did (eg, at the time the CEO informed the company of

[35] ECJ 11 March 2015, Case C-628/13 *Lafonta v Autorite des marches financiers* ECLI:EU:C:2015:162, [2015] Bus LR 483 (*Lafonta*).

[36] ibid at 36.

[37] ECJ 28 June 2012, Case C-19/11 *Geltl v Daimler AG* ECLI:EU:C:2012:397, [2012] 3 CMLR 32 (*Markus Geltl v Daimler AG*).

his unilateral decision to step down). Daimler argued that the information only became sufficiently precise when the supervisory board accepted the resignation and appointed a successor.

In response to a request for a preliminary ruling submitted by the German *Oberlandesgericht Stuttgart*, the ECJ held that:

> in the case of a protracted process intended to bring about a particular circumstance or to generate a particular event, not only may that future circumstance or future event be regarded as precise information within the meaning of those provisions, but also the intermediate steps of that process which are connected with bringing about that future circumstance or event.[38]

This decision means that in the case of dynamic events that develop over time, the issuer, offeror or person seeking admission to trading must make an assessment at each relevant milestone whether that particular milestone in and of itself qualifies as sufficiently precise.[39] The decision in *Daimler* was subsequently codified in MAR.[40] Article 87(2) also references the *Daimler* decision almost *verbatim*.

It is uncertain whether the complex 'Daimler regime' will be part of the MAR and MiCAR market abuse rules much longer. In December 2022, the EC published a legislative package known as the Listing Act.[41] On 8 October 2024, the European Council adopted the Listing Act and it was published on 14 November 2024.[42] The Listing Act contains amendments to the Prospectus Regulation, MAR, MiFID II and MiFIR. One of its purposes is to relax some of the initial and ongoing obligations applicable to listed companies. These amendments introduce a new disclosure regime covering protracted processes. Under the Listing Act, disclosures in a protracted process should not include announcements of mere intentions or updates on the

[38] ibid para 40.

[39] MiCAR, Article 87(3), referring to an intermediate step in a protracted process that shall be 'deemed to be inside information if, in and of itself, it satisfies the criteria of inside information.'

[40] MAR, Article 7(2).

[41] The 'Listing Act' as proposed by the European Commission in 2022 consisted of two proposed Directives and one proposal for a Regulation: (i) Proposal for a Directive of the European Parliament and of the Council on multiple-vote share structures in companies that seek the admission to trading of their shares on an SME growth market (COM(2022) 761 final); (ii) Proposal for a Directive of the European Parliament and of the Council amending Directive 2014/65/EU to make public capital markets in the Union more attractive for companies and to facilitate access to capital for small and medium-sized enterprises and repealing Directive 2001/34/EC (COM(2022) 760 final); and (iii) Proposal for a Regulation of the European Parliament and of the Council amending Regulations (EU) 2017/1129, (EU) No 596/2014 and (EU) No 600/2014 to make public capital markets in the Union more attractive for companies and to facilitate access to capital for small and medium-sized enterprises (COM(2022) 762 final).

[42] Regulation (EU) 2024/2809 of the European Parliament and of the Council of 23 October 2024 amending Regulations (EU) 2017/1129, (EU) No 596/2014 and (EU) No 600/2014 to make public capital markets in the Union more attractive for companies and to facilitate access to capital for small and medium-sized enterprises, *OJ* L2024/2089, Directive (EU) 2024/2810 of the European Parliament and of the Council of 23 October 2024 on multiple-vote share structures in companies that seek admission to trading of their shares on a multilateral trading facility, *OJ* L2024/2810, and Directive (EU) 2024/2811 of the European Parliament and of the Council of 23 October 2024 amending Directive 2014/65/EU to make public capital markets in the Union more attractive for companies and to facilitate access to capital for small and medium-sized enterprises and repealing Directive 2001/34/EC, *OJ* L2024/2811.

various stages of negotiations. The disclosure should only be made after the 'final event' has occurred. For instance, in the context of merger talks, the relevant moment would be when management approves the merger. For other material contracts, the relevant moment would be the agreement on key conditions of the contract.[43]

When proposing the Listing Act, the EU lawmakers recognised that, notwithstanding this further guidance, it will remain difficult to pinpoint the exact moment at which a process that develops over time becomes 'sufficiently precise' for disclosure purposes.[44] For this reason, the European Commission will be authorised to adopt non-exhaustive lists of 'final events' that would trigger a disclosure obligation, including the moment at which the event shall be deemed to have occurred.[45]

The Listing Act does not contain amendments to MiCAR. However, the reasonable expectation is that a similar relaxation will also find its way into the MiCAR market abuse regime at some point. After all, the market abuse regimes of MAR and MiCAR are very similar and MiCAR was supposed to contain a 'light' version of the MAR regime.[46]

9.3.3. Information which has not been Made Public

The element 'which has not been made public' of the definition of inside information is relatively straightforward. Information that is already in the public domain cannot constitute inside information. Examples of public information include publicly disclosed court decisions and grants or withdrawals of governmental permissions. Arguably, inside information that is inadvertently or deliberately leaked outside the restricted circle of insiders does not automatically become public information simply because that information is also circulating outside the limited group of the issuer and its bona fide insiders. Issuers have an obligation to disclose inside information in a prescribed manner ensuring that the information is available to the general public, with limited grounds to delay such disclosure in specific circumstances (see section 9.4.3). To date, no ECJ case law provides further guidance on when information qualifies as not having been made public within the meaning of MAR.

9.3.4. Significant Effect on the Price

The third key element of the definition is that information only qualifies as 'inside information' if, when that information is made public, the disclosure would be

[43] Listing Act Regulation ((EU) 2024/2809), Recital (67) and Article 2(6)(a) (containing amendments to Article 17 MAR).

[44] Listing Act Regulation, Recital (67). On the proposed changes in the Listing Act, see also A Pijls, 'The duty to publicly disclose inside information under the EU Listing Act' (OBLB, 25 April 2024) blogs.law.ox.ac.uk/oblb/blog-post/2024/04/duty-publicly-disclose-inside-information-under-eu-listing-act.

[45] Listing Act Regulation, Recital (67) and Article 2(6)(f) (containing amendments to Article 17 MAR).

[46] MiCAR, Recital (95).

likely to have a significant effect on the price of the relevant crypto-asset or on the price of a related crypto-asset. This analysis requires a mental exercise. To determine whether an issuer must disclose a particular fact (Article 88(1)) or whether an investor may trade while having certain knowledge of the issuer that the general public does not have (Article 89(1)), the issuer or investor should predict what the impact of that knowledge would likely be.

In enforcement situations, the context is different. Regulators or prosecutors benefit from knowing what the price movements have been. In fact, unusual price movements are often the trigger to investigate in the first place. However, even then, it may be difficult to determine whether the relevant information did in fact have a significant impact on the price for the purposes of MiCAR. For example, this challenge arises in cases where the general market trend was downward due to developments affecting the crypto market as a whole, yet the price of the affected crypto-asset remained stable; or in the event that the price of the crypto-asset was moved by multiple factors, which can make it difficult to determine the relative weight of each factor, including inside information that was disclosed.

The term 'significant effect on the price' does not refer to significance in the quantitative, mathematical sense. It is therefore not decisive whether the price movement is significant for statistical purposes (although the presence or absence of a statistically relevant price movement could support the argument that there was or was not a significant effect within the meaning of the definition of 'inside information'). Instead, in order to facilitate the determination of significance, Article 88(4) introduces a 'reasonable investor'-test. Information that would be likely to have a significant effect on the price of a crypto-asset is information a reasonable holder of crypto-assets would likely use as part of the basis of that holder's investment decision (ie, the decision to buy or sell crypto-assets or to cancel an existing buy or sell order). This clarification is only partly helpful. It triggers further questions, such as: (i) who is a reasonable holder of crypto-assets; (ii) when is a reasonable holder *likely* to use information as part of his or her decision-making, and (iii) how meaningful should that part be in the overall set of factors that drives his or her decision-making?

Neither MAR nor MiCAR provides further guidance on the reasonable investor test. However, under MAR, courts[47] and regulators[48] have provided examples of events that are typically considered to be inside information. These examples include the following:

- Periodic financial results and material deviations from earlier forecasts.
- Dividend announcements, changes to the dividend date or dividend policy.

[47] See eg the ECJ judgments in the *Lafonta* and *Daimler*, discussed above.

[48] See eg, 'Public disclosure of inside information' (updated July 2017), a publication issued by the Netherlands Authority for the Financial Markets (*Autoriteit Financiële Markten*) and the guidance provided by the German Federal Financial Supervisory Authority (*Bundesanstalt für Finanzdienstleistungsaufsicht*) on their website www.bafin.de/EN/Aufsicht/BoersenMaerkte/Emittentenleitfaden/Modul3/Kapitel1/Kapitel1_2/Kapitel1_2_1/kapitel1_2_1_node_en.html.

- Changes in accounting standards.
- Significant litigation.
- Significant enforcement action by regulators or prosecutors.
- Mergers, acquisitions, joint ventures (to the extent material relative to the size of and impact on the company).
- Material new credit facilities, covenant breaches, early termination of credit facilities by the lenders.
- Key changes in the company's strategy.
- Material reorganisations.
- Changes affecting the rights of shareholders or key features of the shares (including the introduction of anti-takeover measures).
- Insolvency, suspension of payments or dissolution of the company.
- Share buybacks.
- Changes in the composition of the management board or the supervisory board.

These examples have been developed in the context of MAR, where the relevant asset is a financial instrument, typically a listed share or bond issued by a company. In the context of MiCAR, the relevant asset is a crypto-asset. In the case of crypto-assets, there does not necessarily need to be a similar relationship between the price of the crypto-asset and developments affecting the issuer or offeror of the relevant asset, as is commonly the case with listed financial instruments under MAR

When applying seemingly familiar MAR-concepts under MiCAR, it is essential to realise that, while the legal concepts may be the same, the relevant asset and environment are not. Examples of events that could have a significant effect on the price in a specific MiCAR context include, but are not limited to: (i) decisions on the admission to trading on a trading platform for crypto-assets; (ii) changes to the underlying technology or trading methodology, (iii) 'hypes' created on social media to increase the popularity (or damage the reputation) of a crypto-asset; (iv) hacks or other security concerns regarding the systems on which the crypto-asset relies; (v) knowledge of other transactions in the relevant crypto-asset or related crypto-assets; (vi) changes to the properties of a crypto-asset that could affect the value of the crypto-asset; (vii) events affecting confidence in a crypto-asset (eg, a sizable crypto-asset custodian facing financial difficulties, or large scale fraud involving a crypto-asset).[49] The specific properties and dynamics of crypto markets will no doubt lead to the development of MiCAR-specific (and potentially diverging) guidance and decisions in the coming years.

[49] See also Recital (96) of MiCAR, which also refers to the specific characteristics of crypto markets that should be considered in the context of the prevention of market abuse, such as the use of social media, the use of smart contracts for order execution and the concentration of mining pools.

9.3.5. Trading Information

Not only information relating to the issuer or crypto-asset itself may be valuable to others. This is also true for information relating to significant orders or trades in crypto-assets that have not been executed yet. A large buy (or sell) order may have a significant upward or downward impact on the price, especially if the trading volume in the relevant crypto-asset is low. 'Front running' – benefiting from non-public information on an expected large transaction in a crypto-asset that will affect the price of the crypto-asset – is prohibited under MiCAR.[50] For persons involved in the execution of orders in crypto-assets for the account of clients, 'inside information' also means information of a precise nature communicated by a client and relating to that client's pending orders in crypto-assets and which, if it were made public, would likely have a significant effect on the price of those crypto-assets or on the price of a related crypto-asset.[51]

9.4. Public Disclosure of Inside Information – Article 88 MiCAR

9.4.1. General Introduction

For their investment decisions, investors need accurate and timely information that is relevant to them in relation to the crypto-asset they hold or are considering buying or selling. Prompt disclosure of inside information also reduces the risk of insider dealing, as inside information loses its value after it has been made public. Article 88 therefore requires that issuers, offerors and persons seeking admission to trading of a crypto-asset on a trading platform disclose inside information that directly concerns them as soon as possible. The information must be disclosed in a manner that enables fast access and complete, correct and timely assessment of the information by the public. In order to ensure fast access and understanding, the disclosure of inside information cannot be combined with marketing messages or general newsletters. All publicly disclosed information must also be posted on the website of the issuer, offeror or person seeking admission to trading for a minimum period of five years.[52]

9.4.2. Means of Disclosure

MiCAR itself does not contain detailed requirements on how inside information must be made public. These requirements will be laid down in Implementing Technical Standards to be adopted by the Commission, on the basis of a

[50] MiCAR, Article 89(2).
[51] MiCAR, Article 87(1)(b).
[52] MiCAR, Article 88(1).

draft prepared by ESMA.[53] On 3 July 2024, ESMA published its draft of the Implementing Technical Standards referred to in Article 88(4).[54] The standards are very similar to those adopted under MAR,[55] but with some specific variations to account for the unique environment in which the listing of and trading in crypto-assets occurs.[56] These variations mainly relate to the categories of media that can be used to satisfy the obligation to actively disseminate inside information. If adopted in accordance with the draft, issuers must disclose inside information in the following manner:

- The information must be posted on a dedicated section on the website of the issuer, offeror or person seeking admission to trading, accessible to the general public on a non-discriminatory basis, in a downloadable format (eg, as a pdf file) and free of charge.
- Posting inside information on the website (passive dissemination) is mandatory, but not enough. The information must also be 'pushed' by communicating the information to media which are 'reasonably relied upon by the public'[57] (active dissemination).
- 'Media which are reasonably relied on by the public' include traditional media, social media permitting publication in written form and web-based publication platforms. The mix of traditional media and social media was chosen because seasoned crypto investors may rely less, if at all, on traditional media for their information needs, while inexperienced crypto investors may be less familiar with navigating the various and rapidly evolving social media channels.[58] Traditional media includes crypto-specific trade journals as well as traditional financial 'wires' such as Reuters and Bloomberg to the extent that they also cover crypto-assets. The prominent reliance on social media in the draft Implementing Technical Standards as a means to disseminate inside information is a marked difference with the MAR regime. Under MAR, dissemination heavily relies on the use of traditional news outlets and their agents. In the context of the consultation of the draft Implementing Technical Standards, respondents quoted X, Reddit, Telegram and Discord as the most influential social media outlets they consult for crypto-related information.[59] Video platforms such as YouTube and TikTok are unsuitable, as they do not enable publication in written form.[60]

[53] MiCAR, Article 88(4).

[54] Draft Technical Standards specifying certain requirements of the Markets in Crypto Assets Regulation (MiCA) – second package, ESMA75-453128700-1229, 3 July 2024 (Draft ITS).

[55] Implementing Regulation (EU) 2016/1055 of 29 June 2016 laying down implementing technical standards with regard to the technical means for appropriate public disclosure of inside information and for delaying the public disclosure of inside information in accordance with Regulation (EU) No 596/2014 of the European Parliament and of the Council.

[56] Draft ITS, para 308.

[57] Draft ITS, Article 3(2).

[58] Draft ITS, paras 354–362.

[59] Draft ITS, para 358.

[60] Draft ITS, para 371.

9.4.3. Delay of Disclosure

There may be situations in which immediate disclosure would not be in the best interest of the issuer, offeror or person seeking admission to trading and, indirectly, the investors in the relevant crypto-asset. For this reason, these relevant parties are allowed to delay disclosure if all three of the following conditions are satisfied:

- immediate disclosure is likely to prejudice the legitimate interests of the issuer, offeror or person seeking admission to trading;
- delay of disclosure is not likely to mislead the public;
- the issuer, offeror or person seeking admission to trading is able to ensure the confidentiality of the inside information.[61]

9.4.3.1. Legitimate Interest

Under MAR, ESMA has issued guidelines explaining which situations can constitute a 'legitimate interest' under the corresponding MAR regime.[62] Examples of legitimate interests include:

- The issuer is involved in negotiations which could fail if the information would be made public. This would be the case for some negotiations involving mergers or acquisitions, carve-outs, the purchase or sale of material assets and restructurings.
- The issuer is in financial distress and disclosure would put any attempted rescue effort of the issuer at risk.
- The relevant project requires approval of the supervisory board or other corporate body of the issuer (other than the shareholders' meeting) under its constitutional documents or applicable corporate law. That said, this approval must be secured as soon as possible. In this era of modern communication methods, any prolonged delay on this ground will be difficult to justify and exposes the issuer to criticism (or worse) from its investors or the regulator.
- The issuer has developed a new product and the disclosure of that fact is likely to adversely affect the intellectual property rights of the issuer.
- The issuer is planning to acquire or sell a major holding in another entity and the disclosure of that intention is likely to put the transaction at risk.
- A transaction is subject to regulatory approval that contains conditions, and the disclosure of such conditions is likely to put the transaction at risk.[63]

[61] MiCAR, Article 88(2).

[62] ESMA, MAR Guidelines – Delay in the disclosure of inside information, 20/10/2016 | ESMA/2016/1478 (MAR Guidelines).

[63] MAR Guidelines, pp 4–5.

Similar guidelines under MiCAR do not yet exist. The non-exhaustive list of examples set out in the ESMA Guidelines in relation to MAR can serve as inspiration. They also demonstrate that a legitimate interest only exists if disclosure would be detrimental to the issuer, and therefore represents more than a mere inconvenience. Invoking the right to delay disclosure is only available in case of events with a similarly profound impact on negotiations, decision-making or the likelihood of success of transactions.

9.4.3.2. Not Likely to Mislead the Public

The second condition is that the delay of disclosure must not be likely to mislead the public. The issuer, offeror or person seeking admission to trading may not issue conflicting statements or actively deny the undisclosed fact. Similarly, the undisclosed information should not be materially different from information that the relevant party disclosed in the past (including 'guidance' on expected future financial performance), or materially different from market expectations if such expectations were based on messages from such a party.[64]

9.4.3.3. Ensuring Confidentiality

Finally, the duty to disclose will be suspended as long as the issuer can ensure confidentiality of the non-disclosed inside information. If the information leaks, whether as a result of an act or omission of the issuer, offeror or another party, the right to delay disclosure no longer applies. Issuers, offerors and persons seeking admission to trading relying on the right to delay disclosure should therefore be prepared to issue a press release at short notice in the event of a leak. Typically, companies prepare draft press releases for this purpose in advance, and keep these updated as the transaction or other event progresses.

9.4.3.4. Notification

In the event that an issuer has delayed the publication of inside information, the issuer must notify its regulator of the fact that it delayed disclosure in accordance with Article 88(2). This notification must be made immediately after the disclosure of the inside information (Article 88(3)), and not immediately after the decision on the delay. The notification must explain how the three conditions for a lawful delay were satisfied during the period in which disclosure was delayed.[65]

[64] This interpretation is based on the MAR Guidelines, p 5.
[65] MiCAR, Article 88(3).

9.5. Prohibition of Insider Dealing – Article 89 MiCAR

As explained, there can be situations where inside information has not yet been made public, sometimes for prolonged periods of time. Those who are aware of this undisclosed information are not allowed to 'use' this information by trading in the relevant crypto-assets. In a recent and noteworthy example, a former Coinbase product manager and his brother settled insider trading charges with the U.S. Securities and Exchange Commission in May 2023.[66] The Coinbase product manager had knowledge of pending admissions of crypto-assets to the Coinbase platform. The Coinbase product manager shared this information with his brother and a friend, in violation of internal Coinbase policies to treat such information as confidential. Both his brother and his friend traded ahead of the admission to listing, in the expectation that the value of the relevant crypto-asset would increase upon the announcement that the crypto-asset would be admitted to the Coinbase platform. Both brothers face a prison sentence and forfeiture of ill-gotten gains.

The prohibition of insider dealing in MiCAR is broadly worded. It captures buy and sell orders, own account trading and trading for the account of a third party, and the modification and cancellation of pre-existing orders. Failed attempts to trade on the basis of inside information are also caught by the prohibition.[67]

Two separate regimes exist under the insider dealing prohibition of Article 89. A stricter regime applies to persons usually referred to as 'insiders'. For the purpose of MiCAR, insiders are:

- Members of the management board, supervisory board or other similar corporate body of the issuer, offeror, or person seeking admission to trading.
- Persons having a holding in the capital of the issuer, offeror, or person seeking admission to trading.
- Persons with access to inside information in the ordinary course of their employment, profession or duties, or in relation to their role in DLT or similar technology. This broad category typically includes external or internal lawyers or consultants, auditors, certain IT specialists, trading professionals, persons having access to confidential financial information and other persons with access to valuable confidential information, whether on a permanent basis or on an ad hoc basis for the duration of a specific project. In the specific context of MiCAR and crypto-assets, specialists involved in the implementation of changes to the underlying technology could therefore very well qualify as insiders. The categories of persons who qualify as insiders for the purpose of

[66] U.S. Securities and Exchange Commission, 'Former Coinbase Manager and His Brother Agree to Settle Insider Trading Charges Relating to Crypto Asset Securities', Press release 2023-98, 30 May 2023.

[67] MiCAR, Article 89(2).

MiCAR can vary over time and across issuers, offerors and persons seeking admission to trading.

- Persons involved in criminal activities. This category includes hackers or persons stealing or otherwise gaining illegitimate access to inside information (e.g. by stealing a laptop or hacking into document servers).

Persons belonging to these categories are prohibited from using inside information, regardless of whether they were actually aware that the information they had access to constituted inside information. Other persons (ie, non-insiders) are also prohibited from making use of inside information. However, the prohibition only applies to non-insiders to the extent they know, or ought to know, that the information is inside information. This more lenient regime applies in situations such as someone overhearing a confidential conversation in a public place or a person who finds a lost USB-stick or physical document containing inside information. Depending on the circumstances and overall appearance of the document or data (eg, marked 'Confidential' or not), the person trading on the basis of this information may or may not be able to demonstrate that he or she did not know or ought not to have known that the document contained inside information.

The term 'use' in the prohibition suggests a causal link between the trade and the information available to the insider at the time of the trade. Arguably, if an investor is privy to inside information likely to have a positive effect on the price and purchases the relevant crypto-asset, this will at least give the outward appearance of 'use'. However, whether or not a person actually used the information as part of his or her investment decision is ultimately a mental process, which may be difficult, if not impossible, to prove. In the *Spector Photo* case,[68] the dilemma created by restricting the *use* of inside information became apparent. Should 'use' be interpreted as meaning that a competent authority must actually prove subjective use? This would require insight in an investor's actual mental process at the time, which would be difficult to prove. Or can 'use' simply be assumed if a person executes a transaction while possessing inside information? Such a non-rebuttable presumption would, however, be incompatible with the presumption of innocence laid down in the European Convention for the Protection of Human Rights and Fundamental Freedoms (ECHR)[69] and other human rights treaties, as well as national law of individual Member States. The ECJ opted for a middle-ground approach: if an investor possesses inside information and executes a trade, this implies that the investor has used the inside information. Yet this is a rebuttable presumption. If the investor can point to circumstances evidencing that he or she did not use the information, they would not be in violation of the prohibition on insider dealing.

[68] ECJ 23 December 2009, Case C-45/08 *Spector Photo Group NV v Commissie voor het Bank-, Financie- en Assurantiewezen* (*CBFA*) ECLI:EU:C:2009:806, [2009] ECR-I-12073 (*Spector Photo*).

[69] ECHR, Article 6(2).

9.6. Prohibition of Unlawful Disclosure of Inside Information – Article 90 MiCAR

Persons having access to inside information must not only refrain from using such information to their own benefit; they must also refrain from disclosing this information to others.[70] Similarly, these insiders shall not recommend that others buy or sell the relevant crypto-asset, or amend or cancel existing orders in the crypto-asset.[71] Careless treatment of documents or files containing inside information could also amount to a violation of Article 90.

As in the case of the prohibition on insider dealing, separate regimes exist for insiders and non-insiders. Non-insiders who may have gained access to inside information inadvertently must not pass this information on to others or recommend trades to others if they know or ought to know that the information is inside information.[72]

In the ordinary course of fulfilling their duties, insiders may need to disclose inside information to others from time to time. For example, the CEO will need to discuss confidential projects with internal project teams or outside counsel or consultants, and the company's auditor and internal finance department will require early access to interim financial data of the company before it is communicated to the market. These disclosures in the ordinary course of business – and on a 'need to know'-basis – are permitted under Article 90(1).[73]

9.7. Market Manipulation

9.7.1. Market Manipulation in Crypto-asset Markets

The concept of market manipulation is a challenging one to define precisely, yet it essentially encompasses various behaviours that exploit the information function of an asset's market price. Examples of such behaviour include using trading patterns to send misleading signals about the supply and demand for crypto-assets or to secure the price at an artificial level, and disseminating false or misleading information to misguide market participants in their investment decisions and cause mispricing. The aim of such behaviour is for the manipulator to profit from

[70] MiCAR, Article 90(1).

[71] MiCAR, Article 89(3) and (4).

[72] MiCAR, Article 90(2).

[73] For additional guidance on the meaning of disclosures 'made in the normal exercise of an employment, a profession or duties', see ECJ 22 November 2005, Case C-384/02 *Criminal Proceedings against Grøngaard* ECLI:EU:C:2005:708, [2005] ECR I-9939 (*Grøngaard & Bang*), and ECJ 15 March 2022, Case C-302/20 *A v Autorite des Marches Financiers* (*AMF*) ECLI:EU:C:2022:190, [2022] 1 WLR 3036 (*A/AMF*). Both decisions have been rendered under the MAD and MAR-regimes, respectively.

the market conditions that result from his or her acts to mislead other market participants.

Market manipulation has been observed in traditional financial markets since their inception and is probably as old as the financial markets themselves.[74] Predictably, a parallel occurrence of such behaviour has affected the emerging crypto-asset markets from their inception.[75] While traditional financial markets have benefited from centuries of experience and regulatory evolution, the relatively young crypto-asset markets have lacked a comparable level of regulatory maturity.[76]

From the standpoint of manipulators, the advent of crypto-asset markets presented fresh opportunities to deploy familiar strategies that would qualify as market manipulation if executed in traditional financial markets. Not only did these crypto-asset markets introduce a novel instrument in the form of crypto-assets, they also brought forth innovative trading platforms dedicated to these assets. Both novelties accentuated the susceptibility of crypto-asset markets to manipulation. The heightened vulnerability factors due to the uniqueness of crypto-assets and their underlying technology relate to the novelty of the technology used, the complexity of the product, the (in)sensitivity of their valuation to hype (fundamentals), and pseudonymity.[77] Similarly, the distinctive characteristics of crypto-asset trading platforms amplified vulnerability factors such as a lack of regulations (ie, transparency requirements or conflict of interest rules), low liquidity, price volatility, and concentration issues.[78] Collectively, these factors render crypto-asset markets more susceptible to market manipulation than their traditional counterparts. Moreover, the distinct characteristics of crypto-assets and their platforms create an environment that is particularly vulnerable to specific manipulation strategies, such as 'wash trading,' 'spoofing' and 'layering,' and 'pump-and-dump.'[79] These concepts will now be discussed in more detail.

Wash trading is a manipulation technique where the perpetrator artificially inflates trading volume by engaging in trades with itself, resulting in no change in ownership or market risk. This, in turn, creates a deceptive signal regarding the trading volume of the relevant crypto-asset. To illustrate, a manipulator may initiate

[74] See for a complete historical overview of financial market manipulation, J Markham, *Law Enforcement and the History of Financial Market Manipulation* (Routledge, 2014).

[75] See Commission Staff Working Document Impact Assessment accompanied to the MiCAR Proposal (SWD/2020/380 final) (Impact Assessment), para 2.2.3.

[76] For more on the lack of regulation, see D Twomey and A Mann, 'Fraud and Manipulation within Cryptocurrency Markets' in C Alexander and D Cumming (eds), *Corruption and Fraud in Financial Markets* (John Wiley & Sons, 2020) 212–13.

[77] See for these vulnerabilities, Impact Assessment, para 2.2.3; Twomey and Mann (n 76) 212–13 and 214–15; M Mirtaheri, S Abu-El-Haija, F Morstatter, G Ver Steeg and A Galstyan 'Identifying and Analyzing Cryptocurrency Manipulations in Social Media' (2021) 8(3) *IEEE Transactions on Computational Social Systems* 607, 608.

[78] See for these vulnerabilities, Impact Assessment, para 2.2.3; Twomey and Mann (n 76) 212–13 and 214–15.

[79] See Impact Assessment, para 2.2.3. See also for an overview, F Eigelshoven, A Ullrich and D Parry, 'Cryptocurrency Market Manipulation: A Systematic Literature Review' (2021) *ICIS* 2021 Proceedings 1.

a sell order on an exchange and simultaneously execute a matching buy order, generating a deceptive appearance of increased liquidity. Effectively addressing and curbing wash trading necessitates comprehensive insights into individual trades and involved parties. This manipulative trading strategy is notably prevalent in the realm of crypto-assets.[80] To indicate, the proportion of traded volume on non-regulated crypto exchanges flagged as suspicious and likely to be fraudulent is alarmingly high, with numerous studies pointing to an estimated magnitude of 70 per cent.[81] The inherent susceptibility of crypto-asset markets to wash trading can be attributed to their characteristic pseudonymity, which increases challenges related to the precise identification of participants and assessment of their status, including creditworthiness and aggregate exposure.[82] These challenges become even more pronounced in platforms for crypto-assets that adopt a decentralised structure, commonly referred to as decentralised exchanges or DEXs. In such environments, manipulators find it easier to execute wash sales due to the absence of overarching supervision, making it more challenging to discern the identities of market participants.

Spoofing and *layering* represent manipulation strategies employed by traders to exploit order book dynamics and achieve favourable prices. In the context of financial markets, 'spoofing' entails placing deceptive buy or sell orders in the order book with no intention of executing them. To influence market direction, the manipulator floods one side of the order book with a large order or a series of orders, thereby establishing a new best bid or offer, or significantly augmenting liquidity at the existing best bid or offer. Subsequently, within the lifespan of these initial orders or shortly after their cancellation, the manipulator executes a trade on the opposite side of the market, often securing a more advantageous price than would have been possible without the initial orders. On the other hand, 'layering' is a variation of spoofing where the manipulator introduces multiple visible orders on one side of the market across various price tiers. This strategic placement causes the midpoint of the spread to move away from the multiple orders, enabling the manipulator to execute a trade on the opposite side of the market. Both spoofing and layering tactics typically make use of advanced technology, such as bots or algorithms, to ensure timely entry and cancellation of orders.[83]

[80] See generally G le Pennec, I Fiedler, and L Ante, 'Wash Trading at Cryptocurrency Exchanges,' 2021 (43) Finance Research Letters, 101982; L William Cong, X Li, K Tang and Y Yang, 'Crypto Wash Trading' (2022) NBER Working Paper No. 30783; F Victor and A Marie Weintraud. 'Detecting and quantifying wash trading on decentralized cryptocurrency exchanges' (2021) Proceedings of the Web Conference.

[81] Cong et al pointed to a wobbling 70%. See Cong et al (n 80) 23; Pennet et al. used a different methodology, but pointed to a similar percentage. See Pennec et al (n 80) 5. For research pointing to a lesser magnitude (although still above 30%), Victor and Weintraud (n 80).

[82] Pseudonymity refers to the string of letters and numbers that constitute the 'public keys' of self-custody wallets that often do not require any know-your-costumer procedures to be created. This pseudonymity is commonly identified as a 'native risk' to crypto-assets. See ESMA, TRV Risk analysis. Crypto-assets and their risks for financial stability', October 2022, ESMA50-165-2251, p 6.

[83] See for the application of bots and algorithms in the context of crypto-asset markets, DE O'Leary, 'Open Information Enterprise Transactions: Business Intelligence and Wash and Spoof Transactions in Blockchain and Social Commerce' (2018) 25(3) *Intelligent Systems in Accounting, Finance and Management* 148.

Effectively combating spoofing and layering requires detailed information about individual trades and involved parties. However, the pseudonymous nature and the absence of regulatory obligations requiring the identification of participants, such as 'know your customer', in (certain parts of) crypto markets, make it challenging to obtain such information.[84] Consequently, these markets become attractive targets for spoofing and layering activities. A notable example illustrating this vulnerability is the reported surge in Bitcoin's price in 2017, allegedly resulting from a large-scale spoofing orchestrated by a single entity known as 'Spoofy.'[85]

Pump-and-dump is a manipulative strategy characterised by artificially inflating the price of a previously acquired asset through the dissemination of false or misleading information, followed by selling it off to other investors. This fraudulent scheme unfolds in two distinct stages: the 'pump' and the 'dump.' During the 'pump' phase, the manipulator acquires an asset and initiates an aggressive promotional campaign, spreading misleading information to entice other investors to purchase the targeted assets or entering small but multiple purchase transactions, consequently driving up the price. Subsequently, in the 'dump' phase, the manipulator swiftly sells the asset at the inflated price, causing a sudden drop and leaving unsuspecting investors at a financial loss.

Pump-and-dump schemes are especially successful when applied to assets with low market capitalisation and limited trading volume and whose valuation is more sensitive to 'hype' – typically uncertain information regarding non-economic factors indicating what the future value could be, such as popularity – than 'fundamentals' (usually basic, measurable economic information indicating the current value of an asset, such as balance sheet information (i.e. revenue, outstanding assets and debt, earnings, etc.), financial records, and economic outlook).[86] In traditional financial markets, microcap or 'penny' stocks are often vulnerable to such manipulative tactics. Generally, crypto-assets are also susceptible to pump-and-dump schemes.[87] This susceptibility is accentuated by their thinly traded nature and low market capitalisation.[88] Besides, the valuations of crypto-assets are driven less by 'fundamentals' and are more sensitive to hype.[89] Additionally, the

[84] See Twomey and Mann (n 76) 236–37.

[85] O'Leary (n 83) 154.

[86] On the issue of low market capitalisation and low trading volume, see RK Aggarwal and G Wu, 'Stock Market Manipulations' (2006) 79(4) *The Journal of Business* 1915, 1947–48.

[87] See generally JT Hamrick, F Rouhi, A Mukherjee, A Feder, N Gandal, T Moore, and M Vasek, 'An examination of the cryptocurrency pump-and-dump ecosystem' (2021) 58(4) *Information Processing & Management* 102506.

[88] Some studies have shown that typically less popular coins with low market caps and circulation are targeted. See M La Morgia, A Mei, F Sassi and J Stefa, 'Pump and Dumps in the Bitcoin Era: Real Time Detection of Cryptocurrency Market Manipulations' (2020) 29th International Conference on Computer Communications and Networks (ICCCN), Honolulu, HI, USA, 1–9; F Victor, and T Hagemann, 'Cryptocurrency Pump and Dump Schemes: Quantification and Detection' (2019) International Conference on Data Mining Workshops (ICDMW), Beijing, China: IEEE, 244–51.

[89] In the UK, various market participants have stressed the insensitivity of crypto-asset's valuations to fundamentals as a heightened vulnerability factor to market manipulation. See HM Treasury, Future financial services regulatory regime for crypto-assets. Response to the consultation and call for evidence, October 2023, 64–64.

reliability of available information sources plays a pivotal role.[90] While investors in traditional financial markets tend to rely more on information from sources that have credibility and are under some form of public supervision (financial media outlets, newspapers, etc), investors in crypto-asset markets tend to rely more on social media (X, Facebook, Reddit, etc) where it is common to use pseudonyms and supervision is largely absent.[91]

It is also suggested that crypto-asset markets witness a higher incidence of pump-and-dump schemes due to the prevalence of 'pump groups' – organised entities with a hierarchical structure that coordinate pump-and-dump activities.[92] While the underlying mechanics of pump groups may not be novel, certain distinguishing factors set them apart from market manipulations that have typically occurred in traditional financial markets.[93] Notably, these groups use social media as their primary tool, operate on a larger scale, and attract a high level of investor participation.[94] More crucially, pump groups in the crypto space differentiate themselves by not 'abusing' the information function of prices.[95] Unlike traditional market manipulations, these groups refrain from pretending to possess private information or claiming that a coin is undervalued.[96] Instead, pump group administrators openly declare their intention to pump a specific coin by releasing a 'pump signal' and encouraging others to join. Investors, in turn, rush to buy the coin, hoping to capitalise on the upward momentum before the inevitable collapse of the coin's price. The transparency of this scheme raises questions about whether such behaviour should be categorised as market manipulation, as pump groups do not mislead market participants by distorting the information function of market prices.[97]

9.7.2. Prohibition of Market Manipulation

9.7.2.1. General

Article 91 MiCAR imposes a prohibition on market manipulation specifically targeting crypto-assets. This prohibition closely mirrors the provisions outlined

[90] See Twomey and Mann (n 76) 213.

[91] See Twomey and Mann (n 76) 213; Mirtaheri et al (n 77).

[92] See eg A Dhawan and TJ Putniņš, 'A New Wolf in Town? Pump-and-Dump Manipulation in Cryptocurrency Markets' (2023) 27(3) *Review of Finance* 935; Mirtaheri et al (n 77).

[93] The recent 'meme-stock saga' demonstrates that traditional financial markets could be subjected to actions very similar to the workings of pump groups on crypto-asset markets. See for a discussion of the meme stock saga in the context of market manipulation, N Campuzano, 'Gamestop en particuliere beleggers. Eerlijk meegespeeld of marktmanipulatie?' (2021) (09) *Ars Aequi* 900.

[94] For an analysis of the effects of social media, see Mirtaheri et al (n 77). For an explanation of the participation rate of market participants in such 'pump groups', see Dhawan and Putniņš (n 92).

[95] Dhawan and Putniņš (n 92) 936–37.

[96] ibid.

[97] The same question can be raised for similar behaviour in traditional financial markets. See in the context of 'meme-stocks', Campuzano (n 93).

in Article 12 in conjunction with Article 15 MAR, with the primary difference being the substitution of the term 'financial instrument' with 'crypto-asset'.[98] Since these prohibitions align, our analysis of the elements within the market manipulation prohibition in Article 91 MiCAR will rely on interpretations derived from MAR. Hereafter, we will discuss the three categories of market manipulation delineated in Article 91(2): transaction manipulation, deception, and information manipulation.

9.7.2.2. Transaction Manipulation

Transaction manipulation encompasses manipulative practices relying on trading strategies. Article 91(2)(a) defines it as 'entering into a transaction, placing an order to trade, or engaging in any other behaviour which: (i) gives, or is likely to give, false or misleading signals regarding the supply of, demand for, or price of a crypto-asset; (ii) secures, or is likely to secure, the price of one or several crypto-assets at an abnormal or artificial level.' The previously discussed tactics of 'wash trading', 'spoofing', and 'layering' all typically fall within this category.[99] Establishing whether a behaviour qualifies as transaction manipulation involves meeting two specific requirements.

- *Transaction, order or any other behaviour.* The first requirement to identify transaction manipulation involves determining whether the behaviour falls under the category of 'entering into a transaction, placing an order to trade, or engaging in any other behaviour'. This criterion is already fulfilled merely by placing and receiving an order; the actual execution of a transaction or entry into the order book is not necessary.[100] It is argued that even a failure to act, such as a breach of duty in a specific business transaction or order, is covered by the term 'any other behaviour'.[101] While the precise meaning of 'any other behaviour' is not explicitly defined, MiCAR's market abuse regime's material scope includes omissions, which can support interpreting 'any other behaviour' to encompass a failure to act.[102]
- *Effect: (i) gives false or misleading signals, or (ii) secures an abnormal or artificial price level.* The second requirement to establish transaction manipulation

[98] MiCAR, Article 91(1) explicitly prohibits individuals from participating in or attempting to engage in market manipulation, thereby reflecting Article 15 MAR. Article 91(2) and (3) MiCAR describe what constitutes market manipulation, thereby reflecting Article 12 MAR.

[99] See section 9.7.1.

[100] This includes the initial order, follow-up orders, and modifications or the cancellation of active orders. See MiCAR, Article 91(3)(b).

[101] S Kalss, 'Article 12 Market Manipulation' in S Kalss, M Oppitz, U Torggler and M Winner (eds), *EU Market Abuse Regulation* (Edward Elgar, 2021) 172; P Buck-Heeb, *Kapitalmarktrecht*, 9th edn (CF Müller, 2017) para 575; KU Schmolke, 'Artikel 12: Marktmanipulation' in L Klöhn (ed), *Marktmissbrauchsverordnung* (CH Beck, 2018) para 40.

[102] See section 9.2.2.

involves determining whether the transaction, order or other behaviour has one of the effects described in either (i) or (ii).[103]

Effect (i). Concerning the effect outlined in (i), the transaction, order, or other behaviour must give, or be likely to give, false or misleading signals regarding the supply of, demand for, or price of a crypto-asset. Crucial components in identifying transaction manipulation with effect (i) include the concepts of 'signal', 'false' and 'misleading'.

Regarding the 'signal' element, the transaction, order, or behaviour must convey or be likely to convey information related to the supply, demand, or price of the crypto-asset. While every transaction inherently signals market information, the term 'signal' encompasses behaviour that potentially influences the supply, demand pattern, or price of the traded crypto-asset – information that a reasonable investor[104] would consider when making investment decisions.[105] In simpler terms, the transaction or behaviour must stand out in some way from others for an informed market participant familiar with prevailing conditions to draw meaningful conclusions.

The signal from the transaction or order must be 'false' or 'misleading'. It is logical to infer that a correct transaction or order would not generate a false signal. Therefore, the transaction or order itself must be false to produce a misleading signal. Defining a false transaction or order involves scenarios where it is either fabricated – or displayed in the order book but not entered by any party – or is detrimental to price formation, resulting in an artificial price. Both forms of false transactions are already addressed under Article 91(2)(a)(ii) and Article 91(2)(b).[106] Consequently, the primary concern in this form of manipulation revolves around whether a signal is 'misleading'. A signal is deemed misleading if it is likely to create a misconception in a reasonable investor.[107] Even if a signal is not false, it can still be misleading if, when viewed in isolation, it provides an incomplete view of the transaction, the intentions of the investor or instrument's actual conditions due to context or presentation.[108] A classic example of an effect under (i) is observed in

[103] Although Article 92(2)(a) MiCAR may give the false impression that both effects are cumulative (as the word 'or' is missing), this is undoubtedly an error. In MAR, these effects are understood as two alternative effects that could each meet the 'effect' condition instead of cumulative effect. Another strong indication that the word 'or' has been left out mistakenly is that this error emerges in other parts of Article 92(2) as (a), (b) and (c) also seem to be cumulative, while the wording of 92(2) is clear that 'any of the following activities' and not *all* compromise market manipulation.

[104] The 'reasonable investor' is the central standard of European capital market law. It is also used in the context of market abuse, see eg, Recital (1) MAD I. The reasonable investor is unanimously considered to be a rational, adequately informed, attentive, critical and familiar market participant. This refers less to small or private investors but rather more to institutional, informed market participants.

[105] See Kalss (n 101) 173; M Nelemans, *Het Verbod Van Marktmanipulatie* (Kluwer, 2007) 12–13 and 201–205.

[106] See sections 9.7.2.2 and 9.7.2.3.

[107] Kalss (n 101) 173.

[108] See R Raas, 'Marktmanipulatie' in DR Doorenbos e.a., *Handboek Marktmisbruik (Onderneming en recht nr. 104)* (Wolters Kluwer, 2018) para 6.3.2. See Kalss (n 101) 173.

the practice of wash trading, as discussed above. Whereas these transactions are real, wash trades lack certain elements commonly associated with a transaction, such as a change in ownership or transfer of economic risk.

Effect (ii). Regarding the effect outlined in (ii), the transaction, order, or other behaviour must secure or be likely to secure the price of one or several crypto-assets at an abnormal or artificial level. The crucial component in identifying this form of transaction manipulation is the concept of an 'abnormal or artificial price level', with both terms being synonymous. It is sufficient that the artificial price level is attained or is likely to be attained; the duration for which the price remains at the artificial level is not relevant.[109] Furthermore, the observed price effect is not determinative; the price level does not necessarily have to be exceptionally high or low to qualify as artificial. For instance, propping up a price drop or mitigating a price increase can result in an artificial price, even if the price is at or near average or typical levels.[110] An example of an effect under (ii) is observed in the practices of spoofing and layering, as discussed above. Both actions create an artificial price because the orders are not intended to be executed and, thus, do not reflect true demand/supply.

9.7.2.2.1. Examples and Indicators

Despite the clear articulation of the effects in (i) and (ii) outlined above, determining accurately when a transaction or order signals false or misleading information or secures the price at an artificial level based on objective standards remains a formidable challenge. In an attempt to offer guidance, MiCAR presents a few examples of behaviour that unambiguously constitute market manipulation in Article 91(3)(b), which are copied from Article 12(2) MAR. However, while MAR endeavours to enhance clarity by providing a non-exhaustive list of specific indicators of manipulative behaviour associated with the transaction manipulation of financial instruments, MiCAR falls short in this regard.[111] This shortfall is particularly regrettable because a similar non-exhaustive list of indicators could effectively capture the unique characteristics of crypto-assets and their trading platforms, allowing for a nuanced adjustment of the general prohibition of transaction manipulation in the context of crypto-asset markets.

9.7.2.2.2. Justification: Legitimate Reasons

If both requirements outlined in Article 91(2)(a) are met, the action qualifies as market manipulation unless executed for 'legitimate reasons'. The interpretation of 'legitimate reasons' is subjective and should align with the market participant's

[109] See ECJ 7 July 2011, Case C-445/09, ECLI:EU:C:2011:459 *IMC Securities/AFM*, at 30. See also Raas (n 108) 199–200; Kalss (n 101) 173.

[110] See Raas (n 108) 200.

[111] See MAR, Annex I, Section A, and Delegated Regulation (EU) 2016/522, Annex II Section 1.

conduct as recognised by the applicable capital market laws and regulations, adhering to its objectives and purpose while not conflicting with established market principles, structures, mechanisms, and functional conditions.[112] However, MiCAR's clarification on what qualifies as 'legitimate reasons' remains ambiguous. Unlike MAR, MiCAR does not offer 'accepted market practices' as guidance. Under MAR, trading strategies that meet the criteria for transaction manipulation are allowed if executed for 'legitimate reasons' *and* in accordance with 'accepted market practices'.[113] Conversely, Title VI of MiCAR justifies transaction manipulation solely based on proving legitimate reasons without the necessity of adhering to additional accepted market practices.

This divergence can have dual implications. On the one hand, it may be more straightforward to justify transaction manipulation under Article 91(2)(a) MiCAR compared to its MAR counterpart. Given the absence of the accepted market practice as an additional requirement and the EC's intention to make the market abuse regime under MiCAR less burdensome (or more proportional), this interpretation seems reasonable. On the other hand, the absence of accepted market practices introduces uncertainty about what qualifies as a legitimate reason. In MAR, accepted market practices serve as formalised interpretations of legitimate reasons.[114]

9.7.2.3. Deception

Manipulation by deception encompasses various strategies that rely on deceptive practices, including forms of transaction manipulation and information manipulation. Article 91(2)(b) MiCAR defines it as 'entering into a transaction, placing an order to trade, or any other activity or behaviour which affects or is likely to affect the price of one or several crypto-assets, while employing a fictitious device or any other form of deception or contrivance.' A pump-and-dump scheme, which has been discussed above, is a classic example of behaviour falling within this category.[115] To determine if a behaviour qualifies as manipulation by deception, three criteria must be satisfied.

- *Transaction, order, or any other activity or behaviour.* The initial criterion assesses whether the behaviour constitutes 'entering into a transaction, placing an order to trade, or any other activity or behaviour'. This criterion closely aligns with the first requirement for establishing transaction manipulation

[112] Kalss (n 101) 186.

[113] See MAR, Article 12(1)(a) and Article 13. Legitimate reasons and accepted market practices are mutually reinforcing prerequisites. Ultimately, a strong correlation exists between the criteria for recognising a market practice in general and establishing a legitimate reason for an individual market participant in a specific situation. Consequently, it is challenging to derive entirely new criteria or justifications from this interconnection. See Kalss (n 101) 186.

[114] See Kalss (n 101) 186.

[115] A pump-and-dump scheme consists of various behaviours and typically has two stages. The entire scheme is a classic example of manipulation by deception, but each individual stage could also constitute one of the other forms of market manipulation described under Article 91(2) MiCAR.

under Article 91(2)(a).[116] The distinction lies in its inclusivity of 'any other activity', which makes it broader and akin to a catch-all provision.[117]

- *Likely to affect price.* The second criterion necessitates that the transaction, order, activity, or behaviour affects or is likely to affect the price of one or several crypto-assets. As discussed in the context of transaction manipulation, all transactions affect prices, and all orders are likely to influence them.[118] Consequently, this criterion is inherently met by all transactions and orders. Moreover, it extends to encompass other activities or behaviours with potential price effects, such as disseminating information.
- *Deception.* The pivotal and decisive third criterion for establishing manipulation by deception revolves around the use of a fictitious device or any other form of deception or contrivance. The crucial element is 'deception', which refers to conduct capable of misleading a reasonable investor about economic circumstances, such as supply and demand.[119] It is sufficient to establish the potential for deception; the success of the deceptive behaviour is not imperative.

Similar to transaction manipulation, MiCAR fails to provide explicit indicators of manipulative behaviour related to the deployment of a fictitious device, which MAR does.[120] Again, it is unfortunate that MiCAR misses the opportunity to fine-tune the prohibition on market manipulation to the unique characteristics of crypto-assets and their trading platforms. For example, while MAR identifies pump-and-dump schemes as an indicator of manipulative behaviour related to the deployment of a fictitious device or any other form of deception or contrivance, it does not address the specific role of pump-groups.[121]

9.7.2.4. *Information Manipulation*

Information manipulation refers to manipulation tactics that rely on the dissemination of false or misleading information. Article 91(2)(c) describes it as 'disseminating information through the media, including the internet, or by any other means, which gives, or is likely to give, false or misleading signals as to the supply of, demand for, or price of one or several crypto-assets, or secures or is likely to secure, the price of one or several crypto-assets, at an abnormal or artificial level, including the dissemination of rumours, where the person who engaged in the dissemination knew, or ought to have known, that the information was false or misleading.' To establish whether a behaviour qualifies as information manipulation, three criteria must be satisfied.

[116] See section 9.7.2.1.
[117] See also Kalss (n 101) 175.
[118] See section 9.7.2.2.
[119] Kalss (n 101) 174–75.
[120] MAR, Annex I, Section B, and Delegated Regulation (EU) 2016/522 in Annex II, Section 2.
[121] MAR, Annex I, Section B, and Delegated Regulation (EU) 2016/522 in Annex II Section 2(2)(b).

- *Dissemination of information.* The first requirement assesses whether the behaviour involves the 'dissemination of information'. While the term 'information' lacks a precise definition, its broad scope should encompass rumours, value judgments, and news.[122] The concept of 'dissemination' is equally expansive and entails making information, or the likelihood of making it available to the public. It is sufficient for the information to be accessible to individuals through various channels such as newspapers, social media, and blogs.[123] Dissemination can also encompass passive actions, including the omission or concealment of crucial information. For example, one can passively disseminate incomplete information by withholding critical details.
- *False or misleading signals, or likely to secure the price at an abnormal or artificial level.* The second requirement stipulates that 'the information gives or is likely to give, false or misleading signals or is likely to secure, the price at an abnormal or artificial level [...].' Presumably, only false or misleading information can yield deceptive signals or secure the price at an abnormal or artificial level. Thus, this element fundamentally boils down to the presence of 'false or misleading information'.[124] False information diverges from the underlying reality, while misleading information misdirects the recipient.[125]
- *Knew, or ought to have known.* The third requirement introduces a subjective element, necessitating that 'where the person who engaged in the dissemination knew, or ought to have known, that the information was false or misleading'.[126] Determining when a person 'ought to have known' that the information was false or misleading requires a case-by-case assessment, but the threshold for this requirement should not be excessively high.[127]

9.7.3. Observations and Commentary

9.7.3.1. Vulnerability of Crypto-asset Markets to Manipulation not Reflected in MiCAR

The relatively young crypto-asset markets lack the regulatory developments and centuries of experience concerning market manipulation that traditional financial

[122] MiCAR, Recital (48).
[123] MAR, Recitals (47) and (48).
[124] See also M Nelemans, *Het verbod van marktmanipulatie (diss. Tilburg)* (Kluwer, 2007) 76–82.
[125] ibid 164–65.
[126] The UK financial supervisor, the Financial Conduct Authority (FCA), explains this requirement as follows: 'If a normal and reasonable person would know or ought to have known in all the circumstances that the information was false or misleading, that indicates that the person disseminating the information knew or ought to have known that it was false or misleading'. See FCA Handbook MAR, 1.8 Dissemination.
[127] E Avgouleas, *The mechanics and regulation of market abuse. A legal and economic analysis* (Oxford University Press, 2005) 356–57.

markets possess. It is logical that the EC has aimed to extend a level of protection to crypto-asset markets that closely mirrors the safeguards provided to traditional financial markets.[128] However, the EC also argues that it is not just the novelty of these markets that makes them more vulnerable to manipulation. Other factors mentioned include issues regarding low liquidity, high price volatility and concentration, the complexity of the technologies used, and a lack of requirements for crypto-asset trading platforms regarding transparency, conflict of interests, equal access to information and fair pricing.[129] Whether these other factors are the result of the crypto-asset markets' novelty or are additional factors making these markets more vulnerable to manipulation, the question is whether the rules developed to combat market manipulation in traditional financial markets are adequate and sufficient to combat market manipulation in the crypto-asset sector.

9.7.3.2. Failure to Provide Indicators is Missed Opportunity to Finetune Prohibition of Market Manipulation to Crypto-asset Markets

Market manipulation is an offence that is very case-specific. The prohibition must contain open norms that allow it to cover novel forms of unwanted behaviour but simultaneously provide enough certainty to market participants to understand the offence and for regulators to enforce the rules. MAR aims to manage this conflicting nature of the prohibition by supplementing the open norms with certain indicators that give direction and explanation.[130] Yet, as mentioned, MiCAR fails to provide such indicators and misses the opportunity to fine-tune the prohibition initially intended for traditional financial markets to the unique functioning and characteristics of crypto-asset markets. This omission is particularly disappointing, as recognising these distinctions would likely enhance the effectiveness of market abuse regulations for crypto-assets.

9.7.3.3. Manipulation of 'Benchmarks' not Prohibited

Another noteworthy disparity with MAR is that MiCAR omits any reference to the manipulation of benchmarks.[131] This omission may be justified from a formal standpoint, as the definition of a benchmark outlined in both MAR and the Benchmarks Regulation (BMR)[132] inherently pertains to financial instruments,

[128] This alignment is evident in the striking similarity between Article 91 MiCAR and Articles 15 and 12 MAR. The parallels between these provisions highlight the EC's intention to afford crypto-assets a regulatory framework that mirrors the measures implemented in well-established financial markets.

[129] See Impact Assessment, para 2.2.3.

[130] See MAR, Annex I and Delegated Regulation (EU) 2016/522, Annex II.

[131] See MAR, Article 12(1)(d).

[132] Regulation (EU) 2016/1011 of the European Parliament and of the Council of 8 June 2016 on indices used as benchmarks in financial instruments and financial contracts or to measure the performance of investment funds.

thereby excluding crypto-assets.[133] However, from a substantive perspective, it is difficult to justify prohibiting the manipulation of indices, rates, or other values when used for pricing financial instruments but not when used for pricing crypto-assets – especially considering the following arguments supporting the inclusion of a prohibition on the manipulation of 'crypto-asset benchmarks'.

The first argument supporting the inclusion of a similar prohibition in MiCAR is that e-money tokens and asset-referenced tokens seem to exemplify exactly such crypto-asset benchmarks, as their value is determined by one or more fiat currencies or a referenced asset, essentially constituting the 'benchmark'.[134] Under MiCAR, uncertainty arises concerning whether the manipulation of the 'benchmark' used for pricing ARTs is explicitly prohibited. This ambiguity is particularly noteworthy given that MiCAR identifies risks associated with e-money tokens and asset-referenced tokens as potential threats to the financial system.[135] Clarification on this matter is crucial in ensuring regulatory efficacy and addressing potential vulnerabilities in the evolving landscape of crypto-assets.

The second argument in favour of including a similar prohibition for the manipulation of 'crypto-asset benchmarks' is that the crypto-asset market is displaying an increasing familiarity with the benchmark concept. The spot price of some of the more widely used crypto-assets, such as bitcoin (BTC), is increasingly being used as a benchmark, as evidenced by the SEC's recent approval of BTC exchange-traded funds (ETFs) on US exchanges, designating BTC as a benchmark for pricing financial instruments like ETF stocks.[136] It is foreseeable that, in due course, products with a reverse construction – where indices, rates, or other values are being used for pricing crypto-assets – will emerge. Leaving it unregulated may inadvertently foster the creation of such crypto-assets and attract manipulative practices. Historical precedent underscores the tendency of manipulators to exploit unregulated (areas of) markets.

9.7.3.4. Forms of Manipulation Using Decentralised Structure Possibly not Covered

As explained, the notion of market manipulation, as conceived in traditional financial markets, revolves around distorting an asset's market *price* – a centralised

[133] See MAR, Article 3(1)(29) and BMR, Article 3(1)(3).

[134] The value of e-money tokens is determined by referencing to one fiat currency, while the value of asset-referenced tokens could be determined by referencing multiple fiat currencies or other assets. See MiCAR, Article 3(1)(6) and Article 3(1)(7). See also chs 3 and 6.

[135] See Impact Assessment, para 1.1.

[136] See G Gensler, 'Statement on the Approval of Spot Bitcoin Exchange-Traded Products' 10 January 2024 SEC Statement, www.sec.gov/news/statement/gensler-statement-spot-bitcoin-011023; HM Pierce, 'Out. Damned Spot! Out, I Say! Statement on the Omnibus Approval Order for List and Trade Bitcoin-based Commodity-based Trust Shares and Trust Units' 10 January 2024 SEC Statement, www.sec.gov/news/statement/peirce-statement-spot-bitcoin-011023. See also U Bindseil and J Schaaf, 'ETF approval for bitcoin – the naked emperor's new clothes' (*ECB Blog*, 22 February 2024) www.ecb.europa.eu/press/blog/date/2024/html/ecb.blog20240222~0929f86e23.en.html.

concept derived from the aggregate supply and demand of all market participants condensed into a single figure.[137] Consequently, the prohibition of market manipulation has evolved in traditional financial markets to combat practices that exploit this centralised construct. MiCAR adopts the same prohibition. While this prohibition adequately addresses many forms of manipulation for crypto-assets admitted to trading, it fails to encompass the decentralised aspects inherent to crypto-assets. Abusive practices targeting the decentralised nature and functioning of crypto-assets are thus likely not covered by the current prohibition of market manipulation.

For example, it is questionable whether manipulation of a crypto-asset's consensus mechanism – a decentralised aspect governing transaction validation – constitutes market manipulation.[138] Although manipulating the consensus mechanism could alter the crypto-asset's functioning, it may not necessarily impact the pricing mechanism of the 'market'. While behaviour manipulating the consensus mechanism could *also* (indirectly) influence centralised aspects and qualify as a form of market manipulation under Article 91(2), it is crucial to acknowledge that the manipulation of decentralised facets, such as consensus mechanisms, does not inherently constitute an act of market manipulation in and of itself.[139]

9.8. Prevention and Detection of Market Abuse – Article 92 MiCAR

9.8.1. General

In the fight against market abuse, MiCAR goes beyond merely prohibiting specific behaviours and mandating the disclosure of certain information. It imposes an additional obligation on designated market participants to report any suspicions of market abuse to the regulator and to implement measures aimed at preventing and detecting potential market abuse. Article 92 mandates that individuals professionally engaged in arranging or executing transactions in crypto-assets must report any suspicious transactions and establish effective arrangements, systems, and procedures to prevent and detect (attempted) market abuse.[140] Notably, Article 92 draws significant inspiration from the provisions outlined in Article 16 MAR.

[137] See section 9.7.1.

[138] See for the definition of consensus mechanism, see MiCAR, Article 3(1)(3).

[139] In comparison with conventional financial markets, consider a scenario where one issuer (A) undergoes acquisition by another issuer (B), subsequently leading to a modification in the company's strategic direction. While this shift in the company's operations naturally influences the market price of securities issued by issuer (A), it does not inherently constitute market manipulation.

[140] MiCAR, Article 92(1).

9.8.2. Prevention and Detection

The obligation to prevent and detect market abuse in Article 92 is directed at 'any person professionally arranging or executing transactions in crypto-assets'.[141] Notably, MiCAR does not explicitly define this norm addressee.[142] However, MAR uses and defines the similar norm addressee as 'a person professionally engaged in the reception and transmission of orders for, or in the execution of transactions in, financial instruments'.[143] A person is considered 'professionally' engaged when they perform these activities regularly and with the intention of earning income.[144] The scope of Article 92 is extensive, encompassing anyone professionally engaged in arranging or executing transactions in crypto-assets, irrespective of whether such services are offered to clients. This implies that the scope of Article 92 extends beyond CASPs and includes individuals acting on their own accounts.[145]

The scope of Article 92 MiCAR is considerably broader than its counterpart in Article 16 MAR. This extended scope is manifested in two crucial aspects. First, with respect to the norm addressee. Article 16 MAR confines the obligation to *prevent* market abuse to 'market operators' and 'investment firms operating a trading venue'. Under MAR, only the obligation to *detect* market abuse extends to 'persons who professionally arrange or execute transactions'.[146] In contrast, Article 92 MiCAR extends the obligation to *prevent and detect* to include 'persons who professionally arrange or execute transactions', thereby encompassing a wider range of participants than MAR. Second, while Article 16 MAR mandates the obligation to prevent and detect (attempted) insider dealing and (attempted) market manipulation, Article 92 MiCAR imposes an obligation to prevent and detect any form of (attempted) market abuse. Although we believe that it was not MiCAR's intention to extend the obligation to prevent and detect the unlawful disclosure of inside information, it should not be excluded.

Under Article 92, the norm addressee bears the responsibility to both prevent and detect market abuse. Although these obligations are distinct, their close interconnection can make differentiation challenging. Fulfilling the dual obligations of preventing and detecting market abuse necessitates the establishment of 'effective

[141] ibid.

[142] Although one could read it implicitly into various related definitions in Article 3(1) MiCAR, such as 'execution of orders for crypto-assets on behalf of clients' (Article 3(1)(21)), 'placing or crypto-assets' (Article 3(1)(22)), and 'reception and transmission of orders for crypto-assets on behalf of clients' (Article 3(1)(23)).

[143] One of the norm addressees of Article 16 MAR is any 'person professionally arranging or executing transactions' (Article 3(1)(28) MAR). See MAR, Article 16(2). The primary addressees of Article 16 MAR are all market operators (Article 3 (1)(5) MAR) and investment firms operating a trading venue (Article 3(1)(2) MAR). See MAR, Article 16(1).

[144] See F Kusznier, 'Article 16 Prevention and Detection of Market Abuse' in S Kalss, M Oppitz, U Torggler and M Winner (eds), *EU Market Abuse Regulation* (Edward Elgar, 2021) 200.

[145] See also ESMA's vision on this norm addressee in relation to Article 16 MAR. ESMA, Questions and Answers on the Market Abuse Regulation, 25 November 2022, ESMA70-145-111 (17), pp 23–24.

[146] See MAR, Article 16(1)–(2).

arrangements, systems and procedures'.[147] ESMA is tasked with developing draft regulatory standards to precisely define the attributes of such arrangements, systems, and procedures.[148] Potential characteristics to be specified are likely to include continuous monitoring of specific orders for particular types of clients and crypto-assets, scrutiny of the software employed for reading, analysing, and retrieving order book data, and assessment of the capacity used for algorithmic trading.[149]

9.8.3. Reporting

In addition to the aforementioned obligations to prevent and detect market abuse, 'any person professionally arranging or executing transactions in crypto-assets' is further obligated in Article 92 to report suspicious behaviour.[150] More specifically, the reporting obligation extends to suspicion of (an attempt of) committed market abuse concerning: (i) orders and transactions, and (ii) other aspects of the functioning of distributed ledger technology.[151]

Concerning the reporting obligation for (i) orders and transactions that could potentially constitute (an attempt of) market abuse, this requirement also encompasses suspicions related to the cancellation or modification of an order. This parallel obligation can be observed in Article 16 MAR when dealing with financial instruments.[152]

The reporting obligation for (ii) other aspects of the functioning of distributed ledger technology, which may constitute (an attempt of) market abuse, is specific to Article 92 MiCAR and extends the reporting obligation to forms of behaviour other than transactions or orders. In this respect, the reporting obligation under MiCAR is even broader than the equivalent under MAR. MiCAR does not elaborate on or define 'other aspects of the functioning of distributed ledger technology' but offers the consensus mechanism as (merely) one example.[153] However, this example does not clarify the seemingly broad and vague reporting obligation and raises further confusion, as the connection between the functioning of distributed ledger technology – specifically, the consensus mechanism – and forms of market abuse is unclear. How the functioning of the distributed ledger technology and the consensus mechanism could constitute market abuse is not explained or

[147] MiCAR, Article 92(1).

[148] MiCAR, Article 92(2)(a).

[149] See for inspiration Articles 2 and 3 of Delegated Regulation (EU) 2016/957 [2016] OJ L 160/1, complementing Article 16 MAR.

[150] MiCAR, Article 92(1).

[151] ibid.

[152] See for more on the obligation to report suspicious transactions, ESMA Final Report 2015/1455 (2015) 34–36. Kusznier (n 144) 198–201; F 't Hart, 'Preventie en opsporingsplicht' in DR Doorenbos e.a., *Handboek Marktmisbruik (Onderneming en recht nr. 104)* (Kluwer, 2018) 415–18.

[153] The consensus mechanism is defined in Article 3(1)(3) MiCAR as 'the rules and procedures by which an agreement is reached, among DLT network nodes, that a transaction is validated'.

clarified in MiCAR. Besides, the market abuse prohibitions of Title VI MiCAR lack explicit mention of aspects of distributed ledger technology, which further raises uncertainty about whether specific behaviour associated with these aspects is covered under the prohibitions.[154]

The reporting obligation only applies when there is a 'reasonable suspicion'. Although the exact threshold for the reporting obligation remains to be determined, this requirement indicates that there must be some circumstances pointing to prohibited behaviour.[155] The norm addressee must report to the competent authority 'without delay'. This means that once reasonable suspicion has been formed in relation to the behaviour, the norm addressee must immediately report to the relevant competent authority.[156]

9.8.4. Observations and Commentary

Article 92 MiCAR closely mirrors Article 16 MAR but introduces nuanced deviations across its provisions that might initially appear inconsequential. However, upon closer examination, the following deviations in the obligations to prevent, detect, and report market abuse under MiCAR may increase the burden for compliance and disproportionately affect market participants.

First, the *obligation to prevent* under MiCAR encompasses not just market operators and investment firms operating a trading venue as under MAR, but extends to 'any person professionally arranging or executing transactions in crypto-assets'. This broader scope of the obligation to prevent significantly increases the number of entities obligated to uphold preventive measures.

Second, while MAR's *obligation to prevent and detect* pertains to market manipulation and insider dealing, MiCAR directs this obligation to market abuse, potentially including unlawful disclosure.[157] This possible expansion would significantly broaden the spectrum of activities that market participants must actively prevent and detect.

Third, MiCAR's *obligation to report* suspicions of market abuse goes beyond mere transactions, extending to encompass 'other aspects of the functioning of distributed ledger technology'.[158] This addition necessitates not only the monitoring of transactions in crypto-assets but also the monitoring and assessing of the functioning of crypto-assets and their underlying technology.[159] Although ESMA has yet to develop draft regulatory standards setting the precise arrangements, systems, and procedures for reporting, extending the obligation to report

[154] See section 9.7.3.4.

[155] See for factors relevant for determining this threshold: ESMA Final Report 2015/1455 (2015) 35. Kusznier (n 144) 200.

[156] ESMA Final Report 2015/1455 (2015) 35.

[157] See also section 9.8.2.

[158] See also section 9.8.3.

[159] MiCAR, Article 92(2)(a).

suspicious behaviour concerning the functioning of crypto-assets and their underlying technology seems highly disproportionate.

Despite MiCAR's purported aim to establish a less burdensome and more proportionate market abuse regime compared to MAR, the discussed deviations seem to indicate that the obligation to prevent and detect market abuse under MiCAR is broader and more burdensome than under MAR. Market participants should be aware of this.

9.9. Conclusion

This chapter focused on MiCAR's market abuse regime outlined in Title VI. We reviewed the scope of this regime, its various prohibitions, and the obligations related to preventing market abuse involving crypto-assets under MiCAR. For each topic, we provided a detailed analysis, explaining the relevant provisions and their substantive content, with interpretations derived from the MAR where applicable. Additionally, we offered general commentary on key provisions and shared our observations.

The introduction of MiCAR's market abuse regime is a welcome step towards preserving the integrity of the crypto-assets market. This relatively young and rapidly maturing market has become increasingly important for the global economy, but it still faces challenges, particularly in preventing fraud and market abuse. A dedicated legislative framework to address these issues in the EU is essential, and we commend the introduction of MiCAR's regime targeting market abuse in the context of crypto-assets.

However, MiCAR's market abuse framework is not as distinct as it claims to be. In reality, it largely mirrors MAR, with many of its provisions extended to crypto-assets. While we believe that MiCAR's regime will effectively combat the more obvious forms of market abuse within the crypto sector, it does not fully address the gaps that remain in the EU's existing market abuse framework, represented by MAR. This raises the question of why a separate framework was created rather than simply amending MAR to include crypto-assets.

Moreover, the opportunity to craft a more specialised framework tailored to the unique characteristics of the crypto-asset market appears to have been missed. Nevertheless, MiCAR's market abuse regime still holds significant potential. It provides a solid legislative foundation which, with further legislative efforts and active guidance from ESMA, could be fine-tuned to better address the specific needs and challenges of crypto-asset markets.

10

Role and Powers of Competent Authorities, the EBA and ESMA

ELISABETH NOBLE*

10.1. Introduction

Title VII of MiCAR (Articles 93 to 138)[1] establishes the powers available to competent authorities and to the European Banking Authority (EBA) to supervise and enforce the application of the Regulation. Specific powers are also conferred on the European Supervisory Authorities or ESAs (EBA, European Insurance and Occupational Pensions Authority (EIOPA) and European Securities and Markets Authority (ESMA)) to facilitate convergence in supervision and in the classification of crypto-assets.

Notwithstanding the fact that Title VII sets out the familiar 'nuts and bolts' of supervision, it should be regarded a cornerstone of the new regime, equipping relevant authorities with essential powers to share information, to carry out investigations and on-site inspections, and to impose supervisory measures and administrative penalties with a precautionary, remedial and sanctioning effect in the event of suspected or identified infringements of MiCAR. The exercise of these powers in practice will be at the heart of the successful application of the new regime, and instrumental to securing high standards of investor protection, the orderly functioning and integrity of crypto-asset markets and, ultimately, financial stability.[2]

* The views expressed in this chapter are solely those of the author and do not necessarily reflect those of the EBA.

[1] Article and Title references in this chapter are to MiCAR unless otherwise stated.

[2] For a general discussion of the role supervision and enforcement plays in the delivery of effective financial regulation see J Armour et al, *Principles of Financial Regulation* (Oxford University Press, 2016) ch 26 'Supervision and Enforcement of Financial Regulation'.

10.2. Authorities in Scope of Title VII

10.2.1. Competent Authorities

Title VII encompasses provisions relating to competent authorities, the EBA (including in its capacity as a supervisor under MiCAR; see section 10.4), ESMA and, in one instance, EIOPA.[3]

The term 'competent authority' is to be understood as the relevant national authority or authorities designated by each Member State in accordance with Article 93 to perform supervisory tasks under MiCAR, and by each Member State for the application of the second Electronic Money Directive (EMD2)[4] concerning issuers of e-money.[5]

In some Member States, a 'fully integrated' model of supervision applies whereby only one authority is assigned supervisory tasks for the financial sector (eg, the Czech Republic, Denmark, Ireland, Lithuania, Malta, Sweden) whereas in others a twin peak model (eg, Austria, Cyprus, France, Romania, the Netherlands) or multi-peak model (eg, Italy, Spain, Portugal) applies where, respectively, two or more authorities are assigned supervisory tasks. The tasks are typically allocated on a sectoral basis: banking and payments, securities and markets, insurance and pensions.[6] This means that in some Member States an active choice has to be made as to the designation of authorities for the purposes of supervisory tasks under MiCAR. In many cases, the choice follows the traditional sectoral division of tasks. This implies the assignment of supervisory functions and duties with regard to ARTs (Title III) and EMTs (Title IV) to the authority responsible for banking and payments, in view of the uses to which EMTs and (some) ARTs may be put (payments), and the assignment of functions and duties with regard to other crypto-assets (Title II), CASPs (Title V) and market abuse (Title VI) being assigned to the authority responsible for securities and markets (as is the choice expressed in France[7]). However, other divisions of tasks may occur with some Member States perhaps assigning functions and duties across MiCAR to one

[3] Article 97 (promotion of convergence on the classification of crypto-assets).

[4] Directive 2009/110/EC of the European Parliament and of the Council of 16 September 2009 on the taking up, pursuit and prudential supervision of the business of electronic money institutions amending Directives 2005/60/EC and 2006/48/EC and repealing Directive 2000/46/EC (OJ L 267, 10.10.2009, p 7) (as amended).

[5] MiCAR, Article 3(1)(35).

[6] The lists of members of the Boards of Supervisors of the EBA, EIOPA and ESMA further illustrate the allocation of supervisory tasks among the authorities in the Member States: EBA, www.eba.europa.eu/about-us/organisation-and-governance/governance-structure-and-decision-making/board-supervisors/members-and-observers, EIOPA, www.eiopa.europa.eu/about/governance-structure/board-supervisors_en, and ESMA, www.esma.europa.eu/about-esma/governance-structure/board-of-supervisors.

[7] L'Autorité de contrôle prudentiel et de résolution (ACPR) is responsible for the application of Titles III and IV whereas l'Autorité des marchés financiers (AMF) is responsible for the application of other Titles, acpr.banque-france.fr/autoriser/procedures-secteur-banque/agrement-autorisation-ou-enregistrement/emetteur-de-crypto-actifs.

authority, particularly having regard to the emergence of multi-function crypto-asset intermediaries[8] (as known as 'crypto conglomerates'), or assigning functions on a functional basis (eg, consumer protection/conduct of business, and prudential supervision).

Where Member States designate more than one competent authority to carry out supervisory functions and duties under MiCAR, there must be a clear delineation of tasks. A single point of contact must be identified for the purposes of cooperation between competent authorities on a cross-border basis and with the EBA and ESMA (Article 93(2)). The designated authorities are required to be notified to ESMA, and a list of competent authorities is to be maintained on ESMA's website (Article 93(3)).[9] Moreover, by 30 June 2025, Member States are required to notify the European Commission, the EBA and ESMA of the laws, regulations and administrative provisions implementing Title VII, including any subsequent amendments thereof (Article 99). Typically, such laws, regulations and administrative provisions include measures relating to the designation of functions and tasks and 'activation' of the supervisory toolkit (including information gathering, investigations, and enforcement powers) for the relevant authority/authorities, notwithstanding the 'directly applicable' nature of MiCAR.[10]

Importantly, the designation of a national authority for the purposes of MiCAR has implications not only for that Regulation, but also for the purposes of the regulations establishing the ESAs. In particular, the full suite of powers assigned to the EBA and ESMA under their Founding Regulations[11] with regard to competent authorities, including regarding breaches of EU law (Article 17 of the Founding Regulations), actions in emergency situations (Article 18), the settlement of disagreements between competent authorities in cross-border situations (Article 19) and across sectors (Article 20), the building of a supervisory

[8] The term 'multi-function crypto-asset intermediary' is not used in MiCAR. However, it is used in the context of the work of International bodies such as the Financial Stability Board (FSB). For example, see the FSB's November 2023 report 'The Financial Stability Implications of Multifunction Crypto-asset Intermediaries', www.fsb.org/2023/11/the-financial-stability-implications-of multifunction crypto-asset-intermediaries/.

[9] See www.esma.europa.eu/esmas-activities/digital-finance-and-innovation/markets-crypto-assets-regulation-mica.

[10] EU Regulations become binding throughout the EU on their date of application, albeit some changes in national law or regulation may be needed. This can be compared with the position for Directives which need to be incorporated into national law and by such date as specified in the Directive concerned.

[11] Regulation (EU) No 1093/2010 of the European Parliament and of the Council of 24 November 2010 establishing a European Supervisory Authority (European Banking Authority), amending Decision No 716/2009/EC and repealing Commission Decision 2009/78/EC (OJ L 331, 15.12.2010, p 12) (as amended) and Regulation (EU) No 1095/2010 of the European Parliament and of the Council of 24 November 2010 establishing a European Supervisory Authority (European Securities and Markets Authority), amending Decision No 716/2009/EC and repealing Commission Decision 2009/77/EC (OJ L 331, 15.12.2010, p 84) (as amended). As the result of a 'quirk' in the drafting of Regulation (EU) No 1093/2010, as compared to the wording of Regulation (EU) No 1095/2010, a specific amendment to the former was introduced in MiCAR to extend the EBA's powers to competent authorities designated under MiCAR (Article 144).

culture (Article 29), peer reviews (Article 30) and coordination (Article 31), are all extended to competent authorities designated under MiCAR.

10.2.2. EBA, ESMA and EIOPA

For the most part, supervisory tasks under MiCAR are undertaken by competent authorities. However, as noted in chapter eight, the EBA is assigned supervisory responsibilities with respect to:

- ARTs that are determined by the EBA to be 'significant' in accordance with the criteria established in Article 43(1)[12] (including in cases where applicant issuers indicate a wish to be classified as significant on a 'voluntary' basis pursuant to Article 44) (Article 117(1) and (2)); the EBA's direct supervision role is slightly narrower in the case of ARTs issued by credit institutions as the MiCAR requirements applicable to credit institutions are more limited than for other ARTs issued by other types of issuer (Article 17(4)).
- EMTs that are determined by the EBA to be 'significant' in accordance with Article 56 (including in cases where an issuer, or the applicant issuer, voluntarily wishes to be classified as significant pursuant to Article 57). Importantly, the EBA's direct supervision tasks for significant EMTs are limited to cases where the issuer is an electronic money institution; significant EMTs issued by credit institutions remain subject to supervision by the banking supervisor (Article 117(4)). See section 10.4.1.

EIOPA and ESMA do not have any direct supervision tasks under MiCAR. However, ESMA can exercise supervisory and investigative powers under Article 94(1), and under Article 17 of its Founding Regulation,[13] where it identifies an entity as providing crypto-asset services (as defined in Article 3(1)(16)) without the necessary authorisation or registration (Article 110(4) and (5)).

The EBA and ESMA are responsible for promoting supervisory convergence in the application of MiCAR with both specific tasks under that Regulation (eg, Article 95(8)) and in the context of their general objectives and tasks under their

[12] The criteria are further specified in Commission Delegated Regulation (EU) 2024/1506 of 22 February 2024 supplementing Regulation (EU) 2023/1114 of the European Parliament and of the Council by specifying certain criteria for classifying asset-referenced tokens and e-money tokens as significant (OJ L, 2024/1506, 30.5.2024).

[13] Regulation (EU) No 1095/2010 of the European Parliament and of the Council of 24 November 2010 establishing a European Supervisory Authority (European Securities and Markets Authority), amending Decision No 716/2009/EC and repealing Commission Decision 2009/77/EC (OJ L 331, 15.12.2010, p 84) (as amended). Article 17 concerns cases where a breach of EU law is identified. In specific situations where a breach has been identified, ESMA can adopt individual decisions addressed to financial market participants with the objective of remedying the situation in a timely manner. The same power is available to the EBA under the equivalent provision of the EBA's Founding Regulation.

Founding Regulations (section 10.2.1).[14] ESMA has an enhanced role to promote dialogue and convergence with regard to CASPs that are identified as 'significant' in accordance with Article 85.[15] Additionally, all three ESAs have a role to promote convergence in the classification of crypto-assets (Article 97; see section 10.6), including in cases where crypto-assets may be non-fungible,[16] qualify as financial instruments,[17] or as various insurance or pensions products.[18]

To address significant investor protection concerns or threats to the orderly functioning and integrity of markets in crypto-assets or to the stability of all or part of the EU financial system, the EBA and ESMA, along with competent authorities, have available temporary intervention powers (Articles 103 to 106; see section 10.5). Additionally, ESMA has a miscellany of responsibilities to maintain on its website important information including:

- the list of authorities designated by Member States for the performance of supervisory tasks (Article 93(3));
- the register of crypto-asset white papers, and register of issuers of ARTs and EMTs, and CASPs (Article 109);
- the register of entities determined to be providing crypto-asset services in violation of the authorisation requirements in Article 59 and 61 (Article 110).

10.3. Supervisory, Investigative and Enforcement Powers Available to Competent Authorities

In the context of the designation of functions and duties of competent authorities for the purposes of MiCAR, Member States are required to ensure that authorities have available at least the set of supervisory and investigative powers enlisted in Article 94(1) and (3) and the powers to impose appropriate administrative penalties and other administrative measures in relation to infringements (Article 111(1)).

This means that some competent authorities may have available a broader suite of powers, depending on the law establishing the authority and administrative norms in the Member State concerned. Additionally, bearing in mind that an issuer, offeror, person seeking admission to trading, or CASP may be performing

[14] For an illustration of the ESA convergence activities, see the information available on the EBA's website, www.eba.europa.eu/activities/supervisory-convergence/supervisory-convergence.

[15] A CASP shall be deemed significant if it has in the EU at least 15 million active users, on average, in one calendar year, where the average is calculated as the average of the daily number of active users throughout the previous calendar year.

[16] Crypto-assets that are unique and non-fungible are outside the scope of MiCAR (Article 2(3)).

[17] 'Financial instrument' is defined in Article 3(1)(49). Crypto-assets that are classified as financial instruments are outside the scope of MiCAR pursuant to Article 2(4)(a).

[18] Crypto-assets classified, for example, as non-life or life insurance products or pensions products are outside the scope of MiCAR. For the full list of excluded financial products, see Article 2(4).

other regulated activities, it is acknowledged that supervisory and investigative powers deriving from other regulatory measures may be available (Article 94(2)). Moreover, such 'other' powers might be available to authorities other than the competent authority, as may be the case in the context of the supervision of an entity carrying out multiple regulated activities such as crypto-asset service provision and payment services, or a credit institution that issues a significant ART. Competent authorities are required to cooperate with such other authorities performing supervisory tasks pursuant to EU or national law, and with tax authorities and relevant regulatory authorities of third countries (Article 98).

10.3.1. Access to Information

For the purposes of carrying out their supervisory functions and duties under MiCAR, competent authorities must have available the power to require 'any person' to provide information and documents which could be relevant to the performance of such duties (Article 94(1)(a)). Specific powers to require the provision of information in relation to Title VI (market abuse) are also required to be made available (Article 94(3)), consistent with the approach set out in the Market Abuse Regulation (MAR).[19]

The scope is intentionally broad so as to ensure that competent authorities can require information not only from issuers, offerors, and CASPs,[20] but also from other relevant persons, such as members of the management body, staff, shareholders, and third parties, including custodians of reserve assets for ARTs. Such information requests may be ad hoc (eg, in the context of a specific investigation), occasional (eg, requests for data on complaints) or regular (eg, in accordance with any national application of the EBA's own initiative Guidelines to address reporting gaps under MiCAR[21]).

A person shall not be considered to have infringed any contractual, legislative, regulatory or administrative provision, or to be subject to related liability, by virtue of making available to the competent authority information required to be provided in exercise of powers envisaged in Article 94 (Article 94(7)) or in the context of reporting infringements of MiCAR (Article 116).[22] This type of

[19] Regulation (EU) No 596/2014 of the European Parliament and of the Council of 16 April 2014 on market abuse (market abuse regulation) and repealing Directive 2003/6/EC of the European Parliament and of the Council and Commission Directives 2003/124/EC, 2003/125/EC and 2004/72/EC (OJ L 173, 12.6.2014, pp 1–61) (as amended).

[20] As defined in, respectively, point (10), (13) and (15) of Article 3(1).

[21] The EBA's own initiative Guidelines were published for consultation on 15 July 2024, www.eba.europa.eu/publications-and-media/press-releases/eba-consults-guidelines-reporting-data-assist-authorities-their-supervisory-duties-and-significance, and the final version is accessible via the EBA's website: www.eba.europa.eu/regulation-and-policy/asset-referenced-and-e-money-tokens-micar.

[22] Directive (EU) 2019/1937 of the European Parliament and of the Council of 23 October 2019 on the protection of persons who report breaches of Union law (OJ L 305, 26.11.2019, pp 17–56) applies to the reporting of infringements of MiCAR and enlists protections for so-called 'whistleblowers'.

'protected disclosure' provision is not uncommon in EU regulation.[23] It removes potential impediments to the flow of information to the competent authority for reasons of public policy (ie, ensuring the authority has available all relevant information to ensure the effective superintendence and enforcement of regulation applicable for reasons of consumer and investor protection, prudential resilience, market integrity and, ultimately, financial stability). Professional secrecy and data protection requirements apply to competent authorities, to the EBA and to ESMA (Articles 100 and 101).

10.3.2. Complaints from Consumers, Investors and Other Parties

Without prejudice to the complaints handling procedures required to be implemented by issuers and CASPs (Article 31 and Article 71), clients and other interested parties (including consumer associations) may also submit complaints to competent authorities regarding infringements of MiCAR by offerors, persons seeking admission to trading, issuers of ARTs and EMTs, and CASPs. To this end, competent authorities are required to set up procedures for the submission in writing of complaints. Such procedures shall be published on the website of each competent authority and communicated to the EBA and ESMA (the latter also having responsibility to publish on its website links to all the relevant webpages) (Article 108). Member States must also provide, in accordance with national law, that one or more of the following entities may, in the interests of consumers, take action before the courts or competent authorities to ensure the application of MiCAR: public bodies or their representatives, consumer organisations, and professional organisations (Article 113(2)).

10.3.3. Supervisory and Investigative Powers

In addition to powers to require the provision of information[24] and launch investigations or on-site inspections,[25] Article 94 enlists a large number of supervisory powers, some of which can be activated in relation to suspected infringements of MiCAR, and others – in the event of identified infringements. This list is similar to the list of powers set out in Article 69 MiFID II.[26]

[23] For example, a similar provision exists in MiFID II, Article 77(2).

[24] Including information from CASPs which might have an effect on the provision of the services, in order to ensure the protection of the interests of the clients or smooth operation of the market (Article 94(1)(d)).

[25] MiCAR, Article 94(1)(w).

[26] Directive 2014/65/EU of the European Parliament and of the Council of 15 May 2014 on markets in financial instruments and amending Directive 2002/92/EC and Directive 2011/61/EU (recast) (OJ L 173, 12.6.2014, pp 349–496) (as amended).

In the case of suspected infringements, competent authorities must have available, among others, powers to:

- suspend, or require a CASP to suspend, the provision of crypto-asset services for a maximum of 30 consecutive working days on any single occasion (point (b));
- order the immediate cessation of activity, where there is reason to assume a person is providing crypto-asset services without authorisation (point (h));
- suspend an offer to the public or an admission to trading of crypto-assets for a maximum of 30 consecutive working days on any single occasion (point (l));
- prohibit an offer to the public or an admission to trading of crypto-assets where there are reasonable grounds for suspecting MiCAR will be infringed (point (m));
- suspend, or require a CASP operating a trading platform to suspend, trading of a crypto-asset for a maximum of 30 days on any single occasion (point (n));
- cease, suspend or prohibit marketing communications (points (p) and (q)).

In the case of identified infringements of MiCAR, competent authorities must have available, among others, the powers to:

- prohibit the provision of crypto-asset services (point (c));
- make public the fact that a CASP, offeror, person seeking admission to trading or an issuer, fails to fulfil its obligations (point (e) and (r));
- require the amendment of white papers (point (i));
- prohibit the trading of crypto-assets on a trading platform for crypto-assets (point (o));
- require the cessation of an issuance or offer to the public (point (u)).

Additionally, some powers are framed not by reference to suspected or identified infringements but rather by reference to public policy goals. For example, competent authorities must have powers:

- to suspend, or require a CASP to suspend the provision of crypto-asset services where the situation of a CASP would be detrimental to the interests of its clients, in particular retail clients (point (f));
- to require offerors, persons seeking admission to trading, or issuers to include additional information in white papers where necessary for financial stability or the protection of interests of holders of crypto-assets, in particular retail holders (point (k));
- to disclose, or require the offeror, person seeking admission to trading or issuer, to disclose all material information to ensure the protection of the interests of holders of crypto-assets, in particular retail holders, or the smooth operation of the market (point (s)).

The powers may be used singularly or in combination. For example, a competent authority may choose to require a CASP to take remedial action and pay an administrative penalty pursuant to Article 111 (section 10.3.4), and may make public the fact that the CASP has infringed MiCAR.

Moreover, competent authorities may impose supervisory measures with regard to one person with respect to a breach by another. Notably, competent authorities must have powers to suspend or prohibit the provision of crypto-asset services, including where the issuer or offeror has infringed MiCAR (Article 94(1)(b), (l), (n), (q) etc). This ensures that competent authorities have the capability to mitigate risks to investors, including retail holders, specifically through limiting access to the crypto-asset concerned.

The supervisory and investigative powers of competent authorities, including powers to request information, may be exercised directly, in collaboration with other authorities, including authorities responsible for AML/CFT, or via delegation to other authorities (Article 94(5)).

Typically, the competent authority in the 'home Member State'[27] will take the lead in deploying supervisory and investigative powers, including where the competent authority in the 'host Member State'[28] identifies and notifies the home authority of suspected irregularities (Article 102(1)).[29] However, where, despite any actions taken by the home authority, the irregularities persist and amount to an infringement of MiCAR, the host authority may, following notification of the home authority, ESMA and, as appropriate, the EBA, take 'appropriate measures' to protect clients of CASPs and holders of the crypto-assets. This may include preventing the conduct of further activities in the host Member State (Article 102(2)).

Depending on national norms, competent authorities may, or may be required to, exercise some or all of the supervisory and investigative powers by application to national courts (Article 94(4) and (5)(d)).

10.3.4. Administrative Penalties and Administrative Measures

Beyond supervisory and investigative powers, Member States are required, in accordance with national law, to provide competent authorities with the powers to impose appropriate administrative penalties and other administrative measures with regard to specific infringements (Article 111(1)). These infringements include breaches of requirements relating to white papers, reserve assets, and own funds, and market abuse, as well as failures to cooperate of comply with investigations, inspections or information requests pursuant to Article 94(3).

[27] MiCAR, Article 3(1)(33).

[28] MiCAR, Article 3(1)(34).

[29] The EBA must also be notified in the case of suspected irregularities regarding an issuer of an ART or EMT or a crypto-asset service related to such tokens (second sub-paragraph of Article 102(1)).

The types of administrative penalties and measures include public statements, 'cease and desist' orders, administrative fines (Article 94(2)), and temporary bans preventing any member of the management body of a CASP, or other relevant natural person, from exercising management functions in a CASP (Article 111(4)). In cases of market abuse, the administrative measures may include, in addition, the disgorgement of profits gained or losses avoided as a result of the conduct, and withdrawal or suspension of the authorisation of a CASP, and more severe bans and fines than for other infringements (Article 111(5)). However, in any case, Member States have flexibility to confer on competent authorities additional powers, and may provide for higher levels of penalties than those established in Article 111(2) to (5) (Article 111(6)).

A range of factors must be taken into account by competent authorities in determining which, if any, administrative penalty or other measure or combination, shall be imposed. Such factors include the gravity and duration of the infringement, whether the infringement was negligent or intentional, the losses for third parties, the level of cooperation with the competent authority, and the impact of the infringement on the interests of holders of crypto-assets and clients of CASPs, in particular retail holders (Article 111(1)).

In accordance with administrative law and practice, decisions imposing administrative penalties and other measures are required to be fully reasoned, transmitted to the legal or natural person concerned, and subject to a right of appeal before a court (Article 113(1)).

Decisions are required to be published on the website of the competent authority, except where the measure is of an investigatory nature (Article 114(1)) or where publication would jeopardise an ongoing investigation or be disproportionate (Article 114(2)). In such cases the competent authority may determine not to publish, or to publish on an anonymised basis, or at a later stage. The publication of administrative penalties or other measures can have a strong deterrence effect and, by itself, have a sanctioning effect by virtue of the reputational impact for the person subject to the penalty or measure.[30]

Each year competent authorities are required to provide the EBA and ESMA with aggregate information regarding administrative penalties and measures imposed under MiCAR,[31] and ESMA is required to publish that information in an annual report (Article 115(1)). Anonymised and aggregate information must also be provided in relation to criminal penalties, where Member States have exercised their discretion to specify in national law that infringements constitute criminal offences. Where administrative penalties and measures have been imposed but not published by the competent authority, or where they are subject to appeal, the EBA and ESMA must also be notified, and ESMA must maintain

[30] For example, see Raluca A Roman, 'Winners and losers from supervisory enforcement actions against banks' (2020) 60 *Journal of Corporate Finance* 101516.

[31] Simultaneous reporting to the ESAs can also be done at the same time as disclosure to the public (Article 115(2)).

a central database of penalties and administrative measures for the purposes of facilitating information exchange between competent authorities, the EBA and ESMA (Article 115(3)).

10.3.5. Coordination and Cooperation Among Competent Authorities

In the discharge of the functions and duties under MiCAR, competent authorities are required to cooperate with each other, with the EBA and ESMA (Article 95(1) and (8), Article 96 and Article 111(2)), and other relevant authorities (Article 98). The requirement to cooperate encompasses the exchange, without undue delay, of information, including information of a kind set out in regulatory and implementing technical standards adopted pursuant to Article 95(10) and (11) and, in the case of cooperation with the EBA and ESMA, pursuant to Article 96(3).[32] It also encompasses cooperation in the context of supervision, investigation and enforcement actions and, where applicable, criminal proceedings (second subparagraph of Article 95(1) and Article 111(2)). Such a case may arise, for example, in the event of the identification of an entity carrying out a regulated activity without the relevant authorisation, which may be classified as a criminal offence in some Member States (eg, Ireland[33]). Information exchanged between competent authorities that relates to business or operational conditions and other economic or personal affairs is to be treated as confidential and subject to professional secrecy requirements (Article 100). Personal data must also be protected in accordance with the General Data Protection Regulation (GDPR)[34] (see Article 101).

Requests for assistance may be made verbally or in writing, and may arise in the context of information gathering, investigations and on-site inspections (Article 95(3) and (4)). The EBA and ESMA could also be requested to coordinate inspections or investigations where more than one competent authority is involved (Article 95(5)). Competent authorities may refuse a request for assistance only in limited cases, for instance, on grounds of national security, or where such a request may adversely impede an ongoing investigation, enforcement or criminal proceeding (Article 95(2)). Refusals to cooperate, or undue delays, may be reported to ESMA or, where relevant, the EBA (Article 95(6) and (7)). In these cases, the EBA

[32] ESMA's final report on the draft technical standards was published on 25 March 2024 www.esma.europa.eu/sites/default/files/2024-03/ESMA75-453128700-949_Final_Report_MiCA_cooperation_technical_standards.pdf.

[33] For an example of actions taken by the Central Bank of Ireland for a breach of authorisation requirements, see www.centralbank.ie/news/article/warning-notice-central-bank-of-ireland-issues-warning-on-unauthorised-firm-compare-deposit-03-nov-2023.

[34] Regulation (EU) 2016/679 of the European Parliament and of the Council of 27 April 2016 on the protection of natural persons with regard to the processing of personal data and on the free movement of such data, and repealing Directive 95/46/EC (General Data Protection Regulation) (OJ L 119, 4.5.2016, pp 1–88) (as amended).

and ESMA may assist the competent authorities concerned in reaching an agreement as to the way forward and can, as a last resort, address individual decisions to financial institutions or financial sector operators to take such steps as appropriate (Article 19(4) of the Founding Regulations).[35] This power is also applicable in cases where the competent authority in a home Member State disagrees with measures taken by the competent authority of a host Member State pursuant to Article 102(2) (Article 102(3)) (section 10.3.2).

More generally, the EBA and ESMA are required to fulfil a coordination role between competent authorities and across supervisory colleges (section 10.4.2) in order to facilitate a common supervisory culture, consistent supervisory practices, and uniform procedures (Article 95(8)). This requirement is in line with the broader role of the ESAs in promoting supervisory convergence. For example, the EBA and ESMA have the objectives, within the spheres of their respective sectoral competencies, to strengthen international supervisory coordination, and to enhance supervisory convergence.[36]

10.3.6. Cooperation with Third Countries

The crypto-asset sector is inherently cross-border, with a clear presence of internationally active CASPs and issuers of so-called 'global stablecoins'.[37] Effective coordination and cooperation among supervisors globally will be a necessary complement to the emergence of crypto-asset regulation to ensure effective oversight of the crypto-asset sector.

Although MiCAR does not include any third country equivalence regime, it foresees that competent authorities may need to conclude cooperation arrangements with the supervisory authorities of third countries concerning the exchange of information and enforcement of MiCAR (Article 107(1)). A template for such agreements has been developed for use by competent authorities.[38] Again, the EBA and ESMA have a facilitation and coordination function (Article 107(2)) with regard to the development of cooperation arrangements between competent authorities and supervisory authorities of third countries.

[35] Regulation (EU) No 1093/2010 of the European Parliament and of the Council of 24 November 2010 establishing a European Supervisory Authority (European Banking Authority), amending Decision No 716/2009/EC and repealing Commission Decision 2009/78/EC (OJ L 331, 15.12.2010, p 12) (as amended) and Regulation (EU) No 1095/2010 of the European Parliament and of the Council of 24 November 2010 establishing a European Supervisory Authority (European Securities and Markets Authority), amending Decision No 716/2009/EC and repealing Commission Decision 2009/77/EC (OJ L 331, 15.12.2010, p 84) (as amended).

[36] See eg Article 1(5) and Article 8 of Regulation (EU) No 1093/2010 and Regulation (EU) No 1095/2010.

[37] Financial Stability Institute (FSI), Recommendations for the Regulation, Supervision and Oversight of Global Stablecoin Arrangements – Executive Summary (29 February 2024) www.bis.org/fsi/fsisummaries/global_stablecoins.htm.

[38] ESMA's final report on the draft regulatory standards was published on 25 March 2024 www.esma.europa.eu/sites/default/files/2024-03/ESMA75-453128700-949_Final_Report_MiCA_cooperation_technical_standards.pdf.

10.4. Supervisory, Investigative, and Enforcement Powers Available to the EBA

MiCAR confers on the EBA direct supervision functions.[39] Unlike the position for competent authorities where national law may confer on the relevant authority a broader suite of supervisory, investigative and enforcement powers than specified in EU law (as evidenced by the formulation of Article 94(1)), the powers of EU agencies are defined by EU law. Accordingly, MiCAR confers on the EBA a broad range of supervisory, investigative and enforcement powers, which are very similar to those available to ESMA in its supervisory capacities, including under the Regulation on OTC derivatives, central counterparties and trade repositories (Regulation (EU) No 648/2012).[40]

10.4.1. Scope of the EBA's Supervisory Responsibilities and Tasks

As noted in section 10.2.2, MiCAR confers on the EBA supervisory responsibilities with respect to:

- ARTs that are determined by the EBA to be 'significant' in accordance with the criteria established in Article 43(1)[41] (including in cases where applicant issuers indicate a wish to be classified as significant on a 'voluntary' basis pursuant to Article 44);
- EMTs that are issued by electronic money institutions and are determined by the EBA to be 'significant'.

The EBA's supervisory responsibilities vary not only by reference to type of issuer (credit institutions and other types of issuer in the case of significant ARTs, and electronic money institutions in the case of significant EMTs), but also by reference to substantive requirements applicable to issuers.

For significant ARTs, the EBA 'takes over' from the competent authority and is responsible for supervising compliance by the issuer with the applicable Title III requirements (which are narrower for credit institutions than for other types of ART issuers (Article 17(4)) and shall exercise all of the powers conferred on competent authorities under Articles 22 to 25, 29, 33, 34(7) and (12), 35(3) and (5),

[39] For completeness, although outside the scope of this book, it is noted that the EBA, along with the other ESAs, also has direct oversight powers in relation to 'critical ICT third-party providers' designated under DORA.

[40] Regulation (EU) No 648/2012 of the European Parliament and of the Council of 4 July 2012 on OTC derivatives, central counterparties and trade repositories (OJ L 201, 27.7.2012, pp 1–59).

[41] The criteria are further specified in Commission Delegated Regulation (EU) 2024/1506 of 22 February 2024 supplementing Regulation (EU) 2023/1114 of the European Parliament and of the Council by specifying certain criteria for classifying asset-referenced tokens and e-money tokens as significant (OJ L, 2024/1506, 30.5.2024).

36(10) and Articles 41, 42, 46 and 47 (Article 117(2)). This means, for example, that the EBA may require the issuer to stop issuing ARTs used widely as a means of exchange, to adjust own funds, or make changes to the reserves, recovery and redemption plans. The EBA also has access to supervisory reporting, audit reports and can make assessments regarding the suitability of members of the management body (where the issuer is not a credit institution). Should the issuer of the significant ART also carry out other regulated activities, these remain subject to supervision by the relevant authority – the national authority or the ECB in relation to some credit institutions in Member States participating in the Banking Union pursuant to the Single Supervision Mechanism (SSM).[42]

For significant EMTs issued by electronic money institutions, the EBA's role is more limited, and concerns supervising compliance with the requirements under Articles 55 and 58. Essentially this means that the supervision of the issuer (ie, electronic money institution) is shared with the competent authority under the EMD2.[43] For the purposes of supervision, the EBA shall exercise the powers conferred on competent authorities under the same articles as cited above for significant ARTs.

Responsibilities for authorisation remain within the scope of competent authorities, except in the case of withdrawals of authorisation where the EBA can withdraw the authorisation of the issuer of a significant ART in the event the EBA finds an issuer to have committed an infringement of MiCAR (Article 24 and point (l) of Article 130(1)). This power is not available with respect to issuers of significant EMTs[44] (recalling that EMTs can be issued only by entities authorised as credit institutions or electronic money institutions). However, the EBA has available other powers to impose supervisory measures (Article 130(2)).

In discharging its supervisory tasks, the EBA is required to act in close cooperation with other relevant authorities, including the prudential supervision authority (which may be the ECB in the case of a SSM credit institution issuing ARTs), the competent authority for the purposes of the EMD2 regarding the supervision of electronic money institutions, and other competent authorities, including in cases where the issuer also carries out crypto-asset services pursuant to Title V (Article 115(2) and (7)).

For the purposes of preparing EBA decisions in relation to the performance of supervisory tasks under MiCAR, the EBA is required to establish a crypto-asset

[42] Council Regulation (EU) No 1024/2013 of 15 October 2013 conferring specific tasks on the European Central Bank concerning policies relating to the prudential supervision of credit institutions (OJ L 287, 29.10.2013, pp 63–89).

[43] Directive 2009/110/EC of the European Parliament and of the Council of 16 September 2009 on the taking up, pursuit and prudential supervision of the business of electronic money institutions amending Directives 2005/60/EC and 2006/48/EC and repealing Directive 2000/46/EC (OJ L 267, 10.10.2009, p 7) (as amended).

[44] Only Article 24(3) (limit on issuance) is applied under Article 117(4).

committee (Article 118), which, in accordance with international best practices,[45] is intended to provide a designated forum to support the performance by the EBA of its direct supervision tasks. This is not the first time the EBA is mandated to establish an internal committee to perform specific tasks.[46]

On a case-by-case basis, the EBA may choose to delegate specific supervisory tasks to the relevant competent authority (Article 138) which is also an option available to ESMA with regard to the performance of its supervisory tasks under the Regulation on OTC derivatives, central counterparties and trade repositories (European Market Infrastructure Regulation or EMIR).[47] Such delegation may be exercised, for example, for reasons of administrative efficiency, for example, in the context of a wider information gathering, investigations, or on-site supervision of the issuer whether that issuer also carries out other regulated activities. Prior to the delegation, the EBA must consult the competent authority concerned (Article 138(2)) and the costs incurred by the competent authority shall be reimbursed by the EBA with the funding drawn from supervisory fees paid to the EBA pursuant to Article 137. More generally, the costs incurred by the EBA in relation to its supervisory tasks under Article 117 (and with regard to supervisory colleges established under Article 119; section 10.4.2) are to be funded through fees levied on issuers subject to the EBA's direct supervision (Article 137).[48] The amount to be charged to issuers of significant ARTs and significant EMTs is to be proportionate to, respectively, the size of the reserve assets and size of issuance, and is further particularised in a delegated act adopted by the European Commission pursuant to Article 137(3).[49]

10.4.2. Supervisory Colleges

Notwithstanding the fact that the EBA's direct supervision role is limited, in the case of significant EMTs, to those issued by electronic money institutions, the EBA is required to establish supervisory colleges for issuers of all significant ARTs and EMTs (Article 119).

[45] See, for example, Principle 2 of the Basel Committee on Banking Supervision 'Core principles for effective banking supervision', most recently updated in April 2024, www.bis.org/bcbs/publ/d573.pdf. For a discussion of principles and practices of good supervision, see T Adrian et al., 'Good Supervision: Lessons from the Field' (2003) IMF Working Paper No. 2023/181, www.imf.org/en/Blogs/Articles/2023/09/18/financial-stability-needs-supervisors-with-the-ability-and-will-to-act.

[46] For example, see Article 127 (EBA Resolution Committee) BRRD.

[47] Regulation (EU) No 648/2012 of the European Parliament and of the Council of 4 July 2012 on OTC derivatives, central counterparties and trade repositories (OJ L 201, 27.7.2012, pp 1–59).

[48] The Legislative Financial Statement (LFS) accompanying the Proposal for MiCAR emphasises the need for the supervisory tasks of the EBA to be fee-funded, eur-lex.europa.eu/legal-content/EN/TXT/?uri=CELEX%3A52020PC0593.

[49] Commission Delegated Regulation (EU) 2024/1503 of 22 February 2024 supplementing Regulation (EU) 2023/1114 of the European Parliament and of the Council by specifying the fees charged by the European Banking Authority to issuers of significant asset-referenced tokens and issuers of significant e-money tokens (OJ L, 2024/1503, 30.5.2024).

The colleges are to be established, chaired and coordinated by the EBA (Article 119(1) and (7)) and composed of a broad membership including ESMA, various competent authorities responsible not only for the supervision of the most relevant CASPs but also entities acting as custodians for reserve assets, the ECB and, where relevant, the national central banks, and relevant supervisory authorities of third countries (Article 119(2) and (3)).[50] The breadth of membership acknowledges the high interconnectedness of the crypto-asset ecosystem in terms of the distribution and use of significant ARTs and EMTs, including in the context of crypto-asset exchanges and trading platforms, and also with the traditional financial system via reserve composition and custody requirements.

The supervisory colleges are intended to facilitate the exchange of information with a view to deepening supervisory cooperation across ecosystems for the issuance, circulation, and redemption of significant ARTs and EMTs, to agree the voluntary entrustment of tasks among members, and to prepare non-binding opinions pursuant to Article 120 (Article 119(5)). Opinions are not mandatory. However, the college may choose to issue non-binding opinions on a wide range of issues, such as reassessments of significance, decisions to require issuers to hold higher own funds, changes in the business model of an issuer, changes to white papers, recovery and resolution plan updates, as well as the imposition of envisaged corrective or supervisory measures pursuant to Article 130, supervisory task delegation by the EBA pursuant to Article 138, and changes to college membership (Article 120(1)). This approach departs from the role of colleges in more traditional supervisory settings (for example, under Article 16 of the Capital Requirements Directive (CRD IV))[51] and most probably reflects a legislative intention to promote from 'day 1' a cross-jurisdictional and cross-disciplinary approach to the supervision of significant ARTs and EMTs and their wider ecosystems. The opinions, albeit non-binding, can include recommendations aimed at addressing shortcomings of any measure envisaged by the EBA or competent authorities. Where the EBA or a competent authority does not agree with an opinion of the college, they must explain their reasons for significantly deviating from the opinion or recommendation (Article 120(2) and (4)).

[50] In determining the membership of each college, the EBA shall act in accordance with the regulatory technical standards adopted under Article 119(8). The EBA's Final Report on the draft regulatory technical standards was published on 19 June 2024, www.eba.europa.eu/publications-and-media/press-releases/eba-publishes-regulatory-products-under-markets-crypto-assets-regulation-0.

[51] Directive 2013/36/EU of the European Parliament and of the Council of 26 June 2013 on access to the activity of credit institutions and the prudential supervision of credit institutions and investment firms, amending Directive 2002/87/EC and repealing Directives 2006/48/EC and 2006/49/EC Text with EEA relevance (OJ L 176, 27.6.2013, pp 338–436). Article 116 CRD IV (colleges of supervisors) sets out a narrower set of functions for the college as compared to the college arrangements in MiCAR, including sharing information, ensuring the consistent application of the prudential framework to entities within the banking group, and taking joint decisions on the application of specific prudential requirements (see, in particular, Article 113 CRD IV).

10.4.3. Supervisory and Investigative Powers

As explained in the introduction to section 10.4, EU agencies derive their powers from EU law, rather than national laws. For this reason, MiCAR confers on the EBA a wide range of powers to ensure the EBA can carry out its supervisory responsibilities effectively. These powers are set out in Articles 122 to 132 and broadly replicate the powers Member States are required to make available to their competent authority as summarised in section 10.3.

The cornerstone of effective supervision is access to information. Therefore, MiCAR makes provision for the EBA to access information through exchange with competent authorities (Article 125) and with other parties. In particular, the EBA's ability to request and receive information is not limited to the issuers within its scope of supervision. Rather, the EBA and competent authorities are expected to exchange information related to a wide range of legal or natural persons (Article 125(1))[52] and the EBA may request directly information from a similarly broad range of persons, including CASPs and custodians of reserve assets, where the information is necessary to enable the EBA to carry out its duties. Persons receiving such requests are required to comply (Article 122(4)) and failures to conform with EBA decisions can be subject to periodic penalty payments or fines (Article 122(3)).

Requests for information, whether ad hoc, pursuant to EBA decisions under Article 122, or in the context of investigation and onsite inspections, cannot require the disclosure of information that is subject to legal privilege (Article 121).

In addition to the ability to request information, the EBA may carry out investigations (Article 123) and on-site inspections at the business premises of the issuers of significant ARTs and significant EMTs (Article 124). In all cases the competent authority in the Member State where the inspection is to be carried out shall be notified before the commencement of the on-site inspection. However, prior notice need not be provided to the issuer where the conduct and efficiency of the inspection so require (Article 124(3)). The supervisory college established under Article 119 shall be informed of any findings that might be relevant for the execution of the tasks of the colleges (second sub-paragraph of Article 123(1) and second sub-paragraph of Article 124(1)). Where persons do not provide information in the context of an investigation or do not cooperate with an onsite inspection, periodic penalty payments may be imposed under Article 132 (Article 123(2) and Article 124(5)) and fines may be imposed in relation to the provision of incomplete or misleading information (Article 123(2)).

[52] Competent authorities may only refuse to act on a request to exchange information, or to cooperate in the carrying out of an investigation or on-site inspection in limited circumstances (see Article 125(2)).

The EBA may, in accordance with national law, be required to seek authorisation by a court in a Member State before requesting specific reports or data (eg, records of telephone or data traffic) or before launching an on-site inspection (Article 123(5) and Article 124(4)).

In seeking information, or carrying out an on-site investigation, the assistance of the relevant competent authority can be requested (Article 124(6)). In terms of cooperation and information exchange with supervisory authorities established in third countries, and with other authorities, including tax and law enforcement authorities, the EBA is empowered to enter into administrative agreements on the exchange of information, and to disclose information and cooperate (Articles 126 to 128). Professional secrecy obligations apply to the EBA, its employees and contractors (Article 129).

Where issuers of significant ARTs and significant EMTs within the scope of EBA supervision have been found to have infringed MiCAR, the EBA is empowered to impose a wide range of supervisory measures (Article 130(1) and (2)). These measures include cease and desist orders, fines or periodic penalty payments, warnings, and powers to withdraw authorisation (in this latter case the powers are available only with respect to issuers of significant ARTs (Article 130(1)(l)). As well as targeting supervisory measures at the issuer, the EBA has the power to impose other measures, such as requiring a CASP operating a trading platform that has admitted a significant ART or EMT to suspend trading in the event of suspected infringement of MiCAR, or to prohibit trading in the event of a confirmed infringement (points (f) and (g) of Article 130(1) and (2)).

When adopting the supervisory measures, the EBA is required to take into account the nature and seriousness of the infringement and various factors (Article 130(3)) and, before imposing the measures, it is required to inform various authorities, including the relevant central bank where the significant ART or significant EMT references an official currency (Article 130(4)–(5)). Finally, in terms of process, the EBA needs to communicate any decision to impose supervisory measures to the issuer, to the relevant competent authority and to the European Commission (Article 130(6)). Decisions on supervisory measures must be published on the EBA's website unless such disclosure would seriously jeopardise financial stability or cause disproportionate damage to the parties involved (Article 130(6)).

10.4.4. Administrative Penalties and Measures

Consistent with the powers required to be made available to competent authorities pursuant to Article 111, the EBA has the power to impose on issuers of significant ARTs and significant EMTs fines and periodic penalty payments (Articles 131 and 132).

10.4.5. Procedural Rules, Hearings and Rights of Appeal

The EBA is required to appoint an 'independent investigation officer' (IIO) to investigate alleged infringements and to submit its findings to the EBA for consideration prior to the EBA determining whether to take supervisory measures or impose fines (Article 134).[53] The IIO must not have been involved directly or indirectly in the supervision of the issuer and shall perform its functions independently from the EBA (Article 134(1)). Additionally, before taking its decision, the EBA is required to give the person concerned the opportunity to be heard, except where urgent action is needed (and on an interim basis) in order to 'prevent significant and imminent damage to financial stability or to the holders of crypto-assets, in particular retail holders' (Article 135(2)).

Persons subject to EBA decisions, including decisions regarding the provision of information, decisions on the application of supervisory measures, can be referred to the EBA's Board of Appeal, and along with decisions on fines and periodic penalty payments, can be reviewed by the Court of Justice in accordance with Articles 60 and 61 of the EBA's Founding Regulation (Article 122(3)(g), Article 130(7)(c), Article 136).

10.5. Intervention Powers Available to Competent Authorities, EBA and ESMA

Intervention powers are available to competent authorities (Article 105), along with temporary intervention powers for the EBA and ESMA to address significant investor protection concerns, threats to the orderly functioning and integrity of markets in crypto-assets, or to the stability of the whole or part of the financial system in the EU (Articles 103 to 106). These powers are modelled on similar powers set out in Articles 40 to 42 MiFID II,[54] which have been used rarely to date at the European level,[55] but have been used at the national level and subject to ESMA and the EBA coordination and convergence role.[56]

[53] At the time of writing, the EBA has not published any information about its approach to sanctions and enforcement, including regarding the IIO. However, the information on ESMA's website with regard to its approach to the supervision of specific types of entity (outside the scope of MiCAR) is illustrative, www.esma.europa.eu/esmas-activities/supervision-and-convergence/sanctions-and-enforcement.

[54] Similar powers are also available to competent authorities and to EIOPA under Regulation (EU) No 1286/2014 of the European Parliament and of the Council of 26 November 2014 on key information documents for packaged retail and insurance-based investment products (PRIIPs) OJ L 352, 9.12.2014, pp 1–23.

[55] In 2018 ESMA exercised its intervention powers to prohibit binary options and restrict contracts for differences to protect retail investors, www.esma.europa.eu/sites/default/files/library/esma71-98-128_press_release_product_intervention.pdf.

[56] For a discussion on the utility of intervention powers, see V Colaert, 'The MiFIR and PRIIPs Product Intervention Regime: In Need of Intervention?' (2020) 17 *ECFR* 99.

10.5.1. Intervention Powers Available to Competent Authorities

A competent authority may prohibit in, or restrict from, its Member State, the marketing, distribution or sale of certain crypto-assets or crypto-assets with certain features, or a type of activity or practice related to crypto-assets (Article 105(1)).[57] It is important to emphasise that the powers extend to crypto-assets as broadly defined in Article 3(1)(5). This means that competent authorities may exercise the powers with regard to crypto-assets regardless of whether they are ARTs, EMTs or some other type of crypto-asset, and regardless of who is the issuer or offeror, or from where the issue, offer, or admission to trading takes place. There is no limit on the duration of the prohibition or restriction, but the competent authority must revoke the prohibition or restriction where the conditions for the imposition are no longer satisfied (Article 105(6)).

Bearing in mind that the intervention powers are essentially backstop powers complementing the supervisory and administrative measures available to competent authorities, MiCAR sets out the set of conditions that must be satisfied in full in order for the competent authority to impose the prohibition or restriction (Article 105). Among other conditions, the competent authority must be satisfied on reasonable grounds that: (a) a crypto-asset gives rise to significant investor protection concerns or poses a threat to the orderly functioning and integrity of markets in crypto-assets or to the stability of the whole or part of the financial system within at least one Member State, and (b) existing regulatory requirements under EU law applicable to the crypto-asset or crypto-asset service concerned do not sufficiently address the risks and the issue would not be better addressed by improved supervision or enforcement of existing requirements.

Save for exceptional cases where urgent measures are needed (Article 105(4)), a competent authority must not impose a prohibition or restriction, unless at least one month's notice is given to all other competent authorities and, as the case may be, to ESMA and the EBA (Article 105(3)). These arrangements are identical to those specified in Article 42 MiFIR. Additionally, as under MiFIR, the EBA (in relation to ARTs and EMTs) and ESMA are required to perform a facilitating and coordinating role in relation to measures taken by competent authorities and, in particular, should ensure that the measures are justified, proportionate and, where appropriate, consistent (Article 106(1)). To this end, the relevant ESA is required to issue an opinion assessing whether the measure is justified and appropriate. Such an opinion must be made public (Article 106(2)). Examples of opinions can be found on ESMA's website with regard to intervention measures by national authorities under MiFIR.[58] The opinions are non-binding and where a competent authority acts in a manner contrary to an opinion, a notice must be immediately published on its website 'fully explaining its reasons'.

[57] The prohibition or restriction may also be applied on a precautionary basis before a crypto-asset has been marketed, distributed or sold to clients (second sub-paragraph of Article 105(2)).

[58] ESMA Opinions on the proposed exercise of intervention powers by national authorities, www.esma.europa.eu/investor-corner/product-intervention.

10.5.2. Temporary Intervention Powers Available to EBA and ESMA

In accordance with Article 9(5) of the EBA and ESMA Founding Regulations:[59]

- the EBA may temporarily restrict or prohibit the marketing, distribution or sale of ARTs or EMTs, or a type of activity or practice related to ARTs or EMTs (Article 104(1));
- ESMA may temporarily restrict or prohibit the marketing, distribution or sale of crypto-assets other than ARTs or EMTs, or a type of activity or practice related to crypto-assets other than ARTs or EMTs (Article 103(1)).

In comparison to the intervention powers available to competent authorities (discussed above) which, in exceptional cases, can be exercised on an urgent basis in order to prevent any detrimental effects arising from a crypto-asset or activity or practice (Article 105(4)), the restriction or prohibition by the EBA or ESMA cannot be imposed on such a basis.

The intervention powers can be exercised only where three conditions are determined to be satisfied, namely: (a) the proposed prohibition or restriction addresses a significant investor protection concern or a threat to the orderly functioning and integrity of markets in crypto-assets or to the stability of the whole or part of the financial system in the EU, (b) the regulatory requirements under EU law do not address the threat at issue; (c) a relevant competent authority has not taken action to address the threat at issue or the actions that have been taken do not adequately address that threat. The criteria and factors to be taken into account in determining whether there is a significant investor protection concern or threat to the orderly functioning and integrity of markets in crypto-assets or to the stability of whole or part of the financial system are particularised in the European Commission delegated acts adopted pursuant to Article 103(8) and 104(8).[60]

Before deciding to exercise the intervention powers, the EBA and ESMA shall notify the relevant competent authorities of the intended measure (Article 103(4) and 104(4)). No minimum timeframe is provided for such notifications.

Any decision to impose a prohibition or restriction shall be made public on the website of the relevant ESA and shall prevail over any previous measure taken by the relevant competent authorities on the same issue (Article 103(7) and Article 104(7)). The decision must be reviewed at appropriate intervals, but no

[59] Regulation (EU) No 1093/2010 of the European Parliament and of the Council of 24 November 2010 establishing a European Supervisory Authority (European Banking Authority), amending Decision No 716/2009/EC and repealing Commission Decision 2009/78/EC (OJ L 331, 15.12.2010, p 12) (as amended).

[60] Commission Delegated Regulation (EU) 2024/1507 of 22 February 2024 supplementing Regulation (EU) 2023/1114 of the European Parliament and of the Council by specifying the criteria and factors to be taken into account by the European Securities Markets Authority, the European Banking Authority and competent authorities in relation to their intervention powers (OJ L, 2024/1507, 30.5.2024).

less frequently than every 6 months (Article 103(6) and Article 104(6)) and can be referred to the Board of Appeal of the relevant ESA and to the Court of Justice of the European Union.[61]

10.6. Powers Available to EBA, EIOPA and ESMA to Promote Convergence in Crypto-asset Classification

In addition to the supervisory convergence tasks attributed to the EBA and ESMA under MiCAR, Article 97 confers on the EBA, EIOPA and ESMA specific responsibilities to promote convergence in the classification of crypto-assets. These are important tasks in view of the classification challenges extensively described in chapter four. Overall, the performance of tasks under Article 97(2) to (4) is expected to result in further interpretive guidance benefitting both the industry and competent authorities and complementing the ESMA Guidelines under Article 2(5)[62] and the joint ESA Guidelines under Article 97(1).[63]

10.6.1. Dialogue and Exchange of Views on Classification

In accordance with the mandate for the ESAs to promote a 'common supervisory culture',[64] Article 97(2) requires the ESAs to 'promote discussion' among competent authorities on the classification of crypto-assets, including those excluded from the scope of MiCAR pursuant to Article 2(3) (ie, crypto-assets that are unique and not fungible with other crypto-assets). Tools available to the ESAs in this context include establishing coordination groups, promoting effective bilateral and multilateral exchange of information, establishing training programmes, and developing handbooks.[65] Other tools can also be developed as appropriate.

[61] Articles 60 and 61 of the EBA's Founding Regulation.

[62] A consultation paper on the draft Guidelines was published by ESMA on 29 January 2024, www.esma.europa.eu/document/consultation-paper-draft-guidelines-conditions-and-criteria-qualification-crypto-assets. The Guidelines are on the conditions and criteria for the qualification of crypto-assets as financial instruments as defined in Article 3(1)(49).

[63] A consultation paper on the draft Guidelines was published by the ESAs on 12 July 2024, www.eba.europa.eu/publications-and-media/press-releases/esas-consult-guidelines-under-markets-crypto-assets-regulation. The Guidelines set out a standardised test for the classification of crypto-assets, as well as a template for the explanation and legal opinion regarding the classification which is required to accompany, respectively, the crypto-asset white paper under Title II, and the white paper for the ART under Title III.

[64] Article 29 of the Founding Regulations of the ESAs (Regulation (EU) No 1093/2010, Regulation (EU) No 1094/2010, and Regulation (EU) No 1095/2010) requires each of the ESAs to 'play an active role in building a common [EU] supervisory culture and consistent supervisory practices, as well as in ensuring uniform procedures and consistent approaches throughout the Union'.

[65] ibid.

The need for discussion and a common approach, including on the topic of non-fungibility, is likely to become more acute in the context of increasing experimentation with, and roll out of, asset tokenisation applications for tangible and intangible assets and potential qualification as NFTs.[66]

10.6.2. Opinions on Crypto-asset Classification

At the request of competent authorities, the ESAs can provide opinions on the classification of crypto-assets (Article 97(3)), including those excluded under Article 2(3). The opinions are to be issued in accordance with Article 29 of the ESA Founding Regulations,[67] adopted by the Board of Supervisors of the respective ESA in accordance with Article 43 of the Founding Regulation on simple majority (first sub-paragraph of Article 44 of the Founding Regulations), and made public. The opinions are not binding but are expected to carry interpretive weight.

Interestingly, the role for the ESAs under Article 97(3) is very similar to the role for the EBA and ESMA under Article 20(5) (opinions on the classification of a crypto-asset as an ART), albeit the timeframe for issuing the opinion is 15 working days from receipt rather than 20 days.

10.6.3. Annual Reports

Annually, the ESAs are required to publish a report on the performance of their tasks under Article 97(2) and (3), identifying any difficulties in the classification of crypto-assets and divergences in the approach of competent authorities (Article 97(4)). These reports are expected to be taken into account by the European Commission in the context of the preparation of its report on the application of MiCAR which is due by 30 June 2027 and may be accompanied by a legislative proposal as appropriate (Article 140(1) and (2)(b)).

10.7. Conclusion: Assessing Title VII and Looking Ahead

Title VII confers on competent authorities and the EBA a wide range of critical powers to supervise and enforce the application of MiCAR. The success of this regime will rest on proactive surveillance and, where appropriate, enforcement activity.

[66] See further ESMA, Consultation Paper on the draft Guidelines on the conditions and criteria for the qualification of crypto-assets as financial instruments, ESMA75-453128700-52, 29 January 2024, www.esma.europa.eu/document/consultation-paper-draft-guidelines-conditions-and-criteria-qualification-crypto-assets and the final version is available via ESMA's webste: www.esma.europa.eu.

[67] Article 29 of the Founding Regulations of the ESAs (Regulation (EU) No 1093/2010, Regulation (EU) No 1094/2010, and Regulation (EU) No 1095/2010).

Perimeter surveillance and enforcement challenges are expected to arise, in particular taking account of the non-traditional distribution channels for crypto-assets, including a web of centralised and decentralised intermediaries for which enhanced monitoring tools will be essential. It will be important to identify if an entity is carrying out activities in scope of MiCAR and to enforce the perimeter accordingly.

Cross-sectoral cooperation and coordination (for example issuer-CASP, issuer-reserve custodians, CASPs and payment service providers) will be essential to the success of any information-gathering, investigations and enforcement activities in view of interconnectedness within the crypto-asset sector, and with the traditional financial sector. Moreover, cross-border coordination and cooperation is also likely to be crucial as competent authorities and the EBA, in its supervision capacity, grapple with the activities of globally active issuers (including of so-called 'global stablecoins') and service providers.

Within the EU, the EBA and ESMA, in accordance with their general objectives, appear strongly committed to promoting convergence in the application of MiCAR, and thus the level playing field, from 'day 1' of its application.[68] However, global arbitrage risks remain ever-present as some crypto-asset market participants continue to shape-shift around the introduction of new crypto-asset regulations in leading financial centres, including the EU. The absence of a third country equivalence regime may mean that regulatory frictions could arise as jurisdictions apply the requirements to globally active entities and groups in the context of implementing global standards.[69]

In view of the anticipated challenges in crypto-asset classification, the ESAs can expect to be busy in the discharge of their tasks to promote convergence in classification, particularly given the complexities of the MiFID/ART classification as described in Chapter 4, anticipated growth in asset tokenisation, and market dynamism. Intervention powers, on the other hand, are expected to be applied relatively infrequently based on experience from other contexts,[70] as current crypto-asset markets appear to present no immediate threats to the orderly functioning of the financial system. However, serious threats to investors cannot be ruled out based on past misdemeanours in the market.

[68] For example, see the EBA's statements of 12 July 2023, www.eba.europa.eu/publications-and-media/press-releases/eba-encourages-timely-preparatory-steps-towards-application. See also the EBA's statement of 5 July 2024, www.eba.europa.eu/sites/default/files/2024-07/7dcd9ce9-96e3-4c5c-8d86-39d7784d1f03/EBA%20statement%20on%20Application%20of%20MiCAR%20to%20ARTs%20and%20EMTs.pdf.

[69] FSB, 'High-level Recommendations for the Regulation, Supervision and Oversight of Global Stablecoin Arrangements' (17 July 2023) www.fsb.org/wp-content/uploads/P170723-3.pdf. Also, FSB, 'High-level Recommendations for the Regulation, Supervision, and Oversight of Crypto-Asset Activities and Markets' https://www.fsb.org/wp-content/uploads/P170723-2.pdf.

[70] See, eg, ESMA data on the exercise of intervention powers under MiFID II www.esma.europa.eu/investor-corner/product-intervention.

11

Excluded Topics and Future Regulation

LODEWIJK VAN SETTEN

11.1. Introduction

MiCAR seeks to provide a regulatory framework for two distinct realms of activities: (i) the issuance of crypto-assets, and (ii) the provision of crypto-asset services. The previous chapters of the book covered both realms extensively. This chapter explores MiCAR's regulatory perimeter across each realm, and focuses on 'excluded topics', or rather, topics that have, at least in the original version of MiCAR, not been specifically brought into its scope. Regarding token issuance and token delineation, the key concepts that will be examined in this chapter are the notions of 'representation of value' and 'fungibility'. In respect of the service provider delineation, the key concepts discussed in this chapter are the notions of decentralisation and certain specific activities, such as borrowing and lending, which are not in within MiCAR's perimeter.

11.2. The MiCAR Perimeter Defined by Reference to the Properties of a Token

MiCAR's stated objective is to regulate 'markets in crypto-assets',[1] which, logically, means, first, to regulate issuers of crypto-assets, and second, to regulate firms that by way of business provide certain services in respect of the issued crypto-assets. MiCAR's perimeter, therefore, principally turns on the question whether a particular digital asset is a 'crypto-asset' within the meaning of MiCAR.

MiCAR defines 'crypto-asset' as 'a digital representation of a value or of a right that is able to be transferred and stored electronically using distributed ledger technology or similar technology'.[2] The MiCAR notion of a 'digital representation

[1] MiCAR, Recital (6): 'A dedicated and harmonised framework for markets in crypto-assets is therefore necessary at Union level in order to provide specific rules for crypto-assets and related services and activities that are not yet covered by Union legislative acts on financial services'.

[2] MiCAR, Article 3(1)(5).

of a value or of a right' is anchored in the 'web3' concept of 'distributed ledger technology or similar technology'.[3] 'Web2'-supported digital representations of value or rights, such as e-money or a bank balance, would and should not be a MiCAR crypto-asset. 'Distributed ledger technology' is defined by MiCAR by reference to several different components: a 'distributed ledger', meaning a form of duplicated recordkeeping shared between 'DLT network nodes' who together form a network that operates a 'consensus mechanism', a certain type of protocol, to validate and update the record shared and duplicated across all nodes.[4] In short, to be a MiCAR crypto-asset, the 'digital representation of a value or of a right' must manifest in the form of a blockchain record or must have been created using similar distributed network technology.

The defining feature of distributed network technology is that the network subject matter data is hosted on a distributed basis by a network of participating nodes. Each node has a copy of the relevant subject matter data, which it cannot, independently or jointly with other nodes, alter. Changes to the network subject matter data can only occur through state changes initiated by network users who exercise their entitlements via private key operations.[5] Distributed ledger technology, also referred to as 'DLT', allows the creation of an independent record of units of a certain kind and description that are allocated to one or more 'network addresses' or, by way of shorthand web3 jargon, 'wallet addresses'. Once one or more units of a certain type and description are allocated to a wallet address, only the holder of that wallet's private key can request changes to the unit balance recorded at or in respect of that wallet address, for example, by requesting a 'transfer' to another wallet address.

[3] References to 'web1' are references to technology that facilitated the internet of information, where the 'new thing' was that the operator of a website could publish information, but which did not permit interaction with internet users. 'Web2' technology and cryptography introduced interaction by enabling secure transactions between website operators and users, based on software and data hosted and controlled by the 'web2' website operator. Blockchain technology and cryptography, first pioneered by the Bitcoin network, introduced secure peer-to-peer transactions between internet users based on software and data hosted on a shared and distributed basis and is known as 'web3'.

[4] MiCAR, Article 3(1)(1)–(4).

[5] Note that 'distributed ledger technology' is a composite technology consisting of several layers, each layer featuring specific interactive functionalities. The stack includes, without meaning to be exhaustive: the *network layer* (which facilitates, among other matters, the messaging between nodes in the network and ensures data synchronisation across the network), the *consensus layer* (which, in essence, determines how nodes agree on the state of the ledger), the *data layer* (which supports the maintenance of the distributed ledger, that is, it is the structure used to store transactions and state information on a distributed basis – which can be a blockchain, or another type of distributed ledger – and ensures immutability and chronological ordering of transactions), the *protocol layer* (which defines how transactions are formatted, broadcast, and validated across the network and includes cryptographic algorithms for signing and verifying transactions), the *incentive layer* (the design of economic incentives to encourage participation and honest behaviour in the network, which includes reward mechanisms for the nodes and, can include mechanisms for protocol upgrades, decision-making processes, and resolving disputes), the *application layer* (this in essence is one level up in the stack, and contains smart contracts), and the *interface and API layer* (a further level up in the stack, and includes tools and libraries for developers to interact with the blockchain, and the wallets and user interface software).

Token balances are created at two different levels in the DLT stack: at protocol level ('protocol tokens') and at the application, or smart contract level ('application tokens').[6] Protocol tokens are created as an intrinsic part of the blockchain protocol to provide utility at blockchain operational level. Application tokens are created one level up in the stack to provide utility within the smart contract ecosystem ('dApps') and facilitate interactions and transactions at that level. The utility of application tokens is limited only by the limits on their design or use objectives.

Not all tokens that are created using DLT are necessarily MiCAR crypto-assets. To be a MiCAR crypto-asset, the token must be of a type and description that constitutes a 'representation of a value or of a right that is able to be transferred and stored electronically'. Taking these conditions in turn:

- *Transferability.* Recital (17) puts beyond doubt that tokens that cannot be transferred to other holders are not MiCAR crypto-assets. Transferability and storage conditions are defined by DLT programming, either at the core protocol level in case of protocol tokens or at smart contract level in case of application tokens. The programming supports the creation, storage, and controlled mutations of the ledger that shows the token balance. Tokens that are programmed to be accepted only by the issuer or the offeror and that cannot be transferred peer-to-peer using DLT, therefore, are excluded from MiCAR.
- *Value.* MiCAR does not provide guidance on how to test whether a token represents a 'value'. Presumably, the concept of 'value' has an economic connotation, which suggests that the token must have economic utility to be a MiCAR crypto-asset. Economic utility of an asset is commonly understood to mean that the asset can be exchanged for goods, services, or other assets. If a token functions as a medium of exchange, store of value, or unit of account, the value test would be relatively straightforward. Most protocol tokens – the tokens issued at protocol layers such as Bitcoin, Ethereum, Solana, Tezos, etc., function by their very nature as mediums of exchange and often also as a unit of account. It is probably true that exceptionally decentralised protocol tokens, such as Bitcoin, that are widely held and traded in a liquid and well-developed market, may also be justifiably characterised as a store of value.

  The value test can also be relatively straightforward for certain types of fungible application tokens. For instance, if the economic utility of an application token is defined by its intrinsic functionality as part of the dApp stack that operates as an exchange, lending, or investment platform or some other form of decentralised finance (DeFi) platform, that type of application token would have properties similar to those of protocol tokens. The DeFi application token

[6] Each type of token serves a distinct role within the DLT ecosystem. Protocol tokens, such as Ether (ETH) or Bitcoin (BTC), function as currency to pay for transaction fees (gas fees) on the blockchain, ensuring the execution and validation of transactions and smart contracts. They are integral to the consensus mechanisms and often play a role in governance, allowing holders to vote on protocol upgrades and other critical decisions. Transaction requests involving protocol tokens result in changes to the state of the wallet address. Application tokens are created at smart contract level.

would function as a medium of exchange and unit of account, possibly even as a store of value, so that the value test would ordinarily be the same. Protocol tokens and application tokens whose utility is defined solely by intrinsic functionality as part of the dApp stack have no function outside the blockchain on which they are created. This type of token may be referred to as a 'function token'. Function tokens are protocol tokens and application tokens that are used only to facilitate the execution of a function within the relevant blockchain ecosystem, mostly to serve as a form of value transfer. Function tokens only have blockchain intrinsic utility and their economic value must derive from their economic utility within the blockchain ecosystem.

- *Right.* MiCAR does not provide guidance on how to test whether a token is a 'digital representation of a right' that can be transferred and stored electronically using DLT. It is not clear whether the reference to 'a right' in Article 3(1)(5) of MiCAR has a legal connotation, or not. If a legal right is required, it would imply a limitation to rights enforceable *in personam* or *in rem*. In the case of blockchain function tokens that only have on-chain utility, it would be difficult to distinguish a legal right against a person or in relation to an asset. Conceptually, a blockchain function token cannot be characterised as a legally enforceable right against the blockchain network, as the network is not a person against whom or which a right can be exercised, unless one would wish to indulge in constructive partnership or multi-party agreement theories, which would be stretching reality. The absence of legal relationships between the nodes and the holder of a token who means to effect a token transaction, seems quite plain.[7] Blockchain function token entitlements and permissions are *de facto* entitlements programmed in the code of the relevant stack, and not *de jure* entitlements. Consequently, assuming that the reference to a 'right' in MiCAR is a reference to a legal right, any attempt to bring function tokens into the MiCAR remit, therefore, would ordinarily have to be based on a 'value' argument.

On the basis that the reference to a 'right' in MiCAR is a reference to a legal right and not to the *de facto* entitlements that a holder of a private key can exercise in respect of the DLT protocol, the intention of the legislator appears to be to capture application tokens that are not merely function tokens and, somehow, are connected to an 'off-chain' asset or claim. If a smart contract is

[7] See also 'Initial VAT reflections on non-fungible tokens', observations of the Value Added Tax Committee (Article 398 of Directive 2006/112/EC), *Question Concerning the Application of EU VAT Provisions* (Working Paper No 1060, 21 February 2023) at 10: 'However, identifying the existence of a direct link between the gas fee paid and the publication on the digital ledger is not straightforward due to the difficulty in establishing the existence of a legal relationship between the one requesting minting to be done and the network validators involved in the said publication'. Consistent with that finding, the automatic creation of protocol tokens by a blockchain protocol to reward nodes for services is not intended to be within the MiCAR perimeter. See Recital (26): 'In order to ensure a proportionate approach, no requirements of this Regulation should apply to offers to the public of crypto-assets […] that are automatically created as a reward for the maintenance of a distributed ledger or the validation of transactions in the context of a consensus mechanism.'

programmed with the intention to record rights against a person, or interests in or rights in respect of, tangible property, such as commodities, or intangible property, such as intellectual property, the question arises whether the application token is issued such that some form of legally enforceable entitlement is created in the hands of the token holder.

The process of creating records relating to an off-chain *in personam* right or *in rem* interest by way of token issuance is commonly referred to as 'tokenisation' of that right or interest. Prima facie, MiCAR appears to consider all forms of tokenisation of rights or interests as 'crypto assets' because the tokens by their mere existence and purpose as a record would arguably 'represent' in some form a right or interest. MiCAR expressly excludes certain tokenisations from its scope. For instance, if the *lex societatis* of a privately held company permits the creation of a smart contract-based shareholder register, the tokens would arguably 'represent', in web3 jargon, the 'real world asset', that is, the shares. *In casu*, the tokenised real world assets are also 'financial instruments' within the meaning of the exclusion under Article 2(4)(a),[8] which provides that MiCAR does not operate on tokenised real world assets and claims that fall within the scope of the existing traditional financial services regulatory, in web3 jargon, 'TradFi', framework. Further, Article 4(3)(c) and (d) provides that MiCAR does not apply to token offerings of functional (as opposed to economical) utility tokens where the embedded entitlement concerns access to an existing good or service, or if the holder of a crypto-asset has the right to use it only in 'exchange for goods and services in a limited network of merchants with contractual arrangements with the offeror'.[9]

In conclusion, transferable tokens that are function tokens, which, if they have 'value', that is, economic utility, would usually be MiCAR crypto-assets. Second, tokenised real world assets or claims, unless explicitly excluded from MiCAR's scope, would also be likely to be within MiCAR's scope if the tokens are programmed to be peer-to-peer transferable. There is a legitimate question, though, whether the wholesale treatment of all real world asset tokenisations as MiCAR crypto assets is the correct interpretation in all circumstances. Should any form of real world asset tokenisation that is not expressly excluded by MiCAR always be interpreted to be a MiCAR crypto-asset? Recital (9) observes that financial services legislation 'should be guided by the principles of 'same activities, same risks, same rules' and of technology neutrality'. If that is true, then logically, if there has been a policy decision under the TradFi framework not to bring a particular asset class

[8] See generally on the concept of 'financial instruments' within the context of MiCAR, European Securities and Markets Authority (ESMA), *Consultation paper – On the draft Guidelines on the conditions and criteria for the qualification of crypto-assets as financial instruments* (29 January 2024, ESMA75-453128700-52). See also M Lehmann and F Schinerl, 'The Concept of Financial Instruments: Drawing the Borderline between MiFID and MiCAR' (2024) 171 EBI Working Paper Series, papers.ssrn.com/sol3/papers.cfm?abstract_id=4827376.

[9] MiCAR, Recital (26).

within its scope, then the mere fact that the asset class is made accessible by using blockchain technology to register ownership should not alter that policy outcome. For instance, spot commodities trading is mostly unregulated under the TradFi framework. Blockchain technology is well-suited to simplify the recording of a settlement of a spot trade in commodities. Does the fact that DLT is used to record ownership rights and facilitate settlement of spot trades mean that the activity must now be regulated under MiCAR? That conclusion seems to be inconsistent with the technology neutrality principle espoused by Recital (9). On application of the principle 'same activities, same risks, same rules', tokenised commodities spot trading should not necessarily be an activity that is in scope of MiCAR.[10]

The lack of contemplation of the different types of tokenisation by MiCAR seems to rest on an implied premise that each and every token is in some form an asset in its own right so that the off-chain asset or claim that the token relates to somehow now displays transformed properties. As such, a drafting decision seems to have been taken that each transferable fungible token that is not caught by the TradFi regulatory framework, should, by default, be caught by MiCAR.[11] However, that approach does not take into account the fact that not all tokens are necessarily independent objects of property themselves. An English law example may illustrate the point.

Under English law, the transfer of a property interest that is an equitable interest in an asset is effected by way of assignment, which must be in writing and must be signed.[12] There appears to be consensus among English jurists that a statutory signature requirement is 'highly likely to be capable of being met by means of a private key', because an 'electronic signature which is intended to authenticate a document will generally satisfy a statutory signature requirement, and a digital signature produced using public-key cryptography is just a particular type of electronic signature'.[13] Equally, the updated smart contract state recorded as part of the relevant blockchain 'can be said to be representing or reproducing words

[10] See also M Lehmann, 'MiCAR – Gold Standard or Regulatory Poison for the Crypto Industry?' (2024) 160 EBI Working Paper Series, papers.ssrn.com/sol3/papers.cfm?abstract_id=4692743, explaining that 'regulations which are technology neutral will not favour certain products or services over others, but maintain a level playing field between competing products or services.' Lehmann provides an example of a voucher to use cloud space, which is recorded on a centralised database. Even if such vouchers are fungible and actively traded, they remain unregulated. Yet if such vouchers are recorded on a DLT, they are likely to fit the MiCAR's definition of 'crypto-assets', and therefore be regulated by MiCAR's rules (eg, an obligation to publish a white paper).

[11] This implied premise can be observed in the ESMA Consultation Paper on the conditions and criteria for the qualification of crypto-assets as financial instruments. The Consultation Paper appears to assume throughout that the mere fact that DLT is used to tokenise off-chain assets is sufficient to create a 'crypto-asset'.

[12] Section 53(1)(c) of the Law of Property Act 1925 (England and Wales) says that 'a disposition of an equitable interest or trust subsisting at the time of the disposition, must be in writing signed by the person disposing of the same, or by his agent thereunto lawfully authorised in writing or by will'.

[13] See UK Jurisdiction Taskforce of LawTech UK (UKJT), *Legal Statement on the issuance and transfer of digital securities under English private law* (February 2023), para 130.

and be made visible on a screen or printout is likely to fulfil a statutory writing requirement'.[14]

The legal mechanism whereby the holder of a legal right or interest in an asset is identified by reference to a token is sometimes referred to as 'stapling'.[15] In the case of stapling by way of a smart contract-maintained register of property interests, the balance of tokens recorded in a wallet address is not itself an object of property. A share certificate may be said to 'represent' the share, but it would not be considered an object of property. If the smart contract-maintained register is ultimately controlled by a person who functions as a registrar, including the power to rectify any errors, the fact that the smart contract-based register/record is principally updated on a decentralised basis through token holder transactions does not change the legal nature of the operations. The use of the smart contract based registry does not change the legal nature of the interest in and assignment of the real world asset, a conclusion that is generally incompatible with the recognition of any tokens deployed in the system as the object of property independent of the real world asset.[16] If the token balance were itself the object of property, it would transform the stapled property interest notwithstanding that the DLT is intended to be used only to evidence entitlement (as a certificate would) and to create a mechanism to transfer the tokenisation subject matter property (as a written instrument of assignment would). However, where the intention is to embed the tokenisation subject matter property into the token and transform that property into a form of negotiable bearer instrument, the conclusion could be different. Overall, the starting point ought to be that smart contract-based ownership records must be characterised as a record only, and not as somehow creating independent objects of property, unless there is clear evidence of an intention to embed the tokenised property into the token so that it ceases to be an independent object of property. The token balances are better characterised as a recording and execution mechanism, electronic documentary evidence of equitable interests and their assignments, not as independent assets of some kind. Therefore, in these circumstances, the token smart contract and the resulting token balances should not be characterised as a crypto-asset within the meaning of MiCAR. The token record demonstrates a legal right, but does not itself confer or embody it and as such, cannot be said to be representing it, in the same way that a shareholder register does not embody the share, nor the value attributable to the share. The tokens should not be assumed to fall within MiCAR's definition of a crypto-asset solely by virtue of their form or technology.

The lack of consideration at the EU legislative level of the nature and properties of tokenisation is not characteristic of MiCAR only. It is instructive to note that the EU regulation that permits securities market infrastructure operators to use tokenisation to facilitate securities settlements powered by DLT, the 'DLT Pilot

[14] ibid para 130.
[15] ibid para 84.
[16] ibid paras 67 and 68.

Regime Regulation',[17] does not address the distinction between the token and the linked security at all. The DLT Pilot Regime Regulation aims to allow for the testing of DLT market infrastructures that deal with tokens that qualify as financial instruments for regulatory purposes. Article 2 of that regulation defines 'DLT financial instrument' as 'a financial instrument that is issued, recorded, transferred and stored using distributed ledger technology'. As a TradFi regulatory instrument, the DLT Pilot Regime Regulation would not be expected to intervene in domestic property laws. Surprisingly, however, the regulation also fails to provide any guidance on the expected treatment of DLT financial instruments as a composite of a token and an issued security under domestic property and company laws. By overlooking this complexity and, in doing so, framing regulatory asset safeguarding requirements through a broad reference to the need to safeguard the DLT financial instrument,[18] the DLT Pilot Regime Regulation creates a lot of uncertainty about how a tokenisation structure can be compliant with its provisions.

Having said that, even if tokenisation does not create the token as an object of property in its own right, it is conceivable that the potential of tokenisation to transform the tradability of an asset class could warrant bringing that activity within the scope of MiCAR. This would be the case even though that type of asset class is presently not within the scope of the traditional finance (TradFi) framework. Tokenisation enables fractional ownership, which increases accessibility of an asset class. Smart contracts operate as a central depository in respect of the tokenised asset that can be accessed directly, which reduces the need for intermediaries. That in turn reduces credit and settlement risks, lowers transaction costs, and speeds up the settlement process. On the back of those advances, tokenised assets can be listed and traded on digital platforms that operate around the clock, allowing global access. These innovative features increase the pool of potential investors who may invest in an asset and substantially enhance liquidity of that asset class, thus transforming its economic features.

If a token is admitted to or accessible for trading on trading venues, it would be appropriate to consider that token, at least from a regulatory policy perspective, as an independent 'asset' and a crypto-asset for the purposes of MiCAR.[19] However,

[17] Regulation (EU) 2022/858 of the European Parliament and of the Council of 30 May 2022 on a pilot regime for market infrastructures based on distributed ledger technology and amending Regulations (EU) No 600/2014 and (EU) No 909/2014 and Directive 2014/65/EU.

[18] See eg Article 7(5) of the DLT Pilot Regime Regulation, which provides, among other matters, that '[o]perators of DLT market infrastructure shall segregate the funds, collateral and DLT financial instruments of the members, participants, issuers or clients using the DLT market infrastructure, and the means of access to such assets, from those of the operator as well as from those of other members, participants, issuers and clients'. It is not clear whether this means that the asset tokens need to be segregated, that the underlying security must be segregated, or that both must be segregated.

[19] See in this context the consideration in Recital (26) of MiCAR, which notes in respect of tokens that are used 'only in exchange for goods and services in a limited network of merchants with contractual arrangements with the offeror' and therefore excluded from MiCAR, that the limited network exemption 'should cease to apply when the offeror, or another person acting on the offeror's behalf, communicates the offeror's intention of seeking admission to trading or the exempted crypto-assets are admitted to trading'.

the mere tokenisation of an asset should not automatically imply that the token is a MiCAR crypto-asset. There is a need for a more detailed perimeter policy response, which considers economic transformation parameters and minimum hurdles. In essence, tokens that simply tokenise existing assets without significantly altering their economic characteristics should be excluded from MiCAR's scope.

11.3. MiCAR Perimeter Delineation Based on Token Non-fungibility and Free Drops

Tokens were originally only created as a class of *n* identical tokens,[20] meaning that the protocol or smart contract that 'mints' the tokens is programmed to supply a certain number of identical tokens of a certain type and description. In the case of *n* supply of protocol or application tokens, the tokens are fungible, meaning, they are a kind of property of which one unit is indistinguishable from any other unit. Further innovation of smart contracts has led to the development of a type of application token that is created as an indivisible token that has a unique token ID. To create and deliver a unique and indivisible token, the token contract is programmed to issue a unique token ID that is mapped to the token holder's blockchain address and permits inspection and confirmation that the balance in the token contract of the linked address is 0 (the address does not control the unique indivisible token) or 1 (the address controls the unique indivisible token).

These types of unique and indivisible tokens are typically referred to as 'non-fungible tokens' or 'NFTs'.[21] The reference to non-fungibility is meant to distinguish the NFT from a token that is created as part of a class of *n* identical tokens. Nevertheless, whether an asset is fungible depends on its economic properties, not on its technical properties. 'Fungibility' is commonly understood to mean that, subject to the context of a given transaction, the asset in question is a kind of property of which one unit, in terms of an obligation owed by one party to another, is indistinguishable from any other unit, so that a duty to deliver one unit is considered to be performed by the delivery of an equivalent unit.[22] Notwithstanding, the mere fact that an application token is created by the smart contract as an 'NFT', thus as a unique token and not as a class of *n* identical tokens, does not necessarily

[20] Here, '*n*' stands as a placeholder for an integer that can be varied or generalised. In this case, it refers to the variability of the token supply programmed in the smart contract code.

[21] Prominent examples of NFT use cases can be found in the art sector. These examples include Beeple's 'Everydays: The First 5000 Days'. In March 2021, digital artist Beeple sold this NFT for over USD 69 million at Christie's auction house. The artwork is a collage of 5,000 images that Beeple created daily over 13 years. Another example is Pak's 'The Merge'. Sold on the NFT marketplace Nifty Gateway in December 2021, this artwork amassed over USD 91 million through a unique sale of multiple tokens representing shared ownership.

[22] This description is accepted under English law, see E McKendrick (ed), *Goode on Commercial Law: Fifth Edition* (Penguin, 2017) 2.89.

mean it is not a fungible token. In a similar vein, banknotes are uniquely identifiable through their number. However, banknotes are undeniably fungible.

MiCAR provides that 'crypto-assets that are unique and not fungible with other crypto-assets' are excluded from its scope.[23] The use of the non-fungibility terminology implies that the token must be an NFT in technical terms, as opposed to being part of a class of identical tokens. It must also not be readily exchangeable for another NFT. Recital (11) observes that the 'mere attribution of a unique identifier to a crypto-asset is not, in and of itself, sufficient to classify it as unique and non-fungible. The assets or rights represented should also be unique and non-fungible in order for the crypto-asset to be considered unique and non-fungible.' To understand what that means in practice, Recital (10) helpfully points out that MiCAR is not intended to apply to 'crypto-assets that are unique and not fungible with other crypto-assets, including digital art and collectibles', because the 'value of such unique and non-fungible crypto-assets is attributable to each crypto-asset's unique characteristics and the utility it gives to the holder of the token.' Importantly, Recital (10) continues to note that:

> While unique and non-fungible crypto-assets might be traded on the marketplace and be accumulated speculatively, they are not readily interchangeable and the relative value of one such crypto-asset in relation to another, each being unique, cannot be ascertained by means of comparison to an existing market or equivalent asset. Such features limit the extent to which those crypto-assets can have a financial use, thus limiting risks to holders and the financial system and justifying their exclusion from the scope of this Regulation.

The simple fact that an NFT has potential investment value or is the subject of speculation are not conditions that would bring the NFT within scope of MiCAR.

In summary, the answer to the question of whether an NFT is non-fungible in MiCAR terms depends on the use case for the NFT.[24] If the NFT is created to serve as a certificate of licensee rights to use certain linked creative content in a particular manner, such as a visual file that may be displayed by the NFT owner, even in the case of a series of NFTs referencing the same content, number 1 in the series is not considered readily exchangeable for a subsequent number in the series. This is no different in the context of physically printed art, although it should be noted that MiCAR observes that the 'issuance of crypto-assets as non-fungible tokens in a large series or collection should be considered an indicator of their fungibility.'[25] If the NFT were to be issued as a series of NFTs that are used to certify co-ownership to, for instance, a commingled fund of gold bars deposited

[23] MiCAR, Article 2(3).

[24] See MiCAR, Recital (11) ('This Regulation should also apply to crypto-assets that appear to be unique and non-fungible, but whose de facto features or whose features that are linked to their de facto uses, would make them either fungible or not unique. In that regard, when assessing and classifying crypto-assets, competent authorities should adopt a substance over form approach whereby the features of the crypto-asset in question determine the classification and not its designation by the issuer').

[25] MiCAR, Recital (11).

at a warehouse, even as the NFTs are uniquely numbered as part of a series like physical certificates of deposits, the NFTs in that series would be entirely fungible and would not be in scope of the MiCAR exclusion of Article 2(4). The mere attribution of a unique identifier to a crypto-asset is not, in and of itself, sufficient to classify it as unique and non-fungible. The assets or rights represented by an NFT should also be unique and non-fungible in order for the crypto-asset to be considered unique and non-fungible. In a similar vein, it is possible to fractionalise an NFT by depositing it in a smart contract by way of a vault and then issue co-ownership tokens against that deposit. Recital (11) of MiCAR clarifies that the 'fractional parts of a unique and non-fungible crypto-asset should not be considered unique and non-fungible.'

NFT 'free drops', also known as 'airdrops', have become a popular marketing and community engagement strategy in web3 to promote brands and increase visibility. By distributing NFTs for free, projects can attract attention and generate 'buzz' within the target crypto community. Free drops can also help build and strengthen a community around a project. The idea is to reward early supporters or active community members with free NFTs to foster loyalty and engagement with a web3 project. The subject matter of free drop NFTs is diverse due to the broad range of creative content underpinning them. Free drop NFTs can range from digital art and collectibles to gaming assets and educational content. An early example of free drops were the 'CryptoPunks', a series of 10,000 unique, algorithmically generated characters, each with distinct traits and identifiers. CryptoPunks were originally given away for free to anyone with an Ethereum wallet. The only cost involved was the network transaction fee (gas fee) required to claim them. A CryptoPunk's distinct attributes and appearance contribute to their scarcity and, in turn, to their value. As the concept of NFTs gained popularity and CryptoPunks became recognised as one of the first NFT projects on the Ethereum blockchain, their value increased significantly. Over time, some CryptoPunks have sold for significant amounts of money, with rare types (like aliens, apes, and zombies) fetching particularly high prices.

It is not immediately obvious how the CryptoPunks would be treated under MiCAR if they were issued as a series of 10,000 NFTs today. However, even if they were considered to be fungible enough to fall within the scope, the drop would probably have the benefit of the MiCAR free drop exclusion set out in Article 4(3)(a). This article provides that offers to the public of crypto-assets other than asset-referenced tokens or e-money tokens are excluded if 'the crypto-asset is offered for free'. The exclusion is heavily qualified by a subsequent paragraph, which provides that 'a crypto-asset shall not be considered to be offered for free where purchasers are required to provide, or to undertake to provide, personal data to the offeror in exchange for that crypto-asset, or where the offeror of a crypto-asset receives from prospective holders of that crypto-asset any fees, commissions, or monetary or non-monetary benefits in exchange for that crypto-asset.' It seems obvious that the offering of an NFT in exchange for some form of monetary or non-monetary benefit would disqualify it from falling under the 'free drop exclusion'. It is less obvious that this should be true for free drops in exchange for personal data, which would defeat the most common objective of the free drop, that is, community building. It may be that the mere connection of a wallet, as a public address that is not without further effort identifiable as personal to any key holder, is not considered personal data within the meaning of MiCAR. This qualification certainly prevents collection of email addresses or other personal data against a free drop.

11.4. Delineation of the CASP Perimeter: Token Financing Transactions

TradFi financial assets (equity, debt, and derivative instruments)[26] are fungible property because financial assets are a kind of property of which one unit, in terms of an obligation owed by one party to another, is indistinguishable from any other unit, so that a duty to deliver one unit is considered to be performed by the delivery of an equivalent unit. Fungibility supports liquidity because it does not matter which particular unit is transferred pursuant to a transaction, as long as that unit is of a certain type and description. This means that the holder of the financial asset can exit that position through sale of the financial asset, and a successor holder can assume the position. Fungibility of an asset class also enables its use for financing transactions. All financing transactions, whether fiat financing or securities financing, rely on the notion that the financed party acquires the supplied asset as owner in consideration for an obligation to return assets of the same type and description. In short, the fungibility of financial assets is the essence of modern finance.

Tokens are typically created and supplied as fungible assets. Accordingly, like financial assets and money, token positions can be easily traded in and out of, and tokens can be used for financing transactions, be that in the form of a loan, a repo contract, a swap, or, indeed, any other form of collateralised or uncollateralised financing transaction. MiCAR seeks to regulate professional services that have tokens as their subject matter. Consequently, if a person, by way of a professional business, provides investment management, investment advisory, brokerage, custody, exchange, transfer, or order transmission services to clients in the EU in relation to MiCAR crypto-assets, that person must be authorised as a crypto-asset services provider or 'CASP'.

Notably, the scope of the activities of a crypto-asset service provider (CASP) does not reference 'lending and borrowing' of crypto-assets, nor the 'taking of

[26] A financial asset, in economic terms, is a medium through which the person acquiring that asset provides capital to the real economy in return for an expectation of future benefits, see Z Bodie, A Kane and A Marcus, *Investments and Portfolio Management*, 9th edn (McGraw-Hill Higher Education, 2011) 30.

deposits' from the public.[27] Recital (94) states that MiCAR 'should not address the lending and borrowing of crypto-assets, including e-money tokens, and therefore should not prejudice applicable national law.' A policy decision has been taken to assess the need to regulate this type of activity at EU level at a later point in the development of DLT and crypto-assets.[28]

Crypto-asset deposit-taking and lending, 'token banking', therefore, are not within the MiCAR perimeter. Neither are crypto-asset lending and borrowing transactions. TradFi financing transactions, instead of being documented as a loan, may be documented as a funded swap or repo under suitable forms of master agreements. Arguably, if the subject matter of the funded swap or repo were crypto-assets, these transactions would be considered crypto-asset financing transactions outside MiCAR's scope and any TradFi regulatory framework, depending on the interpretation of the word 'exchange' in the definition of 'crypto-asset service' in Article 3(1)(16) of MiCAR as a spot exchange transaction.[29]

11.5. Delineation of the CASP Perimeter: DeFi[30]

Smart contracts can be programmed to create, hold, transfer, or perform other actions in relation to crypto-assets. Consequently, the obvious ramification of smart contract technology is its ability to create a platform that permits multilateral execution of financial transactions with tokens, that is, enables token owners to trade, exchange, lend, and borrow tokens, and use tokens as collateral.

[27] Lending can occur through centralised platforms such as Nexo and Ledn, or decentralised finance (DeFi) applications such as Aave, Compound, and MakerDAO, which enable peer-to-peer lending and borrowing through smart contracts, eliminating the need for intermediaries. Borrowers obtain crypto-assets by providing collateral, often exceeding the loan amount to mitigate risk. Similar to the rationale for lending and borrowing of TradFi assets, this allows access to liquidity without selling holdings, leveraging crypto-asset positions, and engaging in various trading strategies. Lenders can earn additional tokens or rewards by providing liquidity to DeFi protocols ('yield farming').

[28] The recital notes the 'feasibility and necessity of regulating such activities should be further assessed.' Article 142 provides that the Commission in consultation with the EBA and ESMA must by 30 December 2024 'report to the European Parliament and the Council on the latest developments with respect to crypto-assets, in particular on matters that are not addressed in this Regulation, accompanied, where appropriate, by a legislative proposal.' The report must include '(a) an assessment of the development of decentralised finance in markets in crypto-assets and of the appropriate regulatory treatment of decentralised crypto-asset systems without an issuer or crypto-asset service provider, including an assessment of the necessity and feasibility of regulating decentralised finance; and (b) an assessment of the necessity and feasibility of regulating lending and borrowing of crypto-assets.'

[29] See the definition of 'crypto-asset service' in Article 3(1)(16) of MiCAR, which lists the following crypto-asset services: (a) providing custody and administration of crypto-assets on behalf of clients; (b) operation of a trading platform for crypto-assets; (c) exchange of crypto-assets for funds; (d) exchange of crypto-assets for other crypto-assets; (e) execution of orders for crypto-assets on behalf of clients; (f) placing of crypto-assets; (g) reception and transmission of orders for crypto-assets on behalf of clients; (h) providing advice on crypto-assets; (i) providing portfolio management on crypto-assets; (j) providing transfer services for crypto-assets on behalf of clients.

[30] Certain parts of this section are based on L Van Setten, 'DeFi platforms: delineating the regulatory perimeter' (2023) Butterworths Journal of International Banking and Financial Law (2 November 2023).

The platform includes the infrastructure needed for clearing of the transactions, transferring the various tokens by way of settlement of the mutual delivery obligations, and holding and administering the transferred tokens directly at the user's blockchain address (meaning the platform is 'non-custodial').[31] The set of smart contracts that underpin the platform can be coded to operate autonomously, automatically executing actions as programmed. This can increase efficiency, reduce costs, and minimise the potential for human error relative to traditional finance's market infrastructure.[32] A smart contract can also be coded to take data (eg, a price feed) from an external source called 'oracles'.[33] Acceptance and validation of a transaction initiated by a wallet holder with a smart contract will lock the performance of that transaction into the smart contract. The smart contract is programmed to effect the transfer of the relevant crypto-assets to or from the relevant wallet addresses upon satisfaction of the coded conditions. Smart contract-based application platforms whose functionality permits the initiation, execution, and performance of these types of financial token transactions are referred to as 'decentralised finance' or 'DeFi'.[34]

The most important DeFi platforms to date are lending platforms.[35] In these constellations, smart contracts are used to replace the intermediary institutional balance sheet and automate the execution and settlement of loans. The DeFi lending platforms, such as Compound and Aave, allow users to lend or borrow funds directly to or from a smart contract. Interest rates can be set algorithmically based on supply and demand. A user-lender can connect their wallet to deposit the token they wish to supply to a particular smart contract-maintained pool. In return, the user-lender receives an equivalent amount of a deposit token. For example, depositing DAI via the Aave platform will give you aDAI. The deposit tokens represent the supplied token and accrue interest in real-time, reflected by an increase in the balance of the deposit token. The typical DeFi loan is disbursed in stablecoin tokens, while the collateral consists of riskier unbacked tokens.[36]

Another important category of DeFi platforms comprises the decentralised exchanges, or 'DEX'. Order Book DEX such as dYdX permit the matching of buy and sell orders in a smart contract-operated order book, much in the way of a traditional finance exchange trading engine. Automated Market Maker DEX such as Uniswap permit users to connect their wallet to contribute token pairs to a smart

[31] See R Auer et al, 'The Technology of Decentralized Finance (DeFi)' (2023) BIS Working Papers No 1066, www.bis.org/publ/work1066.htm.

[32] For a helpful analysis of how a decentralised smart contract functions, see B Ramamurthy, *Blockchain in Action* (Manning Publications, 2020) 22–29.

[33] In the context of smart contracts, an oracle is any data source for reporting information external to the blockchain network, where that data is used by the smart contract to execute transactions. On oracles and oracle risks, see C Harvey, A Ramachandran and J Santoro, *DeFi and the Future of Finance* (Wiley, 2021) 23, 137.

[34] See K Schuler, AS Cloots, F Schär, 'On DeFi and On-Chain CeFi: How (Not) to Regulate Decentralized Finance' (2024) 10(2) *Journal of Financial Regulation* 213.

[35] OECD, 'Why Decentralised Finance (DeFi) Matters and the Policy Implications' (2022) 27.

[36] See IOSCO Decentralized Finance Report, OR01/2022, March 2022, at 11. See also Harvey, Ramachandran and Santoro (n 33) 69ff.

contract that operates as a token pair pool. Pricing of the token pair exchange rate is determined algorithmically based on the ratio of the tokens in the pool. The idea is that if the pool's exchange rate is off market, users will reduce the spread by way of arbitrage transactions with the pool. These are all types of smart contract-based sets of applications that facilitate peer-to-peer token trading between users with minimal centralised intermediary functionality.[37] The user can typically earn returns from trading activities and from commission-like income generated because of the deposit of tokens into a smart contract. The smart contract-based execution and asset holding mean that the operator, the person or persons who deploy the smart contracts and maintain the application set, typically do not control the users' transactions or their tokens.[38] DEX Aggregator platforms such as 1inch can assist users in sourcing liquidity from various DEXs to offer users the best trading rates.

TradFi regulation is framed on the identification of an accountable actor, that is, the person who conducts the activities that are within the regulatory perimeter, and who must therefore apply for authorisation and comply with prudential and conduct of business rules in conducting that regulated activity. DeFi platforms, in their purest form, are arranged such that a great deal of the accountable effort is automated through software, that is, a set of smart contracts that are part of a blockchain that is run independently on a decentralised network. Once deployed successfully at their own unique public network address, the smart contracts become an immutable part of the particular blockchain and can be accessed directly by knowledgeable users of wallet software without the need for intermediation. The immutability of the program code means that it cannot be changed or updated, except, importantly, to the extent that the smart contract is programmed to give certain permissions to an administrator network address.[39]

Subject, therefore, to any such administrator rights, the decentralised nature of the blockchain network ensures that the smart contract's operations are not controlled by any single party, significantly reducing execution and non-performance risks, but also, correspondingly, eliminating accountability for the operation of the smart contracts. Accordingly, where a certain token that can be transacted through a DeFi platform is a financial instrument within the meaning of operative TradFi regulatory framework, or a virtual or crypto-asset within the meaning of applicable anti-money laundering and countering the financing of terrorism (AML/CFT) rules,[40] or specialist crypto legislation such as MiCAR, the

[37] OECD (n 35) 36; Harvey, Ramachandran and Santoro (n 33) 95ff.

[38] IOSCO Decentralized Finance Report (n 36) 14.

[39] A smart contract administrator address refers to a specific blockchain address (or account) that holds special permissions to manage and control certain aspects of the smart contract with the administrator private key.

[40] As outlined in Financial Action Task Force (FATF, 2012-2023), International Standards on Combating Money Laundering and the Financing of Terrorism & Proliferation. Recommendation 15 requires that virtual asset services providers (VASPs) be regulated for AML/CFT purposes, that they be licensed or registered, and subject to effective systems for monitoring or supervision. 'Virtual assets' are defined as 'a digital representation of value that can be digitally traded, or transferred, and can be used for payment or investment purposes'.

prevailing argument is that there is no accountable actor to hold responsible for the offering and operations of the DeFi platform in question, and therefore, that the autonomous operations of the set of deployed DeFi smart contracts are not within the regulatory perimeter.

MiCAR states in that context that a crypto-asset service activity is in its scope if the services are 'provided or controlled, directly or indirectly, by [the CASP], including when part of such activities or services is performed in a decentralised manner.'[41] It continues to note that '[w]here crypto-asset services are provided in a fully decentralised manner without any intermediary, they should not fall within the scope of this Regulation.' That means that where smart contracts and other dApps are used to provide custody, exchange, transfer, or order transmission services, but the dApp stack is ultimately controlled by an operator, the use of the dApps to deliver the service does not provide the operator with a safe harbour from the regulatory framework.[42] Similarly, just as the use of DLT for tokenisation purposes does not automatically imply that the token is an object in its own right, the fact that DLT is used to provide a virtual asset service does not mean that service is not controlled by an accountable actor, also referred to as 'on-chain centralised finance (CeFi)'.[43] The question is where the line is to be drawn between a platform that is essentially a CeFi platform that uses smart contract components to provide virtual asset services, and DeFi proper, where the originators of the set of smart contracts are merely developing and deploying software as a public utility. How much decentralisation is enough decentralisation for the purposes of MiCAR?

To examine decentralisation, one must look at the complete stack, that is, all the layers that underpin the dApp-based services. The smart contract innovation essentially turns a network that operates eligible blockchain technology into a public computer that can be used for any programmable purpose. The search for an accountable actor in the context of DeFi should therefore start with the network. Critical to the notion of decentralisation is the nature and character of the network of validator nodes that maintain the distributed ledger, such as, for instance, the Bitcoin network that maintains the Bitcoin blockchain. Decentralisation implies that control is distributed among independent nodes of the network and decisions are made by the nodes cooperating in accordance with the network consensus protocol. As a result, decentralised networks, provided that enough independent

[41] MiCAR, Recital (22).

[42] UK's HM Treasury observes in a recent Consultation Paper that regulators 'should be able to apply rules to persons who maintain significant control or influence over a DeFi arrangement or protocol providing cryptoasset services and activities. To illustrate this point further, the objective is not to regulate the activity of developing software, but if software developers go on to maintain, run and operate systems used for regulated financial activities (e.g. exchange, lending) then they should be subject to financial services regulation'. HM Treasury, *Future financial services regulatory regime for cryptoassets – Consultation and call for evidence* (February 2023) 11.7.

[43] See R Rettig, M Mosier and K Gilman, 'Genuine DeFi as Critical Infrastructure: A Conceptual Framework for Combatting Illicit Finance Activity in Decentralized Finance' (2024) 13, papers.ssrn.com/sol3/papers.cfm?abstract_id=4607332.

nodes actively participate, are more resistant to censorship and are more resilient as there ought to be no single point of failure. If one or several validator nodes fail, the rest of the network can still function and maintain its integrity.[44]

Although a high number of independent and active validator nodes with meaningful geographic distribution normally indicates a good level of decentralisation of the network, assessing decentralisation is more nuanced than that single factor. In the context of a blockchain protocol that operates a proof-of-work (PoW) consensus mechanism, such as the Bitcoin protocol, the 'hash rate' is an important decentralisation level indicator. The term 'hash rate' refers to the number of hash calculations performed by validator nodes, known as Bitcoin 'miners', within a given period. When the network hash rate is generated by many independent miners, it indicates a good level of decentralisation of the PoW network. This is because it denotes the absence of a dominant miner or group of miners making unilateral decisions that could undermine the integrity or consensus of the PoW network.

In the context of a blockchain protocol that operates a proof-of-stake (PoS) consensus mechanism, which is now the dominant consensus model among the prevailing blockchain protocols other than Bitcoin, the concept of hash rate does not have the same meaning as in PoW networks. The PoS validation and network security process is not based on CPU power spent but on the length of time and the number of protocol tokens staked by a validator.[45] Accordingly, in a PoS blockchain protocol, the even distribution of stakes among many independent and active validator nodes is considered a good indication of proper decentralisation.

MiCAR refrains from offering further guidance on the matter of decentralisation in respect of a DLT network. In contrast, a recent Bill, the *Financial Innovation and Technology for the 21st Century Act*, known as 'FIT21',[46] adopted by the U.S. Congress (House of Representatives), is very specific about the notion of decentralisation in the context of DLT. FIT21 puts the requirement that no single entity has control over the system at the heart of the decentralisation test for the DLT network. Section 25(A) FIT21 requires that, during the previous 12-month period, no individual or group must have had the unilateral authority to control or materially alter the blockchain system's functionality or operation, nor restrict its use

[44] A decentralised network must be distinguished from a distributed network, which denotes a network architecture based on the allocation of specific data and computing resources across a number of nodes. In a distributed network, each node is responsible for performing a specific task or set of tasks and the nodes communicate with each other to complete the overall task. A distributed network is designed to scale task performance and engineer higher fault-tolerance. In that context, the better term would be 'decentralised ledger technology', but the term 'distributed ledger technology' seems to be prevailing.

[45] CPU power refers to the capability and performance of a Central Processing Unit (CPU), which is the primary component of a computer responsible for executing instructions from programs and performing calculations.

[46] H.R. 4763 – 118th Congress (2023–2024): *Financial Innovation and Technology for the 21st Century Act.* Introduced in House on July 20, 2023. Passed House on May 22, 2024, www.congress.gov/bill/118th-congress/house-bill/4763.

by others. Section 25(B) FIT21 stipulates that no digital asset issuer or affiliated person can own 20 per cent or more of the digital asset units or control 20 per cent or more of the voting power, which will be relevant for PoS DLT systems. Section 25(C) FIT21 observes that any contributions to the blockchain's source code must address vulnerabilities, maintenance, or other technical changes and must be adopted through a decentralised governance system. Section 25(D) FIT21 requires that the digital assets should not have been marketed to the public as investments, and finally, Section 25(E) mandates that all units issued through the blockchain system must be end-user distributions.

These five components collectively aim to maintain and promote the decentralised nature of blockchain systems. They aim to test whether there is (i) control by any single entity, (ii) sufficiently broad distribution of ownership and voting power, (iii) community involvement in code development and governance so that enhancements and fixes are vetted and approved collectively rather than controlled centrally, (iv) speculative marketing rather than promotion of the use of digital assets for functional purposes, supporting the development and use of decentralised applications and services, by (v) the ultimate users. Although MiCAR-specific criteria are still yet to be formulated, the considered approach of FIT21 could be persuasive when testing for decentralisation.

Next in line to be examined as a potential accountable on-chain CeFi actor in the context of a DeFi platform is the originating team, incorporated or otherwise, which deployed and may maintain the set of smart contracts. The originating team very often not only deploys the set of DeFi smart contracts but also provides centralised web-based user interfaces (UIs), that is, a front-end, user-facing component of the DeFi application stack. UIs display relevant information from the smart contracts and allow users to send transactions, view data, and interact with the smart contract functions. If the UI application operates such that the UI provider effectively intermediates between the user and the DeFi smart contracts, the UI operator could be a CASP on grounds that it serves as an arranger or person receiving and transmitting orders from users to the DeFi platform.[47] Similarly, if the originating team coded the set of DeFi smart contracts such that it can be controlled through administrator private keys that permit the controller to amend and upgrade the smart contract code and its operational features, assuming the originating team operates as a business, the originating team's activity would very likely be a CASP activity, and the platform should therefore be characterised as a CeFi platform.

Smart contracts can be designed without access rights so that once the smart contract is deployed, it is immutable except through exploitation of bugs and code errors. Further, UIs can be decentralised, relying on technologies like IPFS

[47] MiCAR, Article 80 (Reception and transmission of orders for crypto-assets on behalf of clients), but also eg, Paragraph 14A(1) of the UK's Money Laundering, Terrorist Financing and Transfer of Funds (Information on the Payer) Regulations 2017, which includes 'arranging or making arrangements with a view to' within in the regulatory perimeter.

(InterPlanetary File System) for hosting front-end files, or it can be offered by way of software as a service, where the UI provider offers the application for downloading and local operating. It may be that the UI provider earns a royalty for use of the software IP, but that is not the same as earning a fee for intermediary activities. In cases where the DeFi smart contracts are not controlled by the originating team and the UI is not heavily centralised but offered as a tool for user by way of licensed software, it would be difficult to construct an argument that brings what is essentially a software provider into the CASP perimeter. To do so would require legislative intervention, which would bring the provision of wallet software or the deployment of DeFi smart contract sets within the CASP definition as a specified regulated activity.

In a case that is very much on that point, certain deceived users of the Uniswap DeFi exchange platform sought to hold the originating team, Universal Navigation Inc. trading as 'Uniswap Labs', liable for their losses on several grounds. Access to the Uniswap pools is available through a Uniswap Labs-developed UI, and through wallet application extensions that permit direct access to the pools without relying on intermediaries or needing permission. Plaintiffs argued, among other matters, that Uniswap Labs controls the token transactions in the Uniswap pools. While the court accepted, without making a finding, the assertion that the tokens in question were securities for US securities regulation purposes, it observed that plaintiffs' argument that Uniswap Labs somehow sold the tokens as unregistered broker-dealers was not sustainable, because the court considered the set of Uniswap pool smart contracts to be mere software tools made available to the users at their discretion. 'Looking at the allegations [...], it defies logic that a drafter of computer code underlying a particular software platform could be liable under Section 29(b) for a third-party's misuse of that platform.'[48] The court declined 'to stretch the federal securities laws to cover the conduct alleged' and concluded 'that Plaintiffs' concerns are better addressed to Congress than to this Court.'[49]

On the other hand, the US Commodities Futures Trading Commission (CFTC) recently issued orders against originating teams of three different DeFi platforms that facilitate token derivatives trading.[50] Unlike the Uniswap platform, where users self-create pools or access pools created by other users, the originating teams of the platforms that are the subject matter of the CFTC Orders, as stated by the CFTC, retained control over the DeFi, ie, the 'ability to update relevant smart contract code to adjust how the smart contracts operated in order to, among other things, suspend trading or prevent users from depositing collateral.'[51] Importantly,

[48] *Risley, e.a. v Universal Navigation Inc., d/b/a Uniswap Labs, e.a*, Case No. Case 1:22-cv-02780-KPF (S.D.N.Y. Aug 29, 2023) storage.courtlistener.com/recap/gov.uscourts.nysd.577791/gov.uscourts.nysd.577791.90.0.pdf.

[49] ibid.

[50] CFTC Issues Orders Against Operators of Three DeFi Protocols for Offering Illegal Digital Asset Derivatives Trading (7 September 2023) www.cftc.gov/PressRoom/PressReleases/8774-23.

[51] Commodity Futures Trading Commission, *Re Deridex, Inc.*, CFTC Docket No. 23-42 (7 September 2023).

unlike Uniswap Labs, the originating teams also earned fees directly from the trading contracts. Essentially, therefore, the CFTC is arguing that these platforms are CeFi platforms operated by an accountable actor, and not DeFi platforms.

A third category of potential accountable actors that are typically part of the DeFi platform are the smart contract-based token operated governance structures commonly known as 'Decentralised Autonomous Organisations' or 'DAOs'. Many DeFi platforms have implemented a DAO layer as part of the DeFi platform. The aim is to offer users of the DeFi platform governance tokens that usually enable them to vote via the DAO smart contract structure and so have a say in the platform's development, and, importantly, changes to the DeFi smart contracts. Not all DeFi platform have a full-fledged DAO governance structure in place, especially in their early stages, when the developers might retain control over the protocol to develop the platform without going through a lengthy governance process. Some DeFi platforms offer hybrid structures that incorporate certain DAO components but also retain some centralised control or decision-making processes, eg, for reasons of efficiency or security.

A DAO's legal characterisation depends on the specific facts and circumstances of its operation. US federal courts have not struggled to decide in preliminary findings that a DAO could be a general partnership or unincorporated association if certain facts and circumstances support that finding – most notably, that token holders can participate in the management or profits of the DAO operations – and accordingly, that such DAO token holders may be held liable jointly for the DAO's decisions and actions.[52] However, where the DAO operates like a club of the DeFi users, offering users governance rights without profit sharing, the nature of the DAO changes from a commercial enterprise to user community engagement. The purpose of a governance DAO is to permit users of the DeFi platform to vote on protocol upgrades, parameter adjustments, and other strategic decisions. Its aim is to generate use of the DeFi platform by engaging the users in community-driven proposals and consensus with a view to user experience optimisation. That way, the DAO governance mechanism ensures that the DeFi platform evolves in a manner that reflects the community's collective interests. The governance process is typically public, and users can track the progress and status of each proposal, including discussions, voting results, and implementation status. Such DAOs, if the DAO token ownership is properly distributed, would pass the decentralisation test. Here, too, the FIT21 criteria could offer a meaningful and persuasive test.

In conclusion, under MiCAR, a CASP ought not to be identifiable in the context of DeFi proper, and it is likely that, for instance, no CASP would be identified in connection with a DeFi platform that is substantively similar in its set up and operations to the Uniswap platform. Equally, if control of the DeFi platform for all material intents and purposes is in the hands of a user-driven governance

[52] *Sarcuni v bZx DAO*, Case No. 22-cv-618-LAB-DEB, 2023 WL 2657633 (S.D. Cal. 27 March 2023), and *Commodity Futures Trading Commission v Ooki Dao*, Case No. 3:22-cv-05416-WHO (N.D. Cal. 20 December 2022).

DAO that meets the requisite decentralisation standards, neither the DAO nor the development team ought to be identified under MiCAR as a CASP. To bring DeFi proper within the MiCAR regulatory perimeter, statutory intervention will be required. Conversely, if a platform arranges for token transaction execution and settlement through a set of smart contracts, the development teams as the platform operators or the DAO, if it were a for profit DAO, could be held responsible as a CASP on the grounds that either or both arrange the transactions and/or control and profit from the platform.

11.6. Conclusion

The MiCAR framework defines its regulatory scope based on the characteristics of tokens, such as transferability, representation of value, and the legal characterisation of the rights associated with these assets. As argued in this chapter, not all tokens created with the use of DLT should qualify as MiCAR crypto-assets. The latter must meet specific criteria related to their functionality and economic utility. We have pointed out that tokens that simply tokenise existing assets without significantly changing their economic nature should be excluded from MiCAR's scope. Any other conclusion would risk being inconsistent with the principle of technology neutrality underpinning MiCAR. The exclusion of unique and non-fungible tokens (NFTs) from its scope equally reflects an understanding that the economic characteristics of NFTs differ from those of fungible tokens typically used in financial transactions.

This chapter also investigated the concept of decentralisation, which plays a crucial role in terms of delineating MiCAR's regulatory perimeter. Thus, the provision of crypto-asset services in a fully decentralised manner without any intermediary falls outside this regulator perimeter. In practice, determining whether an arrangement (eg, a DEX or a crypto-lending platform) is fully decentralised may be complicated and would require the assessment of all relevant circumstances. In any case, the use of DLT to deliver a crypto-asset service should not by itself indicate the requisite level of decentralisation or the absence of a centralised intermediary.

12

The UK Regulatory Regime for Crypto-Assets

SIMON GLEESON

12.1. Introduction

Regulating crypto-asset activity is now a global business, and, despite the wide divergence of starting-points of the different authorities, it is interesting to see that they converge in practice in a remarkably similar set of principles and standards. The EU, first out of the gate with MiCAR, has chosen a single legal instrument covering the offering of crypto-assets, establishment of asset-backed tokens generally, and the provision of services in respect of those instruments. The US, late to the start but coming up rapidly, is proceeding with two separate measures – the GENIUS Act,[1] which regulates the creation and issue of stablecoins, and the CLARITY Act,[2] which establishes a provisional registration regime for digital commodity exchanges, brokers, and dealers, until full CFTC registration is implemented. However, whereas the EU model seeks to exclude crypto-assets from the financial regulatory framework, the US model, although it explicitly provides that crypto-assets are not securities, explicitly allocates responsibility for the supervision of crypto-asset intermediaries to the CFTC.

This convergence represents a surprisingly strong degree of global regulatory consensus on the tools of crypto-asset regulation, as set out in IOSCO's Policy Recommendations for Crypto and Digital Asset Markets.[3]

The UK has, on the face of it, adopted a diametrically opposite approach to MiCAR. Whereas MiCAR establishes a completely new legislative framework which, although modelled on existing securities legislation, is formally separate from it, the UK has simply included crypto-assets within its existing securities regulatory framework. This broadly means that whereas the EU must proceed by

[1] At the time of writing a Senate Bill – s 394–119th Congress (2025–2026).

[2] At the time of writing, a bipartisan proposal introduced by the US House Committees on Financial Services and Agriculture. This bill is an iteration of a previous proposal (FIT 21).

[3] CR01/2023 of May 2023.

inclusion, deciding which parts of the securities framework it wishes to include in the MiCAR regime, the UK must proceed by exclusion, deciding which parts of its securities framework it is prepared to disapply to crypto-asset business. Instinct would suggest that this will lead to overregulation in the UK, where regulatory conservatism will result in the application of inappropriate requirements by default, and underregulation in the EU, where the blank canvas created by MiCAR will take time to fill in. This should give the EU a substantial competitive advantage over the UK in this area.

Before embarking on a discussion of the regulation of this market, it may be helpful to consider its actual composition. At the time of writing, the global crypto-asset market is valued at around \$3.5trn (roughly equal to the market capitalisation of the London Stock Exchange).[4] 60 per cent of this value (\$2.1trn) is attributable to Bitcoin, with a further 9 per cent (\$ 350bn) to Etherium. Total stablecoin issuance is \$230bn (roughly 7 per cent of total), although growing rapidly. Of this amount, 65 per cent consists of USDT[5] and 26 per cent of USDC.[6] The vast majority of the trading in these instruments (90 per cent) occurs over centralised trading platforms (CEXs), with the largest of these – Binance – having a market share of 40 per cent. Trading on decentralised platforms ('DEXs') is less than 10 per cent of all trading in these assets.

12.2. The UK Legislative and Policy Framework

Given the absence of a single policy document, it may be helpful to begin by identifying the building-blocks with which UK policy in this area has been constructed.

The 'foundations', as it were, have been around for some time. From 10 January 2020 the UK Financial Conduct Authority (FCA) became be the Anti-Money Laundering and Countering Terrorist Financing (AML/CTF) supervisor for firms carrying on certain crypto-asset activity.[7] The practical effect of this was that crypto-asset businesses conducted in the UK were required to be registered with the FCA.[8]

The next step was the regulation of financial promotions of crypto-assets in the UK. By section 69 of the Financial Services and Markets Act 2023 (FSMA 2023),[9]

[4] Crypto figures in this paragraph are derived from the IMFs Crypto Assets Monitor Q2 2025, www.imfconnect.org/content/dam/imf/News%20and%20Generic%20Content/GMM/Special%20Features/Crypto%20Assets%20Monitor.pdf.

[5] Operated by Tether. USDT is currently 81% backed by US Treasuries, short-term assets and overnight repo.

[6] Operated by Circle. USDC is currently entirely backed by cash, overnight repo and US Treasuries.

[7] By the Financial Services and Markets Act 2000 (Financial Promotion)(Amendment) Order 2023, SI 2023/612.

[8] Under the Money Laundering, Terrorist Financing and Transfer of Funds (Information on the Payer) Regulations 2017, SI 2017/692.

[9] Which took effect as from 8 October 2023 by the Crypto-asset Financial Promotions Instrument 2023.

qualifying crypto-assets were brought within the FCA's remit, so that the FCA now regulates all marketing of crypto-assets to UK consumers, regardless of where the firm doing the marketing is based or what technology is used to make the promotion. FSMA 2023 also introduced measures that would permit the regulation of crypto-assets more generally. However, these measures are facilitative – they create a statutory framework which enables the various regulators to regulate, but do not oblige them to do so. The current policy debate is therefore as to what regulations should be put in place within this framework.

After some consultation, HM Treasury (HMT) produced, in October 2023, a policy document entitled 'Future financial services regulatory regime for crypto-assets: Response to the consultation and call for evidence', (the 'Response'), and the FCA produced a Discussion Paper entitled 'Regulating Crypto-assets Phase 1; Stablecoins'.[10] The latter remains the primary policy framework document for the UK. The Response was accompanied by a separate HMT document entitled 'Update on Plans for the Regulation of Fiat-backed Stablecoins' (the 'Update'), which suggested that fiat-backed stablecoins would be regulated through the Payment Services Regulator. This plan has since been abandoned,[11] although the Bank of England will be responsible for supervision systemic payment systems using stablecoins.

This work proceeded in parallel with discussions on the introduction of a UK Central Bank Digital Currency (CBDC). In February 2023 the Bank of England and HMT jointly produced a discussion paper on how such an instrument might work, and in January 2024 they produced a response to that paper[12] setting out the design principles which would apply to the construction of such a product if it were to go ahead.

In December 2024 the FCA produced a discussion paper[13] setting out its proposals for regulating the offering of crypto-assets in the UK – in effect, replicating the existing securities offering regime, including applying market abuse and inside trading rules. The legal basis for this approach was based on the idea that HMT would prohibit any public offer of crypto-assets that was not made through a UK regulated trading platform. This legislation has not yet appeared.

In early 2025 draft legislation was provided, both as to statute and as to regulatory rulebooks. On 29 April 2025 HMT published near-final draft legislation[14] varying the existing regulatory perimeter to bring crypto-assets fully within it

[10] FCA, DP 23/4, November 2023.

[11] Announced by HMT in 'Keynote address at the Tokenisation Summit: UK government approach to tokenisation and regulation' of 21 November 2024. This speech contained a number of important policy announcements.

[12] 'Response to the Bank of England and HM Treasury Consultation Paper: The digital pound: a new form of money for households and businesses?' January 2024.

[13] FCA, Regulating Crypto-assets: Admissions & Disclosures and Market Abuse Regime for Crypto-assets (DP 24/4).

[14] The Financial Services and Markets Act 2000 (Regulated Activities and Miscellaneous Provisions) (Crypto-assets) Order 2025.

(the 'Order'), along with a policy note setting out the objectives of the legislation.[15] At the same time the FCA produced two policy documents setting out proposed rules text – CP25/14 on stablecoin issuance and crypto-asset custody and CP25/15 on a proposed prudential regime for crypto-asset firms.[16] These were accompanied by a discussion paper setting out the framework for the conduct of business rules which will apply to service providers.[17]

The current agenda for the development of the UK regime is as follows. There will be a series of further consultation papers setting out draft rules for different aspects of the regime, with the aim of having a complete draft rulebook ready by early 2026. There will then be a lead-in period before the rules go live, which should in principle be before the end of 2026.

In parallel with this legislative programme, the capacity has been created for the creation of 'sandboxes' – that is, arrangements whereby existing law and/or regulation is disapplied for the purposes of a particular product development.[18] Sections 13 to 17 of The Financial Services and Markets Act 2023 give HM Treasury the power to create 'sandboxes' to test particular financial infrastructure technologies, and such regulations may disapply existing laws for this purpose. The first of these (the 'Digital Securities sandbox') was implemented into law on 8 January 2024,[19] and opened for applications on 30 September 2024.[20] It is expected that more may follow.

12.3. The Regulatory Perimeter – Products

The core of the UK regulatory architecture is the Financial Services and Markets Act 2000 (FSMA 2000). Section 22 of FSMA 2000 sets out on broad terms that it applies to the assets and activities identified in the Financial Services and Markets Act 2000 (Regulated Activities) Order 2001[21] (the 'RAO'). The current position is that a broad definition of Crypto-assets has been inserted into section 22,[22] which reads:

> 'crypto-asset' means any cryptographically secured digital representation of value or contractual rights that—
>
> (a) can be transferred, stored or traded electronically, and

[15] Future financial services regulatory regime for crypto-assets (regulated activities), HMT April 2025.

[16] Implementing in part the policies set out in DP 23/4.

[17] FCA 'Regulating Crypto-asset Activities' DP 25/1 (May 2025).

[18] The policy thinking behind this proposal is elaborated on in HMTs 'Digital Securities Sandbox: Response to Consultation' of November 2023.

[19] By The Financial Services and Markets Act 2023 (Digital Securities Sandbox) Regulations 2023, SI 2023/1398.

[20] See the Bank of England and FCA, 'Joint Policy Statement and Final Guidance' of 30 September 2024. This was produced alongside Bank of England 'Guidance on the operation of the Digital Sandbox', which sets out the details of the processes involved.

[21] SI 2001/544.

[22] By FSMA 2023, s 69.

(b) that uses technology supporting the recording or storage of data (which may include distributed ledger technology).

This enables language to be added to the RAO to specify certain crypto-assets as investments. This is done in the Order by designating certain crypto-assets as 'Qualifying crypto-assets'. The relevant provisions are Articles 88F and 88G of the RAO.[23] These define qualifying crypto-assets and qualifying stablecoins, and are as follows:

> 88F. – (1) Subject to paragraphs (2) to (4), a 'qualifying crypto-asset' is a crypto-asset which is—
>
> (a) fungible; and
> (b) transferable.
>
> (2) For the purposes of paragraph (1)(b), the circumstances in which a crypto-asset is to be treated as 'transferable' include where—
>
> (a) it confers transferable rights; or
> (b) a communication made in relation to the crypto-asset describes it as being transferable or conferring transferable rights.
>
> (3) Subject to paragraph (4), a qualifying crypto-asset includes a crypto-asset that is a qualifying stablecoin.
>
> (4) A crypto-asset does not fall within paragraph (1) if it is—
>
> (a) a specified investment crypto-asset, excluding the operation of—
>   (i) article 74A (electronic money); and
>   (ii) article 88F (qualifying crypto-assets);
> (b) electronic money;
> (c) fiat currency;
> (d) central bank digital currency; or
> (e) a crypto-asset that—
>   (i) cannot be transferred or sold in exchange for money or other crypto-assets, except by way of redemption with the issuer; and
>   (ii) can only be used in the following ways—
>   (aa) it allows the holder to acquire goods or services from the issuer; or
>   (ab) it allows the holder to acquire goods or services within a limited network of service providers which have direct commercial agreements with the issuer
>
> 88G. – (1) Subject to paragraph (2), 'qualifying stablecoin' means a qualifying crypto-asset that—
>
> (a) references a fiat currency; and
> (b) seeks or purports to maintain a stable value in relation to that referenced fiat currency by the issuer holding, or arranging for the holding of—
>   (i) fiat currency; or

[23] As inserted by Art 3(10) of the Order (n 14).

(ii) fiat currency and other assets, irrespective of whether the holding of a fiat currency other than the one referred to in sub-paragraph (a) or other asset contributes to the maintenance of that stable value.

(2) Qualifying stablecoin does not include a crypto-asset comprising or representing a claim for the repayment of a sum of money received by way of deposit, within the scope of article 5 (accepting deposits), excluding the operation of article 9AZA (sums in exchange for qualifying stablecoin), by an authorised person that has Part 4A permission to carry on the regulated activity specified by article 5.

Note that the last element of this definition has the effect of taking tokenised bank deposits outside the scope of the definition of qualifying stablecoin.

There are also some exclusions – notably Article 9AZA, which provides that 'A sum is not a deposit for the purposes of article 5 (accepting deposits) if it is immediately exchanged for qualifying stablecoin, within the scope of the regulated activity specified by article 9M (issuing qualifying stablecoin in the United Kingdom).' This was inserted to address a concern that stablecoin issuers could potentially be treated as taking deposits if they received money for investors as part of a new issuance and did not immediately create the relevant stablecoin.

12.4. The Regulatory Perimeter – Activities

12.4.1. Stablecoin Issuance

The major innovation in the Order is that it brings issuers of qualifying stablecoins (but not other crypto-assets) within the scope of the regulatory perimeter. The relevant provisions are Articles 9M and 9N of the Order:[24]

9M. – (1) Issuing a qualifying stablecoin in the United Kingdom is a specified kind of activity.

(2) For the purposes of paragraph (1), issuing means a person ('A'), established in the United Kingdom, carrying on any of the following activities—

(a) offering, or arranging for another to offer, a qualifying stablecoin created by or on behalf of A for sale or subscription;
(b) undertaking, or arranging for another to undertake, to redeem a qualifying stablecoin created by or on behalf of A; or
(c) carrying on, or arranging for another to carry on, activities designed to maintain the value of the qualifying stablecoin created by or on behalf of A.

(3) For the purposes of paragraph (2)(a), the activity includes where the person ('A') accepts an invitation from another person ('B') for B's purchase of a qualifying stablecoin.

[24] Inserted by Art 3(5) of the Order (n 14).

(4) For the purposes of paragraph (2)(b)—

(a) 'undertaking' includes where the person ('A') has assumed (by contractual assignment, variation, operation of law or by any other similar mechanism) an undertaking to redeem a qualifying stablecoin created by, or on behalf of, another; and

(b) in the situation given by sub-paragraph (a), A is to be treated as having created the qualifying stablecoin.

(5) For the purposes of paragraph (2)—

(a) where the person ('A') is a member of the same group as the person that created the qualifying stablecoin, or on whose behalf the stablecoin was created, then that qualifying stablecoin is to be treated as having been created by or on behalf of A;

(b) the creation of a qualifying stablecoin includes the design of that qualifying stablecoin.

9N. The regulated activity specified by article 9M (issuing qualifying stablecoin in the United Kingdom) does not include the following—

(a) the creation, including the design, of a qualifying stablecoin;

(b) the minting of a qualifying stablecoin, such that it first exists as—

  (i) an identifiable asset on the blockchain; and

  (ii) in a transferable form.

Given that the creation of a pool of assets backing such a stablecoin would prima facie constitute a collective investment scheme ('CIS') in the UK, it has been necessary to include a carve-out for this activity by the insertion of a new Article 3A into the CIS regime.[25] This reads:

> 3A. – (1) Arrangements do not amount to a collective investment scheme where they constitute arrangements where money or assets are held as the backing assets or the stabilisation mechanism for a qualifying stablecoin.

Because of defective drafting in the Alternative Investment Fund Managers Directive[26] (AIFMD) (which the UK, post-Brexit, has chosen not to correct), it is also necessary to include a provision in the UK implementation of that directive, the Alternative Investment Fund Managers Regulations 2013, to include a new Regulation 3 to the effect that the management of such a pool does not constitute conducting the regulated activity of acting as an alternative investment fund manager.

12.4.2. Operating a Qualifying Crypto-asset Trading Platform

The operation of a qualifying crypto-asset trading platform is a specified kind of activity.[27] A 'qualifying crypto-asset trading platform' means a system which

[25] Financial Services and Markets Act 2000 (Collective Investment Schemes) Order 2001, SI 2001/1062.

[26] 2011/61/EU.

[27] RAO, Art 9T, inserted by Art 3(5) of the Order (n 14).

brings together or facilitates the bringing together of multiple third-party buying and selling interests in qualifying crypto-assets in a way that results in a contract for the exchange of qualifying crypto-assets for:

(a) money (including electronic money); or
(b) other qualifying crypto-assets.

The border between stablecoins and e-money is not always clear. In the UK, by the Electronic Money Regulations 2011,[28] 'electronic money' is defined (in regulation 2(1)) as:

> electronically (including magnetically) stored monetary value as represented by a claim on the electronic money issuer which—
>
> (a) is issued on receipt of funds for the purpose of making payment transactions;
> (b) is accepted by a person other than the electronic money issuer; and
> (c) is not excluded by regulation 3.[29]

The UK approach to this regime is simply to exclude it. A new Regulation 3ZA is inserted into the Electronic Money Regulations 2011[30] to provide that:

> 3ZA. – (1) For the purposes of the definition of 'electronic money' in regulation 2 (interpretation), 'stored monetary value' does not include—
>
> (a) qualifying stablecoin;
> (b) money or assets held as the backing assets or the stabilisation mechanism for a qualifying stablecoin;
> (c) a crypto-asset comprising or representing a claim for the repayment of a sum of money received by way of deposit, within the scope of article 5 (accepting deposits) by an authorised person that has Part 4A permission to carry on the regulated activity specified by that article.

12.4.3. Custody of Qualifying Crypto-assets

An interesting feature of the Order is that it provides a new definition of custody of crypto-assets which is distinctly different from that which is applied to custody of other types of assets. The relevant provision, inserted into the RAO, is:[31]

> 9O. – (1) The following are specified kinds of activity—
>
> (a) the safeguarding of qualifying crypto-assets or relevant specified investment crypto-assets on behalf of another; or
> (b) arranging for one or more other persons to carry on that activity.

[28] SI 2011/99.
[29] That is, limited use tokens and electronic communications networks transactions of less than £40.
[30] Inserted by Art 9 of the Order (n 14).
[31] RAO, Art 9O, inserted by s 3(5) of the Order (n 14).

(2) For the purposes of paragraph (1)—

(a) 'safeguarding' means circumstances in which a person ('C') has control of the crypto-asset through any means that would enable C to bring about a transfer of the benefit of the crypto-asset to another person, including to C;
(b) 'on behalf of another' includes where that other person has—
   (i) both legal and beneficial title;
   (ii) the beneficial title only; or
   (iii) a right against C for the return of a qualifying crypto-asset or relevant specified investment crypto-asset.

(3) For the purposes of paragraph (2)(a), the means by which C may have control include—

(i) holding or storing of the means of access, or part of the means of access, to the crypto-asset;
(ii) appointing one or more other persons to hold or store the means of access, or part of the means of access, to the crypto-asset under an arrangement operated by C.

(4) For the purposes of this article—

(a) a 'relevant specified investment crypto-asset' means a specified investment crypto-asset that is a—
   (i) security; or
   (ii) contractually based investment.
(b) references to a qualifying crypto-asset or a relevant specified investment crypto-asset include the means of access to that crypto-asset;
(c) references to the 'means of access' to a crypto-asset include—
   (i) a private cryptographic key to that crypto-asset; and
   (ii) one or more parts of that private cryptographic key.

A 'specified investment crypto-asset' means a crypto-asset that is a specified investment, as specified within Part III of RAO (specified investments), including where the crypto-asset is a right to or an interest in such a specified investment within Article 89 of RAO (rights to or interests in investments).

The question of what is meant by 'control' in this context is a matter of private law. The best guide to the details of its interpretation is the UNIDROIT 'Principles on Digital Assets and Private Law'.[32]

The use of the idea of 'control' as the basis for this regulated activity necessitates a large number of carve-outs. The most significant is Article 9P of RAO, which addresses the situation where a custodian and an intermediary are members of the same group, and the intermediary arranges custody of the crypto-asset for a customer. The effect of the exclusion is that the intermediary is not treated as a custodian of the crypto-asset, even if they have a degree of control over it. Arrangements are also carved out where an intermediary has control of a

[32] Published October 2023, see www.unidroit.org/wp-content/uploads/2024/01/Principles-on-Digital-Assets-and-Private-Law-linked-1.pdf.

crypto-asset for the purposes of settling a transaction (RAO, Article 9R), where the controller has control by virtue of being an agent of the owner (RAO, Article 9S(1)), or where the person has control for some reason other than that they hold themselves out as being a service provider in relation to qualifying crypto-assets (RAO, Article 9S(2)).

12.4.4. Dealing in Qualifying Crypto-assets as Principal

Article 9U[33] of RAO provides that 'Buying, selling, subscribing for or underwriting qualifying crypto-assets as principal is a specified kind of activity'. It is a good general principle of market regulation that unregulated customers should be able to deal in the market concerned without having to obtain authorisation to do so. Consequently, having specified that all dealing as principal is a regulated activity, it is necessary to provide very substantial carve-outs from this basic provision. The basic approach is the same as for investments – a person who deals in investments is not required to be authorised provided that they do not hold themselves out as a market-maker, a dealer or an underwriter, and do not 'regularly solicit members of the public' to deal in qualifying crypto-assets ('the public', in this case, being defined as more or less anyone other than an authorised person).[34]

It is specified (RAO, Article 9W(1)) that this activity does not include the creation, including the design, of a qualifying stablecoin, the minting of a qualifying stablecoin, such that it first exists as: (i) an identifiable asset on a blockchain; and (ii) in a transferable form. Article 9W(2) and (3) of RAO lists a further group of exclusions:

> 9W(2) .... (a) activity where the qualifying crypto-asset is bought, sold, or subscribed for no consideration;
>
> (b) the distribution of a qualifying crypto-asset that was automatically created as a reward for the maintenance of the distributed ledger or the validation of transactions; or
>
> (c) activity where the qualifying crypto-asset is—
>
> (i) issued by; and
> (ii) sold to or subscribed for by an employee or partner of, the person carrying on the activity;
>
> (d) the non-public sale or transfer by a person ('A') of a qualifying crypto-asset—
>
> (i) created and minted by, or on behalf of, A; and
> (ii) having as its sole purpose the raising of capital by A.
>
> 9W(3) The regulated activity specified by article 9U does not include any transaction into which a person ('A') enters as principal with another person ('P') if P is also acting as principal within the scope of the regulated activity specified by article 9U, and—
>
> (a) A and P are members of the same group; or
> (b) A and P are, or propose to become, participators in a joint enterprise, and the transaction is entered into for the purposes of or in connection with that enterprise.

[33] Inserted by s 3(5) of the Order (n 14), as are all the RAO Articles referred to in this section.
[34] RAO, Article 9V(1).

(4) The regulated activity specified by article 9U does not include activity which is a regulated activity specified in—

(a) article 9M (issuing qualifying stablecoin in the United Kingdom);
(b) article 9T (operating a qualifying crypto-asset trading platform);
(c) article 9Z7 (qualifying crypto-asset staking).

12.4.5. Dealing as Intermediary

This is prescribed by Articles 9X[35] (dealing as agent) and 9Z (arranging deals) of RAO. There is an interesting quirk of the UK regime which is copied through into the crypto-asset regime. This is that the UK defines arranging deals as not only 'making arrangements for another person to buy, sell, subscribe for or underwrite a qualifying crypto-asset',[36] but also 'making arrangements with a view to a person who participates in the arrangements buying, selling, subscribing for or underwriting qualifying Crypto-assets'.[37] This latter is, in the securities world, taken to catch market service providers (such as trade confirmation, settlement checking and infrastructure service providers). The general summary of this requirement in the securities world is that this clause catches 'necessary providers' – that is, those who provide services without which the market either would not exist at all or would function very differently.

In the crypto world, there are of course a relatively large number of participants whose activities are necessary, but who are not investment intermediaries. As a result, there are a relatively large number of exclusions from Article 9Z of RAO. These are contained in Article 9Z6:

9Z6. – (1) The regulated activity specified by article 9Z (arranging deals in qualifying crypto-assets) does not include a person engaging in the following activities—

(a) the creation, including the design, of a qualifying stablecoin;
(b) the minting of a qualifying stablecoin, such that it first exists as—
    (i) an identifiable asset on the blockchain; and
    (ii) in a transferable form.

(2) The regulated activity specified by article 9Z does not include—

(a) activity where the qualifying crypto-asset is bought, sold, or subscribed for no consideration;
(b) the distribution of a qualifying crypto-asset that was automatically created as a reward for the maintenance of the distributed ledger or the validation of transactions; or
(c) activity where the qualifying crypto-asset is—
    (i) issued by; and
    (ii) sold to or subscribed for by an employee or partner of, the person carrying on the activity.

[35] Inserted by s 3(5) of the Order (n 14), as are all the RAO Articles referred to in this section.
[36] RAO, Art 9Z(1).
[37] RAO, Art 9Z(2).

(3) The regulated activity specified by article 9Z does not arrangements made by a person ('A') where—

(a) A is a member of a group and the arrangements in question are for, or with a view to, a transaction which is or is to be entered into, as principal, by another member of the same group; or

(b) A is or proposes to become a participator in a joint enterprise, and the arrangements in question are for, or with a view to, a transaction which is or is to be entered into, as principal, by another person who is or proposes to become a participator in that enterprise, for the purposes of or in connection with that enterprise.

(4) The regulated activity specified by article 9Z does not include a regulated activity specified in—

(a) article 9M (issuing qualifying stablecoin in the United Kingdom);
(b) article 9T (operating a qualifying crypto-asset trading platform);
(c) article 9Z7 (qualifying crypto-asset staking).

12.4.6. Staking

The UK has included staking as a separate regulated activity in Article 97Z of RAO. It is notable that the process of platform operators staking pools of assets belonging to their customers was regarded as potentially falling within the UK fund regime,[38] and that regime has now been amended to make clear that operating staking pools does not constitute operating a collective investment scheme.[39] 'Staking' is defined as 'the use of a qualifying crypto-asset in blockchain validation',[40] and 'blockchain validation' means the validation of transactions on:

(a) a blockchain; or
(b) a network that uses distributed ledger technology (DLT) or other similar technology, and includes proof of stake DLT consensus mechanisms.[41]

Further exemptions are included for introducing a person to an authorised person[42] and for making arrangements which enable parties to communicate.[43]

[38] FCA, DP 25/1 para 6.5.

[39] The Financial Services and Markets Act 2000 (Collective Investment Schemes) (Amendment) Order 2025, SI 2025/17, which inserts a new paragraph 22 into the Schedule to the Financial Services and Markets Act 2000 (Collective Investment Schemes) Order 2001, which states that 'arrangements for qualifying crypto-asset staking' are excluded from the meaning of collective investment schemes (CIS) as defined under FSMA 2000.

[40] RAO, Art 9Z7.

[41] RAO, Art 9Z7.

[42] RAO, Art 9Z8.

[43] RAO, Art 9Z9.

12.5. The Regulatory Perimeter – Territorial Scope

There are two elements to this. The first is the question of how non-UK issued crypto-assets can get into the UK in the first place, and the second is how and whether they can be dealt in when they get there.

12.5.1. Public Offers

The essence of the restriction on non-UK crypto-assets getting into the UK is the rule that they cannot be publicly offered in the UK unless they are admitted to trading on a UK regulated trading platform – the UK has no equivalent of the MiCAR provisions that permit crypto-assets to be publicly offered in the EU without being admitted to an EU trading platform if an appropriate white paper is prepared and published.[44] The UK rule is not, of course, a complete prohibition on sales of non-UK crypto-assets, but only of sales of those assets conducted in a particular way. The definition of a 'public offer' is set out in section 102B of FSMA 2000. (based on Article 2(d) of the Prospectus Regulation).[45] The FSMA 2000 definition reads:

> (1) For the purposes of this Part there is an offer of transferable securities to the public if there is a communication to any person which presents sufficient information on—
>
> (a) the transferable securities to be offered, and
> (b) the terms on which they are offered,
>
> to enable an investor to decide to buy or subscribe for the securities in question.

Public offers do not include offers made exclusively to professional investors, and there are some other exemptions in the securities world (for example, private sales, offers to employees, exchange offers &c) but we have yet to find out which of these will be imported into the UK's cryptoregulatory framework. As the FCA have fairly pointed out, one of the effects of the drafting of this definition is that, simply by not disclosing the identity of the offeror, any resulting communication in respect of securities can be taken outside the scope of this definition, since without that information the communication concerned cannot constitute 'sufficient information'.[46] To be fair, the FCA has made clear that it does not regard this as a sensible approach to the regulation of product sales, and indicated that it will be unsympathetic to such arguments.[47] Even the FCA has limited scope to operate

[44] MiCAR, Art 4.
[45] (EU) 2017/1129.
[46] FCA Primary Markets Technical Note of May 2022 Primary Market/TN/601.3.
[47] FCA Report – Quality of Advice on Structured Investment Products, 27 October 2009.

in contravention of the clear words of the law, but it seems clear that the FCA is likely to take any attempt to provide services to UK retail investors in crypto-assets which are not admitted to trading on a UK venue to be in breach of this new regime.

When a crypto-asset is admitted to trading on a UK regulated trading platform, it, its issuer and the platform will become subject to regulatory obligations. The obligations on the issuer (and potentially the platform) largely replicate the MiCAR 'white paper' requirements.[48]

12.5.2. Secondary Trading

It is therefore possible for crypto-assets which have not been admitted to trading on a UK platform to circulate within the UK. However, it will be very hard for a UK non-professional investor to transact in them. UK regulated intermediaries will be prohibited from dealing in such crypto-assets with retail investors,[49] so his only hope will be to try and deal directly with an overseas provider. This, of course, raises the question of whether such a provider would be permitted to deal with him.

The ordinary UK rules as to territorial scope are rewritten for crypto-assets. The basis of UK financial regulation is that what is regulated is business done from the UK or into the UK.[50] In principle, therefore, any non-UK person who deals with ordinary UK persons falls within the scope of FSMA 2000. This problem is dealt with by the regime for securities known as the 'Overseas Persons Exemption (OPE)',[51] which (broadly) exempts from UK regulation an overseas person who deals with a UK person where the parties have communicated in a way which does not contravene UK law (broadly, where the overseas party has not engaged in regulated financial promotion in the UK). This provision permits the UK to operate as an international financial centre, since in general, communications between institutional and professional investors do not contravene the regulated financial promotion. Communications with retail investors, however, do, and since the market for crypto-assets is currently primarily a retail market, the question of the application of the OPE to it is a matter of some difficulty. HMT has elected to cut this Gordian knot by disapplying the OPE to transactions in crypto-assets. However, in order to avoid turning the UK into an international pariah in this regard, it has been forced to come up with an alternative exemption. This is set out in the new subsection 6A of section 418 of FSMA 2000.[52] This

[48] DP 24/4, paras 2.24 and 2.25, cf MiCAR, Art 19.
[49] CP 25/15, para 2.18.
[50] FSMA 2000, s 19.
[51] RAO, Art 72.
[52] Inserted by Art 4(3) of the Order (n 14).

addresses the question of when an overseas firm should be treated as engaging in activities in the UK. It reads as follows:

> (6A) The ninth case is where—
>
> (a) the person ('P') is carrying on a regulated crypto-asset activity and, in doing so, is involved directly or indirectly in the sale, or subscription of, a qualifying crypto-asset to, or by, a consumer ('C') in the United Kingdom, and
>
> (b) there is no other person who is—
>
> (i) authorised to carry on a regulated crypto-asset activity of a kind referred to in subsection (6B)(a) or (b),
>
> (ii) carrying on that activity in relation to the sale or subscription, and
>
> (iii) in doing so is acting as an intermediary between P and C.
>
> (6B) In subsection (6A), a 'regulated crypto-asset activity' means a regulated activity specified by the following articles of the Regulated Activities Order —
>
> (a) article 9T (operating a qualifying crypto-asset trading platform),
>
> (b) article 9U (dealing in qualifying crypto-assets as principal),
>
> (c) article 9X (dealing in qualifying crypto-assets as agent),
>
> (d) article 9Z (arranging deals in qualifying crypto-assets).
>
> (6C) The tenth case is where the person is—
>
> (a) carrying on a regulated activity specified in—
>
> (i) article 9O (safeguarding of qualifying crypto-assets and relevant specified investment crypto-assets) of the Regulated Activities Order, or
>
> (ii) article 9Z7 (qualifying crypto-asset staking) of the Regulated Activities Order,
>
> (b) is doing so directly or indirectly on behalf of a consumer in the United Kingdom, and
>
> (c) in the case of a regulated activity specified by article 9O, is not carrying on the activity at the direction of a person who is authorised to carry on a regulated activity of that kind.
>
> (6D) In subsections (6A) to (6C)—
>
> (a) 'consumer' means an individual who is acting for purposes outside those of any trade, business or profession carried on by the individual;
>
> (b) 'directly' means without an intermediary;
>
> (c) 'indirectly' means through an intermediary;
>
> (d) 'Regulated Activities Order' means the Financial Services and Markets Act 2000 (Regulated Activities) Order 2001;
>
> (e) where a term that is used is also used in Chapter 2B (crypto-assets) of Part 2 (specified activities) of the Regulated Activities Order, then it has the same meaning as that given in that Chapter.

This creates something of an 'elephant trap' for non-professional UK crypto-asset market participants – if they are not acting for the purpose of a trade, business or profession, non-UK service providers are effectively prohibited from dealing with them. However, by designating themselves as acting pursuant to such a trade they open themselves to adverse tax treatment by the UK revenue authorities. There is probably a sliver of hard standing between Article 9U of RAO and section 418(6A) of FSMA 2000, but the size and shape of this sliver is yet to be determined.

A likely consequence of this would be that most non-UK platforms and all non-UK stablecoin issuers will seek to geofence UK retail customers away from their platforms and instruments. This in turn will mean that UK retail investors who wish to participate directly in the global crypto-markets will be obliged to deal through DEXs,[53] and may well find their trading confined to those tokens which do not have an identifiable issuer.

This approach is in line with the UK's general policy of trying to prevent retail investors investing in anything other than a small group of regulated products. One way of looking at this is that the FCA had largely succeeded in squeezing UK retail investors out of the existing markets,[54] and are alarmed that the existing ease of access by retail investors to crypto-asset trading platforms is driving an upsurge in retail investment which is not intermediated by regulated firms. The economics of this are not difficult to understand – the UK regulatory system places a very significant burden of compliance costs and potential compensation liabilities on any person who deals with retail customers, and these costs are necessarily passed on to those customers. It is unsurprising that investors wanting to invest but being unwilling to pay these costs have flocked to an alternative investment venue which does not impose such (or, apparently, any) charges.

It seems unlikely in practice that the FCA will be prepared to engage in a face-off with a large and active UK retail investor base. This is supported by the inclusion in the policy documents of warm words about the undesirability of cutting UK investors off from global liquidity pools,[55] since that would significantly increase their costs of dealing, and – not coincidentally – significantly incentivise UK investors to find ways to circumvent a regime, which they would perceive as acting strongly against their own interests. The likely end-point – as suggested in the HMT response to consultation itself[56] – will be for the UK to create a series of 'temporary' ad hoc exemptions for global liquidity pools which are operated in jurisdictions which meet international standards pending the establishment of formalised deference/equivalence arrangements. Whether the United States will have any interest in establishing any such formalised arrangements remains to be seen.

[53] For example, Uniswap.

[54] UK retail investment in listed equities and mutual funds is famously the lowest in the G7 – see 'Tell Sid and Tell Him Again' (Aberdeen, January 2025).

[55] 'Response' 4.29.

[56] 'Response' para 4.28.

12.6. Issuance of Stablecoins

There are two primary requirements placed on UK issuers of stablecoins. One is the requirement to have appropriate capital.[57] This in practice comes down to a requirement for such an issuer to have capital equal to 2 per cent of the average qualifying stablecoin in issuance.[58] The other is the requirement that the issuer must be prepared to redeem all coins on demand by the end of the next business day following the receipt of the demand.[59]

The major innovation for the UK in this regard is the provision that assets held by a stablecoin issuer will be held on a statutory trust for the coin owners.[60]

The key point here is that there are broadly two regulatory mechanisms which can be used to deal with assets administered by a regulated firm for the benefit of clients. One is the depository model used for funds – a third-party depositary is appointed to hold the funds concerned directly for the end-investors. The primary claim of the investors is against the depository, and the manager has a mere right to instruct the depository as to how the resulting pool is to be invested. The other is the investment firm model as set out in (inter alia) MiFID.[61] In this case the assets placed with the firm belong to the firm, and the investors have a mere claim against the firm. However, the firm is required to place the assets concerned with a third-party custodian, on terms that if the firm fails, those assets will be held for the clients. This is the client asset model (known in the UK as the CASS model, after the relevant section of the FCA rulebook).[62]

The UK, having considered the imposition of the depository model,[63] has elected to impose the CASS model. The effect of English Law is that the pool of assets maintained by the firm is held on a statutory trust for the clients[64] – an arrangement which provides a very high level of protection for those clients collectively. The quid pro quo for this is that stablecoin issuers are subjected to the full breadth of the CASS rules (including the appointment of a 'CASS oversight officer'), including the rules on daily reconciliations and other book-keeping measures. These measures are widely regarded as bureaucratic and onerous.

Finally, there is the issue of the obligations of issuers towards retail token holders. The FCA say that they will impose the 'consumer duty' on issuers.[65] However,

[57] As set out in FCA CP 25/15, 'A prudential regime for crypto-asset firms'.

[58] CP 25/15, para 4.27. This is the same level of requirement as is imposed by MiCAR (Art 35(1)(b)).

[59] Although regulators would have the power to defer this in emergencies – DP23/4, para 3.48; CP 25/14, paras 3.135–3.139.

[60] See CP 25/14, paras 3.82–3.90.

[61] Markets in Financial Instruments Directive 2004/39/EC.

[62] FCA Handbook, Client Assets Sourcebook.

[63] See DP 23/4, paras 3.35–3.38.

[64] FSMA 2000, s 137B(1)(a) has the effect that such a trust arises where it is provided for in FCA rules.

[65] DP 23/4, para 4.2.

it appears that this will be in the form of a general obligation to design products and communicate in a fair and open manner. There is therefore (as yet) no sign of a formal set of consumer obligations imposed on issuers in respect of specific holders as there is in MiCAR.[66]

As noted above, the initial intention of the UK was that stablecoins used for payment which are deemed to be 'systemic' should be jointly regulated by the FCA and the Bank of England, and to this end provisions have been included in the Banking Act 2009 setting out the type of crypto-asset which the Bank could regulate on this basis. This relates to 'digital settlement assets' (DSAs). These are defined as follows:[67]

> 'digital settlement asset' means a digital representation of value or rights, whether or not cryptographically secured, that—
>
> (a) can be used for the settlement of payment obligations,
> (b) can be transferred, stored or traded electronically, and
> (c) uses technology supporting the recording or storage of data (which may include distributed ledger technology).
>
> In this section, 'digital settlement asset' includes a right to, or an interest in, a digital settlement asset.[68]

'DSA service provider' is defined as follows:

> a person who provides one or more services in relation to a payment system that includes arrangements using digital settlement assets where—
>
> (a) the person creates or issues the digital settlement assets involved in the payment system,
> (b) the person provides services to safeguard, or to safeguard and administer, digital settlement assets including their private cryptographic keys (or means of access),
> (c) the person is directly involved in any of the activities mentioned in paragraphs (a) or (b),
> (d) the person is a digital settlement asset exchange provider,
> (e) the person sets rules, standards, or conditions of access or participation in relation to the payment system, or
> (f) the person provides any service that facilitates, or supports, a transfer of money or digital settlement assets to be made using the payment system, including any infrastructure provider in relation to the system.[69]

'digital settlement asset exchange provider' is defined as follows:

> a person who provides one or more of the following services, including as creator or issuer of any of the digital settlement assets, by—

[66] MiCAR, Art 14.

[67] Text inserted in s 182 (Interpretation of Payment System) of the Banking Act 2009 by para 4 of Sch 6 to the FSMA 2023.

[68] Banking Act 2009, s 182(4A).

[69] Banking Act 2009, s 182(5A).

(a) exchanging, or arranging the exchange of—
  (i) digital settlement assets for money,
  (ii) money for digital settlement assets,
  (iii) digital settlement assets and money for digital settlement assets, or
  (iv) digital settlement assets and money for money,

(b) exchanging, or arranging the exchange of, one digital settlement asset for another, or

(c) operating an automated process to carry out any of the activities mentioned in paragraphs (a) and (b).[70]

The interesting thing about this definition is that, unlike that in the FSMA, it is not confined to cryptographically secured assets. The point here is that it is considered undesirable within the payments regulatory framework to have two separate regimes, one for crypto-tokens and another for other forms of tokens. As HMT explain, 'A "digital settlement asset" comprises … those digital assets that can be used for the settlement of payments … [and] it therefore covers other digital assets that can be used for the settlement of payments, as well as crypto-assets used in payments.'[71]

Where an FCA authorised DSA service provider is recognised as systemic by HM Treasury, and thus should be supervised by the Bank of England, the Bank of England becomes the primary supervisor.[72] However, the firm will continue to be regulated by the FCA for conduct. The Payment Systems Regulator[73] will also regulate such fiat-backed stablecoin firms for competition, innovation and access purposes.

The logic of giving the Bank of England a regulatory role in addition to the FCA is that the Bank's focus is primarily on avoiding problems concerning the interaction of DSAs and the existing bank deposit system. However, for providers that are not deposit-takers, the designation of the provider as systemic will enable the Bank of England to deal with the insolvency or financial collapse of these entities by applying the Financial Market Infrastructure Special Administrative Rules (the FMI SARs).[74] These rules restrict the powers of persons other than the Bank in relation to the insolvency of infrastructure companies, and enable the Bank to exercise a degree of control over the way in which such failures are managed. However, as the Bank itself points out 'the modified FMI SAR is not a resolution regime, so it will not have the range of tools to facilitate continuity of service

[70] Banking Act 2009, s 182(5B).

[71] HM Treasury, 'Consultation and Call for Evidence on the future financial services regulatory regime' (February 2023) para 2.2.

[72] It derives its powers in this regard from Part 5 of the Banking Act 2009. A new s 184A (inserted by FSMA 2023) provides that a DSA service provider may be specified by a recognition order, and s 185A sets out the criteria which must be satisfied before such an order is made.

[73] Under Part 5 of the Financial Services (Banking Reform) Act 2013. A new s 41(2A), (inserted by FSMA 2023) expands the scope of the term 'payment system' to systems dealing with DSAs.

[74] Implemented for existing Financial Market Infrastructures by Part 6 of the Financial Systems (Banking Reform) Act 2013.

in the way that resolution regimes do for the largest deposit-takers. In addition, the timeliness of payout by issuers will be dependent on the speed with which administrators are able to make such payout.'[75]

12.7. Custody of Qualifying Stablecoins

The regime for custodians of qualifying crypto-assets tracks that for issuers fairly closely. Most importantly, the existing UK rules for client assets (the CASS rules described above) will be applied to assets held in custody in the same way as they are applied to the backing pool for a stablecoin. This means that such assets will be held on a statutory trust for the customers of the custodian on its failure. There has been some debate as to whether client assets should be held in separate accounts, but the FCA has decided that multiple clients assets will be permitted to be held in 'omnibus' accounts.[76] Again the full panoply of CASS requirements will be imposed on the custodian.

There are two specific issues on which FCA is currently undecided. One is as to the use of client assets. In existing securities legislation, this is generally permitted for institutional clients only subject to strict safeguards, and broadly prohibited for retail clients.[77] However, FCA note that in the current crypto markets it is common for custodians (usually as platform providers) to have use of client assets for purposes of staking, collateral or for lending purposes,[78] and that imposing the existing securities rules would cause significant disruption to existing business models. It is therefore in search of a policy.

The second issue is structural separation. After the failure of FTX, the idea of structural separation of client custody activities has become more prevalent in the crypto world, but there is still considerable debate as to whether this is necessary or desirable, and whether sufficiently robust internal procedures could be employed. The FCA clearly leans towards requiring structural separation of trading platforms and custody service provision, but is seeking further input on this issue.[79]

Another of the significant differences between the EU and the UK regimes is as regards capital requirements. The UK has decided that it should impose on both crypto issuers and custodians the capital requirements imposed on investment firms generally by the UK adopted text of the EU Regulation on the Prudential Requirements of Investment Firms[80] (IFPR). Two of these – the base

[75] Bank of England, 'Dear CEO' letter of 6 November 2023, www.bankofengland.co.uk/-/media/boe/files/prudential-regulation/letter/2023/november/innovations-in-the-use-of-deposits-emoney-and-regulated-stablecoins.pdf.
[76] CP 25/14, para 4.26.
[77] DP 23/4, para 5.2.1.
[78] DP 23/4, para 5.23.
[79] DP 23/4, para 5.52.
[80] (EU) 2019/2033.

minimum requirement and the requirement for 13 weeks' operating expenses – are uncontroversial. The third, however, is an issue for hot debate. IFPR provides that investment firms generally should face a third requirement, known as the K-Factor, which scales with the business of the firm. The FCA suggests that it will impose this requirement on custodians of crypto-assets, at a level of 0.04 per cent of average assets held in custody, which is equal to the requirement that would be imposed on an investment firm holding client assets in segregated accounts.[81] However, the UK 'double-counts' this requirement – this, if an investment firm delegates the management of a custody pool to a third party authorised custodian, both the third party and the stablecoin issuer will have to maintain the relevant level of capital in respect of it.[82]

12.8. Operating a Crypto-asset Trading Venue

The crypto trading platforms which exist today are generally one-stop shops, providing trading, dealing, custody and provision of credit to customers of all kinds.[83] The regulatory structure that the UK has created for trading venues effectively marries the MiFID regime for Regulated Markets and Multilateral Trading Facilities with the listing regime. The MiFID element is clearest in the requirement that the operator functions on a non-discretionary basis[84] (ie, is a passive venue provider), that the platform provider cannot trade on its own platform,[85] and that it must assume client obligations to any retail client to whom it gives access.[86] At the same time, it will be required to accept the liabilities of a regulated market as quasi-listing authority, being required to approve any crypto-asset which it admits to trading, and presumably having some degree of regulatory liability for non-disclosures by issuers of such crypto-assets. HMT and the FCA helpfully suggest that the trading platforms concerned might achieve this by establishing a branch of the trading platform in the UK along with a separate UK established and authorised subsidiary which could take on these regulatory liabilities, thereby effecting a degree of separation between the platform itself and the other activities.[87] It is also notable that FCA propose that such platforms should be subject to the majority of rules which apply to MTFs, such as those relating to algorithmic trading[88] and market-maker agreements,[89] which would constitute fairly major changes to the

[81] See FCA Handbook, MIFIDPRU 4.8 (K-CMH requirement).
[82] CP 25/15, para 4.43.
[83] DP 25/1, Annex 2 (p 66).
[84] DP 25/1, para 2.41.
[85] DP 25/1, para 2.49.
[86] DP 25/1, paras 2.24–2.26.
[87] DP 25/1, para 2.13.
[88] DP 25/1, paras 2.27–2.32.
[89] DP 25/1, paras 2.33–2.37.

business model of the firms concerned. It is also fair to say that these measures are not perceived as particularly useful in the markets to which they currently apply.

12.9. Broker/Dealers

The broker-dealer regime proposed by the FCA is at heart a straightforward copy of that which is imposed on MiFID broker-dealers – order handling and best execution[90] and execution venue rules[91] will all be imposed. Intermediaries will be subject to post-trade transparency requirements,[92] and there seems to be some idea of imposing pre-trade transparency obligations (as for MiFID Systematic Internalisers[93]) as well.[94]

The thing which should give pause in this regard is therefore the fact that the crypto-asset market as it is today is not generally an intermediated market[95] – users predominantly have direct access to trading venues. However, if the proposal discussed above to impose client obligations on UK platforms who grant direct access to retail investors is implemented, it seems likely that this access will cease, and retail business will be forced through an intermediated channel. This is likely to have significant costs for customers – it is proposed that intermediaries will be subject to the full burden of the UK rules relating to suitability, the RDR rules on charging for advice, and the Customer Duty with its accompanying obligations to provide monetary compensation to customers who lose money. It is, however, fairly clear that the FCA wish to see all UK retail crypto-asset business passing through regulated intermediaries. A part of this may well be that they propose to use this to block any access by UK retail investors to overseas crypto-assets not listed on a UK regulated trading platform. This is to be accomplished by banning intermediaries from dealing with UK customers in any such crypto-asset.[96]

12.10. Market Abuse

The basic structure of UK market abuse regulation is that if a person anywhere in the world takes an action whose consequence is to manipulate the price of an asset traded on a UK trading venue, that person breaks UK law as regards market manipulation. The obvious starting point for the UK would therefore be to apply this approach to crypto-assets. Unfortunately, the effect of such an approach would

[90] DP 25/1, para 3.19.
[91] DP 25/1, para 3.30.
[92] DP 25/1, para 3.58.
[93] Markets in Financial Instruments Regulation, Art 14 (EU 2014/600).
[94] DP 25/1, para 3.59.
[95] DP 25/1, para 3.4.
[96] DP 25/21, para 3.18.

be to require UK venues to perform a global policeman role for which they are highly unlikely to have either the resources or the necessary information. In the securities markets, it is reasonable for trading venues to be required to monitor trading on their venues and to identify possible manipulation. In the crypto markets, by contrast, UK trading venues will be unlikely to see more than a small proportion of the total trading in some of the larger crypto-assets. It therefore seems unreasonable to expect such venues to monitor the entire global market in order to identify manipulation.

The HMT proposals for the crypto market suggested introducing a market abuse regime for crypto-asset trading based on elements of the Market Abuse Regulation (UK MAR[97]) regime which currently applies to financial instruments.[98] The market abuse offences would apply to all persons committing market abuse on a crypto-asset that is admitted (or requested to be admitted) to trading on a UK crypto-asset trading venue. This would apply regardless of where the person is based or where the trading takes place. The proposed regime would entail obligations for certain market participants – thus, for example, crypto-asset trading venues would be expected to detect and disrupt market abuse behaviours, and crypto-asset market intermediaries would have obligations placed on them, in particular around the handling of inside information.[99]

This has been translated by the FCA into an almost complete transplant of the existing MAR regime.[100]

There are two major parts to the market abuse regime – insider dealing and market manipulation.

12.10.1. Insider Dealing

It is very hard to understand the logic behind the FCA's position on insider dealing. It is hard to imagine circumstances in which dealing in a pure or fiat-based crypto-asset could be based on inside information,[101] since it is almost impossible to imagine what sort of information could have this characteristic as regards the price of these assets. The FCA can only come up with two possibilities, one being information that a particular asset might be about to be admitted to trading, and the other being information held by an intermediary or platform provider about future orders.[102] However, despite the fact that it is virtually impossible to see what this regime might capture, it is nonetheless proposed that there should

[97] This is the UK version of (EU) 2014/596.
[98] Response, para 9.1.
[99] Response, para 9.1.
[100] DP 24/4, ch 4.
[101] Although, in a tribute to human ingenuity, there has been at least one case of insider dealing in crypto-coins (*SEC v Wahi*, settled 30 May2023, SEC 2023-98).
[102] DP 24/4, para 3.20.

be a disclosure obligation,[103] a central announcement venue,[104] and potentially a requirement for the maintenance of 'insider lists'.[105]

This regime is likely to raise a difficult issue for issuers and trading platforms. Trading platforms are not only permitted but positively encouraged to prepare and file disclosure documents for third party crypto-assets in order to bring them onto their platforms. However, if a UK trading platform does this, the issuer of the crypto-asset concerned will become subject to the full weight of these restrictions, and will have no way to protect itself from any subsequently arising liability. It is possible that this may lead to such issuers seeking actively to prevent UK trading platforms from admitting them to trading in this way.

The only area here where there seems to be serious doubt is as to 'MEV' strategies. HMT give the following example:

> … with proof-of-stake (PoS) and proof-of-work (PoW) mechanisms, pending transactions may be queued in a publicly visible waiting area called a memory pool, or 'mempool', until a miner or validator selects them to be incorporated into a transaction block. Miners and validators have found ways to profit from what is called Maximal Extractable Value (also referred to as Miner Extractable Value, in each case 'MEV'). strategies. These strategies may involve excluding, or reprioritising transactions from the mempool. This can result in sub-optimal outcomes for investors and may create opportunities for frontrunning or at least frontrunning-like behaviour.[106]

It is a reasonable subject for debate as to whether these strategies – which are currently common – should be prohibited or not, and, if so, how such a prohibition might operate.[107]

12.10.2. Market Manipulation

The risk of market manipulation in crypto-asset markets would seem considerably greater than in the securities markets, as the crypto markets are both less transparent and more fragmented than traditional markets. This fragmented and incomplete trading data could enable the exploitation of individual participants.

The FCA's approach to market manipulation appears to rely on requiring trading platform providers and intermediaries to maintain 'rigorous' systems and controls to detect it and to be 'pro-active' in implementing them.[108] However, in order to know that market abuse is occurring, it is necessary for at least trading venues to have more or less real-time information as to what trading is being done

[103] DP 24/4, paras 3.29–3.30.
[104] DP 24/4, paras 3.31–3.43.
[105] DP 24/4, paras 3.69–3.72.
[106] Response 9.3. This issue is considered further in R Auer, J Frost and JM Vidal Pastor, 'Miners as intermediaries: extractable value and market manipulation in crypto and DeFi' (2022) 58 *BIS Bulletin*.
[107] DP 24/4, para 3.50.
[108] DP 24/4, paras 3.62 and 3.65.

in the market as a whole for the relevant crypto-asset. Establishing this would involve a fairly high degree of information sharing between trading venues and the UK regulator. FCA do accept that this is only likely to be feasible if there is a considerable amount of cross-platform information sharing.[109]

12.11. Other Issues

12.11.1. Insolvency

In the case of firm failure, the standard corporate insolvency procedures under the Insolvency Act 1986 (eg, liquidation and administration under Schedule B1) will be applicable to UK issuers of fiat-backed stablecoins. Part XXIV of FSMA 2000 provides the FCA with specific powers to intervene in insolvency procedures of this kind in order to protect consumers, and these provisions will be extended to apply to failures of issuers of fiat-backed stablecoins in or from the UK. For issuers designated as systemic the Financial Market Infrastructure Special Administration Regime (FMI SAR) will apply.

The FCA's powers under Part 24 of FSMA 2000 will also be extended to custodians of UK issued fiat-backed stablecoins, so that the FCA has the same rights to participate and protect consumers in an insolvency process as it does for other FCA supervised firms. Likewise, the Government intends to apply the FMI SAR, with modifications, as the primary regime to be used in the event of the failure of a systemic DSA custodian.

12.11.2. Settlement Finality

HM Treasury have also undertaken to clarify the application of the Settlement Finality Regulations 1999 (SFRs).[110] The purpose of the SFRs is to mitigate the potential systemic impact of a participant in a system becoming insolvent. This is achieved by Bank of England designation of the relevant system under the SFRs, which protects the designated system and its participants against the adverse operation of certain provisions of UK insolvency law. Under the existing SFRs, only a system for the clearing or execution of transfer orders/instructions: (i) involving the transfer of money or the assumption or discharge of a payment obligation, and/or (ii) involving the transfer of title to or an interest in 'securities' (defined by reference to existing categories of authorised financial instruments) can apply

[109] DP 24/4, para 3.64.

[110] Financial Markets and Insolvency (Settlement Finality) Regulations 1999, SOI 1999/2979, implementing Directive 98/26/EC of the European Parliament and of the Council of 19 May 1998 on settlement finality in payment and securities settlement systems.

for designation. HM Treasury therefore intends to vary the SFRs to enable a system involving the transfer of DSA to be designated under these regulations.[111] However, this task is not as straightforward as it appears, because key concepts such as references to a 'system operator' responsible for the operation of the system and 'book-entry' records and the maintenance of 'accounts' may not map straightforwardly onto DSA systems.

12.11.3. Central Bank Digital Currency

The UK authorities (and in particular the Bank of England) are investigating the development of CBDCs without expressing any particular enthusiasm for the project. The Bank of England and HMT have produced a joint paper setting out their thoughts on how a UK CBDC might operate,[112] and the policy issues which arise in the context of the CBDC project are currently undergoing detailed consideration. However in a recent speech the Governor of the Bank of England, Andrew Bailey, said

> [Are there] reasons why in the retail space, digital payments need to be done in a newly created Central Bank Digital Currency? A priori, I think the answer to this is that commercial bank money – i.e. banks – is the best home for such innovation. But if for some reason innovation in unlikely to happen, then the central banks have to decide whether they are the only game in town. For me, this justifies why we must continue to prepare for retail CBDC. We have not yet seen enough evidence that the innovation will happen in commercial banks. As central banks, we should be thoroughly engaged to encourage, and if necessary, provide such innovation – but there is no good reason to be proprietorial on this.[113]

A UK CBDC would fall outside the definition of 'qualifying Crypto-asset',[114] and would require its own regulatory architecture.

12.11.4. Lending and Staking

The essence of staking is that an owner of a crypto-asset agrees to immobilise it for a specified period of time, and permit a third party (a 'validator') to treat that crypto-asset as their own for the purpose of validating transactions.[115] Some of the fee received by the validator is then shared with the provider of the staked

[111] Response, 4.8.

[112] 'Response to the Bank of England and HM Treasury Consultation Paper: The digital pound; a new form of money for households and businesses?' (HMT, January 2024).

[113] 'The future of money and payments – speech by Andrew Bailey Given at Group of Thirty's 39th Annual International Banking Seminar, Washington' (26 October 2024).

[114] RAO, Art 88F(4)(d).

[115] Staking is only possible for those coins which employ a 'proof of stake' validation mechanism. It therefore only applies to some crypto-assets.

crypto-assets. Some cryptocurrency exchanges offer staking services, handling the staking process on a blockchain network and distributing staking rewards to participants. Staking is in many respects similar to lending, but it has the essential distinction that the crypto-asset owner never loses ownership of the crypto-asset.

The FCA have a number of concerns in this area. One – technological resilience and third-party dependency is universal across the industry – but creates a special vulnerability in this context because of the risk of 'slashing'.[116] Another is the safeguarding of staked crypto-assets. FCA would like to require segregate a single customer's crypto-assets into a single wallet for each staking product.[117] More nebulously, there are expressed concerns about 'customer understanding'. Precisely what anyone is expected to do about this is unclear, but the idea that a 'key features' document[118] will help seems far-fetched.

12.11.5. Decentralised Finance (DeFi)

This is an issue which HMT readily accepts is too difficult to be tackled by any regulator in isolation, and it will wait for further progress to be made at the international level before seeking to regulate DeFi per se.[119] However, the question as to how to approach arrangements of this kind is a live one.

The term 'DeFi' refers to arrangements where multiple users use programmes on their own computers (decentralised apps or ('dApps')) to interact with other users on a Blockchain. The interactions are made possible via 'smart contracts' – open sourced, codified sets of rules which automatically execute and record transactions on the blockchain when certain parameters are met. Once entered into, smart contracts are immutable. This arrangement enables users to transact with each other without centralised decision making from intermediaries.

The problem that DeFi creates for regulators is that there appears to be nothing to regulate. It is a general principle of financial regulation not to regulate end-users, and it would be a category error to regulate providers of software as if they were the providers of the services which that software enables its users to access. The problem, however, is that the proposition that we regulate centralised finance (CeFi) but not DeFi immediately runs into problems in that there is in reality a continuum of business models between the two.[120] Thus, although the regulation of DeFi itself may be put off until a later day, the question of how to distinguish CeFi from DeFi – that is, to distinguish arrangements where a person is providing

[116] See DP 25/1, para 6.6.
[117] DP 25/1, para 6.31.
[118] Proposed in DP 25/1, para 6.28.
[119] 'Response' 11.28.
[120] K Schuler, AS Cloots and F Schär, 'On DeFi and On-Chain CeFi: How (Not) to Regulate Decentralized Finance' (2024) 10(2) *Journal of Financial Regulation* 213; OECD, 'Why Decentralised Finance (DeFi) Matters and the Policy Implications' (19 January 2022); S Aramonte, W Huang and A Schrimpf, 'DeFi Risks and the Decentralisation Illusion' (2021) *BIS Quarterly Review* 21.

a service from arrangements where they are merely providing software – is live today.

HMT therefore identify five main features that separate CeFi from DeFi:[121]

- Self-custody. In DeFi only the owner has possession of the private key to access their private keys.
- Autonomy. DeFi is reliant only on the execution of transactions through smart contracts.
- Transparency. DeFi activity is recorded on a public blockchain and based on open sourced code.
- Composability. This concerns interoperability of DeFi protocols and dApps.
- Control. DeFi by its nature is decentralised and controlled by a network of users; CeFi is controlled by a single person/small, centralised group.

The other question which arises in this context is as to what 'decentralised' means in practice. In particular, since DeFi arrangements are not covered by the regulatory regime, it is entirely possible that there may well be a rush to develop DeFi functionality. FCAs position is as follows

> When DeFi involves the proposed regulated activities, and where there is a clear controlling person(s) carrying on an activity, then these activities will be covered by the regime, for example, services that involve an identifiable intermediary or entity that has control over business operations and product features.[122]

12.11.6. Tokenised Bank Deposits

Today bank deposits form the vast majority of the money held and used by people and businesses in the UK. However, most large deposit-takers have been exploring the use of new technologies in accepting deposits, for example the 'tokenisation' of deposits. The regulation of tokenised deposits will be separated from the regulation of fiat-backed stablecoins. This is because tokenised deposits are covered by the existing deposit taking activity in Article 5 (accepting deposits) of the RAO.

It is not always easy to distinguish a bank issued crypto-asset from a tokenised bank deposit – there is a useful report from the EBA discussing the difference.[123]

The protections available to retail depositors in particular reflect the importance for financial stability of ensuring confidence in deposits and – by extension – in deposit-taking institutions. Alongside deposits, non-deposit forms of digital money or money-like instruments are increasing in availability. Protections for

[121] 'Response' 11.14.
[122] DP 25/1, para 7.4.
[123] EBA Report on Tokenised Deposits, December 2024, EBA/REP/2024/2.

retail holders of e-money and regulated stablecoins differ from those for retail depositors. Thus, in the same way that FSCS protection will not be available in respect of regulated stablecoin issuers or custodians[124] – in particular, holders of bank issued stablecoins will not be protected by the deposit protection scheme in the same way as ordinary depositors, since such stablecoins do not fall within the definition of 'deposit' under Article 5 of the RAO.

This confusion is perceived as posing a systemic threat to the financial system more broadly. The concern is that if customers cannot clearly distinguish between bank deposits and holdings of bank-issued digital money, the result may be a collapse of confidence in the UK banking and payments systems generally.

The Bank of England has therefore written to UK regulated banks[125] to set out a number of measures intended to avoid this outcome. These are:

> First, deposit-takers should ensure that deposit-taking entities only provide innovations in digital money to retail customers in the form of deposits. If deposit-takers or their groups want to issue e-money or regulated stablecoins to retail customers, then this should be done from separate non-deposit-taking and insolvency-remote entities, ensuring that: (i) they have distinct branding to the deposit-taker; and (ii) their failure would not have adverse impacts on the rest of the deposit-taking group and the continuity of its deposit-taking services. We recognise that a small number of deposit takers have already issued e-money to retail customers from a deposit-taking entity. These deposit-takers should engage with the PRA on how they intend to mitigate the risk of contagion and restructure their activities as soon as practicable. The PRA recognises such deposit-takers may need time to adjust and will adopt a proportionate approach to implementation.
>
> Second, where a firm without a deposit-taking permission has issued e-money or regulated stablecoins to retail customers and seeks a deposit-taking permission, we expect them to transition their UK customers to deposits at the new deposit-taking entity as soon as practicable; and to engage with the PRA on their plans to do so.
>
> Third, where a deposit-taker intends to innovate in the way that it takes deposits from retail customers (e.g. by taking 'tokenised' deposits), we expect this to be done in a way that meets the PRA's rules for eligibility for depositor protection under the FSCS. Deposit-takers must also ensure they meet the single customer view and exclusions view requirements in respect of such deposits. Deposit-takers considering such innovations – especially innovations such as transferable 'tokenised' deposit claims, where they may find it more challenging to meet these rules – should inform their supervisor of their intentions. The PRA will continue to monitor potential risks and risk mitigants for such innovations as more applications and use cases emerge, and may apply additional expectations for them in due course.

These expectations will also be applied to international deposit-takers with UK branches.

[124] FCA DP 23/4, para 7.43.

[125] 'Dear CEO' letter of the 6 November 2023 (n 75).

12.11.7. Advice

The question of whether the giving of advice as regards crypto investments, and the management of crypto portfolios, should be a regulated activity, is a surprisingly difficult one. Part of the problem is that the UK's current investment advice regime requires regulated advisors to be experienced, competent and qualified, and for them to assess that an investment is suitable before making a recommendation. However, the price and value of an unbacked crypto-asset is driven by speculative investment decisions, rather than market fundamentals which can be objectively assessed. This is in contrast to traditional financial assets; even for high-risk investments such as illiquid securities, advisors at least have experience and qualifications to conduct due diligence on the corporate issuer (eg, through assessing projected growth plans). It would be very difficult to require an investment advisor to meet these criteria for crypto-asset investment advice.

As a result, HMT will reconsider this issue at a later date in the light of what is learned from the FMI Sandbox initiative. While crypto-assets are outside of scope, the sandbox will enable firms to experiment with DLT, to provide the services that underpin financial markets. Accepted firms will be able to set up an FMI that utilises new technology within the sandbox, while being subject to modified legislative requirements (where the existing requirements act as a barrier to using new technology).[126]

12.12. Comparison of the UK and MiCAR Approaches to Crypto-assets

12.12.1. Legislative Structure

The UK and EU processes regarding crypto-asset regulation are to some extent illustrations of convergent evolution – different authorities, presented with the same problem, are very likely to produce very similar solutions. However, the differences between them are non-trivial.

The UK and the EU begin with a very similar definition of crypto-asset, so the scope of the two regimes should be very broadly similar. However, the policy and legislative approaches to be taken are very different. Whereas MiCAR is a standalone legislative framework, aimed at creating a separate regime for crypto-assets, the UK intends to regulate this area through an extension of the scope of existing financial regulatory tools. Thus, whereas MiCAR regulates the issuance of crypto assets, the use of stablecoins and the abuse of crypto-asset markets under a single regulatory schema, the UK will achieve these ends by extending the public offers regime, the payment services regime and the market abuse regimen respectively.

[126] Response, paras 12.5–12.6.

This will mean that the question of whether a particular instrument constitutes a 'financial instrument' for MiFID II purposes or not will be more important in the EU than in the UK. This is because in the EU, the MiFID II and MiCAR regimes will exist separately side by side, so the characterisation of an instrument as a 'financial instrument' or not will determine almost every aspect of the rules applicable to it. In the UK, by contrast, the approach of extending existing rules to cover new types of crypto-asset is likely to render this distinction less all-embracing in its consequences – although it will still have significant consequences.

12.12.2. Issuance of Crypto-assets

MiCAR regulates the issuance and offering of crypto-assets to the public in the EU, along with the admission of such assets to trading platforms. The UK prohibits the offering of crypto-assets to the public unless the asset is admitted to trading on a UK regulated trading platform, but does not impose regulatory obligations[127] directly on issuers of crypto-assets per se. However, both regimes will require a disclosure document to be prepared and published when a crypto-asset is offered to the public or admitted to listing on a publicly accessible trading platform. MiCAR describes the required document as a 'white paper', whereas the UK does not use the term. However, once the detailed requirements for the contents of such a document are settled, it seems very unlikely that either the UK or the EU requirements will be satisfied by the white papers currently prepared for crypto-asset issuance. In the EU, in principle, there must be an identifiable legal person who is the offeror for every issue. The UK seems to be less prescriptive, but still requires some person to take responsibility for the offer document.

A significant distinction between the EU and the UK approaches to offer documentation is that the MiCAR approach is based on the idea that the contents of the offer document are prescribed at a high level in MiCAR itself, and then fleshed out in detail by ESMA.[128] That said, for non-stablecoin crypto-assets, MiCAR does not require a white paper to be approved by a listing authority prior to publication. The UK, by contrast, proposes that responsibility for approving the contents of the issue document should be with the regulated trading venue on which the crypto-asset is to be admitted to trading.

12.12.3. Stablecoins

MiCAR sets out requirements for asset-referenced tokens and electronic money tokens. Both MiCAR and the UK identify the possibility to designate certain

[127] Apart from disclosure obligations.

[128] ESMA, Consultation Paper, Technical Standards specifying certain requirements of Markets in Crypto Assets Regulation (MiCAR) – second consultation paper, ESMA75-453128700-438 (5 October 2023).

stablecoins as 'significant', and subject them to a higher level of regulation and to supervision by the banking regulator. Issuance of any such stablecoin will be subject to prior approval by a competent authority, and, where the issuer is a credit institution, a detailed set of rules will regulate that institution's conduct, marketing, communication, governance, organisational and prudential requirements in respect of its issuance business. The UK will regulate the use of what it describes as 'Digital Settlement Assets', but will focus on the use of these assets within the payment system as well as their creation and transfer. Current UK policy effectively prevents UK credit institutions from issuing stablecoins unless the stablecoin is issued by a legal entity which is separate from the regulated bank and is clearly distinguishable as a separate produce from the deposits offered by those banks.

There is a clear distinction between the policy orientations of the UK and the EU as regards stablecoins. The UK seems positively enthusiastic to see fiat-backed stablecoins in circulation as payment media, whereas the EU places a series of formal restrictions on any such circulation. It seems likely that the reason for this is that the ECB is engaged in a significant push to create and issue a CBDC – the 'digital Euro' – and it is likely that both it and the European Commission are therefore unenthusiastic about encouraging the development of a private sector competitor. This is most clearly manifested in the MiCAR provisions to the effect that when the estimated quarterly average number of transactions involving a stablecoin is greater than EUR 1 million, or where the daily value of transactions using it is greater than EUR 200 million, further issuance of the relevant coin will be banned.[129] The UK has almost exactly the opposite position, taking the view that the development of a CBDC should only be undertaken if the private sector fails to take the opportunity to develop new and improved payment mechanisms.

12.12.4. Authorisation

MiCAR adopts the MiFID II classification of services, and broadly provides that any service that would require MiFID authorisation if provided in respect of a MiFID financial instrument will require authorisation if provided in respect of a crypto-asset. It also provides for services to be provided by an undertaking who is not a legal person provided that customers are provided with equivalent legal protections. The UK's approach in this area is more nuanced. Certain services, such as intermediation, are identified as requiring regulation, and the existing authorisation framework will be applied to them. Others, such as investment advice and arranging transactions, are identified as requiring further work before any rules can be made or applied. It is only in the area of custody that the UK accepts that

[129] MiCAR, Art 23. For context, in the second half of 2022, the 29 retail payment systems within the euro area processed around 29.4 billion transactions with a combined value of €23.5 trillion. ECB, 'Payments statistics: first half and second half of 2022' (9 November 2023).

a wholly new regime will have to be constructed to apply across both stablecoins and other crypto-assets.

Another interesting distinction is that the UK regulates dealing as principal in crypto-assets, whereas MiCAR does not. The effect of this is that the UK has to carve back the scope of this regulated activity to exclude persons who do not hold themselves out as securities dealers. The EU, by contrast, has to grapple with the question of when a principle dealer provides a sufficiently publicly available service to qualify as a provider of CASP services to clients.

12.12.5. Financial Promotion

This is an area where the UK's approach has always diverged from that adopted in EU legislation. The general EU approach is to regulate advertising in respect of offers of securities and certain other products, but on a piecemeal product-by-product basis. The UK has a general 'financial promotion' regime which applies to all communications in respect of a wide variety of different types of financial product and instruments. The difference is that whereas the EU approach identifies with some precision the communications which it restricts, the UK approach is based on a broad prohibition of communications of any kind, accompanied by a broad set of exclusions within which advertisers may operate. Both the UK and the EU will apply their traditional approaches to crypto-asset marketing.

12.12.6. Location Requirements

MiCAR requires a service provider to be a legal person resident in the EU before they can be authorised to provide services in the EU, and it expects that person to have its place of effective management in the EU. The UK, by contrast, is open to offshore firms operating through a UK-authorised branch, provided that the UK authorities are satisfied that UK customers are appropriately protected.

12.12.7. Trading Venues

Operators of trading venues under MiCAR will be subject to broadly similar rules to those which are applied to trading venues under MiFID II – in particular, operators of platforms will be prohibited from dealing on their own account on their platforms.[130] They will, however, be allowed to engage in matched principal trading with appropriate client consents. The effect of the MiCAR provisions, taken as a whole, is to seek to force trading venue operators into the mould of MiFID II venues. The UK

[130] MiCAR, Art 76(5).

approach is somewhat different. The UK begins by accepting that the crypto-asset trading venues which exist today are very different from those which exist in the securities world. In particular, many crypto venues have vertically integrated models in which they may take custody of participant funds, issue their own securities, extend credit to members, or act (in effect) as a central clearing counterparty. The UK takes the view that it should be possible to accommodate structures of this kind within the existing regulatory architecture provided that sufficient attention is paid to the existence and resolution of conflicts of interest, although they acknowledge that some conflicts may prove irresolvable and will have to be prohibited.

12.12.8. Staking

MiCAR does not provide for the regulation of crypto-lending or staking platforms. The UK, however, proposes to regulate these, although these proposals are currently at an early stage of development.

12.12.9. Cross-border Business

Crypto-asset service providers authorised under MiCAR will be authorised by the competent authority in their home Member State, and will therefore be passported to operate in other EU states, and to establish branches. However, since the main centres of the crypto-asset markets are outside both the EU and the UK, the primary question as regards cross-border business is the extent which it will be possible for customers in the UK or the EU to access these markets and venues.

MiFID II deals with this issue by setting out provisions governing the terms on which non-EU firms may be able to provide services into the EU ('third country' provisions). MiCAR has no such provisions.[131] This means that persons located in a non-EU jurisdiction and wishing to actively promote and/or advertise their services to clients in the EU will have to obtain full authorisation in an EU Member State, which in turn will necessitate establishing a subsidiary in that state and conducting their business through that subsidiary. The UK, by contrast, seems to be prepared to permit non-UK firms to do regulated business in the UK, provided they do so through a branch.

Unlike other EU financial legislation, MiCAR does not contain a mutual recognition mechanism. The UK, by contrast, expresses the hope that major jurisdictions will be prepared to enter into mutual recognition arrangements with each other that will permit seamless cross-border activity, and purports to be prepared to enter into such arrangements.[132]

[131] The MiFID reverse solicitation exemption is explicitly excluded from MiCAR by Art 61.
[132] Response 4.28 to 4.32.

12.12.10. Custody

Both the EU and the UK accept that custody of crypto-assets requires differential regulation from that which applies to securities custody, and both therefore provide for special regimes applicable to custody of crypto-assets. Both regimes require a degree of segregation, and grapple with what this means in practice. The primary difference between the two approaches involves liability. Following the existing EU model for securities, MiCAR imposes full liability on custodians for the loss of securities (up to the value of the securities). The UK, by contrast, takes the view that custodians should only be liable for loss of securities where the loss is attributable to the default of the custodian – thus, where securities are misappropriated or otherwise lost for reasons to do with manipulation of the digital ledger or other factors entirely outside the custodian's control, the custodian will not be liable for the loss.

However, this distinction may be more apparent than real. Although Recital 83 of MiCAR contains a ringing declaration that crypto-asset service providers (CASPs) should be held liable for any losses for their clients resulting from an ICT incident such as a 'cyber-attack, theft, or malfunction', the second subparagraph of Article 75(8) on custody appears to explicitly relieve CASPs of any liability when those losses are associated with, 'incidents not attributable to the crypto-asset service provider includ[ing] any event [... occurring] independently of the operations of the crypto-asset service provider, such as a problem inherent in the operation of the distributed ledger that the crypto-asset service provider does not control'. ESMA interprets this to mean that CASPs using permissionless DLT infrastructure that they do not control or manage (ie, no contractual arrangement exists) are exempted from this liability. Consequently it may well be that the UK and the EU, having started from different places, will end up fairly close.

12.12.11. Market Abuse

Both the EU and the UK begin from the existing regime created under the Market Abuse Regulation,[133] and seek to apply a broadly similar regime to crypto-assets. Operators of crypto-asset trading venues are required to develop systems and controls and procedures to identify and investigate suspected market abuse.

12.12.12. Transition and Grandfathering

This is an area where the EU takes a considerably more permissive approach than the UK. Credit institutions and investment firms in the EU need simply notify their

[133] Regulation (EU) No 596/2014.

national competent authority to obtain authorisation to perform those crypto-asset services which align with their existing permissions. An 18-month delay (starting with the date of publication of MiCAR) will be granted as regards the issuance of crypto-assets and, importantly, limited requirements will be applicable to crypto-assets other than stablecoins that were admitted to trading on a crypto trading platform before MiCAR's entry into force. By contrast, the UK will require all firms to apply for authorisation to perform the newly regulated activities, and there is to be no grandfathering for pre-existing crypto-assets.

12.13. Conclusion

The UK and the EU have taken very different regulatory approaches to the development of crypto-asset markets, with the EU seeking to channel the market by pre-emptive regulation, whilst the UK adopts a wait and see approach. This is in part driven by the fact that the EU has determined that crypto-asset regulation should be a separate division of regulation, subject to its own rules, whereas the UK seeks wherever possible to maintain a 'level playing field' between crypto and traditional investments and investment activities. This divergence presents a fascinating natural experiment as to the extent to which pre-emptive regulation helps or hinders the development of new products and services, and future developments will be fascinating to watch.

13

Conclusion

ILYA KOKORIN, LOUISE GULLIFER AND MATTHIAS HAENTJENS

13.1. MiCAR – A Breakthrough Legal Instrument

MiCAR was adopted on 31 May 2023 and became fully effective in all Member States as of 30 December 2024. It is a directly applicable legal instrument, relevant to traditional market players such as banks, investment firms and investment funds, national and EU supervisors, as well as 'new' market participants such as issuers of crypto-assets and crypto-asset service providers.

MiCAR was adopted as part of a package of legal instruments focused on the crypto industry, alongside the DLT Pilot Regime Regulation, which creates a testing regime and a legal framework for trading and settlement in tokenised securities[1] and the revised Transfer of Funds Regulation, which requires crypto-asset service providers to accompany transfers of crypto-assets with information on the originators and beneficiaries, with the ultimate goal of fighting money laundering and terrorist financing.[2] Together, these regulations have created the first major and highly developed legal framework for crypto-assets and their market and service infrastructures in the EU. MiCAR is the central piece of this complex regulatory framework and, as such, its adoption is a significant step towards a global regulatory response to the crypto markets. In a relatively short period of time, the EU managed to establish a monumental piece of legislation, creating a harmonised regime for crypto-assets across 27 Member States. It was adopted with the objective of facilitating legal certainty and promoting a level playing field, curbing regulatory arbitrage and moral hazard. It is likely to serve as a standard or at least a source of inspiration for legislation in other countries.

Spanning more than 160 pages and comprising 119 recitals, 149 articles and 6 annexes, and supplemented by numerous Level 2 acts (Regulatory Technical

[1] Regulation (EU) 2022/858 of the European Parliament and of the Council of 30 May 2022 on a pilot regime for market infrastructures based on distributed ledger technology, and amending Regulations (EU) No 600/2014 and (EU) No 909/2014 and Directive 2014/65/EU.

[2] Regulation (EU) 2023/1113 of the European Parliament and of the Council of 31 May 2023 on information accompanying transfers of funds and certain crypto-assets and amending Directive (EU) 2015/849.

Standards (RTS) and Implementing Technical Standards (ITS)) and Level 3 supervisory guidelines, MiCAR raises multiple questions. It may be difficult to understand and apply in practice. The chapters in this book seek to shed light on the goals of MiCAR, clarify its scope and key terms, and provide an explanation of the main rules for issuers of crypto-assets, crypto-asset service providers and crypto-asset services. The book aims to offer a critical assessment of potential weaknesses, uncertainties and possible bottlenecks in the effective regulation of the crypto industry.

In this conclusion, we highlight some of the criticisms raised in the different chapters of this book, summarise remaining open questions and uncertainties, and discuss specific policy choices made by the European legislator.

Section 13.2 below examines the complex interplay between MiCAR and existing rules and regulations, stressing both external complexity (complexity in relation to other EU laws), and internal complexity (complexity within MiCAR's provisions). Section 13.3 focuses on MiCAR's general approach, which is largely based on the methods, tools and strategies adopted in 'traditional' financial law. Several chapters of the book question whether this 'copy-and-paste' approach adequately responds to the unique characteristics of crypto-assets and their infrastructure. Section 13.4 analyses another complex interplay: the interplay between regulatory and private law. While MiCAR is primarily an instrument of administrative (public) law, some of its provisions aim to produce outcomes under (national) private law. Different private law aspects of MiCAR are pinpointed throughout the book. Section 13.5 deals with the regulatory objectives of MiCAR and notes that, when designing rules for the new crypto market, the EU legislator had to balance various policy objectives, while being guided by the overarching principle of proportionality. Whether a particular rule strikes the correct, ie, proportionate balance, is a question that frequently appears in the chapters of this book.

MiCAR creates a relatively comprehensive regulatory framework for crypto-assets, crypto-asset issuers and CASPs for all Member States of the EU, but it is not the only regulatory model available. Section 13.6 discusses the approaches to regulating the crypto industry in the UK and the US, and compares them with the EU approach. Finally, section 13.7 outlines the topics excluded from MiCAR and explores future steps the EU may or should take to promote safe and efficient markets in crypto-assets.

13.2. Complex Interplay with Existing Rules and Regulations

A consistent application of MiCAR by supervisory authorities and market participants alike relies, first and foremost, on a uniform understanding of how 'crypto-assets' are defined. It must therefore first be questioned whether a given crypto-asset falls within another category of regulated financial products, and thus within the scope of 'traditional' financial regulation such as the Prospectus Regulation, Market Abuse Regulation, MiFID II or MIFIR. The answer to this question is not always straightforward (see section 3.3.3). This ambiguity may create opportunities for regulatory arbitrage. ESMA has been tasked with publishing guidelines on the conditions and criteria for the qualification of crypto-assets as financial instruments,[3] but it remains to be seen whether this implementing legislation can bring uniformity to the delineation of the scope of MiCAR and existing financial regulation.[4] Even if we assume that ESMA's guidelines will bring clarity with respect to the definition of MiFID II financial instruments, they will not extend to other types of financial products excluded from MiCAR's scope. The 'delineation problem' between the respective scopes of application of MiCAR and other legal instruments was highlighted in chapter three. In that chapter, Paech argues that '[i]n the absence of guidelines, divergences comparable to those described in relation to financial instruments may emerge and even be more pronounced.'[5]

Second, it must be questioned how MiCAR interacts with other EU instruments. While crypto-assets that qualify as financial instruments are excluded from the scope of MiCAR[6] and thus fall within the scope of EU's 'traditional' financial markets legislation, MiCAR is not insulated from such 'traditional' financial law. In fact, it is inextricably linked to various pieces of existing EU financial law instruments. For example, as observed in chapters three and six, a significant part of the E-Money Directive (EMD2) applies to electronic money tokens (EMTs), although certain provisions of this directive are overridden by specific provisions of MiCAR. One example of an overridden provision is Article 11 EMD2, which governs the issuance and redeemability of e-money and does not apply to EMTs. Instead, issuance and redeemability of EMTs are exclusively governed by Article 49 MiCAR. Yet, EMD2's rules on initial capital, own funds, permitted activities, and fund safeguarding do continue to apply to issuers of non-significant EMTs.

This patchwork of rules creates a complex and potentially unclear relationship between the various regulatory instruments. It also raises serious concerns regarding technology neutrality of MiCAR. For instance, EMTs are not subject to the same rules as 'traditional' electronic money, while in substance they are very similar to e-money. According to Paech, this setup contributes to frictions and creates a potential for regulatory arbitrage. It 'poses significant challenges in terms of predictability, applicability, and international compatibility, lacking the

[3] See ESMA, Final Report, Guidelines on the conditions and criteria for the qualification of crypto-assets as financial instruments, 17 December 2024.

[4] DA Zetzsche, RP Buckley, DW Arner and MC van Ek, 'Remaining regulatory challenges in digital finance and cryptoassets after MiCA', Study requested by the ECON Committee, May 2023, p 16, concluding that '[e]ven if the framework is developed, over time, only some NCAs will find themselves in the position to enforce the classification criteria (if any) consistently.'

[5] Section 3.3.3.1 of this book.

[6] MiCAR, Article 2(4)(a).

clarity and consistency needed to set international standards.'[7] Perhaps, a better approach would have been to extend the scope of EMD2 to cover EMTs, with targeted amendments where necessary.

Chapter seven points out other complex relationships: those between MiCAR and the Payment Services Directive (PSD2) and the Digital Operational Resilience Act (DORA). PSD2 is the EU's primary regulatory framework for retail payments, aimed at creating a single market for payments across the EU. DORA aims to strengthen the information and communication technology security of financial entities to protect them against cyber risks. Kokorin observes that in order to make payment transactions related to the crypto-asset services they provide (particularly those relating to EMTs), CASPs must be licensed as payment institutions under PSD2. In fact, many CASPs may need both a MiCAR licence and a PSD2 licence to operate, because they engage in transactions involving fiat currencies and hold customer funds.[8] Alternatively, they can choose to outsource the payment services to a third-party provider authorised under PSD2. CASPs fall within the scope of DORA, a new EU instrument that establishes an EU-wide regulatory framework for managing ICT risks in the financial sector. Kokorin highlights that some of DORA's requirements such as setting up backup systems and restoration and recovery procedures and methods, may be difficult to implement and reconcile with the operational models of some CASPs, given the limits of interoperability across DLT networks and the lack of control by CASPs over permissionless decentralised governance arrangements.[9]

In addition to the intricate interplay with pre-MiCAR instruments – referred to as *external* complexity – MiCAR is notable for its *internal* complexity. There is a complex interplay between different titles and provisions within MiCAR itself. This brings us back to the issue of asset classification.[10] MiCAR outlines three distinct frameworks for the issuance and public offering of crypto-assets (Titles II, III, and IV) and for the provision of crypto-asset services (Title V). The applicable framework, along with the related regulatory requirements, is determined by the classification of the crypto-asset in question. Under MiCAR, a 'crypto-asset' is either an EMT, ART, significant EMT, significant ART, or a crypto-asset that is neither an EMT nor an ART. Title V applies to all crypto-assets under MiCAR. It is crucial for market participants and supervisors to adopt a common approach to determining the status of a crypto-asset under MiCAR. In light of far-reaching legal consequences, it should be clear whether a specific crypto-asset is a Title II crypto-asset, whether it is a utility token or another Title II crypto-asset, an EMT or ART. However, even when this determination is correctly made, internal

[7] Section 4.2 of this book.

[8] On the interplay between MiCAR and PSD2, see further Letter from John Berrigan, 'Interplay between MiCA and PSD2 – Possible 'no action letter' by the EBA', 5 December 2024.

[9] Section 7.3.3 of this book.

[10] See ESAs, Consultation Paper on Draft Guidelines on templates for explanations and opinions, and the standardised test for the classification of crypto-assets, under Article 97(1) of Regulation (EU) 2023/1114, ESA 2024 12, 12 July 2024.

complexity remains. A good example is the regulation of significant issuers of EMTs and ARTs, and significant CASPs – entities that pose particular risks, including systemic risk. For example, in chapter eight, Machacek notes that significant EMTs are subject to a complex, fragmented legal regime, comprising general EMT rules applicable to all EMTs, rules designed for ARTs, and bespoke rules specifically created for significant EMTs.[11]

The internal and external complexities just described could lead to legal uncertainties and impose an additional compliance burden on market players, particularly affecting start-ups and SMEs, which must navigate an already complicated and multi-layered regulatory environment. The development and crystallisation of this regulatory landscape will be further influenced by the growing body of Level 2 implementing legislation.

13.3. Crypto-specificity and a Copy-Paste Approach

MiCAR, to a substantial extent, builds on existing paradigms and approaches found in EU capital markets and banking regulations. When reading MiCAR, a sense of *déjà vu* is therefore difficult to avoid. Commenting on MiCAR's provisions concerning the obligations of ART issuers in chapter six, Maume observes that most of them are mere copies or adaptations of existing rules found in MiFID II and EU banking and payment services regulation.[12] This 'copy-and-paste' approach is a characteristic feature of MiCAR and has also been noted in other chapters of the book.

Chapter five highlights the many similarities between the white paper requirements for Title II crypto-assets and the prospectus requirements for transferable securities under the Prospectus Regulation. This information disclosure obligation seems reasonable, because disclosure and transparency are in line with the efficient market hypothesis and should in theory promote informed decision-making. According to Marjosola and Salo-Lahti, the 'required content and form of the crypto-asset white paper and the publication process are broadly similar to the EU prospectus regime.'[13] For instance, in a similar way to the Prospectus Regulation, MiCAR requires that the white paper be accompanied by a summary. As the Prospectus Regulation does for securities, MiCAR also distinguishes between primary and secondary issuances.

Chapter seven points out that the legal regime for CASPs is similar to that applicable to investment firms under MiFID II. This regime concerns, inter alia, obligations to act in the best interests of clients, avoid conflicts of interest, ensure best execution of orders and a suitability assessment. MiCAR imposes on crypto

[11] Section 8.3.1 of this book.
[12] Section 6.2.4.1 of this book.
[13] Section 5.3.2 of this book.

intermediaries authorisation, conduct of business and prudential requirements similar to those of traditional financial intermediaries. In view of the critical importance of centralised intermediaries in crypto markets such as crypto exchanges, wallet service providers, crypto-advisers, and the recent experience of the Crypto Winter, we believe this regulatory approach is largely justified. The same applies to the rules aimed at preventing fraud and market abuse. Regulators must establish and enforce robust measures to combat market abuse, ensuring fairness and protecting investors. In chapter nine, Campuzano and Raas make it clear that the regulation of market abuse under MiCAR is almost identical to the corresponding prohibitions and obligations in the existing market abuse regime for financial instruments laid down in MAR. Both instruments prohibit insider dealing, unlawful disclosure of inside information, and various forms of behaviour that qualify as market manipulation.

As the crypto-asset markets are relatively young, there are no extensive legal frameworks or centuries of regulatory experience compared to traditional financial markets. It is therefore understandable that the European Commission has sought to implement protections for crypto-asset markets that closely resemble those already in place for traditional financial markets. To some extent, the parallels with established EU financial law standards and rules were unavoidable. Indeed, such parallels can be beneficial, because some legal concepts and the rationale behind them are well-suited for crypto-assets and have already been long-established and tried. Examples of those principles are the obligation of service providers to act honestly, fairly and professionally in the best interests of clients. Therefore, their inclusion in MiCAR can draw on existing interpretations, which facilitates legal certainty and saves costs.

At the same time, MiCAR does not fully replicate the rules found in other EU instruments. For example, the Prospectus Regulation requires supervisory approval of a prospectus prior to the issuance of transferable securities, whereas MiCAR does not mandate such approval for Title II crypto-assets. This reflects a more lenient treatment of these crypto-assets. MiCAR also introduces a bespoke, consumer law-type tool in the form of the right of withdrawal for retail purchasers. According to Marjosola and Salo-Lahti, the 14-day withdrawal right 'is transplanted from EU consumer contract law' and is 'alien to EU financial law'.[14] Another example of crypto-specific regulation is the regulation of stablecoins such as ARTs. Maume describes it as the regulation 'that deviates most from the established concepts of financial markets regulation', which makes it 'a bit of a conceptual novelty.'[15] Crypto-specific rules have also been examined in chapter seven of this book. Among these is the requirement for crypto-asset service providers who offer custody services to technologically segregate crypto-assets held in custody. Technological segregation is introduced in addition to more 'traditional' forms of

[14] Section 5.6 of this book.
[15] Section 6.1.2 of this book.

asset segregation, such as operational and legal segregation applicable in relation to intermediated securities. Pursuant to the technological segregation requirement, customer crypto-assets must be held through separate blockchain addresses from the CASP's own crypto-assets.

The above begs the question: Is MiCAR sufficiently crypto-specific? In other words, does it adequately account for the technological, organisational, and economic attributes of crypto businesses? In this respect, one may reasonably question whether the prevailing 'copy-and-paste' approach effectively addresses the unique characteristics of crypto-assets, as well as the risks and needs of markets in crypto-assets. The rules on market abuse may be a case in point. MiCAR recognises that since issuers of crypto-assets and CASPs are often SMEs, it would be disproportionate to apply all of the provisions of MAR.[16] However, as noted by Campuzano and Raas in chapter nine, the market abuse title of MiCAR almost verbatim copies the provisions of MAR.[17] Moreover, it does not include certain exemptions found in MAR, such as those for buy-back and stabilisation programmes.

The European Commission's intention was to design a distinct market abuse framework for crypto-assets. This goal has been justified by the peculiarities of crypto-asset markets, including the uniqueness of crypto-assets and their underlying technology, the complexity of crypto products, the (in)sensitivity of their valuation to hype (fundamentals), and their pseudonymity. However, this goal does not seem to have been fully realised with MiCAR. While regulatory frameworks targeting new market developments may consist of both novel and 'repurposed' rules, it must be realised that existing rules should be adapted or completely replaced by new ones when new categories of assets or services pose new and different risks.

13.4. Complex Interplay of Public and Private Law

MiCAR does not aim to harmonise private law across EU Member States. Instead, its rules are first and foremost rules of administrative or regulatory nature, the violation of which typically leads to public law consequences in the form of sanctions imposed by a supervisory authority. The powers of these authorities, both national and European, have been examined by Noble in chapter ten. Nevertheless, upon a closer look, it becomes clear that MiCAR has implications for private law (and vice versa), or at least will serve as a catalyst for the adoption of certain rules and strategies to achieve desired – private law – effects.

As an example, chapter seven discusses the obligations of CASPs, one of which is to implement the legal segregation of crypto-assets held in custody for clients

[16] MiCAR, Recital (95).
[17] Section 9.1 of this book.

to ensure that these assets do not become part of the CASP's insolvency estate.[18] According to Kokorin, this constitutes a specific private law outcome that can only be achieved through relevant – national and largely unharmonised – property and insolvency laws.[19] In the same vein, MiCAR requires crypto custodians to make adequate arrangements to safeguard the 'ownership rights' of clients. However, not all national legal systems in the EU do recognise property rights in crypto-assets.[20] Among other rules that appear to have a private law purpose is the rule in Article 75(4), which relates to the situation where 'changes to the underlying distributed ledger technology or any other event likely to create or modify a client's rights'. This article provides that a client should be entitled to any crypto-assets or any rights newly created, unless otherwise agreed with the CASP. This is an example of a rule couched in regulatory language which leaves it unclear whether, and if so how, the desired effect is to be achieved under private law. Because the rule is included in an article that sets out regulatory obligations of a CASP, it seems that the entitlement to newly created crypto-assets or rights is a right against the CASP as opposed to any other party, but whether it is a contractual right or some other type of right is unclear.

The private law aspects of MiCAR are discussed in other chapters as well. Chapter six examines MiCAR's requirements for ART issuers concerning the reserves of assets. Maume explains that the regulation of reserve assets aims to ensure that the creditors of the issuer (other than the holders of the ARTs to which the reserve assets relate) and the third-party custodian have no claim against these assets. Whether ART holders have any right in the reserve assets will depend on how the relevant ART is set up, as well as on the applicable law. In practice, it may turn out that the holders of the ART are mere general unsecured creditors of the issuer and have no proprietary rights in the relevant reserve assets. Unless the holders of the stablecoin have a proprietary right in the assets, they will only be protected if the issuer has no other creditors and the reserve assets are preserved from dissipation. For this reason, Maume notes that the extent to which legal segregation regarding the reserve of assets is effective and capable of protecting the rights of stablecoin holders 'remains a question of national property and insolvency laws, which might need to be amended while implementing MiCAR.'[21]

[18] MiCAR, Article 75(7).

[19] Section 7.4.1.3 of this book.

[20] I Tirado and L Gullifer, 'Proprietary rights and digital assets: a 'modest proposal' from a Transnational Law perspective' (2025) 87(2) *Law and Contemporary Problems* 211; D Zetzsche, J Sinnig, A Nikolakopoulou, 'Crypto custody' (2024) 19(3) *Capital Markets Law Journal* 207, 226, noting that 'the obligation to safeguard the ownership rights is undermined when it is not certain, from a private law perspective, that the clients actually have ownership rights over the custodied crypto-assets and whether their nature is contractual or proprietary.'; I Kokorin, 'Crypto Insolvencies and the Limits of a Contract and Contract Law' (2023) 6 *European Review of Private Law* 1245, 1268–69, arguing that '[t]o establish a firm foundation for customers' proprietary interests in intermediated crypto-assets, it may be essential to supplement MiCAR with a comprehensive private law framework [...].'

[21] Section 6.2.9.1 of this book.

The relationship between a crypto-asset and an off-chain asset or claim that this crypto-asset may relate to is analysed in chapter eleven. In it, Van Setten argues that not all uses of DLT and smart contracts to record entitlements to, and transfers of, off-chain assets involve crypto-assets that are independent objects of property. For example, when DLT is used to record entitlements in a legal entity as a registrar would typically do, this activity does not automatically fall under MiCAR.[22] On the other hand, when there is an intention to embed an off-chain asset into a crypto-asset, the private law conclusion would be different. However, as Van Setten points out, the question of what the regulatory response should be to the 'tokenisation' of off-chain assets should depend on the economic features of the resulting assets and markets, and not on their private law characterisation.

A number of provisions in MiCAR refer to applicable law. For example, the reserve of assets backing stablecoins must be legally segregated from the issuer's estate 'in accordance with applicable law'.[23] The same applies to the legal segregation obligations of crypto custodians.[24] ESMA, in its Draft ITS regarding forms, formats and templates for crypto-asset white papers, suggests that issuers of crypto-assets must include information about the law applicable to the crypto-asset in the white paper.[25] Yet neither MiCAR nor Level 2 acts contain rules of private international law and they do not specify how applicable property, insolvency and company law should be determined. However, this determination is key to achieving legal segregation and thus protecting the rights of parties in various crypto-asset arrangements. The problem is that typical connecting factors for choice-of-law rules, such as the location of activities or assets, are generally not suitable for proprietary issues related to crypto-assets. Using such factors would be impractical and inconsistent, because crypto-assets are intangible and lack any physical location.[26]

Private law is thus critical for consumer and investor protection, legal certainty for market participants, and for the determination of the exact scope of MiCAR. This is why we argue that to provide a solid basis for customers' proprietary rights in crypto-assets, it is necessary to complement MiCAR with a robust and harmonised private law and private international law frameworks. For this purpose, inspiration can be drawn from the work produced by standard-setting organisations, such as UNIDROIT. In 2023, UNIDROIT published the UNIDROIT Principles on Digital Assets and Private Law (Principles).[27] These Principles have been designed to facilitate transactions in digital assets and are meant to help countries to 'enable their private laws to be consistent with best practice and international standards

[22] Section 11.2 of this book.

[23] MiCAR, Article 36(2).

[24] MiCAR, Article 75(7).

[25] ESMA, Final Report, Draft Technical Standards specifying certain requirements of the Markets in Crypto Assets Regulation (MiCA) – second package, ESMA75-453128700-1229, 3 July 2024.

[26] See eg A Bonomi, M Lehmann and S Lalani (eds), *Blockchain and Private International Law* (Brill, 2023).

[27] UNIDROIT Principles on Digital Assets and Private Law, www.unidroit.org/instruments/digital-assets-and-private-law/.

in relation to the holding, transfer and use as collateral of digital assets.'[28] Among other things, they provide that a digital asset can be the subject of proprietary rights[29] and contain rules for the determination of law applicable to proprietary issues in respect of crypto-assets.[30]

We acknowledge that harmonisation of property and private international law rules concerning property is notoriously difficult. Nevertheless, we believe it to be crucial for the achievement of MiCAR's goals.

13.5. Complex Balancing between Regulatory Objectives

MiCAR pursues several policy objectives, including consumer and investor protection, market integrity, financial stability, and the development of crypto-assets and the broader use of DLT, particularly by start-ups and SMEs. As observed by Kokorin in chapter two, whereas these policy objectives do not inherently contradict each other, in some contexts, MiCAR appears to give priority to one objective over another. This complex balancing of goals is evident in various provisions of MiCAR. It is a different question, however, whether these provisions strike a fair and reasonable balance.

The regulation of stablecoins can be taken as a case in point. In chapter six, Maume poses the question of whether MiCAR's approach to stablecoins will facilitate an EU system for stablecoin payments or, instead, isolate the European crypto-payment market from the rest of the world.[31] He argues that the chosen approach is demanding, creates a privileged position for incumbent financial institutions[32] and could prevent smaller start-ups from entering the EU crypto market. MiCAR enforces stringent rules and requirements for stablecoin issuers, regardless of their risk profile or business model. The proportionality of this one-size-fits-all approach should be scrutinised. Maume believes a more tailored approach would have been preferable, balancing the need to ensure investor protection and financial stability while simultaneously fostering entrepreneurship and the development of novel technologies.

According to Maume, 'MiCAR approach obviously prioritises stability through business size over the innovative power of start-ups.'[33] Paech emphasises that the legislator's intention was to curb the rise of potentially global stablecoins, such

[28] ibid p 9.
[29] ibid Principle 3.
[30] ibid Principle 5.
[31] Section 6.1.2 of this book.
[32] See also M Lehmann, 'MiCAR – Gold Standard or Regulatory Poison for the Crypto Industry?' (2024) 160 EBI Working Paper Series, papers.ssrn.com/sol3/papers.cfm?abstract_id=4692743, arguing that it is 'unlikely that the stablecoin sector in the EU will feature start-ups; more probably, it will be dominated by incumbent behemoths.'
[33] Section 6.1.3 of this book.

as Facebook's Libra/Diem – the project that never succeeded.[34] This is especially evident in the regulation of so-called 'super-significant' stablecoins, denominated in a currency that is not an official currency of a Member State. Should these stablecoins pass a specified threshold of 'significance', their issuers may be required to stop issuing them.[35] By creating this limitation, MiCAR effectively imposes a hard cap on super-significant stablecoins. This cap serves to protect monetary transmission channels and the monetary sovereignty of the EU and its Member States. The preservation of monetary sovereignty is a unique, public-interest-driven goal, which takes priority over other objectives pursued by MiCAR.

In contrast to the stringent regulation of stablecoins, Marjosola and Salo-Lahti note that Title II of MiCAR, which addresses non-stablecoin crypto-assets, is less prescriptive, aims to support innovative and inclusive financing methods, particularly for SMEs (especially those issuing utility tokens) and generally establishes proportionate, risk-based rules.[36] For instance, while MiCAR mandates the publication of Title II crypto-asset white papers, it does not require their prior approval by a competent authority. This is a significant difference from the regulation of stablecoins. It also does not impose prudential requirements on issuers of Title II crypto-assets. It appears that, with respect to Title II crypto-assets such as payment tokens like Bitcoin and utility tokens such as Filecoin, the EU legislator aimed to widen investment opportunities for investors, promote new sources of funding for start-ups and early-stage companies, and increase the efficiency of payments – objectives aligned with the broader goal of developing crypto-assets and expanding the use of DLT.

Interestingly, both the chapter on stablecoins and the chapter on Title II crypto-assets note that MiCAR blurs the boundary between the primary and secondary markets.[37] This is because it imposes an ongoing obligation on crypto-asset issuers to modify already published crypto-asset white papers in the event of significant changes.[38] In this regard, Maume observes that the ongoing white paper modification and disclosure obligations could prejudice the legitimate interests of the issuer, while Marjosola and Salo-Lahti argue that these obligations 'constitute a cumbersome way of implementing a type of continuous disclosure obligation.' The imposition of an ongoing, potentially indefinite, obligation to modify a white paper creates a significant burden for crypto-asset issuers, especially those that are SMEs.

When it comes to addressing market abuse under MiCAR, Campuzano and Raas question the proportionality of the chosen approach.[39] They assert that

[34] On the Libra/Diem project, see DA Zetzsche, RP Buckley, DW Arner, 'Regulating Libra' (2021) 41(1) *Oxford Journal of Legal Studies* 80.
[35] MiCAR, Article 23(1) and Article 58(3).
[36] Section 5.2 of this book.
[37] Sections 5.3.2 and 6.2.2.2 of this book.
[38] MiCAR, Article 12 for Title II crypto-assets and Article 25 for issuers of ARTs.
[39] Section 9.2.3.1 of this book.

MiCAR introduces a legal regime that substantively resembles the regulatory framework of MAR and therefore is hardly adjusted to crypto-assets. They conclude that MiCAR may increase the compliance burden and disproportionately affect market participants. The authors argue that a more nuanced and proportionate approach should have been adopted, taking into account the decentralised aspects inherent in some crypto-assets arrangements and the indicators of behaviour that may constitute market abuse. Chapter nine concludes that MiCAR 'fails to provide such indicators and misses the opportunity to fine-tune the prohibition initially intended for traditional financial markets to the unique functioning and characteristics of crypto-asset markets.'[40]

MiCAR is a complex legal instrument with a broad range of rules, regulatory techniques and policy objectives. This is why it is impossible to make any generalised statement about its approach. In fact, these approaches differ depending on the type of crypto-asset or the services provided by CASPs. Therefore, any assessment should focus on specific provisions, in view of the balancing of conflicting regulatory objectives.

13.6. Different Regulatory Approaches: EU, UK, USA

While MiCAR, together with the DLT Pilot Regime Regulation and the revised Transfer of Funds Regulation may be the first major harmonised legal framework for the crypto industry in the EU, it is not the only possible regulatory response to crypto-assets. The recent report by the World Economic Forum shows that different countries are adopting different approaches to the regulation of crypto-assets, with different timelines for their development and implementation.[41] These notably divergent approaches may help to identify successful regulatory models and areas of weakness, but they are a serious impediment to the effective regulation of the global crypto industry.

MiCAR is a comprehensive piece of legislation, containing requirements for issuers of different types of crypto-assets, general rules applicable to all CASPs and those covering specific crypto-asset services, market abuse prohibitions, and extensive provisions establishing the powers of competent authorities and the EBA to supervise and enforce MiCAR's application. Thus, MiCAR is intended to be the primary legal instrument for the regulation of the crypto industry in the European Union as a whole and to serve as the key point of reference for all crypto businesses. This regulatory approach has certain advantages, as it is accessible, provides a degree of legal certainty and should support harmonised application in the entire EU. However, it is not the only way to regulate crypto-assets.

[40] Section 9.7.3.2 of this book.

[41] World Economic Forum, Insight Report, 'Digital Assets Regulation: Insights from Jurisdictional Approaches' (October 2024) www3.weforum.org/docs/WEF_Digital_Assets_Regulation_2024.pdf.

In comparison to MiCAR, the UK has chosen a gradual approach, initially focusing on fiat-backed stablecoins and crypto promotions. According to Gleeson (chapter twelve), the UK has decided to take a more market-oriented approach, imposing regulation only where clearly necessary.[42] It is also notable that instead of introducing an entirely new, standalone piece of legislation, the UK has opted to extend certain existing frameworks, such as the Financial Services and Markets Act 2000, to accommodate crypto-assets. Thus, while MiCAR regulates the issuance of crypto-assets, including stablecoins, and market abuse involving crypto-assets under a single regulatory framework, the UK seeks to achieve the same regulation by extending the public offers regime, the payment services regime and the market abuse regime, respectively. These different regulatory models may lead to frictions, particularly affecting cross-border offerings of crypto-assets, the admission of crypto-assets to trading on crypto trading platforms and exchanges, and the provision of cross-border crypto-asset services. Apart from different regulatory strategies, there are other notable differences between the UK's approach and that of MiCAR. While MiCAR is fearful of potential risks created by stablecoins resulting in strict rules concerning their issuance, the UK appears to be positively enthusiastic about the circulation of fiat-backed stablecoins as payment media.[43] Another area where the UK's position diverges from that of the EU is crypto-promotions. In the EU, there are different rules for marketing communications, which depend on the specific type of the product or crypto-asset. In contrast, the UK has adopted a broad financial promotion framework that governs all communications related to a wide range of financial products and instruments.

Unlike the EU with its MiCAR, the US currently lacks a comprehensive federal law for crypto-assets. Instead, the US has a fragmented regulatory framework that involves multiple agencies such as the Securities and Exchange Commission (SEC) and the Commodity Futures Trading Commission (CFTC). Several federal legislative proposals have been introduced in recent years that aim to offer clarity to regulatory agencies and market participants on how digital assets are to be regulated. Among these proposals is the Lummis-Gillibrand Payment Stablecoin Act,[44] which seeks to create a comprehensive regulatory framework for the issuance of stablecoins, as well as the management of their reserves and the structure of the market. More recent proposals include the Stablecoin Transparency and Accountability for a Better Ledger Economy (STABLE) Act[45] and the Guiding and Establishing National Innovation for U.S. Stablecoins (GENIUS) Act.[46] However, there is still no comprehensive piece of legislation. Federal agencies

[42] Section 12.10.1 of this book.

[43] Section 12.10.3 of this book.

[44] S.4155 – Lummis-Gillibrand Payment Stablecoin Act, www.congress.gov/bill/118th-congress/senate-bill/4155/text.

[45] H.R.2392 – STABLE Act of 2025.

[46] S.394 – GENIUS Act of 2025.

have therefore taken the lead in addressing the crypto industry and risks posed by it. In doing so, they often rely on the test established by the US Supreme Court in its 1946 *Howey Co.* decision[47] – the so-called 'Howey Test'. This test is used to determine whether a crypto-asset is part of an investment contract that is subject to regulation under US securities laws. Using this test, regulators and courts have concluded that various unconventional investment vehicles qualify as investment contracts.

During the Biden administration, the SEC has initiated a growing number of enforcement actions against crypto-asset service providers, alleging violations of federal securities laws.[48] For example, the SEC charged Coinbase – one of the leading cryptocurrency exchanges – with operating its crypto-asset trading platform as an unregistered securities exchange, broker, and clearing agency.[49] To a significant extent, the fate of crypto-asset firms and crypto-assets, more generally, rests in the hands of supervisory agencies and courts. The active role of federal agencies in the US has been described by some authors as 'regulation by enforcement',[50] which refers to the practice of pursuing legal actions against market participants on a case-by-case basis to establish precedents, instead of rulemaking by legislators. The leading position of government agencies and courts in shaping the legal regime for crypto markets, their reliance on existing financial regulations, and the application of 'traditional' legal tests and precedents – none of which were designed with crypto-assets in mind – characterise the US approach and distinguish it from the approaches adopted in the EU and the UK.

While the US approach may be viewed as flexible and adaptive, it has notable disadvantages compared to the EU approach, including legal uncertainty, unpredictability, potential political influences, and a lack of tailor-made provisions that promote the advantages of crypto-assets and address the specific risks and negative externalities they produce. That said, with the election of Donald Trump as president – who promised to make the US the 'crypto capital of the planet',[51] the

[47] *SEC v W.J. Howey Co.*, 328 U.S. 293 (1946). The Howey Test introduces four criteria for classifying an asset or arrangement as an 'investment contract.' If an asset involves an 'investment of money in a common enterprise, with a reasonable expectation of profits to be derived from the efforts of others', it is considered a security. As a result, it falls under the disclosure and registration requirements of the Securities Act of 1933 and the Securities Exchange Act of 1934.

[48] SEC, Crypto Assets and Cyber Enforcement Actions, www.sec.gov/securities-topics/crypto-assets.

[49] *SEC v Coinbase Inc. and Coinbase Global Inc*, Complaint, 23 Civ. 4738, 6 June 2023, www.sec.gov/files/litigation/complaints/2023/comp-pr2023-102.pdf.

[50] C Brummer, Y Yadav and D Zaring, 'Regulation by Enforcement' (2023) SSRN (forthcoming in the University of Southern California Law Review) ssrn.com/abstract=4405036; CR Goforth, 'Regulation by Enforcement: Problems with the SEC's Approach to Cryptoasset Regulation' (2022) 82 *Maryland Law Review* 107.

[51] White House, Fact Sheet: Executive Order to Establish United States Leadership in Digital Financial Technology, 23 January 2025.

regulatory approach to crypto-assets and crypto businesses in the US is likely to change. What shape the new regulatory framework will take remains to be seen.

13.7. Future Challenges and Regulation

Blockchain technology has always been based on decentralisation. The seminal Bitcoin white paper, for instance, proposed a technological solution to eliminate the need for a 'trusted central authority', such as banks or payment service institutions, in bilateral transactions. Instead, it argued for the creation of a decentralised payment infrastructure through the use of technology.[52] This narrative of decentralisation is often associated with cryptocurrencies and crypto-transactions.[53] However, as is noted in various chapters of this book, modern crypto-markets are dominated by centralised players: issuers of crypto-assets, crypto lenders, exchange or trading platforms, and other crypto-asset service providers. This is why MiCAR focuses on centralised or partially centralised actors and does not extend to situations '[w]here crypto-asset services are provided in a fully decentralised manner without any intermediary.'[54]

However, certain platforms, such as decentralised crypto exchanges (DEXs) and decentralised finance (DeFi) crypto lending platforms, function without a central authority, and use algorithms that are governed in a decentralised manner by the platform's users instead. These algorithms and platforms may escape the regulatory perimeter of MiCAR, but they are not necessarily immune from 'traditional' financial risks related to market abuse, investor protection and money laundering and terrorist financing.[55] These risks have already materialised in practice. For example, in the *Uniswap* case, investors argued that they lost money after investing in what turned out to be 'scam tokens' traded on the DEX. Due to the decentralised nature of the protocol, the identities of the issuers of those tokens

[52] Satoshi Nakamoto, 'Bitcoin: A Peer-to-Peer Electronic Cash System' (2008).

[53] Nick Szabo, Tweet from 4 September 2015 (@NickSzabo4), arguing that '[d]ecentralization is what allows Bitcoin to substitute an army of computers for an army of accountants, investigators, and lawyers.' Nick Szabo is best known for developing a concept of smart contracts in the mid-1990s.

[54] MiCAR, Recital (22).

[55] ESMA, 'Decentralised Finance in the EU: Developments and risks' (11 October 2023) www.esma.europa.eu/document/trv-article-decentralised-finance-eu-developments-and-risks, observing, among other things, that 'although investors' exposure to DeFi remains small overall, there are serious risks to investor protection, due to the highly speculative nature of many DeFi arrangements, important operational and security vulnerabilities, and the lack of a clearly identified responsible party.' The report also highlights various market manipulation issuers characterising DeFi. See also A Born et al., 'Decentralised finance – a new unregulated non-bank system?' (2022) ECB Macroprudential Bulletin, No. 18, www.ecb.europa.eu/press/financial-stability-publications/macroprudential-bulletin/focus/2022/html/ecb.mpbu202207_focus1.en.html.

were unknown, leaving the plaintiffs with identifiable damages but without an identifiable tortfeasor.[56]

While truly decentralised financial arrangements are outside the scope of MiCAR and may represent a relatively small segment of crypto markets, they warrant consideration due to the existing risks to investor protection, market integrity and possibly, to financial stability. In view of these risks, we think regulation of DeFi arrangements should be considered at the EU level in the near future.[57] DeFi also relates to another area currently beyond MiCAR's scope – crypto lending. In fact, as noted by Van Setten in chapter eleven, the most important DeFi platforms today are lending platforms.[58] DeFi lenders such as Compound and Aave enable users to lend or borrow crypto-assets directly through a system of smart contracts. DeFi lending protocols have seen explosive growth, increasing from zero to over USD 50 billion in total value locked in under two years.[59]

MiCAR lacks a dedicated legal framework for crypto lending. MiCAR is explicit that it does 'not address the lending and borrowing of crypto-assets, including e-money tokens, and therefore should not prejudice applicable national law.'[60] However, crypto lending is prone to many classic financial sector vulnerabilities, including maturity and liquidity mismatches, margin calls, fire-sale collateral liquidations and digital bank runs. In fact, the business models of some crypto lenders are similar to those of banks or investment funds.[61] Yet, crypto lenders are not subject to the same requirements as traditional market players, which gives them a competitive advantage. Recent failures of large crypto-lending firms – Voyager, Celsius, BlockFi and Genesis – exposed significant vulnerabilities and highlighted various risks related to their activities.[62] The similarities between crypto lenders and 'traditional' financial institutions do not automatically imply that existing regulatory models are adequate for these relatively new market players. Therefore, we believe the EU should consider

[56] *Risley v Universal Navigation Inc.*, 2023 WL 5609200 (S.D.N.Y., 2023) storage.courtlistener.com/recap/gov.uscourts.nysd.577791/gov.uscourts.nysd.577791.90.0.pdf.

[57] The regulation of DeFi is supported by the recent report prepared for the European Parliament by a group of leading experts in the field. See DA Zetzsche, RP Buckley, DW Arner, MC van Ek, 'Remaining regulatory challenges in digital finance and cryptoassets after MiCA', Study requested by the ECON Committee, May 2023.

[58] Section 11.5 of this book.

[59] S Aramonte, S Doerr, W Huang and A Schrimpf, 'DeFi lending: intermediation without information?' (2022) BIS Bulletin No 57, www.bis.org/publ/bisbull57.pdf. See also G Cornelli, L Gambacorta, R Garratt and A Reghezza, 'Why DeFi lending? Evidence from Aave V2' (2024) BIS Working Paper No 1183, www.bis.org/publ/work1183.htm.

[60] MiCAR, Recital (94). The European Commission is tasked to prepare a report by 30 December 2024, containing an assessment of the necessity and feasibility of regulating DeFi, and lending and borrowing of crypto-assets. See MiCAR, Article 142(2)(b).

[61] E Avgouleas and A Seretakis, 'How Should Crypto Lending Be Regulated Under EU Law?' (2023) 24 *EBOR* 421, 422, arguing that 'the activities of crypto lenders, which involve the taking of deposits in crypto assets and the granting of crypto loans, resemble banking activities.'

[62] On the recent wave of failures of crypto-lending platforms, see I Kokorin, 'The anatomy of crypto failures and investor protection under MiCAR' (2023) 18(4) *Capital Markets Law Journal* 500.

designing regulations specifically for crypto lending to achieve MiCAR's overarching policy goals of ensuring financial stability, market integrity, and investor protection for the entire crypto industry.

13.8. Conclusion

In conclusion, MiCAR must be seen as a highly ambitious initiative that aims to establish a comprehensive and harmonised regulatory framework for crypto-assets across the EU. It represents a far-reaching piece of supranational legislation that focuses on crypto-assets, crypto-asset services and relevant market players. MiCAR's policy goals are to support innovation while safeguarding market integrity, to protect investors and ensure financial stability and monetary sovereignty of the EU and its Member States. By providing such a framework, MiCAR seeks to position the EU as a leader in the regulation of crypto-assets and the infrastructure surrounding them.

As MiCAR became fully applicable only as of 30 December 2024, it is far too early to endeavour to draw any conclusions as to whether it will achieve its goals. Instead, this book sought to explain the key rules of this regulation, highlight its strengths, point out its weaknesses, and offer recommendations on how the provisions of MiCAR should be applied or improved in the future. MiCAR is a complex, multi-layered and evolving instrument that has sparked divergent opinions among commentators. While some scholars praise it as a 'structured and complete legislation on crypto-assets',[63] others emphasise that it 'consists of repurposed material laws'[64] and argue that it results 'in a heavy bureaucratic mix', which can discourage start-ups and cause crypto firms to avoid the EU entirely.[65]

The divergence in views about MiCAR underscores its complex nature, which is shaped by several interplays explored in this chapter: the interplay between MiCAR and existing rules and regulations, the interplay between crypto-specific rules and those borrowed from traditional financial law, the interplay between public and private law, and the interplay between MiCAR's different policy goals. Through further analysis of these interplays, we hope to have given the reader insight into a fascinating and rapidly changing industry, that raises serious questions about fundamental issues of regulation and law.

[63] P Annunziata, 'An Overview of the Markets in Crypto-Assets Regulation (MiCAR)' (2023) EBI Working Paper Series No 158, 1, ssrn.com/abstract=4660379.

[64] P Paech, 'New regulations or novel regulation for crypto assets and DeFi? – The folly of hybrid laws' (2023) SSRN publication, 1, ssrn.com/abstract=4579968.

[65] M Lehmann, 'MICAR – Gold standard or regulatory poison for the crypto industry?' (2024) 61(3) *Common Market Law Review* 699, 726.

INDEX

www.ingramcontent.com/pod-product-compliance
Ingram Content Group UK Ltd.
Pitfield, Milton Keynes, MK11 3LW, UK
UKHW020702280626
472601UK00003BA/31